ALASKA

LISA MALONEY

ARCTIC
Barrow
ALASKA
Arctic Circle
Chukchi Sea
North
RUSSIA
Noatak National Preserve
Cape Krusenstern National Monument
Kobuk Valley National Park
Kotzebue
Bering Strait
Selawik National Wildlife Refuge
Bering Land Bridge National Preserve
Koyukuk National Wildlife Refuge
Nome
Galena
St. Lawrence Island
RUSSIA
U.S.A.
Innoko National Wildlife Refuge
Yukon
Bering Sea
Holy Cross
Yukon Delta National Wildlife Refuge
St. Matthew Island
Bethel
Nunivak Island
Togiak National Wildlife Refuge
Dillingham
Katmai National Park and Preserve
King Salmon
St. Paul Island
Becharof National Wildlife Refuge
Pribilof Islands
St. George Island
Alaska Peninsula
Aniakchak National Monument and Preserve
0
100 mi
0
100 km
Izembek National Wildlife Refuge
Alaska Peninsula National Wildlife Refuge
Alaska Maritime National Wildlife Refuge
Unalaska
The Aleutian Islands

OCEAN
Beaufort Sea
Prudhoe Bay
Slope
Arctic National Wildlife Refuge
Vuntut National Park
NORTHWEST TERRITORIES
Inuvik
Trans-Alaska Pipeline
DALTON HWY
Gates of the Arctic National Park and Preserve
CANADA
U.S.A.
River
Arctic Circle
Porcupine
Mackenzie River
Kanuti National Wildlife Refuge
Yukon Flats National Wildlife Refuge
Circle
DEMPSTER HWY
White Mts. Nat. Rec. Area
Yukon
YUKON TERRITORY
River
Yukon-Charley Rivers National Preserve
Fairbanks
TOP OF THE WORLD HWY.
Nowitna National Wildlife Refuge
Dawson City
Delta Junction
Tok
RICHARDSON HWY
DENALI HWY
River
Denali National Park and Preserve
PARKS HWY
Beaver Creek
KLONDIKE HWY
TOK CUTOFF
Talkeetna
ALASKA HWY
Glennallen
McCarthy
GLENN HWY
Haines Jct.
Whitehorse
Watson Lake
Anchorage
Valdez
Wrangell-St. Elias National Park and Preserve
Kluane National Park
Lake Clark National Park and Preserve
Kenai National Wildlife Refuge
Chugach National Forest
Cordova
Seward
Skagway
Haines
BRITISH COLUMBIA
CASSIAR HWY
Cook Inlet
Homer
Kenai Peninsula
Yakutat
Kenai Fjords National Park
Glacier Bay National Park and Preserve
Juneau
Chichagof Island
Gulf of Alaska
Kodiak
Admiralty Island National Monument
Sitka
Petersburg
Tongass National Forest
Wrangell
Hyder
Kodiak Island
Baronof Island
Misty Fjords National Monument
Stewart
Kodiak National Wildlife Refuge
Ketchikan
Prince of Wales Island
Prince Rupert
PACIFIC OCEAN
Queen Charlotte Islands

Contents

DISCOVER

Alaska

What are the first things that come to mind when you think of Alaska? Steep-walled fjords, charismatic bears, soaring eagles, breaching whales, or glaciers creeping down the side of a mountain and into the sea? Then you're already in tune with some of our state's grandest sights. But there's so much to Alaska that it can't possibly be summed up in just one image—and every part of the state is a little bit different.

In Southeast Alaska the evergreen rainforest dominates the landscape and totem poles stand silent witness to humpback whales, each one the size of a school bus, cavorting in the glacier-fed waters.

Southcentral Alaska and the Interior are a road-tripper's dream clad in boreal forest, with paved two-lane highways leading from Fairbanks—land of gold mining, the midnight sun, and the aurora borealis dancing overhead—to Homer, the pinnacle of Alaskan art, food, and fishing in one small town.

Southwest Alaska holds some of the state's best bear watching on Kodiak Island—also known as Alaska's Emerald Isle—and nearby Katmai National Park. You'll also find some of the continent's best bird-watching at Unalaska/Dutch

Clockwise from top left: baby bear in a tree; St. Nicholas Russian Orthodox Church in Juneau; reindeer at Running Reindeer Ranch; wolf in Denali National Park; seal in Valdez; Denali is North America's tallest peak.

Harbor and on the remote, windy Pribilof Islands, where millions of seabirds and more than half the world's fur seals congregate to breed.

In Arctic Alaska, people are outnumbered by the caribou that migrate en masse between their winter ranges and summer breeding grounds. Small planes are the only way to travel between remote communities that still hold deep roots in traditional Native ways, and dog sleds are still a viable mode of winter transportation, although the iron dog—the snowmobile to anyone else, but "snowmachine" to Alaskans—reigns supreme.

As amazing, exotic, and even otherworldly as Alaska's pristine landscapes may be, our "peoplescapes" are just as special. Alaskans are known for being warm and friendly despite—or perhaps because of—our cold winter temperatures.

Believe it or not, the number of people who visit Alaska every year is more than double our year-round residents. Over one million people visit during the summer alone, and winter vacations in Alaska are starting to catch up in popularity as brave tourists come to see the Iditarod or watch the northern lights dancing in the night sky. We never get tired of seeing people who genuinely enjoy and are awed by their visit to Alaska.

Welcome, and enjoy every moment of your visit to this most remarkable state.

Clockwise from top left: dog sled in Denali National Park; Ketchikan harbor; Santa Claus House, North Pole; foxglove flowers.

NORTH POLE
SANTA'S WORKSHOP
LF & REINDEER LODGE
NORTH POLE

15 TOP EXPERIENCES

1 **Bear Viewing:** Seeing a bear is a guaranteed adrenaline rush (page 31). Visitors have their choice of excellent viewing areas such as **Katmai National Park and Preserve** (page 332), **Admiralty Island** (page 96), and **Sitka's Fortress of the Bear** (page 83).

2 Whale Watching: Don't miss the **orcas** and **humpback whales** in Southeast, especially **Frederick Sound** (page 74).

3 Glaciers: Visit active glaciers while you still can: **Mendenhall** (page 95), **LeConte** (page 73), **Matanuska** (page 163), and **Columbia** (page 228).

4 **Northern Lights:** The dancing aurora borealis lights up Alaska's nighttime skies (page 39).

5 Native Culture: Learn about Alaska's eleven Native cultures and see them alive today (page 50 and page 133).

6 Iditarod: Be a spectator of Alaska's great race at the ceremonial start and the official restart (page 143), or the finish line (page 364).

7 **Denali National Park & Preserve:** Check out the highest peak in North America and the 6-million-acre park around it (page 263).

8 **Hiking, Camping, and Backpacking:** Looking for a wilderness adventure? Start at **Caines Head State Recreation Area** (page 187), **Hatcher Pass** (page 160) or anywhere in the **Southeast** (page 84).

9 **Alaskan Towns:** These wonderful small towns re-define quirky (page 29).

10 Gold Rush History: Visit **Klondike Gold Rush National Historical Park** in Skagway (page 108) or pan for gold with **Gold Daughters** in Fairbanks (page 294).

<<<

11 Wildlife Viewing: Already seen bears and whales? How about **moose** (page 393), **eagles** (page 117), or even **walrus** (page 341)?

>>>

12 Scenic Drives: The best way to see some of Alaska's most beautiful places is on a road trip. Check out the **Seward Highway** (page 167) or scenic highways starting in **Tok** (page 311).

<<<

13 Fishing: Find spectacular fishing throughout the state, but especially in **Homer** (page 215), **Valdez** (page 229), **Petersburg** (page 74), and on **the Kenai River** (page 203).

14 Flightseeing: Take to the air to fully appreciate the incredible Alaskan landscape and majestic **Denali** (page 271).

15 Kayaking: Paddle through the **Columbia Glacier**'s ice field (page 229), the protected waters of **Prince William Sound** (page 176), or **Glacier Bay National Park** (page 106).

Planning Your Trip

Where to Go

Juneau and Southeast Alaska

The lush, temperate rainforest and mild climate of Southeast Alaska's island communities turn outdoor excursions into *Jurassic Park*-style adventures. With waters rich for fishing and whale-watching, and tall trees perfect for ziplining, it's wildly popular with both cruise ship passengers and independent travelers, who make use of the ferry system and convenient connections via plane. **Juneau** is not only the transit hub, but also the state capital and gateway to **Glacier Bay National Park,** where the wildlife outnumbers the people. Other popular stops include **Ketchikan,** with its rich mix of Alaska Native cultures, **Skagway,** which is all about the Klondike Gold Rush, **Sitka,** which exhibits the influence of Russian settlers, and authentic fishing towns like **Wrangell** and **Petersburg.**

Anchorage and Southcentral Alaska

With a population of about 300,000, **Anchorage** contains almost half the state's population and offers a breadth of urban amenities. Go kayaking, hiking, or even flightseeing by day then enjoy big-city comforts by night. If you want the greatest range of Alaska experiences in the shortest time, this is the place to be—a launch pad for trips

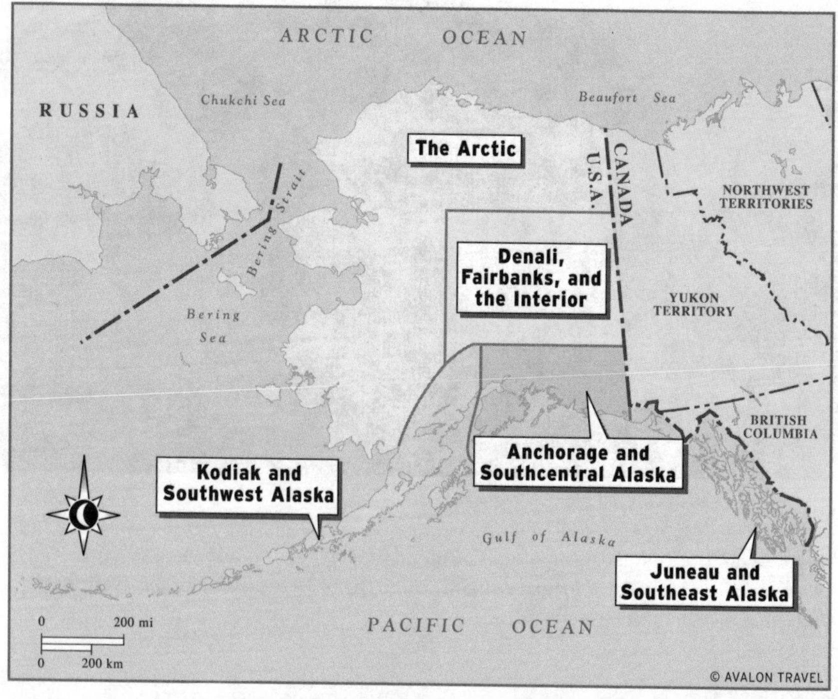

Juneau's downtown harbor

south along the **Kenai Peninsula,** north into the **Matanuska-Susitna Valley,** or east into the spectacular fjords of **Prince William Sound.** Choose from seaside towns like historic **Valdez,** which has survived both the Great Earthquake of 1964 and the *Exxon Valdez;* **Hope,** where hiking and mountain biking await; the cruise port of **Seward,** the fishing meccas **Kenai** and **Soldotna,** and **Homer,** renowned for its thriving art scene.

Denali, Fairbanks, and the Interior

If you want the most varied wildlife-watching, head for **Denali National Park.** You may see Dall sheep, mountain goats, wolves, and maybe even bears here in its wide swaths of untouched wilderness, centered around the highest peak in North America. **Fairbanks** is a fascinating mix of natural history and culture, with everything from Athabascan fiddling and a chance to roam with reindeer. But the busy season is winter, when droves come to see the **northern lights** and quintessentially Alaskan activities like **dog mushing** and **ice art.**

Kodiak and Southwest Alaska

Southwest Alaska's communities are small and remote—so they're perfect for watching wildlife. Alaska's "Emerald Isle," **Kodiak** is popular for **bear-viewing** tours to nearby **Katmai National Park;** it also has a rich Alaska Native heritage. Farther west, **Dillingham** offers unparalleled fishing at the head of the world's most famous **salmon** fishery, **Bristol Bay.** The lush islands of **Dutch Harbor/Unalaska** are a **birder** and **eco-tourist**'s paradise. The **Pribilof Islands** contain some of the state's richest coastline, dotted with colonies of **walruses, seals,** and **seabirds.**

The Arctic

In the **Arctic Circle,** the sun really does vanish for a while in the winter then returns to provide 24-hour light during the summer. This creates an unbelievably lush, short-lived ecosystem. This is also the only part of Alaska where you'll encounter **polar bears.** Remote Arctic communities can be reached only by small plane and preserve deeply rooted **indigenous traditions.**

Travel Lifelines: Roads, Ferries, Planes, and Regional Hubs

one of several water taxis that ferries passengers back and forth across Kachemak Bay

Alaska is more than twice the size of Texas, and our coastline is longer than that of all the other states combined. Yet only 740,000 people live in the entire state. With that few people spread over such a wide area, the lines of transportation and travel are necessarily sparse.

Even our largest cities only have one or two highway links to other communities, part of a road web that extends through Southcentral Alaska and a little bit of the Interior, but not beyond. The rural communities in Western, Southwest, and Arctic Alaska (plus some Interior communities) are off the road system entirely: The only way to get there is by plane or, in a few cases, oceangoing ship.

Alaska's mighty rivers serve as conduits between some of these communities, with boats traveling up and down the rivers in summer. By winter, snowmachines—and sometimes, yes, dog teams—travel the frozen ice that coats the rivers, or range across the land, which becomes much easier to travel once it's covered in snow.

In Southeast, the Alaska Marine Highway System ferries ply the waters between island communities, forming the vital lifeline that keeps people, produce, and everything imaginable—from vehicles to furniture and building materials—moving through the state.

As tenuous as those connections may seem, we make them work. Each region of the state has a hub community, a larger town or city that serves as the center of commerce, travel, and transportation for that part of the state; those hubs, in turn, connect to the state's largest cities, which in turn have the infrastructure for a more robust connection "Outside"—to the world beyond Alaska.

And, truth be told, many of us appreciate the perspective that comes with knowing we live in such a vast, wild state. As inconvenient as our limited connections to the Outside world may sometimes be, they also bring a sense of perspective, togetherness, and belonging. Perhaps that relative isolation is why Alaskans are so good at taking people as they are in the moment and still reliably come to the rescue of someone in need, even in the bigger cities.

Resolution Park in the city of Anchorage

Know Before You Go

High and Low Seasons

High season for most of the state is **mid-June** through **early September.** (In Southeast Alaska, high season starts in May and ends in late September. Southeast's shoulder seasons are April and October.) You'll have the best weather, the richest landscape, most touring and wildlife-viewing opportunities, and the most services available in high seasons—along with the **highest prices.** July and August are the best months for **salmon fishing.**

Save money—and still have a great time—during the **shoulder seasons (May and September).** May is the best time for birding trips. You'll have few to no salmon-fishing options, but **halibut fishing** is good. In Southcentral and Interior Alaska, spring may not start as early as May, but the rainforests of Southeast are always green.

In **Fairbanks,** the high season is actually **winter,** when tourists arrive to watch the **aurora borealis.** The **Iditarod sled dog race** that ends in Nome, draws visitors from all over the world.

Advance Reservations

Book at least **six months ahead** for **high season lodgings** in your price range. If you're aiming for a high-demand lodging, a very small community like Haines, or an annual event like the Iditarod or salmon fishing in July, plan **a year in advance.** The most spectacular **wildlife-viewing opportunities,** such as visiting the Walrus Islands State Game Sanctuary, require you to secure a **permit** that may sell out **nine or more months in advance.**

If you're planning to bring a **car** on the **Alaska state ferry system** or want a cabin **berth,** book as early as possible—**six months or more in advance.** Last-minute **walk-on spots** are almost always available.

Best of Alaska

Because Alaska is so big and the logistics of transport are challenging, it can take three weeks to hit the highlights. To plan a shorter trip, choose one or two regions from the following itinerary.

Plan additional rest time (or time cushions in case of weather delays) into your trip as you think you'll need it.

Southeast

Most Southeast Alaska communities are on islands, so travel takes place almost exclusively by sea or air. Ferries work more like a bus line than a cruise, stopping at each community for just long enough to load and unload passengers, cargo, and cars.

That means that if you choose to disembark, you're committed to staying for at least a couple of days until the next ferry comes through. With that in mind, the following itinerary features more air travel. (Unlike ferries, the planes come and go at regular intervals.)

DAY 1

Arrive by flight (or ferry) to **Ketchikan,** the first port of call for seagoing visitors to Alaska. Ketchikan has the highest concentration of standing **totem poles** of any community in the state, so spend half a day exploring the many parks and museums where they stand. Top the day off with a two-hour **flightseeing** trip to stupendous **Misty Fjords National Monument** (or, if you don't like small planes, go fishing or take the only snorkeling tour in Alaska), then end your day with a stroll along picturesque **Creek Street,** where the historic buildings stand on stilts over a creek that flows right through downtown Ketchikan. Turn in early for a good night's sleep.

DAY 2

If the timing works out for an early-morning ferry, take the six-hour ferry ride to **Wrangell.** If there is no early ferry, catch the morning Alaska Airlines flight to Wrangell instead, then take an afternoon bear-viewing trip to the **Anan Creek Wildlife Observatory.** This special place mostly showcases black bears, but sometimes you'll get to see brown bears fishing here, too. When you get back to Wrangell, take the time to visit the **Chief Shakes Tribal House** (which you can enter for a fee, prior arrangements required) and take the mile-long walk to **Petroglyph Beach State Historic Park,** where ancient petroglyphs are still out in the open. Get an early dinner (the few restaurants in Wrangell all close early) and get an early night's rest at your hotel.

DAY 3

Take the morning flight to **Juneau,** the state's capital and the air transit hub of Southeast Alaska. This should leave you time to check into your hotel and stop by the spectacular **Walter Soboleff Center** in downtown Juneau, then

If You Have...

One week: Spend your time in Southeast, where you can experience a condensed version of all the things that make Alaska great: beautiful scenery, rich wildlife, Native culture and art, friendly people, and small, authentic, hard-working communities.

Two weeks: Combine a week in Southeast with either Southcentral or Interior Alaska for the second week. If you're most interested in fishing, hiking, more coastal cruises, or sampling Alaska's best food, head for Southcentral. If you want to learn more about gold rush history, see the northern lights, or tour Denali National Park, head for the Interior.

Three weeks: Follow the three-week itinerary or consider adding excursions to Southwest Alaska or the Arctic.

along Ketchikan's famous Creek Street

catch a shuttle bus—or rent a car—and visit the beautiful **Mendenhall Glacier.** Many visitors also love riding the **Mount Roberts Tramway** in downtown Juneau, which carries you 1,800 feet up Mount Roberts to walking trails, a small gift shop, and beautiful views over Juneau and the Gastineau Channel, which runs between Juneau and the neighboring island suburb of Douglas. The tramway runs later into the evening than the shuttle buses to the glacier, so leave it for last.

DAY 4

On your second day in Juneau, take a big adventure. For most people, this will be a one-day **bear-viewing** tour to nearby **Admiralty Island,** which has the densest population of **brown bears** in the world, as well as one of the longest bear-viewing seasons. If you're intent on seeing these massive, shaggy, and beautiful apex predators, this is one of the best places to do it. If you'd rather see humpback whales—also known as the ballerinas of the seas—go **whale-watching** instead. Southeast is the only place in the world where you might get to see humpback whales bubble-net feeding, a cooperative behavior in which several whales work together to "round up" a school of fish in a net made of air bubbles, then lunge up through the middle of the net to gulp the fish down.

DAY 5

Leave Juneau for an overnight trip to **Skagway.** Take the five-hour ferry ride (a jet is not an option here, although you could book a small plane shuttle) and spend an afternoon in the **Klondike Gold Rush National Historical Park.** There are lots of historical buildings and shops to explore, some lovely day hikes in the area, an interesting brothel tour in the **Red Onion Saloon,** and a dinner theater show, **The Days of '98 Show.** Spending the night here will give you a little bit of a rest day, plus a chance to take a scenic train ride in the morning.

DAY 6

Take a morning tour on the historic, narrow-gauge **White Pass & Yukon Route Railroad,** then head back to Juneau on the ferry. If your ferry gets into Juneau early, you can squeeze in one more short day tour (try **fishing, kayaking,**

Klondike Gold Rush National Historical Park

or **ziplining**), or spend the afternoon browsing the wonderful locally owned shops downtown. End your day by hopping an evening flight from Juneau to the gorgeous island community of **Sitka.**

DAY 7

Spend the day exploring **Sitka National Historical Park,** which has many beautiful totem poles and a **cultural center** where you can meet and chat with Alaska Native artisans. There are also many **historical Russian buildings** scattered throughout town; they're run as **mini museums** and are typically open during business hours. Spend the night here.

DAY 8

Take a rest day or, if you're still feeling energetic, book a **whale-watching** or **fishing** trip, or explore some of Sitka's wonderful **hiking trails.** Take the evening flight from Sitka to Anchorage.

Anchorage and Southcentral

Southcentral is the heart of Alaska's rudimentary road system, which means it's much easier to get around on your own schedule. That said, the distances between towns often come as a huge surprise to visitors—for example, it takes most people eight hours to drive from Anchorage to Fairbanks. If you don't want to rent a car, there is usually limited shuttle service between communities along the Kenai Peninsula (see *Transportation* in each community listing for details), although that will force you to extend your itinerary by at least a couple of days to accommodate the shuttle schedules.

DAY 9

Visit the **Anchorage Museum at Rasmuson Center** and the **Alaska Native Heritage Center;** you can easily spend most of the day at these two sights. Top it off by renting a bike and pedaling the 11-mile **Tony Knowles Coastal Trail** to Kincaid Park, where you have very good chances of seeing a **moose,** then enjoy dinner in one of Anchorage's excellent restaurants before you turn in for the night.

DAY 10

Get up early to rent a car, if you haven't already, and make the scenic five- to six-hour drive (depending on traffic and photo/rest stops) to **Homer** for some of the state's best food, fishing, and art, all in one place. Once you get to Homer check into your hotel and spend the afternoon exploring the **Homer Spit,** a narrow, four-mile peninsula containing some of the state's best art galleries, gift shops, and restaurants. Don't forget to stop by the iconic **Salty Dawg Saloon** to pin your signed dollar bill to the wall.

DAY 11

Start your second day in Homer at the small but spectacular **Pratt Museum,** then take a stroll along **Bishop's Beach,** which is much nicer for walking and less crowded than the Spit. Your options for the rest of the day include a **fishing or sea kayaking trip** or, if you're more of a landlubber, take **a guided nature tour** across Kachemak Bay with the Center for Alaskan Coastal Studies. But don't miss the chance to take the 5pm *Danny J* ferry to **Halibut Cove** (this is a small, private ferry, not an Alaska Marine Highway System ferry), where you can have dinner in the world-famous **Saltry Restaurant** before heading back to Homer for another night.

DAY 12

Get up early for the 4.5-hour drive to **Seward.** Once there, take a half-day **sightseeing, whale-watching,** and **wildlife viewing cruise** through beautiful **Kenai Fjords National Park.** If you're here in very early spring, this is one of your best chances for seeing migrating **gray whales**—but, as always, nothing is guaranteed. The captain will usually point out the ruins of old World War II coastal emplacements, too, although you can't get very close to them from the water. Stay in Seward for the night.

DAY 13

You have two missions today: One, stop by the **Alaska SeaLife Center** and take a **behind-the-scenes tour** so you can get up close and personal with the **animals** at this education, conservation, and rehabilitation center for all manner of aquatic wildlife, from octopi to sea lions and seabirds. Two, take a half-day tour to **Caines Head State Recreation Area.** You'll paddle kayaks out to the beach, then take a moderate hike to explore the old WWII-era **Fort McGilvray.** Finally, make the three-hour drive north to Anchorage and spend the night there.

the Salty Dawg Saloon

Interior Alaska

Interior Alaska is a mix of easy road access (primarily to Fairbanks, Alaska's second largest city) and remote communities, like the tiny, traditional village of Anaktuvuk Pass, which can only be reached by air. Gold-mining history, the wonderful day tours out of Fairbanks, and the sheer experience of exploring a remote part of the state tend to be the biggest draws here, although in the last few years Fairbanks has really come into its own as a hip, happening place to be, with lots of food, art, and music for city-minded visitors to enjoy.

DAY 14

There's no rush today, as long as you make the 2.5-hour drive north from Anchorage to quirky little **Talkeetna** in time to spend the afternoon exploring the shops along Main Street. Go ahead and spend the night there to enjoy the way Talkeetna turns back to its quaint, quirky self once the tourist buses leave. There's often great live music at the **Fairview Inn.**

DAY 15

Drive another 2.5 hours north to **Denali National Park and Preserve** and spend the day exploring the park's three **visitor centers,** touring the park's working **sled dog kennels,** and either day **hiking** or taking a short **day tour** in the park; your options include **horseback riding, ATV tours, flightseeing, white-water rafting,** and ranger-guided **hikes.** Turn in early at your hotel or campground near the park entrance—tomorrow will be a long day!

the ice museum at Chena Hot Springs Resort

DAY 16

Take a **shuttle bus ride** into the park. You can choose between shuttle buses that drive the entire length of the 92-mile road or just part of it. Make sure you have your binoculars handy and camera ready for great **wildlife and landscape photo ops.** Once the adventure is over, turn in for a good night's sleep and another early start the next day.

DAY 17

Make the 2.5-hour drive north to **Fairbanks** and check out a few of its best attractions. Stop by **Gold Daughters** to try your hand at Fairbanks's most **authentic gold-panning** experience, then visit the **Pipeline Viewing Station,** which is just across the highway, for an up close and personal view of one of the state's most impressive engineering accomplishments. Then spend 2.5 hours on an astonishingly fun nature walk among a herd of reindeer at **Running Reindeer Ranch** before you cap off the evening by catching the hilarious **Golden Heart Revue dinner show** in the Alaska-themed **Pioneer Park.**

DAY 18

Choose between a relaxing day trip to **Chena Hot Springs Resort** (about 60 miles east of Fairbanks) or exploring a remote stretch of **Interior Alaska.** Your options include booking a day tour to the nearby village of **Anaktuvuk Pass** (which includes a flight in a small plane); riding along on a bush mail flight with Warbelow's Air; or booking a fly/drive adventure up the **Dalton Highway,** AKA the Haul Road, north of the Arctic Circle. Settle into your Fairbanks hotel as early as possible; you'll make another long drive tomorrow.

DAY 19

In the morning, stop by downtown Fairbanks and do a little shopping, then visit the gleefully kitschy **Santa Claus House** in **North Pole, Alaska** (about 20 minutes outside of Fairbanks) as you start your **six-hour drive** southeast to **Valdez.** This small community of about 4,000 people has seen many of Alaska's most historic moments, from the gold rush to the Great Earthquake of 1964 and the *Exxon Valdez* oil spill in 1989. Make sure you stop to take in **Worthington Glacier,**

Bridal Veil Falls, and **Horsetail Falls** on the way into town.

Back to Southcentral

DAY 20

Take a boat tour from Valdez to the massive **Columbia Glacier,** one of the largest and most active tidewater glaciers in the world. If you'd rather, you can book a kayaking tour to paddle through the glacier's massive ice field, but you won't get as close to the glacier's face.

DAY 21

Stop by the **Valdez Museum;** it's easy to spend the whole morning here and at the **Valdez Museum on Hazelet.** Make sure to ask about the scale models of **Old Town Valdez.** You'll pass a marked turnoff for the Old Town Valdez townsite on your way back out of town. It's about a six-hour drive back to Anchorage (or Fairbanks) to catch your flight back home tomorrow.

TOP EXPERIENCE

Alaska's Top Towns

Every Alaska town is surrounded by spectacular natural beauty. But it's their determinedly individual and often quirky nature, combined with a hardworking ethic that kicks into overdrive during our long summer days that really makes them special.

SOUTHEAST

Petersburg was founded by Norwegian fishermen. It remains a hardworking fishing community to this day, and visitors love that authenticity and the lack of the glitzy shops that often accompany cruise ports (page 72).

Ketchikan houses the state's highest concentration of totem poles and an impressive stretch of local shops and artists overlooking picturesque Creek Street, where the historical houses stand on stilts over the water (page 48).

Sitka is a beautiful port city with locally owned shops, great fishing and whale-watching, and a phenomenal historical park where you can walk the trails among totem poles or visit with Alaska Native artisans as they demonstrate their art. Don't forget to visit the many historical Russian buildings in town too, which are maintained as mini museums (page 80).

SOUTHCENTRAL

Valdez is one of the most pleasant small towns in Alaska, with some of the state's prettiest scenery, biggest history and friendliest people all in one place. This is as close as you can get to rural Alaska without leaving the road system (page 222).

Homer packs some of the state's best artists, food, and fishing all into one place, along with the highest density of water taxis that I've ever seen. The small, isolated seaside communities of Seldovia and Halibut Cove are just a short boat ride away (page 211).

Seward is sometimes characterized as "a drinking town with a fishing problem." For many visitors, it's the perfect mix of tourist amenities, beautiful seaside scenery, and just a few city comforts. There are also some interesting World War II artifacts within a short boat ride and hike of the town (page 181).

INTERIOR

Talkeetna remains the idealized standard of quirky Alaska towns. Visitors often come here just to wander Main Street, but don't miss out on a chance to ride the fabled Hurricane Turn Train or take a flightseeing trip around 20,210-foot Denali (page 252).

SOUTHWEST

Kodiak feels like a gritty big city set in island paradise—but if you love fishing or bears, this charming town, with clusters of wonderful shops and restaurants, is the place to be. The helicopter flightseeing over Alaska's Emerald Isle is absolutely breathtaking (page 321).

ARCTIC

Nome, the most cosmopolitan town in the region, is worth a visit to see the Iditarod finish in March. By summer, this is a lovely community for birding and driving the scenic roads (page 360).

Best Hikes

The hiking is phenomenal throughout Alaska, but the deeper you go into the wilderness, the higher the level of skill and preparation you'll need. Here are the best hikes that combine scenery, interesting terrain, and reasonable access all in one.

Southeast Alaska

Petersburg has some lovely **remote hiking trails** that can be accessed by water taxi. One of the toughest—but also one of the most beautiful—is the **Cascade Creek Trail,** which runs 4.1 miles between the seaside public-use Cascade Creek Cabin and Falls Lake, poised high above the shoreline in the temperate rainforest.

Most of the hiking in **Tongass National Forest,** which essentially covers Southeast Alaska, offers a similar feel: The trails are beautiful but remote, and you need either a car or a water taxi to get to most of them. Some of the most beautiful exceptions include the trails near **Mendenhall Glacier** in **Juneau** (the crowds dissipate once you walk a mile or two) and the lovely 3.5-mile (one-way) **Perseverance Trail,** which includes a turnoff to a viewing point over **Ebner Falls.**

Some of **Ketchikan**'s best hikes include the **Deer Mountain Trail,** an out-and-back hike into the alpine that skilled and well-prepared hikers can turn into a 14-mile traverse, and the milder 4.8-mile **Lunch Creek Trail.**

Finally, **Sitka** has a ridiculous number of hiking trails in comparison to its population, although you'll need to hire a water taxi to get to some of them. Local favorites include the **Indian River Trail** (4.5 miles one-way), whose trailhead you can reach on the community bus line; the pretty walk to **Mosquito Cove** (just 1.5 miles, but you can link it up with other trails); and the stiff climb up **Mount Verstovia** (2.5 miles one-way).

Southcentral Alaska

The **Lost Lake Trail** near **Seward** is a 15-mile thru-hike with some of the most beautiful scenery you'll ever see. Lost Lake itself (at about the midway point) is the highlight, and you can easily spend one or two nights simply exploring the rolling tundra and other lakes nearby.

The **Mineral Creek Trail** in **Valdez** offers a 12.2-mile round-trip stroll to an old stamp mill, but it's the spectacular scenery—lush, *Jurassic*

path leading into lush and green rainforest in Tongass National Forest

Bear Viewing

a black bear at Anan Creek Wildlife Observatory near Wrangell

You'll find bears all over Alaska, but the ideal place for a bear-viewing trip is a coastal location where food is plentiful and the human presence is carefully managed.

The plentiful food means bears tolerate each other—and us—much more easily, while managing the human presence means we become predictable to the bears, so they're less likely to see us as a threat or anything interesting at all. That's safer for both us and the bears, and also means we get to see them acting naturally.

The most iconic destination for bear viewing is **Katmai National Park and Preserve** in Southwest Alaska. You'll also find the famous **McNeil River State Game Sanctuary** and **Lake Clark National Park** here.

But these are far from the only places you can go to see brown bears playing, tending their young, and feeding on fish. A day van tour out of Kodiak (the city) gives you very good opportunities of seeing at least one or two bears, while a multiday trip to the remote **Kodiak Brown Bear Center,** on the other end of Kodiak (the island) lets you observe the largest brown bears in the world in a small-group setting.

Bear viewing is also a popular activity in Southeast Alaska. **Admiralty Island,** near Juneau, has one of the world's highest concentrations of **brown bears;** in fact, the bears outnumber the humans. If you'd rather see bears in a somewhat more controlled setting, **Sitka's Fortress of the Bear** is an educational center that rescues orphaned bears (at the time of this writing, it has eight resident bears).

Black bears are plentiful in Southeast too, and although they're smaller and not quite as brazen as brown bears, viewing them is a thrill too. Sometimes you'll even get to see that rarest of sights: black and brown bears fishing together, both lured by plentiful **salmon runs.** Some of the best places for black bear viewing are **Anan Creek Wildlife Observatory** near Wrangell, plus a few lesser-known places on **Prince of Wales Island.**

If you want to see **polar bears,** there is a chance you might see them at **Point Barrow,** near the Arctic city of Barrow. But your very best chance of spotting a polar bear is on a trip to the tiny village of **Kaktovik** in the **Arctic National Wildlife Refuge.**

Park-worthy greenery dotted with frothy waterfalls—that really makes it stand out. You can shorten the hike by a few miles if you're comfortable driving on the rough, unmaintained road, which also doubles as a trail, or if you hitch a ride on a passing ATV.

Perhaps the best short hike in the state, the 5-mile **Portage Pass Trail** out of **Whittier** offers stunning views almost from the word "go," with the glacier on one side and shimmering Passage Canal on the other. Although there are a few challenging spots with uneven footing, most reasonably active individuals can make it up to the top without too much trouble.

If you want to feel like you're on a grand adventure without going too far from civilization, take a water taxi across Kachemak Bay from Homer and hike the 3.2-mile (one-way) **Grewingk Glacier Trail,** where you can picnic at the edge of a glacial lake while hardly breaking a sweat on the way in. For a little bit more of a challenge, hike out via the moderate to challenging **Saddle Trail,** which is only another mile long. (You'll have to arrange for the water taxi to pick you up at the Saddle trailhead.)

Hatcher Pass, north of Wasilla and Palmer, offers some of the best "drive-up tundra" hiking you'll find anywhere in the state. Because you can get up above treeline—or very close to it—before you even leave your car, you're treated to sweeping vistas that extend for miles. **April Bowl** (2.5 miles round-trip) and the 11-mile round-trip hike to the beautiful blue-green **Reed Lakes** are two of the best hikes here.

For visitors willing to brave the rough, unpaved 60-mile road in to McCarthy (Southcentral Alaska), the 4-mile round-trip hike out to the **Root Glacier** is absolutely splendid. Although you can go by yourself, it's great fun to hire one of the local guide services, which can take you hiking on the glacier itself or even **ice climbing.**

Southwest Alaska

For most visitors, unguided hiking around Kodiak—the largest city in Southwest Alaska—isn't a great idea because of the profusion of bears. You're better off taking a guided van tour for bear viewing, or walking the trails in **Fort Abercrombie State Historical Park,** which is full of World War II relics.

Unalaska, on the other hand, is a real haven for hikers who might be concerned about bears—because there aren't any! Consider making the 2.2-mile (one-way) hike up **Mount Ballyhoo** in the **Aleutian World War II National Historic Area,** or the 3-mile round-trip trek on the **Peace of Mind Trail** to **Beaver Inlet,** on the far side of the island. Remember that you'll need to purchase a **land-use permit** from the Ounalashka Corporation, which owns this land, before you set out.

Interior Alaska

At first glance, Fairbanks seems to be lost in rolling hills covered with trees. But you'll find a few very picturesque hikes here, including the 15-mile loop around **Granite Tors,** a series of unusual granite towers that are slowly being revealed as the earth is etched away around them, and the 3.7-mile loop to **Angel Rocks.**

trail in Fort Abercrombie State Historical Park

Best Scenic Drives

Alaska doesn't have many roads, but what it lacks in quantity is made up for in quality. Each of the following drives showcases Alaska's natural beauty. And often, the destination at the end of the road is every bit as interesting as the journey it took to get there.

These are all one-way drives. That means you'll have to retrace your route on the return trip, but that's hardly a problem. After living here for almost 30 years, I can tell you that the only thing better than taking these beautiful drives once is taking them twice.

Southcentral Alaska

SEWARD HIGHWAY

127 MILES

The coastal drive from **Anchorage to Seward** snakes along the coastline before ascending **Turnagain Pass** and eventually winding back to sea level through a series of beautiful—and enormous—alpine lakes.

Hatcher Pass

60 MILES

The inland drive from **Anchorage to Hatcher Pass** does take you through some pretty scenery, but it's the last 15 miles, which follow the winding, tree-lined **Little Susitna River** before bursting into the tundra where you can see for miles, that are really the most beautiful.

Valdez

257 MILES

The drive to **Valdez** is arguably the most beautiful. It takes about six hours to get there from either Fairbanks or Anchorage, and while the first couple hundred miles are pretty, it's the last 26-mile drive through **Thompson Pass** and **Keystone Canyon**—which helps earn Valdez its nickname as **"land of the waterfalls"**—that will really take your breath away.

looking down above Hatcher Pass

Interior Alaska

TOP OF THE WORLD HIGHWAY

185 MILES

Open seasonally, the **Top of the World Highway** runs 185 miles (about a six-hour drive) north from **Tok** and east into Canada's **Dawson City.** For real road-trip cred, make this an enormous loop by driving south to **Whitehorse** and then coming back on the **Alcan Highway,** for a total loop distance of about 900 miles or 20 hours of driving. Along the way, you'll see plenty of beautiful scenery, of course, but this sort of drive is more for the pleasure—and pride—of saying you've done it.

The Alaska Railroad

The **Alaska Railroad** is a viable means of moving between the communities of Anchorage, Seward, Whittier, Talkeetna, and Fairbanks. Taking the train might be a little slower than a car, but you're free to sit back and take in the scenery with no worries about construction or traffic delays.

Also, whether by accident or design, the rails occasionally diverge from the roadway and give you a glimpse of something special, such as the incomparable **Spencer Glacier Whistle Stop** on the train from Seward to Anchorage.

Although it's not a point-to-point train, the **Hurricane Turn Train** out of Talkeetna is another perennial favorite with both tourists and locals. The Hurricane Turn Train combines lighthearted, tourist-friendly narration with very practical flag stop service to a few small, isolated communities. It also serves as a "bus" for locals who are heading out to remote cabins or other areas to hunt, paddle, or camp.

But that's not all the Alaska Railroad has going for it. It also runs **specialty trains** that cater to locals but can be a lot of fun for visitors, too. They include a **ski train**—a chartered train to go cross-country skiing in the backcountry—a **girls' night out train,** a **blues train** with live music and an overnight stay in Seward, a **beer train,** and a **Halloween train** that includes an overnight stay at the delightful Alyeska Resort. Check alaskarailroad.com for more information on these and the other Alaska Railroad trains, and if you're coming for a special event train, book well ahead of time; they always sell out.

Alaska Railroad in Seward

The Inside Passage

The Inside Passage is the most popular destination in Alaska for cruise ships. The island communities, beautiful landscape, and great whale-watching are all custom-made for travel by sea.

But not everybody is cut out for cruise ship life. Independent travelers can take the Alaska Marine Highway System ferries through Southeast instead.

Here's a sample of what a (mostly) ferry-based Southeast itinerary might look like, starting with your arrival in Ketchikan after either a short plane ride from Seattle, Washington or a two-day ferry ride from Bellingham, Washington.

Day 1

Check into your hotel in Ketchikan and spend the day touring the town's more than 80 totem poles, including the lovely **Totem Bight State Historical Park** (almost 10 miles northwest of downtown—you can get there on the bus). You can also take a short drive or bus ride to nearby Saxman and watch master carvers at work. Take your lunch break at **The Point,** a lovely waterside café/art gallery with light fare like sandwiches, quiches, and cookies, and stop in at the **Southeast Alaska Discovery Center** on Main Street before it closes in the late afternoon, then snag dinner in the **Heen Kahidi Dining Room and Lounge** at the Cape Fox Lodge. Ask for a table with a view.

Day 2

Start your second day in Ketchikan with a couple of adventures. Your options include a saltwater or freshwater fishing trip, sea kayaking, day hiking, ziplining, flightseeing over spectacular **Misty Fjords National Monument,** or, believe it or not, snorkeling. You'll have time for two shorter adventures or one long day trip for kayaking or fishing. If you're a reality-TV buff, book a half-day **Bering Sea Crab Fishermen's Tour** aboard the *Aleutian Ballad*, which you may recognize from the early seasons of the Discovery Channel reality TV show *The Deadliest Catch*. Once the excitement is over, kick back and relax: You can get a good

one of the totem poles at Totem Bight State Historical Park

seafood dinner in the cozy little **New York Café,** which has an old-timey speakeasy feel, or snag casual Asian-American food with a waterfront view at the **Waterfront Restaurant,** then head for the **Sourdough Bar & Liquor Store** to scope out the shipwreck photos or play a game of pool.

Day 3

Before leaving Ketchikan, take a stroll along historic **Creek Street,** set on pilings above the creek, and prepare for your six-hour ferry trip to Wrangell. The ferry schedule varies so much, it's hard to say when you'll be arriving in Wrangell, so it's best to call your travel day a rest day, too. Day hiking or walking near the harbor or strolling along Creek Street are both great ways to fill your day until it's time to leave Ketchikan. Don't forget to shop for a few souvenirs, too; Ketchikan, Juneau, and Sitka offer the best shopping in Southeast.

Day 4

On your first full day in Wrangell, snag an early breakfast at the **Diamond C Cafe** and then head for the city docks—right in the middle of town—where you can hop on a boat bound for the remarkable **Anan Creek Wildlife Observatory.** The observatory allows you to watch and photograph black bears—and sometimes brown bears, too—feeding on salmon. That's not the brown stream bottom you're seeing; that's the backs of thousands of salmon massing to make their run upstream. Restaurants close early in Wrangell, so grab dinner early. **Zak's Cafe,** which offers at least one seafood option in its rotating menu every day, is a favorite.

Day 5

Make the easy one-mile stroll (or drive) from downtown Wrangell to **Petroglyph Beach State Historic Park,** where you can see ancient rock petroglyphs still lying in the open on the beach. On the far end of town, you'll find the historic **Chief Shakes Tribal House,** which you can enter for a fee and with advance notice. Then hop on the ferry for a three-hour ride to **Petersburg** through the winding Wrangell Narrows. If the ferry comes early in the day, you'll have time to snag dinner at the **Joan Mei** restaurant, a local favorite just across from the ferry terminal that serves Chinese food. From there, it's a pleasant one-mile walk, drive, or cab ride into Petersburg, where, if it's still early, you can wander the

getting up close and personal with humpback whales aboard Whale Song Cruises out of Petersburg

surprisingly picturesque streets and take pictures in front of the totem poles outside city hall. If you're feeling tired, turn in early to rest up before your whale-watching tour the next day.

Day 6

In Petersburg, book an all-day **whale-watching** tour to Frederick Sound, which boasts an unbelievable profusion of humpback whales feeding and playing. The small boat harbor, which is where you'll board your tour, sits right up against downtown Petersburg. Some day trips also include kayaking and a short hike. Once the tour's over, you should still have time to snag dinner at **Inga's Galley** (it's a modest setting, but the seafood is great), then stroll Petersburg's main street, fittingly called Nordic Drive, and do a little shopping.

Day 7

While you're still in Petersburg, be sure to visit the magnificent tidewater **LeConte Glacier;** it's a half-day tour by small boat out of the Petersburg harbor. Once you're back in town you'll have plenty of time to visit the Sons of Norway hall and the fishermen's monument and dragonboat *Valhalla,* both of which are very close to the harbor, then walk up the hill to the **Clausen Memorial Museum,** which documents the early days of this Norwegian-founded settlement. Tomorrow's ferry ride to Juneau often comes at odd hours, so don't be shy about turning in early to rest up.

Day 8

Make the eight-hour ferry trip north to Juneau. Keep your eye out for more humpback whales as you pass through Frederick Sound again! If your ferry gets in early, you'll have time to get a head start on browsing some of downtown Juneau's many excellent gift shops. (Watch out for Franklin Street near the cruise shop docks—there are a few local shops there, but most are not locally owned.) You also have several great dinner options along Seward Street, including Mexican fusion cuisine at **V's Cellar Door** or fusion cuisine built on locally harvested seasonal ingredients at **The Rookery.**

From this point on, you have several options. You can continue exploring Southeast by catching an Alaska Airlines jet to Sitka or taking the ferry to Haines, Skagway, or Gustavus (which is the gateway to the spectacular, wild waters of Glacier Bay National Park). You can also reach Haines, Skagway, and Gustavus by small plane (there is no jet service in either community).

Day 9

While in Juneau, book a bear-viewing day tour to nearby **Admiralty Island,** which has the highest concentration of brown bears on the planet. You'll get there by floatplane, and the trip lasts 6-8 hours. If you still have energy once you get back, you can finish exploring the many wonderful shops that are just past "cruise ship alley" in downtown Juneau. Again, your nicest dinner options are on Seward Street, but if you're feeling adventurous, hike up the hill to **Gourmet Grub,** a tiny hole-in-the-wall restaurant with the best pelmeni (Russian dumplings/ravioli) I've ever had. Want some nightlife? Head to the turn-of-the-20th-century bar in the **Alaskan Hotel** for live music late on a weekend night, or hit the iconic **Red Dog Saloon.**

Day 10

On your last day in Juneau, spend the morning at the lovely **Mendenhall Glacier.** If you drive yourself, there's a $5 admission fee; if you take one of the shuttle buses from the cruise docks, admission is included in the price of your ticket. If you enjoy the adrenaline rush of heights, Juneau also has a very popular **zipline.** From this point on, you can choose one or more of the following multi-day excursions to round out your two-week trip through Southeast.

Excursion: Haines or Skagway

Take a four-hour ferry ride to **Haines,** where you can take a day or two to soak up some of Alaska's most beautiful scenery in a laid-back small-town setting. You can also take a cultural tour in the nearby Chilkat Indian village of Klukwan, and if you're here between October and February, you can see thousands of eagles congregating in the open waters of the **Alaska Chilkat Bald Eagle Preserve.**

If you want a little more excitement than Haines has to offer, head to **Skagway** instead, which is a one-hour ferry ride from Haines or a five-hour ferry ride from Juneau. (The ferry often stops in Haines on the way, but it isn't there long enough for you to get out and explore.) The biggest attractions in Skagway are the bustling boardwalks of the **Klondike Gold Rush National Historical Park** and a scenic ride on the historic **White Pass & Yukon Route Railroad.** If the ferry times line up just right, you can do both activities with a one-night stay in Skagway. If you're in a real rush, you can also catch a small plane back to Juneau.

Once you're done in either town, the ferry can take you back to Juneau where you can continue onward (or home). Or, if you've brought your vehicle with you on the ferry, you can make the long drive north across the border into Canada, then west to cross the border back into Alaska. Haines and Skagway are the only two Southeast communities connected to the continental road system, and the distance is nothing to sneeze at: It's 440 miles of beautiful scenery from Haines to Tok, and 495 miles from Skagway to Tok.

Excursion: Gustavus and Glacier Bay National Park

Hop a small plane to the small community of **Gustavus,** or take a five-hour ferry ride, and spend a few days lounging in a wilderness lodge and taking boat or kayak tours into the wild and remote waters of **Glacier Bay National Park.** Be warned that there are no ATMs or banks in Gustavus, and you'll get most of your food from your hotel or lodge. You'll have just a few tour companies to choose from, but the offerings, including half-day whale-watching cruises and half- or full-day trips for kayaking and fishing, are all phenomenal.

When you're ready, head back to Juneau aboard a ferry or small plane and plan your travels (or trip home) from there.

Excursion: Sitka

There are three ways to get to **Sitka.** Many cruise ships stop here, and you can also get here by ferry from Juneau, although it's about a 10-hour ride aboard a regular ferry. Fast ferry service is only sometimes available from Juneau to Sitka, so the easiest way to get here is often by plane.

Once you reach Sitka you can easily spend half a day exploring **Sitka National Historical Park,** which has three parts: outdoor trails through the forest with totem poles at intervals; a visitor center that houses a museum and educational exhibits about totem poles; and the **Southeast Alaska Indian Cultural Center,** where you can watch master crafters demonstrate their traditional arts. The setting is small and intimate, so you can also ask them questions or get a close-up look at what they're doing. Your other activity for the day should be a 2.5-hour cultural tour led by Sitka Tribal Tours, which might come with an opportunity to watch traditional Tlingit dancing at the **Sheet'ka Kwaan Naa Kahídi Community House** ("The community house for the people of Sitka"). Get a weekday dinner at the Larkspur Cafe or snag pizza, wings, and salad at the new local favorite **Mean Queen.**

If you have a second day to spend in Sitka, consider making a morning trip to the **Fortress of the Bear,** a nonprofit educational center that houses orphaned bear cubs until they can be transferred to another sanctuary. There are also historical Russian buildings in town that are maintained as mini museums, including the **Russian Bishop's House** and the 1848 **St. Michael the Archangel Cathedral.** As you're waiting on your flight out of the Sitka airport, grab a slice of pie at **The Nugget** restaurant (it's in the airport, before security). The cream pies are very good.

You can either fly back to Juneau or Ketchikan to continue your adventures in Southeast, fly to Anchorage or Fairbanks to explore Southcentral or the Interior, or catch one of the two nonstop flights from Sitka to Seattle as you work your way back home.

Chasing the Northern Lights

the northern lights over the ice museum at Chena Hot Springs

The enchanting phenomenon known as the northern lights, or aurora borealis, is caused by charged particles from the sun striking Earth's atmosphere. The lights occupy an important place in the legends and mythology of every culture that evolved under their gaze. They've been viewed as healing spirits, the dancing spirits of our ancestors, animal spirits dancing in the sky, or human spirits playing ball.

Whatever their spiritual implications, the northern lights are beautiful. Even longtime residents will rush outside in their pajamas if a friend calls or texts to say the lights are shining. Unfortunately the lights are unpredictable and only visible when skies are dark and clear (**October through April** are the best months), so there's no guarantee you'll see them while you're here—but if you take three or four days and use the following tips, you'll have great odds:

- **Plan your visit in Nome, Fairbanks, or a community farther north (like Barrow);** all three are at a high enough latitude to see the lights overhead. You might still see the lights in more southerly parts of Alaska, but they're more likely to shine low on the horizon and may even be blocked by mountains.

- **Get as far away as you can from the city lights and any other light pollution.** The darker the sky, the clearer your view of the lights will be. That's one reason why Chena Hot Springs (page 304) is such a good place for viewing the northern lights. It's 60 miles out of town and offers heated viewing areas where you can watch for the lights all night long.

- **Ask for a wake-up call.** Most hotels under the "aurora oval" (the latitude at which the aurora shines overhead) will happily let you know if the aurora comes out. You can also check the University of Alaska Fairbanks Geophysical Institute's aurora forecast at www.gi.alaska.edu/auroraforecast.

- **Be patient.** The northern lights don't shine every night, but if you spend three nights under the aurora oval—when it's dark enough to see them, and you're actively looking for them—you have at least an 80 percent chance of seeing them.

Want to take a great photo of the northern lights? Set your camera to the longest exposure possible, choose an object to be silhouetted in the foreground (it adds interest), and use a tripod if at all possible. Bonus points if you can set the shutter to a two- or three-second delay, so the motion of your pushing the button doesn't blur the image.

Explore the Interior

People come to Interior Alaska for the gold-mining history, dog mushing, the northern lights—and Denali National Park.

Day 1

Welcome to Fairbanks! As you get settled, take the time to visit **Gold Daughters** and learn how to pan for gold from a pair of talented women who grew up giving demonstrations to tourists. Don't miss the **Pipeline Viewing Station** just across the highway, where you can get up close to the 800-mile pipeline that transfers crude oil from Prudhoe Bay to Valdez. Next, if you love Christmas, make the 20-minute drive southeast to the year-round **Santa Claus House** in **North Pole,** Alaska. End the day at **Pioneer Park,** filled with historical buildings, mining equipment, an all-you-can-eat salmon bake, and a hilarious dinner theater show about the history of Fairbanks. Let the front desk at your hotel know you'd like to be woken up if the **northern lights** come out.

Walk with reindeer through the boreal forest at Running Reindeer Ranch.

Day 2

Choose your big adventure for the day: If you want a day of relaxation, head out to **Chena Hot Springs** for hot springs and an **ice museum.** If you want a more extreme adventure, you can book a **day trip** to a more remote area: Fly out to the traditional, isolated village of **Anaktuvuk Pass** for a day tour to learn more about Alaska Native culture, or get up very early to fly halfway up the **Haul Road** (aka the Dalton Highway) and then drive back with **Northern Alaska Tour Company.** You can also hitch a ride on the mail plane to a rural village with **Warbelow's Air.** You won't get to spend any real time in the village(s)—the plane just drops off the mail then takes off again. But getting to flit out to a remote village in a small plane is still a fun, exciting experience for many people.

Day 3

Book a morning tour at the **Running Reindeer Ranch,** where you get to take a short nature walk with a herd of reindeer running wild around you; it's perfectly safe but surprisingly exhilarating, and you'll learn a lot about the domesticated cousin to Alaska's wild caribou. Next, stop by the stunning **Museum of the North** at the **University of Alaska Fairbanks.** Then head downtown to visit **The Crepery** for one of Fairbanks's best lunches, and a stop by the **Alaska House Art Gallery** for a glimpse at the region's best Alaska Native art.

That evening, make the 2.5-hour drive south to **Denali National Park and Preserve,** get settled in your hotel or campground.

Day 4

Take either a narrated tour bus or a shuttle bus ride into **Denali National Park and Preserve.** The difference is more than just narration; shuttle buses will stop for photo ops and to let people hop on and off, while the narrated tour buses only stop for photo ops. There are many shuttle and tour bus trips into the park every day, each of them of varying length; you get to choose if you want to spend five hours on a "short" trip or twelve hours on a bus ride that goes all the way to the end of the road. Wildlife sightings are never guaranteed—after all, the animals are wild and wander as they please—but most visitors are still eager for a chance to see bears, caribou, moose, and wolves in the wild. If you take one of the shorter rides, you'll have time for a short day hike before you check out the restaurants near the park entrance. If you have a car, get dinner at the **49th State Brewing Company** in nearby **Healy;** it has the bus that was used for filming ***Into the Wild*** set up so you can take selfies or photos to your heart's content. It also offers shuttle service to the carless for a nominal fee.

Day 5

Check out the park's three visitor centers, if you haven't already, and visit their working kennel of sled dogs, or book a **day tour** of your choice. Options include everything from white-water rafting to horseback rides, dog cart rides, ATV rides, and ziplining. Then make the 2.5-hour drive south to **Talkeetna.**

Day 6

Once you've arrived in Talkeetna, it's time to book that **flightseeing** trip around **Denali,** using one of the small airlines that also ferry climbers back and forth to Denali base camp. If you don't like small planes you have lots of other **day tour** options, including a **jet boat ride** on the mighty rivers nearby, **fishing,** or **ziplining.** End your day with live music at the **Fairview Inn** or a great dinner at **Mountain High Pizza Pie, Twister Creek Restaurant,** or the **Wildflower Cafe;** they're all excellent.

Day 7

Hop on the **Hurricane Turn Train,** a delightful narrated trip on one of the nation's last flag stop trains. When you get back, make it a point to wander the shops along **Main Street** (they're all locally owned) before you make the drive back to Fairbanks or south to explore Southcentral.

sightseeing in Denali National Park and Preserve

Alaskan Cruise Ports of Call

a cruise ship docks in Whittier

So you've booked a cruise to Alaska? Congratulations! The cruise line will handle all the transportation logistics for you, but here are some tips on how to spend your time on land.

First and most important tip: **Don't be late** getting back to the ship. Unless you've booked a small, intimate cruise where all the staff and passengers know each other's names within the first hour, your cruise ship will leave without you if you're late, in which case you'll have to hop a flight or a boat to the next port to catch up. A range of shore excursions may have been included in the price of your cruise or offered as optional add-ons. These tour companies work closely with the cruise lines to make sure you're back in plenty of time to catch your ship's departure.

If you're looking for a more up-close, personalized experience of that day's destination, book with one of the **independent, local tour companies** that probably aren't included in your cruise line's roster. Many will be able to get you back in plenty of time to catch your cruise on the way out (always ask to be sure), and they almost always offer smaller groups and a more in-depth experience.

Many (though not all) of the shops featured in your shipboard handout aren't local Alaskan shops at all, and most of them aren't selling Alaska-made goods, either. Quite a few of them sell imitation Alaska Native artwork that is carefully marketed to make you think you're getting an authentic souvenir. If you want to see the **local shops,** where you can buy **authentic Alaska Native artwork,** usually from someone who actually lives in town year-round and can tell you about its life and culture, walk a couple of extra blocks past "cruise ship alley"—the lineup of international stores that are ubiquitous in any cruise line terminal, from Alaska to the Caribbean.

Spot the local shops by looking for fairly uniform signs or stickers on the storefronts that say things like "We live here year-round" and "Owned by an Alaskan family." Unfortunately, some imposters in the busiest ports have started advertising themselves as locally owned, using signs that mimic those used by the actual residents. But said imposters are still pretty easy to identify because the moment you come in the door, you'll be met by a hard sell. Locals will always be happy to answer any questions you have about the authenticity of their goods or biographical information about the people who made them. You can also look for the Silver Hand and Made in Alaska labels; see *Essentials* for more information on what these mean and what they look like.

Finally, when it comes to choosing your Alaska cruise, pay special attention to **how much time you have in port.** It's tempting to try and see as much as you can in a short period of time, but with just a few hours, you can't get a feel for the authentic culture. If that's one of your priorities, pick a couple of ports where you want to spend more time and tailor your cruise journey around them. That might mean starting or ending your cruise in those towns, or choosing a smaller cruise that tends to offer more time in port than the big ships. Either way, you're in for the trip of a lifetime.

Juneau and Southeast Alaska

Look for ★ to find recommended sights, activities, dining, and lodging.

Highlights

★ **Totem Bight State Historical Park:** Just outside Ketchikan you can see more than a dozen totem poles and a splendid traditional community clan house (page 50).

★ **Misty Fjords National Monument:** The 2.2-million-acre national monument encapsulates the best of Southeast Alaska's dramatic terrain in one place, with steep fjords, dramatic mountain peaks, majestic glaciers, and stunning waterfalls (page 51).

★ **Anan Creek Wildlife Observatory:** Anan Creek hosts one of the world's largest returns of pink salmon, creating the perfect opportunity for you to see black bears and grizzly bears together (page 68).

★ **Whale-Watching:** You have great odds of seeing whales, along with other plentiful marine wildlife, in uncrowded Frederick Sound near Petersburg (page 74).

★ **Sitka National Historical Park:** Walk into history among looming totem poles, ancient Tlingit fortifications, and memories of the early Russian settlers (page 83).

★ **Mendenhall Glacier:** Visit Southeast's most popular (and accessible) glacier for unparalleled hiking, photo ops, and maybe even a chance to see a bear (page 95).

★ **Bear Viewing at Admiralty Island National Monument:** Feeling brave? Take a guided trip to get up close and personal with brown bears (page 96).

★ **Glacier Bay National Park and Preserve:** Experience untouched wilderness amid 3.3 million acres of rugged mountains, glaciers, fjords, and temperate rainforest (page 102).

★ **Klondike Gold Rush National Historical Park:** Stop at Alaska's most-visited national park to learn about the last great rush for gold (page 108).

★ **Ride the White Pass & Yukon Route Railroad:** Don't miss a chance to ride a scenic, historic narrow-gauge railroad that dates back to the gold rush days (page 110).

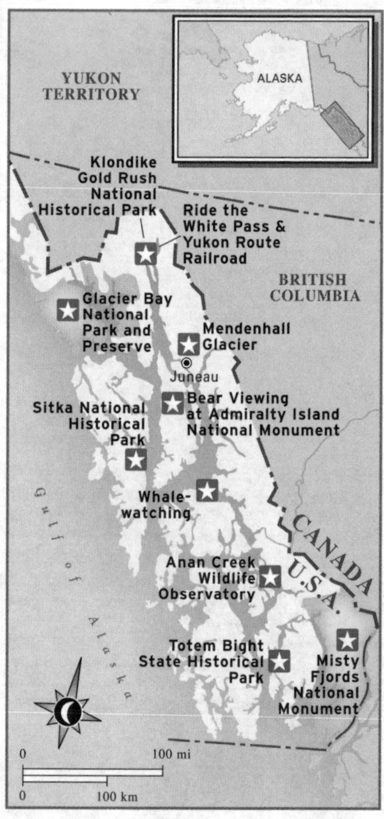

Southeast Alaska draws the vast bulk of visitors to the state—in part because it's so close to the Lower 48 states and Canada, and also because it's accessible to cruise ships, which account for more than 50 percent of tourist traffic into Alaska.

In a single visit to Southeast Alaska you can see craggy, dramatic fjords; glaciers tumbling into the sea; and remote communities accessible only by sea and air, where life is slow and simple . . . until the fish are running. You'll also see lots of wildlife, including bears fishing for salmon and humpback whales bubble-net feeding—a learned behavior that you won't see anywhere else in the world.

Southeast Alaska is also rich in Alaska Native history, culture, and art. It's home to the Tlingit, Haida, and Tsimshian peoples, and there are opportunities to see traditional singing, drumming, and dancing, or to watch Native artisans demonstrate their fine art and tell cultural stories.

If you're interested in gold rush history, Ketchikan and Skagway—the most southerly and most northerly communities in Southeast, respectively—should be on your list. And no matter what sort of outdoor recreation you love, from hiking to paddling and fishing for all of Alaska's iconic species, including salmon, halibut, and grayling, you'll find it in Southeast.

Technically speaking, all of Southeast Alaska is the "Inside Passage," a series of zigzagging channels that protect the islands from the open waters of the sea. It's often easiest, however, to think of this region's most consistent ferry route—from Ketchikan north through Wrangell, Petersburg, Juneau, Haines, and Skagway, then back again—as the core of the Inside Passage.

These communities are the best equipped to provide comfort and services to tourists, and they're also easier to reach: Northbound and southbound Alaska state ferries service them every few days, and all of the towns mentioned except Haines and Skagway receive daily flights from Alaska Airlines.

Previous: the ferry *Matanuska* from Wrangell; a black bear at Anan Creek Wildlife Observatory.
Above: a totem pole at Petersburg city hall.

Juneau and the Inside Passage

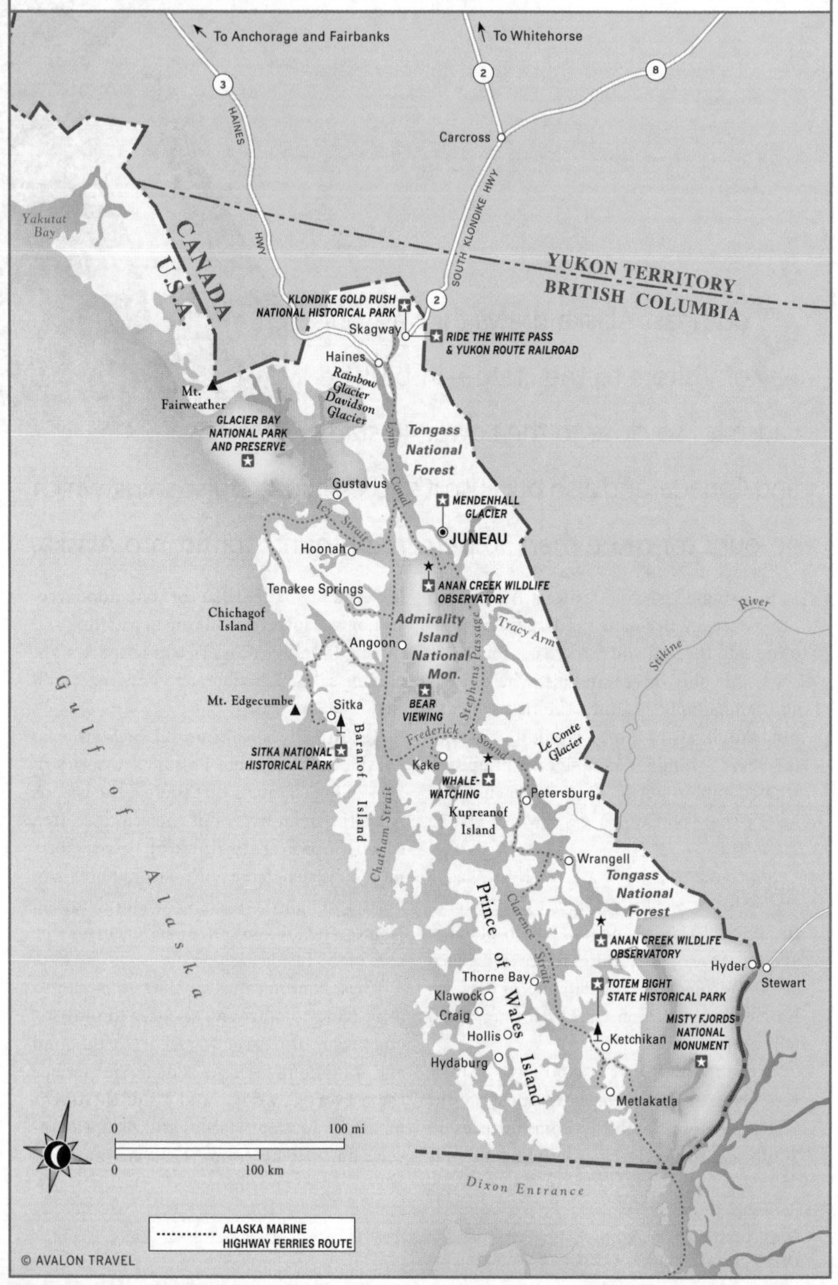

Ride the Alaska Marine Highway System Ferries

For the isolated communities of Southeast and Southwest Alaska, the **Alaska Marine Highway System (AMHS)** (800/642-0066, ferryalaska.com) ferries are a literal lifeline, offering affordable transport of cargo (including fresh produce), people, and their luggage. In Southwest communities and those Southeast communities not served by frequent Alaska Airlines flights, the only transport alternative to the ferry is buying a seat on a small to midsize plane, which can easily cost a thousand dollars for a round-trip ticket.

The AMHS has 11 vessels of various sizes plying a route that totals 3,500 miles, and it's designated as an official Scenic Byway; it even receives federal highway funds! Each ferry has indoor seating, a "solarium" (covered outdoor seating, often with heat lamps to take off the chill), and uncovered outdoor viewing decks. All seats are first-come, first-served when you board, although cabins can be reserved in advance.

The solariums on the larger ferries have reclining plastic loungers. They're a very popular space to camp out in your sleeping bag, especially on ferries that run overnight; the fresh air and the hum of the ferry engine make for a great night's sleep. Line up early—usually about an hour before the ferry is scheduled to depart—if you want to snag one of those seats.

You can almost always buy—or change—a walk-on ferry ticket at the last minute, and it doesn't cost much to take a bike along for easy transport in port towns. But if you're traveling with a car or have your heart set on a certain type of cabin, plan to buy your tickets a minimum of six months ahead of time. Otherwise, you might find that one or more legs of the ferry run you want are already booked up.

You can bring pets on the Alaska Marine Highway System ferries, but it's not necessarily much fun for them or you. Your pets must be in a suitable crate or in your car, and they're restricted to the car deck, which you can only visit while the ship is in port or during 15-minute breaks granted by the captain every eight hours or so on long trips. See ferryalaska.com for more details on pet policies.

To build a complicated ferry itinerary, pick one attraction—say, a trip to Gustavus, which only has ferry traffic a couple days out of the week—and plan your trip around that. Or, start with the basic ferry run up and down the core of the Inside Passage (Ketchikan-Wrangell-Petersburg-Juneau-Haines-Skagway), which gives you time to spend a couple of days in each community; then build out any side trips from there.

PLANNING YOUR TIME

Because you can only travel between Southeast Alaska communities by plane or boat, travel delays are inevitable. They may happen because of weather that keeps a boat or plane from setting out, or because of mechanical problems.

It's easier to take those delays in stride if you've left a couple of days of flex time in your schedule, along with enough room in your budget to cover an emergency hotel stay until things get sorted out. Travel insurance can really save your bacon. Even if nothing goes wrong, having that flex time makes it easier to enjoy the relaxed, easygoing pace of life in the small Alaska towns you'll visit.

May through September is typically the high season in Southeast; you can get some great deals if you're willing to travel in the shoulder season (mid-April and late September or early October), although if you want to see humpback whales or catch a lot of salmon you'll want to be here late June through early August.

While cruise ship docks are positioned to mainline visitors into each city's downtown shopping area, in some communities the ferry terminal and airport may be miles away from downtown (and miles away from each other, too). Mass transit to/from the ferry and airport ranges from limited to nonexistent, depending on the community. If you're not driving a car, booking into a hotel with a free ferry or airport shuttle on the first and last days of your trip makes things a whole lot easier.

Ketchikan

Much of everyday life in Ketchikan revolves around tourism and the fishing industry; once upon a time, lumber was a big economic driver, too. The town itself is eye-catching, stretching several miles along the shore, with steep staircases and roads creeping up the sides of the mountain.

But what really gets visitors' attention is the profusion of totem poles—you'll find more standing poles here than anywhere else in the world, backed by a rich heritage in living Alaska Native culture and unparalleled opportunities to watch some of the world's best Native artisans at work in nearby Saxman and the small Tsimshian community of Metlakatla, on neighboring Annette Island.

But that's not all you'll find in Ketchikan: This sprawling, sometimes gritty city of more than 8,000 is all about making a living from the ocean. If you're not hanging out by the docks watching fishing boats and cruise ships come in, you can stroll the notorious former red-light district and its "Married Man's Path," or watch salmon flinging themselves up the salmon ladder that sits right in the heart of town. There's a strong arts scene, too.

Temperatures in Ketchikan are mild by Alaska standards, with highs typically hitting at least in the 60s from June through August; even the shoulder months of April, May, October, and November usually yield temperatures into the 50s; in winter, low temperatures barely dip below freezing. Bring your rain jacket, waterproof boots, and some warm layers, though—Ketchikan gets more than 140 inches of precipitation per year, well over four times the national average.

Many attractions are year-round, but there's more availability from April to the end of October.

SIGHTS

Dolly's House Museum

Like most Alaskan towns, Ketchikan was once a wild and lawless place—a fact that's well reflected in the town's former red-light district, a strip of shops on pilings over Ketchikan Creek, which runs through the middle of town. Look for plaques explaining each building's history, or visit the last Creek Street bordello left standing: tiny **Dolly's House Museum** (24 Creek St., 907/225-6329, $10). It might be a little bit of a tourist trap, but if you have the money to burn it's a fun, fascinating way to spend a few minutes.

Deer Mountain Hatchery

You don't have to pay to watch one of Creek Street's biggest attractions: salmon flinging themselves onto, and eventually over, the salmon ladder (look for signs along Creek Street), a series of rock "steps" that make it easier for them to reach their upstream spawning grounds. Even after almost 30 years in Alaska, I never tire of seeing this portion of the life cycle repeated, and it always draws a steady stream of visitors to take photos or just enjoy watching the fish.

If you follow signs upstream from the fish ladder, you can walk to the **Deer Mountain Hatchery** (1158 Salmon Rd., 907/225-9606, May-Sept. Mon.-Fri. 8am-4:30pm, call for admission and tour info), where interpretive signs explain the hatchery process and salmon life cycle, and you can view baby salmon waiting to be released back into the wild. The hatchery releases about 100,000 chinook smolt (baby king salmon) into Ketchikan Creek every year. There used to be an Eagle Center here too, but it closed due to funding concerns, and the raptors were transferred to the Alaska Raptor Center in Sitka.

Southeast Alaska Discovery Center

For a one-stop look at Southeast Alaska's stupendous natural and cultural history, including a re-created rainforest and Native fishing

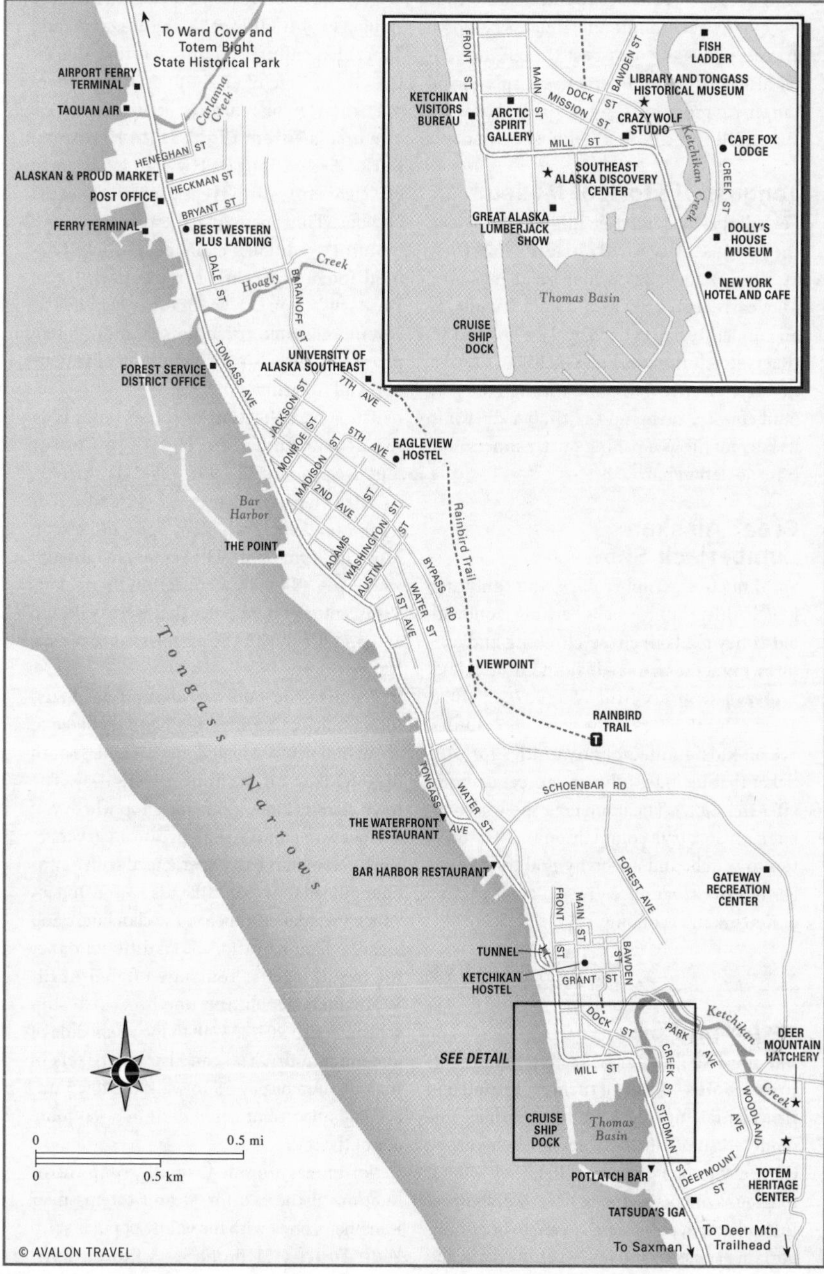
Ketchikan
To Ward Cove and Totem Bight State Historical Park
AIRPORT FERRY TERMINAL
TAQUAN AIR
Carlanna Creek
HENEGHAN ST
ALASKAN & PROUD MARKET
HECKMAN ST
POST OFFICE
BRYANT ST
FERRY TERMINAL
BEST WESTERN PLUS LANDING
DALE ST
BARANOFF ST
Hoagly Creek
TONGASS AVE
FOREST SERVICE DISTRICT OFFICE
UNIVERSITY OF ALASKA SOUTHEAST
7TH AVE
JACKSON ST
MONROE ST
5TH AVE
EAGLEVIEW HOSTEL
MADISON ST
2ND AVE
Bar Harbor
THE POINT
ADAMS
WASHINGTON ST
AUSTIN
Rainbird Trail
BYPASS RD
WATER ST
1ST AVE
Tongass Narrows
VIEWPOINT
RAINBIRD TRAIL
SCHOENBAR RD
THE WATERFRONT RESTAURANT
BAR HARBOR RESTAURANT
FOREST AVE
GATEWAY RECREATION CENTER
FRONT ST
MAIN ST
TUNNEL
KETCHIKAN HOSTEL
BAWDEN ST
GRANT ST
DOCK ST
PARK AVE
Ketchikan Creek
DEER MOUNTAIN HATCHERY
SEE DETAIL
MILL ST
CREEK ST
WOODLAND AVE
CRUISE SHIP DOCK
Thomas Basin
STEDMAN ST
DEEPMOUNT ST
POTLATCH BAR
TOTEM HERITAGE CENTER
TATSUDA'S IGA
To Saxman
To Deer Mtn Trailhead
0 0.5 mi
0 0.5 km
FRONT ST
MAIN ST
DOCK ST
MISSION ST
BAWDEN ST
FISH LADDER
LIBRARY AND TONGASS HISTORICAL MUSEUM
KETCHIKAN VISITORS BUREAU
ARCTIC SPIRIT GALLERY
CRAZY WOLF STUDIO
CAPE FOX LODGE
SOUTHEAST ALASKA DISCOVERY CENTER
GREAT ALASKA LUMBERJACK SHOW
DOLLY'S HOUSE MUSEUM
NEW YORK HOTEL AND CAFE
CRUISE SHIP DOCK
© AVALON TRAVEL

village, visit the stupendous **Southeast Alaska Discovery Center** (50 Main St., daily 8am-4pm, $5 adults). If you don't have time to actually get out into the Tongass National Forest, this is the next best thing. The center also offer films, interactive displays, and ranger-led programs—some for all ages, some specifically for children—almost every day.

Tongass Historical Museum

For a deeper look into Ketchikan's city history, the **Tongass Historical Museum** (629 Dock St., ktn-ak.us/tongass-historical-museum, May-early Sept. daily 8am-5pm, $3 adults, 12 and under free) uses historical photos and artifacts to tell the story of Ketchikan's evolution from Native fish camp through the gold (and copper) rush and the timber days into its current life as a fishing port, cannery, and transportation hub.

Great Alaskan Lumberjack Show

Speaking of the timber days, you can watch ESPN athlete lumberjacks battling it out with old-timey skills like tree-climbing and axe-throwing at the **Great Alaskan Lumberjack Show** (420 Spruce Mill Way, 907/225-9050, alaskanlumberjackshow.com, $37 adults, $18.50 kids, limited opportunities for $125 ticket that includes all-you-can-eat crab fest after the show). The hour-long show is corny but it's also a true competition that's a ton of fun to watch, and a worthy nod to the timber industry that once drove a great portion of Ketchikan's economy.

TOP EXPERIENCE

★ Totem Poles

The most striking sight in Ketchikan is its **totem poles**—some of them still painted in rich, contrasting colors, while others have surrendered some of that color to the weather. Contrary to one popular belief, they are not religious symbols and were never worshipped. Instead, totem poles were carved to honor important people, record noteworthy events, and proclaim the lineage and history of the people who owned them.

There are more than a dozen of these signposts of traditional Tlingit, Haida, and Tsimshian culture standing sentinel all over the city of Ketchikan, but you'll find them particularly concentrated in three places. The first is **Totem Bight State Historical Park** (9883 N. Tongass Hwy., 10 miles north of Ketchikan), which is easily accessed on the city bus. This open-air park also contains a beautiful traditional clan house. Tucked behind Totem Bight park is tiny Potlach Totem Park, where you can see another clan house, several recreated tribal homes, more totem poles, and, surprisingly, a museum of antique cars and firearms.

The next collection of totem poles is in the downtown **Totem Heritage Center** (601 Deermount St., 907/225-3111, ktn-ak.us/totem-heritage-center, $5 (12 and under free); May-Sept. daily 8am-5pm, off-season Mon.-Fri. 1pm-5pm). The center is a museum where you can view a collection of precious 19th-century totem poles that were collected and preserved with the permission of Alaska Native elders.

Finally, you can see about two dozen totem poles in **Saxman,** a Native village of about 400 people located just 2.5 miles south of Ketchikan on the Tongass Highway. The town also includes a carving shop where you can see some of Alaska's greatest carvers at work. Saxman is best experienced with a two-hour guided tour ($35, $18 kids 12 and under), which includes entrance to the clan house and a short demonstration of traditional dancing in full regalia. Tours are offered April-September, depending on the cruise ship schedule; call 907/224-4846 for a schedule of upcoming tours. You can also buy tickets in the gift shop or pay $5 to walk the town unaccompanied—but you'll definitely get more out of the tour.

For an easy, guided, small-group introduction to the rainforest and totems near Ketchikan, book with the wildly popular **Wild Wolf Tours** (131 Front St., wildwolftours.

totem pole in Ketchikan's Totem Bight State Historical Park

com, adults $59-79, children under 12 $39-59). This Native-owned family business conducts small-group two- and three-hour walking tours on easy nearby trails, where you can learn about native plants and their traditional uses, then visit a totem park and clan house. Sampling of a few traditional foods (salmon and seaweed) is included.

Tours

Ketchikan's well-developed tourism industry offers some unique—and highly enjoyable—ways of experiencing its combination of land and water. If you don't mind riding in a large bus, a lot of visitors love the **Ketchikan Duck Tour** (511 Borch St., 907/225-9899, akduck.com, from $49), a 90-minute ride through town—and then through the water—on an amphibious bus.

You can board the crabbing vessel *Aleutian Ballad* straight from downtown Ketchikan for a **Bering Sea Crab Fishermen's Tour** (888/239-3816, alaskacrabtour.com, from $169 adult, $109 12 and under). This ship was made famous when, during season 2 of the Discovery Channel's *Deadliest Catch* show, it was walloped by a 60-foot rogue wave that slammed it onto its side and nearly sank it. Don't worry: You're going to stay in the calm waters of the Inside Passage and enjoy a protected seating area while the fishers—sometimes including familiar faces from the TV show—haul up a catch and place specimens into a live viewing/touch tank for you to explore.

For the opposite end of the water-based expedition spectrum, you can also drive your own 14-foot inflatable Zodiac on a guided sightseeing excursion with **Ketchikan Outdoors** (2868 S. Tongass Hwy., 907/617-1820, ketchikanoutdoors.com, $169). Each boat holds four, so if you have a small party, you'll get to share.

RECREATION

Wilderness Tours

HELICOPTER TOURS

Most people automatically think "small plane" when the topic of Alaska flightseeing comes up, and it's certainly the prevailing mode of transportation—especially if you want to cover any distance at a reasonable rate of speed. But for low, slow tours that get you in close to the attractions and offer many options for landing, there's nothing like a helicopter trip. **Ketchikan Helicopters** (855/858-4354, ketchikanhelicopters.com) offers helicopter flightseeing through Ketchikan fjords from $229 per person, with an optional landing at 1,000-foot **Totem Falls** ($249) and heli-supported fishing, hiking, and wildlife viewing.

★ MISTY FJORDS NATIONAL MONUMENT

Just 22 miles to the east of Ketchikan, the 2.2-million-acre **Misty Fjords National Monument** epitomizes everything people imagine when they think of Alaska: snow-capped peaks, steep fjords, glaciers, and plunging waterfalls, all shaped by the massive ice sheets that covered this area as recently as 17,000 years ago. You can visit

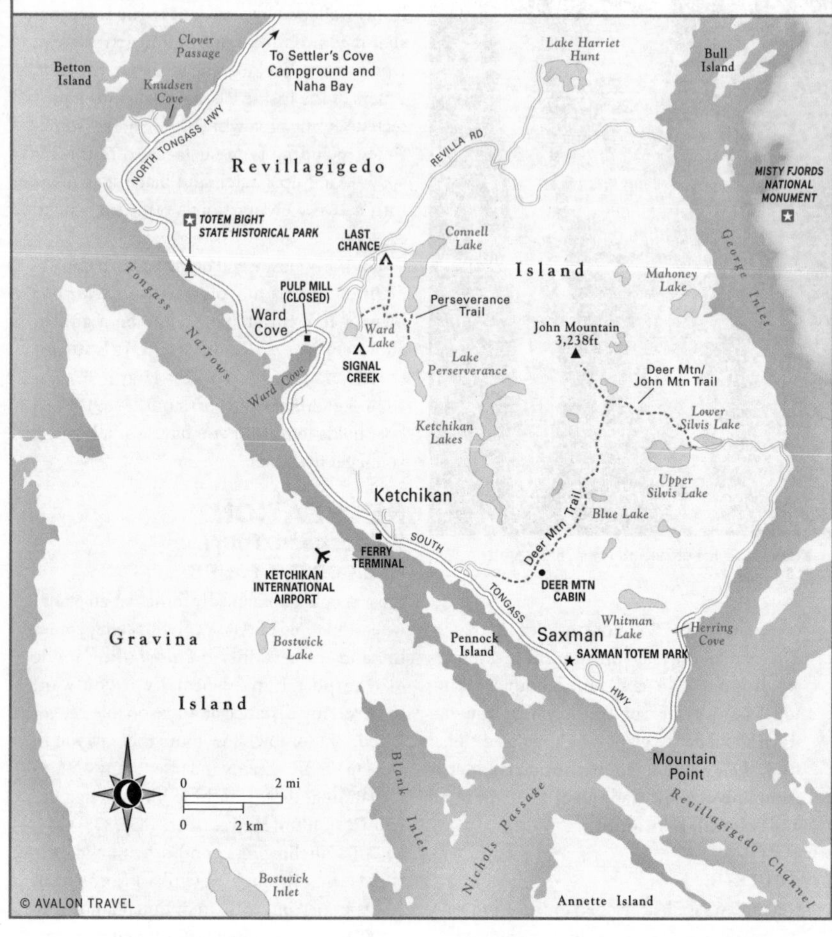

Misty Fjords by floatplane or on a cruise tour through Behm Canal; aside from the stunning scenery and sheer rocks walls rising thousands of feet, keep your eyes open for wildlife like orcas, porpoises, mountain goats, and bears.

You have an enormous array of flightseeing providers to choose from, many of which also offer flights to other regional attractions that are too far away to reach by boat from Ketchikan, like the Anan Creek Wildlife Observatory. The following are some of the best, known for their attention to safety and careful handling of nervous flyers. Each of the providers listed also offers fly-in fishing trips and transport to and from public-use cabins in the area. Prices listed are for two-hour excursions, although many offer shorter and longer trips as well; discounts are often given for children under 12 and for end-of-season travel in September.

- **Alaska Seaplane Tours** (866/858-2327, alaskaseaplanetours.com, from $229, also offers bear viewing on Prince of Wales Island)

- **Family Air Tours** (907/247-1305, familyairtours.com, from $239)
- **Island Wings** (888/854-2444, islandwings.com, from $239, also offers trips to Anan Creek and Traitor Cove bear observatories as well as hiking tours)
- **Misty Fjords Air** (877/228-4656 or 907/225-5155, mistyfjordsair.com, from $249)
- **Mountain Air Service** (907/821-2500, mtnairservice.com)
- **SeaWind Aviation** (877/225-1203 or 907/225-1206, seawindaviation.com, from $229, also offers Traitors Cove and Prince of Wales Island bear viewing)
- **Taquan Air** (4085 Tongass Ave., 800/770-8800 or 907/225-8800, taquanair.com, from $269, also offers trips to Anan Creek)

Note: Misty Fjords often lives up to its name with wind, rain, and limited visibility, and there have been fatalities attributed to flightseeing trips that went out in poor flying conditions. Play it safe and don't push a pilot to fly in borderline weather, no matter how correctly disappointed you might be to miss out. This is where having a flex day or two planned into your trip comes in really handy; it's worth it!

BLACK BEAR VIEWING

Most of Alaska's high-profile bear viewing is of brown bears—after all, who wouldn't want to see the largest land predator living? But black bear viewing is also immensely popular. If you're interested in ticking off another member of the bear trifecta, you can watch these more shy, secretive bears fishing in August and September at Margaret Bay/Traitors Cove.

Although you can get here by boat, the ride is long and often rough—it's much more fun to take a 20-minute floatplane ride from Ketchikan, followed by a guided outing with one of the following providers. Heads up: You'll need to walk more than a mile from the dock to the bear-viewing observatory.

- **Island Wings** (888/854-2444, islandwings.com, from $365)
- **Mountain Air Service** (907/821-2500, mtnairservice.com)
- **SeaWind Aviation** (877/225-1203 or 907/225-1206, seawindaviation.com, from $359)
- **Taquan Air** (4085 Tongass Ave., 800/770-8800 or 907/225-8800, taquanair.com, from $369)

Island Wings and Taquan Air also offer fly-in bear viewing at the **Anan Creek Wildlife Observatory** near Wrangell, potential for black and brown bears). SeaWind Aviation and **Alaska Seaplane Tours** (866/858-2327, alaskaseaplanetours.com) offer black bear viewing on nearby **Prince of Wales Island,** which has yet to be deluged by crowds.

Water Sports

Believe it or not, there's exactly one commercial snorkeling operation in Alaska, and it's in Ketchikan. **Snorkel Alaska** (907/247-7782, snorkelalaska.com) takes groups of up to 25 people snorkeling in near-shore waters off Mountain Point where you can see starfish, sea urchins, jellyfish, sea cucumbers, kelp, and, of course, fish. The water is surprisingly warm by Alaska standards—up to 65 degrees by midsummer—and thick 7mm wetsuits, including boots, gloves, and a hood, ensure you won't get cold. Participants must weigh between 80 and 260 pounds for the wetsuits to fit.

Another unusual way to experience Ketchikan is **Alaska Sea Cycle Tours** (907/821-2728, alaskaseacycletours.com, from $155 adult, $85 child), a combination history/sightseeing ride down the coast on pedal-powered pontoon boats. That's right—you're the engine.

Of course, paddling is enormously popular here and gives you unparalleled opportunities for sightseeing and, with any luck at all, wildlife viewing. Two of the best family-owned, small-group sea-kayaking outfitters that really take their time and give you the full experience are **Ketchikan Kayak Company** (407 Knudson Cove Rd., 907/225-1272, ketchikankayakco.com, from $129 for 4 hours in Clover Pass, discounts for parties of 5 or more) and **Southeast Sea Kayaks Alaska** (800/287-1607, kayakketchikan.com, from $89 adult for 2.25 hours around Ketchikan, $169 for 4-hour Orca Cove trip, discounts for children 6-15). Both companies limit group sizes, so they tend to sell out early.

Ketchikan Kayak Company also offers combination electric bike and hike tours, multiday kayak fish expeditions into Misty Fjords National Monument, and outfitting services if you're experienced enough to DIY a paddling trip in Alaska's cold, fast-moving coastal waters.

Ziplining

Alaska Canopy Adventures (4085 Tongass Ave., alaskacanopy.com, starting at $189) offers two Ketchikan ziplines, both booked through spiritofalaskatours.com: an Eagle Creek tour out of Herring Cove with eight ziplines and three aerial bridges, topping out at 135 feet above the forest floor; and a Bear Creek Zipline Adventure, which showcases panoramic mountain, forest, and ocean views from eight ziplines on huge western hemlocks, ending with a rappel.

The **Southeast Exposure Outdoor Adventure Center** (rainforestcanopyzipline.com) also offers zipline tours, with eight separate ziplines and another eight aerial traverses. It caters to the cruise lines, so you can expect larger groups.

Hiking

You can access several easy hiking trails from Ketchikan's road system. One of the best is **Rainbird Trail,** a 1.3-mile walk with views over the water and three trailheads in town. From the cruise ship docks, it's a steep walk up Schoenbar Road; turn left onto 3rd Avenue. The trailhead will be on the north side of the road. The second trailhead is close to 3rd Avenue and Washington Street; take a steep staircase up to the trail. The third trailhead is at the rear of the University of Alaska Southeast parking lot. If you start in town, you can take the bus back from the university.

The **Married Man's Trail,** made famous as the "back way" access to brothels over Ketchikan Creek, isn't a wilderness experience, but many visitors still find it a charming trip due to its history. It starts at the Cape Fox Lodge (800 Venetia Ave.) before heading downhill to the creek and ending at Park Avenue, a distance of less than 0.25 mile.

For a wilder walk through the rainforest, the 4.8-mile **Lunch Creek Trail** begins at the terminus of the North Tongass Highway, 18 miles north of town. You have two options here: Turn right to stay on the 4.8-mile Lunch Creek Trail, which mostly parallels the creek through looming rainforest, or hang a left to intersect the **Lunch Falls Loop,** which offers views of the falls, the creek, and a couple of side trails for beach access.

Perhaps the most-hiked trail in all of Ketchikan, the **Deer Mountain Trail** starts at the end of Ketchikan Lakes Road and winds three miles uphill through old-growth forest, gaining 3,000 feet of elevation and offering a couple of great lookout points near the one-mile and two-mile points along the way. The trail branches about 0.5 mile before the summit: Go right for the summit, or go left for the Deer Mountain A-frame shelter (first-come, first-served).

This trail continues up and over the mountain for a serious backcountry trek to **Silvis Lakes**—about 14 miles and, for most people, a two-day trip. I highly recommend contacting the U.S. Forest Service visitor center in Ketchikan, the **Southeast Alaska Discovery Center** (50 Main St., 907/228-6234, May-Sept., Mon.-Fri. 8am-4pm), before trying anything like this; Alaska trail conditions and signage are highly variable and maintenance frequency often varies with funding.

Fishing

Ketchikan is the salmon capital of the world, with huge runs coming back to its protected waters; you'll also find great freshwater fishing for steelhead (best in the spring shoulder season), Dolly Varden, and grayling. Stellar saltwater fishing for halibut, red snapper, lingcod is just a short boat ride away. You'll get excellent freshwater fishing for salmon just returned from the ocean July-September, but you're not allowed to catch kings in freshwater here; those have to come from the ocean.

The Alaska Catch (2417 Tongass Ave., 907/617-9585, thealaskacatch.com, 4-hour excursion from $180) is one of the most popular saltwater fishing charters; they also offer water-taxi service to remote forest service cabins. Also extremely popular is family-owned **Baranof Fishing** (headquartered at the end of Main St., 877/732-9453, exclusivealaska.com), which offers salmon and halibut fishing, with good multispecies fishing from mid-June to mid-August. Both operations limit their group sizes, so you don't have to worry about jockeying for a pole or for fishing space.

For freshwater fishing, book a combination saltwater/freshwater fishing trip with Captain Rob of **Classic Alaska Charters** (907/225-0608, alaskafishingcruises.com). He's originally from the Midwest but has been guiding fishing in Alaska for more than 30 years. He also offers overnight charters so you can catch your limit one day, then start all over again with a fresh limit the next day.

You can also book a multi-day sea-kayak fishing expedition—truly a trip highlight for the dedicated angler—with **Ketchikan Kayak Company** (407 Knudson Cove Rd., 907/225-1272, ketchikankayakco.com).

For a DIY fishing trip, some of the most popular spots with road access are the saltwater **Herring Cove** (a nine-mile drive to Wood Rd., at the end of the S. Tongass Hwy.), for kings, and **Ward Lake** (about six miles north of town), which has a late-July run of silvers. Always consult a copy of the local fishing regulations (available at adfg.alaska.gov) before you go. For more diverse fishing opportunities, book a heli-supported fishing trip with **Ketchikan Helicopters** (855/858-4354, ketchikanhelicopters.com) or charter a boat or plane taxi to remote waters.

Remote Cabins

Floatplane companies that offer tours to **Misty Fjords National Monument** also offer transport to cabins. Round-trip transport for the entire plane can easily cost $1,000 or more but makes for a one-of-a-kind experience and can be split between members of your party. All the boat-based Ketchikan fishing services also offer water-taxi service.

The area around **Josephine Lake Cabin** on neighboring Prince of Wales Island is known for quartz and epidote crystals; make sure you respect private mining claims in the vicinity. It's also a stupendous place for seeing black-tailed deer and black bears, but there are no fish in the lake. An aluminum skiff with oars is available, and kayaking is also popular.

Manzanita Lake Cabin is 28 miles northeast of Ketchikan on Revillagigedo Island, located beside a spectacular series of cascading waterfalls and surrounded by old-growth spruce, hemlock, and cedar. An aluminum skiff with oars is available for exploring the lakeshore. Opportunities abound for wildlife viewing, including bears, deer, moose, mountain goats, and beavers. Fishing is great for cutthroat trout, Dolly Varden, and kokanee (landlocked sockeye) salmon.

Wistanley Island Cabin (on an island off Behm Canal in Misty Fjords National Monument) has lots of destinations for adventurous sea kayakers and good wildlife viewing for bears, moose, goats, etc. as well as aquatic wildlife, including porpoises, orcs, humpbacks, sea otters, and seabirds. Saltwater fishing is an option.

On **Ella Lake** is a cabin with lots of rooms for kids to run, set back from the lake in old-growth forest. Near the cabin are a cobble beach and a white-sand beach. Wildlife viewing includes black bears, black-tailed deer, and beavers, and birding is popular. An aluminum skiff with oars is available. Ella Lake has excellent fishing for kokanee salmon, cutthroat trout, and Dolly Varden.

There are more than 100 Forest Service cabins in the area, all of them stupendous—these are just some of the highlights. They are all primitive accommodations with no services; usually there is no cell service and no connection to the outside world while you're there. You need to bring the oil for the heater and all other gear to keep yourself safe and warm. **Alaska Wilderness Outfitting** (3857 Fairview Ave., 907/225-7335, alaskawilderness.com) rents just about everything you need for a backcountry cabin excursion, from life jackets to fishing gear, camping gear, and outboard motors.

ENTERTAINMENT AND EVENTS

Bars

Ketchikan looks and feels safe for visitors—but the locals will tell you that if you wander into the wrong places, it's a rough scene. Because of that, steer clear of the Totem Bar (314 Front St.), where that rough reputation is very well-earned.

The **Sourdough Bar & Liquor Store** (301 Front St., 907/225-2217, daily 8am-2am) is much more fun and sometimes has live music. While you're there, check out the shipwreck photos on the walls or try your hand at pool, darts, and shuffleboard. Also fun—and friendly—is **The Asylum** (522 Water St., 907/220-0809, daily 8am-2am), with 16 draft beers, Wi-Fi, pool, darts, pinball, themed parties, a DJ, and a double-decker beer garden. As a bonus, you can order food from the Burger Queen next door straight from your server and have it brought out to you.

Other occasional live music venues include **The Point** (25 Jefferson Way #102, 907/225-2858, thepointketchikan.com, Mon.-Sat. 9am-4pm) and **New York Café** (907/247-2326, 207 Stedman St., Sun.-Thurs. 7am-8pm, Fri.-Sat. 7am-9pm); sometimes the latter has a $5 cover on music nights.

Events

For information about most of Ketchikan's events, check out the **Ketchikan Area Arts and Humanities Council** (ketchikanarts.org). You can count on the **Blueberry Arts Festival** taking place the first full weekend in August. This fun community celebration on Main Street includes music, dancing, and country-style events like a fun run, a big slug contest/race, a community art project, and a blueberry-pie-eating contest, along with lots of arts and crafts booths—if you're looking to shop for keepsakes, this is a good time to come.

A similar event, the **Winter Arts Faire,** takes place the Friday and Saturday after Thanksgiving (the last weekend in November), and it's indoors, at the **Ted Ferry Civic Center** (888 Venetia Ave., 907/228-5655) and the **Cape Fox Lodge Shaa Hit Banquet Room** (800 Venetia Ave., 866/225-8001).

First Friday is a big deal in Ketchikan, too—but it only happens twice a year. On the First Friday in May, the Ketchikan Area Arts and Humanities Council offers a **Celebration of the Sea Art Walk** (5pm-8pm); on the First Friday in December, it organizes a **Winter Art Walk** (5pm-8pm); see the full calendar of events at ketchikanarts.org. If you miss out on those outings, you can always download the **Ketchikan Art Walk** app to your smartphone and take your own walk at your convenience.

Every third Friday of the month from January to September, the **Haida Descendant Dancers** showcase traditional dancing in the Totem Bight clan house (9883 N. Tongass Hwy., 10 miles north of Ketchikan) 6:30pm-7:30pm.

SHOPPING

The array of aggressive, borderline-fraudulent sellers close to Ketchikan's cruise ship docks is dismaying, but the good news is that they're outnumbered by great local shops that sell all manner of arts and crafts, including fine art from true Alaska Native master craftspeople. The trick is just getting past the frauds to the real deal, and I've vetted the following shops to make sure they are who they say they are.

Let's cover authentic Alaska Native artwork first, since it's what so many of the fraudulent shops try to duplicate. Be sure to stop by **Arctic Spirit Gallery** (318 Mission St.,

Creek Street in Ketchikan

907/228-2277, arcticspiritgallery.com). It offers a selection of beautiful Northwest Coast and Alaska Native art, and the curators can tell you all about the artists who created each piece. Even if you're not looking to buy, it's worth a stop just to see the beautiful art, and it'll help give you an idea of the difference between real Alaska Native artwork and the crudely made frauds. The shop next door, **Scanlon Gallery** (318 Mission St., 907/247-4730, scanlongallery.com), is owned by the same family. It doesn't sell Alaska Native art, but instead represents a number of fine local and Alaskan artists.

For another source of authentic Native art that's so beautiful you should go just to marvel at it, visit **Alaska Eagle Arts** (5 Creek St., Suite 3, 907/225-8365, alaskaeaglearts.com), the gallery of Marvin Oliver, a Quinault/Isleta-Pueblo artist, professor of American Indian studies and art at the University of Washington, and adjunct curator of contemporary Native American art at the Burke Museum. His larger pieces are museum quality and priced accordingly, but you'll also find smaller gifts like jewelry, stationery, and blankets. Again, you'll get a great example of the difference between fine Native art (with a strong contemporary twist) and the imitations sold elsewhere.

For a gallery full of traditional Northwest Coast Native art (which includes Alaska Natives plus some tribes from Canada and the Pacific Northwest), go to **Crazy Wolf Studio** (633 Mission St., 907/225-9653, crazywolfstudio.com).

Creek Street Shops

You'll find many excellent shops on one side or the other of Creek Street, built into boardwalks that crisscross back and forth across the water. They're almost all locally owned, and many of them offer great handmade Alaskan goods.

Right next to Alaska Eagle Arts over Creek Street is the funky art gallery **Soho Coho** (5 Creek St., 907/225-5954, trollart.com), which houses a delightful collection of original art, prints, shirts, books, fossils, pottery, and other great gifts.

For Alaskan books and a charming selection of gifts, visit **Parnassus Books & Gifts** (105 Stedman St., 907/225-7690, Mon.-Thurs. 8am-5pm, Fri. 8am-6pm, Sat. 9am-5:30pm, Sun. 9am-4pm). **Alaska Northern Lights** (203B Stedman St., corner of Stedman St. and Creek St., 907/617-6067) offers a great collection of jewelry, Alaska-made soap and salves, local photography, children's gifts, and Alaskan artwork.

Sam McGee's (18 Creek St., 907/225-7267) also offers an extensive array of Alaska-made gifts, especially herbal soaps, salves, and other inexpensive treats that make great gifts. If you like what it sells, you'll find a similar selection on the main drag at its sister store (or should that be "brother store"?), **Blasphemous Bill's** (100 Main St., corner of Mill St., 907/220-9898).

For those who prefer to make their own crafts, the **Hive Bead & Yarn Shoppe** (716 Totem Way #1, 907/225-9161,

Made in Alaska

Like many active cruise ship ports around the world, Ketchikan has attracted a collection of international shops near the docks that carry inexpensive, generic goods that have little or nothing to do with Alaska. Unfortunately, many of those shops in Ketchikan also sell imitation Alaska Native art, using a combination of aggressive and misleading sales tactics to trick travelers into thinking they're getting an authentic product.

Please *do* shop carefully in Ketchikan, but please *don't* let knowing there are some frauds out there discourage you from shopping with the many fine local merchants that are just past—and sometimes even mixed in with—the misleading shops. There are many fine, creative items in all price ranges that you can only get here.

You can identify authentic goods by looking for the Silver Hand and Made in Alaska stickers and by paying attention to the seller's sales tactics; if sellers are aggressive, intimidating, or distracting with you, or seem unwilling to give direct answers, they're not selling authentic goods. True local shops will be thrilled to have a discerning traveler in their store, and will happily tell you all about the artists whose work you are admiring.

thehiveonthecreek.com) offers local knitting and quilt patterns, as well as some finished local art.

FOOD

For lunch or coffee, locals love **The Point** (25 Jefferson Way #102, 907/225-2858, thepoint-ketchikan.com, Mon.-Sat. 9am-4pm), which is a combination of waterside café and a gallery showcasing local artists. They offer great homemade soups and other light fare, including sandwiches, quiche, and cookies; check Facebook for lunch specials, valid 11am-2pm.

The **New York Café** (211 Stedman St., 907/247-2326, Sun.-Thurs. 7am-8pm, Fri.-Sat. 7am-9pm) feels like an old-timey hotel bar. The menu is heavy on seafood, and the salads are as good as it gets in Ketchikan, with local produce whenever possible. It can get crowded—which means slow service and sometimes a $5 cover—on evenings when live music is on. They also have a few breakfast options and a selection of Pacific Northwest wines and Alaska microbrews, and good coffee, too.

One of the best quick salmon meals you can get is from **Upcreek Salmon Co.** (133 Stedman St., 206/724-4765, mid-May-Sept., daily 11am-4pm), a brand-new operation that offers just one option: $14 for a slab of spice-rubbed, just-caught king salmon that's as big as your hand, roasted corn on the cob, and handmade coleslaw. It's worth it. The fish will come just barely cooked through, unless you specify otherwise.

If you don't mind rubbing shoulders with lots of other tourists just off a cruise ship, the ultimate in iconic Alaska seafood experience is the **George Inlet Lodge Crab Feast** (907/225-6077, catchcrabs.com, May-Sept. daily, often serving 6:45am-9pm, $69 adult, $59 for 12 and under). The location is as important as the feast of Dungeness crab; the lodge is an old cannery bunkhouse that was moved 90 miles to the current location at an old gold mine. You'll have to take a boat to get there, so expect the experience to last almost three hours.

Some of the best fish chowder and fresh fish-and-chips you'll ever have is at the little hole-in-the-wall **Alava's Fish-n-Chowder** (420 Water St., next to the tunnel between berth 2 and berth 3, 907/617-5328, daily 11am-5pm or later during the summer, reduced hours in winter), where they "don't serve breakfast because they're out catching lunch."

The spectacular views don't stop there: Also right on the water is the **Bar Harbor Restaurant** (55 Schoenbar Ct., 907/225-2813, Mon.-Thurs. 10am-3pm and 5pm-8pm, Fri.-Sat. until 9pm, opens at 9am Sun., $25). They serve an eclectic menu, with basics like fish-and-chips and some nicer seafood and crab entrées to go with the views; beer and wine are available.

The **Burger Queen** (518 Water St., 907/225-6060, Sun.-Mon. 11am-3pm, Tues.-Sat. 11am-7pm, $10-20) is a good-natured "relatively quick food" place that's been around for decades. The burgers are some of the best you'll ever have, the fish-and-chips is great, and the milk shakes are really good too. It's right next door to the Asylum Bar, so you can order the food from the bar and have it delivered if you like.

For the novelty factor or good, cheap burgers and seafood sandwiches, head for **Rose's Caboose** (4761 N. Tongass Hwy., 907/225-8377, Tues.-Sat. 11am-6:45pm, under $10), which is built into an actual train caboose. They serve great hand-scooped milk shakes, too, with indoor and outdoor seating where you might get to see floatplanes taking off.

Heen Kahidi Dining Room and Lounge in the Cape Fox Lodge (800 Venetia Ave., 866/225-8001, breakfast Mon.-Fri. 7am-11am, Sat.-Sun. 7am-1:30pm; lunch daily 11am-2pm, limited bar menu until 5:30pm; dinner Sun.-Thurs. 5pm-9pm, Fri.-Sat. 5pm-10pm; lunch $16, dinner $28) serves seafood, bison burgers, and reindeer sausage. Some tables have amazing views out over the treetops and the service is usually good.

The **Waterfront Restaurant** (1245 Tongass Ave., 907/225-5400, Mon.-Sat. 11am-8pm, entrées $16) is owned by the same family that used to run the Galley Restaurant, offering good Asian-American food (mostly Chinese, Filipino, and some burgers) at very reasonable prices. The spectacular view over the Tongass Narrows doesn't hurt, and this is a good place for cheap lunch ($11).

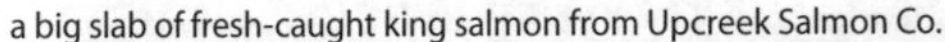

a big slab of fresh-caught king salmon from Upcreek Salmon Co.

The **Green Coffee Bean Co.** (7206 N. Tongass Hwy., 907/247-5621, tgcbc.com, Mon.-Sat. 6am-5pm, Sun. 9am-4pm, closed holidays) is on the cozy side of things, with a few booths and tables. It serves a wide variety of original blends and single origin blends, plus a great tea selection and a smattering of baked goods.

Groceries

There are two grocery stories convenient to downtown Ketchikan. You'll find the best selection at **Safeway** (2417 Tongass Ave., 907/228-1900, daily 5am-midnight), followed by longtime independent grocer **Tatsuda's IGA** (633 Stedman St., 907/225-4125, daily 7am-11pm). Prices range widely depending on how hard items are to ship, from about on par with Anchorage to double the price.

ACCOMMODATIONS

Cape Fox Lodge (800 Venetia Ave., 866/225-8001, capefoxlodge.com, from $215) is the nicest hotel in town, set on a steep wooded hill overlooking downtown Ketchikan; the service is very good and the bar often has live music. The decor is a blend of rustic and modern, with beautiful examples of Alaska Native artwork lining the walls, good Wi-Fi access, free parking, and a free airport/ferry shuttle. Water views over the Tongass Narrows are available from separate lodges (and for a fee, of course). A funicular car (a small tram car set on rails instead of cables) takes hotel guests down to street level for free, although it isn't always working. Non-guests can ride the car up for the restaurant—or to check out the artwork or the restaurant—for $2.

The **Inn at Creek Street & New York Hotel** (207 Stedman St., 907/225-0246, thenewyorkhotel.com, from $119) encompass a small boutique hotel, a few inn rooms overlooking historic Creek Street, and a couple of vacation rentals. The clean, homey rooms (each with its own handmade quilt), accommodating owners, free Wi-Fi, and away-from-the-docks downtown location all make this the best bargain for the dollar in town. Shuttle service for the ferry and airport is usually available, but call to verify. The setting for most of the rooms (right over Creek Street) is noisy during the day but peaceful at night once the crowds clear out.

The **Best Western Plus Landing Hotel** (3434 Tongass Ave., 800/428-8304 or 907/225-5166, from $225) is right next to the ferry terminal, but a couple miles out of downtown—so you'll need to either have a car or plan to take the bus, which runs about once an hour in each direction. Amenities include a fitness center, free Wi-Fi, and limited courtesy shuttle service, so call first to make sure the shuttle will be able to meet your plane or ferry. There are also two restaurants on-site, although they don't match up to the food you can get downtown.

Ketchikan has two hostels. The **EagleView Hostel** (2303 5th Ave., 907/225-5461, eagleviewhostel.com, Apr.-Oct., from $28, linens and towels included) is essentially a converted home. It has stunning views and is within a mile of the Alaska Marine Highway System ferry terminal, and a little under two miles from the airport ferry—but the walk includes a very steep hill, and if you want to visit downtown, you'll have to take the bus or rent a car. Heads up: There's no real common room and the owner is notoriously picky about behavior, but if you're tidy, follow the house rules, and take some time to chat, you'll probably be okay. Deposits are by check or money order only.

The **Ketchikan Hostel** (400 Main St., 907/225-3319, ktnumc.org/hostel, May-Aug., from $20, managers available 7am-9am and 6pm-11pm) is located in the First United Methodist church, smack in the middle of downtown, and has a calm, open atmosphere in clean but spartan accommodations. On the downside, if you don't have a sleeping bag you'll need to rent linens, there's a daytime lockout, and you'll share the kitchen space with the church's breakfast ministry to the homeless. Sometimes you'll end up sharing a dorm with people who are obviously using the hostel as long-term accommodations, too—a fact that makes some visitors uncomfortable.

Fishing Lodges

A few fishing lodges in Ketchikan offer the

Alaska version of an all-inclusive experience: For most packages, your food, gear, transportation, and processing are all included, in addition to the lodging. One of the best is **Salmon Falls Resort** (16707 N. Tongass Hwy., 907/225-2752, salmonfallsresort.com), which has newly renovated rooms and a newly improved restaurant; the food and service are both now excellent, and the lodge is about a 30-minute drive from downtown Ketchikan. For prices starting from $1,010 for three days, you get lodging and meals; make that $2,295 for three days and you get lodging (including a private bathroom), meals, and two days of fully guided fishing in one of the resort's cabin cruisers.

If you have an experienced group, you can't beat the private chalets, rental boats, and both guided and unguided trips from **Chinook Shores** (119 Potter Rd., 907/225-6700, chinookshores.com)—but because you're renting a chalet or beach house that sleeps up to six, this isn't for solo travelers. The accommodations are clean, comfortable, and reasonably modern, with private bathrooms, fully equipped kitchens, free Wi-Fi, and cable TV. Experienced anglers can purchase a self-guided fishing package that includes a rental boat, starting at $1,230 for three days and three nights (you pay for fuel, make your own meals, and process your own fish), or fully guided packages begin at $2,050 for three nights of lodging and two days of fishing.

Also excellent is the **Waterfall Resort** (800/544-5125, waterfallresort.com) on nearby Prince of Wales Island, an old salmon cannery that's been refitted with lovely, comfortable rooms sporting incredible water or forest views. **Sportsman's Cove Lodge** (800/962-7889, alaskasbestlodge.com), also on Prince of Wales Island, offers rustic but comfortable accommodations (think bear skins and carved fish on the walls) just a short floatplane ride away. Both lodges offer some of the best sportfishing, service, and—just as important—food you'll get on the island.

Camping

If you have a vehicle or don't mind riding the hourly bus, you can sleep in the Signal Creek or Last Chance campgrounds, six miles north of Ketchikan in **Ward Lake Recreation Area** (reservations tel. 877/444-6777, recreation.gov, $10). Signal Creek has 24 units surrounded by the spruce, hemlock, and cedar giants of the rainforest, with water and pit toilets available. Last Chance Campground straddles Last Chance Creek and sits right next to Ward Creek, making it a great place for fishermen. It has 19 drive-in units, 17 of which are fully accessible.

Past the reach of the bus system, lovely forested **Settlers Cove Campground** (Milepost 18, N. Tongass Hwy., no reservations, 35-foot RV size limit, $15) is 18 miles north of town and links in to Ketchikan's system of hiking trails, most notably Lunch Falls and Lunch Creek. It has an unusual (for Alaska) sandy beach. Pit toilets and water are the only amenities.

INFORMATION AND SERVICES

The **Berth 2 visitor center** (Mission St. and Front St., 800/770-3300 or 907/225-6166, visitketchikan.com) is open year-round; during the summer it's open seven days a week 8am-6pm or 6:30pm. During the winter, hours are typically Monday-Friday 8am-5pm.

Like most Southeast communities, Ketchikan has excellent cellular coverage through AT&T and Verizon, although the service probably won't be as fast as you're used to. If you use other carriers, it's best to inquire about their service before your trip.

The **PeaceHealth Ketchikan Medical Center** (3100 Tongass Ave., 907/225-5171, peacehealth.org/ketchikan-medical-center) is a level IV trauma center with a 24-hour emergency room; enter the emergency room from Carlanna Lake Road.

Visitors are always surprised by the limited Wi-Fi availability in Southeast communities (and Alaska in general). However, most Ketchikan cafés and bars offer Wi-Fi access with a purchase, and most hotels offer complimentary Wi-Fi that is, by Alaska standards, reasonably fast.

You won't find any gas stations right in downtown Ketchikan, but they're just a couple of miles away: Try the **Safeway gas station** (2417 Tongass Ave., 907/228-1900) or **Chevron Westside Services** (2425 Tongass Ave., 907/225-5700) to the north of Ketchikan, or **South Tongass Services** (2852 S. Tongass Hwy., 907/225-6696) to the south. **Lighthouse Tesoro Services** (10730 N. Tongass Hwy., 907/247-2244) and Chevron Westside Services both offer repair service too.

The **Ketchikan post office** (3609 Tongass Ave., 907/225-9602, Mon.-Fri. 8:30am-5pm) is right next to the ferry terminal; there's another one in **Ward Cove** (7172 N. Tongass Hwy.)

Ketchikan has a number of ATMs. Two 24-hour **Wells Fargo** ATMs are located inside branches (409 Dock St., 907/225-2184, and 2415 Tongass Ave., 907/225-4141). **KeyBank** also offers a branch with an ATM to the north (2501 Tongass Ave., 844/433-2068).

TRANSPORTATION

Many people see Ketchikan as a remote location, but it's actually one of the best-connected communities in Southeast. It's only a 90-minute flight from Seattle, Washington and receives five **Alaska Airlines** (800/252-7522, alaskaair.com) flights every day, some of them going on to Juneau and some turning back to Seattle.

That's not the only transport surprise here: The Ketchikan airport is actually located on a separate island. The airport is on Gravina Island, while Ketchikan is on Revillagigedo Island. The two are linked by a short ferry ride across the Tongass Narrows; the one-way fare is $6 for a walk-on passenger ($3 for ages 6-11, 5 and under free) and $7 for most cars and vans, payable on the airport side of the water. Taxicabs meet the airport ferry on the Ketchikan side of the water. The ferry leaves the Ketchikan side of the narrows at 15 and 45 minutes after the hour, starting at 6:15am; it departs the airport side of the strait on the hour and half past, with the final departure at 9:30pm.

Ketchikan's main ferry terminal is about two miles north of town on the North Tongass Highway; if you don't have a car, you can hop a bus into town. The ferry terminal sees incoming traffic from **Alaska Marine Highway System** ships (800/642-0066, ferryalaska.com) heading north from Bellingham and Prince Rupert, or south from Wrangell. The AMHS also runs a twice-daily ferry shuttle for the 45-minute trip between Ketchikan and nearby Metlakatla five days a week, and **Inter-Island Ferry Authority** ships (866/308-4848, interislandferry.com) offer daily passenger and vehicle service running from Hollis (on Prince of Wales Island) to Ketchikan and back again.

Once you're in town, the **Ketchikan Bus** (907/225-8726, kgbak.us/Transit, $1 adult, $0.50 students, day pass $2) offers excellent service given the size of the community, including transport to the ferry terminal and the airport. Service is reduced somewhat on Sunday, with extra runs added on Friday and Saturday evenings.

During tourist season (May-early Sept.), the free **Salmon Run Bus** runs 20-minute loops (daily 7am-7pm) through downtown Ketchikan; just look for the bus with brightly painted fish on it.

You have four rental car services to choose from in Ketchikan: **First City Car Rental** (907/225-7368), **Budget Rent a Car** (907/225-6003), **Alaska Smart Rentals** (907/225-1753), and **Alaska Car Rental** (907/225-5000). Most downtown parking is free for two hours; if you want to park longer, you can purchase a one-day permit for $5 at city hall (334 Front St., 907/225-3111). You can also rent bikes from **Ketchikan Town Bike Rental** (1224 Tongass Ave., near the cruise ship docks). Bike rentals are available by the half day ($20 for less than four hours) or the full day ($30).

Taxicabs all should charge the same rate: $3.70 for flag drop and $3.50 per mile after that. Try **Alaska Cab** (907/225-2133) or **Sourdough Cab** (907/225-5544).

Prince of Wales Island

If you like your road trips rustic and remote, with only tiny communities along the way, it's time to start planning a trip to **Prince of Wales Island.** This 2,231-square-mile island—the fourth largest in the nation, behind Kodiak, Hawaii's Big Island, and Puerto Rico—has more than 1,500 miles of roads passing through tiny communities like Craig, Coffman Cove, and Thorne Bay (an easygoing commercial fishing town).

Most of those roads are old logging roads in various states of disrepair that present what I like to call "true adventure driving"; most visitors focus on the approximately 250 miles of paved and maintained gravel road around the island, including a state scenic byway that basically bisects the island from Hydaburg in the southeast to Point Baker in the northwest. Bring a car charger for your cell phone; you'll need it.

Of course, before you start driving, you have to get your car there. The **InterIsland Ferry Authority** (866/308-4848, interislandferry.com) offers a single round-trip (three hours each way) between Ketchikan and **Hollis,** a small community on Prince of

Southern Southeast Alaska

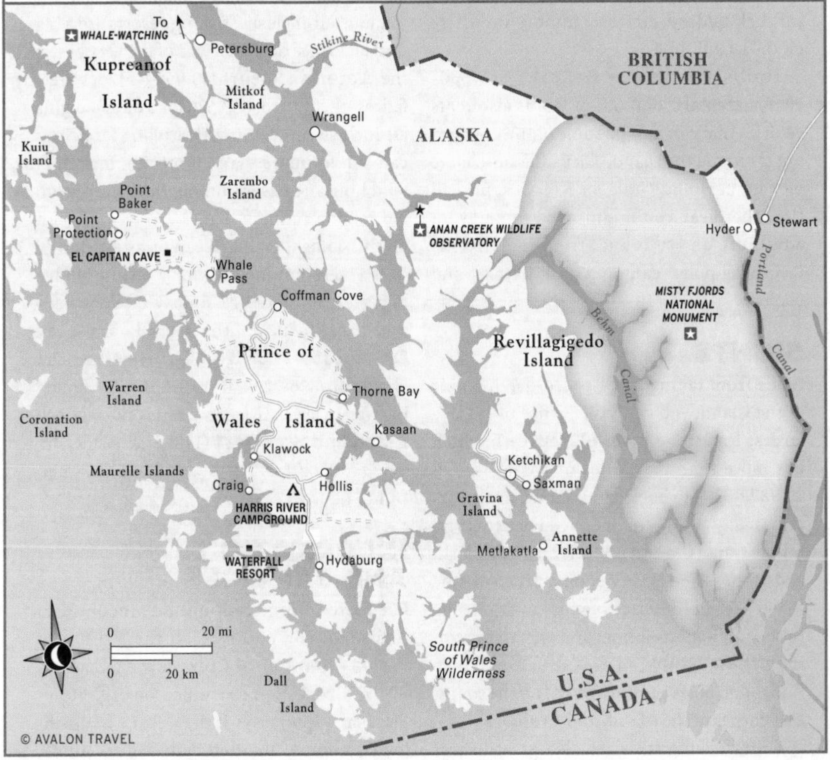

Wales Island, most days of the week. There are no regular services at the ferry terminal; **Island Ride** (907/401-1414) provides transport from the terminal, but you must make advance reservations. If you're renting a car, you're best off renting from either of two businesses on Princes of Wales, which have vehicles that can handle the local roads.

The community of **Craig** (about 1,250 people) is your ideal base camp on this island; it's centrally located and has the most services to offer. Craig is about a 30-mile or 45-minute drive from Hollis, and just seven miles from **Klawock,** which has the island's only official airport. If you're going carless, you can take one of the daily flights from almost every one of the small airlines flying out of Ketchikan then rent a car from **Rainforest Auto Rentals** (405 JS Dr. Ste. 195, 907/826-2277, craigakcarrentals.com, from $80/day). They're located in Craig but can set up a rental car pickup/drop-off point almost anywhere on the island.

Hollis Adventure Rentals (907/530-7040, harentals.com) out of Hollis also rents vehicles that can handle some of the unpaved roads around the island. They offer no-charge pickups at Hollis, Craig, or Klawock, plus all the other gear you might need to enjoy an adventure on the island, from rental skiffs to fishing poles, camping gear, kayaks, and coolers.

SIGHTS

Aside from taking a self-paced driving tour of the island, you can visit Prince of Wales's largest limestone cave, **El Capitan,** which has more than two miles of passages; call 907/828-3304 to book a tour. You can also explore many miles of maintained Forest Service hiking trails (**Cavern Lake Trail** on the north end of the island is very popular); explore the totem park in **Klawock,** a village with strong roots in Tlingit tradition; and visit the standing **Whale House** in **Kasaan.** You'll also find totem poles in **Hydaburg,** on the southeast corner of the island, and **Craig.**

Bear-viewing trips are also great in this area. **SeaWind Aviation** (877/225-1203 or 907/225-1206, seawindaviation.com) and **Alaska Seaplane Tours** (866/858-2327, alaskaseaplanetours.com) offer crowd-free opportunities to see black bears on Princes of Wales Island (the trips set out from Ketchikan).

FOOD

The tiny communities around Prince of Wales Island all have some sort of food for sale, but just one restaurant distinguishes itself from the others: **Zat's Pizza** (420 Port Bagial Blvd., Craig, 907/826-2345, lunch and dinner, call for hours, $24) serves great pizza, calzones, and even ice cream. You can buy groceries at the **AC Value Center** (504 Front St., 907/826-3394, daily 7am-8pm), but brace yourself for high prices.

FISHING AND ACCOMMODATIONS

Remote, all-inclusive fishing resorts are a big deal on Prince of Wales. One of the very best is the **Waterfall Resort** (800/544-5125, waterfallresort.com, from $3,620 for 3 days/4 nights all-inclusive, including floatplane fare). You can fish for more than 20 species, including wild king and silver salmon, then sleep in an old salmon cannery that's been refitted with lovely rooms sporting ocean or forest views.

If you're not looking for a fishing lodge experience, there are some excellent bed-and-breakfasts on the island. Try cozy **Dreamcatcher B&B** (1405 E. Hamilton Dr., Craig, 907/826-2238, from $125); it has amazing water views. Also good is the oddly named **A Bed and Breakfast** (1401 Sunnyside Dr., Craig, 907/401-3131, abedandbreakfast.net, from $125).

INFORMATION AND SERVICES

For more information on the amenities in this small community, call the **Prince of Wales Chamber of Commerce** (Klawock, 907/755-2626, princeofwalescoc.org, Mon.-Fri. 10am-3pm) or visit the website to download a copy of the detailed visitors guide.

Gas is typically available in the communities of Craig, Klawock, Naukati, Thorne Bay, Coffman Cove, and Whale Pass, but for anything outside of Craig and Klawock, it's best to call ahead first and verify availability.

METLAKATLA

Metlakatla, on neighboring **Annette Island,** is a thriving Tsimshian community and the only Indian reservation in all of Alaska. You can now easily visit Metlakatla as a day trip, thanks to twice-daily shuttle service from the *Lituya,* part of the **Alaska Marine Highway System** (800/642-0066, ferryalaska.com). Currently service is available Thursday-Monday, but the ferry schedule fluctuates in accord with state funding, so always double-check before planning your trip.

Two providers offer cultural day tours in Metlakatla: **Metlakatla Tours** (907/886-8687), which includes traditional Tsimshian dancing in full regalia, and **Laughing Berry Tours** (907/886-4133), a narrative tour by a member of the local Native community. **Laughing Berry Gifts** (505 Milne St., 907/225-4133) and **House of the Wolf** (end of Breakwater Rd., 907/225-1937) are a couple of gift shops worth a visit.

Accommodations and Services

If you decide to stay overnight, the **Metlakatla Inn** (3rd Ave., 907/886-3456, from $99) is excellent, with comfortable, clean rooms, reasonably fast Wi-Fi, friendly hosts, and a full-service restaurant on the first floor. A grocery store, **Leask's Market** (48 Western Ave., 907/886-4881, Mon.-Fri. 10am-6pm, Sat. till 5:30pm, Sun. noon-5pm), is nearby. For a B&B, book the **Tuck 'Em Inn** (574 Hillcrest Rd., 907/886-6611).

Finally, to rent a vehicle, contact **Laughing Berry Car Rentals** (505 Milne St., 907/886-4133 or 907/723-9835).

Wrangell

Wrangell—located on an island of the same name—is a sleepy little town of about 2,500 people, with a natural deepwater port that hasn't seen a big cruise ship since about 2005. That's when the cruise lines started stopping in Prince Rupert, Canada, which bumped Wrangell off the small-port itinerary and sliced some 200 jobs, eliminating about 30 percent of the town's revenue in one swoop.

The community drew together and rebounded, though, and tourism remains one of the primary economic drivers; this is still a very popular stop for small cruise ships and independent travelers. Visitors appreciate the chance to get a taste of authentic small-town Alaska life, and Wrangell's nearby attractions—including the LeConte Glacier and Anan Creek Wildlife Observatory—are some of the best in the state.

The other mainstays of Wrangell's economy are commercial fishing, processing, and a marine haulout with a 300-ton lift.

Summer temperatures in Wrangell typically peak in the 60s through June, July, and August, with about 80 inches of average annual rainfall—a little less than other Southeast communities. Fall is wet and windy, and winter temperatures are mild, dipping below freezing often enough to generate some lingering snow. If you're not on a small cruise ship, the only ways to reach Wrangell are by Alaska state ferry or Alaska Airlines jet.

SIGHTS

James & Elsie Nolan Center

You'll find the Wrangell visitor center and museum in the **James & Elsie Nolan Center** (296 Campbell Dr., 907/874-3770, May-mid-Sept., Mon.-Sat. 10am-5pm, reduced winter hours, museum $7, discounts for children and seniors). As is usually the case, Alaska's smallest museums are often its best, so be sure to make time for a look into Wrangell's colorful past.

a boardwalk overlook in Wrangell's small-boat harbor

Chief Shakes Tribal House

From the Nolan Center, take Brueger Street south to Shakes Street, then cross a short bridge to the **Chief Shakes Tribal House,** an exact replica of a 1700s-era traditional high-caste Tlingit communal housing and community space. You'll see a few totem poles here, and more in the **Totem Park** at the intersection of Front and Episcopal Streets. The house is usually closed but may be opened on request for a small admission fee. Direct inquiries to the Wrangell Cooperative Association (907/874-4304).

Petroglyph Beach State Historic Site

You can get another look into the past on Wrangell's beach at **Petroglyph Beach State Historic Site** about 0.5 mile north of town via Evergreen Avenue. (There's no

the Chief Shakes Tribal House

Wrangell

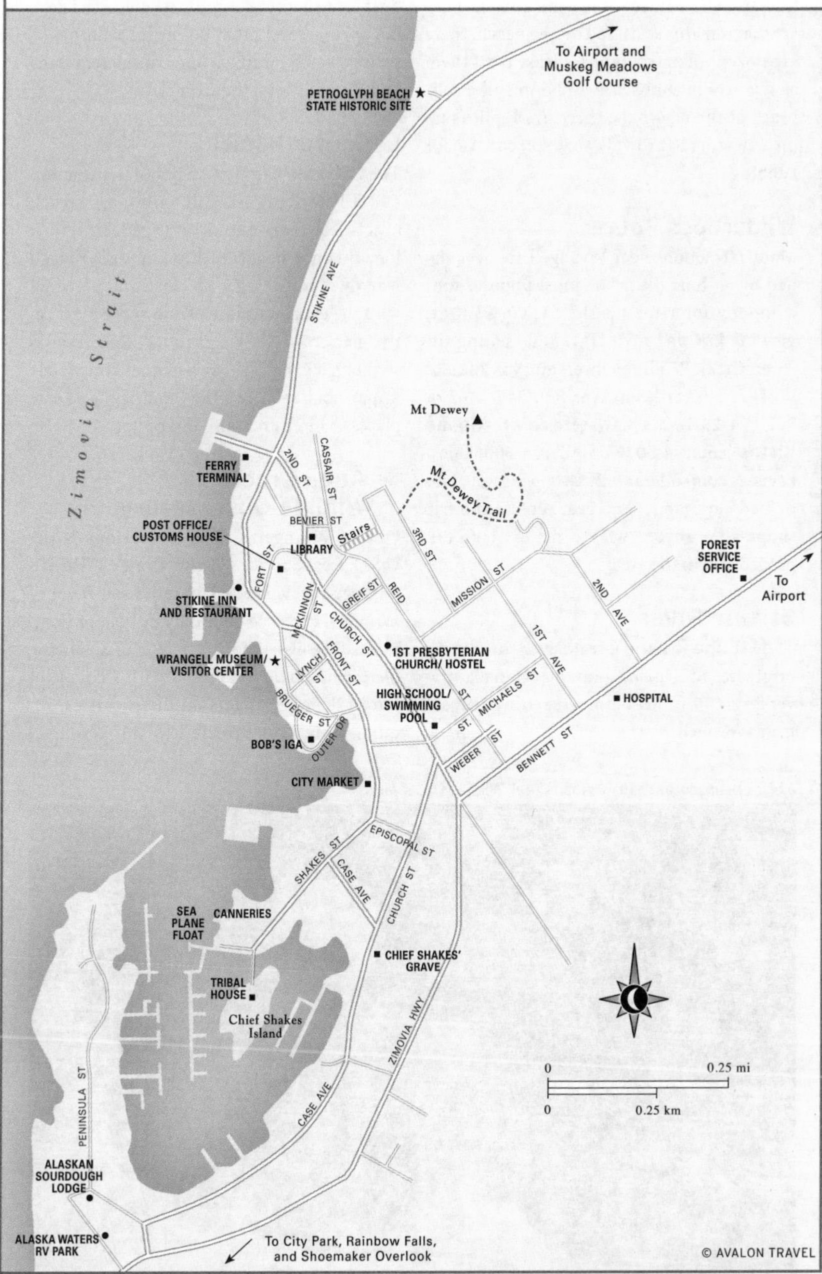
To Airport and Muskeg Meadows Golf Course
PETROGLYPH BEACH STATE HISTORIC SITE
Zimovia Strait
STIKINE AVE
Mt Dewey
Mt Dewey Trail
FERRY TERMINAL
2ND ST
CASSAIR ST
BEVIER ST
POST OFFICE/ CUSTOMS HOUSE
LIBRARY
Stairs
3RD ST
FOREST SERVICE OFFICE
To Airport
FORT ST
STIKINE INN AND RESTAURANT
MISSION ST
2ND AVE
GREIF ST
REID
MCKINNON ST
CHURCH ST
1ST PRESBYTERIAN CHURCH/ HOSTEL
1ST AVE
WRANGELL MUSEUM/ VISITOR CENTER
LYNCH ST
FRONT ST
ST. MICHAELS ST
HIGH SCHOOL/ SWIMMING POOL
HOSPITAL
BRUEGER ST
BOB'S IGA
OUTER DR
WEBER ST
BENNETT ST
CITY MARKET
EPISCOPAL ST
SHAKES ST
CASE AVE
CHURCH ST
SEA PLANE FLOAT
CANNERIES
CHIEF SHAKES' GRAVE
TRIBAL HOUSE
Chief Shakes Island
ZIMOVIA HWY
0
0.25 mi
0
0.25 km
CASE AVE
PENINSULA ST
ALASKAN SOURDOUGH LODGE
ALASKA WATERS RV PARK
To City Park, Rainbow Falls, and Shoemaker Overlook
© AVALON TRAVEL

sidewalk, but it's an easy walk and drivers are considerate.) Go during a reasonably low tide and you can scout for the ancient rock art that remains scattered on the beach; there are dozens of petroglyphs. Please treat them as if you're in a museum and don't take rubbings of the originals; there are replicas up on a viewing boardwalk that you can use for rubbings.

Wilderness Tours

Many attractions near Wrangell are best visited by jet-boat tour. The most popular tour company for trips up the **Stikine River,** viewing **LeConte Glacier,** and visiting the Anan Creek Wildlife Observatory is **Alaska Waters** (107 Stikeen Ave., 800/347-4462 or 907/874-2378, alaskawaters.com). **Alaska Vistas** (866/874-3006 or 907/874-3006, alaskavistas.com) offers all three trips as well, plus guided kayak tours and gear rentals and trip support for anyone who wants to do an unguided trip in the area.

Stikine River

The **Stikine River** ("Great River" in Tlingit) originates in British Columbia, Canada, traversing 400 miles before reaching the sea near Wrangell. This massive river has carved a braided passage through wild, beautiful valleys; one of the best ways to see it is a jet-boat tour that'll take you past glaciers, lakes, hot springs, and often bountiful wildlife. In spring, watch for migrating trumpeter swans and shorebirds on the river flats.

LeConte Glacier

The **LeConte Glacier**—a popular attraction out of Petersburg—is still within easy reach of jet-boat tours out of Wrangell. In return for a thrilling boat ride through the Wrangell Narrows, you can get up close and personal with the enormous face of one of the most active glaciers in Alaska. Every so often, it sheds so much ice that the bay becomes completely impassable; seals use the floating ice as safe places to birth and raise their pups.

★ Anan Creek Wildlife Observatory

One of Wrangell's chief attractions is the U.S. Forest Service's **Anan Creek Wildlife Observatory,** located 30 miles southeast of Wrangell and accessible only by boat or floatplane. The observatory consists of a viewing platform and a photo blind with a couple of Forest Service rangers on the premises; inquiries are best directed to the Wrangell

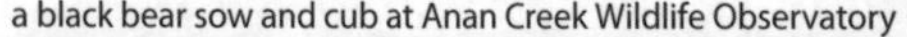

a black bear sow and cub at Anan Creek Wildlife Observatory

Ranger District of the Tongass National Forest (907/874-2323). Anan Creek is unusual because it offers a great chance to see black bears fishing. Brown bears come here too, lured by one of the largest pink salmon runs in the state. Often, what looks like algae in the water is actually the fish, packed so densely side by side that they completely obscure the creek bottom.

The chance to see black and brown bears together is highly unusual, as is the chance to see bears walking by right on the other side of the viewing deck railing; a photo blind gets you right down to the water level, where the bears are fishing. Access during peak viewing season (July and August) is by permit only ($10), and only 60 permits are issued per day, with 36 going to commercial tour operators and 24 to private individuals. You can reserve the nearby public-use cabin **Anan Bay Cabin** (accessible by water only, 877/444-6777, recreation.gov).

If you come to Anan Creek on your own, you must be prepared for close-distance, unexpected bear encounters, both on the 0.5 mile boardwalk leading to the observatory and at the observatory itself. The bears grudgingly tolerate the human presence for the same reason they tolerate each other: All those fish are worth it. But they are still wild, and if you're not thoroughly comfortable handling face-to-face encounters with massive, unpredictable wildlife on your own, you should come with a guide service. One of the closest—and thus most convenient—is the excellent **Alaska Waters** (107 Stikine Ave., 800/347-4462, alaskawaters.com, from $315 pp), based in Wrangell.

RECREATION

You'll find all five species of salmon in waters near Wrangell, plus trout, steelhead, and even halibut. Ply the island streams or shoreline on your own by picking up a fishing license and local regulations at the **Alaska Department of Fish and Game** (215 Front St., 907/772-5231, adfg.alaska.gov) or purchasing a license online. **Night N Gale Charters** (509/951-1373, nightngalecharters.com) specializes in ocean-fishing trips out of Wrangell; multi-tour operator **Alaska Waters** (107 Stikine Ave., 800/347-4462 or 907/874-2378, alaskawaters.com, starting at $325) is also very popular for ocean-fishing trips.

Wrangell has some great hikes. Take time for the **Mount Dewey Trail** (starts near Mt. Dewey Ln. and 3rd St.)—about 0.25 mile of steep staircase that gives you great views over the town and waterside—or hike the 0.8-mile trail to **Rainbow Falls** (trailhead at Mile 4.5, Zimovia Hwy., south of town). The Rainbow Falls Trail can be linked with a longer traverse into camping opportunities in the high country, and the same trailhead also offers access to the **Institute Creek** and **Wrangell High Country Trails**. Get more information at the U.S. Forest Service visitor center, which is appended to the **James & Elsie Nolan Center** (296 Campbell Dr., 907/874-3770, May-mid-Sept. Mon.-Sat. 10am-5pm, winter Tues.-Sat. 1pm-5pm).

Residents of Wrangell and nearby Petersburg carry out a friendly, ongoing rivalry on Wrangell's nine-hole regulation golf course and driving range, **Muskeg Meadows** (next to the airport, 907/874-4653, wrangellalaskagolf.com). The first United States Golf Association (USGA)-rated golf course in Southeast, Muskeg Meadows comes with a few unusual rules. For example, ravens often steal golfers' balls, thinking they're eggs; if this happens to you and there's a witness, you can replace the ball without penalty.

Some excellent **Forest Service cabins** are accessible by boat from Wrangell (see recreation.gov for more information). For a truly unusual outing, charter a boat to visit **Chief Shakes Hot Springs,** 28 miles northwest of Wrangell up the Stikine River, with enclosed and open-air redwood hot tubs and dressing rooms; **Breakaway Adventures** (888/385-2488 or 907/874-2488, breakawayadventures.com) can get you there. Try to avoid weekends and holidays during the summer, when the place gets unusually crowded.

EVENTS

For such a small community, Wrangell has a number of events that attract interest throughout the evening, including its five-day **Bearfest** at the end of July (alaskabearfest.org), which features educational lectures, nature walks, music, community activities, and tours of the Anan Creek Wildlife Observatory; the **Stikine River Birding Festival** in late April (stikinebirding.org), which features birding tours, educational activities and community activities; the annual **King Salmon Derby** that kicks off in mid-May (wrangellchamber.org).

SHOPPING

All of Wrangell's businesses are locally owned, and most guide services also offer small gift shops where you can get quality apparel and some Alaska-themed items like insulated water bottles, but the rest of the town's shops have a very practical bent. In fact, most of them are hardware stores. Your best shot at a gallery is **Watercolors of the Pacific Northwest** (off the corner of Stikine Ave. and Front St.), featuring paintings by "Marine Artist" Brenda Schwartz-Yeager.

The **Wrangell Museum** (296 Campbell Dr., 907/874-3770, summer hours May-mid-Sept., Mon.-Sat., 10am-5pm; winter hours are Tues.-Sat., 1pm-5pm) in the James & Elsie Nolan Center has a good gift shop that, in addition to maps, books, and a smattering of gifts, also sells garnets that local youth have mined from the "Garnet Ledge," a deposit located seven miles away on the mainland. Make sure to ask for a brochure on the ledge's history; it's been set aside for use only by the youth of this region, who often still meet cruise ships to sell their garnets. If you want to visit the ledge, you'll have to charter a private boat to get there.

FOOD

Wrangell offers just a few places to eat out. The **Stikine Restaurant** (Stikine Inn, 107 Stikine Ave., 888/874-3388 or 907/874-3388, stikineinn.com, $20) is the best for dinner; it's beloved for its burgers, hand-cut steaks, and local halibut fish-and-chips. Waterfront patio seating, a full wine list, and a cocktail menu are available. A new addition to the Stikine Inn, the **Stik Cafe** (daily 6:30am-6pm), offers baked goods, sandwiches, soup, and a few breakfast options, along with some of the best coffee in town.

The town favorite for breakfast and lunch is the **Diamond C Cafe** (223 Front St., 907/874-3677, daily 7am-2pm, $12); it's famous for its Diamond C Hash. **Zak's Cafe** (316 Front St., 907/874-3355, Mon.-Sat. 11am-7pm) is also very popular; every day it offers a new soup, salad, and dessert, with at least one seafood option.

Groceries are available in two places, both of which close early. The prices and selection are best at **Wrangell City Market** (423 Front St., 907/874-3333, wrangellcitymarket.com, Mon.-Sat. 8am-6pm), where you can get a sampling of almost anything you'd expect in a big-city market—but said sampling is very small. Prices range wildly from on par with Anchorage to 50 percent more. Your other option is **Bob's IGA** (223 Brueger St., 907/874-2341, bobswrangell.iga.com, Mon.-Sat. 8am-6pm, closed major holidays).

ACCOMMODATIONS

Wrangell offers just one hotel: the **Stikine Inn** (107 Stikine Ave., 888/874-3388 or 907/874-3388, stikineinn.com, from $156 for a street-side room, from $180 for a waterside room). The beds are comfortable, and each room has cable TV, a coffeemaker, and Wi-Fi.

A second high-volume option (by Wrangell standards, anyway) is the **Alaskan Sourdough Lodge**, aka the **Harding Lodge** (1104 Peninsula St., 800/874-3613 or 907/874-3613, akgetaway.com, from $120). It offers new beds, continental breakfast, a free shuttle to/from the airport and ferry terminal, and cable TV/Wi-Fi. Some of the rooms can sleep as many as six people, so if you have a group, this is a great option.

For budget travelers, the **Wrangell Hostel** (220 Church St., 907/784-3534, $20/night for a dorm) is run out of the Presbyterian Church; single-sex dorm rooms and a family room are available. Be warned that Google Maps deposits you somewhat east of where the church actually is; look for the white steeple with a cross on it. You'll sleep on either small inflatable mattresses or cots and share the kitchen and common area with churchgoers during their services and events, but they're easygoing and have no lockout policy. Linens, towels, and use of an aging washer/dryer are available for a small fee. Hostel managers are not very responsive to phone calls, but you should try to make reservations to guarantee your spot—be sure to leave a message.

Wrangell has 15 miles of paved roadway to explore and more than 100 miles of forest roads. If you're here with an RV, you have two options: The tiny **Alaska Waters RV Park** (Mile 1.2 Zimovia Hwy., corner of Berger St., $30 for up to 32 feet, $40 for over 32 feet) offers a few spots with some of the speediest Wi-Fi on the island. **Shoemaker Bay RV Park** (Mile 4.5 Zimovia Hwy., 907/874-2444) offers more RV spaces ($20-30, some electrical hookups) and a few tent spots.

INFORMATION AND SERVICES

The **Wrangell Medical Center** (310 Bennett St., front desk 907/874-7000 Mon.-Fri. 8am-5pm, call 911 for medical emergencies) maintains a small, 24-hour emergency room, with a registered nurse on duty and a physician on call. Patients with serious medical emergencies are often medevaced to either Harborview Medical Center in Seattle or one of the hospitals in Anchorage.

Wrangell has one **post office** (112 Federal Way, 907/874-3714, Mon.-Fri. 9am-5pm, Sat. 10am-noon) and two gas stations: **LNM Services** (21 Front St., 907/874-3687) and the **Alpine Mini Mart** (930 Zimovia Hwy., 907/874-2361).

Banking services and 24-hour ATM access are available at **Wells Fargo** (115 Front St., 907/874-3341, wellsfargo.com, Mon.-Thurs. 9am-5pm, Fri. 9am-5:30pm) and at the regional **First Bank** (224 Brueger St., 888/540-8585 or 907/874-3363, firstbankak.com, Mon.-Fri. 9am-5pm).

As is usual in Southeast Alaska, the public library is your best chance at free Wi-Fi. Visit the **Irene Ingle Public Library** (124 2nd St., 907/874-3535, wrangell.com/library, Mon. and Fri. 10am-noon and 1pm-5pm, Tues.-Thurs. 1pm-5pm and 7pm-9pm, Sat. 9am-5pm) to get connected.

TRANSPORTATION

There are just two ways to get to Wrangell: daily flights from Juneau and Seattle on **Alaska Airlines** (800/252-7522, alaskaair.com) or by boat. The airport is about 1.5 miles from downtown Wrangell. As there's no mass transit, you'll have to call a cab, or your hotel may offer a shuttle. The **Alaska Marine Highway System** (800/642-0066, ferryalaska.com) terminal is right in the middle of town, and ferries ply the waters of the Inside Passage every few days, heading northbound from Bellingham, Washington, and Prince Rupert, British Columbia, or southbound from Petersburg. Once you're in town, there's just one taxi company: **Northern Lights Taxi** (907/874-4646), which offers 24-hour cab service throughout town.

Petersburg

The small town of **Petersburg** (population 3,200) on **Mitkof Island** comes by its nickname of "Little Norway" honestly; it was founded when Norwegian fishermen selected it as an ideal site for cannery work, using drifting icebergs from the nearby LeConte Glacier to preserve their catch.

Petersburg remains a hardworking fishing town; some visitors can be a little put off that some residents would rather keep working than take the time to chat, while others love this extra touch of authenticity. It's not that residents are unfriendly—they're just busy pursuing the same lifestyle the original founders of Petersburg pursued.

Keep an eye out for sea lions in the harbor

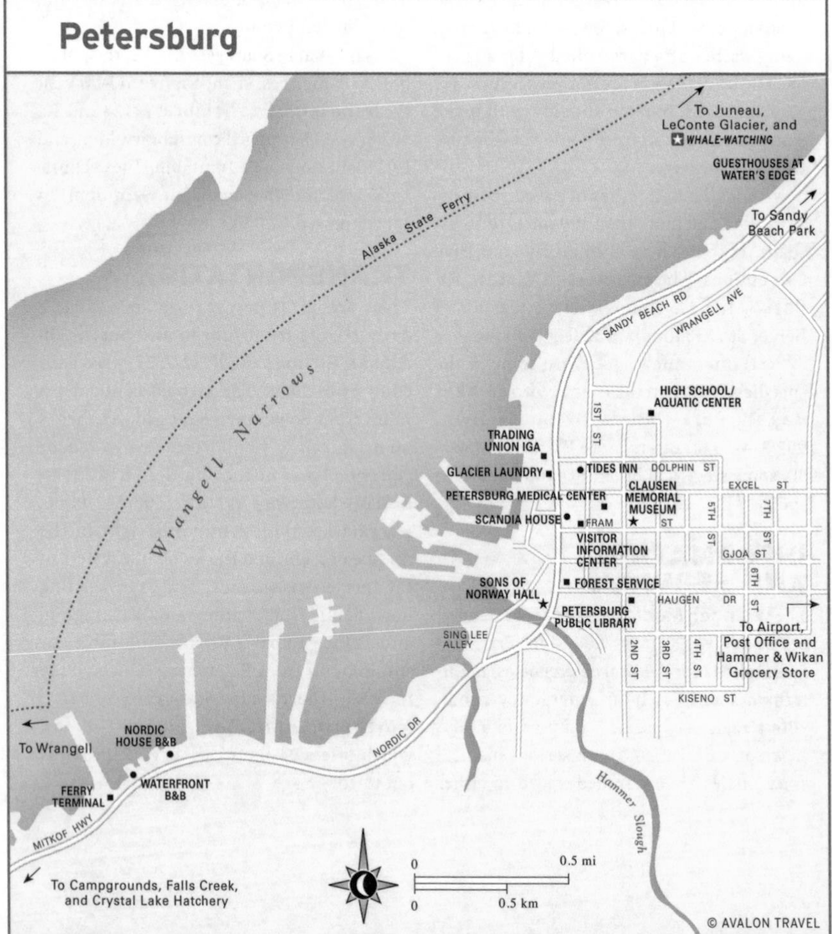

Sea lions make use of a buoy near Petersburg harbor.

or lounging on harbor buoys. These clever animals have become a famous nuisance because they have figured out when fishermen would be tossing fish scraps from the dock and started rearing aggressively out of the water, demanding to be fed. Storing the scraps in barrels, which are then dumped at sea, resolved the conflicts.

Temperatures here are mild, topping out in the 60s from June through August, with typical winter highs in the upper 30s. Petersburg receives about 110 inches of rainfall every year, so remember your rubber boots (or other waterproof footwear) and a good rain jacket.

Petersburg is a very popular stop for small cruise ships whose passengers want a glimpse of authentic, unpretentious Alaska life in a real fishing town. If you're coming on your own, there are two easy ways to get here: the state ferry system, which runs through town every few days on the way from Juneau to Ketchikan and vice versa, or on the daily Alaska Airlines flight.

SIGHTS

Weather allowing, everybody gets the same views of the famously daunting and only rarely climbed 9,500-foot **Devil's Thumb,** a distinctive near-vertical mountain that looks a bit like upward-jutting shards of crystal. Petersburg is also known for its **public art;** keep an eye out for art stamped into the sidewalks, rosemaling (Norwegian flower painting) on the storefronts, and old salmon labels on trash cans. The latter might sound a little odd, but the effect is really quite charming.

TOP EXPERIENCE

LeConte Glacier

LeConte Glacier is one of the most active and most-studied glaciers in Alaska. It is just 15 miles from Petersburg by boat, and it's the source of icebergs that sometimes make it all the way to the Wrangell Narrows (the waters just outside Petersburg) before they melt away. That ice is part of the reason Norwegian settlers chose this place for a town—before the days of ice machines, it was an easy way to preserve their catch. Both Whale Song Cruises and Tongass Kayak Adventures offer tours to see the glacier, and, again, you have the choice between a fast jet boat or a trip that can combine paddling with glacier viewing.

Leikerring Dancers

If you're coming on a small cruise ship, you may be met at the docks by the **Leikerring Dancers** in the **Sons of Norway Hall** (23 Sing Lee Alley, petersburgsons.org), performing traditional Norwegian dance to welcome you to town; unfortunately, independent travelers don't get such a fanfare. It's still worth a stop to see the picturesque Sons of Norway hall, though, as well as the **Fishermen's Memorial** and the surprisingly diminutive dragonboat ***Valhalla,*** both right beside the hall.

Clausen Memorial Museum

Leave time to stop by the **Clausen Memorial Museum** (203 Fram St., 907/772-3598, clausenmuseum.com, May-Sept. Mon.-Sat. 10am-5pm, limited winter hours; $5 adults, $3 youth/students and seniors, free 12 and under). It documents the early days of Petersburg's fishing history and shows artifacts from the traditional Tlingit people who lived in this area; ask to see the Fresnel lighthouse lens and Petersburg's first *bunad* (a traditional Norwegian dress that's tied closely to the place from which each pattern originates).

WILDERNESS TOURS

For two of Petersburg's biggest sights, **whale-watching** and the **LeConte Glacier,** you need to book a tour—but it's well worth the cost. Two of the best providers are **Whale Song Cruises** (office at 207 N. Nordic Dr., in the office supply store, 907/772-9393 or 907/772-3724 evenings, whalesongcruises.com) and **Tongass Kayak Adventures** (907/772-4600 or text 907/518-0076, tongasskayak.com).

the dragonboat *Valhalla,* outside the Sons of Norway Hall

TOP EXPERIENCE

★ Whale-Watching

When you take a July whale-watching tour in **Frederick Sound,** just 30 miles north of Petersburg, your boat may be surrounded by more than a dozen humpbacks feeding, diving, and even breaching. They don't eat when they breed in the warm waters to the south, so, once they migrate to these northerly waters, life is all about packing on as much blubber as possible from the rich food sources, including herring and krill. Sometimes you'll see orcas, porpoises, and other marine mammals, too, along with the historic **Five Finger Lighthouse.**

Captain Ron Loesch of Whale Song Cruises has a fast, 600-horsepower jet boat that lets you get out to Frederick Sound quicker and spend more time with the whales; Captain Scott Roberge of Tongass Kayak Adventures can blend whale-watching with kayaking and lunch stops ashore, giving you the chance to explore the beach in a place where few people have ever set foot.

TOP EXPERIENCE

FISHING

Fishing is one of the most popular pursuits out of Petersburg; after all, that's what this town was founded on, and it remains one of the biggest economic drivers for the community. To catch your own fish, contact **Secret Cove Charters** (907/772-2866, secretcovecharters.com) for saltwater salmon and halibut fishing trips at great prices, and **Petersburg Sportfishing** (707/208-0613, petersburgsportfishing.com) for saltwater fishing and freshwater fly fishing. For independent travelers who are up to handling a skiff in the challenging currents and rocks of the Wrangell Narrows, **Jensen's Boat Rentals** (907/772-4635 or 907/518-0121, jensensboatrentals.com) offers 18- to 22-foot rental skiffs by the day or the week, starting at $140/day for an 18-foot skiff.

RECREATION

The waters off Petersburg are great for **kayaking,** with one huge caveat: You must be competent enough to handle not just the cold water but also the high tidal differential and strong currents that constantly ebb and flow in the Wrangell Narrows. Time it right, and you can ride the rising tide up into creeks or deeper into the narrows, then coast back out on the current; if you venture too far south, you might just find the tide sweeping you down toward Wrangell instead of back toward Petersburg.

Confident paddlers can rent gear from one of the most experienced outfitters in town, **Tongass Kayak Adventures** (907/772-4600, tongasskayak.com); for those who aren't up to going it solo, guided kayaking trips, from day tours to multiday expeditions, are also offered.

Here's another unusual way to pass the time in Petersburg: Take a **Bella Vista Garnet Mine Tour** (907/772-3818, garnethouse.com, from $65); you'll be transported by van to a roadside garnet mine and loaned the tools to mine your own, which you then get to keep.

Petersburg is right in the midst of **hiking** trails and public-use areas in the Tongass rainforest, both along its roads and on neighboring islands, accessible only by boat or floatplane. Two of the most popular places nearby include **Eagle Roost Park** (just outside town on N. Nordic Dr.), with a viewing platform and an access trail for tide-pooling at low tide, and **Sandy Beach Picnic Area** (3 miles southeast of town on Sandy Beach Rd.), where you can search for ancient petroglyphs, prehistoric fish traps, and wildlife in the tidepools.

Also very popular are **Blind River Rapids** (Mitkof Highway, 14 miles south of Petersburg), where a boardwalk provides access to fishing or just makes for a pleasant stroll, and **Ohmer Creek Trail** (Mitkof Highway, 22 miles south of Petersburg), a two-mile loop through old-growth forest, part of which is wheelchair accessible. Very hardy locals go fishing and swimming at **Blind Slough** (Mitkof Highway, 15 miles south of Petersburg), which has some delightful wheelchair-accessible picnic tables under a covered

A humpback whale flashes its tail in Frederick Sound while passengers on a small cruise ship look on.

shelter. If you're here during the winter, you may see hundreds of trumpeter swans passing through between mid-October and early December, and locals ice-skating on the same water in December and January—if it freezes, which isn't always the case.

Finally, for adventurous travelers who are comfortable in the backcountry, Petersburg makes a great launching-off point for backcountry **public-use cabins** in the 1.6-million-acre Petersburg Ranger District, just a tiny fraction of the 17-million-acre **Tongass National Forest.** The really hardy can access the **Raven's Roost** cabin, which sits atop a mountain behind the airport, after 4.2 miles of steep, muddy, challenging hiking.

More popular is beautiful **Cascade Creek Cabin** on Thomas Bay (accessible only by boat or floatplane). If you're feeling especially intrepid, you can take a floatplane or helicopter in to the **Swan Lake Cabin,** high in the peaks of the Cosmos Range, then make a ridiculously steep, slippery, and challenging hike of about four miles down to the Cascade Creek Cabin on the **Cascade Creek Trail.** This trail exemplifies the most rugged of barely maintained Alaska hiking trails, and traversing it one-way takes most fit people a full day of effort. Alternatively, you can also walk the relatively easy first 0.25 mile of this trail to the first falls along Cascade Creek. Either way, any time you head out to one of these remote cabins, you should always stop by the **Petersburg Ranger District Office** at 12 N Nordic Dr (907/772-3871) for updated information.

Visit the **U.S. Forest Service Petersburg Visitor Information Center** (19 Fram St., 907/772-4636) for detailed information on local trails and cabins, and don't be shy about consulting an experienced guide/water taxi like Scott Roberge at **Tongass Kayak Adventures** (907/772-4600, tongasskayak.com). Those are your best tools for finding a cabin that's a good fit and getting you there.

EVENTS

One of Petersburg's most iconic events is the **Little Norway Festival** (petersburg.org), a four-day, mid-May celebration of its Nordic heritage and the beginning of the fishing season. Festivities include a parade, art shows, music, dancing, forest walks, traditional Norwegian foods and dancing, and some silly events like a herring toss.

Other big events include the **Rainforest Festival** in early September (akrainforest.org), which includes films, field trips to

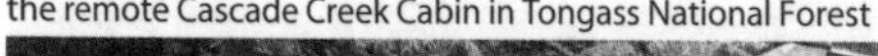
the remote Cascade Creek Cabin in Tongass National Forest

attractions like the LeConte Glacier, foraging for natural foods, art shows, and educational walks about the Tongass Rainforest. The Memorial Day **Salmon Derby** in late May (907/772-3646 for more information) is a four-day event with lots of family fun in addition to the fishing competition.

SHOPPING

Every shop in Petersburg is locally owned. The best gallery in town is **Miele Gallery & Framing** (211 Nordic Dr. 907/772-2161, Mon.-Sat. 9:30am-5:30pm, Sun. 10am-2pm), which carries a tasteful selection of handcrafted-only items, many of them from local and Alaska artists.

Lee's Clothing (212 N. Nordic Dr., 907/772-4229, Mon.-Fri. 9am-6pm, Sat. 9:30am-5:30pm, Sun. noon-4pm) sells outdoor clothing brands like Patagonia, along with a selection of beautiful Norwegian sweaters; they're a little pricey but make a stunning gift or the perfect souvenir of your time in Little Norway.

Sing Lee Alley Books & Gifts (11 Sing Lee Alley, 907/772-4440, Mon.-Sat. 9:30am-5:30pm, Sun. 10am-4pm) has a delightful mix of Alaskan titles, new releases, and gifts, along with some authentic Alaska Native art; they have a children's room filled with educational books, activities, and gifts, too.

Finally, for crafty souls, **Frontier Yarn and Fibre** (607 Excel St., 907/518-0233) has a selection of yarn and sewing supplies, plus quirky T-shirts and other gifts.

FOOD

For a community of its size, Petersburg has a pretty good selection of casual-dining options. As you'd expect, freshly caught seafood figures prominently on most menus.

Located across from the ferry terminal, **Joan Mei** (1103 S. Nordic Dr., 907/772-4221 or 907/772-4222, Tues.-Sat. 11:30am-8:30pm, Sun. 8am-8pm, $12-16) offers great Chinese food and some American meals, including hamburgers.

Your other top options are in the heart of downtown. The best food in town, including freshly caught seafood, local eggs, and local vegetables whenever possible, is at **Inga's Galley** (104 N. Nordic Dr., 907/772-2090, Mon.-Fri. 11am-7pm, Sat. 11am-2pm, $12), a small outdoor stand with a covered, heated dining area in case of rain.

Coastal Cold Storage Fish Market (306 N. Nordic Dr., 907/772-4177, deli daily 6am-2pm, $11-14) offers excellent seafood options; lunch service starts at 11am, and the shop stays open until 5pm for seafood purchases (dining ends at 2pm). They also offer retail seafood sales, and they'll ship.

Another downtown option that's particularly popular with the younger crowd is **Papa Bear's Pizza** (219 N. Nordic Dr., 907/772-3727, papabearspizza.com, Mon.-Sat. 11am-8pm, $20-25).

Two nice full-service coffee shops in town offer locally made baked goods and a bare-bones breakfast and lunch menu: **Java Hus** (110 N. Nordic Dr., tucked right against Scandia House, 907/772-2626, Mon.-Sat.

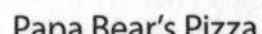

Papa Bear's Pizza

6am-5pm, Sun. 7am-3pm) and **Glacier Express** (400 Nordic Dr., 907/772-4141, Mon.-Sat. 6am-6pm, Sun. 6am-5pm).

For groceries, head to the **Trading Union IGA** (402 N. Nordic Dr., 907/772-3881, tradingunion.iga.com, Mon.-Sat. 7am-7pm, Sun. 9am-5pm, closed major holidays). Prices range widely here, from as good as (or even better than) Anchorage up to twice as much on items that are heavy or bulky, which means higher shipping costs.

ACCOMMODATIONS

There are two reasonably comfortable hotels in downtown Petersburg: **Tides Inn** (307 N. 1st St., 800/665-8433, tidesinnalaska.com, from $115, $10 per extra person) and the **Scandia House** (110 N. Nordic Dr., 800/722-5006 or 907/772-4281, scandiahousehotel.com, from $120, $10 per extra person). Both offer complimentary transportation to/from the airport and ferry terminal and a free continental breakfast. The Tides Inn also has free Internet, laundry facilities on-site, and kitchenettes in some rooms. The Scandia House charges a fee for their high-speed Internet.

Petersburg has excellent B&Bs. Two of the best are **Nordic House Bed and Breakfast** (806 S. Nordic Dr., 907/772-3620, nordichouse.net, from $97) and **Waterfront Bed and Breakfast** (1004 S. Nordic Dr., 907/772-9300, waterfrontbedandbreakfast.com, from $95), which is just a block from the ferry terminal. It has five bedrooms, each with a private bath, laundry facilities on-site, and a full breakfast. Each room booked in Petersburg is subject to a 10 percent tax.

For RV travelers, the **Trees RV Park** (Mile 10.2 Mitkof Hwy., south of Petersburg, 907/772-2502, thetreesrvpark.com, summer daily 9am-7pm, winter daily 10am-6pm) offers a laid-back ambience, tucked in the trees within walking distance of salmon streams and the ocean. They can accommodate RVs up to 50 feet and have 13 sites, 7 of which offer full service (water, sewer, and electricity; $30) and 6 of which offer just water and electricity ($20). There's also a rental cabin with an electric fireplace ($40). Coin-operated showers and laundry are available in the on-site general store.

Tent campers with a vehicle will find some limited accommodations at the Forest Service's **Ohmer Creek Campground,** 22 miles south of Petersburg on the Miktof Highway—but there are essentially no services due to budget cuts. The good news is that there are no fees for the 10 camping sites either (two of them are accessible). Help preserve the camping experience for others by packing your trash out with you.

INFORMATION AND SERVICES

The **Petersburg Visitor Information Center** (1st St. and Fram St., 866/484-4700 or 907/772-4636, petersburg.org, summer Mon.-Sat. 9am-5pm and Sun. noon-4pm, winter Mon.-Fri. 10am-2pm) is a great place to stop for brochures on local attractions and activities. Make sure you ask for walking tour brochures on public art installations and the historic canning labels that you see wrapped around trash cans in town. (The latter might sound a little silly at first, but they are actually quite striking and charming, and I will admit to amassing quite a collection of trash can photos as a result.)

For medical care, the **Petersburg Medical Center** (emergency room on N. 2nd St. between Excel and Fram, 907/772-4299 for the clinic or 911 for ambulance service) offers a 24-hour emergency room staffed by the community's four family practice physicians; serious cases will be medevaced to larger communities, which can include Anchorage or Seattle.

Drop your postcards at the **post office** (1201 Haugen Dr., 907/772-3121, Mon.-Fri. 9am-5:30pm, Sat. 2pm-4pm). The best banking and ATM option for most visitors is **Wells Fargo** (201 N. Nordic Dr., 907/772-3833, wellsfargo.com, Mon.-Thurs. 9am-5pm, Fri. 9am-5:30pm). There are also three—count them, three!—local credit unions within about two blocks on the same street.

For free Wi-Fi, the **Petersburg Public**

Travel with a Viking

If you've ever found yourself wishing you could have someone to arrange and troubleshoot an itinerary for you as the cruise ship lines do but still preserve the authentic Alaskan experience, there's a solution: **Viking Travel** (101 N. Nordic Dr., Petersburg, 800/327-2571 or 907/772-3818, alaskaferry.com, Mon.-Fri. 10am-6pm, Sat. 10am-5pm), a small, independent travel agency based in Petersburg.

Viking Travel deals only with local tour operators and serves as a booking agent for the state ferry system and Alaska Airlines, so you can have all the authentic travel you want with none of the logistical headaches. They take care of it all for you, and if your plane or ferry is delayed, they'll have your itinerary fixed before your buddies finish lining up for customer service.

Viking Travel also arranges travel with independent, local tour operators throughout the state, including the Arctic and all the way from Fairbanks down to Homer on the road system.

Travel delays are a fact of travel in Alaska, especially in Southeast, where both air and sea travel can be affected by bad weather and equipment problems. It's not a matter of if you'll be affected, but when. Even if you didn't originally use Viking Travel to book your itinerary, if you run into a scheduling snafu that you can't solve on your own, give them a call—they can probably help.

Library (14 S. 2nd St., 907/772-3349, psglib.org, Mon.-Thurs. 11am-8pm, Fri.-Sat. 11am-6pm) is your best bet. You can also get free Wi-Fi with a purchase from Java Hus, Glacier Express, and Papa Bear Pizza, all located downtown.

For gas, **Petersburg Motors** (10 N. 2nd St., 907/772-3223) is downtown; **Petro Express** (901 S. Nordic Dr., 907/772-4251) and **Southeast Island Fuel** (902 S. Nordic Dr., 907/772-3740) are south of town. The latter also offers vehicle repairs.

Glacier Laundry (309 N. Nordic, 907/772-4144) is open 6am-7pm some days, 24 hours on others; it all depends on which boats are in the harbor.

TRANSPORTATION

Petersburg is easy to reach with twice-daily **Alaska Airlines** (800/252-7522, alaskaair.com) jet service to Seattle, Juneau, and Anchorage, and service every couple of days by ferries from the **Alaska Marine Highway System** (800/642-0066, ferryalaska.com), heading north to Juneau and south to Wrangell. The ferry terminal is about a mile away from downtown Petersburg; some hotels offer a shuttle service, or call the wonderfully named **Viking Shuttle Taxi** (907/722-2222). The airport is about three miles from downtown Petersburg.

There are two places to rent a car, both hotels: an **Avis** located in the **Tides Inn** (307 N. 1st St., 907/772-4716, daily 7am-8pm) and at **Scandia House** (110 N. Nordic Dr., 800/722-5006 or 907/772-4281, scandiahousehotel.com, $70/day, unlimited mileage).

Ferry Through the Wrangell Narrows

Between Petersburg and Wrangell, and extending a short distance north of Petersburg, are the **Wrangell Narrows.** This narrow stretch of water was dredged and blasted during World War II to create a shortcut for navy ships under way, and it still has to be dredged periodically to keep it open.

The passage is too tight for big cruise ships to manage; only the state ferries, small cruise ships, and smaller tour, fishing, or personal boats make the serpentine trip through the narrows. At night, solar panels help light up the navigation markers like the inside of a pinball machine—if you're sleeping in a cabin near the engine room of your ship, you'll probably be happier watching from above deck, closer to the fresh air and farther from the noise.

This transit is especially fun if you're lucky enough to be on a jet boat. Some passengers say they see more wildlife—including land species—in this stretch of water than during any other part of their trip. Lately, humpback whales—which typically stick to Frederick Sound, north of the narrows—have started making their presence known here, too.

Sitka

One of Southeast Alaska's crown jewels, Sitka is located on Baranof Island in the massive Tongass National Forest. The town feels much smaller than its population of 9,000, which, believe it or not, makes it the third-largest community in Southeast.

Visitors love that they can get here on cruise ships of any size (including giant ocean liners), but almost everything is locally owned. Many businesses stay open year-round, proud to showcase the area's mix of Tlingit and Russian heritage and Sitka's robust creative community. However, if you're coming here to shop, be warned that many businesses close down entirely on Sunday, even during the peak season.

The climate in Sitka is mild, with average summer highs in the low 60s, and winter weather is rainy and mild, with temperatures topping out in the high 30s. Because it's located in the temperate rainforest, Sitka sees rain often, with an average of 95 inches of precipitation annually. June-August tend to be the drier months, although that's becoming more unpredictable as the climate changes. Happily, even on overcast days the island is beautiful, as long as you're dressed for the wet, breezy weather; overcast days often make for great whale-watching.

Fishing and tourism are the biggest economic drivers here. More than 100 million pounds of seafood are processed in Sitka every year, representing a first wholesale value of more than $80 million. Anywhere from 100,000 to 300,000 visitors pass through the port every year, mostly in the summer.

SIGHTS

Historical Sites

Sitka packs an amazing number of historical

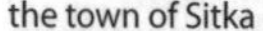

the town of Sitka

Sitka

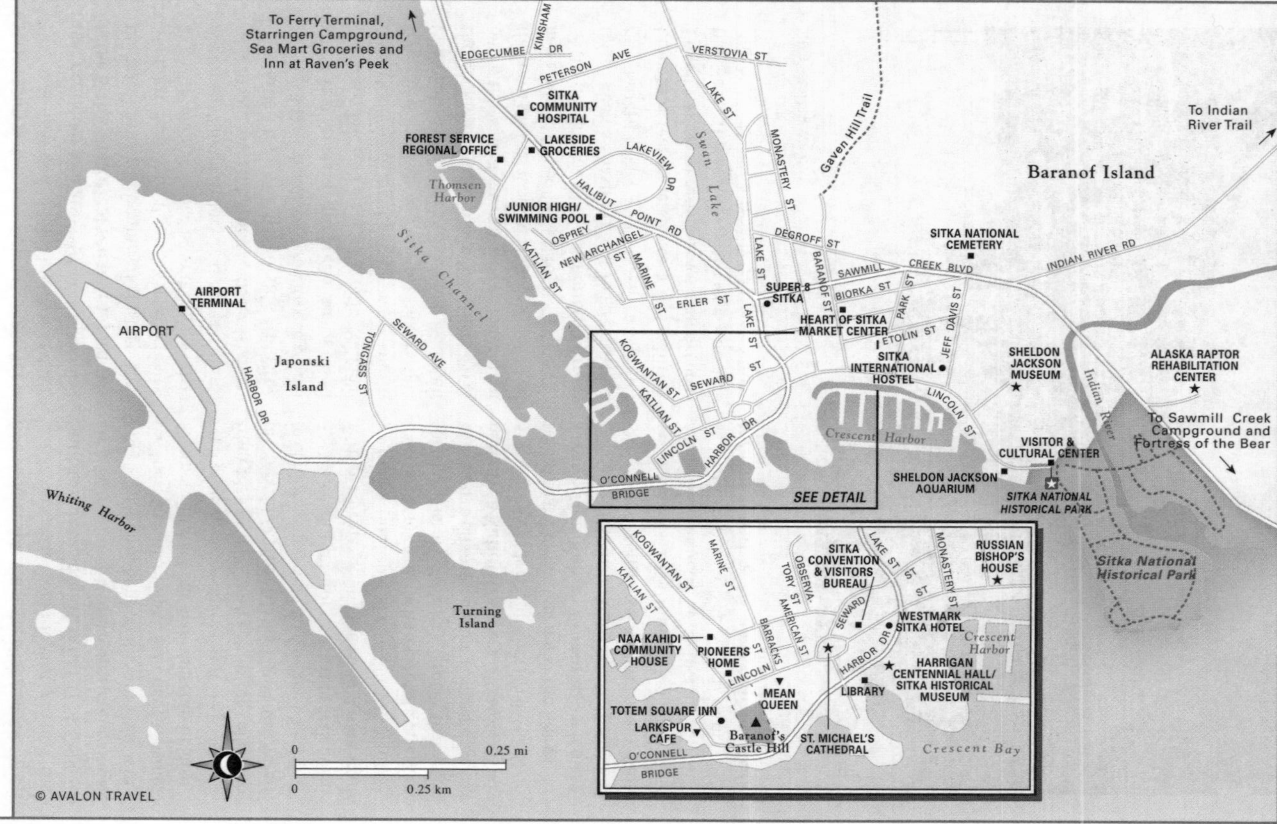
To Ferry Terminal, Starringen Campground, Sea Mart Groceries and Inn at Raven's Peak
EDGECUMBE DR
KIMSHAM
PETERSON AVE
VERSTOVIA ST
LAKE ST
SITKA COMMUNITY HOSPITAL
FOREST SERVICE REGIONAL OFFICE
LAKESIDE GROCERIES
LAKEVIEW DR
Swan Lake
MONASTERY ST
Gaven Hill Trail
To Indian River Trail
Baranof Island
Thomsen Harbor
HALIBUT POINT RD
JUNIOR HIGH/ SWIMMING POOL
OSPREY
NEW ARCHANGEL ST
MARINE ST
DEGROFF ST
SITKA NATIONAL CEMETERY
Sitka Channel
KATLIAN ST
BARANOF ST
SAWMILL CREEK BLVD
INDIAN RIVER RD
AIRPORT TERMINAL
SUPER 8 SITKA
BIORKA ST
PARK ST
ERLER ST
AIRPORT
TONGASS ST
SEWARD AVE
HEART OF SITKA MARKET CENTER
ETOLIN ST
JEFF DAVIS ST
Japonski Island
HARBOR DR
KOGWANTAN ST
SEWARD ST
SITKA INTERNATIONAL HOSTEL
SHELDON JACKSON MUSEUM
Indian River
ALASKA RAPTOR REHABILITATION CENTER
LINCOLN ST
To Sawmill Creek Campground and Fortress of the Bear
Crescent Harbor
VISITOR & CULTURAL CENTER
O'CONNELL BRIDGE
SHELDON JACKSON AQUARIUM
SEE DETAIL
SITKA NATIONAL HISTORICAL PARK
Whiting Harbor
Sitka National Historical Park
SITKA CONVENTION & VISITORS BUREAU
RUSSIAN BISHOP'S HOUSE
OBSERVA. TORY ST
AMERICAN ST
BARRACKS ST
Turning Island
WESTMARK SITKA HOTEL
NAA KAHIDI COMMUNITY HOUSE
PIONEERS HOME
HARRIGAN CENTENNIAL HALL/ SITKA HISTORICAL MUSEUM
MEAN QUEEN
LIBRARY
TOTEM SQUARE INN
LARKSPUR CAFE
Baranof's Castle Hill
ST. MICHAEL'S CATHEDRAL
Crescent Bay
0
0.25 mi
0
0.25 km
© AVALON TRAVEL

sights—and sites—into a very small area. Start at the visitor center in **Harrigan Centennial Hall** (330 Harbor Dr., 907/747-3225, Sun.-Fri. 9am-5pm, Sat. 11am-3pm May-Sept.). Just next door and also part of the complex is the **Sitka Historical Museum** (formerly the Isabel Miller Museum, sitkahistory.com, Mon.-Fri. 9am-5pm, limited weekend hours, $2), with photos, artifacts, and displays that document Tlingit history in the area.

A lovely, paved harbor walk leads about 0.75 mile along the harborside from the Harrigan Hall visitor center, with occasional signs that explain the area's history and economy. The trail ends at the Sitka National Historical Park, a highlight. If you head north into town instead, you can see picturesque Swan Lake Park, which has a small ladder on the dock to help swimmers pull themselves out of the water (you can see the water from the town's roundabout at Halibut Point Road and Sawmill Creek Boulevard).

On the far side of the visitor center from town, keep a sharp eye out for **Baranof's Castle Hill** (corner of Harbor Road and Lincoln Street), the site of a fort built by Tlingit natives to resist the Russian occupation; later, this was the place where ownership of Alaska was officially transferred from Russia to the United States. The trail to the top of the hill is fully accessible and has interpretive panels explaining the site's history.

0.5 mile away from the visitor center, the **Sheldon Jackson Museum** (104 College Dr., 907/747-8981, museums.state.ak.us, mid-May to mid-Sept. daily 9am-5pm, winter Tues.-Sat. 10am-4pm, summer $4, winter $3, under 18 free), the state museum in Sitka, represents Alaska Native cultures in transition from 1888 to 1898, with a stunning collection of everything from Alaska Native watercraft to clothing, tools, and ceremonial objects.

Cruise ship visitors are often welcomed with performances by the **New Archangel Dancers** (multiple venues, newarchangeldancers.com, $10), who celebrate Alaska's Russian history with folk dances that were common in Sitka during the 1700s and 1800s; or the **Naa Kahídi Dancers** (sitkatours.com, $10/adult, $5/kids 12 and under), who perform traditional Tlingit dancing at the **Sheet'ka Kwaan Naa Kahídi Community House** ("The community house for the people of Sitka") (200 Katlian St., 907/747-7137). Both performances last 30 minutes, and tickets are available 30 minutes in advance at the door.

You can pair a Naa Kahídi dance performance with a 2.5-hour **cultural tour**

Sitka's harbor walk

led by **Sitka Tribal Tours** (sitkatours.com, 907/747-7137), a nonprofit founded by the Sitka Tribe of Alaska. Cruise ship passengers, book through your deck excursion office; independent travelers, book through **Viking Travel** (800/327-2571 or 907/772-3818, alaskaferry.com, Mon.-Fri. 10am-6pm, Sat. 10am-5pm), a small, independent travel agency based in Petersburg. The cost for independent travelers is about $70 including the dance performance.

Historic buildings around town make it easy to view Sitka's long Russian history, including the 1842 **Russian Bishop's House** (103 Monastery St., 907/747-0110, 9am-5pm daily), once home to the most famous and beloved of Russian Orthodox missionaries in this area, Ioann Veniaminov, who was later canonized as St. Innocent. Entry downstairs is free; to access the refurbished living quarters upstairs, pay $4 for a short tour.

For a look at the full glory of a Russian Orthodox church, go to the 1848 **St. Michael the Archangel Cathedral** (240 Lincoln St., 907/747-8120, oca.org/parishes/oca-ak-sitsmk, 9am-4pm May-Sept. when cruise ships are docked). For a $5 donation you can see the altar and beautiful, ornate icons, several of which are credited with the powers of miracles and healing. There's also a small gift shop.

Sitka Sound Science Center

The **Sitka Sound Science Center** (SSSC, 834 Lincoln St., 907/747-8878, sitkascience.org, Mon.-Sat. 9am-4pm, gift shop Tues.-Sat. 9am-4pm, $5) is a modest facility that has a huge impact on aquaculture and fisheries research around the world and science education in Sitka. It has a fascinating touch tank aquarium inside and a great little gift shop (complete with a chowder cart run by one of Sitka's best restaurants, Ludvig's Bistro) in a building next door. The SSSC also offers tours of the adjacent Sheldon Jackson hatchery, where they rear and release coho (silver), chum (dog), and pink (humpy) salmon, or you can walk a boardwalk around the hatchery and check out a few signs.

Alaska Raptor Center

If you're in Sitka for long enough, you'll hear the high-pitched chattering of bald eagles and probably see them either swooping over the harbor or perching in the trees. When an eagle is injured in this area it's taken to the **Alaska Raptor Center** (1000 Raptor Way, 800/643-9425 or 907/747-8662, alaskaraptor.org, summer daily 8am-4pm, winter Mon.-Fri. 10am-3pm). Located on 17 acres, this center rehabilitates and researches Alaska's raptors, and provides education services to visitors and locals. Tours are available May-September and include a chance to see two dozen "raptors in residence."

Fortress of the Bear

For a different type of bear-viewing experience, rent a car or catch a $10 shuttle from the downtown visitor center to the **Fortress of the Bear** (4639 Sawmill Creek Rd., 907/747-3550 or 907/747-3032, fortressofthebear.org, 9am-5pm daily May-Sept., 10am-4pm Sat. and Sun. Oct-April, closed during hibernation Nov.-Feb., $10 adults, $5 children 7-18, free children under 7, $10 round-trip shuttle), a nonprofit education center that houses orphaned bear cubs until they can be transferred to an appropriate zoo or sanctuary. It's a great chance to see bears in a simulated version of their natural habitat. You can also take the local bus (weekdays only) to the Gary Paxton Industrial Park, which is just a short walk from the Fortress of the Bear.

★ Sitka National Historical Park

Every visitor should come to **Sitka National Historical Park** (visitor center at 103 Monastery St., 907/747-0110, nps.gov/sitk, May-Sept. daily 8am-5pm, Oct.-Apr. daily 9am-3pm, free) to see the past, present, and future of Alaska Native history in this area. Traditionally, totem poles were allowed to fall and decay in the natural course of events, but with the increasing understanding that historic poles must be preserved as part of a cultural legacy, a number of Tlingit and Haida totem poles were brought here to be preserved.

You can walk miles of Totem Trails around the park buildings to see historic totem poles set against the area's rich greenery (there's a free audio tour—use your cell phone or ask for an audio pen inside the main building), or even walk to the remains of a wooden fort (the Kiks.ádi fort site) where the Native Tlingit people of this area staged their last open resistance against the Russians in the 1804 Battle of Sitka.

Inside the main building, you can tour indoor exhibits of Tlingit regalia and historic photographs, watch one of the documentaries in the theater, and visit the **Southeast Alaska Indian Cultural Center** (accessed through the park visitor center) to watch Alaska Native master craftspeople demonstrate their art in its full cultural context. You can also borrow a kids' beach discovery kit from the rangers behind the desk, then head out to the beach, which is exposed by tides.

Sitka National Historical Park is at its best when you allow yourself some time to really soak things in (at least half a day). Leave yourself the time and space to read the interpretive signs about how totem poles are being preserved, to take the audio tour so you understand the symbols on each pole, and to really visit with—and listen to—the artisans in the cultural center, who are the most authentic windows possible not only into their fine art and its history, but also the culture that ultimately drives their work and holds it all together.

TOP EXPERIENCE

HIKING

Sitka offers an extensive trail system for **hikers;** the most accessible are the 1.5 miles of **Totem Trails** in Sitka National Historical Park (nps.gov/sitk), starting at the visitor center. Some other popular trails include:

The **Indian River Trail** (4.5 miles one-way) is an easy (by Alaska standards) stroll through the coastal rainforest with views of the Sisters Mountains and Indian River Falls at the end. The trail gains only 1,000 feet gradually throughout its length. Because salmon run in this river in the fall, be especially careful about bear encounters. The trail starts within walking distance of downtown Sitka (take Sawmill Creek Road to Indian River Road, watch for the trailhead parking lot at the end of the road). The trailhead may or may not be signed, but there is an obvious wheelchair-accessible gravel trail that briefly parallels the road before heading into the woods. The trailhead is also serviced by the community bus line.

Totem Trail in Sitka National Historical Park

The 1.5-mile **Mosquito Cove Trail** sports some stairs and slippery, uneven surfaces, but is otherwise an easy nature walk with lots of wildlife sightings and tidepools to explore once you reach the cove. The trail is sometimes closed due to high bear activity, but you have good chances of seeing brown bears even if no signs are posted; see *Essentials* for more information about wildlife safety. Find the trailhead 0.75 mile north of the ferry terminal or seven miles north of downtown Sitka at the north end of Halibut Point Road.

Finally, the climb up **Mount Verstovia** (2.5 miles and 2,550 feet of elevation gain, one-way) is a stiff, challenging hike that starts two miles east of downtown Sitka on Sawmill Creek Road. The parking lot is tiny—it only holds a couple of cars—but you'll get stunning views from the shoulder of the mountain. Not all hikers will be comfortable climbing on to the very steep, exposed peak, but you don't need to; once you're above treeline, a whole world of beautiful views opens up. Look for soaring eagles overhead and take a good plant book (see recommended reading in *Resources*) to help you identify the many tiny tundra plants and flowers.

See the website of local nonprofit **Sitka Trail Works** (907/747-7244, sitkatrailworks.org) for more information on these trails and many others, including some that are accessible by boat or floatplane only. They also offer guided hikes on most weekends of the year, on a donation basis for shorter hikes on the road system or $100 for all-day treks that include water transport.

RECREATION

Sitka Sound, the protected waters off Baranof Island just outside Sitka, offers an easy introduction to spectacular marine wilderness. **Sitka Sound Ocean Adventures** (look for a big blue bus at Crescent Harbor, east of Lincoln St., 907/752-0660, kayaksitka.com) is hands down the most popular tour company here, offering paddling trips, whale-watching, and a trek to World War II fortifications; they also rent gear and offer water taxi service, if you have the skills to DIY a trip in remote wilderness. Prices start at $79 for a 2.5-hour paddling tour, with discounts for children.

Gallant Adventures (907/738-2855, gallantadventures.com, starting at $125 for a 2.5-hour wildlife tour) is also extremely popular for whale-watching, wildlife tours, puffin watching on St. Lazaria Island, and even mountaineering expeditions. They also offer a trip to Goddard Hot Springs and its hand-built wooden baths, accessible only by boat or floatplane, and long expedition cruises aboard the 65-foot seaworthy wooden vessel *Gallant Girl*.

When the **fishing** in Sitka is good, it's really good. The island creates plenty of sheltered waters with ready access to the open sea

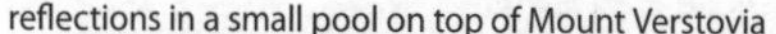

reflections in a small pool on top of Mount Verstovia

and a steady stream of fish; salmon, halibut, lingcod, and rockfish are common species on the ocean, while freshwater fly-fishing trips can bring in salmon, trout, char, and steelhead. June through September is usually the best season for salmon, with kings being especially good in June and silvers (coho salmon) becoming more predominant in the late months.

Many guiding outfits in this area prefer to book multiday trips with lodging included; two of the best are **Angling Unlimited** (primarily saltwater fishing, 4256 Halibut Point Rd., 800/297-3380 or 907/747-3736) and **Baranof Wilderness Lodge** (primarily freshwater fishing, Warm Springs Bay, 800/613-6551, flyfishalaska.com). For day trips, **Sitka Alaska Outfitters** (105B Monastery St., 907/966-2301, sitkaalaska-outfitters.com) offers guided fly-fishing excursions or can outfit you for an unguided excursion. **SeaMarine** (907/738-3724, sitkaseamarine.com) is one of the few charters offering day trips for saltwater fishing.

ENTERTAINMENT AND EVENTS

Sitka is a small town, but its fine arts community is incredibly strong. At the forefront is the **Sitka Summer Music Festival** (alaskaclassics.org), which has been estimated to contribute some $1 million to the local community every year. The festival runs in four weeklong segments, Tuesday-Saturday, every June, featuring world-class classical musicians from around the world. See the website for a full list of concerts and events for the coming year.

For a more informal music experience, you'll find a local jam session around noon on Sunday in the **Larkspur Cafe** (2 Lincoln St., 907/966-2326, Tues.-Sat. 8am-10pm, Sun. 9am-2pm); the café also hosts live music some evenings, and it has a small gift shop for the local public radio station.

The **Mean Queen** (205 Harbor Dr., 907/747-0616, daily 11:30am-2am) offers a full bar with cocktails and at least one $3 beer every day.

Ernie's Old Time Saloon (130 Lincoln St., 907/747-3334, generally 11am-10pm Sun.-Mon., Tues. till 11pm, Wed.-Thurs. till 1am, Fri. till 2am, Sat. till midnight) is just what it sounds like—an old-timey saloon environment close to downtown and the cruise ship docks.

SHOPPING

Sitka is unique among Alaska's larger cruise ship ports of call because almost every store is locally owned, including those right along the waterfront. Many shops stay open past their advertised hours when cruise ships are in town. Even the fine-jewelry store—**Baranof Jewelers** (200 Lincoln St., 907/966-4000, baranofjewelry.com)—is locally owned (their business cards say Park City, Utah, because they also run a year-round operation there, but they started in Sitka and manufacture their own jewelry). Ask about their Sitka-specific whale tail designs.

For the best selection of local artists all in one place, go to the **Island Artists Gallery** (205B Lincoln St., 907/747-6536, islandartistsgallery.com, typically open until 5 or 6pm, see website for hours), a cheery local co-op that sells everything from crafts to prints. Another excellent gallery showcasing diverse local art is the **Fishermen's Eye** (239 Lincoln St., 907/747-6080).

An interesting find is **Wintersong Soap Company** (321 Lincoln St., 907/738-8949 or 888/819-8949, wintersongsoap.com), a Sitka-based company that makes their own soaps using local botanical ingredients. Their soap is sold in gift shops throughout Alaska, but it's a treat to visit their headquarters. Also popular is **Old Harbor Books** (201 Lincoln St., 907/747-8808, oldharborbooks.net, Mon.-Fri. 10am-6pm, Sat. 10am-5pm, Sun. 11am-3pm), a quirky independent bookstore with a tasteful collection of sweets and other gifts.

If you quilt or sew, or know somebody who does, be sure to stop by **Abby's Reflection Apparel & Quiltworks** (231 Lincoln St., 907/747-3510, abbysreflection.com, daily 10am-6pm, from 9am on cruise ship days), where crafters of all persuasions are thrilled to discover Alaska-crafted patterns, including patterns for wall hangings with authentic formline (Southeast Native) designs created in collaboration with Tlingit master carver Tommy Joseph, and exclusive fabrics depicting wildlife and scenes of daily life in Sitka. Joseph offers his own creations and artwork from others in **Raindance Gallery** (205 Monastery St., 907/623-0705, daily 8am-5pm).

You'll find more high-end, authentic Alaska Native artwork at **Indian Village Artists** (428 Kaagwaantaan St., 907/747-5857, indianvillageartists.com); look for walrus ivory carvings, silver jewelry, and a very creative use of furs, all packed into this tiny storefront. **Sitka Rose Gallery** (419 Lincoln St., 888/236-1536 or 907/747-3030, sitkarosegallery.com, summer daily 8:30am-5:30pm, winter Tues.-Sat. 11am-5:15pm) also sells some high-end Alaska Native artwork, along with more contemporary sculpture, wall art, and jewelry. Although not all of their products bear the Silver Hand logo, the artists are identified and you can request bio sheets on their background.

You'll also find excellent gift shops in the **Sitka Sound Science Center** (834 Lincoln St., 907/747-8878, sitkascience.org, gift shop Tues.-Sat. 9am-4pm) and the **Sheldon Jackson Museum** (104 College Dr., 907/747-8981, museums.state.ak.us, summer daily 9am-5pm daily).

The Russian American Company stocks a vast variety of nesting dolls in their **Random House shop** (134 Lincoln St., 800/742-6228 or 907/747-6228, summer Mon.-Sat. 10am-5:30pm, Sun. 10am-4pm); I'd be wary of their Alaska Native art offerings, though, because I'm not so sure they're authentic.

FOOD

If you're coming by air, make a point of stopping for pie at the airport restaurant, **The Nugget** (600 Airport Dr., 907/966-2480, summer daily 5am-8pm, winter daily 8am-8pm daily, $13-17). The pie there is so good, some people on local flights deliberately book themselves for a stopover in Sitka just so they can grab a piece; personally, I prefer the cream pies to the berry pies.

The **Mean Queen** (205 Harbor Dr., 907/747-0616, daily 11:30am-2am, $25) has quickly become a local favorite for pizza, wings, and salad; it has a full bar with cocktails and offers at least one $3 beer a day. On the other end of the spectrum, tiny **Ludvig's Bistro** (256 Katlian St., 907/966-3663,

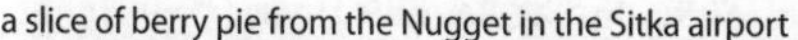
a slice of berry pie from the Nugget in the Sitka airport

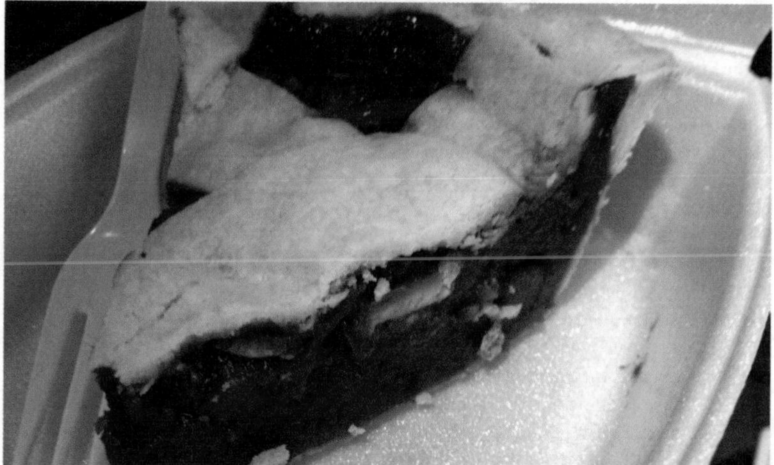

ludvigsbistro.com, May-mid-Sept. evenings, reduced bistro hours Feb.-Apr., year-round wine bar and gallery; see website for full hours, $35) is a long-cherished local spot for high-end Mediterranean cuisine and great fresh, local seafood.

On the cheap (but good) eats end of things, the **Larkspur Cafe** (2 Lincoln St., 907/966-2326, Tues.-Sat. 8am-10pm, Sun. 9am-2pm, $13-16) offers great sandwiches, live music, and a small gift shop that benefits the local public radio station. **North Sister Crepes and Juice Co.** (inside the Homeport Eatery, 209 Lincoln St., 907/738-5824, Tues.-Fri. 8:30am-3pm, Sat. 9am-3pm) offers organic crepes, superfood smoothies, and freshly pressed juices.

Kenny's Wok & Teriyaki (210 Katlian St., 907/747-5676, Mon.-Fri. 11:30am-9pm, Sat.-Sun. noon-9pm, delivery daily noon-9pm, $12) is the best of Sitka's Asian fusion options.

Groceries

You can buy groceries at the **Heart of Sitka Market Center** (210 Baranof St., 907/747-6686, daily 5am-midnight); prices vary widely from what you'll find in Anchorage to twice as much, and produce comes in on the ferry, so it's hard to find really fresh fruits and vegetables. There's an ATM inside the lobby. Your other option is **Sea Mart Grocery** (1867 Halibut Point Rd., 907/747-6266, daily 7am-11pm). You can get fresh, local produce at the **Sitka Farmers Market,** held sporadically on Saturdays throughout the summer at the **Alaska Native Brotherhood Founders Hall** (235 Katlian St.); see sitkalocalfoodsnetwork.org for an updated listing of open days and times.

ACCOMMODATIONS

Cruise ship passengers often stay at the **Westmark Sitka Hotel** (330 Seward St., 907/747-6241, westmarkhotels.com, from $245), which offers the town's most luxurious lodgings; amenities include complimentary airport shuttle, free Wi-Fi, a fitness center, free parking, and two restaurants.

Independent travelers may prefer the **Totem Square Inn** (201 Katlian St., 866/300-1353 or 907/747-3693, totemsquarehotelmarina.com, from $229), with clean and basic but well-kept rooms along with free Wi-Fi, complimentary airport shuttle, a fitness center, and free parking.

Walking down the price ladder, another option is the **Super 8 Sitka** (404 Sawmill Creek Rd., 907/747-8804, wyndhamhotels.com, from $172). You won't be right on the waterfront, but you're within a quick, easy walk of Swan Lake Park and a grocery store (the Heart of Sitka Market Center), and just a short walk from most downtown attractions.

For budget travelers, the **Sitka International Hostel** (109 Jeff Davis St., 907/747-8661, 8:30am-10am and 6pm-10pm, $24-29/bunk, $15 children 12 and under, $65 for a double private room) is generally a friendly place staffed by volunteers from around the country and the world; they offer free Wi-Fi, a couple of bunk options, and a limited choice of private rooms. The hostel is generally clean but has some quirks—for example, sometimes the people in the neighboring room control the radiator in your room, the beds are creaky, and there's no easy way to access upper bunks.

One of the best bed-and-breakfasts in Sitka, **Inn at Raven's Peek** (4260 Halibut Point Rd., 907/738-0140), accommodates just one party at a time. They offer a Master's Suite (from $145 pp), extra bunk housing in the "Mate's Quarters" if need be (from $72.50 pp), and a charming treehouse (from $190 pp); substantial extra charges apply for each additional guest. Amenities include high-speed Wi-Fi, breakfast service, a private sauna and hot tub, and beautiful views over Sitka Sound in a quiet, secluded location.

INFORMATION AND SERVICES

You should have decent cell service in Sitka from large providers like AT&T and Verizon, although there are a few patchy spots in coverage, especially as you move out of town. You may notice a drastic difference in coverage between being inside and outside buildings, or even depending on which side of the building you stand on.

You'll find Sitka's main visitor center in the **Harrigan Centennial Hall** (330 Harbor Dr., 907/747-3225); they may offer some temporary luggage holds, as do some hotels, but always double-check first. **Public bathrooms** are available just down the street, in the public library (320 Harbor Dr.) and in the Sitka National Historical Park on the far end of Lincoln Street.

The **Sitka Community Hospital** (209 Moller Ave., 907/747-3241) offers a 24-hour emergency room, and the small **police department** is on Lake Street (304 Lake St. #102, 907/747-3245 for dispatch, 911 for emergencies). Keep Fido on a leash; there is an enforced leash law here.

There's an ATM inside the lobby of the **Heart of Sitka Market Center** (210 Baranof St., 907/747-6686, daily 5am-midnight), but you're less likely to be charged an extra fee if you take the short walk to **Alps Credit Union** and their 24-hour ATM (401 Halibut Point Rd.).

You can get Wi-Fi access with a purchase in most cafés and bars, and some restaurants. The best free Wi-Fi access is at the **Kettleson Memorial Public Library** (320 Harbor Dr., 907/747-8708, Mon.-Fri. 10am-8pm, Sat. 10am-6pm). There are two post offices; the most convenient to downtown is on Lincoln Street (338 Lincoln St., Mon.-Sat. 8:30am-5:30pm).

Planning an outdoor trip? Visit **Russell's Outdoor Store** (208 Lincoln St., 907/747-6970, Mon.-Fri. 9am-6pm, Sat. 9am-5pm, Sun. noon-4pm) for camping gear, stoves and fuel, clothing, boots, and shoes.

TRANSPORTATION

You can only reach Sitka by air and sea. Traditionally, the **Alaska Marine Highway System**'s fast ferry ***Fairweather*** (800/642-0066, ferryalaska.com), which cuts the usual 10-hour ferry trip from Juneau down to less than 5, has been the most economical and convenient means of getting here. However, fast ferry service is continually on the chopping block as the state budget shrinks, so it's worth considering air travel at least one way to get here, or planning your Southeast ferry schedule—which is generally more flexible in other locales—around your trip to Sitka.

Sitka's **Rocky Gutierrez Airport,** which is served by **Alaska Airlines** year-round (800/426-0333, alaskaair.com) and **Delta Airlines** (800/221-1212, delta.com) during the summer, is actually on neighboring Japonski Island; the two are connected by a bridge, and it's a breezy, 1.5-mile walk from the airport to downtown Sitka. Almost every hotel offers free shuttle service to and from the airport, or a taxi costs about $9. You can also book a small plane trip from Juneau to Sitka on **Alaska Seaplanes** (907/789-3331, flyalaskaseaplanes.com).

The ferry terminal is about seven miles out of town; you can catch a shuttle with **Sitka Tours** (907/747-5800, sitkatoursalaska.com, $6-8 one-way or $10 round-trip) or hire a taxi.

Sitka has several taxi companies, all of which should charge the same fare: **Hank's Taxi** (907/747-8888), a 24-hour small operation that runs a Toyota Prius; **Baranof Taxi** (907/738-4722, daily 8am-5pm, Fri.-Sat. until 2am); and **Sitka Cab** (907/738-5002).

Car rentals are available from locally owned **Sitka Car Rental** in the middle of downtown (907/738-2282, sitkacarrental.com, personalized pickup and drop-off service). If you want to rent at the airport, your terminal options are **Avis** (907/966-2404, avis.com) or locally owned **North Star Rent-a-Car** (800/722-6927, northstarrentacar.com).

There is one official mass transit bus in Sitka, **The Ride** (907/747-7103, ridesitka.com, $2, $1 seniors, children, and disabled). It runs three routes weekdays 6:30am-7:30pm (closed on major holidays): A one-hour loop to the northwest along Halibut Point Road, a one-hour loop east along Sawmill Creek Road, and a half-hour loop through downtown and over the bridge to the airport. Look for the blue buses.

Juneau

With a population of about 33,000, Juneau is Alaska's third-largest city and the capital to boot. Although it is technically part of the mainland, Juneau is, for all intents and purposes, an island. Soaring mountains, massive icefields, and a distinct lack of local interest in being connected to a highway system mean there is no road connecting Juneau to other communities; you can only reach Alaska's capital by sea or air.

Every year, the Alaska Marine Highway System takes one of its ocean-worthy ferries—usually the *Tustumena*—out of regular rotation to bring state legislators and their families to Juneau, then ferry them back once the legislative session is over.

Juneau has five neighborhoods: downtown Juneau, where the cruise ships dock; Douglas, a small suburb on a neighboring island that's connected by a bridge; then, moving northwest, Lemon Creek, Auke Bay, and the Mendenhall Valley. A bus system connects all five neighborhoods, but for visitors without a car, it's much easier to stay in downtown Juneau. You can take a shuttle bus to the one big tourist attraction outside downtown, the Mendenhall Glacier.

Temperatures in Juneau typically peak in the 60s from June through August, and winter highs hover around freezing in December and January. Overcast days and periodic rain showers are common, but the average annual precipitation of 62 inches is surprisingly low for a city that's smack in the middle of a temperate rainforest.

Accessibility for travelers with disabilities is a challenge for exploring downtown Juneau. Most streets have excellent sidewalks, but the town is built right into a mountainside, so grades are very steep and sometimes equally steep staircases—which are actually considered streets!—offer the only pedestrian shortcuts.

SIGHTS

Some of Juneau's most remarkable sights are smack in the middle of downtown. Pick up a walking map at the big **Visitor Information Center** at the cruise ship docks on Franklin Street or at the **Marine Park Kiosk** (right beside the public library at 292 Marine Way). Both locations are seasonal—when the cruise ships leave town in September, they shut down.

While in town, keep an eye out for beautiful Alaska Native art built—or painted—right into the buildings. One of the most striking examples is on city hall on Marine Way, between Shattuck Way and South Seward Street: It's a painting of Raven and all the clan animals looking on as the first (Tlingit) human is born from a clamshell.

Walter Soboleff Center

A stunning sight is Sea Alaska Heritage Center's new **Walter Soboleff Center** (105 S. Seward St., 907/463-4844, sealaskaheritage.org, Mon.-Fri. 7:30am-5:30pm, $5). The building itself is a work of art inside and out, with massive panels carved by master artists from the Tlingit, Haida, and Tsimshian traditions. Inside, the exhibits showcase award-winning Alaska Native artwork and treasured regalia that has been passed down through family lineages. At the very core of the center is a traditional clan house that's quite literally built of some of the finest Alaska Native art in the world.

Alaska State Museum

A must-see tribute to Juneau and Alaska's past, present, and future is the newly renovated **Alaska State Museum** (395 Whittier St., 907/465-2901, museums.alaska.gov, daily 9am-5pm, summer $12 or $11 seniors/active duty military, winter $5 or $4 seniors/active duty military, 18 and under always free),

Juneau

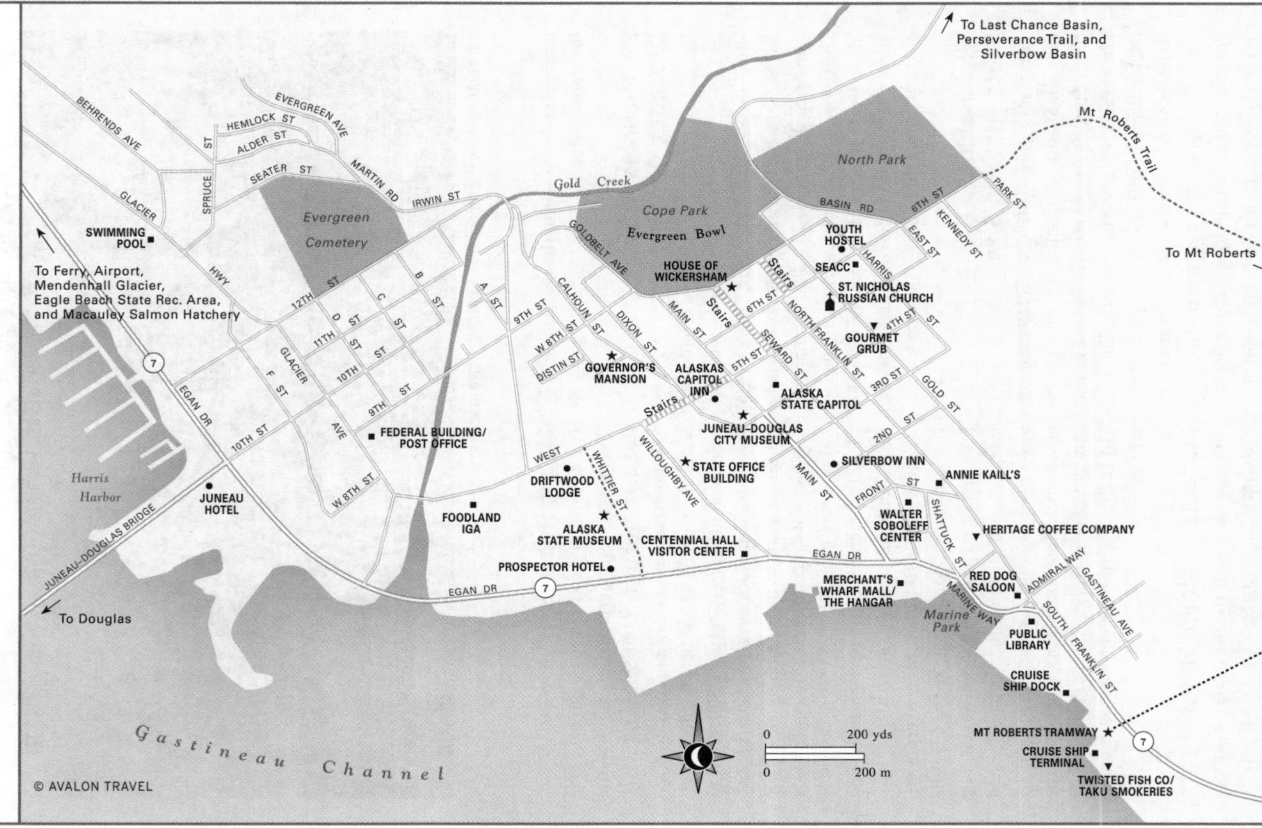
To Last Chance Basin, Perseverance Trail, and Silverbow Basin
Mt Roberts Trail
To Mt Roberts
BEHRENDS AVE
EVERGREEN AVE
HEMLOCK ST
ALDER ST
SPRUCE ST
SEATER ST
MARTIN RD
IRWIN ST
GLACIER HWY
Gold Creek
North Park
Cope Park
Evergreen Bowl
Evergreen Cemetery
SWIMMING POOL
To Ferry, Airport, Mendenhall Glacier, Eagle Beach State Rec. Area, and Macauley Salmon Hatchery
12TH ST
11TH ST
10TH ST
10TH ST
9TH ST
9TH ST
W 8TH ST
W 8TH ST
D ST
C ST
B ST
A ST
F ST
GLACIER AVE
GOLDBELT AVE
BASIN RD
6TH ST
PARK ST
KENNEDY ST
EAST ST
HARRIS
YOUTH HOSTEL
SEACC
HOUSE OF WICKERSHAM
Stairs
Stairs
Stairs
6TH ST
5TH ST
4TH ST
3RD ST
2ND ST
FRONT ST
NORTH FRANKLIN ST
SEWARD ST
MAIN ST
MAIN ST
CALHOUN ST
DIXON ST
DISTIN ST
GOLD ST
ST. NICHOLAS RUSSIAN CHURCH
GOURMET GRUB
GOVERNOR'S MANSION
ALASKAS CAPITOL INN
ALASKA STATE CAPITOL
JUNEAU-DOUGLAS CITY MUSEUM
FEDERAL BUILDING/ POST OFFICE
WEST WILLOUGHBY AVE
WHITTIER ST
DRIFTWOOD LODGE
STATE OFFICE BUILDING
SILVERBOW INN
ANNIE KAILL'S
Harris Harbor
JUNEAU HOTEL
FOODLAND IGA
ALASKA STATE MUSEUM
CENTENNIAL HALL VISITOR CENTER
WALTER SOBOLEFF CENTER
SHATTUCK ST
HERITAGE COFFEE COMPANY
EGAN DR
EGAN DR
EGAN DR
7
PROSPECTOR HOTEL
MERCHANT'S WHARF MALL/ THE HANGAR
RED DOG SALOON
ADMIRAL WAY
GASTINEAU AVE
MARINE WAY
Marine Park
SOUTH FRANKLIN ST
PUBLIC LIBRARY
JUNEAU-DOUGLAS BRIDGE
To Douglas
CRUISE SHIP DOCK
MT ROBERTS TRAMWAY
CRUISE SHIP TERMINAL
TWISTED FISH CO/ TAKU SMOKERIES
Gastineau Channel
0 200 yds
0 200 m
© AVALON TRAVEL

the beautiful new Walter Soboleff Center in downtown Juneau

where you'll find one of the best accounts of the state's history.

St. Nicholas Russian Orthodox Church

Juneau has several smaller historical buildings that are well worth a visit, among them the **St. Nicholas Russian Orthodox Church** (326 5th St., stnicholasjuneau.org, summer daily 1pm-5pm, short tours offered for a donation). The church's exterior is slowly succumbing to the moisture of the rainforest around it, but the interior remains beautiful, with gilt icons and ornate paneling that conceals the altar space.

Wickersham State Historic Site

The fascinating **House of Wickersham** (213 7th St., mid-May-late Sept. Sun.-Thurs. 10am-5pm) is more properly known as the **Wickersham State Historic Site.** This was the home of one of Alaska's most preeminent statesmen and scholars, James Wickersham, who also happened to be a wildly adventurous mountaineering judge—just the person to travel through rural Alaska and clean up a corrupt court system.

Mount Roberts Tramway

For a fun new perspective on Juneau, ride Southeast's only aerial tram, the **Mount Roberts Tramway** (490 S. Franklin St., 888/461-8726, mtrobertstramway.com, May-Sept., all-day pass $33 adult, $16 youth 6-12, kids 5 and under free). It rises 1,800 feet from the cruise ship docks to a perch in the lush rainforest, partway up Mount Roberts. At the upper end of the tramway there's a gift shop, a rudimentary café, a theater that shows short films and sometimes live performances, and several miles of great hiking trails.

Some people feel the tram is overpriced. If you'd rather, you can make the 1.5-mile hike up the mountain from downtown. The steep, often slippery trail starts near the end of Basin Road, which is about a mile from the cruise docks; look for blue signs indicating the Mount Roberts trailhead. If you spend at least $10 at the top, you can ride the tram down for free.

Macaulay Salmon Hatchery

You can walk in to the **Macaulay Salmon Hatchery** (2697 Channel Dr., 907/463-4810, dipac.net, summer Mon.-Fri. 10am-6pm and

Vicinity of Juneau

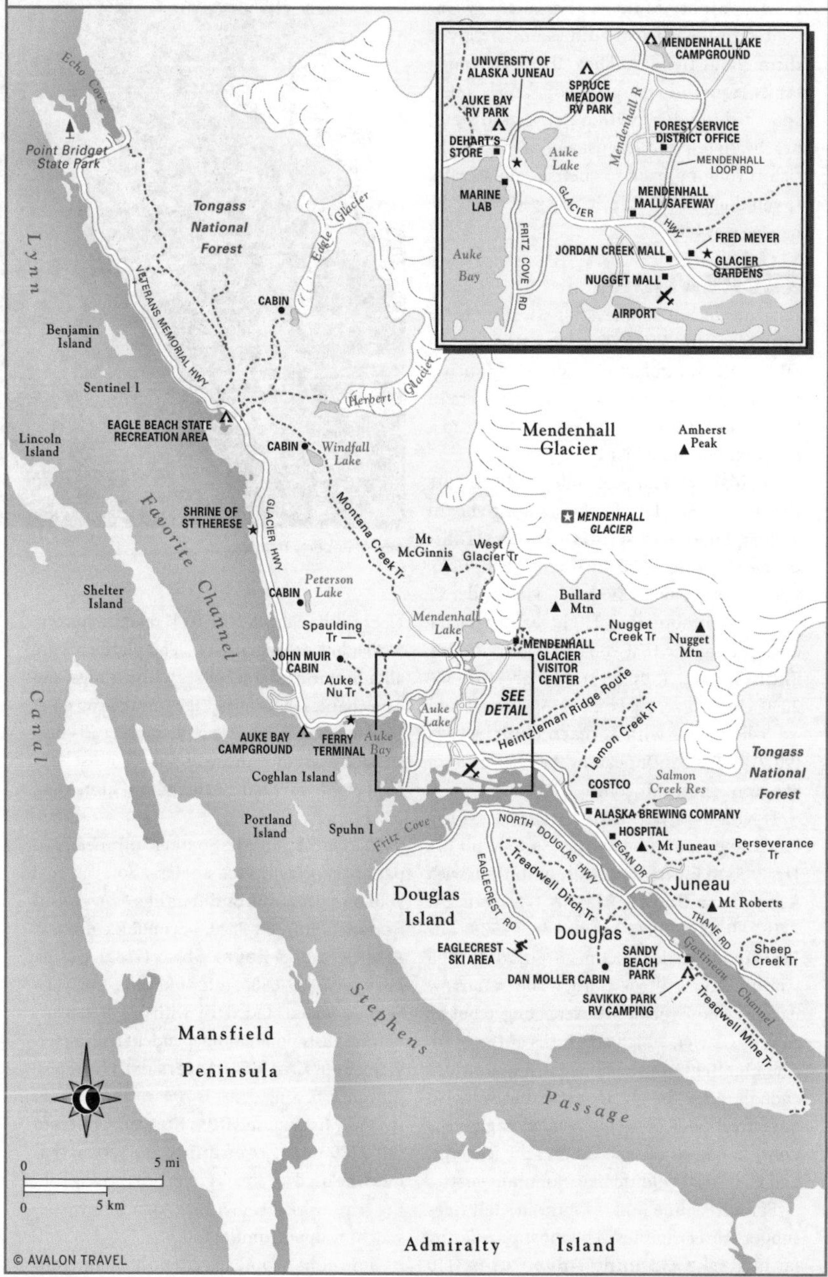

Sat.-Sun. 10am-5pm, winter by appointment, $5 adults, $3 for 12 and under). Fifteen- to twenty-minute tours of the hatchery, included in the price of admission, are given throughout the day. They also have touch tanks, aquariums, a gift shop, and a small sport fishing dock with a gear rental stand nearby. In July and August you can watch the fish thronging back to their home stream. If you don't have a car, it's easy to reach the hatchery by bus.

RECREATION

Juneau is one of Southeast's hottest spots for **flightseeing.** After all, what better way to take in the rainforest-clad slopes, dramatic fjords, and glistening blue-green waters of this part of the world than from the air in a helicopter or small plane?

Popular excursions include the 40-minute Five-Glacier Seaplane Exploration trip aboard a floatplane from **Wings Airways/Taku Glacier Lodge** (2 Marine Way, 907/586-6275, wingsairways.com, $219 adult, $188 under 12 years); a combination flightseeing/glacier dogsledding trip that you can book with **Era Flightseeing** (800/843-1947 or 907/586-2030, eraflightseeing.com, $735/4 hours); and a 1.5-hour tour with **Temsco Helicopters** (907/789-9501 in Juneau or 907/983-2100 in Skagway, temscoair.com).

If you'd rather take in the stunning landscape from the sea, book a tour up the **Tracy Arm Fjord,** southeast of Juneau, with **Adventure Bound Alaska** (76 Egan Dr. #110, 800/228-3875 or 907/463-2509, adventureboundalaska.com, $160 adult, $95 youth). This is a true fjord, a sheer, narrow passage whose rock walls were gouged out by Sawyer Glacier, which still lurks at the head. The highlight of the trip is pulling up close enough to see the glacier calve, but you also have great odds of seeing whales, eagles, sea lions, hundreds of seals among the icebergs, and terrestrial wildlife like mountain goats.

For adrenaline junkies, Juneau's tall trees support three ziplines. The most popular by far is **Alaska Ziplining Adventures** (110 N. Franklin St., 907/321-0947, alaskazip.com, $149 adult, $99 ages 8-12). The platforms are all fully enclosed treehouses with railings, and a mechanical braking system means you don't have to put your hands on the cable at all—just sit back and enjoy the ride. Guests must be at least eight years old and weigh no more than 250 pounds.

Mount Roberts Tramway

Like most areas in Southeast, Juneau is a paradise for dedicated anglers. You can rent your own gear from outfitters like **Above and Beyond** (907/364-2333, beyondak.com) and **Alaska Boat & Kayak Shop** (11521 Glacier Hwy., 907/789-6886, juneaukayak.com, May-Sept.), or take a guided trip with one of Juneau's outrageously popular independent fishing services. **Bear Creek Outfitters** (907/723-2663, juneauflyfishing.com) is one of the best for fly-in fly fishing, and **Rum Runner Charters** (907/789-5482, rumrunnercharters.net) is much beloved for small-group oceangoing fishing trips, which sometimes turn into whale-watching opportunities too.

Juneau has some excellent **hiking** trails

that you can access straight from downtown. Two of them start from Basin Road. The **Perseverance Trail** (3 miles one-way, 1,000 feet of elevation gain) starts from the end of Basin Road and offers great mountain views as well as views of Ebner Falls, plus access to several other trails. The **Mount Roberts Trail** (4.5 miles one-way, almost 4,000 feet elevation gain) starts shortly before the end of Basin Road and takes you up past the upper Mount Roberts tram building, all the way to the top of the mountain.

It might seem counterintuitive, but **stand-up paddleboarding** (SUP) is gaining traction in Alaska. You can rent SUPs and wetsuits from **Blue Nose Surf** on Douglas Island (2126 2nd St., 907/957-2996, bluenosesurf.com) or book one of their **guided tours** (offered five days a week, locations vary, from $80, lesson and rental included). Kayakers can rent from **Alaska Boat & Kayak Shop** (11521 Glacier Hwy., 907/789-6886, juneaukayak.com, May-Sept.).

TOP EXPERIENCE

★ Mendenhall Glacier

For some of the most spectacular photo ops of your life, drive or take one of the continuously running shuttle buses from the cruise ship docks ($30 round-trip) to the **Mendenhall Glacier Visitor Center** (6000 Glacier Spur Rd., 907/789-0097, fs.usda.gov, May-early Sept. daily 8am-7:30pm, reduced winter hours, $5). If you're on a super-tight budget, the city bus will get you the intersection of Glacier Spur and Mendenhall Loop—about 1.5 miles from the visitor center—for just $2 ($1 ages 6-18). You'll have to walk the rest of the way.

It's easy to spend a full afternoon here, especially if you take one of the excellent hiking trails (trail guide available in the visitor center). Two of the most popular highlights include the two-mile round-trip hike to the massive curtain of water that is **Nugget Falls** (you can see it from the visitor center deck) and the shorter, 0.03-mile walk down to **Photo Point,** where you can get completely unobstructed views of the glacier's face.

Visitors also linger on the boardwalks over nearby **Steep Creek,** a stream that draws spawning salmon and, sometimes, black bears that catch and eat the fish. Wildlife sightings are very much hit-or-miss, though; it's safe to call this the most challenging bear-viewing area in the state.

Some of the most iconic images taken in

a guided glacier trekking trip on Juneau's Mendenhall Glacier

this area come from the Mendenhall Glacier ice caves, which are inherently unstable and dangerous to explore. The safest option is to admire from a distance; if you must explore inside the caves, hire a guide service like **Above & Beyond Alaska** (907/364-2333, beyondak.com, $219 and up for an all-day trek, $299 for a hiking/paddling combo) and **Mendenhall Glacier Ice Caves Adventure** (800/892-5504, mendenhallicecaves.com, $289 for a 5-hour tour), which have the technical skills and familiarity to guide you into the safest parts of the ice caves.

If you'd rather pitch a tent than stay in a hotel, one of the most popular and accessible campgrounds is 600-acre **Eagle Beach State Recreation Area** (Mile 29 Glacier Hwy., 907/465-4563). The campground has 16 primitive campsites (35-foot RV limit) and three walk-in sites, plus access to a white-sand beach with great beachcombing in the intertidal areas. Three nearby primitive Alaska State Parks **public-use cabins** sleep 4-8 at a cost of $55 per night: Saturday Creek Cabin, Berry Patch Cabin, and Marten Cabin. See dnr.alaska.gov/parks/cabins/south for reservations and more information on these cabins and the other eight public-use cabins near Juneau, five of which are accessible only by boat or floatplane.

The waters around Juneau are heavenly for sea kayakers. One of the best kayak outfitters/rental shops around is **Alaska Boat & Kayak Shop** (11521 Glacier Hwy., 907/789-6886, juneaukayak.com, May-Sept.), and one of the most popular paddling trips is the water trail between Point Bridget and Oliver Inlet on **Admiralty Island,** which has the highest population density of brown bears in the world. If you're not thoroughly comfortable dealing with bear encoutners in the wild, connect with a service like **Above & Beyond Alaska** (907/364-2333, beyondak.com), which also operates the Alaska Boat & Kayak Shop, for a fun guided outing.

Whale-Watching

You'll find spectacular whale-watching in almost every Southeast Alaska community. Orcas (killer whales) are common here, but even more common are agile humpback whales, the ballerinas of the ocean, which come here to feed nonstop as they rebuild the blubber reserves they lost while fasting at their summer breeding grounds.

If you're especially lucky you may see them bubble-net feeding, a learned, cooperative behavior that's only done in this part of the world, and only during a few weeks in July. The whales swim around a school of herring, blowing bubbles to create a curtain that hems them in. Then, on an audible signal from the lead whale (which you can hear if your tour boat puts a hydrophone in the water), they all surge up through the net, gulping down their trapped meal.

You'll find numerous whale-watching tours in Juneau, and they're all good. One of the best local operations is **Juneau Tours** (907/523-6095, juneautours.com, from $110 for 3-5 hours), because they put you on a relatively small boat, which means you're closer to the water and the whales and won't have to take your photos over the heads of a big crowd. They offer copious complimentary puns to go along with the narrated tour.

★ Bear Viewing at Admiralty Island National Monument

Admiralty Island lives up to its original name—Kootznoowoo, or "Fortress of the Bears" in Tlingit—with the highest concentration of brown bears in the world. The island holds an estimated 1,500 brown bears at a density of one bear per square mile.

The best place to see the bears is at the **Pack Creek Bear-Viewing Area,** where the bears have become accustomed to humans and focus their energy on catching fish instead. They're still wild, though, so you have to follow a strict set of rules, including storing your food and other "smellable" items in bear-proof lockers near the site entrance. Access is by permit only (call 877/444-6777 or visit recreation.gov for permit information). Twenty-four permits per day are allowed during peak season in July and August ($50 adult, $25 for under 16 and over 61); half of those go to commercial operations and half are reserved for private individuals.

For most people, the smartest, safest, and easiest way of visiting Pack Creek is with a guide. Three guide services are authorized to run single-day trips to the viewing area:

- **Above & Beyond Alaska** (907/364-2333, beyondak.com, also offers multiday paddle trips and outfitting)
- **Bear Creek Outfitters** (907/723-2663, juneauflyfishing.com)
- **Pack Creek Bear Tours** (907/209-5432, packcreekbeartours.com)

For those who have the skills and experience to negotiate the nearby land and water on their own, you can charter a floatplane from one of these authorized float taxi services. Camping is available on neighboring islands, and gear rentals are available from Above & Beyond Alaska (907/364-2333, beyondak.com). You can charter a flight with one of the following air services:

- **Admiralty Air Service** (907/796-2000, admiraltyairservice.com)
- **Alaska Seaplanes** (907/789-3331, flyalaskaseaplanes.com)
- **Ward Air** (907/789-9150, wardair.com)
- **Wings Airways** (907/586-6275, wingsairways.com)

ENTERTAINMENT

Juneau locals voted the early-20th-century bar in the **Alaskan Hotel** (167 S. Franklin St., 800/327-9347, thealaskanhotel.com) as the best live music venue in town. It usually has **live music** every night (Sun.-Wed. 4pm-7pm and Thurs.-Sat. 9:30am-2am).

The iconic **Red Dog Saloon** (278 S. Franklin St., 907/463-3658, reddogsaloon.com, Tues.-Sat. 9am-11pm, Mon. 11am-11pm), where you can get a side of excellent pub grub (burgers, sandwiches, pizza, etc.) with your music, is also popular. **Rockwell** (109 S. Franklin St., 907/463-4340, 11am-10pm or later most days) offers a dinner menu with its shows.

SHOPPING

Juneau has many shops that sell imported, mass-produced replicas of Alaska Native art but only a few sell the real deal. If you only have time to visit one shop, head straight for the **Sealaska Heritage Store** (105 S. Seward St., Ste. 201, 907/586-9114, sealaskaheritage.org, summer daily 9am-8pm, winter Mon.-Fri.

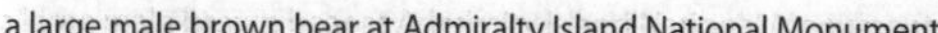

a large male brown bear at Admiralty Island National Monument

10am-6pm and Sat. 10am-5pm), the storefront counterpart to the beautiful **Walter Soboleff Center**. Everything you see for sale will be authentic, and some pieces are truly museum quality. On the first Friday of most months, they also have artists demonstrating (and selling) their art in the Soboleff Center.

One of the most distinctive shops selling Alaska Native art is **Trickster Company** (224 Front St., 907/780-4000, trickstercompany.com), a hip boutique run by formline artist Rico Worl; you'll find everything from skateboard decks to playing cards, beautiful silver jewelry, and *Star Wars* shirts with Alaska Native art on them.

Another good shop is the massive **Mt. Juneau Trading Post** (151 S. Franklin St., 907/523-8100 or 907/586-3426, mtjuneautradingpost.com), where you can choose from a wide variety of Alaska Native and Eskimo artwork and a number of gifts—from fingerless gloves to water bottles and greeting cards—that are decorated with Native motifs. However, I'm not so sure their collection of tiny, rough-hewn totem poles is really authentic.

For the best selection of fine arts and crafts in town, many of them made by Alaskan or Alaska-connected artists, go to **Annie Kaill's** (244 Front St., 907/586-2800, anniekaills.com, Tues.-Sat. 9am-7pm, Sun.-Mon. 10am-7pm). The eclectic selection—everything from paintings to stoneware, clothing, and even jelly beans—shows excellent taste, and it's won a number of "best gallery" awards in recent years. For another great collection of local art, head to the **Juneau Arts & Cultural Center** (350 Whittier St., 907/586-2787, jahc.org/jacc).

To see a true icon of Alaskan art, take time to visit the **Rie Muñoz Gallery** (2101 Jordan Ave., 907/789-7411. riemunoz.com, Tues.-Sat. 11am-5:30pm) in the Nugget Mall near the airport. Muñoz, who died of a stroke in 2015, remains much beloved by the community for her bright, joyful watercolors depicting scenes from everyday Alaska life.

There's a strong element of Russian history in Alaska, too. For authentic handcrafted Russian goods, steer toward the **House of Russia** (389 S. Franklin St., 800/770-2778). The owner makes yearly trips to Russia to purchase handmade goods, with an emphasis on *matryoshka* nesting dolls.

FOOD

Considering its (small) size and isolation, Juneau offers a stupendous selection of good restaurants within an easy walk of downtown hotels. For the adventurous, **The Rookery** (111 Seward St., 907/463-3013, therookerycafe.com, Mon.-Fri. 7am-9pm, Sat. 9am-9pm, $16) has won several "best restaurant" awards in local newspaper polls for its fusion cuisine built of locally harvested, seasonal ingredients. The menu usually changes several times a week.

V's Cellar Door (222 Seward St., 907/586-6870, vscellardoor.com, daily 11am-9pm, $12-20) offers another type of adventure: Mexican fusion cuisine that often incorporates elements of Korean food, like Korean short ribs and kimchi rice. The can't-miss item here is "shrubs," a vinegar infusion of herbs or fruit that can be made into a "just sweet enough" soda or mixed in with your favorite drink. They also have a great $3 Taco Tuesday.

If steak or seafood is more your game, the world-class chef at **Salt** (200 Seward St., 907/780-2221, saltalaska.com, daily 10am-10pm, small plate $15, large plate $35) offers modern, casual cuisine that'll be right up your alley, plus an extensive wine and cocktail list. For a less adventurous (but still delicious) take on seafood, **Tracy's King Crab Shack** (300 S. Franklin St., 907/723-1811, kingcrabshack.com, daily 10:30am-8:30pm, king crab $26-120) offers king crab by the leg and an award-winning crab bisque, plus beer and wine.

Hangar on the Wharf (2 Marine Way, 907/586-5018, hangaronthewharf.com, daily 11am-10pm, $15-25) offers seafood, pub grub, great views over the water, and one of the best microbrew selections in town.

Juneau also has some excellent cafés. If you like ice cream, run—don't walk!—to the tiny, cozy **Coppa** (917 Glacier Ave. #102,

stuffed French toast in Juneau's Sandpiper Cafe

907/586-3500, coppa.biz, Mon. Fri. 6:30am-6pm, Sat. 8am-6pm), which has a small selection of ultra-creamy homemade ice cream. They also offer espresso, tea, soup, sandwiches, salads, and baked goods at reasonable (for Alaska) prices.

On the restaurant side of the café coin, two local favorites are **Capital Café** (Westmark Baranof Hotel, 127 N. Franklin St., 907/463-6208, Mon.-Fri. 6:30am-2pm, Sat.-Sun. 7am-2pm, $12-15), which offers all things breakfast and lunch, including creative skillets, scrambles, and seafood; and the **Sandpiper Cafe** (429 W. Willoughby Ave., 907/586-3150, daily 6am-2pm, $12-14) which is far nicer (and busier) than it appears from the outside. Make sure you check the specials board.

For inexpensive eats, **Pel'meni** (2 Marine Way, blue building, cash only, 11:30am-usually past midnight on weekends) is hard to beat. For around $7, you get a big serving of the Russian equivalent of ravioli with your choice of meat or potato (the veggie option). But the even more rickety hole-in-the-wall **Gourmet Grub** (408 Gold St., also open late) is even better. Trust me: It's worth the hike up the hill, bringing exact change in cash, and the sometimes interminable wait for the oven to warm up; try calling ahead for takeout.

If you can't decide on a single restaurant, consider booking a walking history/tasting tour with **Alaskan Food Tours** (907/780-3663 or 855/780-3663, alaskanfoodtours.com, from $129).

The local coffee-roasting chain is **Heritage Coffee Roasting Company**; they have a huge, comfortable, and very popular coffee shop in the middle of downtown (130 Front St., 907/586-1087, heritagecoffee.com, daily 6am-7:30pm); see the website for a list of other locations around town. They used to offer unlimited Wi-Fi at their flagship downtown location, but too many tourists essentially camped out there on rainy days, so now they limit it to 15 minutes of Wi-Fi with a purchase. You might be able to get longer access at some of their other cafés.

Groceries

There are three supermarkets in Juneau, but just one of them is downtown: **Foodland IGA** (615 W. Willoughby Ave., 907/586-3101, foodlandiga.com, daily 6am-10pm), which is within easy walking distance of many hotels. It also has a pharmacy, as do **Safeway** (3033 Vintage Blvd., 907/523-2000, carrsqc.com, daily 24 hours, limited holiday hours) and **Fred Meyer** (8181 Glacier Hwy., 907/789-6500, daily 7am-11pm).

ACCOMMODATIONS

For budget travelers who don't mind hiking up one of Juneau's steep hills, the downtown **Juneau Hostel** (614 Harris St., summer daily 8am-9am and 5pm-11pm, closes at 10:30pm in winter, $12) is a well-run bargain with kitchen access, free Wi-Fi, and coin-op laundry machines downstairs. There is a daytime lockout 9am-5pm, and you're asked to do one quick chore and leave your shoes in the lobby; stays are limited to five nights.

The next step up in bargain

accommodations downtown, the motel-style **Driftwood** (435 W. Willoughby Ave., 800/544-2239 or 907/586-2280, dhalaska.com, from $123, $140 with kitchenette, add $20/night for pets) looks worn down on the outside, with duct tape holding some of the window screens in place. It's much better on the inside: dated, but clean and comfortable. The staff is friendly and helpful, there's free Wi-Fi plus a few coin-op laundry machines, and the complimentary 24-hour shuttle to/from the airport and ferry is a huge help. Some rooms have kitchenettes. The Driftwood is also right next to the Sandpiper Cafe, a local favorite for breakfast and lunch. A liquor store on the other side can get loud during weekends, so bring earplugs.

The Prospector (375 Whittier St., 907/586-3737, prospectorhotel.com, from $119) is a great bargain for smaller parties, with free Wi-Fi, a grocery store just next door, and just a short walk to downtown's main attractions. The interior is dated and a little spartan, but a huge step up from the Driftwood. The rooms are comfortable and clean, and the staff is helpful, friendly, and very efficient. They don't offer shuttle service to the ferry and airport but will help you coordinate with other guests to share a cab.

For families, business travelers, or anyone who's planning to stay awhile, the **Juneau Hotel** (1200 W. 9th St., 907/586-5666, juneauhotels.net, from $184) has enormous suites at a very reasonable price considering the location (most downtown attractions are less than a mile away), with free Wi-Fi and a free airport/ferry shuttle. They also offer free passes to the nearby Alaska Club fitness center and complimentary freezer storage for your fish and game.

If you need a hotel close to the airport, the **Frontier Suites Airport Hotel** (9400 Glacier Hwy., 907/790-6600, frontiersuites.com, from $169), with clean, comfortable rooms and suites, is just a five-minute drive from the Mendenhall Glacier. Amenities include free Wi-Fi, a fitness facility, on-site laundromat, free airport/ferry shuttle, and freezer storage for your fish and game.

One of the nicest balances of comfort and price in Juneau, the **Silverbow Inn** (120 2nd St., 907/586-4146, silverbowinn.com, from $109) is a boutique downtown hotel with a rooftop garden and hot tub, free Wi-Fi, private bathrooms, and a full breakfast; there's an excellent bakery and restaurant on the bottom floor, with apartments on the second and third floors.

For a top-shelf B&B experience, you just can't beat **Alaska's Capital Inn** (113 W. 5th, 888/588-6507, alaskacapitalinn.com, from $265). The carefully restored, four-floor, gold-rush-era mansion is just up the hill from downtown, and each room comes with a king- or queen-size bed, a private bathroom with luxurious toiletries, and other amenities such as private sitting areas, whirlpool tubs, and fireplaces. The breakfast is to die for. If you make one lodging splurge in all of Southeast, this should be it.

Also thoroughly splurge-worthy is the historic 1915 **Jorgenson House** (635 Alder St., 907/723-4202, jorgensonhouse.com, from $360), a quiet, restful luxury B&B located just outside the downtown area. The accommodations verge on boutique hotel territory, with four suites, a three-course breakfast, and gourmet meals that have earned it a mention on *Top Chef*.

For a more affordable B&B experience without sacrificing the quality of your stay, **Gould's Alaska View B&B** (3044 Nowell Ave., 907/463-1546, from $120) offers a quiet, safe, one-bedroom apartment rental just across the channel from Juneau on Douglas Island. Full continental breakfast and Wi-Fi are provided, along with all the amenities you'd expect in any hotel.

INFORMATION AND SERVICES

Public bathrooms are available in the downtown **Juneau Public Library** (292 Marine Way, 907/586-5249, juneau.org/library,

Mon.-Thurs. 11am-8pm, Fri. 1-5pm, Sat.-Sun. noon-5pm), **City Hall** (Marine Way and S. Seward St.), and the **Juneau Arts & Culture Center** (350 Whittier St.), as well as the **Capital Transit Center** (292 Marine Way), and the upper and lower terminals for the **Mount Roberts Tram** (just past the cruise docks—you can't miss the overhead cables).

Juneau's **Bartlett Regional Hospital** (3260 Hospital Dr., 907/796-8900) is a level 4 trauma center with a 24-hour emergency room.

Gas stations and vehicle repair shops are plentiful. If you're renting a car from the airport, **Mike's Airport Express** (9190 Glacier Hwy., 907/789-9476, daily 24 hours) is a good place to gas up; they also do repair work. The **Fred Meyer** (8181 Glacier Hwy., 907/789-6500) and **Safeway** (3033 Vintage Blvd., 907/523-2000) stores also have fuel centers. If you're downtown, **Tesoro** (920 W. 10th St.) and **Capital Service** (810 Glacier Ave., 907/586-4822) are both convenient.

Visitors to Juneau are often surprised to find that Internet bandwidth is limited (and expensive) in Alaska; that's why most places don't offer free unlimited Wi-Fi, and many businesses close to the cruise ship docks have begun portioning out Wi-Fi in 15-minute vouchers, available only with a purchase. Coffee shops a little farther from the cruise ship docks—and sometimes bars, too—are more easygoing about how long you can spend on their Wi-Fi after a purchase, because they're less likely to be besieged by passengers seeking Internet on rainy days.

As is almost always the case in Southeast Alaska, the downtown **Juneau Public Library** (292 Marine Way, 907/586-5249, juneau.org/library, Mon.-Thurs. 11am-8pm, Fri. 1-5pm, Sat.-Sun. noon-5pm) is the best place to get free Wi-Fi and computer access; it's on the top floor of a public parking garage, very close to the cruise ship docks. Also close by is the **Douglas Branch Library** (1016 3rd St., 907/364-2378, Mon.-Wed. 2pm-8pm, Thurs. 11am-5pm, Fri.-Sun. 1pm-5pm), just across the bridge on Douglas Island.

You can also get Wi-Fi access at the **Alaska State Library** (395 Whittier St., 907/465-2920, library.alaska.gov, Mon.-Fri. 10am-4:30pm for Wi-Fi and computers on the 8th floor, Mon.-Fri. 8am-5pm in the atrium for Wi-Fi only).

TRANSPORTATION

Juneau is essentially landlocked—trapped between the water on one side and steep mountains topped with massive icefields on the other. It's best to think of it as an island, because the only ways you can get there are by air and sea. Juneau has multiple arrivals from the **Alaska Marine Highway System** (800/642-0066, ferryalaska.com) state ferry system every day, and multiple **Alaska Airlines** (800/252-7522, alaskaair.com) flights from Anchorage, Seattle, and smaller Southeast communities.

The cruise ship docks are smack in the middle of downtown Juneau, but the airport is about 8 miles away and the state ferry dock is about 13 miles away. The small but capable Juneau bus system, **Capital Transit** (downtown transit center at 292 Marine Way, 907/789-6901, juneau.org/capitaltransit, $2 adult) can take you to the airport during daylight hours, but not to the ferry. A typical early morning taxi fare from downtown Juneau to the ferry is $35-40; in the daytime when there's more traffic, fares can reach as high as $75. Most hotels are good about trying to help guests who are all going to the ferry terminal connect to share a taxi.

There are three taxi companies: **Glacier Taxi and Tours** (907/796-2300, glaciertaxiandtours.com), **EverGreen Taxi** (also includes Capital Cab and Taku Taxi, 907/790-5555, evergreentaxi.com), and **Juneau Yellow Cab** (907/790-4511). I prefer Glacier Taxi and Tours, as do many locals; they're much more relaxed about letting you share a taxi with other people heading the same direction.

★ GLACIER BAY NATIONAL PARK AND PRESERVE

Glacier Bay National Park and Preserve encompasses an enormous 3.3 million acres of land and water—that's larger than the state of Alabama. Its craggy, snowcapped mountains, towering spruce and cedar trees, and rich waters are hardly unique in Alaska, but this park is remarkable for several reasons.

The first is the pristine nature of the waters and lands; the waters, in particular, are some of the richest in the world, and Glacier Bay is one of the largest protected biosphere preserves in the world. Second, the solitude—cruise ships do visit the bay, but they never dock, and access during peak months is controlled by a free permit system.

Third, it's been less than 300 years since an enormously thick glacier covered much of this land. The bay was uncovered by a stunningly fast series of advances and retreats. Finally, this place is a rich, integral part of the Tlingit Alaska Native tradition, and park officials work closely with the tribes. One of their most notable successes was the opening of the Xunaa Shuká Hít clan house in August of 2016; this is the first permanent clan house in Glacier Bay since Tlingit villages were destroyed by a rapid glacier advance more than 250 years ago.

Permits for Boating and Camping

Glacier Bay is a very popular destination for private boat owners. During the peak months, June-August, private boat owners must secure a free permit to enter the waters of Glacier Bay and Bartlett Cove. Each permit is good for up to seven days, and you must apply within 60 days of your planned arrival date. Don't dillydally, though—permits often "sell out" quickly from mid-June to early August.

If you want to camp in Glacier Bay May-September—whether in the established campground or the backcountry— you need a free permit too. See nps.gov/glba for more information on both types of permits.

Tours in Glacier Bay

The tour operators listed for Gustavus also offer day trips and longer expeditions into Glacier Bay. The only scheduled day tour in the park is the Glacier Bay Tour out of the **Glacier Bay Lodge** (179 Bartlett Cove, 888/229-8687, visitglacierbay.com), which also offers a water taxi for backpackers and kayakers heading deep into the park. **Glacier Bay**

the shores of Glacier Bay National Park and Preserve

Glacier Bay National Park and Preserve

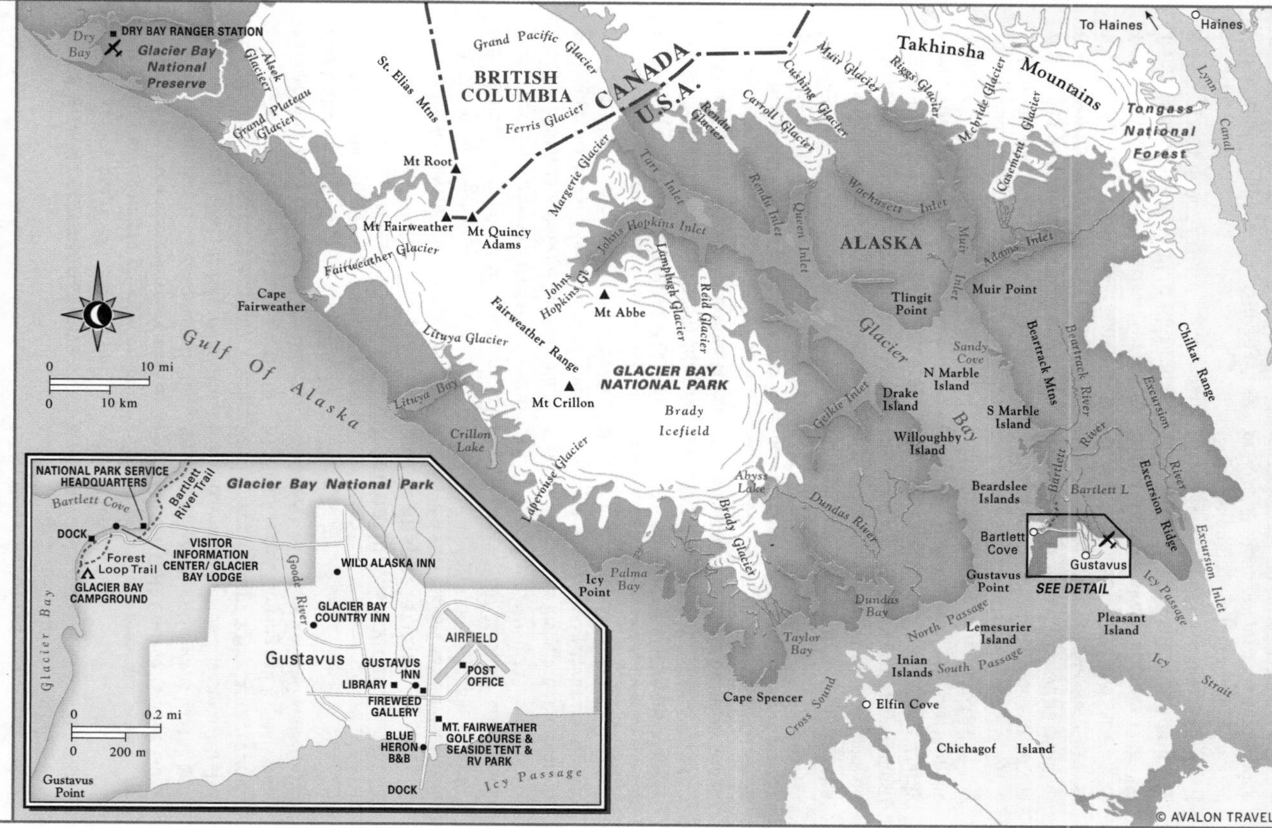

Adventures (907/697-2442) offers a cruise aboard the park-permitted research yacht, the *Steller*.

Food and Accommodations

Unless you're prepared to drive out to Gustavus, you're going to get all your food in Glacier Bay from wherever you're staying. The clear winners in this department are the **Gustavus Inn at Glacier Bay** (800/649-5220, gustavusinn.com, from $225), which serves freshly caught seafood along with the harvest from a full garden, and the **Glacier Bay Country Inn** (35 Tong Rd., 480/725-1158, glacierbayalaska.com, from $298 for lodging)—call before 4pm for reservations—whose three-course meals have been featured in *Bon Appétit, Saveur,* and *Food & Wine*.

If you want to get away from your lodging, you have a couple of food options in **Gustavus**. The **Fireweed Gallery, Coffee and Tea House** (3 Wilson Rd., 907/697-3013, gustavusgallery.com, Mon.-Sat. 6am-8pm, Sun. 8am-4pm) offers a little bit of everything, from high-end coffee and tea to great local gifts, baked goods, milk shakes, and crepes. The **Clove Hitch Cafe** (1250 Gustavus Rd., Tues.-Thurs. 11am-2pm and 5pm-8pm, Fri.-Sat. 11am-2pm and 4:30pm-8pm) offers plain diner-style food in generous portions for breakfast, lunch, and dinner, with pizza on Friday and Saturday nights.

The only hotel-style accommodations are in **Glacier Bay Lodge** (179 Bartlett Cove, 888/229-8687, visitglacierbay.com, from $260). It also houses the official Glacier Bay Visitor Center and interpretive exhibits on its second floor.

More modestly priced accommodations can be had without sacrificing quality: The **Blue Heron B&B** (907/697-2293, blueheronbnb.net, from $125) is excellent and offers a full breakfast and free courtesy van transfer. Also excellent is the **Wild Alaska Inn** (855/977-2704 or 907/697-2704, glacierbay.biz, from $119).

For tent campers, the **Glacier Bay Campground** offers serene tent camping with fantastic views over the water. Sites are free, but you need to register at the Visitor Information Station near the private docks and pick up a free camping permit May-September. The campground does offer bear-resistant food caches.

If you prefer four roofs and a wall, the **Fairweather Golf Course** (1 State Dock Rd., 907/697-2214) in Gustavus has the best bargains, with budget rentals from $60. It also has the **Seaside Tent & RV Campground,** which offers tent camping and RV slots with hot showers, restrooms, and fresh water (from $20).

Information, Services, and Transportation

There are no ATMs or banks in Gustavus or Glacier Bay. To rent a car, contact **Bud's Rent-a-Car** (907/697-2403); for taxi service, call **TLC Taxi** (907/697-2239, glacierbaytravel.com/tlctaxi). For more information on general services in Gustavus and Glacier Bay, contact the **Gustavus Visitors Association** (907/697-2454, gustavusak.com) or the **Glacier Bay Lodge Visitor Center** (907/697-2661).

You can only get here by air or water. Cruise ships enter the bay but don't dock; meanwhile, the **Alaska Marine Highway System** ferry (ferryalaska.com, 800/642-0066) offers weekly service, and **Alaska Airlines** (800/252-7522 or alaskaair.com) offers seasonal jet service, usually June-August. Both the ferry terminal and airport are fairly close to Gustavus; it's about 10 miles from the center of town to the entrance to Glacier Bay National Park.

If you want a small-plane adventure you can take a year-round flight with a small regional carrier: **Wings of Alaska** (Gustavas 907/697-2201, Juneau 907/789-0790, wingsofalaska.com), **Alaska Seaplanes** (907/789-3331, flyalaskaseaplanes.com), **Admiralty Air Service** (907/796-2000), **Ward Air** (8891 Yandukin Dr., Juneau, 800/478-9150 or 907/789-9150), or **Fjord Flying Service** (877/460-2377 or 907/697-2377).

GUSTAVUS

Unless you're on a flightseeing trip out of nearby Haines, almost every visit to the stupendous wilderness that is Glacier Bay National Park and Preserve starts in the 440-person community of Gustavus, which is just 10 miles from the park entrance. Gustavus is a picturesque little town with a big, beautiful beach—great for beachcombing—that's bordered by towering spruce and hemlock trees.

Recreation

If you're not going straight to Glacier Bay, it's worth booking a 45-minute van tour through **Strawberry Point Tours** (907/209-1200) to get to know the town and surrounding land. Hikers can head straight for the 2,600-acre **Gustavus Forelands Preserve** (at end of Glen's Ditch Road), where the 2.5-mile **Nagoonberry Loop** trail takes you through this unusual stretch of flatlands, perched in the midst of some of the craggiest glacier-carved scenery you'll find anywhere in the world. Look for sandhill cranes congregating in the wetlands during the fall.

Although Glacier Bay National Park and Preserve is the biggest draw in the area, Gustavus has some charming recreation opportunities of its own, including the 9-hole **Mount Fairweather Golf Course** and driving range (1 State Dock Rd., 907/697-2214, $15/9 holes, $24/18 holes). It's surrounded by mountains on all sides and has several holes bordering the waters of **Icy Straits** (the waters that access Glacier Bay, and one of Alaska's richest marine environments). Keep your eyes peeled for wildlife both on land and in the water.

WHALE-WATCHING

Whale-watching is phenomenal in the waters of Glacier Bay and Icy Straits; from late June through September, humpback whales focus on nothing but eating as much as they can, stocking up on blubber before they migrate to their warm-water breeding grounds, where they'll fast until their return next year. You'll see many fascinating behaviors, from lunge feeding to breaching, spy hopping, lob-tailing, and even bubble-net feeding, a learned, cooperative behavior that only happens in this part of the world. You have great odds of seeing other wildlife too, from orcas to sea lions, Dall porpoises, and numerous waterbirds.

Two of the best whale-watching tours in these waters are the half-day, naturalist-narrated **"Taz" Cross-Sound Express**

a humpback whale lunge feeding in Glacier Bay National Park

(888/698-2726 or 907/321-2303, taz.gustavus.com), which also offers water-taxi services for kayakers and backpackers (the deck is large enough to handle large groups of kayaks), and the half-day **Wild Alaska Charters** tour (855/997-2704 or 907/697-2704, glacierbay.biz/whale-watching.html, from $140), which never takes more than six passengers at a time.

TOP EXPERIENCE

SEA KAYAKING

Sea kayaking is also enormously popular, both in and around the park. **Glacier Bay Sea Kayaks** (907/697-2257, glacierbayseakayaks.com) has a concession for full- and half-day trips inside the park and also provides gear rentals and trip-planning assistance to paddlers who are experienced enough to go without a guide. The **Beardslee Islands** are a popular destination, with great beach camping and wildlife viewing. Another great destination is Muir Arm in the park; you can use the daily Glacier Bay Tour boat from **Glacier Bay Lodge** as a water taxi to cut days off your paddling time in these glacier-clad waters.

On the other end of the spectrum, the folks at **Alaska Mountain Guides** (800/766-3396 or 801/742-0100, alaskamountainguides.com), based in nearby Haines, are renowned for their guided expeditions of five days or more. **Spirit Walker Expeditions** (800/529-2537, seakayakalaska.com) is also very popular for longer trips throughout the northern portion of Southeast Alaska. If you book with a different provider, make sure they have the proper permits to actually go into the waters of Glacier Bay.

FISHING

The waters of Glacier Bay and Icy Straits are enormously productive, so it's no surprise that this is one of the best places in the world for fishing. Better yet, the isolated location means you won't have to battle crowds. If you don't want to commit to an all-inclusive, multi-day fishing trip with **Glacier Bay Sportfishing** (907/697-3038, glacierbaysportfishing.com, lodging at the Gustavus Inn, from $2,400 for 3 days/4 nights), you can book anywhere from a half-day to five-day trip with **Taylor Charters** (801/647-3401, taylorchartersfishing.com).

Skagway

Skagway is all about the glamorous days of the 1898 Klondike Gold Rush, when miners, scoundrels, and working ladies all flocked to the north in hopes of striking it rich. Those who weren't actively mining for gold were "mining the miners," so to speak, making their living in support of the prospectors.

One of the most-recognized characters of that day is Jefferson "Soapy" Smith, a smooth-talking gentleman scoundrel who earned his nickname by selling $0.05 cakes of soap that supposedly had dollar bills—and sometimes hundred-dollar bills—tucked into the wrapper. But when customers opened the package, they'd find only the soap.

All the action in Skagway takes place within an eight-block radius of the cruise ship docks, on the wide boardwalks of the Klondike Gold Rush National Historical Park. The entire town is a historic site, but pay close attention to the century-old wooden storefronts: Some of them have been turned into tiny museums showcasing photographs, artifacts, and re-creations of historic Skagway, while others have never fallen out of use at all.

Heads up: Almost everything you can see or do in Skagway is seasonal, opening in April and closing down in September once the cruise ships leave, with very limited shopping and services available year-round.

SIGHTS

For most tourists, the **Skagway Convention & Visitors Bureau** (245 Broadway,

Skagway

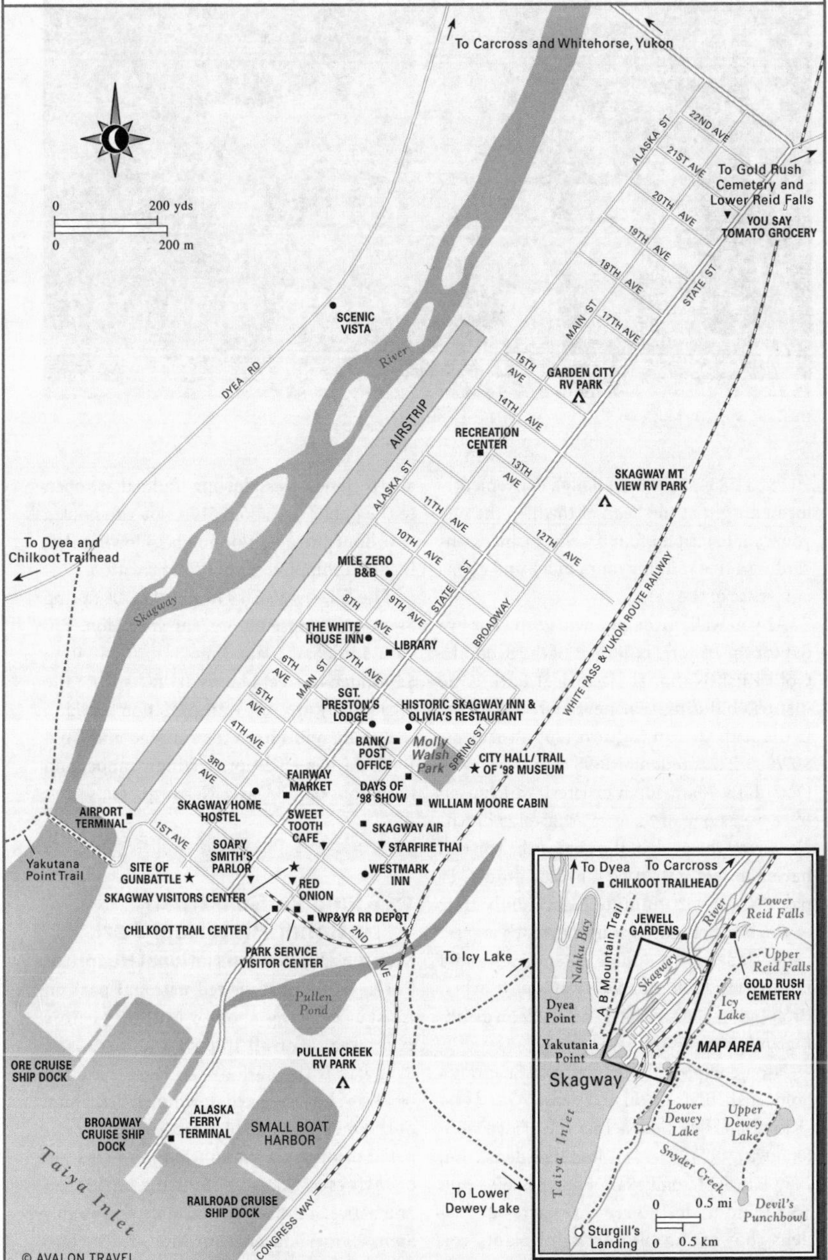
To Carcross and Whitehorse, Yukon
0 200 yds
0 200 m
SCENIC VISTA
River
DYEA RD
AIRSTRIP
To Dyea and Chilkoot Trailhead
Skagway
ALASKA ST
22ND AVE
21ST AVE
20TH AVE
19TH AVE
18TH AVE
17TH AVE
15TH AVE
14TH AVE
13TH AVE
12TH AVE
11TH AVE
10TH AVE
9TH AVE
8TH AVE
7TH AVE
6TH AVE
5TH AVE
4TH AVE
3RD AVE
1ST AVE
2ND AVE
MAIN ST
STATE ST
BROADWAY
SPRING ST
WHITE PASS & YUKON ROUTE RAILWAY
To Gold Rush Cemetery and Lower Reid Falls
YOU SAY TOMATO GROCERY
GARDEN CITY RV PARK
RECREATION CENTER
SKAGWAY MT VIEW RV PARK
MILE ZERO B&B
THE WHITE HOUSE INN
LIBRARY
SGT. PRESTON'S LODGE
HISTORIC SKAGWAY INN & OLIVIA'S RESTAURANT
BANK/ POST OFFICE
Molly Walsh Park
CITY HALL/ TRAIL OF '98 MUSEUM
FAIRWAY MARKET
DAYS OF '98 SHOW
WILLIAM MOORE CABIN
AIRPORT TERMINAL
SKAGWAY HOME HOSTEL
SWEET TOOTH CAFE
SKAGWAY AIR
STARFIRE THAI
Yakutana Point Trail
SITE OF GUNBATTLE
SOAPY SMITH'S PARLOR
WESTMARK INN
RED ONION
SKAGWAY VISITORS CENTER
WP&YR RR DEPOT
CHILKOOT TRAIL CENTER
PARK SERVICE VISITOR CENTER
To Icy Lake
Pullen Pond
PULLEN CREEK RV PARK
ORE CRUISE SHIP DOCK
BROADWAY CRUISE SHIP DOCK
ALASKA FERRY TERMINAL
SMALL BOAT HARBOR
RAILROAD CRUISE SHIP DOCK
Taiya Inlet
CONGRESS WAY
To Lower Dewey Lake
© AVALON TRAVEL
To Dyea
To Carcross
CHILKOOT TRAILHEAD
Nahku Bay
A B Mountain Trail
JEWELL GARDENS
River
Lower Reid Falls
Upper Reid Falls
GOLD RUSH CEMETERY
Dyea Point
Icy Lake
Yakutania Point
MAP AREA
Skagway
Lower Dewey Lake
Upper Dewey Lake
Snyder Creek
Devil's Punchbowl
0 0.5 mi
0 0.5 km
Sturgill's Landing

the Skagway City Museum

907/983-2854, 8am-5pm daily), conveniently located right at the head of town, is the one you want to visit for tour brochures, maps (including a free walking tour guide), and a general sense of the area.

As you walk through town, keep your eye out for the historic buildings of the Klondike Gold Rush National Historical Park. One historic building that never fell out of use is the **Red Onion Saloon** (205 Broadway, 907/983-2222, redonion1898.com, Apr.-early Oct., daily 10am-10pm or later), which used to serve as one of Skagway's 80-plus brothels during the peak of the gold rush. You can have a decent pub-style lunch or dinner, or pay $10 for a 20-minute, adults-only tour of the brothel museum upstairs. It's a great time—laden with double entendres—and a fascinating look into Skagway's past, when Prohibition had absolutely no effect on drinking and prostitution.

For a complete departure from Skagway's gold rush history, visit **Jewell Gardens** (Klondike Hwy., just across the bridge from Skagway, 907/983-2111, jewellgardens.com, May-late Sept., daily 9am-5pm, $12.50 adult, $6 12 and under) to see three acres of gardens showcasing the variety of plants you can grow in this part of Alaska. The grounds also include a glassblowing studio that's open to the public; for about $100, you can book a two-hour introduction to glassblowing that includes shipping of your final creation.

The Skagway City Museum (700 Spring St, skagwaymuseum.org, summer Mon.-Fri. 9am-5pm, Sat. 10am-5pm, Sun. 10am-4pm; $2, under 12 free) houses artifacts from the area's many uses as a transportation corridor, including relics from the railroad and Gold Rush days, a traditional Tlingit canoe, and numerous other Alaska Native artifacts.

TOP EXPERIENCE

★ Klondike Gold Rush National Historical Park

Klondike Gold Rush National Historical Park is the most-visited national park in Alaska, drawing about a million visitors every year. For all intents and purposes, Skagway *is* the park—or at least the eight blocks of boardwalked downtown are. Some of the most notable historic buildings peppered through the park include a re-creation of **Jefferson "Soapy" Smith's parlor** (on 2nd between Broadway and State, daily 9am-5pm, $5 for a docent tour Mon.-Fri. or free Sat.-Sun.); the **Moore Homestead** (5th and

early morning in Klondike Gold Rush National Historic Park, before the streets fill with tourists

Spring, daily 10am-5pm), the first building in Skagway before the gold rush; the **Mascot Saloon Museum** (3rd and Broadway, daily 9am-5pm); and the **Junior Ranger Activity Center** in the **Pantheon Saloon** (4th and Broadway, Mon.-Fri. 10am-noon and 1pm-3pm).

The National Park Service's **Klondike Gold Rush National Historical Park Visitor Center & Museum** (2nd and Broadway, nps.gov/klgo, daily 8:30am-5:30pm) offers more detailed information on area trails and historic sights, along with activities, including a free 45-minute walking tour of Skagway's historic district, a free 25-minute film on the Klondike Gold Rush, and free 90-minute walking tours of nearby Dyea town site, a ghost town that once served as the start of the Chilkoot Trail for gold-hungry miners. (Note: You're responsible for your own transportation to/from Dyea, which is a little more than nine miles from Skagway.) Tickets are free but required; get them from the visitor center or recreation.gov.

RECREATION AND ENTERTAINMENT

No trip to a historical gold rush town would be complete without a visit to the resident vaudevillian musical production, **The Days of '98 Show** (907/983-2545, thedaysof98show.com, May-Sept., $20 daytime show, $22 evening show), which tells the story of Jefferson "Soapy" Smith, Skagway's most notorious con man.

If you're here to hike the 33-mile Chilkoot Trail, you must pick up your trail permit in the **Chilkoot Trail Center** (on Broadway between 5th Ave. and 6th Ave., June 1-Labor Day, daily 8am-5pm). This is also where you'll watch your bear awareness video and get a trail orientation.

There are other pleasant trails around town. One of the most popular hikes is out to the **Gold Rush Cemetery** (head north on State St. and follow signs); from there, you can hike to **Lower Reid Falls,** for a total distance of four miles round-trip. The one-mile hike to **Lower Dewey Lake** (or a 3.6-mile loop around it) is also popular. Beware of trains on the way to the trailhead, which you reach by walking alongside the tracks for about 360 feet, heading north from where the White Pass & Yukon Route train tracks cross the road. There's also a great scenic overlook about two miles out of town on Dyea Road (cross the bridge and follow the signs for Dyea).

You can get more information about other trails in the **Klondike Gold Rush National Historical Park Visitor Center** (2nd and Broadway, nps.gov/klgo, May-Sept., daily 8:30am-5:30pm).

★ White Pass & Yukon Route Railroad

If you love trains, make sure to leave time to ride the historic 1898 narrow-gauge **White Pass & Yukon Route Railroad** (WP&YRR, 231 2nd Ave., 800/343-7373, wpyr.com). The cars and engines are all lovingly restored, either original to the era or faithful re-creations of the same technology that was used to pioneer a most difficult route past mountains, glaciers, tunnels, and old railroad trestles.

Two of the WP&YRR's most popular trips are the summit excursion (a 3-hour, 3,000-foot climb through the Tongass rainforest to the summit of White Pass, $119 adult, $59.50 child) and their train/bus connection through Carcross in Canada's Yukon territory, retracing the same journey that hopeful prospectors took to the Klondike in 1898 ($235-329 adult, $117.50-164.50 child, depending on return method). Both trips cross into Canada, but because you never get off the train for the first trip, you don't need a passport on the summit excursion. You do need a passport for the second trip; see cic.gc.ca/eng-lish/information/inadmissibility for more information about entering Canada and their laws.

But the train isn't just a historical showpiece. It also serves as a shuttle service for Chilkoot Trail hikers heading back to their point of origin and offers flag stop or prebooked service to several trailheads plus the U.S. Forest Service's Denver "cabin" (a railroad caboose that's been repurposed into a public-use cabin), and to the Bennett campground in Canada's Yukon Territory.

SHOPPING

Skagway's Broadway Street is basically one long gift shop. Some of the stores are the sort of generic jewelry or gift stops you'll find near any cruise ship port anywhere in the world—but if you can look past them, the town is flush with local gifts and art. Look for "Made in Skagway" signs in the windows to denote shops that sell local goods, or start with some of the following shops. As with most businesses in Skagway, they're almost all open seasonally (May-September, sometimes April-September depending on weather and cruise ships), and almost all close early—around 5

one of the engines of the historic narrow-gauge White Pass & Yukon Route Railroad

or 6pm—but may stay open later if big cruise ships are in town.

Alaska Artworks (555 Broadway, 907/983-3443) stocks only art from Alaskan or Alaska-related artists, including carvings, photos of the northern lights, and some authentic Alaska Native art. **Kirmse's** (500 Broadway, 907/983-3773) offers everything from fossilized walrus tusks to carvings and jewelry. **Klondike Tours** (3rd and Broadway, 907/983-2075, klondiketours.com) has two gift shops side by side. One offers almost exclusively Alaska-made goods, including some authentic Alaska Native artwork; the other offers Alaska-themed items like T-shirts and cute baby onesies.

For a broad selection of local and regional art, much of it contemporary, visit **Taiya River Arts** (2nd and Broadway), with mostly jewelry and personal accessories; **A Fine Line Alaskan Gifts** (5th and Broadway), which has several dozen Alaska artists in one shop; **Nature's Creations** (6th and Broadway), where all items are handmade; and **Inspired Arts** (555 Broadway, 907/983-3885).

Corrington's Alaskan Ivory (5th and Broadway) has two locations that sell a mix of replica and exquisitely authentic Alaska Native artwork. Their 3rd and Broadway location also houses the small, private **Museum of Alaskan History,** which showcases pieces of Skagway and Alaskan history and gives a little background on the Corringtons' Arctic Trading Post in 1970s Nome, where they first started trading for Alaska Native artwork; they still return to some of the villages to trade.

BearHead Photography by Barrett Hedges (7th and Broadway, 931/581-3521) offers stunning, National Geographic-quality photographs of Alaska wildlife in his storefront. If you're of the crafting persuasion, **Rushin' Tailor's QuiltAlaska** (370 3rd Ave., 800/981-5432 or 907/983-2397, quiltalaska.com) offers its own Alaska-themed quilt patterns and a few Alaska-made quilts for sale, and its sister shop **Aurora Yarns** (near 7th and Broadway on 7th, 800/981-5432 or 907/983-3707, aurorayarnsofalaska.com, May-Sept. most days 9am-5:30pm) sells fiber art, supplies, and qiviut, the finely combed underwool of the musk ox.

Another thing to be aware of is "reproduction" Alaska Native artwork, which is usually made in China or Indonesia. Some stores stock these imitations side by side with authentic Alaska Native artwork, presumably to meet demand for inexpensive Alaska-themed goods; others have ivory carvings that are beautifully done, but not by Alaska Native artists. If the artist's background is important to you, just ask the shopkeeper and pay attention to *how* they answer. If they're clear, direct, and complete in their response, they have nothing to hide.

FOOD

If you're here for the atmosphere, chow down on decent pizzas, sandwiches, and drinks in the **Red Onion Saloon** (205 Broadway, 907/983-2222, redonion1898.com, $12); the bartenders almost always dress in period garb, and you may hear some hooting and hollering during tours of the upstairs brothel museum.

If you're more interested in the food than the ambience, head for **Olivia's Restaurant** (7th and Broadway, 907/983-2289, $20) at the Historic Skagway Inn. They use local crab, wild meat, and garden-fresh vegetables whenever possible to turn out delicious food at reasonable prices; take a peek into the garden to see where your dinner may be coming from. They serve drinks, too, and offer both indoor and outdoor seating.

Another good option is the **Chilkoot** (3rd and Spring, 907/983-6000, westmarkhotels.com, $33), the restaurant inside the Westmark Inn Skagway. They offer generous portions at fair prices.

Locals almost always recommend the **Sweet Tooth Cafe** (315 Broadway, 907/983-2405, daily 6am-2pm, Wed. and Sat. 9pm-1am) for conventional breakfast fare; they also offer burgers and seafood. I'm more partial to the sandwiches and smoothies at **Glacial Smoothies and Espresso** (336 3rd Ave.,

the Red Onion Saloon

907/983-3223, glacialsmoothies.com, Mon.-Fri. 6:30am-4pm, Sat.-Sun 7am-3pm). Both cafés offer box lunch options you can take on your excursions.

Thai food is ridiculously popular in all of Alaska, and that goes for Skagway too. The locals all love **Starfire Thai Food** (4th and Spring, 907/983-3663, starfirealaska.com, summer Mon.-Sat. 11am-10pm, Sun. 2pm-10pm, closed in winter, $18).

The only grocery store in town is the **IGA Fairway Market** (4th and State, 907/983-2220, Mon.-Sat. 8am-8pm, Sun. 9am-6pm), which manages to include a little bit of everything, including produce, although the selection will seem extremely limited compared to what you'd find in a road system city like Anchorage, Fairbanks, or even Juneau. Expect to pay up to 50 percent extra on items, because of the shipping cost and relatively limited demand.

ACCOMMODATIONS

Sgt. Preston's Lodge (866/983-2521, sgtprestonslodge, from $97) is an old army barracks that's been repurposed into a hotel, with 40 rooms that are clean, comfortable, and recently renovated, despite the exterior's tired looks. Most rooms include a microwave and refrigerator, and free Wi-Fi makes this one of the biggest bargains in town—when the Wi-Fi works. They also offer a free shuttle to/from the ferry dock, although it's only about 0.25 mile away.

Your other hotel option in town is the more expensive **Westmark Inn Skagway** (3rd and Spring, 907/983-6000, westmarkhotels.com, from $159, steep discount for AAA or CAA members). The rooms are basic but usually clean, and Wi-Fi is available in the bar and lobby. Rooms facing the bar or main entrance can get particularly noisy.

If you're here for the authentic gold rush experience, you'll love staying at the **Historic Skagway Inn** (7th and Broadway, 888/752-4929 or 907/983-2289, skagwayinn.com, $139-239), a former brothel. The building is old, but for many visitors that's part of the charm, and the staff is very accommodating. Each of the 10 small, quaintly furnished rooms bears a woman's name; most have en suite bathrooms, but the cheapest rooms have a half bath in the room and shower down the hall. Amenities include free shuttle service, full breakfast, Wi-Fi, and satellite TV in the lobby (not the rooms). They also have fridge and freezer space available; 12 and under stay free.

The **Swaying Spruce guest cabins** (Mile

0.2 Dyea Rd., 907/983-2674, swayingspruce.com, Apr.-Oct., $50-125) are ridiculously popular. Located just a couple miles out of town, they offer courtesy airport and ferry pickup and drop-off, free bicycles for guests to use, and a barbecue and firepit; they'll also handle tour bookings for you if you like.

Another great hideaway in the woods just out of town is **Skagway Bungalows** (Mile 0.5 Dyea Rd., skagwaybungalows.com, $125). The two bungalows are extremely clean and make a nice, private getaway in the trees just outside town. Each has a large bed, covered deck, full bathroom, microwave, refrigerator, and electric kettle. The Ravin cabin has a double futon to sleep more people.

Skagway's favorite small B&B is the homey **White House** (8th and Main, atthewhitehouse.com, $139-159, discounts for multiple nights and in winter), with a Sealy Posturepedic bed, mini fridge, cable TV, and free Wi-Fi in every room. Breakfast is a modest self-serve buffet. Wallpaper and handmade quilts make the place even homier, and each room gets a private bath.

If you're hiking the Chilkoot Trail or just want to get out of town, the **Chilkoot Trail Outpost** (Mile 8.5 Dyea Rd., 907/983-3799, chilkoottrailoutpost.com, $165-195) is a bed-and-breakfast seven miles out of town. The great owners offer huge breakfasts, a barbecue gazebo, a campfire, free Wi-Fi, comfortable beds, and charming cabins.

There are several options for campers. What you sacrifice in ambience at **Pullen Creek RV Park** (501 Congress Way, 844/983-3884 or 907/983-3884, pullencreekrvpark.com, May-Sept. 15), you get back in convenience and waterfront views. It's right beside the ferry dock and just about a block away from downtown Skagway. Showers, restrooms, water and electrical hookups, and a dump station are available; it has some tent sites, but you'll feel out of place in all the big rig bustle. Big rigs are welcome.

Another close-to-town option is **Garden City RV Park** (15th and State, 907/983-2378), an older park with basic gravel pads. The restrooms and showers are clean, staff is friendly and helpful, and it's a short walk to town.

To really get away from it all, the **National Park Service Dyea Campground** (907/983-9200 for park headquarters, $10 per site per night, check or exact change in cash required, no reservations) offers both vehicle and walk-in camping with pit toilets and fire pits. This is a primitive, wooded, riverside campground, so no hookups are available and you'll need to provide your own firewood and drinking water, and pack your trash out. Some tent sites are available. The campground is 0.5 mile from the Chilkoot Trail trailhead, and it's just a short drive or bike ride from the old Dyea townsite.

INFORMATION AND SERVICES

Public bathrooms are available throughout Skagway. There are three along Congress Way, the road that leads into town from the cruise ship docks; another at the airport terminal; two on 3rd Avenue, on either side of Broadway; another at the Klondike Gold Rush National Historical Park Visitor Center (2nd and Broadway); and more in the Skagway City Museum and the Skagway Public Library (769 State St.).

Your best contact for general information is the **Skagway Convention & Visitors Bureau** (245 Broadway, 907/983-2854, summer daily 8am-5pm). There is a small **medical clinic** (350 14th Ave. between State and Broadway, 907/983-2255, 907/983-2025 for on-call nurse practitioner after business hours, Mon.-Fri. 7am-7pm, Sat. 10am-6pm). A **gas/diesel station** at 2nd and State has a **laundromat** downstairs. The gas station and laundromat are open daily 7am-7pm during the summer, with limited hours—usually Tuesday-Sunday—during the winter.

Wi-Fi is more of an issue here than in some Southeast communities. If you have a smartphone that can double as a personal hotspot, that'll be faster than anything you can get in town.

The only real place to get free Wi-Fi is at the **Skagway Public Library** (769 State St., 907/983-2665, Mon.-Thurs. 10am-9pm, Fri. 10am-7pm, Sat. and Sun. 1pm-5pm). There are three computers you can use for Internet access. Please respect the library's rules about quiet spaces and no food or drink. A few merchants offer Wi-Fi access if you make a purchase, but some places that previously advertised Wi-Fi now refuse because they've been overwhelmed with requests.

Your next best bet for Internet access is the Internet café in the **Seaman Center** (375 2nd Ave., 907/983-9503), where you can pay $5 for one hour of Internet access on their computers.

TRANSPORTATION

Downtown Skagway only covers eight blocks, with wide sidewalks and slow traffic that's used to pedestrians—so it's easy to get around on foot. A **Smart Shuttle** bus (smart-ak.com, May-Sept., daily 7am-9pm) makes continuous rounds of downtown Skagway, including the ferry and airport terminals; they pass by each stop every 30 minutes. Pay $5 for an all-day pass and hop on and off at your convenience or $2 for a single trip.

If you've arrived by ferry or plane and want to rent a car, you have three options: **Avis** (3rd and Spring St., 907/983-2247, May-mid-Sept., daily 7am-8pm daily) is your only option if you want to drop your car off at another rental location around the state. If you're staying local, you can rent from family-owned **Sourdough Car Rentals & Tours** (350 6th St., 907/983-2523) or **Alaska Green Jeep Tours** (480 Broadway, 907/983-3512, alaskagreenjeeptours.com, daily 8am-6pm). The latter comes with an audio CD that narrates your own self-guided tour of the area.

Your other vehicle option is a bike: Rent from **Sockeye Cycle Co.** (381 5th Ave., 907/983-2851, cyclealaska.com, from $21 for 2 hours, $42/day, tandem bikes available), which also has an office in Haines, or book them for bike-based tours in either location.

Getting There

Skagway is one of two Southeast Alaska communities you can reach by road (the other is Haines). Skagway sits at the end of the **Klondike Highway,** just under three hours (109 miles) south of **Whitehorse** in Canada's Yukon Territory. It's about a 15.5-hour drive from Anchorage (812 miles) and 31 hours (1,608 miles) from Seattle. Both routes take you through Canada, so you'll need your passport. See *Essentials* for more information. Wherever you're coming from, leave yourself plenty of time to enjoy the stunningly beautiful drive.

Skagway is a frequent stop on the cruise ship circuit, of course, and independent travelers can get here easily on the **Alaska Marine Highway System (AMHS)** (800/642-0066, ferryalaska.com). Skagway is a little more than an hour from Haines by regular ferry (30 minutes on the occasional fast ferry runs) and 5 hours from Juneau on a direct ferry run, or 2.5 hours on the fast ferry.

Your other travel options are to book a flight on a small airline out of Juneau—**Wings of Alaska** (Skagway 907/983-2442, Juneau 907/789-0790, wingsofalaska.com) or **Alaska Seaplanes** (907/789-3331, flyalaskaseaplanes.com)—or to hop a one-way ride on the **Fjord Express** shuttle service (800/320-0146, alaskafjordlines.com), a fast catamaran that runs from Skagway to Haines, then on to Juneau; a one-way fare is $130 adult, $115 child, or do an out-and-back day cruise, including six hours in Juneau, for $169 adult, $139 child. That's almost three times the cost of an AMHS ferry ticket, but the daily runs are convenient. No vehicles allowed.

Haines

History runs deep in tiny Haines, which has a population of about 1,370 people. Originally called Dei-Shu or "end of the trail" in Tlingit, this town received its English name in honor of the first missionary to arrive in the area, Francina Haines. This is also the place of the first known meeting between white men (Russian fur traders) and Tlingits in 1741, and the site of a fort that was constructed to shore up the U.S. position in ongoing border disputes with Canada.

Nowadays, the fort is mostly privately owned homes, restaurants, lodgings, galleries, and shops—in other words, it's been assimilated right into the town. But don't get too distracted by the shopping. There's nowhere else on earth that you can experience this type of tranquility in such amazing scenery. Heads up: Many amenities run only from mid-May to mid-September.

SIGHTS

Towns don't come any more picturesque than Haines. Let's start with the mountains that stand in any direction you look. Looking east across the Lynn Canal (which is one of the longest and deepest fjords in the world), you'll see the Coast Mountains. To the south (on your right) is the Chilkat Range, to the north (your left) are the Takshanuk Mountains, and behind the town are the Takinsha Mountains.

Haines has beautiful rivers, too, where you can watch both people and bears fishing for the immense bounty that is salmon returning from the sea. The Chilkat River runs past Haines to the west and southwest, while the Chilkoot River is to the north. But the natural scenery isn't done yet. If you take Mud Bay Road through Chilkat State Park to the west of town, you'll get beautiful views of the Rainbow and Davidson Glaciers, lingering remnants of

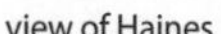
view of Haines

Haines

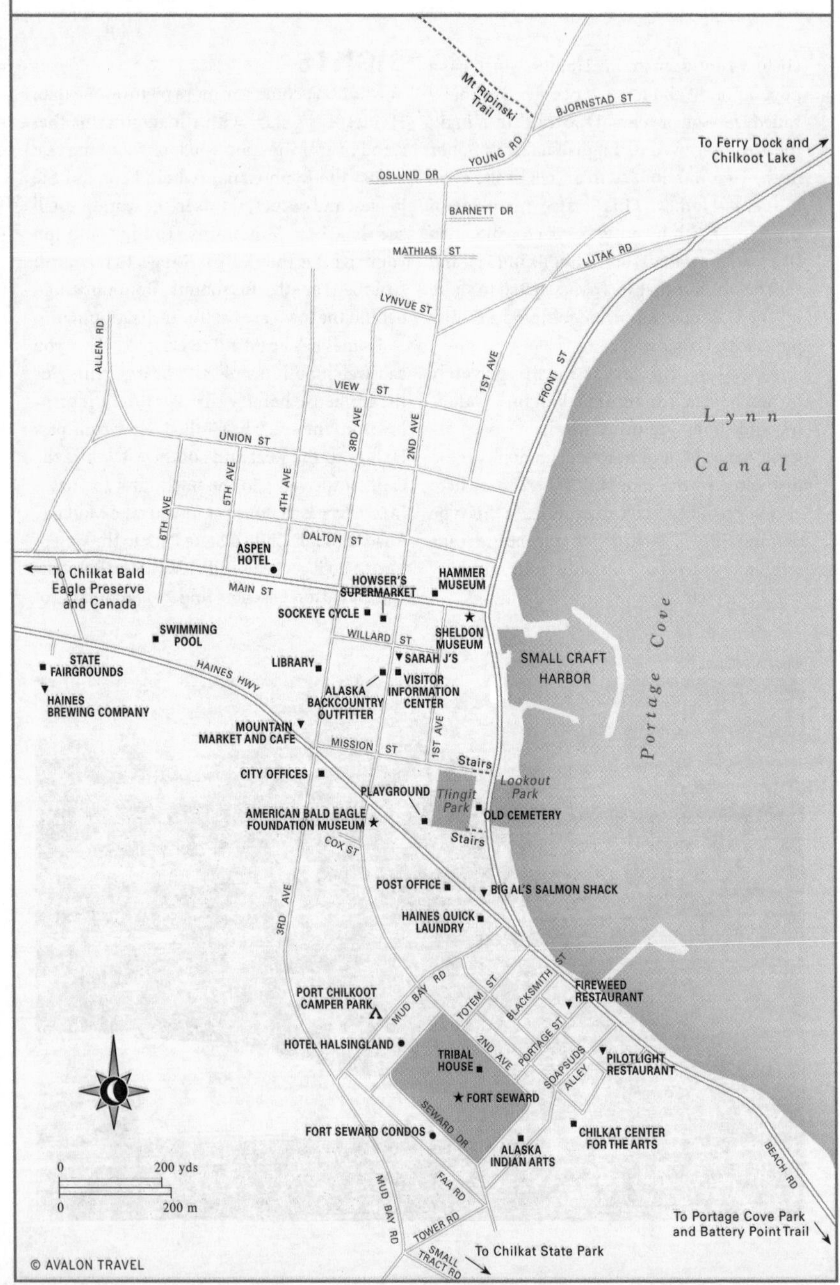
Mt Ripinski Trail
BJORNSTAD ST
YOUNG RD
To Ferry Dock and Chilkoot Lake
OSLUND DR
BARNETT DR
MATHIAS ST
LUTAK RD
LYNVUE ST
ALLEN RD
1ST AVE
FRONT ST
VIEW ST
3RD AVE
2ND AVE
Lynn Canal
UNION ST
6TH AVE
5TH AVE
4TH AVE
DALTON ST
ASPEN HOTEL
HAMMER MUSEUM
To Chilkat Bald Eagle Preserve and Canada
MAIN ST
HOWSER'S SUPERMARKET
SOCKEYE CYCLE
SWIMMING POOL
WILLARD ST
SHELDON MUSEUM
SMALL CRAFT HARBOR
Portage Cove
STATE FAIRGROUNDS
HAINES HWY
LIBRARY
SARAH J'S
VISITOR INFORMATION CENTER
HAINES BREWING COMPANY
ALASKA BACKCOUNTRY OUTFITTER
MOUNTAIN MARKET AND CAFE
MISSION ST
1ST AVE
Stairs
CITY OFFICES
Lookout Park
PLAYGROUND
Tlingit Park
OLD CEMETERY
AMERICAN BALD EAGLE FOUNDATION MUSEUM
Stairs
COX ST
POST OFFICE
BIG AL'S SALMON SHACK
3RD AVE
HAINES QUICK LAUNDRY
BLACKSMITH ST
MUD BAY RD
TOTEM ST
FIREWEED RESTAURANT
PORT CHILKOOT CAMPER PARK
PORTAGE ST
HOTEL HALSINGLAND
2ND AVE
TRIBAL HOUSE
PILOTLIGHT RESTAURANT
SOAPSUDS ALLEY
FORT SEWARD
SEWARD DR
FORT SEWARD CONDOS
CHILKAT CENTER FOR THE ARTS
ALASKA INDIAN ARTS
BEACH RD
0
200 yds
0
200 m
MUD BAY RD
FAA RD
TOWER RD
To Portage Cove Park and Battery Point Trail
SMALL TRACT RD
To Chilkat State Park
© AVALON TRAVEL

the massive ice sheets that sculpted this landscape. Another very popular photo stop is Picture Point, off Lutak Road.

TOP EXPERIENCE

Alaska Chilkat Bald Eagle Preserve

If you've come to Alaska looking for eagles, you're in luck. The **Alaska Chilkat Bald Eagle Preserve,** a 48,000-acre preserve of lands along the Chilkat, Kleheni, and Tsirku Rivers, was created to preserve critical habitat for the world's largest concentration of bald eagles. The best viewing point is on the Haines Highway from mile 18 to mile 24 (including the very traditional Tlingit village of Klukwan), where you can see eagles congregating along the Chilkat River flats in late fall and winter. Viewing is best from October through January.

American Bald Eagle Foundation

Eagle fans will also enjoy a stop by the **American Bald Eagle Foundation** (113 Haines Hwy., 907/766-3094, May-Sept., Mon.-Fri. 9am-5pm, Sat. noon-4pm, reduced winter hours, $15 adult, $12 senior and military, $8 15 and under), which consists of a lovely natural history museum and a staffed raptor center where you can visit with almost a dozen "avian ambassadors," some of which are eagles. Admission is less December-April.

Kroschel Films Wildlife Center

Want up-close, guaranteed wildlife sightings? You can book a tour to visit the **Kroschel Films Wildlife Center** (907/766-5464, kroschelfilms.com, May-Sept. and occasional winter tours), famously featured on National Geographic's *Expedition Wild,* in the heart of the eagle preserve.

Museums

Don't miss a chance to visit the **Sheldon Museum & Cultural Center** (907/766-2366, Mon.-Tues. and Thurs.-Fri. 10am-5pm, Wed. 9am-5pm, Sat. 1pm-4pm), with its exhibits of pioneer history, Tlingit culture, and nearby Fort Seward; it also has an excellent gift shop.

There's another museum in town: It's safe to say Haines has the only **Hammer Museum** (108 Main St., 907/766-2374, Mon.-Fri. 10am-5pm, Sat. 10am-2pm, $5 adult, child 12 and under free) in the world. This odd little building commemorates the world's very first tool in all its varieties—from Egyptian to Australian

the Alaska Chilkat Bald Eagle Preserve

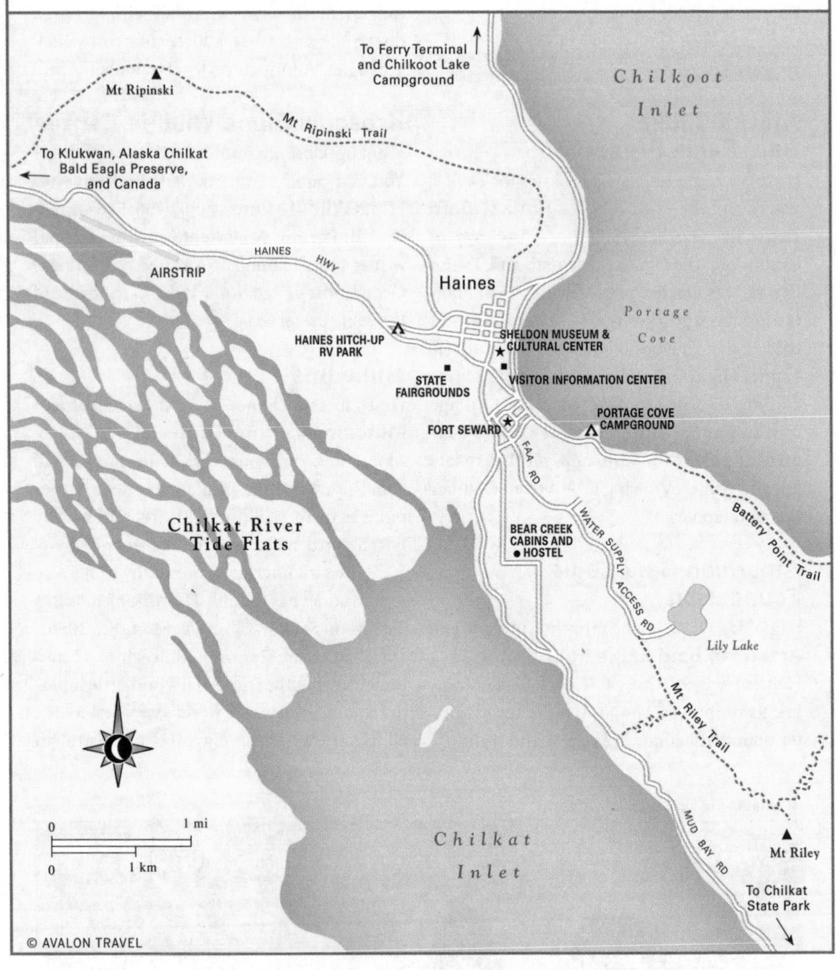

and of course American—and has been a favorite with visitors since its founding in 2002.

Haines Packing Company

Although it's not an official museum, the **Haines Packing Company** (Mile 5.5 Mud Bay Rd., 907/766-2883, hainespacking.com, mid-April-early Nov.) is one of the oldest cannery sites in Southeast Alaska; they've been processing seafood since 1917. You can explore the docks, watch boats unload, and see the processing line at work through large windows—then visit the gift shop for your own takeaway fish.

If you're taking the ferry or a cruise ship in to Haines, keep an eye out for the historic **Eldred Rock Lighthouse,** a red-roofed building that has safeguarded the path to the community since 1905. Its Fresnel lens now resides in the Sheldon Museum, and the Eldred Rock Lighthouse Preservation Association is working to restore and preserve the building.

Klukwan

Located 22 road miles northwest of Haines, Klukwan is a small, very traditional Tlingit Indian village, one of the best places to learn about traditional culture in this region of Alaska. Visit the **Jilkaat Kwaan Cultural Heritage Center** (9 Chilkat Ave., 907/767-5485, jilkaatkwaanheritagecenter.org, Mon.-Fri. 10am-4pm, Sat. 1pm-4pm, reduced hours starting in Sept., $15 adult, $7.50 child 12 and under) to learn more about Southeast Alaska Native culture, language, and history, including a chance to visit with master wood-carvers in residence. You can also take a Jilkaat Kwaan Cultural Tour (offered several times daily May-Sept.; walk in or call 907/767-5485 for tour times) to learn more about traditional architecture, fish processing methods, and arts.

The heritage center also functions as the visitor center for the **Alaska Chilkat Bald Eagle Preserve** and houses the **Bentwood Box Gift Shop,** where you can shop for a one-of-a-kind example of traditional and contemporary Alaska Native art, plus a selection of other Alaska-made products.

You can also sign up for a twice-a-summer salmon camp, where you'll learn both traditional and contemporary methods of harvesting salmon and take a share of fish home; attend a storytelling and dance demonstration in the traditional clan house; or sit down to a gourmet, locally grown and harvested lunch in the Hospitality House.

RECREATION

Haines has a couple of companies that offer guided **brown bear and eagle viewing** as well as **guided raft/kayak trips** in the Alaska Chilkat Bald Eagle Preserve and Chilkoot Lake: **Alaska Nature Tours** (111 2nd Ave. S, 907/766-2876, alaskanaturetours.net), which also offers hiking trips and kayak/canoe rentals, and **Rainbow Glacier Adventures** (877/766-3516 or 907/766-3576, tourhaines.com).

Chilkat Guides (170 Sawmill Rd., 907/766-2491, raftalaska.com, multi-day excursions available) and **Haines Rafting Company** (907/314-0340, hainesrafting.com) also offer daily raft trips through the bald eagle preserve and multiday excursions, while **Chilkat River Adventures** (907/766-2050, jetboatalaska.com) will take you on a jet-boat ride up the river.

Alaska Nature Tours also runs **Alaska Backcountry Outfitter** (907/766-2876, alaskanaturetours.net), a year-round shop for gear rentals and maintenance on everything from hiking, camping, and climbing gear to paddling equipment.

All three airlines that provide small-plane service to Haines also offer **flightseeing** services: **Alaska Seaplanes** (4 Mile Haines Hwy., 907/766-3800, flyalaskaseaplanes.com, scheduled flights and charters), **Harris Aircraft Services** (877/966-3050 or 907/966-3030, harrisaircraftservices.com), and **Wings of Alaska** (800/789-9464 or 907/766-3020, fjordflying.com). You can also book a glacier flightseeing trip with **Mountain Flying Service** (907/766-3007, mountainflyingservice.com) or take a flightseeing trip to legendary Glacier Bay National Park (just 15 minutes away by air) with **FlyDrake** (121 2nd Ave., 907/766-3679, flydrake.com).

Fishing

For saltwater fishing, **1st Choice Charters** (907/314-0681 or 320/224-7646, fish1stchoice.com) offers four- and six-hour charters in addition to two-hour sightseeing trips, or try **I Fish Haines Alaska** (907/314-0735, ifishhainesalaska.com). For freshwater fishing, try **Chilkoot Lake Tours** (1069 Haines Hwy., 907/314-3179, chilkootlake.com) and **Fly Guides** (907/209-0816, haineflyfishing.com).

For DIY trips or to buy your fishing license and pick up local regulations, contact **Outfitter Sporting Goods** (Mile 0 Haines Hwy., 907/766-3221) and **Alaska Sport Shop** (420 Main St., 907/766-2441, oleruds.com). The latter even sells some groceries.

If you drove here and aren't planning on taking your car on the ferry farther south, you might enjoy a day cruise on **Alaska**

Fjordlines (800/320-0146 or 907/766-3395, alaskafjordlines.com) into Juneau, where you can spend a few hours exploring before catching the return trip.

Golf

Haines has a par 36 nine-hole golf course, **Valley of the Eagles Golf Links and Driving Range** (Mile 1.5 Haines Hwy., 907/766-2401, hainesgolf.com, 9 holes $22, day pass $38), where a bear with a fish in its mouth can be considered a legitimate hazard to play. You're more likely to see the tracks of moose and bears than the animals themselves. The course hosts a few competitions throughout the summer, so if getting to play is important to you, it's best to call ahead and guarantee availability. Alaska's long summer days mean that during the peak season, daylight playing hours can start as early as 3am and go as late as 10pm.

Winter Recreation

Winter is a beautiful time of year to visit Haines, when you can enjoy plenty of snow under bright blue skies. Because it's so far south, Haines has nearly six hours of daylight on the winter solstice. Both **Alaska Nature Tours** (111 2nd Ave. S, 907/766-2876, alaskanaturetours.net) and **Rainbow Glacier Adventures** (877/766-3516 or 907/766-3576, tourhaines.com) offer winter sightseeing and wildlife-viewing trips.

For snow activities, contact **Alaska Heli-Skiing** (877/754-4246, alaskaheliskiing.com) and **Southeast Alaska Backcountry Skiing** (907/766-2009, skiseaba.com) for some of the best heli-supported skiing and snowboarding anywhere in the world. **Snowmachining** (the Alaskan word for snowmobiling) is also very popular here; if you have the skills to ride the Alaskan backcountry, contact **Over the Top Motor Sports** (907/766-3855 or 907/303-5053) for rentals.

ENTERTAINMENT AND EVENTS

Despite its relatively remote location, Haines is the gathering place for the **Southeast Alaska State Fair** (907/766-2476, seakfair.org), four days of fun in late July every year. In August, attend the **Celebration of Bears** (bearfoundation.org), and in mid-November, attend the **Alaska Bald Eagle Festival** (907/766-3094, baldeagles.org), a celebration of the peak in wintertime gatherings of eagles, with seminars, tours, and family-friendly events.

If you're looking for a good sports bar, head to the **Bamboo Room Restaurant and Pioneer Bar** (11 2nd Ave. N, restaurant 907/766-2800, bar 907/766-3440, bamboopioneer.net), a full-service sports bar and restaurant that's famous for its halibut and chips. They also have live music on most weekends.

The **Fogcutter Bar** (122 Main St., 907/766-2555, fogcutterbar.com) offers lots of Alaska beers on tap, along with pool and darts, although you'd do well to avoid it when a big cruise ship is in town—it gets packed to the gills quickly. On other days, it's a fun, friendly place to converse and maybe chat up a few locals. Meanwhile, the **Fort Seward Saloon** (Mile 0 Haines Hwy., 877/617-3418 or 907/766-2009, Wed.-Sun. 5pm-2am, fortsewardlodge.com) offers all the old-timey ambience you could want.

SHOPPING

You'll find beautiful examples of traditional Native cultural crafts at **Alaska Indian Arts** (13 Ft. Seward Dr., 907/766-2160, Mon.-Fri. 9am-5pm), which is as much a cultural center as an art gallery. The carving studio is open to the public during business hours, and the director offers a cultural history lecture for a donation; call to book.

For the best collections of artwork by locals, visit **Art on Main Street** (219 Main St., 907/303-0222, alaskaartsconfluence.org) and **Cottage Arts** (46 Portage St., 907/766-2031, Apr.-Dec.). You can see the locals creating their art right in front of you at **Extreme Dreams Fine Arts Studio-Gallery** (2nd and Dalton, 907/766-2097, extremedreams.com).

If you're one of the many who love independent bookstores, **The Babbling Book** (223

Main St., 907/766-3356) is well worth a visit. For seafood, you can choose between two year-round shops: **Dejon Delights Alaska Smokery and Gourmet Gifts** (Bldg. 37, Portage St., 800/539-3608 or 907/766-2505, dejondelights.com) and **Bell's Store** (22 2nd Ave. N, 800/446-2950 or 907/766-2950). You can also visit the gift shop at **Haines Packing Company** (Mile 5.5 Mud Bay Rd., 907/766-2883, hainespacking.com, mid-Apr.-early Nov.).

For nature buffs, gourmet cooks, and those "impossible to shop for" people, **Second Nature** (121 2nd Ave. N, 907/766-2992) offers Chilkat Valley mushroom products, field guides, foraging tools, raw honey, beeswax candles, and the like.

FOOD

The most popular restaurant in town is the **Fireweed Restaurant** (37 Blacksmith Rd., 907/766-3838, fireweedrestaurant.com, lunch May-Sept., Wed.-Sat. 11:30am-2:30pm, dinner Mar.-Sept., Tues.-Sat. 4:30pm-9pm, $30), where the ever-changing menu focuses on fresh, local ingredients. Everything from pizza to salad is excellent, and the windows look out over the ocean. Be ready to wait for a table when the cruise ships are in. Nominally serving Italian cuisine, Fireweed is run by a Cordon Bleu-trained chef.

If the Fireweed is closed or too busy, try **The Pilotlight** (31 Tower Rd., 907/766-2962, Mon. and Wed.-Sun. 5pm-9pm, Sat.-Sun. 9:30am-2pm, $15-20). This new addition to the community opened in 2016, but they hit the ground running with an adventurous menu that includes elk and venison. That said, the real standout is the seafood menu, especially a phenomenal salmon bisque.

The **33-Mile Roadhouse** (Mile 33 Haines Hwy., 907/767-5510, daily 10am-7pm, 33mileroadhouse.com) offers such great soup, pie, and burgers that it regularly draws locals on the 60-plus-mile round-trip just to eat; the seafood is really good, too.

Big Al's Salmon Shack (Haines Hwy., across the street from the post office, 907/766-2883, Mon.-Sat. 11am-7pm, $10-15) offers no frills, but then again they don't need any to dress up their excellent fresh fish-and-chips and fish sandwiches; have a seat on the outdoor picnic tables and look out over the water where the fish was just caught. Service is fast, until it gets crowded.

Sarah J's Espresso Shoppe (25 Portage Dr., 907/766-2928, Mon.-Fri. 6:30am-4pm, Sat. 7:30am-4pm, $10) offers great sandwiches, espresso, and soft-serve ice cream.

For organic and natural foods, plus a full espresso bar and café foods including sandwiches, soups, and tortilla wraps—plus wines and spirits—visit **Mountain Market & Cafe** (Main St. between Front St. and 1st Ave., 907/766-3340, mountain-market.com, Mon.-Fri. 7am-7pm, Sat. 8am-5pm, Sun. 9am-5pm, $10).

Rusty Compass Coffeehouse (116 Main St., 907/766-3941) has great homemade pastries, soup/salad lunches that run $10-13, excellent coffee, and some gifts to shop for.

GROCERIES

The biggest supermarket act in town is **Howsers IGA Supermarket** (209 Main St., 907/766-2040, howserssupermarket.iga.com, Mon.-Sat. 8am-8pm, Sun. 10am-7pm).

ACCOMMODATIONS

It's hard to go wrong with accommodations in Haines. Almost everything is small enough for you to receive personal attention from the owner(s), and many properties have lovely views of the water. Summer prices are surprisingly modest, too, when compared to typical Alaska lodging fees. Lodgings are subject to a borough tax of 5.5 percent and 4 percent lodging tax. Cell phone navigation will often steer you wrong here—and there are cell phone "black holes" where you'll lose service—but lodgings offer driving directions on their websites.

The only nice traditional hotel in Haines is **Aspen Suites Hotel Haines** (409 Main St., 866/483-7848 or 907/766-2211, aspenhotelsak.com/haines, from $159), which opened in June 2015. Amenities include free Wi-Fi, a business center, a fitness room, kitchenette studios, and coin-op laundry. It's a comfortable, basic hotel.

Bear Creek Cabins and Hostel (1 Mile Rd., 907/766-2259, bearcreekcabinsalaska.com, $20 bunk, $68 private four-person cabin, $120 six-person family cabin) is a mile south of town. It offers hostel bunks with separate men's and women's dorms, private cabins, and a couple of group cabins; the cabins are all heated. There are no lockouts, and use of camp showers and kitchen is free. Dogs are allowed with some conditions. There's Wi-Fi. The facility books up far in advance, so reserve as early as possible.

The **Beach Roadhouse** (731 Beach Rd., 866/741-3060 or 907/766-3060, rooms from $115, cabins from $145, weekly rate available) is in a wooded setting—not directly oceanside—that's quiet, with lots of birdsong. Amenities include free Wi-Fi and flat-screen TVs. The two rooms have kitchenettes and private bathrooms, and the three cabins have fully stocked kitchens.

If you're here for all the right reasons—to enjoy the quiet, fresh air and views of lovely Lynn Canal—the clean and spacious **Fort Seward Condos** (4 Ft. Seward Dr., 907/766-2708, fortsewardcondos.com, from $160 for one bedroom, two-night minimum required) offer all of the above with one-, two- and three-bedroom suites that sleep up to five people in former officer quarters of the fort. A stay in this nationally registered historic landmark, built in 1903, is a real bargain for a group, and a good price for singles, too. You get a fully equipped kitchen, in-house laundry, and Wi-Fi.

The **Chilkoot Haven B&B** (800/572-8006 or 907/314-0466, chilkoothaven.com, $159/night in peak season) is located on Chilkoot State Road, 11 miles from Haines and 5 miles from the ferry terminal. This three-room bed-and-breakfast is perched on a bluff just 100 feet from the Chilkoot River, giving you expansive views of bears, eagles, and fishermen along with Haines's natural beauty.

The **River House** (3 River Rd., 907/766-3849, riverhousehaines.com, lower unit $125, upper unit $175, both $275) is a homey little cottage a mile from downtown at the mouth of the Chilkat River. You can rent one or both of the one-bedroom suites, each of which has a queen bed and its own private bath. The upper unit has a wood stove and full kitchen, Wi-Fi, and satellite TV; the lower unit has a washer and dryer, kitchenette, and a two-night minimum. The cottage is close to the beach, with great views of the river and mountains (the views are best from the upper unit). It's wonderfully quiet here, due in no small part to the lack of cell phone service (but you will have access to a landline phone).

Camping

For RV travelers, **Haines Hitch-Up RV Park** (off Main St. between Allen and Union, 907/766-2882, hitchuprv.com, May 15-Sept. 15 weather permitting) offers clean, all-grass sites set back a ways from the wind and cruise ship crowds that sometimes hit the dock area, but you're still close to everything downtown. Amenities include free showers, Wi-Fi, sewer, and cable TV, with lots of room to back in or pull through. They book up quickly June-August.

The **Portage Cove State Recreation Site campground** (1 Mile Beach Rd.) offers a handful of tent-only campsites ($10/night) right on the shoreline close to downtown Haines. You get great water views, and access is by bicycle or walk-in only, so this is a great reprieve for tent campers who want to get away from RVs.

For RV camping in downtown Haines, **Port Chilkoot Camper Park** (123 Mud Bay Rd., 800/542-6363 or 907/766-2000, Apr.-Oct.) is set on a nice wooded lot, with more than 40 RV sites (many with full or partial hookups but no on-site gas, propane, or dump) and 26 tent sites.

INFORMATION AND SERVICES

The **Visitor Information Center** (122 2nd Ave., 800/458-3579 or 907/766-2234,

Mon.-Fri. 8am-5pm, Wed. till 6pm, Sat.-Sun. 9am-4pm) sometimes stays open late when cruise ships are in town; make sure to ask for pamphlets on local hiking trails and the more than a dozen totem poles you'll see around town. Drop off postcards at the local post office (55 Haines Hwy., 907/766-2930, Mon.-Fri. 9am-5pm, Sat. 1pm-3pm).

You'll find public restrooms spaced along Front Street, with one near the small boat harbor, another at the Haines/Skagway fast ferry dock, and a third in Tlingit Park, near where Front Street meets the Haines Highway.

One of the most convenient gas stations in town is the **Tesoro** (900 Main St., 907/766-3776), which also offers auto service. If you can't quite make it into town (or need to gas up on your way out), the **33-Mile Roadhouse** (33 Mile Haines Hwy., 907/767-5510, 33mileroadhouse.com, daily 10am-7pm) also offers gas.

TRANSPORTATION

Getting There

Haines is one of two Southeast Alaska communities you can reach by road (the other is Skagway). Haines is 756 miles (a little more than 14 hours) from Anchorage, or 32 hours (1,627 miles) from Seattle. To get there, you must drive through Canada.

Like most Southeast communities, Haines sees its fair share of cruise ships. The local dock can only handle one large ship at a time, though, so it's ideal for cruise ship travelers who don't want to outnumber the local population or independent travelers trying to avoid the crowds. The big ships almost always dock in the front half of the week, so your odds of avoiding them entirely are best if you come on a Friday or Saturday, or consult the cruise ship docking schedule posted on visithaines.com.

The **Alaska Marine Highway System** ferry (800/642-0066, ferryalaska.com) is a true lifeline for this town; during the Alaska State Fair in late July, the four-hour run from Juneau to Haines is absolutely packed with revelers. The ferry terminal (907/766-2111, 2112 Lutak Rd.) is about 4.5 miles south of town. There's a separate downtown dock for the **Haines Skagway Fast Ferry** (39 Beach Rd., 888/766-2103, 907/786-2100, hainesskagwayfastferry.com), which runs 45-minute trips between Skagway and Haines, with multiple departures daily.

Big airlines like Alaska Airlines don't fly in to Haines, but several small airlines offer scheduled flights from the **Haines Airport** (Mile 4 Haines Hwy.), connecting you to other Southeast communities, including Juneau, Skagway, and Gustavus. They include **Alaska Seaplanes** (4 Mile Haines Hwy., 907/766-3800, flyalaskaseaplanes.com, scheduled flights and charters), **Harris Aircraft Services** (877/966-3050 or 907/966-3030, harrisaircraftservices.com), and **Wings of Alaska** (800/789-9464 or 907/766-3020, fjordflying.com).

Getting Around

Downtown Haines is easy to walk, but there are so many attractions a few miles out of town that it's good to have a car or a bike. **Sockeye Cycle Co.** (24 Portage St., 877/292-4154 or 907/766-2869, cyclealaska.com) offers bike rentals and guided day trips. You can also rent a bike from **Mike's Bikes and Boards** (Mile 0 Haines Hwy., 907/766-3232). If you want a little more power, **Tour de Scooter** (41 Haines Hwy., 832/264-6068, tourdescooter.com) rents 50cc engine scooters.

If you'd rather ride in a car, **Anytime Taxi and Tours** (907/303-9246 or 907/303-8984) meets every incoming ferry, or you can rent from three providers: **Avis** (13 Ft. Seward. Dr., 800/542-6363 or 907/766-2733) now operates year-round, as does **Captain's Choice Car Rentals** (2nd Ave. and Dalton, 800/478-2345 or 907/766-3111, capchoice.com). You can also rent vehicles from **Lynn View Lodge & Cabins** (1299 Lutak Rd., 907/766-3713 or 512/789-3198) at hourly, daily, weekly, and monthly rates.

Anchorage and Southcentral Alaska

Anchorage and the communities around it—collectively known as Southcentral Alaska—hold more than half of Alaska's entire population, with most of those people housed in Anchorage itself.

That relative density translates to more roads, more services, and a much wider variety of everything, from food to accommodations, shopping and tours.

Residents in and around Anchorage sometimes catch grief from other Alaskans for living in "the big city," but for many visitors and residents, that urban appeal in an Alaska setting is a big draw. You can go from black-tie dining (although Alaska's notoriously easy-going dress code means you'll probably see jeans there too) or a movie theater with fully reclining easy chairs to cycling or hiking in true wilderness conditions, all within about a half-hour drive of the city. As a bonus, the drives heading south of Anchorage to the Kenai Peninsula are some of the prettiest in the state.

Don't let the density and ease of transport in and around Anchorage fool you. This is still Alaska, so bears, moose and other spectacular wildlife can pop up at any time; and although Southcentral has many more roads than in most of the state, transport corridors are still very limited, with just one road leading south of Anchorage and one road leading northeast of town.

Because it's located on and near Alaska's southern coast, Southcentral enjoys a relatively mild climate, with summer temperatures peaking in the 60s, 70s, or, in the last few years, even reaching into the 80s. High temperatures during the winter typically average around 20 degrees. The farther south you go along the Kenai Peninsula or along the shores of Prince William Sound, the wetter the climate will be; in fact, Thompson Pass, located just outside of Valdez, is the snowiest place in Alaska.

PLANNING YOUR TIME

Southcentral is by far the easiest part of Alaska to get around in; everything is connected by the highway system and car rentals

Previous: sea otters near Valdez; sea kayaking in Prince William Sound. **Above:** jellyfish on the beach at Caines Head State Recreation Area.

Look for ★ to find recommended sights, activities, dining, and lodging.

Highlights

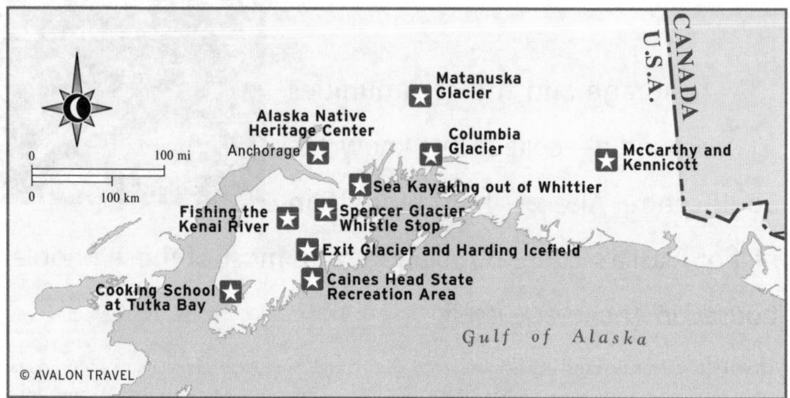

★ **Alaska Native Heritage Center:** This comprehensive visitor center showcases traditional Alaska Native culture, arts, and lifeways; don't miss the tour of traditional village buildings (page 133).

★ **Spencer Glacier Whistle Stop:** This one-of-a-kind backcountry destination is a lakeside glacier accessible only by train (page 136).

★ **Matanuska Glacier:** Take a guided trek or ice-climbing adventure on this convenient roadside glacier (page 163).

★ **Sea Kayaking out of Whittier:** These calm, protected waters are an easy proving ground for beginning kayakers, with scenery dramatic enough that even experienced paddlers will be rapt (page 176).

★ **Exit Glacier and Harding Icefield:** A relatively easy trail leads right up to the toe of Exit Glacier. The fit and adventurous can also hike five miles straight up a mountainside that overlooks the massive Harding Icefield (page 184).

★ **Caines Head State Recreation Area:** Near Seward, explore old World War II ruins or take a five-mile coastal hike to an accessible backcountry cove (page 187).

★ **Fishing the Kenai River:** Tackle shoulder-to-shoulder combat fishing on your own, or hire a guide to take you down the Russian and Kenai Rivers, Alaska's most famous freshwater salmon fisheries (page 203).

★ **Cooking School at Tutka Bay:** Just across the bay from Homer, world-famous Le Cordon Bleu-trained chefs teach their art in a repurposed crabbing boat, originally a World War II troop carrier (page 214).

★ **Columbia Glacier:** Take a boat tour to one of the world's largest tidewater glaciers. This massive wall of ice is so large, it blots out the sky (page 228).

★ **McCarthy and Kennicott:** This tiny, quirky, and stubbornly isolated town and the neighboring "ghost mine town" are the epitome of tranquil small-town Alaska life—if you can stomach the rough, unpaved drive in (page 240).

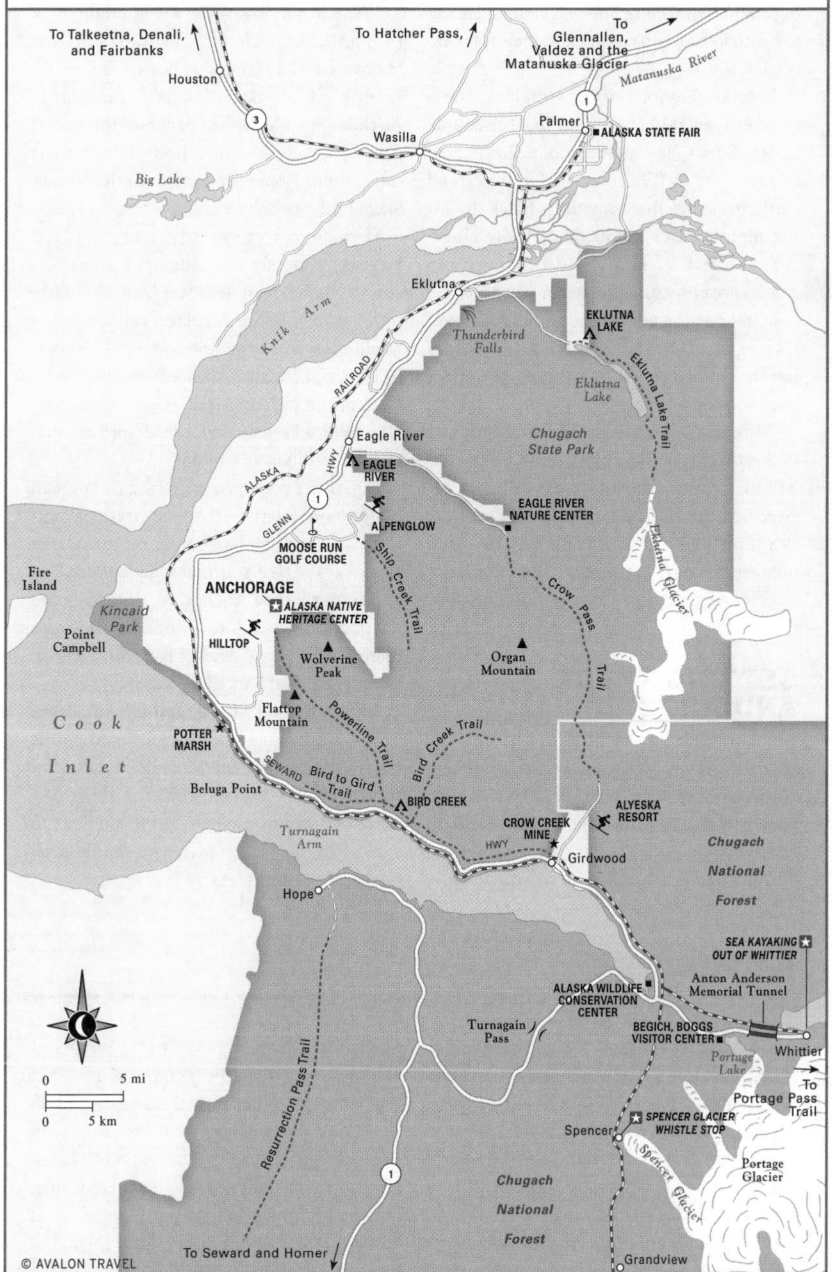
Anchorage and Vicinity
To Talkeetna, Denali, and Fairbanks
To Hatcher Pass,
To Glennallen, Valdez and the Matanuska Glacier
Matanuska River
Houston
Wasilla
Palmer
ALASKA STATE FAIR
Big Lake
Eklutna
Knik Arm
Thunderbird Falls
EKLUTNA LAKE
Eklutna Lake
Eklutna Lake Trail
ALASKA RAILROAD
Eagle River
EAGLE RIVER
GLENN HWY
Chugach State Park
ALPENGLOW
EAGLE RIVER NATURE CENTER
MOOSE RUN GOLF COURSE
Ship Creek Trail
Eklutna Glacier
Fire Island
ANCHORAGE
ALASKA NATIVE HERITAGE CENTER
Kincaid Park
Point Campbell
HILLTOP
Wolverine Peak
Organ Mountain
Crow Pass Trail
Flattop Mountain
Powerline Trail
Bird Creek Trail
Cook Inlet
POTTER MARSH
SEWARD HWY
Bird to Gird Trail
Beluga Point
BIRD CREEK
ALYESKA RESORT
CROW CREEK MINE
Turnagain Arm
Girdwood
Chugach National Forest
Hope
SEA KAYAKING OUT OF WHITTIER
ALASKA WILDLIFE CONSERVATION CENTER
Anton Anderson Memorial Tunnel
Turnagain Pass
BEGICH, BOGGS VISITOR CENTER
Whittier
Portage Lake
To Portage Pass Trail
0 5 mi
0 5 km
Resurrection Pass Trail
SPENCER GLACIER WHISTLE STOP
Spencer
Spencer Glacier
Portage Glacier
Chugach National Forest
To Seward and Homer
Grandview
© AVALON TRAVEL

are readily available, although expensive. (Even if you have elite status with one of the big chain rental companies, it's worth checking with locally run companies; their rates are often less pricey.)

However, any long-distance highway travel in Southcentral requires at least a couple hours of flex time to account for delays caused by slow-moving RVs, construction zones, and traffic accidents that sometimes block the entire highway. In extreme cases, those blockages can last for hours. Most highways in Alaska are only two lanes wide, except for occasional passing zones, and in most parts of this region there are no alternative routes—just the one highway connecting communities like beads on a string.

Also, any airborne or waterborne activities in Southcentral, like flightseeing or glacier/wildlife cruises, can still be cancelled or delayed because of the weather. Usually, a day of flex time is enough to account for this—and because this part of the state is so (relatively) interconnected, there's always something else to spend that time on at the end of your trip.

GETTING THERE AND AROUND

You can reach Southcentral Alaska by road, air, or sea. If you arrive on a cruise, ships usually dock in either Seward or Whittier, then transport you to other communities aboard luxury motorcoaches or by train car. If Seward or Whittier is the endpoint of your cruise, you can also rent a car and drive to any of the other communities in this region.

If you're coming by ferry, you might dock in Whittier or in Homer. The Alaska Marine Highway System ferries do not serve Seward. From Whittier, your best bet for transport to Anchorage—which then becomes the hub of your Southcentral exploration—is taking the train. From Homer, you can take the Homer Stage Line van service.

If you're coming by air, flying into Ted Stevens Anchorage International Airport puts you in the heart of Southcentral. This busy international hub is regularly ranked in the world's top five or six international airports in terms of freight. Alaska Airlines, Delta, United, and Iceland Air offer year-round service, with seasonal service from airlines that include JetBlue and Condor.

Finally, if you're coming by car, you can either hang a left at Tok (the first community past the Canadian border on the Alaska Highway), drive southwest to Glennallen and from there to Anchorage, or keep going northwest from Tok to Fairbanks and from there drive south to Anchorage, with a stop in Denali National Park along the way.

Even though it's the largest city in Alaska by far, Anchorage has a very limited public transportation system. Most day tours offer shuttle service or start within walking distance of downtown hotels, but if you want to explore off the beaten path, you should definitely rent a car.

Anchorage

Almost half of Alaska's 735,000 people live in one sprawling city: Anchorage. The only legitimately "big" city in the entire state, Anchorage is surrounded by Cook Inlet and Turnagain Arm to the west, Joint (Air Force and Army) Base Elmendorf-Richardson to the north, and the front range of the beautiful Chugach Mountains on the east and south.

Just two roads lead into and out of town—the Glenn Highway to the northeast and the Seward Highway to the south—but that's enough to make Anchorage the hub of the state's rudimentary road system, which stretches north to Fairbanks and south to the artsy town of Homer on the Kenai Peninsula. (Alaska highways do have numbers which is how your GPS will probably know them, but locals use the names instead.)

Anchorage's port receives more than 95 percent of the freight coming in to Alaska, and the downtown rail depot is the central hub for the Alaska Railroad's passenger trains. Although the Alaska Railroad doesn't connect to any Outside rail networks, it does offer delightful sightseeing, transport between some of the region's prettiest and most interesting communities (Seward, Anchorage, Talkeetna, and Fairbanks), and, in the case of the Hurricane Turn Train out of Talkeetna, great insight into some of Alaska's most charming quirks.

Add all those big-city perks up, and it's no surprise that Anchorage residents sometimes get grief from other Alaskans for living away from the rest of the state's relatively rustic, rural lifestyle. We may have more than our fair share of big-box stores, but this is still a beautiful and exciting place to live or visit, with lots of shopping, entertainment, and cultural opportunities you won't find elsewhere in the state. We even have urban bears, with an estimated 250 black bears and 60 or so grizzly bears living within the city limits, along with plenty of moose, especially in the winter.

One of Anchorage's biggest distinguishing features is its abundance of green space: There are more than 120 miles of tree-lined paved bike trails in town and another 87 miles or so of non-paved hiking trails, many of which become ski or skijoring trails in the winter (skijoring is like dog-sledding without a sled. The skier is pulled by one, or sometimes two, attached to a towline). It only takes about a 30-minute drive to mainline yourself into the wilderness of "true" Alaska, and Flattop Mountain—which sits just on the city limits—is both the most-climbed mountain in Southcentral and one of the hottest spots for wilderness rescues because people forget just how wild it can be. In short, don't underestimate this sprawling, tree-filled town: It's still Alaska!

SIGHTS

Natural Landmarks

If you're coming by plane from the Lower 48 or Southeast Alaska, most flight paths are over the beautiful **Chugach Mountains**—ripple upon ripple of snow-clad peaks or rolling green tundra topped with craggy gray rocks, depending on the season—and then give you an overview of the coastline along **Turnagain Arm,** which borders Anchorage to the south. The two-lane highway that hugs the coast of the arm is the **Seward Highway,**

the moon rising over the Chugach Mountains and the Anchorage skyline

Anchorage

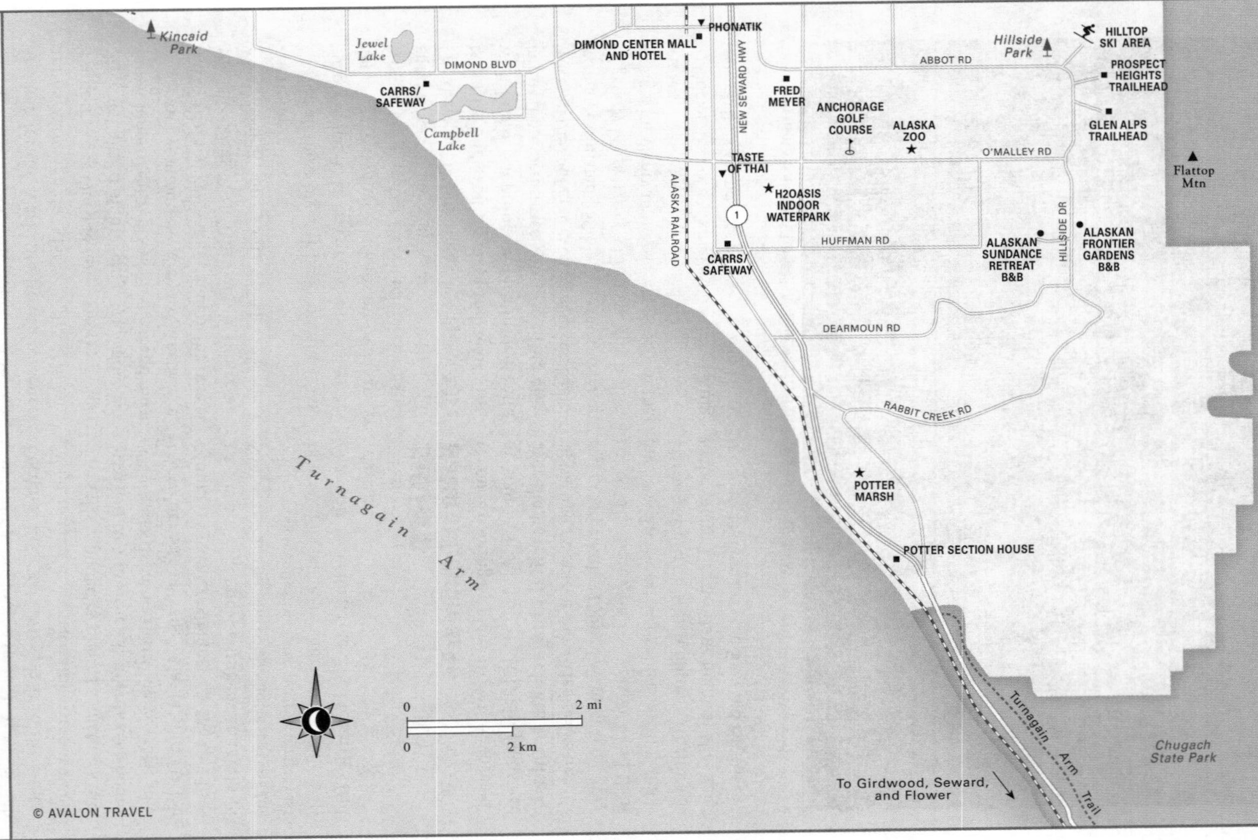

Kincaid Park
Jewel Lake
DIMOND BLVD
DIMOND CENTER MALL AND HOTEL
PHONATIK
CARRS/ SAFEWAY
Campbell Lake
NEW SEWARD HWY
ALASKA RAILROAD
FRED MEYER
ANCHORAGE GOLF COURSE
ALASKA ZOO
ABBOT RD
Hillside Park
HILLTOP SKI AREA
PROSPECT HEIGHTS TRAILHEAD
GLEN ALPS TRAILHEAD
O'MALLEY RD
Flattop Mtn
TASTE OF THAI
H2OASIS INDOOR WATERPARK
1
HUFFMAN RD
CARRS/ SAFEWAY
ALASKAN SUNDANCE RETREAT B&B
HILLSIDE DR
ALASKAN FRONTIER GARDENS B&B
DEARMOUN RD
RABBIT CREEK RD
Turnagain Arm
POTTER MARSH
POTTER SECTION HOUSE
0
2 mi
0
2 km
Turnagain Arm Trail
Chugach State Park
To Girdwood, Seward, and Flower
© AVALON TRAVEL

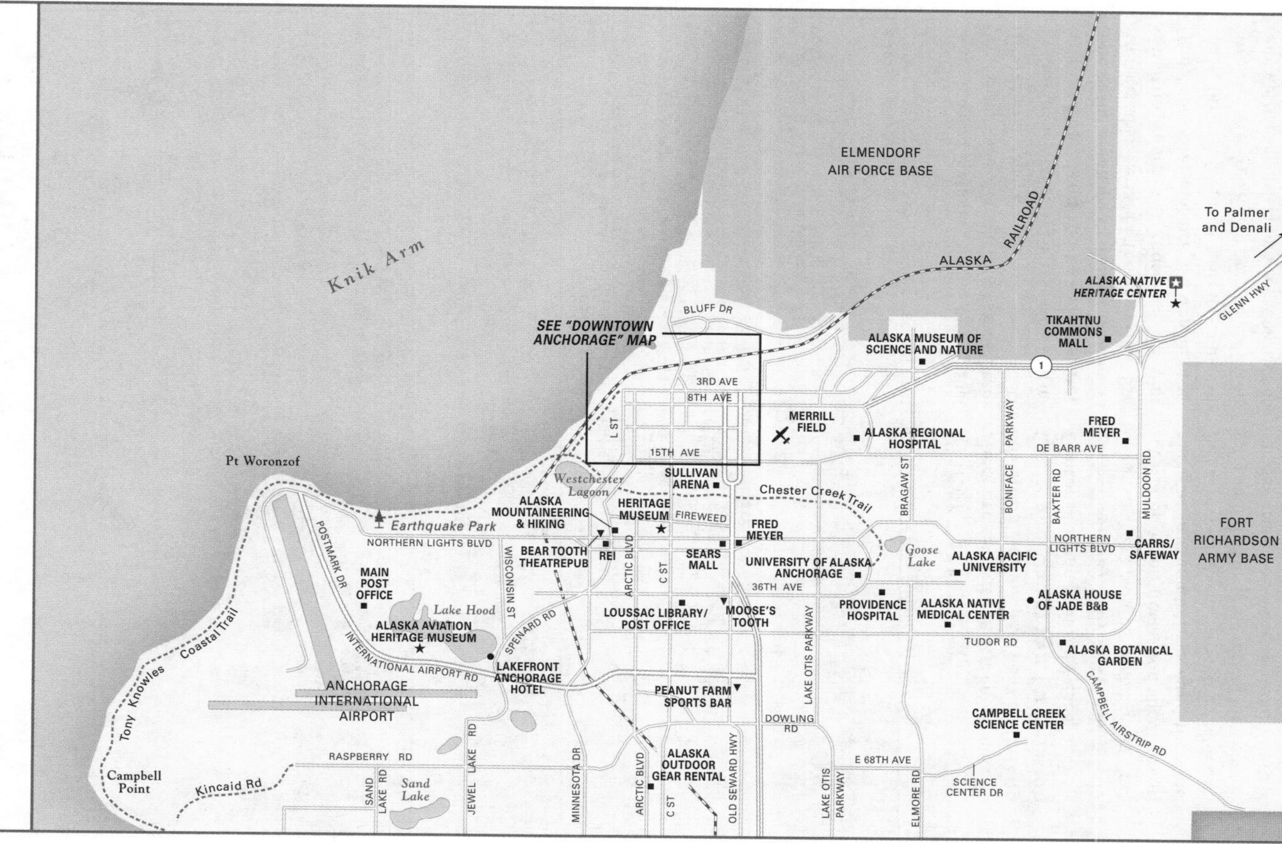
ELMENDORF AIR FORCE BASE
To Palmer and Denali
Knik Arm
ALASKA RAILROAD
ALASKA NATIVE HERITAGE CENTER
GLENN HWY
BLUFF DR
SEE "DOWNTOWN ANCHORAGE" MAP
TIKAHTNU COMMONS MALL
ALASKA MUSEUM OF SCIENCE AND NATURE
1
3RD AVE
8TH AVE
L ST
MERRILL FIELD
ALASKA REGIONAL HOSPITAL
PARKWAY
FRED MEYER
DE BARR AVE
15TH AVE
Pt Woronzof
SULLIVAN ARENA
Westchester Lagoon
Chester Creek Trail
BRAGAW ST
BONIFACE
BAXTER RD
MULDOON RD
FORT RICHARDSON ARMY BASE
ALASKA MOUNTAINEERING & HIKING
HERITAGE MUSEUM
FIREWEED
Earthquake Park
FRED MEYER
NORTHERN LIGHTS BLVD
POSTMARK DR
NORTHERN LIGHTS BLVD
BEAR TOOTH THEATREPUB
REI
ARCTIC BLVD
C ST
SEARS MALL
UNIVERSITY OF ALASKA ANCHORAGE
Goose Lake
ALASKA PACIFIC UNIVERSITY
CARRS/ SAFEWAY
MAIN POST OFFICE
WISCONSIN ST
36TH AVE
Lake Hood
LOUSSAC LIBRARY/ POST OFFICE
MOOSE'S TOOTH
PROVIDENCE HOSPITAL
ALASKA NATIVE MEDICAL CENTER
ALASKA HOUSE OF JADE B&B
ALASKA AVIATION HERITAGE MUSEUM
SPENARD RD
LAKE OTIS PARKWAY
TUDOR RD
ALASKA BOTANICAL GARDEN
Coastal Trail
INTERNATIONAL AIRPORT RD
LAKEFRONT ANCHORAGE HOTEL
Tony Knowles
ANCHORAGE INTERNATIONAL AIRPORT
PEANUT FARM SPORTS BAR
CAMPBELL AIRSTRIP RD
CAMPBELL CREEK SCIENCE CENTER
DOWLING RD
RASPBERRY RD
ALASKA OUTDOOR GEAR RENTAL
E 68TH AVE
Campbell Point
Kincaid Rd
SAND LAKE RD
Sand Lake
JEWEL LAKE RD
MINNESOTA DR
ARCTIC BLVD
C ST
OLD SEWARD HWY
LAKE OTIS PARKWAY
ELMORE RD
SCIENCE CENTER DR

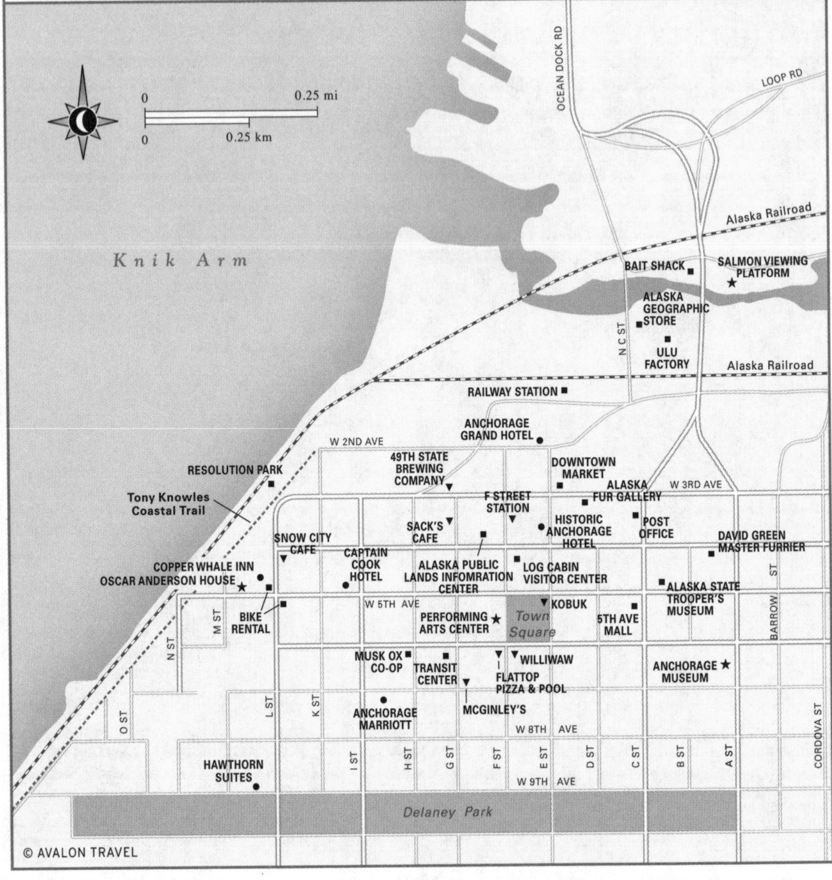

a designated National Scenic Byway that showcases some of Southcentral's most beautiful coastal scenery.

Just to the west of Anchorage you can usually see **Fire Island** and its wind turbines, one of the municipality's first experiments in renewable energy. Farther west is **Mount Susitna,** sometimes known as "Sleeping Lady" for its resemblance to a woman in repose, although it's much easier to distinguish from sea level. You'll get a clear view of it from any west-facing hotel room downtown, or on the **Tony Knowles Coastal Trail.**

Visitor Centers

There are two visitor centers of note in downtown Anchorage. The first, the **Log Cabin and Downtown Information Center** (4th and F, 907/257-2363, anchorage.net, summer daily except major holidays 8am-7pm, reduced winter hours), can set you up with information about almost any tour or community around the state. Just across 4th Avenue from the visitor center, you'll find booking offices for sightseeing day cruises out of Seward and Whittier, plus the very excellent **Salmon Berry Tours**

(514 W. 4th Ave., 907/278-3572, salmonberrytours.com).

The second, the **Alaska Public Lands Information Center** (605 W. 4th Ave., 907/644-3661, alaskacenters.gov, mid-May-mid-Sept., daily 9am-5pm, winter Tues.-Fri. 10am-5pm), has a wealth of information about all things outdoors that take place in Alaska's state and national parks. It also hosts videos in its theater 10am-4:30pm; whoever shows up first gets to choose which film plays.

The Public Lands Information Center used to be the starting point for the free, ranger-led Captain Cook Walking Tour, but that has now been replaced by a walking tour about connecting to Alaska's public lands. The free tours depart at 11am and 3:15pm daily during the summer.

Flightseeing

Flightseeing—that is, sightseeing from the air in a small plane or helicopter—is one of the most glorious adventures you can take out of Anchorage. The two most popular destinations are from Anchorage all the way to **Denali** with **Rust's Flying Service** (800/544-2299, flyrusts.com, from $425 pp) and a trip over the **Knik and Colony Glaciers,** which can be paired with a dog-sledding or kayaking adventure, through **Regal Air** (907/243-8535, regal-air.com, from $265 pp; also available from Rust's starting at $305 pp). Also very popular is flightseeing from the **Knik River Lodge** (29979 E. Knik River Rd., 877/745-4575, knikriverlodge.com) in nearby **Palmer.**

TOP EXPERIENCE

★ Alaska Native Heritage Center

Almost every community in Alaska has some sort of cultural center dedicated to showcasing—and nurturing—the unique Alaska Native culture in that region of the state. But if you can only visit one such center, make it the **Alaska Native Heritage Center** (8800 Heritage Center Dr., 800/315-6608 or 907/330-8000, alaskanative.net, mid-May-mid-Sept., daily 9am-5pm, $24.95 adults, discounts for seniors, veterans, and families, free children under 6) in northeast Anchorage.

This enormous center pools information on each of the five distinct cultural regions throughout the state, with performances of traditional dancing, videos on various aspects of Native culture, and guided tours through life-size recreations of Alaska Native village

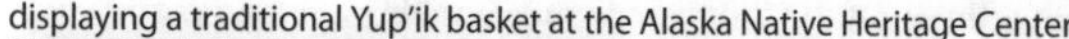

displaying a traditional Yup'ik basket at the Alaska Native Heritage Center

sites (you can also walk through the sites on your own).

The excellent gift shop includes quite a bit of traditional Alaska Native art, and you can sometimes see artisans demonstrating their crafts or teaching them to the next generation. Every so often there are open-enrollment classes where the public can learn traditional arts, too. The heritage center is open daily during the summer season but open only for special community events during the winter.

Anchorage Museum at Rasmuson Center

The **Anchorage Museum at Rasmuson Center** (625 C St., 907/929-9200, anchoragemuseum.org, May-Sept. daily 9am-6pm, reduced winter hours, $15) has always been excellent, but in recent years, under the guidance of CEO Julie Decker, it's really flourished into a cultural and community institution. You'll find ancient Alaska Native artifacts and contemporary master artisans demonstrating their crafts in the Smithsonian Arctic Studies Center; boisterous community events, lectures, and panel discussions; reflections on the state's deep well of history; and an exploration of what it means to be a community of great importance in the Arctic region today.

For the best deal in town, buy the **Culture Pass,** which offers discounted admission to both the Anchorage Museum and the Alaska Native Heritage Center; it includes free shuttle service between them (the pass costs $30 at either facility).

Alaska Aviation Museum

Bush pilots were the lifeblood of transport in the early days of Alaska's statehood, and they're still critically important to rural communities today. The underappreciated **Alaska Aviation Heritage Museum** (4721 Aircraft Dr., 907/248-5325, alaskaairmuseum.org, daily 9am-5pm, $15 adults, discounts for seniors, veterans, and families) explores that history with vintage aircraft, a flight simulator, and historical films.

While at the museum, you can also climb into a restored vintage control tower and watch floatplanes taking off and landing from Lake Hood, the largest and busiest seaplane base in the world; more than 800 planes, a mix of commercial operations and private aircraft, take off and land during a typical day in the summer.

Oscar Anderson House

For a glimpse into everyday life during Anchorage's early "Wild West" days, the Alaska Association for Historic Preservation has lovingly restored and maintained the 1915-era **Oscar Anderson House** (420 M St., 907/274-2336, aahp-online.net), one of the earliest homes built in Anchorage. They offer 45-minute guided tours (Tues.-Sun. noon-4pm, $10 adults, $5 for 12 and under or Alaska residents). Access is currently by tour only. This is a great family experience; the best thing about it is using your surroundings to imagine what life was like, back when Anchorage was little more than a railroad tent camp on the shores of Ship Creek, which still runs through downtown Anchorage. If you'd like to learn more about the city's history, starting with the original Dena'ina inhabitants and progressing all the way through the modern day, pick up a copy of *From the Shores of Ship Creek* by Charles Wohlforth; it's available from most Anchorage bookstores and also on Amazon.com.

Alaska Wildlife Conservation Center

If you want guaranteed wildlife sightings in a natural habitat, head for the 200-acre **Alaska Wildlife Conservation Center** (Mile 79 Seward Hwy., 907/783-2025, alaskawildlife.org, $12.50 adults or 1.5-hour behind-the-scenes tour for $100), a year-round facility that takes in orphaned animals and also works with state and federal agencies to breed animals for reintroduction into their natural habitat. A recent and notable project was the reintroduction of a herd of wood bison, once thought entirely extinct, into the arctic tundra.

along the Albert Loop Trail

There's a nice gift shop too, but the main attraction is the short loop you can walk or drive to see animals including moose, elk, lynx, wolverines, wolves, foxes, and of course bears and eagles in spacious outdoor pens. A schedule of feeding times for each type of animal—always the best time to see them—is listed on the website.

The center is open year-round except for major holidays. Hours vary by the season, but correspond roughly to daylight hours; call or visit the website for season-appropriate schedules.

Eagle River Nature Center

Nature buffs seeking a low-key introduction to Alaska's wilderness should visit the **Eagle River Nature Center** (32750 Eagle River Rd., 907/694-2108, ernc.org); parking costs $5, but admission and most programs are free. Located in Eagle River, a quiet suburb of Anchorage that's surrounded by mountains, this education center is the hub of a system of scenic, mostly flat trails that almost anyone of any age can manage. Docents lead low-key nature walks (June-Aug., Wed.-Sun. 1:30pm).

Other features include a self-guided geology walk on the 3.1-mile **Albert Loop Trail** (the pamphlet costs $1 inside the visitor center), viewing decks where you'll sometimes see moose wading in a beaver pond (or the beavers themselves at work), yurts that can be rented for an overnight stay, and touch exhibits where kids and adults alike can feel furs, bones, and other remnants of animals native to the area.

The center offers educational lectures and hands-on sessions for all ages, on everything from mushroom hunting to medicinal plants. Even the drive out is beautiful, and the trails are always open, even when the center is closed. However, be warned that significant portions of the Albert Loop Trail are closed in the fall to minimize encounters with bears fishing for salmon in the river that gives this area its name.

Alaska Zoo

Perhaps some of you, like me, have mixed feelings about seeing animals behind bars in a zoos. But the **Alaska Zoo** (4731 O'Malley Rd., 907/346-2133, June-Aug. daily 9am-9pm, reduced off-season hours, $15 adult, $7 youth 3-17, discounts for seniors and military) houses only orphaned, injured, and occasionally captive-born animals and works hard to participate in education and conservation efforts, so it's a good way to spend an afternoon. It's also small enough that you can get pretty close to the animals. You'll see many animals that are indigenous to Alaska, including polar, grizzly, and black bears, wolves, coyotes, and foxes, plus a few that don't live here, like beautiful snow leopards.

During the summer, the zoo offers free shuttle service from downtown Anchorage; call or email admissions@alaskazoo.org for a schedule. They also offer daily behind-the-scenes Discovery Tours from mid-May to mid-September ($28 adult, $20 child, including zoo admission).

Alaska Botanical Garden

The **Alaska Botanical Garden** (4601 Campbell Airstrip Rd., daily dawn-dusk, summer $12 adult, winter, $7 adult, discounts for seniors, military, students, and youth) is a nonprofit organization that showcases more than 1,100 species of perennials that are hardy to Southcentral conditions as well as about 150 native plant species. The garden is open year-round daily from dawn to dusk, but if you want to pay admission by credit card you'll have to come during gift shop hours (late May-mid-Sept. daily 10am-4pm, reduced winter hours). The gardens include a plot of herbs and medicinal plants, re-creations of homestead gardens (you might be amazed by what people can grow up here), wildflower gardens, and some short, easy walking trails that might offer chances to see wildlife. There's a king salmon run in a nearby creek, so believe it or not you should be on your best "Bear Aware" behavior, even here—in the heart of the city!

Aurora Borealis

Visitors are sometimes disappointed to find that summer—Alaska's most hospitable season by far—is the worst possible time for seeing the aurora borealis or northern lights. The sky just isn't dark enough. If the aurora is your thing, plan a trip to Fairbanks, Nome, or any community at similar latitude September-April, when skies are dark and the northern lights are more active.

But in the meantime, you can get the next best thing with ***Aurora: Alaska's Great Northern Lights,*** in the Alaska Center for the Performing Arts (621 W. 6th Ave., 907/263-2787, mid-May-Sept., from $15), a 40-minute show that spends about 10 minutes discussing the science behind this amazing phenomenon, then plunges you into a visual riot of dancing northern lights set to music. Some are enthralled by this, others less so, but it's your only chance to see the northern lights during the summer.

Ghost Tours of Anchorage

Both history buffs and supernatural lovers will enjoy the **Ghost Tours of Anchorage** (907/274-4678, ghosttoursofanchorage.com, May-Sept. Tues.-Sun. 7:30pm, $15), an easy, two-hour walking tour through downtown Anchorage. The tour is advertised as not being for young children or those who are highly prone to suggestion, but it's certainly appropriate for older teens. It's a recounting of equal parts of Anchorage's fascinating early history and some of the town's most famous hauntings, including the delightful (and notoriously haunted) Historic Anchorage Hotel. (Don't worry—there are never any intentional scares or "gotcha" moments.) The tour meets at 4th and L outside the Snow City Cafe, proceeds rain or shine, and spends almost the entire time outside, so dress for the weather and light exertion.

Resolution Park

If you're staying downtown, the enormous, multi-tiered deck at **Resolution Park** (3rd and L) is a beautiful place to catch the sunset, and it has a monument to Captain James Cook, the first European to discover this part of the state. However, be aware that when there's not much tourist traffic, this is sometimes a favorite hangout for homeless people.

As long as we're on the subject, please be aware that Anchorage's Downtown Transit Center, located on 6th Avenue between G and H streets, also tends to be a magnet for homeless people and sometimes sketchy behavior. The city is working hard to improve outreach to the homeless and make this area safer, and it's starting to make progress. But for the near future, this will probably continue to be a somewhat rough place.

★ Spencer Glacier Whistle Stop

Every **Alaska Railroad** (800/544-0552, alaskarailroad.com) passenger train travels through some spectacular scenery; but I would argue that the rail system's crowning glory is the **Spencer Glacier Whistle Stop,** a backcountry destination that can only be reached by train. If guests only have time for one adventure before they leave Anchorage, this is where I send them. When you disembark from the train, you're just a short walk from the shore of a lake with Spencer Glacier on the far side, occasionally calving blue ice into the water.

You can walk the trails on your own or with a naturalist guide before you get back on the train. Visitors can also camp overnight if prepared; group campsites must be reserved in advance, or if you're very lucky and adventurous you might be able to reserve the coveted **Spencer Bench public-use cabin,** on a ridge overlooking the glacier—it's about a six-mile round-trip to get there. Make reservations through the railroad (800/544-0552) for summer use. Or you can book a combination tour to paddle among the icebergs and float back toward the road system on the splashy Placer River.

Salmon Berry Tours

A few day tour companies operate out of Anchorage, offering you easy transport and guided accompaniment to some of the area's biggest attractions. That said, locally owned and operated **Salmon Berry Tours** (515 W. 4th Ave., 907/278-3572, salmonberrytours.com) has distinguished itself as one of the very best for its stellar service, excellent trip planning, and superior local knowledge. For almost any adventure you want to have in Southcentral, from dog sledding to wildlife watching, ice fishing, watching the northern lights, or simply being transported from Whittier or Seward to Anchorage with a guided tour thrown in, Salmon Berry can make it happen. They've even developed winter into one of their busiest seasons—a few years ago, that would have been unheard of in Alaska. Be sure to ask about their amazing (and exclusive) Iditarod start parties.

RECREATION

Tony Knowles Coastal Trail

Anchorage has about 120 miles of paved multiuse **bike trails** winding through town. The crowning gem of that network is the 11-mile **Tony Knowles Coastal Trail,** which hugs the coastline of Knik Arm from downtown Anchorage to heavily wooded Kincaid Park, which is also a great place to look for moose. The easiest downtown access points are from

a monument to Captain Cook looks out over the water from Resolution Park

looking down at Spencer Glacier from the Spencer Bench public use cabin

the northeast end of West 2nd Avenue near the railroad depot or from Elderberry Park, just downhill from 5th and L. Even though the trail is paved and sometimes crowded with both locals and visitors out to enjoy the beautiful scenery, the animals are wild, so remember your wildlife etiquette (see *Essentials*).

You can walk the trail, run it, or rent a bike from three downtown businesses (page 155) and pedal the whole length. One important safety warning: Don't venture out onto the mudflats that sit to the coastal side of the trail; you could die. That mud looks and feels solid when the tide is out, but it's made of fine, silty particles that turn to quicksand as the water table rises; it's all too easy to get stuck before you realize what's going on.

If you head east into the trails that run through Anchorage, be aware that there are homeless camps in some of those heavily wooded greenbelts, and the secluded locations sometimes attract people bent on crime. Although this usually isn't an issue during the day when the trail is full of people, it's not the type of place anyone—man or woman—should go alone at night. Happily, the current city administration is taking big steps to address homelessness and a lack of treatment options in Anchorage.

Hiking

Any time you're in Anchorage, look up. Those mountains you see are the front range of the mighty **Chugach Mountains,** and there's at least one established trail to almost every peak you see in the southeast part of town. For directions, trail lists, and maps check dnr.alaska.gov/parks/units/chugach or visit the excellent **Alaska Geographic** store downtown (241 N. C St., 907/274-8440). One of the most popular trailheads is **Glen Alps** ($5 parking fee). Glen Alps has a short, 0.25-mile paved loop that offers great overlooks of Anchorage. This trailhead is also the starting point for the iconic **Flattop Mountain Trail,** a two- to three-hour hike for most people. If you don't have a car to get to the trailhead, you can catch the **Flattop Shuttle** from downtown (334 W. 4th Ave., 907/279-3334, hike-anchorage-alaska.com). Be warned—the trail is often crowded and requires some rock scrambling at the end.

The next most popular trailhead is **Prospect Heights.** There are gentler walks here on a relatively level trail, but it's more wooded, so you don't get as many mountain views. One of my favorite trails from here is the **South Fork Rim Trail,** a gentle two-mile loop that gives you pretty views into a steep little valley carved by South Fork Campbell Creek.

Because these mountains are so close to town, it's easy for people to forget that they're in wild country, but this is still an uncontrolled environment, so always brush up on outdoor safety before you go, including basic etiquette for dealing with wildlife, which is quite common in this valley. In point of fact, if you want to see a moose in Anchorage during the fall, all you have to do is take a pair of binoculars up to the junction where the Powerline Pass Trail meets the Glen Alps access trail and spend a while scanning the valley floor.

If you have children, check out the **Campbell Creek Science Center** (5600 Science Center Dr., 907/267-1247) in southeast Anchorage. There are some lovely, easy hiking trails (get a free trail map inside the center) and a wealth of educational programming, some of it open to the public. Of particular interest, some of the trails pass by old WWII foxholes and fortifications built to protect airplanes. They're not marked, though, so it's best to ask staff to point them out on the map.

Mountain Biking

Kincaid Park—at the far end of the Tony Knowles Coastal Trail—has some excellent single-track biking trails, mostly built and maintained by **Single Track Advocates of Alaska** (singletrackadvocates.org); visit the website for downloadable trail maps. You can rent a full-suspension mountain bike from the rental shops downtown (see *Transportation*) or get a higher-end bike from one of Anchorage's full-service bike shops. Kincaid is also one of the best places in town for guaranteed moose sightings, so ride carefully, especially during calving season in May and June; cow moose are notoriously aggressive and protective of their babies.

The Bicycle Shop (1035 W Northern Lts, 907/272-5219, Midtown location or 1801 West Dimond Blvd, 907/222-9953, Dimond Location; bikeshopak.com) has consistently been voted one of Anchorage's best bike shops in local polls. Both locations are typically open Mon.-Fri. 10am-7pm, Sat. 10am-6pm and Sun. 11am-5pm.

During the summer, **Alyeska Resort** (1000 Arlberg Ave., 907/754-2111, alyeskaresort.com) in nearby **Girdwood** transforms some of its ski slopes into lift-assisted mountain biking trails best suited to intermediate and advanced riders, although some sections are perfectly hospitable to beginners as well. You can rent bikes and body armor at the resort and take lessons to suit almost any skill level.

Birding

You'll see birders doing their thing at **Potter Marsh**—just south of Anchorage on the New Seward Highway—year-round. May and August-September are the best times to catch species migrating through; you might see hovering arctic terns, shorebirds like yellowlegs, and even trumpeter swans staging here for their long southbound trips in the fall. Other species that stay all summer long include canvasback ducks, horned and red-necked grebes, northern pintails, and northern harriers. A couple of eagle families routinely nest nearby, too; listen for their high-pitched chittering sounds. (If you hear something that sounds like a loud, squeaky wheel moving quickly back and forth, that's an eagle. The majestic *scree* usually dubbed over a soaring eagle on movie soundtracks is actually the cry of a hawk.)

Unfortunately I don't know of anywhere in town that rents spotting scopes, but if you're a hardcore birder you might have some luck connecting with your fellows at the **Anchorage Audubon Society** (anchorageaudubon.org). They're also a great resource for birding tours, including a series of early-morning walks looking for migratory songbirds in May. The walks start from the **Campbell Creek Science Center** (5600 Science Center Dr., 907/267-1247); watch the Anchorage Audubon Society website for information. Anchorage Audubon also participates in the fabled **Gunsight Mountain**

a fall day on the boardwalk overlooking Potter Marsh

Hawkwatch (hawkwatch.org; search for "gunsight mountain"), where birders gather to establish a count of migrating raptors—including golden eagles and several varieties of hawks—flying through a mountain pass 120 miles northeast of Anchorage.

Another popular spot for a low-key birding adventure, especially if you have the family along, is **Reflections Lake**, a modest but lovely recreation area that's sprung up around a gravel pit that nature naturally filled in. It's now a refuge for migrating and resident waterfowl and shorebirds. There's a pretty, easy loop trail around the lake and slough (a little more than a mile) and an observation tower for spotting wildlife on the neighboring river flats. Bring your binoculars! To get to the lake, drive about 30 miles northeast of Anchorage and watch for signs directing you to Reflections Lake from the Knik River exit.

Fishing

There's great fishing in all of Southcentral, but nothing beats the convenience of being able to fish salmon (including king and silver salmon) out of **Ship Creek**, which runs straight through downtown Anchorage. Just head for the north edge of downtown (follow the decreasing street numbers) and look down the hill; the best fishing is in July and August and you do need a fishing license, which can be purchased in any supermarket or sporting goods store, or online at adfg.alaska.gov. You can also buy your fishing license and rent any fishing gear you need from **The Bait Shack** (212 W. Whitney Rd., 907/522-3474, thebaitshackak.com, call for hours).

A couple of interesting notes: First, that hill didn't exist before the massive magnitude 9.2 earthquake that rocked Southcentral Alaska in 1964; it was created by a ground collapse during North America's largest earthquake ever recorded. Second, the shores of the creek are made up of the same dangerous mud you'll find in the mudflats up and down Cook Inlet; when the tide comes in, the fine, silty particles essentially turn to quicksand. Fishers often end up wallowing in the mud as they try to climb the slippery banks, and sometimes they have to be extricated by the Anchorage Fire Department as the fast-moving tide rushes in toward them. Be very careful.

If you don't want to get stuck in the mud yourself, it's still fun to watch people fishing, or to stroll up a paved multiuse trail and watch fish working their way up the fish ladder to the **William Jack Hernandez Sport Fish Hatchery** (941 N. Reeve Blvd.). During the summer, you can use an observation corridor to take a self-guided tour through the hatchery (daily 8am-4pm).

Your next best salmon-fishing opportunity near Anchorage is **Bird Creek,** at mile 101.6 of the Seward Highway. Watch out for bears; they like to fish here, too, and it's up to you to make sure they don't start associating people with an easy source of fish. See adfg.alaska.gov for more information about dealing with bears while fishing.

The Bait Shack is the most convenient outfitter for fishing Ship Creek, but if you're fishing the other places, try these: **Alaska Outdoor Gear Rental** (7133 Arctic Blvd. #1, 907/830-0232) rents fishing gear along with kayaks, canoes, and camping gear, while **Alaska Tackle Rental** (907/360-6252 or contct@alaskatacklerental.com) will deliver rented fishing gear right to your hotel or RV.

Golf

Even in the heart of Anchorage, golfing in Alaska is an unusual experience that always runs the risk of being interrupted by wildlife ambling across the course. The 18-hole **Anchorage Golf Course** (3651 O'Malley Rd., 907/522-3363, anchoragegolfcourse.com, nonresidents $67.50 for 18 holes) offers lovely views over Anchorage, and on clear days you can see all the way across Cook Inlet to the Alaska Range, including Denali, looming on the far horizon.

A few miles northeast of town, the **Moose Run Golf Course** (27000 Arctic Valley Rd., 907/428-0056, mooserungolfcourse.com, greens fees $39-49) is on military land, although civilians are welcome to play and you don't have to go on base or drive through a gate to get there. This is the world's northernmost 36-hole golf course, with two 18-hole runs: the aptly named Hill Course and Creek Course.

Off-Road Adventures

There's no off-roading in Anchorage proper, but you can drive your own ATV on an **Alaska ATV Adventures** (907/694-4294, alaskaatvadventures.com) sightseeing tour of **Girdwood** and **Bird Creek,** about 45 minutes north of Anchorage, or take an off-roading tour along the shore of beautiful **Eklutna Lake,** north of Anchorage.

Kayaking

Similarly, there is no kayaking in the heart of Anchorage—just a few small lakes that the locals like to paddle around in. But you can book a single or multiday sea kayaking trip with **Alaska Kayak Academy** (2201 E. Palmer-Wasilla Hwy., 877/215-6600 or 907/746-6600, kayakcenterak.com) out of nearby Wasilla; I know firsthand just how competent and patient their instructors are. They also teach classes on the very Alaskan pursuits of packrafting and white-water kayaking, and offer guided packrafting trips.

Skiing, Snowshoeing, and Skating

Anchorage does have a modest ski/snowboard resort in the community-minded, youth-friendly nonprofit **Hilltop Ski Area** (7015 Abbott Rd., 907/346-1446, ski hotline 907/346-2167, hilltopskiarea.org, typically Mon.-Thurs. 3pm-8pm, Fri. 3pm-9pm, Sat. and holidays 9am-9pm, Sun. 9am-5pm); the ski slope is just over 2,000 feet long, with a vertical drop of almost 300 feet. But most serious skiiers and snowboarders head for **Alyeska Resort** in nearby **Girdwood**, where you have much more varied terrain to choose from.

If you're cross-country skiing in Anchorage, however, you have lots of great options, including all the paved multiuse trails in town (which are also used by skijorers, runners, walkers, and winter bikers) and loops of groomed ski trails at **Kincaid Park** (9401 Raspberry Rd.) and **Service High School** (5577 Abbitt Rd.), and even ungroomed trails in parts of **Chugach State Park,** which covers 495,000 acres and numerous trailheads. You can rent skate or classic cross-country ski gear from **REI** (1200 W. Northern Lights Blvd., 907/272-4565), then download a map of local ski trails from the **Nordic Skiing Association of Anchorage** (anchoragenordicski.com/trail-maps). REI sometimes has paper versions of the maps in stock.

If you're not into skiing, **snowshoeing** is another fun way to enjoy Anchorage's expansive green space (or in this case, white space) during the winter, and it's easy to explore among the trees at the same areas people go cross-country skiing in. Just make sure you stay out of groomed ski tracks and trails, which take a lot of effort to create but can be destroyed in minutes by a thoughtless snowshoer. You can rent snowshoes from REI or **Alaska Mountaineering and Hiking** (2633 Spenard Rd., 907/272-1811, alaskaountaineering.com).

Finally, during winters when the Anchorage area doesn't get much snow, locals have started turning to **Nordic ice-skating** as a way to enjoy the outdoors. Nordic ice skates are longer than hockey or figure skates and clip right into your ski boots, so they're warm, comfortable, and efficient for use over long distances. You can rent Nordic skates at Alaska Mountaineering and Hiking. Heads up: There aren't yet any formal resources for determining when it's safe to go skating, except for a skating loop at **Westchester Lagoon** (15th and T), which is hot-mopped and maintained by the city once ice thickness allows.

ENTERTAINMENT AND EVENTS

Because this is Alaska's biggest city, you can select from a full range of entertainment opportunities, from late-night neon bowling to several types of dancing, live music venues, and of course movie theaters. Two of the most notable theaters are the state's first (and so far only) IMAX movie theater, **Regal Tikahtnu Stadium 16** (1102 N. Muldoon Rd., 844/462-7342), and the remodeled **Regal Dimond Center 9 Cinemas** (Dimond Center, 800 E. Dimond Blvd., 844/462-7342), where you can purchase reserved seating in spacious leather recliners.

That said, the very best movie experience in town is at the **Bear Tooth Theatrepub** (1230 W. 27th Ave., 907/276-4200, beartooththeatre.net, $4), where you can watch second-run movies while dining on first-rate pizza, Tex-Mex, and grill food from one of the best restaurants in town. The monthly "First Tap" music events are some of the best parties in town, and they sometimes show sporting events or throwback movies from the 1980s and '90s on the big screen.

Most bars in Anchorage have at least one pool table, but serious players should head straight for **Flattop Pool and Pizza** (600 W. 6th Ave., 907/677-7665, flattopbar.com), which has been voted the city's best place to shoot pool for several years running. The New York-style pizza is pretty good, too.

Breweries are popular all over the state, but it's no surprise that the state's biggest city also draws an extra-large concentration of brewpubs and breweries. Because many (although not all) of these establishments serve food, you'll find them in the *Food* section.

Bars

Downtown's 4th Avenue is lined with small bars, ranging from quaint, *Cheers*-worthy neighborhood hangouts to "Watch out, this is about to get rough." Some travelers love exploring the "strip," but if you're more interested in nailing down a chance for conversation over good beer, much of it locally brewed, check out the brewpubs and breweries listed in the *Food* section.

For a chill hangout, locals head to either **Humpy's Great Alaskan Alehouse** (610 W. 6th Ave., 907/276-2337, humpysalaska.com, Mon.-Thurs. 11am-2am, Fri. 11am-2:30am, Sat. 10am-2:30am, Sun. 10am-2am, kitchen closes at midnight or 1am) or **Bernie's Bungalow Lounge** (626 D St., 907/276-8808, call to verify hours, usually Sun.-Thurs. 2pm-2am, Fri.-Sat. 2pm-3am), which has an undeniable hipster vibe to go with its martini bar, back garden, and frequent live music acts.

If you like your entertainment with a big slice of risque on the side, one of the most popular bars in town hands down is **Mad Myrna's** (530 E. 5th Ave., 907/276-9762, opens at 4pm), a legendary gay bar that offers wonderfully entertaining late-night variety shows. Also of note for LGBTQ travelers is **The Raven** (708 E. 4th Ave., 907/276-9672), the longest-running gay bar on the West Coast.

Although it's not downtown, the "world-famous" **Chilkoot Charlie's** (2435 Spenard Rd., 907/272-1010, koots.com, opens at 10:30am) absolutely must be mentioned because it really has received a lot of well-earned national attention for its eclectic collection of 10 themed bars all under one roof, from the old-school Birdhouse, which is practically wallpapered with lingerie, to the Russian bar (which has some world-class Russian memorabilia) and the cool-cat swing bar. The crowd can be a little questionable sometimes, but the bar itself is a real Alaska gem.

Finally, if you're looking for a sports bar, the clear favorite in town is the **Peanut Farm** (5227 Old Seward Hwy., wemustbenuts.com, Sun.-Mon. 6am-2:30am, Fri.-Sat. 6am-3am, lunch $14, pizza $26). With more than 70 big-screen TVs, they open early during football season and serve breakfast so you'll never go hungry or miss a game. If you ask nicely and bring a few people to buy food and drink, they're very accommodating about putting special events up on their screens as well.

For the more genteel set, **Kinley's Restaurant and Bar** (3230 Seward Hwy., 907/644-8953, kinleysrestaurant.com, lunch Tues.-Fri. 11:30am-4pm, dinner ($28) Mon. and Sat. 5pm-9pm, Tues.-Fri. 4pm-9pm, $15-28) offers a great selection of wine and beer in a classy but relaxed setting, accompanied by very friendly service of excellent seafood and New American cuisine, ranging all the way from lobster ravioli to a chicken-and-waffle dinner.

Finally, the chic, slightly industrial **Tequila 61 Gastropub** (445 W. 4th Ave., 907/274-7678, tequila61.com) offers traditional Mexican flavors with a high-end foodie twist, accompanied by some of the best margaritas in town.

Live Music Venues

Live music can (and does) pop up anywhere in Anchorage, including its two downtown convention centers, but two venues stand out as the liveliest: **Williwaw** (609 F St., 907/868-2000, williwawsocial.com), the newest and largest concert venue in town, regularly brings in national acts and puts on decade-themed dance parties. **The Taproot** (3300 Spenard Rd., 907/345-0282, taprootalaska.com, opens at 4pm) has more of a cozy pub atmosphere and leans toward riotously popular local music acts and jams, with several packed concerts and dances every week.

For a more laid-back listening experience, **McGinley's Pub** (645 G St., 907/279-1782, opens at 11am) hosts two excellent nights of folk music in an Irish-themed pub atmosphere: a small but rip-roaring old-timey music jam on Wednesday evenings, and a long-lived Irish music session on Thursday evenings.

Theater

Anchorage's (and Alaska's) largest venue for live theater is the **Alaska Center for the Performing Arts** (621 W. 6th Ave., 907/263-2787, myalaskacenter.com), where you can see touring national and international acts every season. For more intimate plays, **Cyrano's Off-Center Playhouse** (411 D St., 907/274-2599, cyranos.org) is a beloved local institution.

TOP EXPERIENCE

Iditarod

The 1,000-mile **Iditarod** sled dog race (iditarod.com)—arguably Alaska's most famous winter event—draws competitors from across the nation and the world. This race actually starts twice. The real race starts in Willow on Sunday of the first full weekend in March. **Salmon Berry Tours** (salmonberrytours.

com) puts on wonderful, exclusive parties at the restart.

The day before, however, there's a carnival-like ceremonial start in Anchorage. Teams start downtown and run 11 miles through town on a mix of city streets, multiuse trails, and dedicated mushing trails. Each team carries an "Iditarider"—a passenger in the sled—and the mushers often dress in costumes, fly flags that announce their country of origin, and throw dog booties or candy to children along the route. People from all over the country bid for the privilege of being an Iditarider; see iditarod.com for information.

Bring a folding camp chair if you have one and get there early to stake out the best viewing spots. A sharp dogleg corner from 4th Avenue onto Cordova Street makes for dramatic wipeouts, but almost any vantage on the downtown streets is good; it's also fun to watch the teams zip into the finish line at the Campbell Airstrip, then wrangle their dogs back into the trucks for transport to the next day's restart in Willow.

Festivals

Both residents and visitors alike love the **Anchorage Market and Festival** (3rd Ave. and E St., anchoragemarkets.com, mid-May-mid-Sept. Sat. 10am-6pm, Sun. 10am-5pm), formerly known as the Saturday market. Pickings can be a little thin during the first and last markets of the season, but once this outdoor market gets going it's full of arts and crafts (many of them local), food vendors, and a stage with rotating entertainment acts throughout the day.

Another big winter event in Anchorage is **Fur Rendezvous** (furrondy.net), a two-week street carnival in downtown Anchorage that runs from the last week of February until the Iditarod start. It still serves the original purpose of fur trading and commercial sales, but it also hosts such uniquely Alaskan events as outhouse races, running with the reindeer (our version of running with the bulls), and sprint sled dog races.

If you're a runner, you may already have heard of the **Mayor's Midnight Sun Marathon** (mayorsmarathon.com), which routinely draws runners from all 50 states and about a dozen countries. Contrary to the name, the race is not run at midnight, but it does take place over the weekend of the summer solstice, when Alaska's midnight sun is in full force. Events range from the full marathon to a popular 5K and relay marathon and half-marathon races.

the ceremonial start of the Iditarod

Although they might not technically count as festivals, the **Alaska Railroad** (alaskarailroad.com) runs some wonderful specialty trains, especially in the winter "off" season, and most of them leave from Anchorage. Check the website for the latest special event offerings: They usually include a **ski train** (complete with polka music), a **blues train** that includes an overnight stay in Seward, a couple of **beer- and food-themed trains,** and a spooky **Halloween train** to the Alyeska Resort in Girdwood. If any of these happen to line up with your personal interests, keep an eye on the railroad's website or Facebook page for announcements and book as soon as possible—they always sell out.

SHOPPING

If you only go to one gift shop while you're in Anchorage, make it **The Ulu Factory** (211 W. Ship Creek Ave., 907/276-3119)—it's just a short walk from the downtown railroad depot. Their premier item is one of the most beautiful yet functional gifts you can buy in Alaska: re-creations of the ulu, the crescent-shaped knife traditionally used by several Alaska Native tribes. You can watch the ulus being made, learn how to use them, and shop The Ulu Factory's broad, tasteful collection of other Alaska-made goods and Alaska-themed gifts. Keep an eye out for The Ulu Factory's vintage trolley on downtown streets; it offers free rides to the factory June-August daily 10am-7pm.

The Kobuk (504 W. 5th Ave., 907/272-3626, kobukcoffee.com) offers a similarly eclectic but tasteful selection of gifts in a beautiful, historic trading post; it's also an excellent café. Those gifts that aren't Alaska-made or -themed lean toward old-world international, with items like Swedish wash towels and Russian gift boxes.

If you're looking for authentic Alaska Native creations, it's no surprise that the **Alaska Native Heritage Center** (8800 Heritage Center Dr., 800/315-6608, 907/330-8000, alaskanative.net) has a great gift shop. But believe it or not, the **Alaska Native Medical Center** (4315 Diplomacy Dr., 907/729-1122, anmc.org, Mon.-Fri. 10am-2pm, 1st and 3rd Sat. each month 11am-2pm) also has one of the best gift shops in town. Even if you don't plan on buying anything, it's worth taking a trip through this miniature gallery of fine Alaska Native artwork.

Alaska's arts scene is thriving, perhaps due in part to the long winters. One of the best selections of gift shops actually resides in the ground level of the high-end **Captain Cook Hotel** (939 W. 5th Ave., 907/276-6000, captaincook.com); you don't have to be staying there to wander through and shop. My favorites are **Stephan Fine Arts** (907/274-5009, stephanfinearts.com), a local institution that showcases high-end art almost all made by locals; its sister gallery, **Crest,** right next door, which features more "functional" art items like jewelry and home decor; and the lovely **Boreal Traditions** (907/276-1644) gift shop, where you can admire some of the finest Alaska Native artwork in the country (ask the clerk to point out the glass baskets made by Preston Singletary).

Aurora Fine Art (737 W. 5th Ave., 907/274-0234, aurorafineart-alaska.com) is another excellent pick, packed with an eclectic selection of fine art in multiple mediums, including paint, sculpture, and multimedia.

The rest of downtown Anchorage's best shopping is on 4th Avenue between C Street and G Street. For beautiful Alaska-made gifts that don't lean quite so far into the art spectrum, head for the exquisite **Cabin Fever Gifts** (650 W. 4th Ave., 907/278-3522, cabinfeveralaska.com, Mon.-Fri. 11am-6pm, Sat. 10am-6pm, extended summer hours), which has all things beautiful created here in Alaska, from quilted bags to vests, soap, lovely birch bowls, and pottery. They also own the **Quilted Raven** (415 G St., 907/278-3521, quiltedravenalaska.com) next door, a great place to get Alaska fabrics.

Knitters will appreciate **Wooly Mammoth Yarn and Fiber** (416 G St., 907/278-3524, Thurs.-Fri. 11am-6pm, Sat. 10am-6pm, extended summer hours). The **Octopus Ink**

Gallery (410 G St., 907/333-4657, octopusinkclothing.com, daily 9am-9pm) is also fun; they specialize in simplistic but lovely line art on clothing and a few uniquely useful items, like squishable silicone cups. Finally, my very favorite of downtown's small galleries is the **Katie Sevigny Studio** (608 W. 4th Ave., 907/258-2787, katiesevignystudio.com, Mon.-Thurs. 10am-7pm, Fri.-Sat. 10am-9pm, Sun. 11am-7pm), which has everything from original prints to multimedia, home decorations, and other great Alaska-made art.

There are some excellent shops in a building the locals know variously as the 4th Avenue Marketplace, the Sunshine Mall, or the Post Office Mall, depending on how long they've been around; it's off 4th Avenue between C Street and D Street. The highlight is **Laura Wright's Alaskan Parkys** (411 W. 4th Ave., 907/274-4215), where you can buy *kuspuk*-style parkas off the rack in sizes XS to 3X or have one custom-made (As of November 2016 it's unclear if this shop is still open, but it's such a unique attraction that it's worth calling to check).

For a truly unusual Alaska-made gift, visit the **Oomingmak Musk Ox Co-Op** (604 H St., 907/272-9225, qiviut.com, Mon.-Sat. 10am-6pm), where you can buy qiviut—the marvelously fine, light, and soft underwool of the musk ox—as raw fiber, yarn, and some finished goods. Warning: Because each musk ox yields so little wool, qiviut is pretty pricey! At the opposite end of the price range, **Alaska Wild Berry Products** (5225 Juneau St., 907/562-8858, alaskawildberryproducts.com, summer daily 10am-9pm) offers great Alaska-made candies, gifts, and the world's largest indoor chocolate fountain (it's so big they call it a "chocolate fall" instead)—in its wonderful Anchorage headquarters.

If you came in search of fur or want a warm souvenir to remind you of your visit, several furriers are clustered on 4th Avenue. The biggest name of them all is **David Green Furs** (4th Ave. between A St. and B St., 907/277-9595, davidgreenfurs.com, Mon.-Fri. 9am-6pm, Sat. 9am-5:30pm, Sun. noon-4pm), but make time to stop in at the **Alaska Fur Gallery** (428 W. 4th Ave., 907/274-3877, akfurgallery.com, Mon.-Fri. 9am-5pm, Sat. 9am-7pm, Sun. 9am-9pm) next door, too.

If your primary goal is finding gifts with "Alaska" emblazoned on every surface possible, head straight for the enormous **Polar Bear Gifts** (600 W. 4th Ave., 907/274-4387, polarbeargifts.net, hours vary by season), a longtime stalwart of the downtown gift shop scene.

For Alaskana books, **Title Wave Books** (1360 W. Northern Lights Blvd., 907/278-9283, wavebooks.com, Mon.-Thurs. 10am-8pm, Fri.-Sat. 10am-9pm, Sun. 11am-7pm), an independent bookstore in midtown Anchorage, is your best bet. They sell both new and used books, with a "best of Alaska" display that's usually front and center when you walk in and a locked cabinet of valuable historical Alaska books. The store might be relocating in 2017, so call or check the website to verify the address.

Midtown Anchorage also has an excellent gift shop, **2 Friends Gallery** (341 E. Benson Blvd., 907/277-004, 2friendsgallery.com, Mon.-Fri. 11am-6pm, Sat. 10am-6pm, Sun. 12-5pm). This inviting shop offers an eclectic mix of all things art and gifts, much of it from local artists.

FOOD

Cafés and Bistros

Anchorage has so many excellent cafés (in the truest sense of the word) and coffee shops that I've been forced to distinguish between the two. If coffee, tea, or the Wi-Fi that usually accompanies them is your goal, look to the *Coffee and Tea Shops* section; the cafés listed here are all about the food.

The breakfasts at downtown's **Snow City Cafe** (1034 W. 4th Ave., 907/272-2489, snowcitycafe.com, Mon.-Fri. 7am-3pm, Sat.-Sun. 7am-4pm, $13) are legendary, but it's good for a late lunch too. The downside to that well-earned popularity is that the place is usually packed—but if you can stomach a short wait, the quick, efficient staff will get you seated before long. Everything is good, but the omelets and scrambles are particularly popular.

Also downtown, the European-inspired **Sack's Cafe** (328 G St., 907/274-4022, sackscafe.com, Mon.-Fri. 11am-2:30pm, Sat.-Sun. 9am-2:30pm, also Tues.-Sun. 5pm-9pm, lunch $16, dinner $30) was a pioneer in the movement for locally sourced, seasonal ingredients. They continue to offer a nice blend of adventurous experiments supplemented by a few safe standards, all marked by their freshness; where else can you get Australian lamb, hog rib chop, confit of duck ravioli, and spectacular Alaska salmon, all in one place? A new executive chef was hired in 2016, and I expect that the same level of freshness, adventure, and quality will continue.

Technically **Fire Island Rustic Bakeshop** (1343 G St., 907/569-0001, fireislandbread.com, Wed.-Sun. 7am-6pm, sandwiches $11) is a bakery, but it feels more like a sunny neighborhood café with a few streetside tables, thanks to the modest menu of ready-made cold sandwiches with non-GMO ingredients that are often organic, too. There's a second location (2530 E. 16th Ave., 907/274-0022), but that one is only accessible if you have a car.

Middle Way Cafe (1200 W. Northern Lights Blvd., 907/272-6433, middlewaycafe.com, Mon.-Fri. 7am-6pm, Sat. and Sun. 8am-6pm, lunch $12-14) in midtown offers a full menu of sandwiches, smoothies, and breakfast. They do a great tuna melt, but you basically can't go wrong if you stick to the sandwich menu or daily specials. They also offer one of the best selections of ready-to-go gluten-free and vegan baked goods in town, and some of their meals are gluten-free and vegan as well. Heads up: Service varies from efficient to painfully slow.

Mediterranean and Italian

If you're looking for fine Mediterranean and North African dining in a casual atmosphere, head immediately to **Aladdin's** (4240 Old Seward Hwy., 907/561-2373, aladdinsalaska.com, Thurs.-Sat. 5pm-9pm, $20), a family-run under-the-radar gem of a midtown restaurant where you'll walk out knowing the owner and his family by name. The food is delicious, authentic, and often deceptively simple, and you can't go wrong with any of the dishes.

Another one of my favorite little places in the middle of town is **Campobello Bistro** (601 W. 36th Ave., 907/563-2040, campobellobistro.com, lunch begins at 11am Tues.-Fri., dinner starts at 5pm Tues.-Sat., $27), where they use fresh ingredients in their

a delicious lunch from Fire Island Rustic Bakeshop

Mediterranean and Italian cuisine, and everything possible is either house made or locally made. Order the calamari.

Seafood

Simon and Seaforts (420 L St., 907/274-3502, simonandseaforts.com, daily 11am-2:30pm and 4:30pm-10pm, Sat.-Sun. opens at 10am, Fri. closes at 11pm, $20-70) is the highest-profile seafood restaurant in town, but I much prefer the teeny-tiny **F Street Station** (325 F St., 907/272-5196, daily 10am-2:30am, $15) for its fresh, wild-caught seafood menu that varies by the season (specials tend to be pricier than the fixed menus, but still entirely fair). This is a favorite haunt for pilots of planes both big and small. The restaurant itself is very small, but the inevitable wait is worth it, and you can sometimes squeeze in at the food bar right beside the open kitchen, where the chefs chat back and forth with you as they work their magic.

Sandwiches

If you're up late and want a sandwich, there is nothing better than the **Brown Bag Sandwich Company** (535 W. 3rd Ave., 907/277-0202, akbrownbag.com, Mon.-Fri. 10am-2am, Sat.-Sun 11am-2am, $10). There's a small bar downstairs, but you get the sandwiches—which would be excellent at any hour—upstairs, and can eat in either place. If your GPS says this place is permanently closed, double-check the address; it's probably pointed toward their old location. Again, you can't go wrong with all the goodness on the menu, but if you like mildly spicy food, check out the Spicy Yeti and Spicy T.B.A. sandwiches.

Coffee and Tea Shops

For a fine coffee shop with some basic food options, head to **Black Cup** (341 E. Benson Blvd., 907/274-0026, cafedelmundo.com, Mon.-Fri. 6am-11pm, Sat. 7am-11pm, Sun. 8am-11pm), which your phone's GPS might still know by its previous name, Cafe del Mundo. The interior has a distinguished European vibe but the service is all mellow, friendly Alaska, with some of the best decor in town, and they're open late.

Also enormously popular is **Kaladi Brothers Coffee Company** (kaladi.com), a local chain with 13 Anchorage cafés and one in Seattle; the chain is known as an active, generous member of the community in general and strikes a laid-back, sleek, wood-furnished vibe. The most convenient Kaladi Brothers location for most visitors is in the downtown Alaska Center for the Performing Arts (621 W 6th Ave, 907/644-7438; Mon. - Fri. 6am-7pm, Sat. 7am-7pm, Sun. 8am-6pm). Another popular local chain is **Steam Dot** (steamdot.com), a café with three locations that uses single-source coffees that are locally roasted and served in a modern-style interior with clean, spare lines reminiscent of an Ikea catalog. The most convenient Steam Dot location is in the downtown Williwaw social center (609 F St, opens at 10am daily; call for closing times).

If you're after a true tea shop with full tea service and all, head to the friendly **Indigo Tea Lounge** (530 E. Benson Blvd., 907/222-1619, indigotealounge.com, Mon.-Fri. 9am-7pm, Sat. 10am-7pm, Sun. 11am-6pm) in midtown Anchorage, where a funky, modern interior design aesthetic blends with the best selection of international teas. Full tea service may not be available every day; reservations are highly recommended.

My favorite coffee shop in all of Anchorage is **The Kobuk** (504 W. 5th Ave., 907/272-3626, kobukcoffee.com, Tues.-Sat. 11am-6pm, café closes an hour before the gift shop). Their old-fashioned cake doughnuts have been quite rightly voted some of the best in America, but their other pastries and sweets are pretty darn good too, especially the turnovers. There isn't much seating and the Wi-Fi isn't reliable, but you can't beat the atmosphere in this cozy little gift shop/café combo that occupies one of the first general stores in town.

If that doesn't sound sweet enough, try the **Alaska Cake Studio** (608 W. 4th Ave., 907/272-3995, Mon.-Thurs. 8:30am-7pm, Fri.

8:30am-9pm, Sat. 10am-9pm, Sun. noon-6pm). It offers a selection of delicious truffles, cupcakes, and single-serve dollops of cake, along with custom cakes and a full selection of espresso drinks. The service is great too.

Finally, **Side Street Espresso** (412 G St., 907/258-9055, Mon.-Sat 7am-3pm, expanded summer hours) is a great neighborhood staple with lots of personality. It's tiny inside, so you might end up making a new friend by sharing your table with somebody new.

Burgers

Who makes the best burgers in Anchorage? It's a long-standing, neck-and-neck race between everybody's favorite Spenard dive restaurant (which wins "Best Burger in Anchorage" in most popular polls), **Tommy's Burger Stop** (1106 W. 29th Pl., 907/561-5696, tommysburgerstop.com, Mon.-Fri. 10:30am-9pm, Sat. 11am-9pm, Sun. noon-6pm, $12), and the slightly more genteel **Arctic Roadrunner** (5300 Old Seward Hwy., 907/561-1245, Mon.-Sat. 10:30am-9pm), which also serves halibut and salmon burgers. Both also offer fantastic homemade milk shakes.

Brewpubs and Breweries

The **Glacier Brewhouse** (737 W. 5th Ave., 907/274-2739, glacierbrewhouse.com, Tues.-Thurs. 11am-10pm, Fri. 11am-11pm, Sat. 10am-11pm, Sun. 10am-9:30pm, Mon. 11am-9:30pm, $20) is a downtown stalwart, for good reason; this upscale brewpub dishes casual fine dining at its best and also does a great job with seafood. (If you want crab legs, they have 'em!) Also popular downtown is **Humpy's Great Alaskan Ale House** (610 W. 6th Ave., 907/276-2337, humpysalaska.com, Mon.-Thurs. 11am-2am, Fri. 11am-2:30am, Sat. 10am-2:30am, Sun. 10am-2am, kitchen closes at midnight or 1am), a chill hangout with a nice back deck and frequent live music.

The **49th State Brewing Company** (717 W. 3rd Ave., 907/277-7727, 49statebrewing.com, daily 11am-1am, Sun. brunch at 8:30am during football season) just opened a second location in Anchorage, taking over the old Snow Goose restaurant and its phenomenal outdoor decks overlooking the inlet. (The other location is in Healy, near Denali National Park.) Try their wonderfully lean, tender, and locally sourced yak meat. They'll also have the best salads in town during the winter, because they're sourcing salad greens that are grown hydroponically in Anchorage.

On the far side of town, the **Midnight Sun**

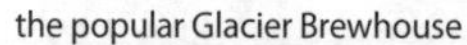
the popular Glacier Brewhouse

Brewing Company (8111 Dimond Hook Dr., 907/344-1179, midnightsunbrewing.com, daily 11am-8pm) offers really good brewpub food, from seafood to sandwiches, wonderful fresh salads, and surprise world cuisine specials, along with their own brews. Show up at 6pm on a Thursday and you can go on a free tour of the brewery.

Due to a quirk of local regulations, certain other classifications of brewing companies are not allowed to serve their own food, but local favorites like **Resolution Brewing Company** (3024 Mountain View Dr., 907/330-4523, resolutionbeer.com, Mon.-Thurs. 3pm-8pm, Fri.-Sun. noon-8pm), which stormed onto the scene a couple of years ago, often station food trucks outside or let you bring your own food to enjoy with good company, Wi-Fi, and their award-winning beer.

Also very popular are the **Alaska Denali Winery** (1301 E. Dowling Rd., 907/563-9434, denaliwinery.info), which specializes in personalized, microbrewed batches of wine, and the **Double Shovel Cider Company** (502 W. 58th Ave., Wed.-Thurs. 4pm-8pm, Fri.-Sat. 3pm-8pm, doubleshovelcider.co), which uses Alaska apples, berries, and syrups in its handcrafted ciders.

Thai

Thai food isn't quite as popular in Anchorage as it is in Fairbanks, but you'll still find plenty of Thai restaurants. Two of the best are **Taste of Thai** (11109 Old Seward Hwy., 907/349-8424, alaskatasteofthai.com, Mon.-Thurs. 11am-9pm, Fri.-Sat. 11am-10pm, closed Mon.-Fri. 2:30pm-4:30pm) in south Anchorage, which combines a slice of authentic Thai ambience with fast, fresh food, and **Thai Kitchen** (3405 E. Tudor Rd., 907/561-0082, thaikitchenak.com, Mon.-Fri. 11am-3pm and 5pm-9pm, Sat. 5pm-9pm, Sun. 5pm-8:30pm) in midtown.

Vietnamese

Vietnamese pho (pronounced "fuh") is a phenomenon in Anchorage. If you want an education in this savory soup, head for **PHOnatik** (901 E. Dimond Blvd., 907/336-8880, Mon. and Thurs.-Sat. 11am-11pm, Tues.-Wed. 11:30am-11pm, Sun. noon-8pm, $14). You can also get pho, plus some of the best spring rolls in town and other Vietnamese food, at longtime local favorite **Ray's Place** (2412 Spenard Rd., 907/279-2932, raysplaceak.com, Mon.-Fri. 10am-3pm and 5pm-9pm, $15).

Pizza

Creative pizza is a big deal in Anchorage, and the **Moose's Tooth** (3300 Old Seward Hwy., 907/258-2537, moosestooth.net, Mon.-Thurs. 10:30am-11pm, Fri. 10:30am-midnight, Sat. 11am-midnight, Sun. 11am-11pm, $24) in midtown remains the undisputed champion in this category. In fact, they're often hailed as one of the best pizzerias in the country, and they also offer a great selection of local beers, many of which come from their own **Broken Tooth Brewing Company.** The best thing about the Moose's Tooth is that they have a (sometimes crazy) pizza for every taste, from the Thai pizza and chipotle steak pizza (two of my favorites) to more conventional pepperoni.

Also popular is downtown's **Fat Ptarmigan** (441 W. 5th Ave., 907/777-7710, fatptarmigan.com, Mon.-Fri. 11am-9pm, Sat.-Sun. noon-10pm, $20). You can (and should) make reservations online. **Hearth Artisan Pizza** (1200 W. Northern Lights Blvd., 907/222-0888, Sun.-Thurs. 4pm-10pm, Fri.-Sat. 4pm-11pm, $20) in midtown is a fairly new addition to the local pizza scene that's still working out some of the kinks but shows a lot of promise; they're owned by the same company that delivers the excellent Middle Way Cafe, which is right next door.

Mexican

Two places in Anchorage have earned a reputation for producing authentic Mexican food. The first is the always fresh and tasty Xalos (xalos.org), which actually has two locations: **Xalos Mexican Grill** (3048 Mountain View Dr., 907/277-1001, Mon.-Sat. 11am-9pm, Sun. 11am-8pm, $12) and **Xalos Burrito Express** (320 W. 100th Ave., 907/782-9994, Mon.-Sat.

11am-9pm, Sun. 11am-8pm, $12). The other is the beloved, longtime community institution **Mexico in Alaska** (7305 Old Seward Hwy., 907/349-1528, mexicoinalaska.com, Mon.-Fri. 11am-9pm, Sat. noon-9pm, $16), which has a short but respectable vegetarian menu that can also be made vegan.

Korean

If you've ever considered Korean food to be bland or boring, do yourself a favor and stop by **VIP Restaurant** (555 W. Northern Lights Blvd., 907/279-8514, Mon.-Sat. 11am-10pm, $20). It's a longtime favorite of the Korean community and anyone connected to it, so you're going to get food so authentic—and dynamic—that you might not recognize much of it. Don't be afraid to ask the servers for suggestions.

Fine Dining

All aspects of Anchorage nightlife—from restaurants to big theater shows—thrive on a casual, inclusive "come as you are" atmosphere. That said, there are several dependable places for a high-end fine-dining experience. The first is the **Crow's Nest** (939 W. 5th Ave., 907/343-2217, captaincook.com, Mon.-Sat. 5pm-midnight, $45) at the top of the Hotel Captain Cook, the nicest hotel in downtown Anchorage. They serve French and New American cuisine, drawing from a 10,000-bottle wine cellar for the perfect pairings with your meal.

For midtown diners, **Jens' Restaurant** (701 W. 36th Ave., 561-5367, jensrestaurant.com, $40) has long been a high-end favorite, serving inventive Continental cuisine. Finally, the **Flying Machine Restaurant** (4800 Spenard Rd., 907/266-2249, millenium-hotels.com) in the Lakefront Anchorage Hotel offers American-influenced Alaska cuisine in a somewhat more relaxed atmosphere.

Food Trucks

Anchorage hasn't *quite* caught up to the food truck trend you'll find in other Pacific Northwest cities, but we're working on it. The list of mobile food vendors (including trucks, carts, and pop-ups) is expanding every year, and a few standouts have emerged as solid leaders of the pack. The best place to find information on their unpredictable whereabouts, prices, and hours is, without fail, on Facebook.

It might sound overly simplistic, but **Bear Mace Bites** sells the best spicy, crispy chicken sandwich in town; it might make your nose run, but it won't make you cry. The halibut sandwiches are pretty darn good, too, and the bright blue truck is awfully hard to miss. **Tasty Traveler** is a little less predictable, but this bright orange truck is also enormously popular for its world-fusion tacos; get the rockfish if you can, and try a few of the creative salsa options.

Cupcakes are definitely a thing up here, and the undisputed queen of cupcakes in Southcentral is still Kastle Sorensen of **Kastle's Kreations,** who won the ninth season of the Food Network's *Cupcake Wars* by incorporating smoked salmon, chives, and lemon into an unusual savory cupcake. You can't miss her bright-pink truck, and like all these vendors she regularly posts her schedule and whereabouts on Facebook.

Challenger to the cupcake title (in my mind, anyway) is **Babycakes Cupcakes,** where they use real, largely organic ingredients to make their cupcakes, which are feather-light, both cake and frosting.

Groceries

Anchorage has **Fred Meyer** (fredmeyer.com) and **Safeway** (safeway.com) grocery stores scattered throughout town; many of the Safeway stores are still branded as **Carrs** (carrsqc.com), the local chain that they bought out when they came into town, and that's what most locals call them as well.

Note: If you're staying in downtown Anchorage, be very careful in the neighborhood of the Carrs (Safeway) grocery store located at 13th and Gambell; it tends to be a hot spot for rough behavior and crime. You'll have a much better experience—and a somewhat more convenient location—if you go to the locally run **New Sagaya City Market** (900 W. 13th Ave., 907/274-6173, newsagaya.com, daily 6am-9pm).

ACCOMMODATIONS

Finding high-quality lodgings in Anchorage is no problem at all, but price and availability can both be serious obstacles during the busy summer system; get the best deals by booking as far in advance as possible, and if you're staying downtown, be sure to factor in the cost of parking. In other parts of town, free parking is almost always guaranteed. All accommodations in Anchorage are subject to a 12 percent bed tax.

Hotels

You'll find your favorite chain names here, including Hilton and Marriott properties. Heads up: The downtown Anchorage Hilton has drawn a number of complaints for not living up to what travelers expect from a hotel of that name, but the smaller Hilton sub-properties around town, including the midtown **Embassy Suites by Hilton** (600 E. Benson Blvd., 907/332-7000, from $340), are very popular. Just be warned that although the Embassy Suites on-demand shuttle will take you to the airport and several downtown locations, it won't take you to the train depot.

If you're on a budget, the all-suite **Anchorage Grand Hotel** (505 W. 2nd Ave., 907/929-8888, anchoragegrand.com, from $99) is one of the best options in downtown Anchorage. The suites are simple but huge and clean, and it's conveniently located for walking almost anywhere downtown.

The **Historic Anchorage Downtown Hotel** (330 E St., 907/272-4553, historicanchoragehotel.com, from $206) is the lovingly restored annex of one of Anchorage's first hotels, with historical photographs of Anchorage lining the hallways. Even if you don't stay here, it's worth poking your head in and checking out the photographs in the upstairs hallways. The hotel is also notoriously haunted, although the spooks seem to be mostly benign. Check out the "ghostbook" in the lobby—a record of spook sightings from guests, many of whom had no prior knowledge of the hotel's haunted reputation—and decide for yourself.

For the best accommodations in town, check out the downtown **Hotel Captain Cook** (939 W. 5th Ave., 800/843-1950 or 907/276-6000, captaincook.com, from $310) and the **Sheraton** (401 E. 6th Ave., 907/276-8700, sheratonanchorage.com, from $389). Of particular note, the Hotel Captain Cook has a wonderful day spa and fitness facility that you can purchase day passes for, even if you aren't staying there.

For midtown accommodations close to the airport, the **Lakefront Anchorage** (4800 Spenard Rd., 907/243-2300, milleniumhotels.com, from $220) offers clean, large, and comfortable rooms, many of which offer views out on Lake Hood, the busiest seaplane port in the world. The staff is friendly and the place is very well-run. If you have a car, this is a reasonably central location for any attractions in town, and many travelers prefer it to staying downtown.

If you want a hotel away from both downtown Anchorage and the noise of the airport, consider the clean, comfortable **Dimond Center Hotel** (700 E. Dimond Blvd., 907/770-5000, dimondcenterhotel.com, from $279). Travelers I've spoken to loved their rooms, although they found the front desk service and complimentary airport shuttle to be a little disorganized. This is another centrally located hotel if you have a vehicle, and it's also perched right on top of the city's largest mall and the second-largest transit center for its bare-bones bus system.

Eating out in Anchorage is relatively affordable, but if you'd rather cook for yourself, **TownPlace Suites Anchorage** (600 E. 32nd Ave., 907/334-8000, marriott.com, from $237) offers the benefit of a nice kitchenette and lots of closet space. The midtown location is somewhat off the beaten path, though, so you'll want to have a vehicle to get around.

Hostels

Anchorage hostels may seem like an attractive option, but as a general rule you should steer clear of them and anything labeled as a budget extended-stay hotel. Unfortunately, such accommodations often end up serving as makeshift housing for some of the city's disenfranchised population, and some travelers have been rudely surprised to find that the pretty pictures they saw online had no real bearing on the property they ended up at.

There is just one hostel that I feel comfortable recommending to travelers, with a couple caveats: The midtown **Bent Prop Inn & Hostel** (3104 Eide St., 907/222-5220, bentpropinn.com, from $30 for a bunk bed) is the only hostel in Anchorage that has won TripAdvisor's Certificate of Excellence for five years running. The owners also have a downtown location (700 H St., 907/276-3635) that they took over from the previous owners, but it previously housed a rough crowd and they've had their work cut out to rehabilitate it.

The caveats are that you should ask to stay upstairs in the semi-private apartment if possible; it never houses more than three or four people at a time, and it has an en suite bathroom and full kitchen. You should also book as far in advance as possible—some people reserve a year in advance—and be aware of the hostel's strict no-tolerance policy for alcohol and drugs. There's also a private room with an en suite bathroom and full kitchen for about $100 per night, one of the best deals in town.

Bed-and-Breakfasts

If you want to get away from the big hotel experience entirely, downtown Anchorage's bed-and-breakfasts offer clean, comfortable, and spacious accommodations in the quieter parts of downtown, and prices that often beat the big hotels. The following bed-and-breakfasts are the cream of the crop, but make sure you book early—it's not unusual for rooms to sell out more than six months in advance.

The **Wildflower Inn** (1239 I St., 907/274-1239, alaska-wildflower-inn.com, $159 summer, $89 winter) offers extremely reasonable rates for a stay in its immaculate rooms, many of which come with an adjoining sitting room and futon if you need extra sleeping space. All rooms have private baths; one even has a Jacuzzi tub. This bed-and-breakfast is in a quiet part of downtown, just a short walk from the high-activity city center.

Alaska House of Jade (3800 Delwood Pl., 907/337-3400, alaskahouseofjade.com, from $159) offers five spacious suites, each of them immaculate, with extra beds and beautiful, well-tended gardens. The hosts are wonderful, as are the delicious breakfasts and fresh smoothies.

City Garden Bed and Breakfast (1352 W. 10th Ave., 907/276-8686, citygarden.biz, from $125) is often recommended by other B&B owners when their properties are full. It's centrally located but in a quieter part of downtown, with a gracious, responsive host who makes a wonderful breakfast and can often help you get to and from your train or plane.

Camping and RV Parks

If you're tent camping, there are no two ways around it—you're going to need a vehicle to get you to and from the campground. RV users have it a little easier: You can almost always park in the lots of the biggest big-box stores, although it's polite to speak to the manager first—not every store has enough room in the parking lot to allow this. The massive South Anchorage strip mall that houses Sportsmans Warehouse and Sam's Club, at the intersection of the Old Seward Highway and Dimond Road, is a particular favorite with the RV crowd.

If you want more natural surroundings, however, both tent campers and RV users have two beautiful public campgrounds to choose from near Anchorage. The **Eagle River Campground** (Mile 12.6 Glenn Hwy., 907/746-4644, lifetimeadventure.net, $20) is about 10 miles out of town, to the northeast. It offers 57 campsites with paved parking, only a handful of which can be reserved online. Large RVs are welcome; an on-site dump

making camp in the mountains above Eagle River

station costs $5. You'll never be completely away from the noise of the nearby Glenn Highway, but some of the sites back right onto beautiful river rapids, and there are several big-box stores in the adjoining town, Eagle River, for easy resupply runs.

Also excellent for both tent campers and RV users is the **Bird Creek Campground** (Mile 101.2 Seward Hwy., no reservations, 28 sites $20 each, 35-foot RV limit), south of Anchorage. Again, you'll never be completely free of noise from the nearby Seward Highway, but you get beautiful water views in many sites and are just a short walk from good salmon fishing in **Bird Creek** and the paved, multiuse **Bird to Gird** trail, which runs all the way to Girdwood at a comfortable distance from the highway.

INFORMATION AND SERVICES

Because Anchorage is such a big city, it has a great variety of general services like gas stations and auto repair shops, along with many big-box stores, including **Walmart** and **Safeway,** although the latter is usually branded as **Carrs,** a local chain that Safeway took over when it first expanded into Alaska. Usually, you'll get the best selection and prices on everything from groceries and household goods at **Fred Meyer** (fredmeyer.com).

For general purpose maps and local guidebooks, the **Alaska Geographic Store** (241 N. C St., 907/274-8440, Mon.-Fri. 10am-5pm) has the most comprehensive collection, including USGS quads for your backcountry adventures and a smattering of Alaska nonfiction books.

If you need service or rentals for high-end camera equipment, go to long-time local favorite **Stewart's Photo** (531 W. 4th Ave., 907/272-8581, stewartsphoto.com) downtown.

Hospitals

Three hospitals in town have 24-hour emergency rooms and trauma centers. Most visitors will use either the nonprofit **Providence Alaska Medical Center** (3200 Providence Dr., 907/562-2211, alaska.providence.org) or the for-profit **Alaska Regional Hospital** (2801 Debarr Rd., 907/276-1131, alaskaregional.com). The third center, the **Alaska Native Medical Center** (4315 Diplomacy Dr., 907/563-2662, anmc.org), is intended for use by those with proof of Alaska Native or American Indian descent, but will provide emergency medical care and screening to anybody.

Internet Access

Visitors to Anchorage are often surprised to see that it doesn't have a citywide Wi-Fi network, and the fastest Wi-Fi (and cellular) speeds here are still slow compared to the Lower 48. That said, speeds here are the best in the state—so enjoy it while you have it! You can get complimentary Wi-Fi at almost every hotel in town and just about every coffee shop too, although the latter always prefer if you make a purchase before logging in.

Outfitters

Anchorage has three excellent, full-service gear shops and outfitters in **Alaska Mountaineering and Hiking** (2633 Spenard Rd., 907/272-1811, alaskamountaineering.com), **Mountain View Sports** (11124 Old Seward Hwy., 907/222-6633, mtviewsports.com), and **REI** (1200 W. Northern Lights Blvd., 907/272-4565, rei.com). If you're downtown, however, you may prefer to shop at **Big Ray's Outfitters** (320 W. 4th Ave., 907/279-2401, bigrays.com) or **Sixth Avenue Outfitters** (524 W. 6th Ave., 907/276-0233, 6thavenueoutfitters.com). For all your specific paddling or rafting needs, including rentals, head to **Alaska Raft and Kayak** (401 W. Tudor Rd., 907/561-7238, alaskaraftandkayak.com).

TRANSPORTATION

Getting There

AIR

The easiest way to reach Anchorage is by air; **Ted Stevens Anchorage International Airport** (5000 W International Airport Rd., dot.alaska.gov/anc/index.shtml) receives year-round service from Alaska Airlines, Delta, United, and Iceland Air, with seasonal service from an ever-expanding list of airlines that includes JetBlue and Condor. That said, Alaska Airlines has the most flights here far and away, including nonstop options from Seattle, Portland, Chicago, Phoenix, Los Angeles, and sometimes Salt Lake City. If you're coming from another Alaska community, both **Alaska Airlines** (800/252-7522, alaskaair.com) and **Ravn Alaska** (907/248-4422, flyravn.com) offer extensive flights within the state.

SEA

Every once in a while, small cruise ships dock in the Anchorage port, but the large cruise lines are more likely to put up in Seward or Whittier and send passengers to Anchorage—then beyond—aboard chartered motor coaches or train cars. Your other options for getting here are to put your vehicle on an **Alaska Marine Highway System ferry** (800/642-0066, ferryalaska.com) into Whittier, Homer, or Valdez, or to drive the Alaska Highway from the Lower 48 through Canada, although Anchorage is hardly the first stop on that route.

TRAIN

Unfortunately, **Alaska Railroad** passenger trains (800/544-0552, alaskarailroad.com) are not connected to lines from Canada or the Lower 48. If you're starting out from the Alaska communities of Seward, Whittier, Talkeetna, or Fairbanks, however, the train is a great way to get to Anchorage, and vice versa. It's slower than driving, though.

Getting Around

CAR AND RV RENTALS

Most of the attractions visitors will be interested in are either downtown or can be reached on a day tour. That said, if you want to take advantage of the stellar hiking opportunities in and around Anchorage or enjoy a scenic drive up or down the road system at your own pace, you'll be better off with a rental car. You can choose from almost any major chain, at both the airport and in-city locations, including Hertz, Avis, Thrifty, Dollar, and Enterprise. If you want to do a one-way rental between Seward or Fairbanks, your best bet is Hertz.

If you want to rent from a local chain, the family-run **Midnight Sun Car and Van Rental** (4211 Spenard Rd., 888/877-3585 or 907/243-8806, ineedacarrental.com, summer rates from $65) offers excellent service at reasonable prices. **Alaska Auto Rental** (907/457-7368, 907/457-7368, alaskaautorental.com), also offers one-way rentals throughout the state, with drop-off to a variety of locations, in exchange for a sizable fee. Alaska Auto Rental is also one of the friendliest companies for renting to people under 25 years of age, and they also rent vehicles specially equipped for travel on Alaska's gravel highways—including the **Denali Highway,** the **McCarthy Road,** and the **Dalton Highway** or "Haul Road" north of Fairbanks—which many other rental companies prohibit.

If you're the independent sort, consider flying into Anchorage, then touring through Southcentral and Interior Alaska in a rented RV. These vehicles, which range in size from short campers to almost the size of a motorcoach, combine transportation with a self-contained place to sleep, cook, store your gear, and lounge away rainy rest days with ready access to running water, electricity and a toilet.

You don't need a commercial driver's license to drive an RV in Alaska. That said, stick with something you're comfortable handling on narrow, winding highways, and *always* check your RV rental company's reputation in the Better Business Bureau Northwest listings (bbb.org). Two of the best RV rental companies in Anchorage are **Clippership Motorhome Rentals** (5401 Old Seward Hwy, 800/421-3456 or 907/562-7051, clippershiprv.com), and **A&M RV Center** (2225 E 5th Ave, 800/478-4678 or 907/279-5508, gorv.com).

BUSES

Anchorage does have a bare-bones bus system, the **People Mover** (907/343-6543, peoplemover.org), which includes service to the airport aboard route 7. Unfortunately, the city's immense spread and relatively low population density make it difficult to provide good service citywide, and the Downtown Transit Center is known as a hotbed of unsavory behavior. Hopefully that will change soon, thanks to renewed efforts from the city, but in the meantime, you'll be more comfortable getting around by rental car or taxi.

TAXIS

There are two main taxi companies in Anchorage: **Yellow Taxi** (907/222-2222, alaskayellowdispatch.com) is dominant by far, but there are a few **Checker Cabs** (907/644-4444, akcheckercab.com) as well. As of winter 2016 we don't yet have rideshare services like Uber or Lyft, but Uber in particular is persistently trying to crack the Alaska market.

BICYCLES

Anchorage as a whole isn't a bike-friendly city yet; if you're used to highly bikable cities like Portland, you'll be disappointed. The municipality is working hard to improve that, though, and in the meantime, you can rent a bike for exploring the city's network of paved trails at any of three downtown businesses: **Pablo's Bicycle Rentals** (907/272-1600, pablobicyclerentals.com, May-mid-Sept. daily 8am-8pm) and **Lifetime Adventures** (907/746-4644, lifetimeadventure.net) are both at the corner of 5th Avenue and L Street, and close up shop promptly in mid-September. **Downtown Bicycle Rental** (334 W. 4th Ave., 907/279-5293, alaska-bike-rentals.com) stays open through September and offers hourly, daily, and weekly rental rates.

North of Anchorage

The region immediately north of Anchorage, ending where Talkeetna merges into Interior Alaska, is known as the Matanuska-Susitna Valley or, to locals, simply "the Valley," and it contains two of the state's fastest-growing communities, Palmer and Wasilla. As of 2013, their combined population was about 15,000 people.

This region hasn't developed its full potential for tourist attractions or services—yet!—but it makes a great stopover during long trips north or south between Fairbanks or Tok and Anchorage. If you're driving an RV, you'll find the RV parks and campgrounds here to be much more restful than a big-box store parking lot in Anchorage.

If you enjoy scenic drives and hikes, it's worth taking an entire day with Wasilla or Palmer as your home base to explore nearby Hatcher Pass, and both communities' distance from the big city makes them perfect hosts for some unusual attractions you'd never find in a more urban setting.

WASILLA

There are two visitor centers in Wasilla, one at the **Alaska Railroad Depot** (415 E. Railroad Ave., 907/376-1299, wasillachamber.org), the other in the **Dorothy Page Museum** (323 N. Main St., Tues.-Fri. 9am-5pm, cityofwasilla.com/museum/, $3, 12 and under free, Fri. all ages free), which also showcases Wasilla's history, including the town's past as a railroad, mining, and mushing town, and preserves eight structures from the original townsite.

Sights and Recreation

Most of the year, the **Iditarod Headquarters** (2100 S. Knik Goose Bay Rd., 907/376-5155, iditarod.com, summer daily 8am-7pm, winter Mon.-Fri. 8am-5pm, free) serves as a small museum of mushing memorabilia, with a small theater and dog cart rides daily 9am-5pm during the summer. For another look at mushing history, visit the **Knik Museum and Musher's Hall of Fame** (Mile 13.9 Knik-Goosebay Rd., wkhsocietyorg, mid-April-Oct. Wed.-Sun. 1pm-6pm); the upstairs of this converted pool hall/roadhouse is the hall of fame, while downstairs houses a collection of everyday artifacts from the days when this area was a bustling town called Knik, which gradually faded into obscurity as development was steered toward Anchorage and Wasilla.

Fly fishers love the **Little Susitna River** near Wasilla; for guided trips, **iFishAlaska** (907/357-0131, ifishalaska.com, from $150 pp) will take you out on the Little Su or the Deshka River on a half-day or full-day trip in search of salmon, primarily kings and silvers. Bed-and-breakfast lodging packages are available too.

If you love planes, trains, and automobiles, you'll enjoy a stop by the **Alaska Museum of Transportation and Industry** (3800 W. Museum Dr., 907/376-1211, museumofalaska.org, open Mother's Day-Labor Day), which preserves all the early modes of transit that helped gold seekers, fur trappers, and other Western pioneers forge a path into the state.

Two of the best adventure outfitters in town offer multiday, small-group soft adventure tours throughout Southcentral Alaska, with packages that include lodging, transport, and many meals. You can't go wrong with **Alaskan Tour Guides** (800/795-1438 or 907/746-1438, alaskantour.com) or **Alaska Adventure Unlimited** (3750 N. Caribou St., 907/373-3494, alaskaadventureunlimited.com), which also offers some single-day trips.

Wasilla has two golf courses: the 18-hole **Settlers Bay** course (7307 S. Frontier Dr., 907/376-5466, settlersbay.com), in Alaska's only residential golf community, and the low-key, 9-hole **Sleepy Hollow** course (2721 E. Sleepy Hollow Circle, 907/376-5948, greens fees $16 adult, discounts for seniors, active military, and children).

Matanuska-Susitna Valley

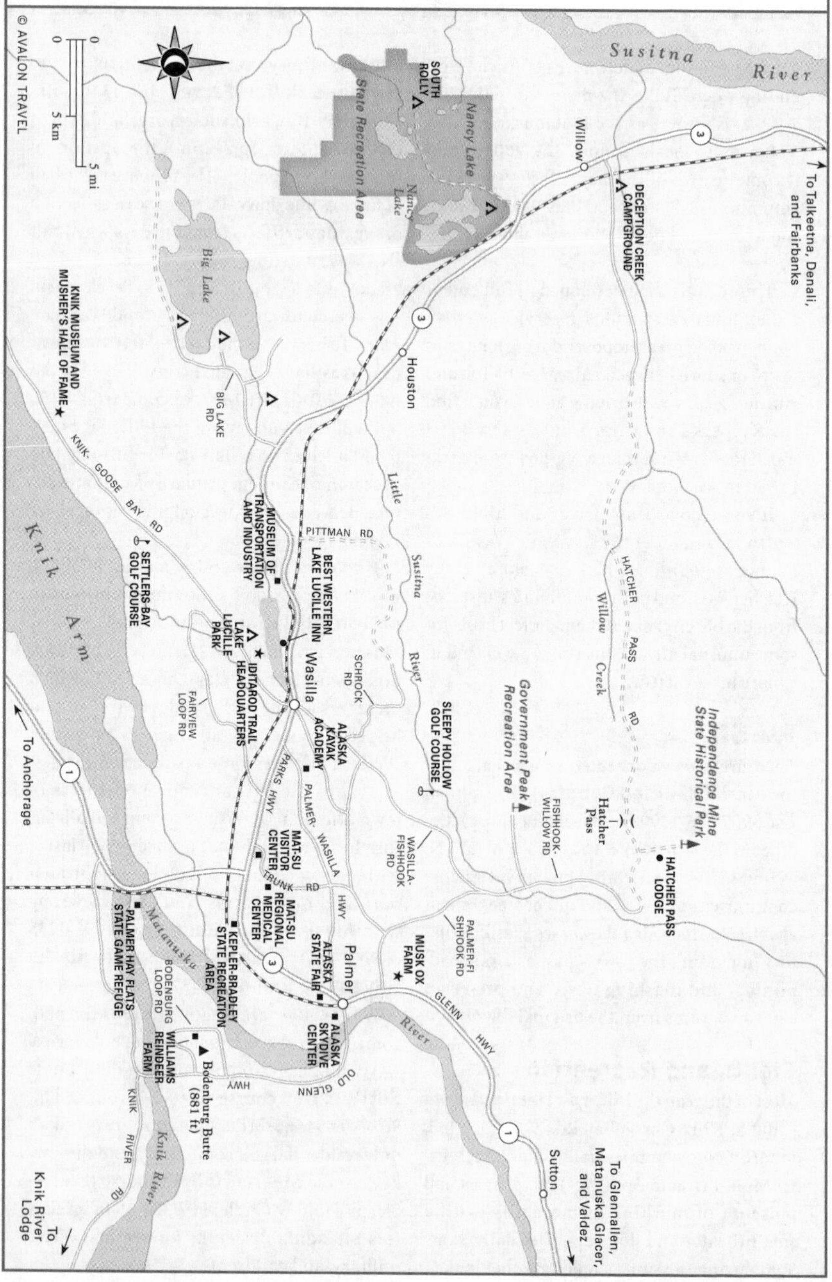

Susitna River
To Talkeetna, Denali, and Fairbanks
Willow
DECEPTION CREEK CAMPGROUND
SOUTH ROLLY
Nancy Lake State Recreation Area
Nancy Lake
Big Lake
KNIK MUSEUM AND MUSHER'S HALL OF FAME
BIG LAKE RD
Houston
Little Susitna River
KNIK-GOOSE BAY RD
SETTLERS BAY GOLF COURSE
Knik Arm
MUSEUM OF TRANSPORTATION AND INDUSTRY
PITTMAN RD
BEST WESTERN LAKE LUCILLE INN
LAKE LUCILLE PARK
IDITAROD TRAIL HEADQUARTERS
Wasilla
SCHROCK RD
FAIRVIEW LOOP RD
HATCHER PASS RD
Willow Creek
Independence Mine State Historical Park
Government Peak Recreation Area
Hatcher Pass
HATCHER PASS LODGE
FISHHOOK-WILLOW RD
SLEEPY HOLLOW GOLF COURSE
ALASKA KAYAK ACADEMY
PARKS HWY
PALMER-WASILLA HWY
WASILLA-FISHHOOK RD
To Anchorage
MAT-SU VISITOR CENTER
TRUNK RD
MAT-SU REGIONAL MEDICAL CENTER
PALMER-FISHHOOK RD
MUSK OX FARM
Palmer
ALASKA STATE FAIR
KEPLER-BRADLEY STATE RECREATION AREA
PALMER HAY FLATS STATE GAME REFUGE
Matanuska River
GLENN HWY
BODENBURG LOOP RD
ALASKA SKYDIVE CENTER
WILLIAMS REINDEER FARM
Bodenburg Butte (881 ft)
OLD GLENN HWY
KNIK RIVER RD
Knik River
Sutton
To Glennallen, Matanuska Glacer, and Valdez
To Knik River Lodge
0 5 km
0 5 mi

Food

FINE DINING

The **Grape Tap** (322 N. Boundary St., 907/376-8466, thegrapetap.com, Tues.-Thurs. 11am-9pm, Fri.-Sat. 11am-9:30pm, $36) is an elegant little wine cellar-themed restaurant with garden seating. The exquisite menu ranges from steak to roast duck, Italian, and, of course, delicious seafood.

THAI

Alaska's love affair with Thai food continues in Wasilla with **Mekong Thai** (473 W. Parks Hwy., 907/373-7690, mekongthaicuisine.com, $16). Their food is some of the best in the state, but their hours are somewhat limited—typically 11am-3pm and 5pm-9pm on most days of the week, but it's best to call or check Facebook before going.

SANDWICHES

Krazy Moose Subs (405 E. Herning Ave., 907/357-8774, Tues.-Fri. 10:30am-6pm, Sat. 10:30am-4pm) is an old-fashioned sandwich shop and enormous community favorite; you can't go wrong with the subs, and the cookies are great too.

GROCERIES

Wasilla has plenty of big-box stores; you'll have no problem getting inexpensive groceries (by Alaska standards, anyway) at both **Fred Meyer** (1501 E. Parks Hwy., 907/352-5000, daily 7am-11pm, may expand hours in summer) and **Carrs** (which is really Safeway; 595 E. Parks Hwy., 907/352-1100, daily 24 hours). Fred Meyer's prices tend to be slightly lower than at Carrs.

Accommodations

Wasilla's highest-end hotel is the lakefront **Best Western Lake Lucille Inn** (907/373-1776, bestwesternlakelucilleinn.com, from $162), which includes a fully equipped fitness club with a sauna and jacuzzi. Note: Not all the rooms have lake views, and it's not always clear from the website which is which—so if you want to see the water, it's best to make your reservations over the phone.

If you'd like to save a few dollars—both on the hotel rate and by cooking for yourself—**Alaska's Select Inn Hotel** (888/357-4768 or 907/357-4768, alaskaselectinn.com, from $149) offers similarly clean, comfortable rooms with fully equipped kitchens.

Services

You'll find plenty of gas and service stations dotted throughout Wasilla, and cellular coverage is excellent here on all providers in the state. Small medical clinics can provide non-emergency services. Hospital services are provided by **Mat-Su Regional Medical Center** (2500 S. Woodworth Loop, 907/861-6000, matsuregional.com) in Palmer, which covers a service area of more than 23,000 square miles.

Transportation

Wasilla is just 44 miles or about a 50-minute drive from Anchorage, first on the Glenn Highway (Alaska Route 1) and then the Parks Highway (Alaska Route 3). If you're coming from farther south on the Kenai Peninsula, this can be a good midway stop on the way to Denali National Park, which is 195 miles and about 3.5 hours farther north on the Parks Highway.

You can also get here on the **Alaska Railroad** train (800/544-0552, alaskarailroad.com) from Anchorage, Talkeetna, Fairbanks, or Denali National Park; the railroad offers daily service in summer and weekend service during the winter.

The **Valley Mover** bus system (907/892-8800, valleymover.org) offers transit between Anchorage and several park-and-ride lots in Wasilla, aimed primarily at commuters; a day pass costs $7, or $5 for a one-way trip. You'll definitely want a car to get around this region, although there's extremely limited bus service (Mon.-Fri. only) among Matanuska Valley destinations, including a few trips between Palmer and Wasilla; see **Mat-Su Community Transit** (907/864-5000, matsutransit.com) for details.

Speaking of commuters; there are a lot of them, and since there's only the one highway route in and out of Wasilla, one accident or stalled vehicle is all it takes to slow traffic to a crawl. Avoid driving (or riding the bus) during rush hour traffic, which extends roughly 7am-8:30am and 4:30pm-6pm, if at all possible.

TOP EXPERIENCE

Hatcher Pass

The unpaved road up to Hatcher Pass usually doesn't open until July, but it's well worth the wait. Hatcher Pass is not a community, but rather exactly what the name suggests: a pass or low point that allows easy passage between two mountain peaks, and one of very few places in Alaska where you can get sweeping views over tundra-clad peaks—seemingly into infinity—while standing right beside your car. For the most part there are no services, and part of the road to the pass is unpaved, with switchbacks, occasional potholes, and no guardrail. However, passenger cars can make the drive with no problem, and you just can't beat Hatcher Pass when it comes to roadside scenery.

Along the way to the pass you'll drive past **Independence Mine State Historical Park** (907/745-2827 for the seasonal visitor center, mid-June to Labor Day as weather allows, $5 day use parking fee), where you can wander a winding footpath among the historical mining camp, where the buildings are all decked out with interpretive signs to help you understand what you're looking at. If you're at all a fan of mining history, this is well worth a stop. A small visitor center and museum just before you start down the trail between buildings has displays on mining in this area (which began more than a decade before the Klondike Gold Rush). This mine produced almost $6 million worth of gold (in early 1900s dollars; it would be more than quadruple that in today's dollars) before gold mining was halted by World War II.

Also obvious from the road will be the A-frame cabins of **Hatcher Pass Lodge** (907/745-1200, hatcherpasslodge.com, from $135 for a private cabin; you'll have to go to the main lodge to use the bathroom). The cabins are very quaint but adequate; it's the location that's the real draw, both for summer sightseeing and winter skiing. In fact the entire region is very popular for sledding, snowboarding, and cross-country skiing, although parts of Hatcher Pass are subject to avalanche hazard, and this is a completely unmaintained area, so you shouldn't recreate here unless you know how to evaluate conditions for avalanche safety.

Independence Mine State Historical Park

While driving to the pass you'll also go by the trailheads for several excellent hikes, including the charming and family-friendly two-mile round-trip trek to **Gold Cord Lake,** where you might see marmots, grounds squirrels, and of course other wildlife including bears, and the turnoff to **Reed Lakes,** an 11-mile round-trip hike that rewards those willing to hop car-sized boulders with pristine blue-green lakes set against glacier-sculpted granite peaks.

To get to Hatcher Pass, take Fishhook Road out of either Palmer or Wasilla (the pass lies between them), or take Trunk Road north from the Parks Highway (before you reach Wasilla) and then follow signs onto Fishhook Road from there. There's limited but adequate parking at the summit, with sweeping views out over Palmer behind you.

A moderately challenging 2.5-mile round-trip hiking trail called **April Bowl** starts just across the road, taking you up a series of switchbacks to a short ridgewalk to the top of Hatch Peak, which only magnifies the lovely views. This hike gives one of the biggest returns on effort in terms of views, but there's an easier outing at the next parking lot, just down the road, where you can take an easy, mostly level stroll around a small lake.

PALMER

Palmer is a farming town—no matter which direction you're coming from, it's hard to miss the massive fields on either side of the road. The flat, fertile land here became Southcentral's center of agriculture thanks in part to a "colony experiment" that moved settlers here from Michigan, Minnesota, and Wisconsin.

You can learn more about this unusual part of Alaska's history in Palmer's refurbished 1935 **Colony House Museum** (316 E. Elmwood Ave., palmerhistoricalsociety.org, summer Tues.-Sat. 10am-4pm, winter tours by appointment, $2 adults). The **Palmer Visitor Information Center**, located inside the **Palmer Museum of History and Art** (723 S. Valley Way, 907/746-7668, palmermuseum.org, free) lets you get any questions answered and take a deeper view into the town's history at the same time, with exhibits on the original colony farms, historical farm equipment, contemporary art, and Palmer's sister city in Japan. One of the biggest highlights for many visitors is the replicas of the giant farm vegetables grown in the Matanuska Valley; the record cabbages for any given year often grow to over 100 pounds, but the other vegetables—including enormous zucchini—are no less impressive.

looking out over April Bowl in Hatcher Pass

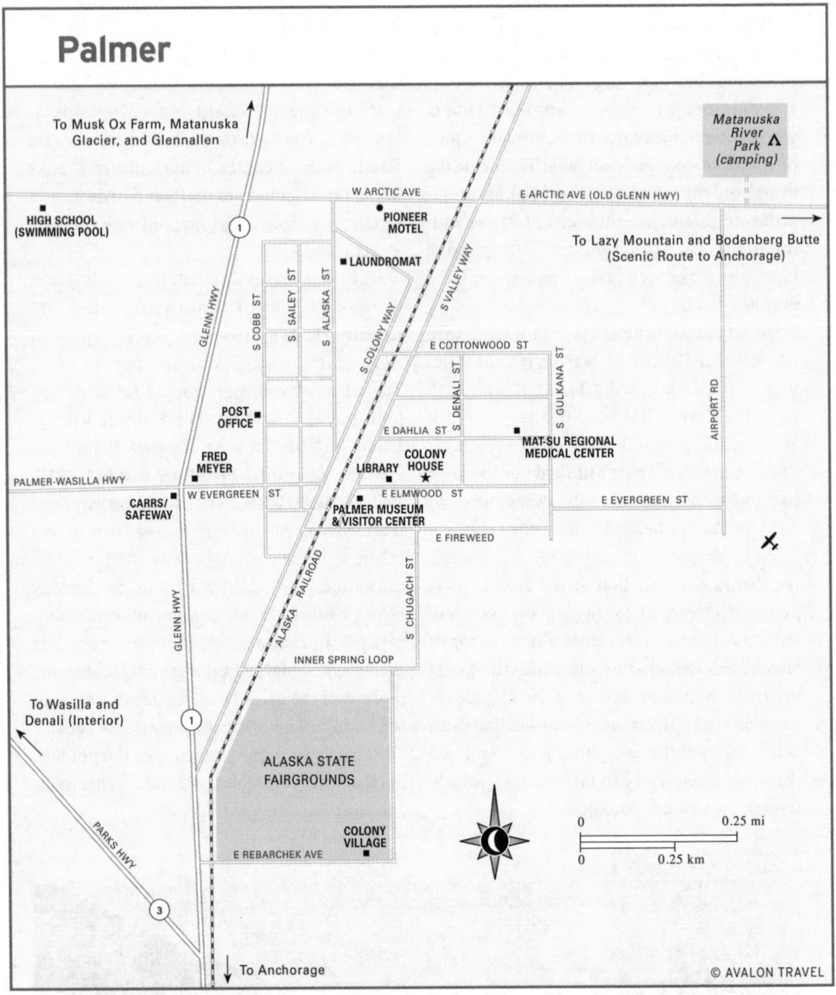

Palmer

Palmer houses two very unusual modern-day farms: At the **Williams Reindeer Farm** (5561 S. Bodenburg Loop, 907/745-4000, reindeerfarm.com, tours offered May-Sept., $9 adults, $7 children), you can take a short walking tour right into the middle of a herd of docile reindeer (domesticated caribou); feed the reindeer, elk, or bison; and cuddle quite a few smaller animals, including chickens and rabbits. They also offer horseback trail rides up a private portion of nearby Bodenburg Butte.

At the **Musk Ox Farm** (12850 E. Archie Rd., 907/745-4151, muskoxfarm.org, limited tours Sept.-Apr., $11 adults, $9 seniors, $5 children), a 45-minute walking tour shows you firsthand how qiviut, the softest, lightest, and warmest wool in the world, is produced from the fine undercoat of musk oxen.

If you'd like to see **Bodenburg Butte** yourself, you can walk right up it from a Mat-Su Borough trailhead on the north side. This diminutive bump, set amid flat fields bordered by tall mountains, offers outsize views of neighboring Pioneer and Matanuska peaks and distant Knik Glacier. The hike is about 1.5 miles and 700 feet of elevation gain one-way; the parking fee is $3 cash or check—bring a pen to fill out the envelope. Directions to the trailhead can be a little hard to find: Take the Old Glenn Highway south of Palmer 5.5 miles to North Bodenburg Loop. Turn left and follow the road 0.5 mile to Morthershead Lane, which leads to the parking lot.

If you're an adrenaline junkie, the **Alaska Skydive Center** (820 E. Airport Rd. Ste. 100, 907/715-4300, alaskaskydivecenter.com, weekends opens at 10am, weekdays by appointment), the only commercial skydiving operation in the state, offers one-off tandem skydives starting from $300.

For a more sedate but no less enjoyable day outside, Palmer offers two golf courses: The USGA handicap-rated 9-hole **Fishhook Golf Course** (2600 N. Palmer-Fishhook Rd., 907/745-7274, fishhookgolfcourse.com), just north of Palmer, and the beautifully scenic 18-hole **Palmer Golf Course** (1000 Lepak Ave., 907/745-4653, palmergolfcourse.com, greens fees from $40, half-price twilight rates), which offers views of majestic Pioneer Peak, the mighty Matanuska River, and even the Knik Glacier. The Palmer Golf Course is consistently rated among *Golf Digest*'s top five courses for the state.

Finally, if you've ever wondered what a 100-pound cabbage looks like, visit Palmer from mid-August to Labor Day for the **Alaska State Fair** (2075 Glenn Hwy., alaskastatefair.org). This isn't terribly different from state fairs the country over, but it's the only place you'll see displays of giant vegetables grown under almost 24 hours of midnight sun.

TOP EXPERIENCE

★ Matanuska Glacier

A short day trip to the northeast from Palmer, the **Matanuska Glacier** (66500 Glacier Park Rd., 907/745-2534, matanuskaglacier.biz) is the only road-access glacier with a maintained trail onto its toe. Glacier-savvy hikers can purchase walk-on access to the glacier for $25 (bring your own crampons). But if you don't know what you're doing, it's best to take a guided trip in summer or winter ($100 pp) or hire longtime local service **MICA Guides** (907/351-7587, micaguides.com, starting at $74). It's safer and you'll see—and understand—more of the glacier; this is truly a once-in-a-lifetime experience if you live in a warmer state.

the Matanuska Glacier

MICA Guides also offers two of Alaska's longest, fastest ziplines through partner company **Glacier View Adventures** (Mile 99 Glenn Hwy., 907/351-7587, glacierviewadventures.com): The 1,500-foot Nitro reaches speeds of 30-40 mph (max weight 235 pounds), and the 2,200-foot G2 dual zip lets you race a friend at speeds up to 45 to 60 mph (max weight 285 pounds). Save by booking both a glacier trip and a zipline. You can also enjoy a truly unusual Alaska experience by booking into one of their canvas "glamping" tents (from $100).

If you don't want to buy access to the Matanuska Glacier itself, stop by the **Matanuska Glacier State Recreation Site** at mile 101 of the Glenn Highway; you'll find 12 campsites ($15; six are for tents only) and a loop trail that overlooks the glacier, with interpretive signs that showcase glacial geology along with a surprisingly sly sense of humor. Day-use parking costs $5, cash or check; bring a pen to fill out the fee envelope.

Food

CAFÉS AND BISTROS

A true local favorite, **Turkey Red Bistro** (550 S. Alaska St., 907/746-5544, turkeyredak.com, Mon.-Sat. 7am-9pm, $20) offers hearty, wholesome Mediterranean-inspired dishes for breakfast, lunch, and dinner, plus baked goods using fresh, locally sourced ingredients whenever possible.

PIZZA

The wildly creative pizza pies at **Humdinger's Gourmet Pizza Co** (173 S. Valley Way, 907/745-7499, humdingerspizza.com) run the gamut from Thai-inspired to Wisconsin cheese, a sweet cherry bomb pizza, and the Chinese-themed General Tso's Revenge.

STEAK

The oddly named **Inn Cafe** (325 E. Elmwood Ave., 907/746-6118, Mon.-Sat. 11am-9pm, Sun. 11am-7pm, $15-35) is actually a quiet little steakhouse that earns rave reviews for its sandwiches and seafood too, all reasonably priced by Alaska standards.

BREWERIES

Almost every town in Alaska has its own craft brewery; in Palmer, it's the very popular **Arkose Brewery** (650 E. Steel Loop, 907/746-2337, arkosebrewery.com, Mon.-Sat. noon-7pm). Free tours are offered sporadically—call for days and times—or you can belly up to the bar and try one of their brews. No food is served, but you're welcome to bring your own.

GROCERIES

There are two big-box grocery stores in Palmer: **Fred Meyer** (650 N. Cobb St., 907/761-4200, daily 7am-11pm) and **Carrs/Safeway** (664 W. Evergreen Ave., 907/761-1400, daily 5am-1am). If all goes as planned, the Fred Meyer store will be moving just a few blocks down the street in March of 2017.

Accommodations

Make the most of the MatSu Valley's quiet ambience by staying in the delightful **Alaska's Harvest Bed and Breakfast** (2252 N. Love Dr., 907/745-4263, from $119), just two miles out of town. Each room comes complete with a kitchenette and complimentary continental breakfast, but it's the big, cozy, comfortable rooms and beautiful grounds that really capture visitors' attention.

If you'd like to stay for a while, the **Knik River Lodge** (29979 E. Knik River Rd., 877/745-4575 or 907/745-5002, knikriverlodge.com, from $135) makes the perfect base for adventure travel, or for just enjoying your stay in a gorgeous mountain setting that feels remote, even though it's just a short drive from Palmer. The rustic cabins are rustic but not at all rough, with comfortable beds and en suite bathrooms; Wi-Fi is available in the main lodge. Outdoor excursions include helicopter flightseeing over the mighty Knik Glacier, dogsledding, skiing, hiking, and kayaking amid icebergs in a glacier lake, with fine dining in the on-site **Raven's Perch Restaurant.**

Services

You'll find plenty of gas and service stations throughout Palmer, which also houses the **Mat-Su Regional Medical Center** (2500 S. Woodworth Loop, 907/861-6000, matsuregional.com), whose 24-hour emergency room serves patients over a 23,000-square-mile area. (Often, patients are brought to the hospital by air ambulance.)

Cell service is excellent, and Wi-Fi can be had in any coffee shop with a purchase; you may also be able to get free Wi-Fi in Fred Meyer (650 N. Cobb St.) and Carrs (664 W. Evergreen Ave.).

Transportation

The only really feasible way of visiting Palmer is by car. It's just a short drive northeast of Anchorage, 43 miles or about 50 minutes on the Glenn Highway, a.k.a. Alaska Route 1. Quite a few workers commute between Palmer and Anchorage on this mostly two-lane highway, so try to avoid the typical rush hours of 7am-8:30am and 4:30pm-6pm whenever possible. Palmer is 275 miles or a five-hour drive southwest of Tok, the first community you hit as you're driving into Alaska from Canada.

There is a railroad depot in Palmer, but it's only infrequently used for passenger trains. **Mat-Su Community Transit** (907/864-5000, matsutransit.com) offers some extremely limited bus service in both Wasilla and Palmer, but in all truth, you really need a car to get around this part of the state.

EKLUTNA HISTORICAL PARK

Eklutna is a tiny Dena'ina Athabascan (Alaska Native) village, with an estimated population of about 70. Despite its small size, this community hosts one of the most interesting attractions in all of Southcentral: The **Eklutna Historical Park** (26640 Eklutna Village Rd., mid-May-mid-Sept., Mon.-Fri. 10am-5pm, $5 adults, 11 and under free, discounts for youth and seniors). Don't miss the guided walking tour that teaches about how the Dena'ina have blended their cultural customs together with those of the Russian Orthodox church. Your tour will include a visit to a historical (and very unusual) "log house" Russian Orthodox cathedral, the new Orthodox church that replaced it, and the colorful, sometimes amazingly realistic spirit houses, which are small structures built over graves to shelter the spirits of the dead and ease their journey into the afterlife.

The Seward Highway

If you have a rental car, make time to drive south of Anchorage along the Seward Highway. (You can't miss it—this is the *only* road that leads south out of town.) This National Scenic Byway offers sweeping views of beautiful mountains and seaside scenery, Alaska-style; depending on the season, it can be full-on summer at highway level while snow- and glacier-clad peaks loom in the near distance.

Perhaps one of the most amazing things about this drive—after the phenomenal views, of course—is that for almost its entire length, you're driving through the protected public lands of first Chugach National Park, then Chugach National Forest and Kenai National Wildlife Refuge. That makes for a profusion of beautiful scenery, surprising wildlife viewing opportunities (keep an eye out for Dall sheep and mountain goats on the cliffs), too many lovely wooded campgrounds to list (almost all first-come, first-served, with nightly fees of $15 or less and plenty of space for both RVs and tent campers), and lots of great hiking trails too.

Sightings of bears and moose along the highway are relatively rare, but they can happen. You're more likely to see eagles soaring

Northwestern Kenai Peninsula

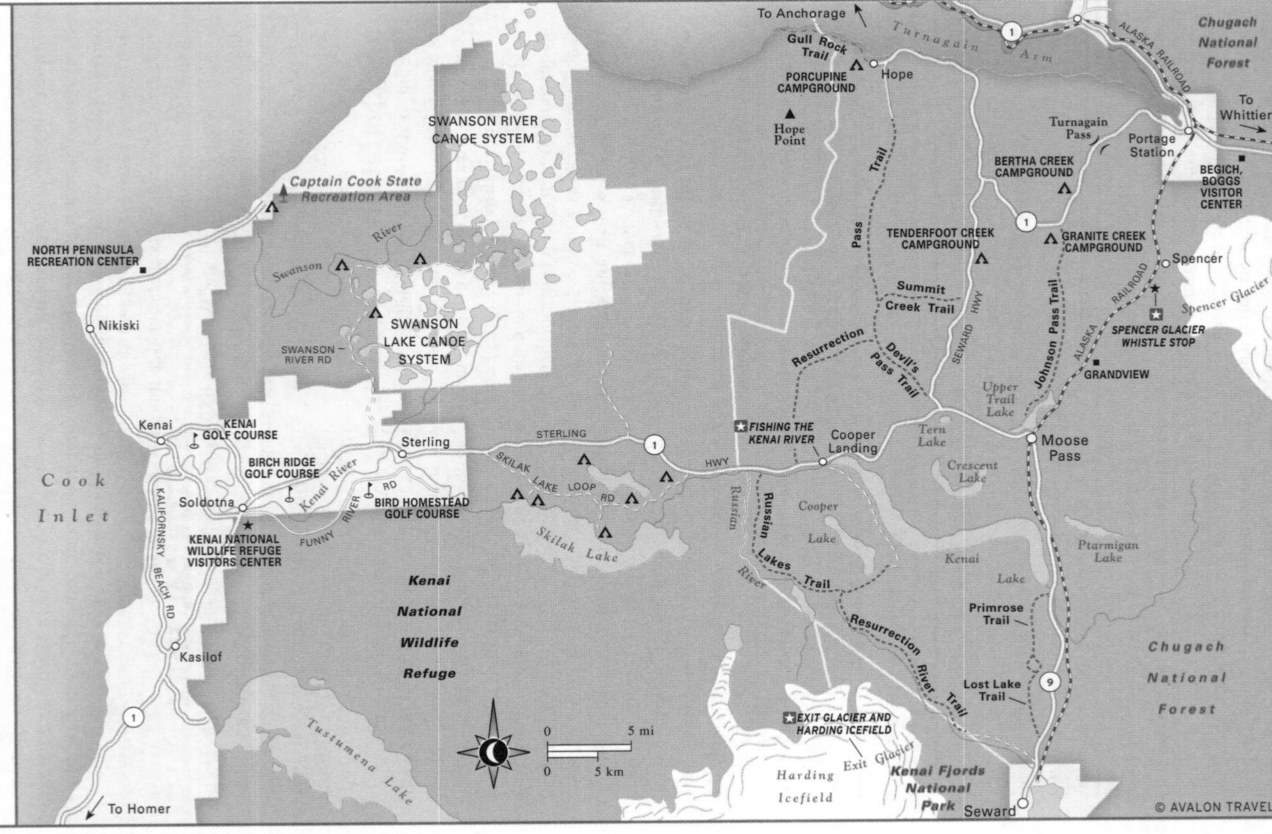

high above the land and water, though, so if you're really set on viewing one, bring your binoculars and pull over at either the **McHugh Creek** picnic area (mile 111 of the Seward Highway) or the **Bird Creek** parking lot (mile 101.6) and scan the skies and nearby trees. It might take a while, but you're sure to eventually see an eagle or two, along with raucous ravens.

TOP EXPERIENCE

DRIVING THE SEWARD HIGHWAY

This narrow, two-lane highway is as dangerous as it is beautiful. Crowds of lumbering RVs and passenger vehicles that slow to take in the views induce travelers in a rush to either tailgate dangerously or, even worse, pass on the many blind corners. Do yourself and everybody else on the road a favor; when you just can't help but slow down to admire the views, pull off to one of the many rest stops instead. And if you have more than five cars stacked up behind you, pull over to let them pass. It's the law (albeit a very poorly enforced one).

The following mile markers (paired with distances from Anchorage) mark the turnoffs to notable communities along the highway. Roadside mile markers start in the coastal town of Seward (mile 0) and continue all the way to Anchorage (mile 127). For a detailed breakdown of mile-by-mile attractions on this and other Alaska highways, the very best reference is *The Milepost* (themilepost.com).

- **Mile marker 90,** 37 miles from Anchorage: Turnoff for the Alyeska Highway, which leads into **Girdwood** (see page 172).
- **Mile marker 80,** 48 miles from Anchorage: Turnoff for the Whittier/Portage Access Road (see pages 176 and 174).
- **Mile marker 56,** 71 miles from Anchorage: Turnoff for the 15-mile cutoff road to the tiny seaside community of **Hope** (see page 179).
- **Mile marker 37,** 90 miles from Anchorage: Turnoff for the Sterling Highway, which leads southwest to **Soldotna, Kenai,** and the blissful seaside haven of **Homer** (page 200 and page 211).
- **Mile marker 29,** 99 miles from Anchorage: The tiny community of **Moose Pass,** population about 200 (page 180).
- **Mile marker 0,** 127 miles from Anchorage: Welcome to **Seward** (page 181)!

the Seward Highway

THE ALASKA RAILROAD

I absolutely love riding trains, so I spend an inordinate amount of time talking about them with others, both locals and visitors alike. Without fail, almost everybody I've spoken to says that one of the Alaska Railroad's routes—the **Coastal Classic,** which runs from Anchorage to Girdwood to Seward—is their favorite. They love that it lets you see almost all the same beauty you'd get while on the Seward Highway—but since you're not driving, you can just sit back and take everything in.

The Coastal Classic also takes you past the **Spencer Glacier Whistle Stop** (see page 136), one of the true highlights of backcountry adventure in Southcentral Alaska, although it doesn't stop there (unless a sodden, desperate camper who missed the first train through manages to wave the conductor down—it's happened before). The whistle stop is not accessible from the roadway, so you're also treated to beautiful backcountry scenery—including those views of Spencer Glacier—that you just can't see any other way.

The Coastal Classic train makes an early start out of Anchorage—usually about 6:45am—but gets you to Seward by roughly 11am and gives you almost seven hours to explore before it heads back. If you don't want to stay the night, you have time for a short day tour and then lunch in town before you get back on the train. For more information, contact the **Alaska Railroad** (800/544-0552, alaskarailroad.com).

CHUGACH STATE PARK

This massive, 495,000-acre park and its 280-plus miles of trails don't receive a lot of attention because it wraps around the state's biggest city, but if you're looking for a quick day hike into beautiful backcountry scenery, you can't beat the access from this park's many trailheads. Excellent hiking guides cover different aspects of this area, although all of them are unfortunately a bit dated: *55 Ways to the Wilderness in Southcentral Alaska,* by Helen D. Nienhueser and John Wolfe Jr., does the best job of highlighting the best trails throughout all of Southcentral, while *50 Hikes Around Anchorage* focuses on opportunities closer to town. (Full disclosure: I wrote that last one.)

Hiking

Chugach State Park has so many trails and recreation sites, it's almost dizzying. The following are some of the best (and easiest for

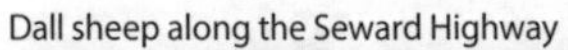
Dall sheep along the Seward Highway

visitors to navigate). Unless otherwise noted, you'll need to pay a $5 per day parking fee; with very few exceptions there is nobody to make change, so bring cash or a check and a pen to fill out the pay envelope.

EKLUTNA LAKE

This massive, blue-green lake is the drinking water reservoir for the city of Anchorage and a favorite place for locals to play. There's a small rental shop run by **Lifetime Adventures** (907/746-4644, lifetimeadventure.net). They offer bikes to explore the broad, 11-mile lakeside trail (ATVs are allowed Sun.-Wed., and riders are usually courteous) and kayaks to paddle the lake. If you're paddling, aim for a calm morning; the lake almost always gets breezy in the afternoon, making the paddle back to shore a lot more difficult. There's also a very nice campground for both RVs and tents; it's first-come, first-served and has no cell service.

Get there by driving 25 miles northeast of Anchorage on the Glenn Highway, then taking the marked turnoff for Eklutna Lake; from there, it's another 15 miles to the lake on a narrow, shoulderless, and winding access road with very few pullouts or turnaround points. If you're driving a big rig, you're going to be committed to going the whole distance before you can turn around.

On the drive in to Eklutna Lake (or perhaps on the way out), make sure you visit **Rochelle's Ice Cream Shop** (37501 Eklutna Lake Rd., 907/688-6201). This seasonal shop (open roughly Memorial Day to Labor Day) is a favorite stop for locals celebrating successful adventures or planning new ones; you can get Alaska-made ice cream or a few other simple foods, like hot dogs and a selection of drinks, and an attached small general store sells firewood and basic camping supplies/travel essentials.

One of the most striking trails is the strenuous but rewarding **Twin Peaks Trail,** which leads 2.5 miles one-way straight up from the lake, giving you a couple of beautiful lookouts over the sprawling lake before ending at an oddly placed observation bench; on a clear day, it should give you views of both East and West Twin Peaks, whose crumbling stone massifs look like they come straight out of Mordor. The ambitious can continue on a well-defined (but unmarked) trail that heads to another overlook of the sprawling lake; a turnoff about 100 feet before that, marked by a large stone cairn, leads up a series of rolling ridges to 5,450-foot Pepper Peak.

a kayak on the shore of Eklutna Lake

Wildfires

As you drive or hike past the McHugh Creek area, you'll see some evidence of a 2016 forest fire that was ignited by an illegal campfire. The area's high winds and rough terrain made it incredibly difficult for crews to fight the fire. Their heroic efforts, combined with the terrain (a double-edged sword that also, fortunately, routed the flames into areas with minimal fuel) finally did contain it—but not before it terrified members of nearby communities, who were rightly worried that the fire might breach their only access road before they had time to evacuate.

More significantly in terms of sheer numbers, the fire was just a couple of ridgelines from sweeping down into the highly forested—and highly flammable—"Hillside" neighborhoods that form part of the Anchorage bowl. Those burn marks are a sobering reminder that even in the state's biggest city, we're still ruled by nature's whim, and the profusion of black spruce trees—a tree that actually needs fire to complete its reproductive cycle, so it goes up like a torch at the slightest touch of flames—makes communities in much of Southcentral and the Interior especially vulnerable.

You can see the dramatic remains of larger fires both north and south of Anchorage. On your way north past Wasilla to Denali, watch for the scorched remains of black spruce on either side of the highway, standing silent sentinel to the 2015 Sockeye fire, which burned 18 square miles of land, destroyed 55 homes in the tiny community of Willow, and cost more than $8 million to suppress.

South of Anchorage, the most devastating fire in recent memory was the 2014 Funny River fire, which burned more than 300 square miles and threatened the small communities of Kasilof, Funny River, and Sterling, along with road access to the entire Kenai Peninsula. (Remember, there's just the one road—the Seward Highway—that goes in and out.)

All three of the fires were human caused, so if there's one big takeaway, it's to please follow rules about having campfires only in designated, permanent fire rings; putting your fires out responsibly (if it's too hot to touch, it's too hot to leave unattended; and understanding that if fires are banned completely during particularly dry or windy conditions, it's for the safety of all of us.

THUNDERBIRD FALLS

This trail is only one mile each way, and almost anybody can handle the broad path and its rolling hills. If the viewing deck over the falls isn't close enough for you, an established footpath will take you right down to the pool at its bottom. There are also quite a few precipitous drop-offs in this area, so make sure to stick to the established pathways. Get there by driving 27 miles northeast of Anchorage on the Glenn Highway, then taking the marked exit for Thunderbird Falls.

EAGLE AND SYMPHONY LAKES

Sometimes referred to as the **South Fork Trail,** this 12-mile, mostly flat round-trip hike roughly parallels South Fork Eagle River on the way to glacier-fed **Eagle Lake** and snowmelt-fed **Symphony Lake;** it's one of the most spectacular trails that's still within easy reach of the road system, and on a sunny weekend day there are enough people on the trail to make even the most nervous hiker feel confident. Because of their different water sources, each lake is a drastically different color: Eagle Lake is a milky turquoise, while Symphony Lake is the deepest blue.

To get there, drive 11 miles northeast of Anchorage on the Glenn Highway. Take the marked exit for Hiland Road and turn right onto Hiland, following it through several name changes until it meets West River Drive.

TURNAGAIN ARM TRAIL

This 9.2-mile (one-way) walk parallels a chunk of the Seward Highway, south of Anchorage, at a respectable distance. It may not be the wildest stretch of trail in Southcentral, but it's one of the most convenient, especially if you have more than one car at your disposal and can arrange a shuttle between the trail's four trailheads. Even if you just go out and back from one of the trailheads, though, the trail offers pretty viewpoints over the water and glimpses into the changing character of the land along the highway, and being close to the road helps keep it within most peoples' comfort level.

The four trailheads are, in order as you depart Anchorage: Potter (mile marker 115), McHugh Creek (mile marker 112), Rainbow (mile marker 108), and Windy Corner, often just called Windy (mile marker 106).

Note: Even though this trail is close to town, bear and moose encounters are very common; in fact, the stretch from Potter to McHugh is consistently one of the "beariest" places I've ever hiked, despite the relatively high foot traffic there. So, always be on your best bear behavior.

BIRD RIDGE

Another very pretty—but very challenging—trail in Chugach State Park is called **Bird Ridge.** The trail, which starts from either of two trailheads at miles 102.1 and 101.6 of the Seward Highway, gains 3,400 feet of elevation in just 2.5 miles. In return for your hard work, you get amazing views out over the inlet and, yes, very good chances of seeing birds—especially eagles—soaring along Turnagain Arm.

BIRD TO GIRD TRAIL

For a gentler outing, walk or pedal a rented bike on the paved, multiuse **Bird to Gird** trail, which actually runs from the tiny roadside community of Indian (mile marker 103.8) to the ski town of Girdwood.

TURNAGAIN ARM

For its first 45 miles or so, the Seward Highway follows a body of water called Turnagain Arm. This narrow finger of water is part of Cook Inlet (named for Captain James Cook, the first European to venture here); because he had to turn his ship again to get out, it was named "River Turnagain," then "Turnagain Arm." Gold was found here in 1896, a year before the well-known Klondike Gold Rush; some of the tiny towns still in existence along the arm were gold rush communities, founded on the banks of the gold-bearing creeks that flowed into Turnagain Arm.

Keep an eye out for **belugas**—small white whales—in the waters of Turnagain Arm. (The juveniles are dark gray.) The belugas often follow salmon, eulachon, and other fish up the arm to feed. Another fascinating characteristic of the arm is its bore tides. Alaska has one of the highest tidal differentials in the world; when the incoming tide comes roaring up the narrow, constricted arm, it creates a standing wave that travels the entire distance and may be a few inches tall or measure up to 10 feet. Roadside pullouts near Girdwood are one of the best places to watch this phenomenon—they get you closer to the water than the better-known viewing points like Beluga Point and Bird Point—and you might also see windsurfers, paddleboarders, and kayakers turning out to ride the wave all the way up the arm.

Beware the Mudflats

When the tide goes out on Cook Inlet, Turnagain Arm, and elsewhere in coastal Alaska, you'll see wide, flat plains of mud that had been concealed by the water. That mud looks and feels solid when the tide is out, but it's made of fine, silty particles that turn to quicksand as the water table rises; it's all too easy to get stuck before you realize what's going on.

Every year, somebody has to be rescued when they disregard posted warning signs, wander out into the mud flats, and become trapped. People have died because the tide came in faster than the rescue equipment could reach them, or by succumbing to the very cold water temperatures before they could be rescued. I can't think of a worse way to go, so please take those warning signs seriously and stay off the flats altogether.

GIRDWOOD

This funky little ski town, about 35 miles (a 45-minute drive) south of Anchorage on the Seward Highway, is a favorite getaway for locals and tourists alike. Much of the town's activity centers around its ski resort, **Alyeska Resort** (1000 Arlberg Ave., 907/754-2111, alyeskaresort.com, from $339), which also happens to be everybody's favorite place to stay in town, thanks to amenities like its luxurious day spa and fitness center, saltwater swimming pool, and a 60-passenger aerial tram that whisks you up 2,300 feet in elevation, almost all the way to the peak of 3,939-foot Mount Alyeska (tram tickets $25 adults, discounts for seniors, children, students, and military; free with hotel stay or Seven Glaciers reservations). If you make it up the challenging 2.2-mile North Face hiking trail, which traces a meandering path from the lower tram terminal to the upper terminal, you can ride the tram down for free.

Sights and Recreation

A very popular hiking trail, the six-mile round-trip **Winner Creek Trail,** also starts at Alyeska Resort and leads to a hand-powered tram over roaring Winner Creek. Make it over that and you'll pop out at a well-marked trailhead on the road to **Crow Creek Mine** (Mile 2.7 Crow Creek Rd., 907/229-3105, crowcreekmine.com, gold panning $20/day, discounts for children, seniors, and military), also accessible from Girdwood, where you can still try your hand at gold panning; two-hour guided tours are also available.

The very end of Crow Creek Road also serves as the trailhead for the **Crow Pass Trail,** a 21-mile hike from here to the Eagle River Nature Center, northeast of Anchorage. If you do only one hike in Girdwood, it should be the first four miles of this trail to overlooks of the Raven Glacier and the Crow Pass public-use cabin, which you can reserve if you're very lucky and plan six months in advance. If you're thinking of doing the entire hike, plan carefully: This is one of the hottest rescue spots for the Alaska Mountain Rescue Group, primarily because of hikers who weren't prepared to handle a swift, wide river crossing and backcountry travel in brushy bear country with limited visibility.

During the summer, Alyeska Resort offers lift-assisted **mountain biking** on a slowly expanding network of groomed trails. By winter, it's in full swing as the state's premier **ski and snowboarding** resort. Lift tickets cost $15-80, depending on time of day and how high up you're riding, with sizable discounts for seniors, military, children, and students. Other popular winter pursuits are **cross-country skiing** on the rolling flats in Girdwood

the upper tram terminal on Mount Alyeska, seen from the North Face hiking trail

proper and snowshoeing in Moose Meadows (look for a park sign on the left as you drive up the Alyeska Highway toward Alyeska Resort).

Flightseeing is a spectacular way to see any part of Alaska. Traveling in a helicopter with **Alpine Air Alaska** (907/783-2360, alpineairalaska.com) makes it extra special because you can and do land almost anywhere, including glacier landings to hike or take a dogsledding excursion in the middle of the summer. Prices start at $270 per person for a 30-minute flightseeing tour and $519 per person for a glacier dog-sledding adventure.

If you're in Girdwood in the winter, you can take a spectacular snowmachine tour with **Glacier City Snowmobile Tours** (877/783-5566, 907/783-5566, snowtours.net); they visit glaciers and old gold mines, or simply tour Alaska's beautiful winter mountains. Prices start at $200 per person for the gold mine tour.

Food

Most dining in Girdwood revolves around the Alyeska Resort, too. The downhill part of the resort contains the **Sitzmark Bar and Grill** (100 Olympic Mountain Loop, 907/754-2111, thesitzmark.com, summer Fri.-Sun. noon-late, expanded winter hours, $14), which serves good pub fare along with famously packed live music shows. At the upper tram terminal you can enjoy fine dining in the **Seven Glaciers** restaurant (907/754-2237, alyeskaresort.com, summer opens daily at 5pm, winter Fri.-Sun. noon-10pm, $50), grab a snack at the cafeteria-style **Bore Tide Deli** (907/754-2111, alyeskaresort.com, late May-mid-Sept. deli daily 11am-5pm, bar noon-8pm, reduced winter weekday hours), or cozy up to the bar. A popular breakfast and lunch place in town is *also* in Alyeska Resort: **Java Haus** (104 Arlberg Ave., 907/783-2827, girdwoodjava.com, $10).

That said, there are some very nice restaurants in and around Girdwood, each with its own distinctive style of cuisine. **Jack Sprat** (165 Olympic Mountain Loop, 907/783-5225, jacksprat.net, Mon.-Fri. 5pm-10pm, Sat.-Sun. 10am-10pm, $21-38) offers international cuisine for both meat eaters and vegans; the menu features organic ingredients, humanely raised meats, and lots of local, sustainably caught seafood. **The Bake Shop** (194 Olympic Mountain Loop, 907/783-2831, thebakeshop.com, summer daily 7am-7pm, winter closed Tues.-Wed.) is one of Girdwood's favorite restaurants, famous for its bread bowls of soup and giant sweet rolls.

New Orleans cuisine in Alaska might seem counterintuitive, but the **Double Musky Inn** (Mile 0.3 Crow Creek Rd., 907/783-2822, doublemuskyinn.com) in Girdwood offers expensive and expansive portions of authentic cuisine made with fresh Alaska seafood.

near Crow Pass, in the mountains near Girdwood

The summer-only **Turnagain Arm Pit BBQ** (Mile 103 Seward Hwy. in Indian, north of Girdwood, 907/202-8393, turnagainarm-pitbbq.com) produces some of Alaska's best barbecue ribs; if you miss the chance to taste them at this location, the company has a year-round restaurant in Anchorage (3637 Old Seward Hwy., 907/202-8010).

Accommodations

If you really want to get away from it all, head for **Alyeska Hideaway** (164 Doran Ln., 907/783-0771, alyeskahideaway.com, from $200 double occupancy), a fully furnished, 640-square-foot cabin tucked at the end of a private road in Girdwood that can accommodate up to four people.

For another beautiful, secluded getaway, book the **Hidden Creek Bed and Breakfast** (739 Vail Dr., 907/783-5557, hiddencreekbb.com, summer rates from $185). They offer three rooms with private bathrooms, while the common area includes a hot tub, an outdoor deck, and a lovely gas fireplace.

For budget travelers, **Alyeska Hostel** (227 Alta Dr., 907/783-2222, alyeskahostel.com, $25 coed bunk, private room from $60, $20 each additional person) offers the lowest rates possible in a clean, sociable environment; showers cost $5. Pets are allowed in their separate cabin rental only.

Transportation

The easiest way to get to Girdwood is, without a doubt, by driving; it's 35 miles south of Anchorage, or about a 45-minute drive once you factor in regular traffic. If you'd rather, you can ride the **Alaska Railroad** (800/544-0552, alaskarailroad.com) trains either from Anchorage (in the morning) or Seward (in the evening).

Once you're in Girdwood, you can use the town's surprisingly good (and, even more surprisingly, free) year-round bus system, **Glacier Valley Transit** (907/382-9908, glaciervalleytransit.com) to get around town and the resort campus.

PORTAGE GLACIER

Technically, Portage—about 10 miles south of Girdwood on the Seward Highway—is a ghost town. The ground it was built on sank more than 10 feet during the 1964 earthquake, swamping the town; you can still see the remains of a few old buildings poking up out of the wetlands on the water side of the highway, along with the skeletons of trees that were essentially mummified by the sudden introduction of saltwater.

That said, Portage still has one major attraction: the glacier of the same name, which unfortunately has receded far out of sight from the multimillion-dollar **Begich Boggs Visitor Center** (Portage Lake Loop, 907/783-2326, fs.usda.gov, mid-May-mid-Sept., daily 9am-6pm, $5 adults, children 5 and under free) that was built to showcase it. The recently renovated visitor center, however, is still worth a visit for its interpretive displays and video history of Chugach National Forest. From there, you can hop on one of the five daily **Portage Glacier Cruises** (800/544-2206, portageglaciercruises.com, from $39 if you provide your own transport, or $90 with transport from Anchorage) aboard the M/V *Ptarmigan,* which will take you around the corner of Portage Lake and very close to the face of the glacier.

These naturalist-narrated cruises are a favorite with visitors who've never been up close to a glacier, and truth be told they're still fun even in bad weather. The only other way to see the glacier is by making a five-mile round-trip hike over Portage Pass; the trail starts in Whittier.

The popular **Byron Glacier Trail** is an easy one-mile hike on a mostly flat, broad trail alongside a rippling creek, leading to the moraine (boulder field) left by Byron Glacier, which has retreated far up the mountainside. There's almost always an ice cave here, created by the piles of snow deposited by frequent avalanches. Explore at your own risk; such caves are always unstable, can collapse at any moment, and have injured (or killed) explorers in the past.

Portage Area

Turnagain Arm
To Anchorage
ALASKA RAILROAD DEPOT
ALASKA WILDLIFE CONSERVATION CENTER
To Seward
Portage River
Chugach National Forest
0 1 mi
0 1 km
PORTAGE HWY
ALASKA RAILROAD
ANTON ANDERSON MEMORIAL TUNNEL
BLACK BEAR
WILLIWAW
NATURE TRAIL
BEGICH, BOGGS VISITOR CENTER
Bear Valley
Explorer Glacier
Placer River Valley
Portage Lake
Portage Pass Trail
To Whittier
Byron Glacier Trail
Portage Pass
To Spencer Glacier and Grandview
Middle Glacier
Byron Glacier
SPENCER GLACIER WHISTLE STOP
Portage Glacier

following the creek to Byron Glacier near Portage

Also enormously popular is the **Trail of Blue Ice,** a five-mile trail that's mostly wide gravel, with boardwalks and bridges to get you over rushing streams as it meanders through. You'll have views of Byron, Middle, and Explorer Glaciers, plus lookouts over spawning salmon at the Williwaw Fish Viewing Platform, and lots of wildflowers along the trail. Heads up: Black bears are sighted here with some frequency. There's just one section of stairs that can present a problem for wheelchair users, who can use an alternative route along the shoulder of the road to bypass that stretch of trail.

If you'd like to stay overnight in Portage, you should be comfortable with camping. Your options are the **Black Bear Campground** (tent and car camping only), **Williwaw Campground** (tents and RVs), and the **Five Fingers Hike-In Camping Area,** all on Chugach National Forest land; they are all first come, first served, and amenities are limited to wheelchair-friendly pit toilets.

If you're staying in an RV, consider the privately owned **Portage Valley Cabins & RV Park** (365 Wyatt's Windy Rd., 877/477-8243 or 907/783-3111, portagevalleyrvpark.com), set back in the woods off Portage Glacier Road. Everything is spotless, the showers are great, the ambience is laid-back and friendly, and the owner can help you organize any day tour you like.

WHITTIER

Whittier is truly one of a kind. Almost all of the town's 200 people live in one 14-story building, Begich Towers, a 1950s Army barracks that also houses the police station, post office, health clinic, grocery store, church, and laundromat. During the harsh winters, when Whittier is lashed by high winds that also dump more than 20 feet of snow, children walk to school (which is in a separate building) through an underground tunnel.

If the idea of living like this entertains you, you should definitely take the time to visit Whittier, if only to say you've been here. You might also be interested in a book on Whittier, *The Strangest Town in Alaska,* by Alan Taylor; it's available in many bookstores and gift shops up and down the Seward and Sterling Highways. Make a whole day out of the visit if you can, though, because there's plenty of excellent hiking, sightseeing, fishing, and kayaking to be had in this little town.

Boat Tours

You can see more than two dozen glaciers from Whittier in just a few hours. Hard to believe? Weather allowing, **Phillips 26 Glacier Cruise** (907/276-8023, phillipscruises.com, early May-late Sept., from $149 pp)—which has one of the most frustratingly memorable jingles in all of Alaska's advertising history—will prove it with a five-hour cruise aboard their high-speed catamaran.

Major Marine Tours (800/764-7300 or 907/274-7300, majormarine.com, from $119 pp plus optional meal) also offers two sightseeing cruises that take you through beautiful, protected Prince William Sound to view actively calving tidewater glaciers. There's no guarantee you'll actually see a glacier calve, but your odds are very good.

For a small-scale, personalized version, consider hiring **Lazy Otter Charters** (look for the green roof near the East Boat Ramp, 800/587-6887 or 907/694-6887, lazyotter.com). They'll let you ride along on a water taxi run as they ferry trekkers or kayakers to a nearby bay, or you can book your own and combine sightseeing, beach landings, and your own paddling trip. They even offer winter glacier-viewing tours.

TOP EXPERIENCE

★ Sea Kayaking

The waters just outside Whittier are calm and protected—the perfect place for sea kayakers of all abilities to explore bays draped in glaciers and populated by humpbacks, orcas, porpoises, and other amazing Alaska wildlife. There are several excellent sea kayaking outfitters in town, including **Paddlers'**

Realm (907/350-2259, paddlersrealm.com) and **Sound Paddler** (877/472-2452, soundpaddler.com).

Both offer single-day and multiday trips, kayaking lessons, and boat rentals if you're experienced enough to handle Alaska's fast-moving tides and cold waters on your own. I recommend Paddlers' Realm for their guided multiday trips; Sound Paddler also rents stand-up paddleboards and teaches you how to use them.

Fishing

The fishing is never bad in Alaska, but out of Whittier, the fishing for halibut, salmon, lingcod, and rockfish is fabulous. Two of the best charters in town are **Crazy Rays Adventures** (1234 Harbor Circle, 907/315-5382, crazyraysak.com) and **Saltwater Excursions** (907/360-7975, saltwaterexcursions.com).

Jet Ski Tours

If you think getting up close to whales is fun on a boat, imagine doing it on a Jet Ski.

Glacier Jetski Adventures (907/830-4001, glacierjetskiadventures.com, from $299 pp) outfits you with protective dry suits and your own Sea-Doo personal watercraft before leading you into the protected, glacier-draped waters of Blackstone Bay. The tour lasts about four hours and group sizes are very limited, so make sure to reserve well in advance.

Hike Portage Pass

Whittier is home to the state's most beautiful short hike: **Portage Pass Trail,** a five-mile round-trip that takes you up and over the 800-foot pass to the shores of the lake that sits at Portage Glacier's feet. Once upon a time you could see the glacier from the visitor center in Portage (which is around the corner from the mountains to your right, as you stand facing the lake), but nowadays, this hike is the only way to see the glacier from land. Even if you only hike the first mile up to the pass, you'll be treated to stunning views of the glacier glistening in the distance and Whittier's brilliant blue Passage Canal behind you.

Although the pass here is only 800 feet high, it's known for fierce weather and brutal winds, so don't bother taking this hike on a day with bad weather. On a sunny day, however, there's nowhere else I'd want to be. The trailhead is the first right turn once you emerge on the Whittier side of the Anton Anderson Memorial Tunnel, marked by a brown Forest Access sign.

Prince William Sound provides tranquil waters that are perfect for sea kayaking.

hiking through Portage Pass, in the hills above Whittier

Food

Whittier has several small restaurants on the harbor; all serve simple dishes with some of the best (and freshest) seafood you'll ever have. My personal favorite is the seasonal **Swiftwater Seafood Cafe** (907/472-2550, swiftwaterseafoodcafe.com, Sun.-Thurs. 11:30am-9pm and Fri.-Sat. 11:30am-10pm starting in mid-May). The same family owns **Varley's Ice Cream and Pizza Parlor** (907/472-2547), which sells pizza by the slice, milk shakes, ice cream, and a small selection of gifts.

Accommodations

You can stay in Begich Towers, just like the locals, if you rent from **June's Whittier Condo Suites** (100 Kenai St. #1506, 907/472-6001, juneswhittiercondosuites.com, $155-450), which are on the top two floors, with stunning views over the water and mountains. You don't need the tower's address; this is the only tall building still in use. The other tall building in town is the Buckner Building, an obviously dilapidated concrete ruin that has been fenced off to keep people from getting hurt in it.

For a more conventional hotel experience, head for the **Inn at Whittier** (5A Harbor Loop Rd., 907/472-3200, innatwhittier.com, from $179), where every clean, spacious room has a view of either mountains or water. If you get stuck on the wrong side of the Anton Anderson Memorial Tunnel when it closes for the night and just want a cheap place to lay your head, you can book at the **Anchor Inn** (100 Whittier St., 877/870-8787 or 907/472-2354, anchorinnwhittier.com), which was once the army communications and headquarters building. The accommodations are clean, with private bathrooms, hot water, and Wi-Fi, but that's about it.

Transportation and Services

Some cruise lines use Whittier as their port of arrival for ground expeditions up and down the Kenai Peninsula. You'll be put on a luxury motorcoach connecting to Anchorage, Seward, Homer, or other communities, and may even be bused up into the Interior as well.

You can also arrive at Whittier on the **Alaska Marine Highway System ferries** (800/642-0066, ferryalaska.com). You don't need a car to get around town, but it's easiest to have one if you intend to explore beyond Whittier. You can rent a car in the seasonal

Avis Alaska office (Lot 8 Small Boat Harbor, 907/440-2847, avisalaska.com, May-Sept., daily 8am-8pm).

If you want to drive to Whittier (or drive out of Whittier), you'll have to queue up to go through the **Anton Anderson Memorial Tunnel,** the longest combined vehicle-railroad tunnel in North America. The tunnel generally opens to vehicular traffic toward Whittier on the half hour, and to traffic out of Whittier on the hour; however, there are sometimes unexpected delays of up to 30 minutes to let trains pass through, then to vent the fumes before cars and trucks can enter.

This isn't the place to plan tight connections, but you do want to be sure you're through before the tunnel closes in the evening; if you miss the last opening, you're going to be spending the night. The last tunnel opening out of Whittier is usually 11pm during the summer, with reduced winter hours, but always double-check the schedule at dot.alaska.gov or by calling 877/611-2586 or 907/566-2244 to be sure.

Once you're through the tunnel, it's about a 90-mile, two-hour drive between Seward and Whittier, or a 60-mile, 90-minute drive between Anchorage and Whittier.

HOPE

The tiny seaside community of Hope, population about 150, was originally a mining camp. Now it's a mecca of camping, hiking, live music, and mountain biking. The only way to get here is by driving: It's about 85 miles or just over 90 minutes from Anchorage, or 72 miles and just under a 90-minute drive from Seward.

There's one small museum here—the **Hope and Sunrise Historical and Mining Museum** (64851 2nd St., hopeandsunrisehistoricalsociety.org, Memorial Day-Labor Day, daily noon-4pm, free, donations welcome). The community library, also open in the afternoons, has a nice gift shop. There is no cell service here, and there might—or might not—be gas to be had at **Pioneer Liquor & Gas** (907/782-3418), just before the end of the road.

Other than that, camping at the U.S. Forest Service **Porcupine Campground** (Mile 18 Hope Hwy., reserveamerica.com, RV and tent camping with great water views) and hiking or biking the 12-mile **Gull Rock Trail** along the coast are the biggest attractions. You can also hike the newly improved **Hope Point Trail,** which goes about 7 miles to the end of the maintained trail, or closer to 12 miles to

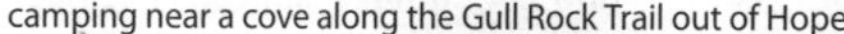

camping near a cove along the Gull Rock Trail out of Hope

the summit, which requires some very limited scrambling.

For adrenaline junkies, **Chugach Outdoor Center** (907/277-7238, chugachoutdoorcenter.com) offers moderate to fierce **white-water rafting** near Hope, all the way up to Class V whitewater in the notorious Six Mile Creek, which drops more than 50 feet per mile on its way out of the mountains. They can also arrange shuttle transport from Girdwood, Cooper Landing, Whittier, and Seward.

Food

The Seaview Cafe (Main and B St., 907/782-3300, seaviewcafealaska.com, mid-May-late Sept. Wed.-Sat., opens at 4pm) offers simple diner food like sandwiches and salads, but the real draw is its stellar live music throughout the summer season. They also offer tent and RV camping if you don't mind being squished in with the other revelers, as well as a few cabin rentals.

Also popular is **Tito's Discovery Cafe** (Mile 16.5 Hope Hwy., 907/782-3274). They have the best pie in the state and are open mid-May through late September, but their hours are sometimes a little unpredictable; call or check their Facebook page before you go. Finally, for your java fix, go to **Turnagain Kayak & Coffee House** (19796 Hope Hwy., 907/907/715-9365, turnagainkayak.com, Tues.-Sun. 8am-2pm), where they'll serve you coffee and tea and happily discuss options for a paddling adventure in other parts of Southcentral.

Accommodations

If you don't want to rough it in one of the campgrounds, there are a couple of wonderful B&Bs to choose from in the Hope area. Book early if you'd like to stay in one of them. The **Black Bear B&B** (63640 Resurrection Creek Rd., 907/782-2202, alaskablackbearbnb.com, from $165, discounts for weekly stays) is a rustic but elegant cabin rental with a full-service kitchen stocked with continental-breakfast-style foods, a stove-heated living area, Wi-Fi, a bathroom with a shower, and three beds in total: a queen bed downstairs and two twin beds in an upstairs loft. **Hope's Hideaway Lodge** (19796 Hope Hwy., 907/764-1910, hopeshideaway.com, from $160 plus one-time $40 cleaning fee) offers comfortable cottage rentals with multiple bedrooms that sleep 5-6, fully equipped kitchens, and full baths.

pie at Tito's Discovery Cafe

MOOSE PASS

Once a railroad construction camp and layover point on the Iditarod Trail, this charming mountain town of almost 200 people makes a good base for day trips into Seward, 30 miles away; it's about 100 miles, or more than a 90-minute drive, south of Anchorage.

Of the two lodges here, the universal favorite is the historic log-built **Summit Lake Lodge** (Mile 45.5 Seward Hwy., 907/244-2031, summitlakelodge.com, from $149 for a small room). The lodge offers homey, rustic but very comfortable accommodations with quilt-covered pillowtop mattresses in log-framed beds. The smallest rooms don't have

TVs, but they all come with a full made-to-order breakfast in the dining room, which also serves lunch and dinner. Even if you don't stay in the lodge, it's worth a stop in their "Shoppe" to sample the ice cream.

A few miles closer to Seward, the **Trail Lake Lodge** (Mile 29.5 Seward Hwy., 907/288-3101, traillakelodge.com, from $115) offers simple rooms with private bathrooms and TVs. People come here not for white glove service, but to cozy up to the best that back-country Alaska can offer; all-inclusive fishing and adventure packages are available, and the Kenai Peninsula Learning Center, which is located at the lodge, offers three- to five-day learning vacations for all ages.

If you're in Alaska to fish, hire a local who was born and raised on the Kenai Peninsula: The guides at **Chugach Backcountry Fishing** in Moose Pass (907/362-1224, chugachbackcountryfishing.com) offer hike-in, fly-in, float and boat-assisted fishing trips throughout the Kenai Peninsula, plus optional lodging.

Seward

Seward, pronounced "SOO-word," is a quaint little fishing town of about 3,000 residents. Tourism is big business here too, so you'll have plenty of lodging options to choose from, but the place has never lost its just-slightly gritty, real Alaska working-town feel.

This beautiful bayside town serves as the gateway to Kenai Fjords National Park, more than 670,000 acres of rugged glacier fjords, just as the name suggests. Interestingly, taking to the water—or to the air—is the easiest way to see the high drama of this park, which has only one road exit point, the Exit Glacier Nature Center.

Like many small Alaska communities, Seward plays an out-sized role in the state's history. Even though the Iditarod sled dog race starts in Anchorage nowadays, the historic race to carry lifesaving diptheria serum to Nome actually began in Seward. It also served as a strategic military port in World War II; you can still see—and sometimes even visit—the ruins of some of the old fortifications.

Finally, like many towns in and around Southcentral Alaska, Seward was battered by the magnitude 9.2 Good Friday earthquake in 1964, the strongest ever recorded in North America. The quake was centered just 95 miles northeast of Seward, and you can still watch a movie in the public library (which doubles as a museum) that documents the destruction it wreaked on the town.

The area surrounding Seward is a fairly mild and wet temperate rainforest, with summer highs in the low 60s, winter highs that linger in the low 30s, and some 72 inches of average rainfall every year.

SIGHTS

Seward Museum

The **Seward Museum** (239 6th Ave., 907/224-3902, cityofseward.us, $5, children 12 and under free) showcases the town's history and a beautiful collection of traditional Native artifacts. It also offers a fine movie, *Waves Over Seward,* that explores the effects of the 1964 earthquake and how the town rebuilt after being ravaged by the resulting tidal wave.

Chugach Heritage Center

The **Chugach Heritage Center** (408 Port Ave., 800/947-5065 or 907/224-5065), inside the historic railroad depot, showcases the natural and Alaska Native history of this region, and also has a good gift shop.

Bear Creek Weir

Every year, the Cook Inlet Aquaculture Association releases millions of salmon smolt into the waters of Bear Lake, then monitors

Seward

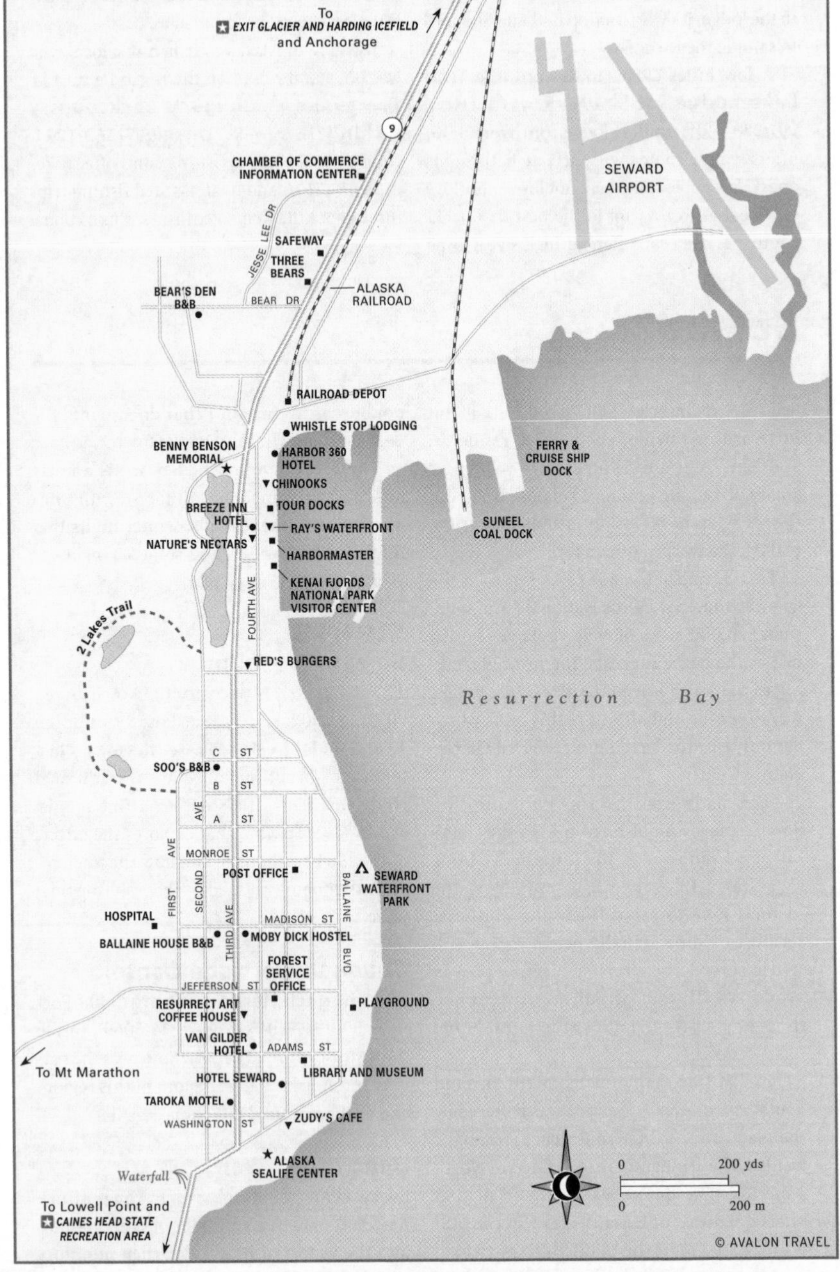
To
EXIT GLACIER AND HARDING ICEFIELD
and Anchorage
9
SEWARD
AIRPORT
CHAMBER OF COMMERCE
INFORMATION CENTER
JESSE LEE DR
SAFEWAY
THREE
BEARS
ALASKA
RAILROAD
BEAR'S DEN
B&B
BEAR DR
RAILROAD DEPOT
WHISTLE STOP LODGING
BENNY BENSON
MEMORIAL
HARBOR 360
HOTEL
CHINOOKS
FERRY &
CRUISE SHIP
DOCK
BREEZE INN
HOTEL
TOUR DOCKS
RAY'S WATERFRONT
NATURE'S NECTARS
SUNEEL
COAL DOCK
HARBORMASTER
KENAI FJORDS
NATIONAL PARK
VISITOR CENTER
2 Lakes Trail
FOURTH AVE
RED'S BURGERS
Resurrection Bay
C ST
SOO'S B&B
B ST
A ST
MONROE ST
FIRST AVE
SECOND AVE
THIRD AVE
POST OFFICE
SEWARD
WATERFRONT
PARK
BALLAINE BLVD
HOSPITAL
MADISON ST
BALLAINE HOUSE B&B
MOBY DICK HOSTEL
FOREST
SERVICE
OFFICE
JEFFERSON ST
RESURRECT ART
COFFEE HOUSE
PLAYGROUND
VAN GILDER
HOTEL
ADAMS ST
To Mt Marathon
LIBRARY AND MUSEUM
HOTEL SEWARD
TAROKA MOTEL
ZUDY'S CAFE
WASHINGTON ST
ALASKA
SEALIFE CENTER
Waterfall
To Lowell Point and
CAINES HEAD STATE
RECREATION AREA
0
200 yds
0
200 m
© AVALON TRAVEL

the previous years' releases when they come back up the creek to spawn. The fish-counting weir makes a great place for visitors to watch the salmon too. The fish—sockeye in late June and July, then silvers from late July to September—are the main attraction, but you might also see waterbirds and even the occasional bear, so use your best wildlife manners. To get to the weir, go to milepost 6.6 of the Seward Highway and turn east onto Bear Lake Road; the weir is just over a half mile farther on the left. Parking is very limited.

Alaska SeaLife Center

Longtime Alaskans who've spent most of their life around marine mammals may not be bowled over by the **Alaska SeaLife Center** (301 Railway Ave., 888/378-2525 or 907/224-7908, alaskasealife.org, summer Mon.-Thurs. 9am-9pm, Fri.-Sun. 8am-9pm, reduced winter hours, adults $21.95, discounts for seniors and children), but for anyone who didn't grow up watching sea lions, seals, puffins, and the like in their natural habitat, a visit to the only permanent marine mammal rehabilitation facility in Alaska is a real treat.

For the price of admission, you can watch seals, sea lions, and other aquatic life swimming right at eye level in enormous aquariums. But the real adventure comes from behind-the-scenes tours (starting at $14.95) and animal encounters (from $24.95/adult and up) that focus on a particular animal—sea otters, seals, puffins—letting you get up close and personal and maybe even participate in feeding or enrichment. These are not tame animals; they're wild animals that are being rehabilitated, or housed if they can't be released back into the wild.

RECREATION

Kenai Fjords National Park

Seward is the gateway to spectacular Kenai Fjords National Park, which gets its name from the true fjords that line the coast—deep, steep-walled, narrow inlets gouged by ancient glaciers, perhaps the predecessors of the 40-some glaciers that now flow out of the park's immense **Harding Icefield.** The **Kenai Fjords National Park Visitor Center** (1212 4th Ave., 907/422-0535, nps.gov/kefj, mid-May-mid-Sept., daily 9am-5pm, Memorial Day-Labor Day, 9am-7pm), near the small boat harbor, contains interpretive displays and an auditorium for showing some of the national park's many films.

There are three easy ways to explore the park: by air on a flightseeing trip; on foot, on some of the state's most spectacular hiking

along the shoreline of Kenai Fjords National Park

trails; or by boat, where you have the added bonus of possibly seeing sea otters, humpback whales, and even gray whales during their March-mid-May migration.

The two most popular day cruise operators are **Major Marine Tours** (1302 4th Ave., 800/274-7300 or 907/274-7300, majormarine.com, from $79 for a 3.5-hour cruise) and **Kenai Fjords Tours** (877/777-4051, kenaifjords.com, from $99 for a 4.5-hour cruise). Both run a similar series of tours from late March-late September, starting at about $80 for a half-day sightseeing cruise and building up to full-day adventures. The biggest difference is that Kenai Fjords Tours is the only company that steps foot onto Fox Island, usually for a lunch or dinner break.

★ EXIT GLACIER AND HARDING ICEFIELD

The modest **Exit Glacier Nature Center** (11.4 miles from Seward on Herman Leirer Rd., often called Exit Glacier Rd., summer daily 9am-7pm) has a small selection of very nice displays about the natural history of the area, especially the glaciers that are still within easy sight.

Parking can be limited during the midday hours (10:30pm-3:30pm), so bring your patient hat or try to time your visit before or after those hours; coming in the morning or afternoon means the light will make the glaciers appear more blue. You can also take the **Exit Glacier Shuttle** (907/224-5569 or 907/224-9225, exitglaciershuttle.com, $10 round-trip), which offers hourly trips to and from the visitor center (call for reservations).

The center sits at the start of the **Exit Glacier Trail,** a series of gentle loops on a broad, mostly level trail, with signs indicating how long ago the glacier covered each portion of the trail. The glacier has retreated drastically in the last few years, but if you're willing to tackle a slightly more strenuous portion of trail, you can still get very close to its toe (the downhill edge).

If you're feeling especially robust and the weather is nice, tackle the roughly 10-mile **Harding Icefield Trail,** which starts from the same trailhead. Note: Most of the park service literature describes the trail as 8.2 miles, but that doesn't take into account a new, massive switchback and the first part of the hike before it diverges from the Exit Glacier Trail.

The hike gains 3,300 feet of elevation on its way to overlooks of the **Harding Icefield,** a massive sheet of ice and snow that spawns some 40 glaciers. This is the hike of a lifetime,

Exit Glacier as it spills out of Harding Icefield

but it's also just as challenging as it sounds. Black bear encounters are fairly common, and weather can change quickly over the icefield.

See *Essentials* for information on how to navigate these hazards, or join a ranger-led hike on either of these trails; see nps.gov/kefj for a schedule of hikes and other ranger-led activities.

If you've ever wanted to hike on a glacier, Exit Glacier is the place to do it—as long as you remember to take the meticulously trained guides from **Exit Glacier Guides** (907/224-5569, exitglacierguides.com) along with you. They offer ice climbing on Exit Glacier (from $195 pp) plus multiday or heli-assisted ice climbing adventures, plus guided hikes and camping trips, including the stunning 15-mile **Lost Lake Trail,** which starts just outside of Seward.

FLIGHTSEEING

The Exit Glacier Nature Center and its nearby hiking trails are the only part of Kenai Fjords National Park that you can reach by road. But there's a whole lot more park out there—670,000 acres of it—that you can take in from the air. Local air charters—all of them excellent—include **Seward Helicopter Tours** (2210 Airport Rd., 888/476-5589 or 907/362-4354, sewardhelicopters.com, from $199 pp), **Marathon Helicopters** (2210-B Airport Rd., 907/224-3616, marathonhelicopters.com, from $175 pp) and **AA Seward Air Tours** (2300 Airport Rd., 907/362-6205 or 907/362-0046, sewardair.com, from $119 pp), which uses small planes.

Hiking and Backpacking

Seward is home to some lovely hikes. Besides the ones in Kenai Fjords National Park (the gentle Exit Glacier hike and the grueling but oh so rewarding Harding Icefield Trail), many hikers walk up **Mount Marathon,** which hosts one of the oldest and most iconic footraces in the nation. They don't take the same route as the racers, though; there's a much less death-defying route starting from the corner of 1st Avenue and Monroe Street. (The race trail starts from the end of Jefferson Street.)

If you're into backpacking (in the camping sense, not the travel sense), one of the most scenic hikes in Alaska starts just outside Seward. **Lost Lake** is just 15 miles from trailhead to trailhead, but most people hike halfway in and spend two nights soaking in the scenery around the lake, which is an enormous, glittering blue jewel set high in the tundra hills. Ideally you should have two cars to shuttle people between trailheads, but in a pinch you can do it with one: Park at the Primrose trailhead (Mile 17 Seward Hwy.), which is farthest from Seward, then call for a cab once you hit the Lost Lake trailhead (Mile 5 Seward Hwy., 5 miles from Seward).

Dog Sledding

Many of the flightseeing services that will take you into Kenai Fjords National Park offer some sort of a glacier dogsled adventure. That said, the hottest mushing attraction around is **Seavey's Ididaride** (12820 Old Exit Glacier Rd., 907/224-8607, ididaride.com, from $69, half-price for children; mid-May-mid-Sept.), where you can spend an hour and a half touring the kennels, cuddling puppies, and taking a two-mile cart or sled ride.

Ziplining

Ziplines have caught on in Southcentral Alaska, and **Stoney Creek Canopy Adventures** (1304 4th Ave., 907/224-3662, stoneycreekca.com, from $149 adults, $119 youth, extra charge for images) makes full use of Seward's towering spruce and hemlock trees for eight ziplines, aerial walkways, and a couple of rappels. This might not be the biggest or fastest zipline in the world, but it's still an awful lot of fun.

Water Sports

With the proper guidance, almost anybody can manage a stable **sea kayak** in the waters of Resurrection Bay, just outside Seward. One of the best outfitters—for both tours and equipment rental if you're experienced enough to DIY—is **Sunny Cove Sea Kayaking** (1304 4th Ave., 907/224-4426, sunnycove.com). Liquid Adventures (411 Port Ave., 907/224-9225, liquid-adventures.com), which offers both paddling and stand-up paddleboard adventures and rentals.

Fishing

Seward is full of excellent fishing charters, to the point that it's very hard to differentiate between them; it's all about finding someone who has an opening—especially if you're trying to go at the last minute, or are a singleton trying to track yourself onto an already existing trip—and then building a relationship with the captain. Before you know it, you'll be a yearly regular.

The following are all excellent companies for salmon, halibut, and mixed species trips:

- **Hill Norvell Alaskan Fishing** (907/321-8905 or 907/321-8886, fishwithhill.com, from $325 pp up to 14 passengers, multi-day trips offered)
- **Crackerjack Sportfishing Charters** (800/566-3912, crackerjackcharters.com, from $285 for halibut or king salmon fishing; affordable lodging specials offered too)
- **Puffin Fishing Charters** (800/978-3346, puffincharters.com, from $325 pp for peak season shared charter)
- **ProFish-n-Sea Charters** (888/385-1312, profish-n-sea.com, from $325 pp for a shared charter)

If you'd like to rent a pole and fish right off the beach, see **Miller's Landing** (13880 Beach Dr., 866/541-5739, millerslandingak.com) or **The Fish House** (1303 4th Ave., 800/257-7760, thefishhouse.net). Both companies also offer fishing charters. Don't forget to buy a ticket for the **Seward Silver Salmon Derby** in mid-August; it's the state's largest fishing competition, with prizes up to $50,000.

Water Taxis and Cabins

Unlike Homer, Seward doesn't have a lot of established hiking trails "across the bay." But that doesn't take away from the fun of exploring little-known coves after a landing craft drops you off, or even staying at a public-use cabin (reservations required).

Some of the most popular cabins in the area are **Derby Cove** and **Callisto Cove** in **Caines Head State Recreation Area** (reservations at dnr.alaska.gov), both of which are set back just enough from the frequent traffic (foot and boat) that goes by in the summer. The Callisto cabin is cut off from the trail, and its freshwater source, at high tides; on the upside, you can watch whales from the cabin deck. Nearby **Thumb Cove** (also dnr.alaska.gov) and its **Spruce Glacier** and **Porcupine Glacier** cabins in Kenai Fjords National Park see much less traffic, although you can only get there by kayaking or taking a water taxi. In all cases reserve the cabins as soon as possible, preferably six months in advance.

Your water taxi options vary according to the season. **Seward Ocean Excursions** (907/599-0499, sewardoceanexcursions.com) is the only water taxi that offers year-round service. Also very helpful is **Alaska Coastal Safari/Seward Water Taxi** (907/362-4101, sewardwatertaxi.com), a one-man operation with a three-person minimum for each trip. The captain isn't very talkative, but he's reliable like clockwork and is often the only water taxi running in the bay in late September.

Another option is **Miller's Landing** (866/541-5739 or 907/331-3113, millerslandingak.com), which has only a two-person minimum for each trip—but their customer service and the accuracy of the information they give out over the phone are really hit or miss. They typically end operations in early September.

Horseback Rides

Horseback tours aren't a very common attraction in Alaska, so they're a real treat when they do crop up. **Bardy's Trail Rides** (907/362-7863, sewardhorses.com, from $113 pp) takes you through country that can be reached only on horseback, including a part of "Old Town"

Seward that was destroyed in the 1964 earthquake; this is a great trip for birders, too. Two departures daily, noon and 3pm, from May through August; check in 20 minutes early.

TOP EXPERIENCE

★ Caines Head State Recreation Area

Caines Head is a rocky promontory overlooking the waters of Resurrection Bay, almost five miles south of Seward. You can hike here along the beach, as long as you time your travel with an adequately low tide so that you can get past two "choke points" that are covered at moderate to high tides. Alaska State Parks recommends hiking the intertidal zone only at low tides of three feet or lower, and leaving the trailhead at least two hours before low tide.

The beach is rocky, and the wet, kelp-covered rocks tend to be very slippery, so never cut the timing close. Once you get to Caines Head you'll have to wait for the next sufficiently low tide before you can head back, so most people choose to spend the night.

If you don't want to camp out at **North Beach** (the part of Caines Head that you first arrive at), you can hire **Alaska Coastal Safari/Seward Water Taxi** (907/362-4101, sewardwatertaxi.com) **or Seward Ocean Excursions** (907/599-0499, sewardoceanexcursions.com) to give you a boat ride there and pick you up later, or book a paddling tour to and from Caines Head with **Sunny Cove Sea Kayaking** (1304 4th Ave., 907/224-4426, sunnycove.com).

ENTERTAINMENT AND EVENTS

It might seem a little sadistic to call a brutal race straight up a mountain and then down again, on surfaces so sheer any sensible person would use a rope and rappel device, "entertainment." But that's exactly what the **Mount Marathon** (mmr.seward.com) race is. Every Fourth of July, men and women participating in the nation's second-oldest footrace reenact a 1915 bar bet to see who could make the fastest three-mile round-trip run to the high point on 4,124-foot Mount Marathon and back again. There's also a shorter juniors race.

Thousands of residents and visitors turn out to cheer the contestants on, a field that often includes Olympians and international ultra-endurance race champions. After all,

North Beach at Caines Head State Recreation Area

World War II History

one of the old gun turrets atop Fort McGilvray

Alaska's Aleutian Islands were an important part of the campaign against Japan during World War II. Attu and Kiska (two of the islands) were the only domestic territory occupied by the Japanese, and Dutch Harbor/Unalaska (another island in the Aleutian chain that was used as a naval base and, later, an airfield) has received appropriate renown for its pivotal role in that region's conflict.

But what many people don't know is that artifacts of World War II are dotted all over Southcentral Alaska, from old fortifications swallowed by the forest around Anchorage's **Campbell Creek Science Center** to the White Alice stations still lingering near communities like **Nome** and abandoned gun emplacements overlooking **Resurrection Bay** that you'll see from a distance if you take a sightseeing cruise out of Seward.

One of the most interesting relics you can visit is **Fort McGilvray** at **Caines Head,** a promontory south of Seward that you can reach on foot, by kayak, or by water taxi. The old fort remains open to the public for exploration (take your headlamp and watch your step), as do the remains of the gun emplacements and numerous ruined concrete bunkers and other structures that make up the entire garrison. A hand-drawn map, now protected from the weather with a cover, helps you make sense of what's left of this military town in the coastal rainforest.

how many other races require that the aid station materials be delivered by helicopter—if they can be sent at all?

Every third Friday in January, people from all over the state—and country—come to Seward for another very unusual celebration: the costumed **Seward Polar Bear Jump** (main.acsevents.org) into Resurrection Bay. People throw themselves into the cold water in their silliest costumes as a fundraiser for the American Cancer Society and Kenai Peninsula Children with Cancer—and because in Alaska, even the shock of cold water immersion is a good excuse for a party.

Like most towns in Alaska, Seward has its own brewing company—the seasonal **Seward Brewing Company** (139 4th Ave., 907/422-0337, sewardbrewery.com, early May-mid-Sept., daily 11:30am-10pm), which serves a very limited pub grub menu ($15) to go with its beer. The **Seward Alehouse** (215 4th Ave., 907/224-2337, daily noon-2am) is very unpretentious. The **Yukon Bar** (201 4th Ave., 907/224-3063, daily noon-2am) is a dive, but that, and the mix of locals and curious tourists, is exactly why people like it so much.

SHOPPING

Believe it or not, one of the very best gift shops in town is in the **Alaska SeaLife Center** (301 Railway Ave., 888/378-2525, alaskasealife.org, adults $22, discounts for seniors and children, summer Mon.-Thurs. 9am-9pm, Fri.-Sun. 8am-9pm). Its Discovery Gift Shop includes a fine selection of eco-friendly products, authentic Alaska Native art, paintings and prints, lots of locally made products, and an expansive kids' section.

You'll also find some excellent gift shops along 4th Avenue near the waterfront, just a short walk from the Alaska SeaLife Center. One high point is **Ranting Raven** (238 4th Ave., 907/224-2228, daily 10am-7pm), an eclectic gallery where the owner can tell you about the person who made anything in the store; they also offer good coffee and treats. **Starbird Studio** (221 4th Ave., 907/224-8770, open summers and holidays) sells Alaska-made prints and art.

For crafters, the **Sew'n Bee Cozy** quilt shop (211 4th Ave., 907/224-7647, sewnbeecozy.com) and the **Flyin' Skein** yarn store (223 4th Ave., 907/224-5648, aflyinskein.com, summer Mon.-Wed. and Fri.-Sat. 11am-6pm, Thurs. 11am-8pm, Sun. noon-5pm) are both excellent. **Cover to Cover Bookstore** (215 4th Ave., 907/224-2525, Mon.-Sat. 10am-6pm) is an exceptional independent bookstore.

If you need an outfitter, stop by **Mountain View Sports** (207 4th Ave., 907/442-0400, mtviewsports.com); they sell name-brand clothing and outdoor gear.

FOOD

Cajun and Creole

Visitors can't always decide whether to be enthralled or sketched out by dining in old train cars. Most go for enthralled, but, either way, eating at the **Train Wreck Restaurant** (411 Port Ave., 907/224-7427, daily 7am-3pm) is an experience, and everyone agrees that the Cajun and Creole food is wonderful.

Coffee Shops

Seward has several excellent coffee shops. **Nature's Nectars** (1313 4th Ave., 907/422-0688, daily 6:30am-3pm) is a town favorite for their great coffee and smoothies, but my top pick is the **Resurrect Art Coffee House Gallery** (320 3rd Ave., 907/224-7161, resurrectart.com, daily 7am-7pm), a Lutheran church that was transformed into a coffee shop (complete with gift shop, an art display, and sometimes live music) when the congregation moved into a new building.

You can get some vegan, vegetarian, and gluten-free options from the **Sea Bean** (225 4th Ave., 907/224-6623, seabeancafe.com, daily 7am-7pm) Internet café. Choose from standard café fare, including paninis, sandwiches, wraps, smoothies, and a few breakfast items.

Sandwiches

Zudy's Cafe (501 Railway Ave., 907/224-4710, zudyscafe.com, usually open Tues.-Sun., hours vary by season) has great sandwiches and desserts in an open café with outdoor seating overlooking the water. The service is great, too, and they have good Wi-Fi.

Hamburgers

The summer-only **Red's Burgers** (302 Van Buren St., $15, cash only) is a big red school bus with outdoor seating. If the inevitable Seward rain arrives, you can sit "inside"—in a big yellow school bus. Heads up: Everything is made to order, so this is not fast food—but the burgers and fries are both worth the wait.

Ice Cream

Alaskans eat the most ice cream per capita of any state in the nation—maybe we're used to the cold? We're equally opportunity lovers of all things sweet, though, so we also love the gelato and handmade candies from **Sweet**

Darlings (204 4th Ave., 907/224-3011, brownandhawkins.com, mid-Mar.-Sept.).

Seafood

In a place like Seward, you can't possibly go wrong with seafood, but **Chinooks** (1404 4th Ave., 907/224-2207, chinooksbars.com, daily 11am-9pm) does it best, with a few other options (mostly steak and burgers) for anyone who doesn't like fish. For a slightly more upscale take on surf-and-turf with beautiful waterfront views, head to **Ray's Waterfront** (1316 4th Ave., 907/224-5606, rayswaterfrontak.com, mid-Apr.-Sept. daily 11am-3:30pm and 4pm-10pm, $35).

Groceries

There is an excellent **Safeway** (1907 Seward Hwy., 907/224-6900, daily 5am-midnight) in Seward, along with **Three Bears** (1711 Seward Hwy., 907/224-2081, daily 7am-9pm), the local version of warehouse shopping, which also has a 24-hour gas station.

ACCOMMODATIONS

The nicest waterfront hotel in town is the **Harbor 360 Hotel** (1412 4th Ave., 888/514-8687, harbor360hotel.com, summer from $295). This isn't five-star lodging, but by small-town Alaska standards it's grand: The rooms are very comfortable, with views right over the harbor in many rooms and the entire town within easy walking distance. It's also dog-friendly, and the helpful staff is really on the ball.

For a locally run lodge experience away from the crowds that develop when cruise ships are in town, book at the **Seward Windsong Lodge** (Mile 0.5 Herman Leirer/Exit Glacier Rd., 877/777-4079 or 907/224-7116, sewardwindsong.com, mid-May-mid-Sept., $270). The rooms are clean and comfortable, and the out-of-town setting is restful, although it's best to book over the phone instead of online to make sure your room has the sort of views you want. An hourly shuttle that runs to the Alaska SeaLife Center and the Seward small-boat harbor makes it easy to get from the lodge to town and back again, even if you don't have a car. Note: This is a two-story lodge, with no elevator access to the second floor.

For a bargain hotel room, book into the "historic" section of the **Breeze Inn** (303 N. Harbor Dr., 888/224-5237, breezeinn.com, summer from $169, winter from $69). These motel-style rooms have exterior entrances and are at street level, so there'll be some road noise; but they're clean and comfortable, with friendly, local staff, in-room refrigerators and coffeemakers, and that grand prize of inexpensive lodging in Alaska, private bathrooms. The Breeze Inn has two other sections with increasingly nicer rooms, some of which offer air-conditioning, mountain views, and sea views (from $229), plus a few Jacuzzi suites. All rooms have Wi-Fi.

For a quieter experience in town, try the **Seward Birdhouse** (433 5th Ave., 907/224-5620, sewardbirdhouse.com, mid-May-mid-Sept., from $275, multiple nights from $250, up to 4 people). This fully furnished vacation rental is just a few blocks from the beach and the historic downtown district; you get a full kitchen, free laundry, on-site parking, cable TV, and Wi-Fi; no pets.

For a less expensive, more rustic getaway, visitors love the **Alaska Creekside Cabins** (welovealaska.com, from $125), which are set off in the woods just 3.5 miles from downtown Seward. Four of the larger (and more expensive) cabins have their own bathrooms; others use a shared bathhouse facility with private shower rooms. Bathroom or not, guests love being able to enjoy rustic accommodations near a salmon spawning creek, without giving up perks like indoor heat and cable TV.

Remote Glamping

If you're here to get away from it all and enjoy as much of Resurrection Bay's wild beauty as possible, you can't beat **Orca Island Cabins** (in Humpy Cove, accessed by water taxi only, 888/494-5846 or 907/362-9014, orcaislandcabins.com). The cabins are rustic yurts that sleep 2-4 people at a time on a queen bed and futon, with solar-powered lights, potable water, a propane cooking range, propane fireplace, a large back deck with a grill, and a private bathroom with a shower.

You'll need to bring your own food; they provide coolers for storage, while you provide the ice. Once you're there, you'll have the use of their fishing gear (buy a fishing license before you go), kayaks, rowboats, and stand-up paddleboards, and there's plenty of firewood for campfires. You have great odds of seeing wildlife—from humpbacks and orcas to Dall porpoises, Steller sea lions, and sea otters—during your stay.

Camping

The best campground in Seward is in the city-run **Seward Waterfront Park,** which runs along the shore from the small boat harbor to the Alaska SeaLife Center. These first-come, first-served sites aren't exactly secluded, but they're grassy and flat, and all you have to do to see the water is turn your head. The fees set by the city are inexpensive, too, considering the location: $10 for tents, $20 for a dry RV site, and $40 for an RV site with water and electric hookups. Cash and debit/credit cards only; no checks accepted and no change given.

There's an RV dump station ($5) on Ballaine Boulevard, the road that runs past the Waterfront Park, just south of the obvious playground and ballfield areas. (For reference, the Alaska SeaLife Center is in the south end of town.)

I recommend against booking the campground at **Miller's Landing** (13880 Beach Dr., 866/541-5739, millerslandingak.com). The sites are piled right on top of each other, and management is entirely disinterested in doing anything about the drunk, noisy campers that always crop up. So if the city campground is full, your next best option for tent camping is the 12-site **Exit Glacier Campground,** a quarter mile before the Exit Glacier Nature Center, which is a 20-minute drive out of Seward. You can also stage your RV in most of the pullouts along this road, as long as you're not blocking traffic.

INFORMATION AND SERVICES

Wi-Fi is available at almost all lodgings in Seward, except the campgrounds. If you still need Wi-Fi access (or a computer connected to the Internet), the **Seward Community Library** (239 6th Ave., 907/224-4082, cityofseward.us, summer Tues.-Thurs. 10am-8pm, Mon. and Fri.-Sat. 10am-6pm) has both. Their hours sometimes change due to funding, and hours are always reduced during winter.

You'll have no problem finding gas stations; there are several just off the highway as you drive into town. One hospital has 24-hour emergency care: **Providence Seward Medical Center** (417 1st Ave., 907/224-5205).

If you need to do laundry, the **Suds n Swirl** (335 3rd Ave., 907/224-3111, daily 8am-10pm) is a decent little laundromat with free Wi-Fi. It used to be the Sip n Spin, a combo café and laundromat, but the café went away when the name changed.

You have several banking and ATM options in Seward. There's a **Wells Fargo** (908 3rd Ave., 907/224-5283, wellsfargo.com, Mon.-Thurs. 10am-5pm, Fri. 10am-5:30pm) branch and ATM, and a **First National Bank of Alaska** (303 4th Ave., 907/224-4200, fnbalaska.com, Mon.-Thurs. 10am-5pm, Fri. 10am-6pm) as well. There is also a **Western Union** money transfer service (1907 Seward Hwy., 800/325-6000, daily 9am-9pm).

TRANSPORTATION

Getting There

Many cruise lines use Seward as their port of call for Anchorage. Once the ship docks, you might spend at least one night in town before being sent north for ground excursions aboard a luxury motor coach.

If you're a ferry buff like I am, you're out of luck here; this is one of the few port cities that the Alaska Marine Highway System does not serve. You also can't fly here; although Seward does have a tiny airport that's put to use for private pilots and flightseeing adventures, there are no scheduled commercial flights.

You can, however, travel between Seward

and Anchorage on the **Alaska Railroad** (800/544-0552, alaskarailroad.com). A one-way ticket for "adventure class" (coach class) starts at around $105 for adults. The train usually leaves Seward around 6pm and arrives in Anchorage a little after 10pm; most downtown hotels will provide a complimentary shuttle from the train depot.

Finally, you can rent a car in Seward and make the drive to any Kenai Peninsula (or even Interior) communities from here. To give you some perspective, it's a 170-mile or 3.5-hour drive from Seward to Homer or 125 miles—about 2.5 hours—from Seward to Anchorage.

If you'd rather let someone else do the driving, you can hire one of several bus services that ply the roads up and down the Kenai Peninsula. The best deal is from **Seward Bus Lines** (888/420-7788 or 907/563-0800, sewardbuslines.net, May-mid-Sept., from $40 for one-way transport to Anchorage or Whittier), with two departures from Seward daily. For an extra $5 they'll also drop you off at the Anchorage airport, any Anchorage hotel, or any Anchorage rental car company.

If you're going to Homer, call **Homer Stage Line** (1242 Ocean Dr., 907/868-3914 or 907/235-2252, stagelineinhomer.com, one-way fare approximately $100), which runs from Homer to Seward and back again June through August once a day on Monday, Wednesday, and Friday. Some limited service may be available in mid-May or mid-September; call to confirm. They also run from Homer to Anchorage, but not from Seward to Anchorage, and the routes are sometimes subject to change.

Getting Around

Alaska Shuttle Service (907/947-3349, alaskashuttleservice.com) offers taxi service within Seward, as well as shuttle and tour service up and down the Kenai Peninsula, usually with a four-person minimum. You can also rent bikes from **Adventure Sixty North** (907/224-2600, adventure60north.com, from $32/day, weekly rentals available), which also happens to be the company that pioneered winter tours into Kenai Fjords National Park.

Kenai Peninsula

The Kenai Peninsula extends south from Anchorage to Homer, a wonderful artsy community that combines the best of the state's food, art, and hospitality. The heart of the peninsula is the Sterling Highway, which diverges from the Seward Highway at mile marker 37. This region may be most famous for its wonderful freshwater fishing for sockeye and king salmon in the Kenai and Russian Rivers, but don't forget to cast a fly for the plentiful rainbow trout, Dolly Varden, and arctic char, too. Much of the Kenai's freshwater fishing is very easily accessible from the roadways; the best in-depth resource is *The Highway Angler* by Gunnar Pedersen, which you can find in most Alaska bookstores and sporting goods stores, or buy it from Amazon.com before your visit.

Fishing isn't the only thing you can do here. The Kenai Peninsula is also a wonderland of opportunities for hiking, backpacking, camping, and mountain biking, almost all of them easily accessed off the road system, just like the fishing. Your drive from Anchorage to Homer travels almost completely through state or federal protected lands, so you're also treated to stunning scenery and, if you get lucky, wildlife—although the relatively dense population and road traffic make the animals more shy and thus difficult to see.

When you first drive out of Anchorage, you'll be passing through Chugach State Park. Once you pass Girdwood, you're in Chugach National Forest. Shortly after you pass through Cooper Landing, you enter the Kenai National Wildlife Refuge, a swath of

Kenai Peninsula

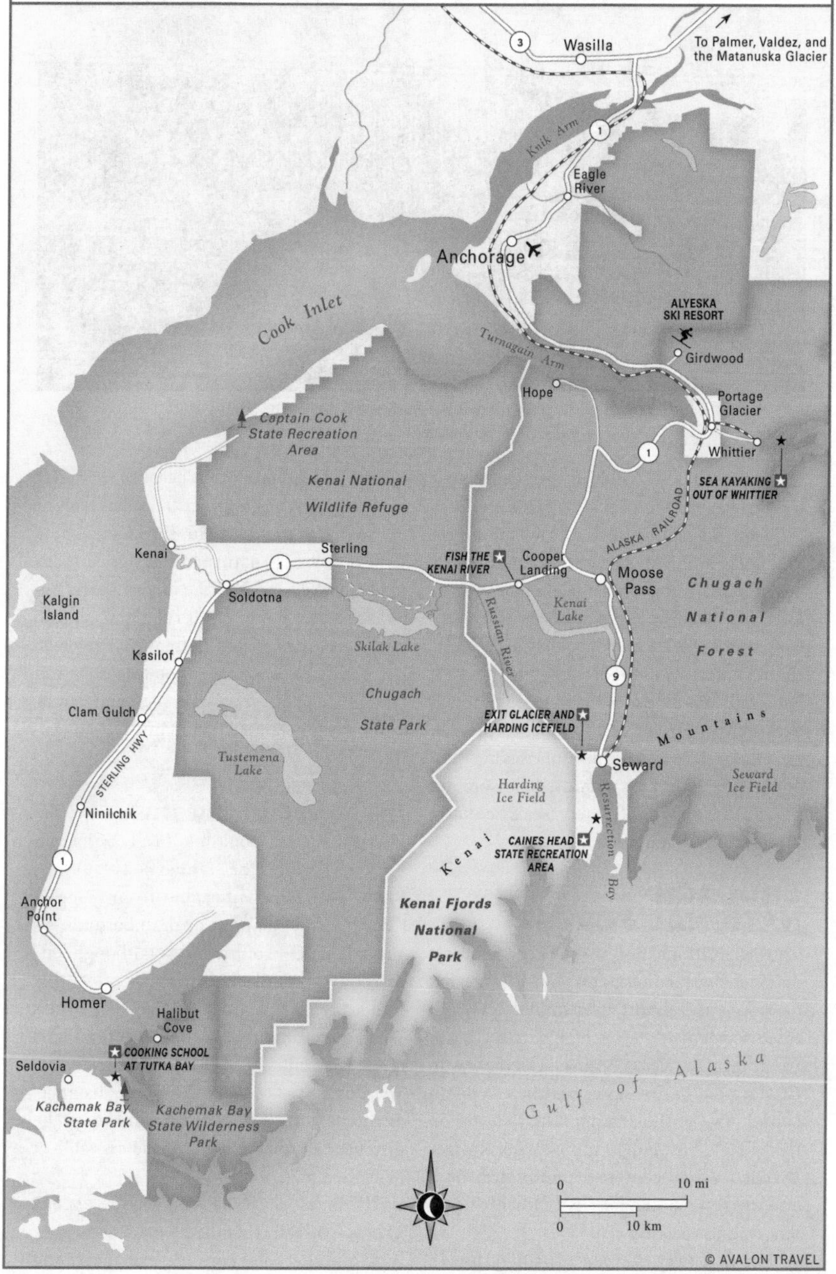

Wasilla
To Palmer, Valdez, and the Matanuska Glacier
Knik Arm
Eagle River
Anchorage
Cook Inlet
ALYESKA SKI RESORT
Turnagain Arm
Girdwood
Hope
Portage Glacier
Whittier
SEA KAYAKING OUT OF WHITTIER
Captain Cook State Recreation Area
Kenai National Wildlife Refuge
ALASKA RAILROAD
Kenai
Sterling
FISH THE KENAI RIVER
Cooper Landing
Moose Pass
Chugach National Forest
Kalgin Island
Soldotna
Kenai Lake
Russian River
Skilak Lake
Kasilof
Chugach State Park
Clam Gulch
EXIT GLACIER AND HARDING ICEFIELD
Mountains
STERLING HWY
Tustemena Lake
Seward
Seward Ice Field
Harding Ice Field
Ninilchik
Resurrection Bay
CAINES HEAD STATE RECREATION AREA
Kenai
Anchor Point
Kenai Fjords National Park
Homer
Halibut Cove
COOKING SCHOOL AT TUTKA BAY
Seldovia
Gulf of Alaska
Kachemak Bay State Park
Kachemak Bay State Wilderness Park
0 10 mi
0 10 km

A field of arctic lupine blooms along the roadside of the Seward Highway.

wilderness that was cobbled together to protect critical habitat for fish and wildlife.

Watch for eagles overhead, look for mountain goats and Dall sheep in the mountains near the road, and keep a particular eye out for moose near the highway once you're away from the ocean. Like all deer, they have a penchant for darting unpredictably into the road, but a half-ton moose is likely to do as much damage to your car as you do to it. Finally, even though the Kenai Peninsula is fairly well-populated by Alaska standards, make sure you stay current on wildlife safety (see *Essentials*); this is still very much a wild place.

CHUGACH NATIONAL FOREST

Chugach National Forest—the northernmost national forest in the country—is so large that it encompasses almost seven million acres and three ranger districts, stretching from Cooper Landing on the Kenai Peninsula all the way to Cordova on the far shores of Prince William Sound. Two of those ranger districts are on the Kenai Peninsula: the Glacier Ranger District, which centers around Girdwood, and the Seward Ranger District, which centers around Seward.

Fire is a very serious consideration in Chugach National Forest, because the forest contains many black spruce trees that evolved to use fire as part of their reproductive process. In essence, nature has designed them to go up like a torch at the merest spark. So, please respect public lands rules and confine your fires to designated, permanent fire rings. Dogs must be restrained or on leash when in established public recreation sites, and mountain biking is allowed on many, but not all, trails.

Hiking and Biking

Perhaps the most iconic hike in all of Chugach National Forest is the 38-mile **Resurrection Pass Trail,** which stretches from Hope to Cooper Landing and is open to both hiking and biking. One of the nicest (although longest) day hikes or bikes that intersects this trail is the 10-mile (one-way) **Devil's Creek Trail,** also sometimes called **Devil's Pass;** it starts at mile 39 of the Seward Highway. You don't have to walk the whole distance, of course, but those who do want to go the distance can reserve the Devil's Pass cabin at recreation.gov.

The lovely, 6.2-mile (one-way) **Crescent Creek Trail** starts at mile 3.5 of Quartz Creek Road and alternates between forest cover and meadows until it reaches the shore of Crescent Lake. You can also reach the lake from the Carter Creek trailhead, but ascending from Crescent Creek is much gentler. Mountain biking is allowed.

The **Russian River** sits on the boundary between Chugach National Forest and the Kenai National Wildlife Refuge. When the salmon are running from mid-June to late July, the river's banks are packed with fishers standing shoulder-to-shoulder; this is called combat fishing. If you don't want to join the combat fishing circus, you can take a 2.4-mile day hike from the Russian River Campground near Copper Landing to **Russian River Falls,** where you have extremely good chances of seeing bears fishing for salmon that are struggling up the stairstep falls to reach their spawning ground. There is a lot of foot traffic on this trail, but you should still be very careful and use full "Bear Aware" precautions to avoid surprising a bear with a close encounter (see *Essentials*).

Camping

Chugach National Forest is dotted with beautiful wooded campgrounds, many situated next to a prominent lakeshore. Granite Creek and Quartz Creek are two of the most popular, and both can be reserved through recreation.gov (877/444-6777). **Granite Creek** (Mile 63 Seward Hwy., early June-early Sept., from $14) has 19 wooded, quiet RV or tent sites; all are back-in sites for RVs, and one accommodates RVs up to 52 feet. **Quartz Creek** (turn onto Quartz Creek Rd. from mile 45.2 of the Sterling Hwy., late May-early Sept., $18-28) offers 45 tent and RV spaces with some pull-through sites. Amenities are limited to drinking water and vault toilets. You can also try your hand at recreational gold panning (bring your own pan) in the tiny, nine-site first-come, first-served **Crescent Creek** campground, which you'll pass on the way to Quartz Creek. During the winter and fall/spring shoulder seasons, if a campground gate is open, camping is allowed on a first-come, first-served basis for free, although you'll also be roughing it without water or trash services, and the toilets might also be locked up.

Another, relatively new amenity for adventurers is the **Manitoba Hut** near Summit Lake; think of it as a backcountry hostel. The hut used to be a circa-1936 mining cabin but was repurposed by the nonprofit Alaska Huts Association in 2012. You can rent a bunk in either of two shared yurts. Each has four single bunks and two double bunks; one of them,

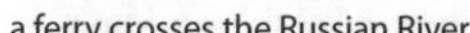

a ferry crosses the Russian River

Toba's Yurt, has a wood stove and allows dogs. The other is heated by a propane stove and does not allow pets. As of 2016, you can also rent the hutkeeper's quarters—a private room with a double bed. There's an outhouse as well as a wood-fired Finnish sauna on-site. This is a popular destination for backcountry skiers, sledders, and families just looking to get away from it all. Prices start at $15 for a single in either yurt or $75 in the hutkeeper's quarters during the week; weekend rates require you to rent an entire yurt ($200) or the hutkeeper's quarters ($90). You can make your reservations up to six months in advance at alaskahuts.org/reservations.

KENAI NATIONAL WILDLIFE REFUGE

Only a few miles down the road from Cooper Landing you'll find yourself in the protected wildlands of the **Kenai National Wildlife Refuge,** a 1.92-million-acre swathe of wilderness habitat that was cobbled together to protect critical habitat for fish and wildlife. (The headquarters are in Soldotna on Ski Hill Rd., 907/260-2820, fws.gov/refuge/Kenai, Memorial Day-Labor Day daily 9am-5pm, off-season Tues.-Sat. 10am-5pm.)

The only real difference in land usage between Chugach National Forest and Kenai National Wildlife Refuge is that while you can ski the refuge's popular hiking trails in the winter, you can't bike on them. Also, while on refuge lands, pets must be on a leash less than nine feet in length and under your control at all times. Fires are allowed in established campground rings and barbecue grates.

The epicenter of easy-access recreation in the Kenai National Wildlife Refuge is Skilak Lake Road, which swoops south from mile 58 of the Sterling Highway to run near the north shore of Skilak Lake, then back north to rejoin the highway at mile 75.3. Be careful when you drive this road; it's minimally maintained and often has terrible ruts caused by large RVs and boat trailers being driven through when the ground is soft. Also, be aware that you won't have cell service once you're on Skilak Lake Road; cell coverage is sporadic at best on the stretch of the Sterling Highway that runs between the two ends of Skilak Lake Road.

Hiking

If you like lakefront walking, you'll love the first mile or two of the 4.5-mile **Seven Lakes Trail.** That distance is one-way, because this is actually a small thru-hike, but if you don't have a second car to park at the first end, you can just hike out until you run out of lakeshore walking, then turn around and go back. The **Engineer Lake** trailhead is at mile 9.4 of Skilak Lake Road (you'll only be able to see the sign if you're coming from the east junction), while the **Kelly Lake** trailhead is at 68.8 of the Sterling Highway.

There are two great public-use cabins at either end of the trail—the Engineer Lake cabin and the Kelly Lake Cabin—both of which come with the use of a rowboat. Reserve them in advance from recreation.gov (877/444-6777).

Also excellent is the **Kenai River Trail,** a 5.5-mile round-trip walk that starts from mile 0.7 of Skilak Lake Road (the mile markers start from the east junction with the Sterling Highway). Some trail guides refer to this as the Upper Kenai River Trail; there is a second trailhead a mile farther into Skilak Lake Road, but if you start from this one you get great views down into the rocky walls of Kenai River Canyon, not to mention great views of the Kenai River itself, which is a striking blue-green color. Be warned that bear encounters are common here, especially when the salmon are running.

Finally, for some of the best lookouts over the region, consider hiking the four-mile round-trip **Skilak Lookout Trail**, which starts at mile 5.4 of Skilak Lake Road, gains elevation relatively gently by Alaska standards, and gives you beautiful, nearly 360-degree views over the refuge.

Also popular is the six-mile round-trip **Fuller Lakes Trail,** which starts from mile 57 of the Sterling Highway; it's a lovely hike through forest to three subalpine lakes.

Camping

Several campgrounds are scattered through the refuge. If you're here during the shoulder season, consider snagging one of the free, first-come first-served spots in campgrounds along Skilak Lake Road; they're open year-round. Your options include **Engineer Lake** (3 sites), **Lower Ohmer Lake** (3 sites), and **Lower Skilak Lake** (14 sites).

During the summer season (mid-May-Labor Day weekend) you'll need to pay fees at a few of the campgrounds on Skilak Lake Road: **Upper Skilak Lake Campground** charges $10 for RVs and $5 for walk-in tent users (25 sites). Also very popular is the **Hidden Lake Campground** (44 sites, $10 during the summer), which also happens to be the largest, with 44 sites. All sights are first-come, first-served.

COOPER LANDING

This tiny town of almost 300 people sits right where Kenai Lake flows out into the Kenai River, one of the most iconic salmon fishing streams in all of Alaska, if not the nation. The Russian River—which flows into the Kenai, just a few miles away, to join its rush to the sea—is also renowned for its salmon fishing.

That said, although fishing is the activity that lures most people here, it's not the only thing to do. Non-fisherfolk can try their hand at stand-up paddleboarding on the lake's relatively placid waters or take a float trip down the river or pony up for a horseback trail ride. During the summer, stop by the tiny log cabin visitor center in Cooper Landing (Mile 48.7 Seward Hwy.) to get oriented.

No matter what brings you here, don't miss a chance to browse the tiny **Cooper Landing Historical Society Museum** (Mile 48.7 Sterling Hwy., 907/598-1042, cooperlandingmuseum.com, mid-May-mid-Sept. Wed.-Mon. noon-5pm or by appointment, donation requested), which continues the trend that Alaska's smallest museums are often among its best. The museum is housed in two historic buildings—one is a 1920s cabin that served as the Cooper Landing post office for almost 40 years, and the other was the local schoolhouse for almost 50 years. Don't miss such treasures as the fully articulated skeleton of a 20-year-old brown bear, furnishings and even musical instruments used by early residents, and an enormous cross-section from a Sitka spruce tree that's estimated to be about 600 years old.

looking down over Kenai Lake and Cooper Landing

Recreation

FISHING

Alaska River Adventures (Mile 48 Sterling Hwy., 907/595-2000, alaskariveradventures.com) is a professional, highly thought-of guide service based out of their own wilderness lodge; they'll put you on the best freshwater streams and rivers in the Kenai Peninsula for species including Dolly Varden and big, beautiful rainbow trout, or guide you on a remote, weeklong wilderness float fishing trip. Lodging starts at $159 for a small cabin, which sleeps up to four, and fishing trips start from $175 per person for a half day or $275 per person for a day; larger cabins and all-inclusive packages are also available.

Another one of the best full-service fishing lodges in town is **Kenai River Drifter's Lodge** (18404 Sterling Hwy., 907/595-5555, drifterslodge.com, from $1,460 for two days fishing and three nights lodging). You can rent a private cabin (comes with kitchenette and private bathroom) or one of the rooms in the lodge; they have shared bathrooms. They specialize in rainbow trout but also fish for salmon and arctic char, and you can purchase guided day fishing trips or lodging only if you don't want the full treatment.

For a B&B-style fishing lodge, head to **Cooper Landing Fish Camp** (Mile 49.6 Sterling Hwy., summer 907/595-3474, winter 907/688-1547, kenaitrout.com, two-night minimum stay, $100), which rents their cabins through vrbo.com. Each cabin has a kitchenette, full linens, front deck, and barbecue; laundry, bathrooms, and showers are in a separate building, with a separate bathroom designated for each cabin.

If you need fishing tackle or gear, you can rent from Cooper Landing's full-service fly and tackle shop, **Kenai Cache Outfitters** (14899 Sterling Hwy., 907/595-1401).

RAFTING

Fishing is the name of the game here—but that doesn't mean it's the only thing you can do in and around Cooper Landing. If you're an adrenaline junkie, **Chugach Outdoor Center** (907/277-7238, chugachoutdoorcenter.com) can arrange shuttle transport for you to enjoy the fierce white water of Six Mile Creek in Hope, which drops more than 50 feet per mile on its way out of the mountains.

If you're not into death-defying white water, **Alaska River Adventures** (907/595-2000, alaskariveradventures.com, from $59/3-hour float, kids 12 and under half price) offers calm, half-day floats down the scenic Kenai River, so you can eyeball the famous combat fishing on the Russian River (which flows into the Kenai) without fear of getting hooked. You might even see some wildlife. Their longer trips include Class II or higher rapids through the rocky Kenai River Canyon and into gorgeous Skilak Lake—a recreation center for the entire region—and a full-day trip that includes a chance to pan gold and try out a sluice box in your search for gold.

KAYAKING

For an even more relaxed water outing, hit up **Kenai Kayak Company** (907/521-0244, kenaikayakco.com, from $75 pp) for a two-hour paddle on pristine **Kenai Lake;** the turquoise waters are stunning, and, although there are no guarantees, the relative isolation gives you decent chances of seeing wildlife like moose and bears, soaring bald eagles, and even leaping salmon. Launch times are flexible but reservations are required; if you've never kayaked before, their instructors will teach you.

You can, of course, take your own kayak into the lake, and some of the lodgings will happily rent or loan you a kayak. But there are a few things you should know first. The water is very cold here, and often it's not a question of swimming ability but the gasp reflex that will kill you if you go in; see *Essentials* for more information on boating safety in Alaska. Next up, Kenai Lake is *big*—it's 22 miles long, and the wind can come up quickly and create large waves. That means you should be in a sea kayak—for extra stability—and think through your trip with the knowledge that you might end up in whitecaps; if you aren't prepared to cope, stick close to shore and the dock.

Food

For some of the best barbecue in all of Alaska, head for **Sackett's Kenai Grill** (16520 Sterling Hwy., 907/595-1827, sackettsgrill.com), where you eat on rough-cut picnic tables indoors. Try the brisket sandwich or the ribs; they also serve pizza, beer, wine, and some freshly baked dessert goodies. Order at the chalkboard on your way into the restaurant.

Gwin's Roadhouse (Mile 52 Sterling Hwy., 907/741-2376, gwinslodge.com) also does an excellent job on food, with rustic, homestyle meals like chicken-fried steak, salmon chowder, and mashed potatoes with the peels still on. **Kingfisher Roadhouse** (19503 Sterling Hwy., 907/595-2861, kingfisherak.letseat.at, summer Sun.-Mon. 5pm-10:30pm, Tues.-Sat. 11:30am-10:30pm) is also excellent, with a similar lineup of rustic lodge food spiced up by a few more adventurous choices like caribou stroganoff.

Despite its humble outside, **Dudes Food Trailer** (35269 King Salmon Dr., 501/209-0851) is probably the best food in Cooper Landing, with touches of several international cuisines creeping into a menu that ranges from baby back ribs to seafood. Whatever the dudes feel like cooking is what you get for the day; try out the reindeer sausage wraps for breakfast. There's just one catch: Their hours are very unpredictable, and rumor is the owner might or might not be back in business for the summer of 2017. So call first, but don't miss the chance to eat here if he's around.

Accommodations

If you don't want to stay in a fishing lodge, your choice of accommodations in Cooper Landing is fairly sparse. The **Alpine Inn Motel** (Mile 48.2 Sterling Hwy., 907/595-1557, kenairivermotel.com, year-round, from $125 summer) might look a little dodgy from the outside (think 1950s roadside motel), but on the inside the rooms are large and very comfortable, simply furnished but spotlessly clean, with kitchenettes, private bathrooms, Wi-Fi, and great blackout curtains. The small gift shop is more like an outfitter, with a selection of outdoorsy clothing, fishing tackle, and practical gifts like baseball caps and coffee mugs.

For the full-service concierge treatment in a rustic lodge, stay in **Gwin's Roadhouse** (Mile 52 Sterling Hwy., 907/741-2376, gwinslodge.com), which offers 17 private cabins (from $140 for a cabin with a private bathroom, from $85 for a "dry" cabin—you walk to the portable toilet) with spotty-to-nonexistent Wi-Fi that's better in the restaurant. The restaurant serves excellent, rustic diner-style food like chicken-fried steak and salmon chowder.

Be warned that even from the cabins, you can hear the frequent live music concerts ($10 cover, $5 for guests); if you don't want to join the party, they have earplugs for you at the front desk. They'll happily help you book any kind of fishing, rafting, gold-panning, or horseback-riding trip you can imagine around Cooper Landing, along with bear viewing, railroad trips, and other activities in the greater Southcentral area.

CAMPING

If you're in an RV or tent and bent on fishing, the best place to stay is the **Russian River Campground** (Mile 54 Sterling Hwy.). It's open late May to mid-September, with 80 reservable sites (recreation.gov, 877/444-6777) for both tents and RVs; this is also a great base camp for area hiking. Amenities include dumpsters, water, picnic tables, and flush toilets. Sites cost $18-28 and do not have electrical hookups.

Transportation

The only bus service to Cooper Landing is the summers-only, several-days-weekly service from **Homer Stage Line** (907/868-3914, stagelineinhomer.com, office hours Mon.-Fri. only, 8am-5pm, no weekends), which stops by Cooper Landing on its runs between Seward and Homer or Anchorage and Homer. Otherwise, you'll have to drive: Cooper Landing is about 100 miles, or an almost two-hour drive, south of Anchorage on the Seward and Sterling Highways, or 120 miles (almost 2.5 hours of driving) north of Homer on the Sterling Highway.

KENAI AND SOLDOTNA

The world-famous Kenai River runs straight through both Kenai and Soldotna—fishing towns that sit just 11 miles apart on Alaska's Kenai Peninsula and are so intertwined, we decided to list them together. In point of fact, both towns claim the world-record king salmon, a 97-pound, 4-ounce monster that was fished out of Honeymoon Cove in Kenai by a Soldotna resident; you can see it on display in the Soldotna Visitor Center.

Kenai sits right on the shores of Cook Inlet, straddling the mouth of the Kenai River, which means you can catch salmon still silver-bright from their ocean voyage. (Salmon start to metamorphose into their breeding form as soon as they hit freshwater.) This town was already the site of a thriving Dena'ina Athabascan Indian village when Russian explorers arrived in 1741; by the late 1700s, the Russians had built a fort to use as a fur trading outpost. Be sure to ask for information on Old Town Kenai walking tours when you stop in at the visitor center.

Soldotna, by comparison, was first opened for homesteading in 1947, with special preference granted to World War II veterans who either slogged in by foot from Moose Pass, some 70 miles away, or walked in after taking a barge to Kenai. Now Soldotna is the hub of traffic in the Kenai Peninsula, poised at the juncture of the Sterling Highway and the Kenai Spur Highway—so if you want the best in big-city comforts from this area, Kenai is your place.

Both Kenai and Soldotna are easy to reach on paved, well-maintained highways (although like most highways in Alaska, they're only two lanes wide). If you decide you want a more remote chance to fish the Kenai River, you can always head to tiny Cooper Landing, which is on the Sterling Highway, 45 miles outside of Soldotna. Cooper Landing is also the best base for fishing the Russian River, which flows into the Kenai just a few miles west of town.

The climate in the Kenai/Soldotna region is one of the mildest and driest in the state, although humidity sometimes hovers around 50 percent—pretty high for Alaska. Summer highs tend to linger in the 60s, and winter highs stay in the 20s. That might not sound like much, but it's a big difference from the -40 temperatures you can expect in the Interior. That said, the most valuable piece of clothing you'll own in Kenai is going to be a pair of knee-high rubber boots to keep your feet dry on your fishing or riverside adventures.

Sights

KALIFORNSKY BEACH

For most of the year, this is a quiet, sandy beach where locals go strolling or beachcombing. (Don't walk on the mud that's exposed at low tide; you could get stuck in what amounts to quicksand.) From August through June, you can access the beach for free from the south end of Spruce Drive (off the Kenai Spur Highway). There's also a good lookout point, with staircase access to the beach, at the south end of Forest Drive.

The beach changes every July, when locals from up and down the Kenai Peninsula, especially Anchorage, flood into Kenai to go dipnetting for sockeye salmon. This unusual fishery is for Alaska residents only, but it's still fun to sit back and watch the circus as families mob both sides of the bank, setting up siege-style camps to support their efforts.

The people doing the fishing put on chest waders and walk waist-deep or farther into the water, holding giant nets in the water that have five-foot-wide hoops and handles that can be more than 20 feet long. The fisher then waits—slowly chilling in the cold water—until a salmon hits their net, at which point they run back to the bank, extract the salmon, pass it to whoever is ready to bleed and fillet it on the spot, then goes back into the water again. Each family gets an allowance of 25 salmon for the first person and 10 more salmon for each additional person in the household, so

Kenai

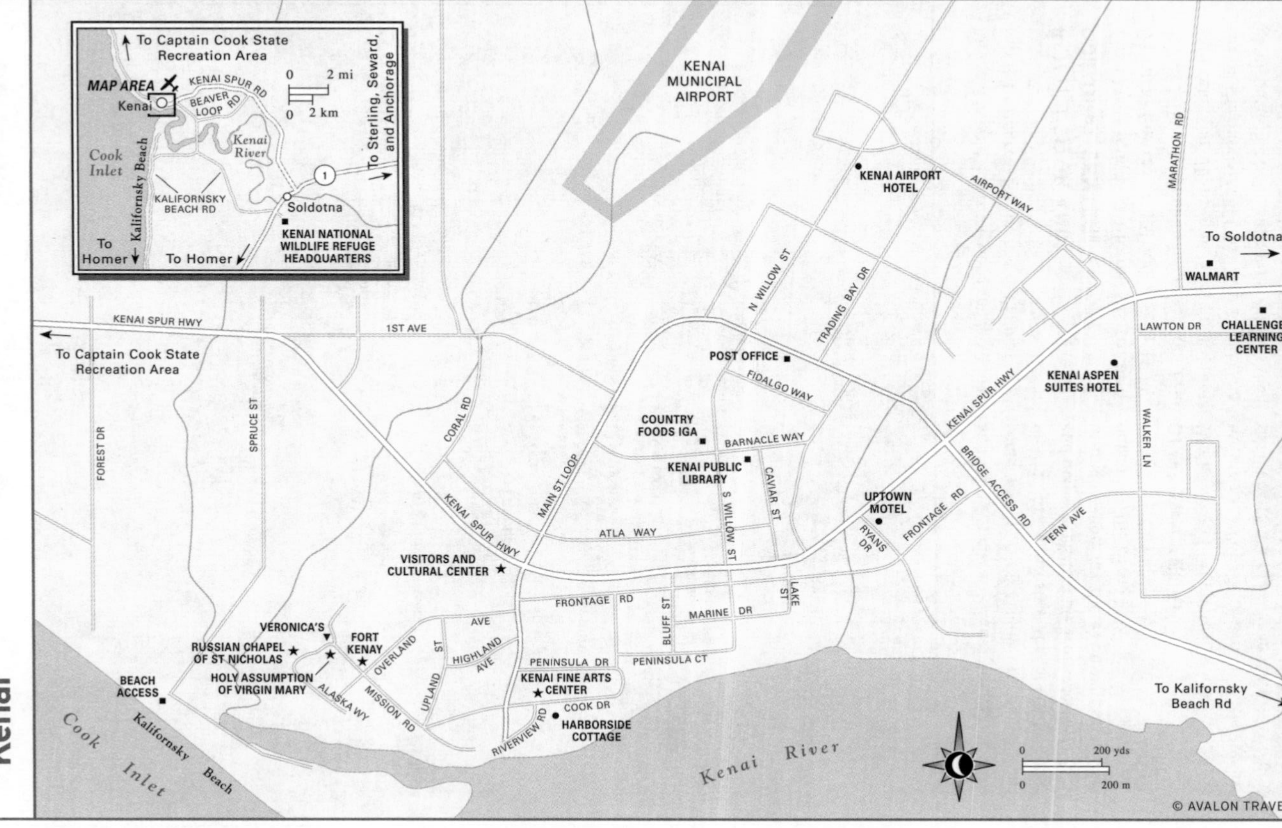
To Captain Cook State Recreation Area
MAP AREA
Kenai
KENAI SPUR RD
BEAVER LOOP RD
0
2 mi
0
2 km
To Sterling, Seward, and Anchorage
Cook Inlet
Kalifornsky Beach
Kenai River
1
KALIFORNSKY BEACH RD
Soldotna
KENAI NATIONAL WILDLIFE REFUGE HEADQUARTERS
To Homer
To Homer
KENAI MUNICIPAL AIRPORT
KENAI AIRPORT HOTEL
AIRPORT WAY
MARATHON RD
To Soldotna
WALMART
N WILLOW ST
TRADING BAY DR
LAWTON DR
CHALLENGER LEARNING CENTER
KENAI SPUR HWY
1ST AVE
To Captain Cook State Recreation Area
POST OFFICE
FIDALGO WAY
KENAI ASPEN SUITES HOTEL
KENAI SPUR HWY
WALKER LN
FOREST DR
SPRUCE ST
CORAL RD
COUNTRY FOODS IGA
BARNACLE WAY
KENAI PUBLIC LIBRARY
CAVIAR ST
BRIDGE ACCESS RD
MAIN ST LOOP
S WILLOW ST
UPTOWN MOTEL
FRONTAGE RD
TERN AVE
KENAI SPUR HWY
ATLA WAY
RYANS DR
VISITORS AND CULTURAL CENTER
FRONTAGE RD
LAKE ST
MARINE DR
BLUFF ST
AVE
VERONICA'S
FORT KENAY
RUSSIAN CHAPEL OF ST NICHOLAS
HOLY ASSUMPTION OF VIRGIN MARY
OVERLAND
ST
HIGHLAND AVE
PENINSULA DR
PENINSULA CT
KENAI FINE ARTS CENTER
BEACH ACCESS
ALASKA WY
MISSION RD
UPLAND
COOK DR
RIVERVIEW RD
HARBORSIDE COTTAGE
To Kalifornsky Beach Rd
Cook Inlet
Kalifornsky Beach
Kenai River
0
200 yds
0
200 m
© AVALON TRAVEL

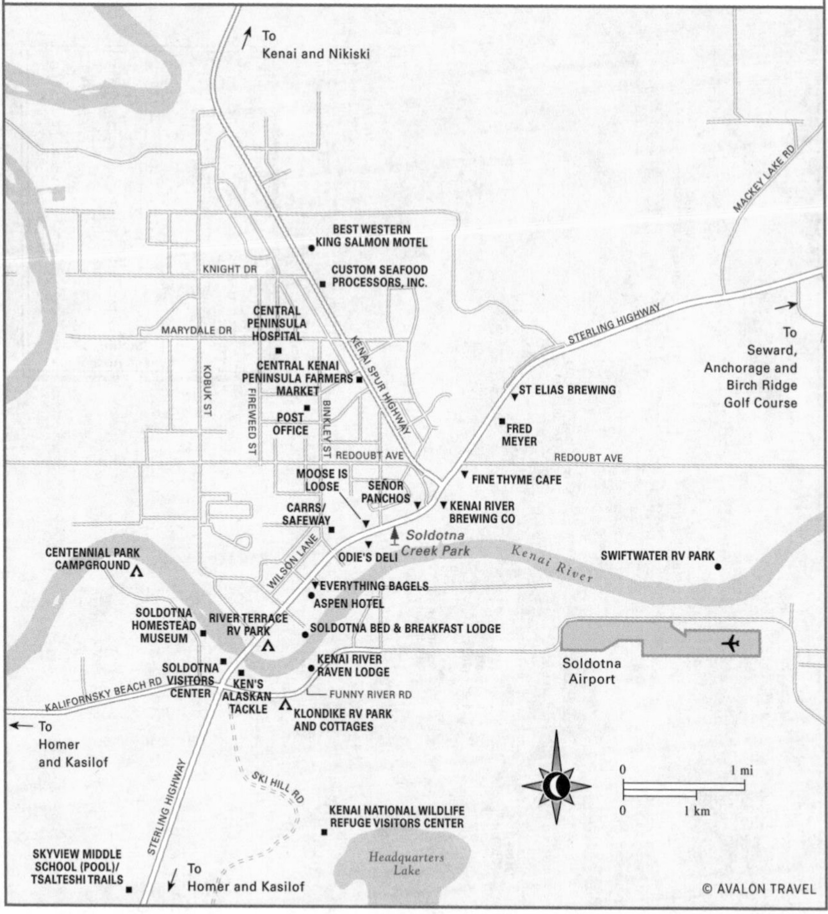

for most people this is a serious endeavor that fills their freezers for the rest of the year.

KENAI VISITOR AND CULTURAL CENTER

The 10,000-square-foot **Kenai Visitor and Cultural Center** (11471 Kenai Spur Hwy., 907/283-1991, kenaichamber.org, Mon.-Fri. 9am-6pm, Sat. 10am-5pm, Sun. noon-5pm) sits on the outskirts of Old Town Kenai. The giant, barn-like building houses exhibits that showcase the flow of influences from Russian and then American occupation, along with contemporary Alaska Native art, many animal mounts, and a gift shop that also sells books and maps. On Saturdays from Memorial Day through Labor Day, there's an artisans market outside on the lawn.

OLD TOWN KENAI

While you're in the visitor center, ask for a walking map of Old Town, and leave yourself an extra hour to take in the town's oldest buildings, including the **Holy Assumption**

of the Virgin Mary Russian Orthodox Church (1106 Mission Ave., 907/283-4122, circa 1895) and the nearby Russian Orthodox **Chapel of St. Nicholas** (circa 1906).

K'BEQ' CULTURAL SITE

The Kenaitze Tribe, the original Dena'ina people of this area, are still a thriving part of this community; they maintain the **K'Beq' Cultural Site** (Mile 52.6 Sterling Hwy., 907/335-7290, kenaitze.org, summer Thurs.-Sun. 10am-4pm, free), very close to Cooper Landing, which teaches about their traditional way of life. Guided tours are available.

SOLDOTNA VISITOR CENTER

The beautiful **Soldotna Visitor Center** (44790 Sterling Hwy., 907/262-1337, visitsoldotna.com, mid-May-mid-Sept. daily 9am-7pm, winter Mon.-Fri. 9am-5pm) houses the world-record, 97-pound king salmon that was fished out of the Kenai River by a Soldotna resident, along with impressive wildlife displays that include brown and black bears, bison, Dall sheep, mountain goats, king crabs, and more.

Be sure to ask for their booklet of wildlife-viewing sites near Soldotna (there are more than 60!), as well as their free fishing rod loan program for children under 16 and their binocular loan program for all ages. The small gift shop's wares include area maps. Don't miss the walking trails that lead out to overlooks of **Headquarters Lake** to the south and link into the **Centennial Trail**—which winds through Centennial Campground—to the north.

SOLDOTNA HOMESTEAD MUSEUM

If you're curious about Soldotna's first homesteaders, you can see examples of their early homestead cabins, handmade utensils, and other pioneer objects in the **Soldotna Homestead Museum** (461 Centennial Park Rd., 907/262-3832, mid-May-mid-Sept. Tues.-Sat. 10am-4pm, Sun. noon-4pm, free but donations accepted). You can walk through the buildings on your own, but the knowledgeable volunteers on hand can answer questions and tell some great stories about the area. Expect to spend at least an hour.

KENAI NATIONAL WILDLIFE REFUGE HEADQUARTERS

The headquarters for **Kenai National Wildlife Refuge** are located in Soldotna (Ski Hill Rd., 907/260-2820, fws.gov/refuge/Kenai, Memorial Day-Labor Day daily 9am-5pm, off-season Tues.-Sat. 10am-5pm). You'll find lots of information about the wildlife and ecosystems in this area, plus hourly movies about Alaska and the region's wild animals. You can also take a self-guided or ranger-led walk on trails that also lead down to Headquarters Lake.

KENAI RIVER

The Kenai River itself is, of course, a major attraction in both towns, although many fishing lodges and other accommodations have claimed much of the riverfront real estate. In Soldotna, the elevated riverside boardwalks along **Centennial Campground** (349 Centennial Park Rd.) are the best place for viewing the water. In Kenai, Kalifornsky Beach takes you right down to the river mouth, and if you take Kalifornsky Beach Road from the Sterling Highway to Kenai, it'll lead you right across a bridge with a designated riverside viewing area on the near side.

Recreation

TOP EXPERIENCE

★ FISHING THE KENAI RIVER

Of all the freshwater fishing in Alaska, the Kenai River is by far the most iconic, especially for its runs of king, sockeye, and silver salmon. That's a mixed blessing, because both day guide and fishing lodge services book up very quickly for the peak months of June and July (schedule your trip at least six months in advance—ideally more) and the rivers are, by Alaska standards, crowded.

On the other hand, guide and lodging

companies in Kenai and Soldotna really have their services down, and both towns offer plenty of big-city comforts and amenities to support your visit (especially Soldotna). When you want a break from freshwater fishing, there's also excellent saltwater fishing for halibut in Cook Inlet.

The good news is that in a region that's so popular and competitive, it's hard to go wrong with day guide services. Your choice of lodging might be able to offer you a discount with their guide service of choice, but if you're booking independently, both of the following are excellent. Most of the fishing lodges under *Accommodations* also offer day trips for anyone (you don't have to be staying there), and, again, their service, crews, and safety records are all excellent.

ACE Fishing Adventures (907/335-2248, acefishn.com) offers freshwater fishing adventures for sockeye, silver, or king salmon, plus year-round fishing for rainbow trout. Prices start from $175 per person for a half-day trip, or $240 per person for a full-day trip, which includes all tackle required and complimentary fish cleaning.

Kenai Riverbend Resort (800/625-2324, kenairiverbend.com) also offers great guided day trips for red, silver, and king salmon, rainbow trout, and Dolly Varden. Saltwater fishing for halibut is also an option. Prices start at $200 for a full-day trip hunting silver salmon or $175 for a half-day king charter. The resort offers lodging and fishing packages too.

If you're fishing on your own, make sure you pick up a copy of the *Soldotna Visitor's Guide* (available at the Soldotna Visitor Center and many local businesses); it lists the best Kenai River fishing spots all the way from Soldotna to the river's mouth in Kenai.

If you don't have your own fishing gear, most accommodations in the area will happily loan or rent you basic equipment. (If you hire a fishing charter, all the gear you need will be included.) If you want to buy your own gear, visit locally owned **Ken's Alaskan Tackle** (44793 Sterling Hwy., Soldotna, 907/262-6870, kensalaskantackle.com), which is just 300 feet from the visitor center, or the **Sportsman's Warehouse** (44402 Sterling Hwy., Soldotna, 907/420-3000, sportsmanswarehouse.com, Mon.-Sat. 9am-9pm, Sun. 9am-7pm, summer hours may expand)

Once you catch your fish, **Custom Seafood Processors** (35722 Kenai Spur Hwy., 907/262-9691, seafoods-direct.com) will process, pack, and FedEx your fish. Smoked

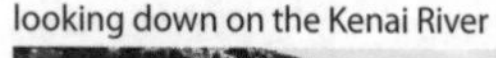
looking down on the Kenai River

A fisherman shows off his catch in the Kenai River.

salmon is absolutely delicious, but creating it takes a lot of work; you can get your fish custom processed and custom cured or smoked at **Tustumena Smoke House** (Mile 101.4 Sterling Hwy., 907/260-3401, tustumenasmokehouse.com), which also sells ready-made Alaska salmon sausage and jerky.

CANOEING

The Kenai National Wildlife Refuge has a couple of great canoe trails, with diverse wildlife-viewing opportunities, including many songbirds, shorebirds, and waterfowl, and good fishing once you're past the most traveled sections of the lakes. Stop at either the refuge headquarters or the Soldotna Visitor Center to get more information about these canoe trails. You can rent a canoe and arrange a shuttle service with **Alaska Canoe & Campground** (35292 Sterling Hwy., 907/262-2331, alaskacanoetrips.com), or if you don't need help with a car shuttle, you can also rent from **Wilderness Way** (44370 Sterling Hwy., summer 907/567-1001, winter 801/782-9696, wildernessway.net, Mon.-Thurs. 10am-6pm, Fri.-Sat. 10am-7pm), a full-service sporting goods store that also sells everything from travel gear to archery and ski equipment.

CAPTAIN COOK STATE PARK

This lovely beach is popular with agate hunters (look for ocean-tumbled rocks that practically glow when the sun hits them), or you can take a picnic lunch to enjoy the views over Cook Inlet and see if you can spot the offshore oil platforms. You'll find the park 25 miles north of Soldotna, at the end of the Kenai Spur Highway. It also sports 53 tent or RV campsites ($12, no RV size limit), with a day-use parking fee of $5 and amenities limited to pit toilets, water, and picnic sites.

NORTH PENINSULA RECREATION CENTER (NIKISKI POOL)

If you're looking for something to do on a rainy day or just need a chance to kick back and rest, the **North Peninsula Recreation Center** (Mile 23.4 Kenai Spur Hwy., 55176 Poolside Ave., 907/776-8800, northpenrec.com) in Nikiski has one of the best pools in the state. It's heated to a balmy 80-plus degrees, has a 136-foot water slide, rain umbrella, and diving area, and ranges in depth from just 1 foot to almost 12 feet deep. There are a few aquatic fitness classes too, including astonishingly difficult classes in log rolling, of all things. A swim pass costs $4, plus $7 for the water slide, or $2 for seniors over 60. Find the pool schedule for lap swim, open swim, and the water slide online.

GOLF

Most Alaska communities have at least one golf course; between them, Kenai and Soldotna have three.

Kenai Golf Course (1420 Lawton Dr., 907/283-7500, kenaigolfcourse.com) is the only full-service 18-hole course on the peninsula, with a driving range, club rental, and both push carts and power carts available. Greens fees are $22 for 9 holes or $32 for 18 holes, with discounts for seniors, juniors, and playing during the weekdays; the course is open May-September daily with 7am-10pm tee times (may be adjusted for daylight).

Birch Ridge Golf Course (42223 Sterling Hwy., 907/262-5270, birchridgegolf.com) in Soldotna is a 9-hole course with separate tee boxes for the front and the back nines. The course offers beautiful vistas of Mount Iliamna and Mount Redoubt, both active volcanoes. Greens fees start at $20 for 9 holes on a weekend and $30 for 18 holes on a weekend, with discounts for seniors, juniors, and playing during the week. Motorized carts and rental clubs are available, and tee times may vary with the length of the daylight hours.

Bird Homestead Golf Course (Funny River Rd., 907/260-4653, alaska-golf.com) is an unpretentious course run by homesteaders. They charge $15 for 9 holes or $24 for 18 holes, with discounts for seniors and juniors. Pull carts, driving carts, and rental clubs are all available; call for tee times.

No matter which golf course you choose, keep an eye out for wildlife, including moose, sandhill cranes, coyotes, wolves, and even the occasional caribou or bear wandering across the course.

Food

STEAK AND SEAFOOD

If you want a substantial meal in a rustic lodge-style atmosphere (translation: dark wood paneling and lots of animal heads on the walls), head for **Louie's Restaurant** in the Uptown Motel (47 Spur View Dr., 907/283-3660, uptownmotel.com). They offer excellent steak and great freshly caught seafood, including halibut, salmon, prawns, and crab legs. If you've never had a salmon steak before (a thick slab of meat cut crosswise through the body of the salmon, instead of filleted along its length), this is the place to try it.

BURGERS

Old school buses are a "thing" in Alaska; I think it's a case of the classic Alaskan ingenuity that inspires us to make use of whatever is available in our surroundings. When you have a big, durable vehicle at your disposal, you use it to shuttle passengers back and forth on remote day tours, stash gear for guiding companies, and, sometimes . . . serve as a restaurant. Case in point, the **Burger Bus** (409 Overland Ave., 907/382-9611, Tues.-Sat. 11am-6pm) is a long-lived favorite that serves the best burgers on the Kenai Peninsula; the onion rings are good too. You may end up eating at outdoor picnic tables. If the weather's bad, it's best to take your burger and run.

CAFÉS AND BAKERIES

For a shot of caffeine, head to **Veronica's Coffee House** (604 Peterson Way, 907/283-2725, veronicascoffeehouse.com, summer Mon.-Wed. 9am-3pm, Thurs.-Sat. 9am-8pm, $16), which serves homemade soup, sandwiches, wraps, quiche, and baked goods in a wonderful old home on a bluff overlooking the mouth of the Kenai River, just across the street from the old Russian Orthodox church. They have live music on Friday and Saturday evenings.

Soldotna's enormously popular **The Moose Is Loose** bakery (44278 Sterling Hwy., 907/260-3036, Tues.-Sat. 6:30am-4:30pm) is legendary for their cinnamon rolls, donuts, and tongue-in-cheek humor; they also sell a few souvenirs.

SANDWICHES

If you've been craving a New York-style bagel, you're not alone. The young founders of **Everything Bagels** (44539 Sterling Hwy., 907/252-8135, everythingbagelsak.com, Mon.-Sat. 7am-2pm, $9) wanted one so badly, in fact, that they started their own bakery. They'll even deliver, but you have to order your handmade bagels at least 48 hours in advance, or shop from their selection of bagels, sandwiches, and salads in store. They also offer coffee and free Wi-Fi.

Some of the best food in Alaska comes from little hole-in-the-wall places; **Fine Thyme Cafe** (43965 Sterling Hwy., 907/262-6620, Mon.-Sat. 9am-5pm) is a fine example. This small shop has great soup and sandwiches (try the corned beef or grilled cheese) and also offers quiche and a few wraps. They recently added an outdoor patio, and if you check their Facebook page you might catch one of their sporadic dinner offerings.

Odie's Deli (44315 Sterling Hwy., 907/260-3255, odiesdeli.com, Mon.-Fri. 8am-8pm, Sat. 9am-4pm, $14) offers enormous, tasty sandwiches, equally big cookies, coffee, and a few breakfast options; you can also build your own sandwich to suit any food restrictions you might have. If you have a free evening, stop by for the pub quizzes on Wednesday and live music on Friday.

MEXICAN

In Soldotna, **Señor Pancho's** (44096 Sterling Hwy., 907/260-7777) offers fresh, flavorful, and authentic Mexican food with great daily specials and an amazing salsa bar.

BARBECUE

Every part of Alaska has its own "most popular" cuisine. In Fairbanks, it's Thai food; in Anchorage, it's Vietnamese pho and pizza; and in the Kenai Peninsula, it's barbecue. You'd be hard-pressed to find a community here that doesn't have some sort of excellent barbecue hut. In Soldotna, visit **Fire House BBQ** (43837 Kalifornsky Beach Rd., 907/252-7747, Tues.-Sat. 11am-8pm, Sun. 11am-4pm). Everything is phenomenal, but don't miss the tender, flavorful brisket and pulled pork.

BREWERIES AND BREWPUBS

You can choose from three breweries and brewpubs in the general Soldotna area. Note that there is a distinction between the two: Brewpubs serve both food and drinks, while breweries only serve drinks and are limited to 36 ounces per person per day for on-site consumption. However, you're welcome to bring your own food to breweries, and they usually promote a very convivial atmosphere.

Just to make things especially confusing, an establishment's name doesn't always make it clear which category it falls into. **St. Elias Brewing Company** in Soldotna (434 Sharkathmi Ave., 907/260-7837, steliasbrewingco.com, summer Sun.-Thurs. 11am-10pm, Fri.-Sat. 11am-11pm, reduced winter hours, $15) is actually a brewpub, with great pizza, salads, and sandwiches.

Kassik's Brewery in nearby Nikiski (47160 Spruce Haven St., 907/776-4055, kassiksbrew.com, daily May-Aug., reduced winter hours) is a modest farmhouse-style brewery. The **Kenai River Brewing Company** (241 N. Aspen Dr., 907/262-2337, kenairiverbrewing.com, Mon.-Sat. noon-7pm) is also a brewery—in both cases no food is served, although you can bring your own, and you can get closed containers of beer to go. Don't miss the Kenai River Brewing Company's fabulous heated, covered patio overlooking the Kenai River Valley.

FARMERS MARKETS

Southcentral Alaska farmers grow some wonderful produce; check out their wares, along with lots of locally made arts and crafts, at the Saturday-only **Central Kenai Peninsula Farmers Market** (Kenai Spur Hwy. at Corral Ave., alaskaartguild.com, June-mid-Sept. Sat. 10am-2pm).

GROCERIES

In Kenai, you can choose from **Country Foods IGA** (140 S. Willow St., 907/283-4834, countryfoodsiga.com, daily 7am-10pm), **Safeway** (10576 Kenai Spur Hwy., 907/283-6300, 24 hours), and a **Walmart Supercenter** (10096 Kenai Spur Hwy., 907/395-0971, 24 hours).

Soldotna has both a **Fred Meyer** (43843 Sterling Hwy., 907/260-2200, daily 7am-11pm) and a **Carrs** (44428 Sterling Hwy. S, 907/714-5400, 24 hours).

Accommodations

If you want a conventional hotel-style experience, your best option in Kenai is the **Aspen Hotels Kenai** (10431 Kenai Spur Hwy., 866/483-7848 or 907/283-2272, aspenhotelsak.com, from $199), which offers clean, spacious suites with fully equipped kitchens, free

Wi-Fi, a fitness center, and a complimentary Seattle's Best coffee bar in the lobby. If you want air conditioning, this is a good place to stay.

Even though its lack of a standalone website might make it seem a little dodgy, travelers in search of a good deal love the **Kenai Airport Hotel** (230 N. Willow St., 907/283-1577, from $159 peak season). The rooms are basic but clean, with free Wi-Fi, cable TV, and private bathrooms; the airport is right across the street. The obvious downside to that is that you'll have to put up with the sound of planes going overhead, but it's not too bad if you get a room on the side away from the airport, and you're within a quick drive of most of the town's attractions. If you want a hair dryer in your room, make sure you ask when you make the reservation; they're only in some rooms.

On the B&B front, one of the very best is the **Red Cabin B&B** (44392 Carver Dr., 907/283-0836, redcabinbandb.homestead.com, from $145 peak season), a stand-alone cabin between Soldotna and Kenai poised on 20 acres of private land and just five minutes from the Kenai River. The cabin's full kitchen is stocked with breakfast food; it has a queen-size bed and a queen-size futon, a private bathroom, and a barbecue grill that's shared with their second property next door, **The Annex** (from $130 peak season), a smaller cabin with a queen bed, full-size futon, and smaller kitchenette with no stove (just a microwave). There's also a private bathroom, but you'll have to use the kitchen sink for the toiletries. Still, The Annex is comfortable and peaceful, and visitors love getting to stay on a working property with dogs and horses nearby. Both properties have Wi-Fi.

I also really like the **Log Cabin Inn** (49860 Eider Dr., Kenai, 877/834-2912 907/283-3653, alaskalogcabininn.com, from $149 peak season); they offer eight clean, comfortable rooms in the main lodge building and three standalone cabins; each room or cabin has its own private bathroom. The cabins are very simple and rustic, with curtains instead of bathroom doors, so they're not for the shy. But they are comfortable, and the three beds (one of them queen size) in each cabin make them a great deal for groups. The Wi-Fi is good in the lodge but questionable in the cabins, but the homemade breakfast—which goes well beyond the usual scrambled eggs and muffins—is excellent, and packed lunches are available for your fishing trips.

Soldotna has a couple of hotel chain options, both with clean and comfortable rooms. **Aspen Hotels Soldotna** (326 Binkley Circle, 866/483-7848 or 907/260-7736, aspenhotelsak.com, from $174) offers the most amenities of the chains in this region, with a business center, fitness center, on-site laundry, kitchenettes in some units, free Wi-Fi, a freezer for storing your fish catch, a swimming pool, and a spa.

Your next best chain option is the **Best Western King Salmon Motel** in Soldotna (35546A Kenai Spur Hwy., 800/780-7234 or 907/262-5857, from $179). They have a fitness center and a large parking lot with plenty of room for big RVs, and they offer a free continental breakfast with waffles, pastries, cereal, yogurt and fruit.

CAMPING

For RV campers or anyone who wants a no-frills lodge room, **Beluga Lookout Lodge & RV Park** (929 Mission Ave., Kenai, 907/283-5999, belugalookout.com, $40-89 for an RV space, monthly and weekly rates available) offers stunning views over the Kenai River and Cook Inlet from many of their 65 full-hookup RV sites, which include water, sewer, electric, showers, Wi-Fi, and cable TV. Many have pull-through access. Other amenities include restrooms, showers, laundry, and fish-cleaning facilities on-site, as well as a picnic pavilion. This is a pet-friendly property, as long as Fido is leashed and you clean up his "deposits."

For those who aren't in an RV or just want a break, Beluga Lookout also rents cabins that sleep up to four people on a queen bed and sleeper sofa, with a private bathroom and kitchenette that includes a microwave.

They also have a few lodge rooms that are more like a standard hotel, with one queen bed, en suite bathroom, cable TV, refrigerator, and great views; prices range from $109 to $159, depending on the season. This is a great place for watching the dipnetting circus on the beach below, and possibly even getting to visit with local dipnetters who've booked into the lodge or cabins.

Soldotna has one of the very best large campgrounds right smack in the middle of town. **Centennial Campground** (349 Centennial Park Rd., soldotna.org, from $20) has more than 220 wooded campsites with fire pits, picnic tables, and pit toilets. Some of the sites are right on the river, but watch out for the tent overflow camping area, where you're literally jammed wall-to-wall with your neighbors. There are no hookups for RVs. More than 800 feet of elevated boardwalk run through the campground, and the trails link up with walkways outside the nearby Soldotna Visitor Center. There's also a boat launch along with a large, wheelchair-accessible boardwalk area for fishing or admiring the scenery.

Swiftwater Park (675 Swiftwater Park Rd., soldotna.org, from $20) is a little more secluded, with 40 campsites set back in the woods along the Kenai River. Amenities include potable water, picnic tables, pit toilets, fire rings, firewood for purchase, and an RV dump station. There are also 800 feet of boardwalk to help you walk or fish along the river's edge without disturbing fragile habitat.

If you want full-service RV hookups, try **Klondike RV Park & Cottages** (48665 Funny River Rd., 800/980-6035 or 907/262-6035, klondikervpark.com, from $46 in peak season), which offers 35 RV sites with electric, water, and sewer connections, just a few minutes from downtown Soldotna. Fourteen of the sites have 50-amp service; they can accommodate rigs up to 60 feet long, and most sites are also wide enough to park your tow vehicle and still deploy your slide-outs. They also rent private cottages that sleep four, with a fully equipped kitchen and private bathroom; rates start at $175 double occupancy during peak season.

FISHING LODGES

It's worth noting that even options with "Bed and Breakfast" in the name still function as fishing lodges, and most of these lodges also offer guided day-fishing trips to the general public.

Kenai Riverbend Resort (45525 Porter Rd., Kenai, 800/625-2324 or 907/283-9489, kenairiverbend.com) is a great lodge that also offers stand-alone fishing charters with a real crackerjack crew, starting from $175 per person for a half-day king charter or $200 per person for a full-day silver salmon charter, or fishing/lodging combos in their nine riverfront cabins or seven lodge rooms. Each cabin sleeps up to six people, with a full kitchen, private bath, television, and sitting area; linens and daily maid service are included. The lodge rooms have log-hewn beds, private baths, and pretty views over the Kenai River. Lodging/fishing package prices start at $1,695 for six nights of lodging and four days of fishing in the shoulder season, plus continental breakfast each day and free fish processing. Peak season rates hit $2,295 for seven nights and five days of fishing.

The Bavarian-inspired, sparkling clean **Alaska Fishing Charters/Soldotna Bed & Breakfast Lodge** (399 Lovers Ln., 877/262-4779 or 907/262-4779, alaskafishinglodges.us, July from $227, rates decrease in other months) has 16 guest rooms perched right on the Kenai River, although most of the river views are screened by tall trees. Guests will enjoy 300 feet of riverfront access, free Wi-Fi, and the option of all-inclusive packages that come with freshwater, saltwater, and fly-out day trips. The hosts speak fluent German, French, Japanese, and English.

Just a few miles outside Soldotna, **Alaska Red Fish Lodge** (32815 Eldorado Way, Sterling, 888/335-4490 or 907/262-7080, alaskaredfishlodge.us, $174 peak season) offers simple, fully furnished and heated cabins with private access to the Kenai River. Each cabin has a private bathroom, TV (with so-so signal), kitchenette, and a barbecue grill, plus parking right outside the front door. There's also a fish-processing center, a shared firepit (the hosts provide the wood), and a fenced play yard for kids. Seven-night double occupancy packages with day tours for fishing and sightseeing (including bear viewing, river rafting, and Iditarod sled dog tours) start at $1,895 per person.

If you're thinking of visiting in the winter or want to get a few miles out of town, **Clam Gulch Lodge** (Mile 119.6 Sterling Hwy., 67260 Sterling Hwy., Clam Gulch, 800/700-9555 or 907/260-3778, clamgulch.com, from $130) near Soldotna has heartbreakingly beautiful views from five lodge rooms that share three bathrooms. They specialize in year-round outdoor activities, including halibut and salmon fishing, dog mushing, snowmachining, and clamming. The friendly hosts make a great breakfast with reindeer sausage, salmon hash pancakes, and the like, and will happily help you plan trips, including fishing, canoeing or kayaking, clamming, and golfing.

Information and Services

Both Kenai and Soldotna have plenty of coffee shops where you can usually get free Wi-Fi when you buy a cup of coffee or tea. You can also get Wi-Fi for free at the **Soldotna Public Library** (235 N. Binkley St., 907/262-4227, soldotna.org/library, Mon., Wed., and Fri.-Sat. 10am-6pm, Tues. and Thurs. 10am-8pm). Another option is the **Kenai Community Library** (163 Main St. Loop, 907/283-43778, kenailibrary.org, Mon.-Thurs. 9am-7pm, Fri. 9am-6pm, Sat. 9am-5pm, closed Sun. during the summer).

The best medical care in the region is at Soldotna's **Central Peninsula Hospital** (250 Hospital Pl., 907/714-4404, cpgh.org), which has a 24-hour emergency room. You won't have any problem finding gas stations or vehicle service in either community.

Each town has a post office: the **Soldotna post office** (175 N. Binkley St., Mon.-Fri. 10am-5pm, Sat. 10am-2pm) and the **Kenai post office** (140 Bidarka St., Mon.-Fri. 8:45am-5pm, Sat. 9:30am-1pm).

Transportation

Ultimately, transportation may be the biggest factor in deciding whether you end up in Kenai or Soldotna. If you want to fly, your only option is Kenai, using the small airline **Ravn Alaska** (800/866-8394 or 907/266-8394, flyravn.com), which has many daily 30-minute flights back and forth to the Anchorage Airport. (If you want to fly from Homer, you have to go through Anchorage first.)

If you're traveling by motorcoach, however, you're going to end up in Soldotna: The Homer **Stage Line** (907/868-3914, stagelineinhomer.com) stops by as part of its Anchorage-Homer and Anchorage-Seward runs. Their passenger vans used to run to Kenai too, but that stop was discontinued because of low demand.

If you're driving yourself, Soldotna is 75 miles (about 90 minutes) north of Homer and 145 miles (just under three hours) south of Anchorage; Kenai is an additional 11 miles or 20 minutes west of Soldotna. If you managed to get to town without a car, there are chain rental agencies at the Kenai Airport, including Avis and Budget. Budget also has an off-site location in Kenai and another in Soldotna, or you can rent locally from **Midway Auto Park Sales & Rentals** (37452 Kenai Spur Hwy., 907/260-3722, midwayautollc.com), which sits between the two towns.

If you need a taxi, **Alaska Cab** (907/283-6000, akcab.com) offers 24/7 service in both Kenai and Soldotna.

Homer

If there's one place in Alaska that exemplifies everything wonderful about the state, it's Homer, a town of about 5,000 poised right at the end of the highway leading south from Anchorage. This little seaside town is still on the road system but feels pleasantly secluded, thanks to the rugged natural beauty all around it. Homer is known for its artsy population, its (literally) world-class food, and its halibut fishing. It's also one of the few places in Alaska where you can walk for miles on a sandy beach. It makes a beautiful launching pad for visiting tiny, almost roadless communities on the far side of Kachemak Bay.

The climate is one of the mildest in the state; summer highs linger in the 60s from July through August, while winter lows bottom out at around 20 degrees. The town is drier than you might expect, with average annual precipitation of just 24.4 inches. But still, it's smart to come prepared for wind, rain, and wet footing. "Alaska sneakers" (calf-high rubber boots) are definitely appropriate.

The town is named for the con man Homer Pennock, who promoted gold mining in the area, but it was coal that was really successful—so successful, in fact, that the locals could and sometimes still do walk the beach, picking pieces of coal right off the sand and using it to heat their homes.

SIGHTS

The Homer Spit

Nothing characterizes Homer like the Spit, a 4.5-mile stretch of sand and rock that stretches away from the mainland into Kachemak Bay, with some of the city's best gift shops, restaurants, fishing charters, and water taxis on both sides of the road that runs its length. Most of them have great views over the water on both sides. There's a paved multiuse trail alongside the road for anyone who wants to bike or run along the spit, a lagoon offers great fishing for kids, and the city campgrounds on both side of the road make great access points for beachcombing at low tide. You can park for free in any lot on the Spit unless otherwise marked, although some of the city lots have time limits for short-term parking.

looking down on Homer and the Spit, stretching out into Kachemak Bay

Homer

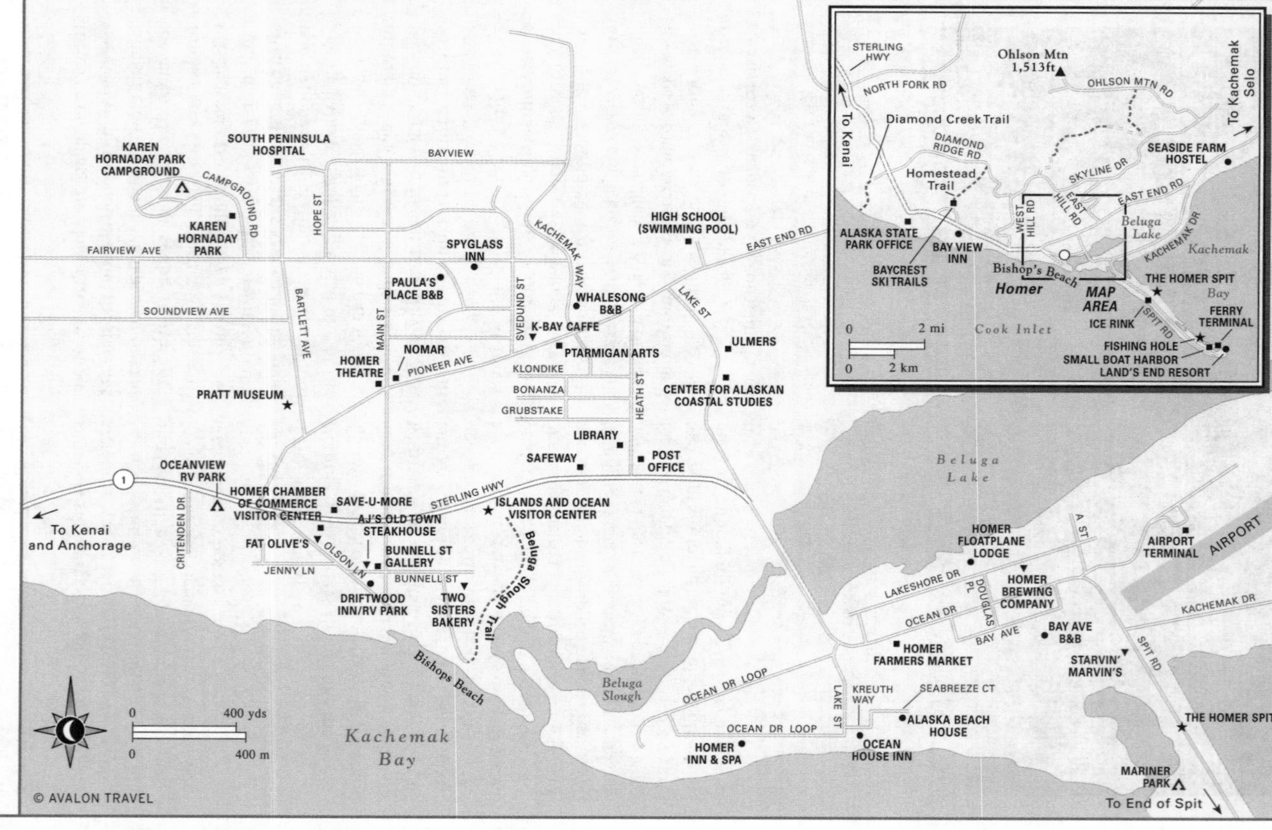
KAREN HORNADAY PARK CAMPGROUND
SOUTH PENINSULA HOSPITAL
BAYVIEW
CAMPGROUND RD
KAREN HORNADAY PARK
HOPE ST
FAIRVIEW AVE
SOUNDVIEW AVE
BARTLETT AVE
MAIN ST
PAULA'S PLACE B&B
SPYGLASS INN
SVEDUND ST
KACHEMAK WAY
WHALESONG B&B
K-BAY CAFFE
PTARMIGAN ARTS
HIGH SCHOOL (SWIMMING POOL)
EAST END RD
LAKE ST
ULMERS
CENTER FOR ALASKAN COASTAL STUDIES
NOMAR
HOMER THEATRE
PIONEER AVE
KLONDIKE
BONANZA
GRUBSTAKE
HEATH ST
PRATT MUSEUM
LIBRARY
SAFEWAY
POST OFFICE
OCEANVIEW RV PARK
HOMER CHAMBER OF COMMERCE VISITOR CENTER
SAVE-U-MORE
AJ'S OLD TOWN STEAKHOUSE
STERLING HWY
ISLANDS AND OCEAN VISITOR CENTER
To Kenai and Anchorage
CRITENDEN DR
FAT OLIVE'S
OLSON LN
BUNNELL ST GALLERY
JENNY LN
BUNNELL ST
DRIFTWOOD INN/RV PARK
TWO SISTERS BAKERY
Beluga Slough Trail
Bishops Beach
Beluga Slough
Kachemak Bay
0
400 yds
0
400 m
© AVALON TRAVEL
Beluga Lake
HOMER FLOATPLANE LODGE
A ST
AIRPORT TERMINAL
AIRPORT
LAKESHORE DR
DOUGLAS PL
HOMER BREWING COMPANY
OCEAN DR
BAY AVE
BAY AVE B&B
KACHEMAK DR
HOMER FARMERS MARKET
STARVIN' MARVIN'S
SPIT RD
OCEAN DR LOOP
LAKE ST
KREUTH WAY
SEABREEZE CT
ALASKA BEACH HOUSE
OCEAN DR LOOP
HOMER INN & SPA
OCEAN HOUSE INN
THE HOMER SPIT
MARINER PARK
To End of Spit
STERLING HWY
Ohlson Mtn 1,513ft
NORTH FORK RD
OHLSON MTN RD
To Kachemak Selo
To Kenai
Diamond Creek Trail
DIAMOND RIDGE RD
SEASIDE FARM HOSTEL
SKYLINE DR
Homestead Trail
EAST END RD
WEST HILL RD
EAST HILL RD
Beluga Lake
KACHEMAK DR
ALASKA STATE PARK OFFICE
BAY VIEW INN
Kachemak
BAYCREST SKI TRAILS
Bishop's Beach
Homer
MAP AREA
THE HOMER SPIT
Bay
ICE RINK
SPIT RD
FERRY TERMINAL
0
2 mi
Cook Inlet
FISHING HOLE
SMALL BOAT HARBOR
LAND'S END RESORT
0
2 km

Bishop's Beach

No doubt the most popular beach in Homer, **Bishop's Beach** sits at the south end of Beluga Place. This is one of the few places in Alaska where, on a warm day, you really can take your shoes off and stroll barefoot in the sand without a care in the world. The beach is so large that despite its popularity, you won't feel crowded. Keep an eye out for coal littering the beach; it looks like burned chunks of wood and washes ashore with every tide. Resist the urge to go into the water—much like in Anchorage, there are dangerous mud flats that could trap and kill you.

Carl E. Wynn Nature Center

The **Carl E. Wynn Nature Center** (Mile 1.5 E. Skyline Dr., 907/235-6667, akcoastalstudies.org, $7, discounts for seniors, youth, and families, visitor center summer daily 10am-6pm, Fri. till 7:30pm) offers miles of easy walking trails through spruce forest and wildflower meadows, with hands-on nature exhibits in the small-cabin visitor center. They offer guided hikes at the center (free with admission, mid-June-Labor Day daily at 10am and 2pm); across the bay at Peterson Bay Field Station (guided hikes from $140 pp adults, including water transport; discounts for children and families); and at the docks on the Homer Spit (June-mid-Aug. daily 1pm and 4pm, small fee applies); look for the "Guided Nature Tours Across the Bay" sign above the check-in hut.

Alaska Islands and Ocean Visitor Center

The lovely, modern **Alaska Islands and Ocean Visitor Center** (95 Sterling Hwy., 907/235-6961, islandsandocean.org, Memorial Day-Labor Day daily 9am-5pm, winter Tues.-Sat. noon-5pm, free) has exhibits and videos showcasing the wildlife of the largest seabird refuge in the world, the Alaska Maritime National Wildlife Refuge. Check the notice board or ask the staff about guided ranger-led hikes in Kachemak Bay State Park, usually held on the first weekend of each month.

Pratt Museum

The **Pratt Museum** (3779 Bartlett Ave., 907/235-8635, prattmuseum.org, $10 adults, discounts for seniors and youth, mid-May-mid-Sept. daily 10am-6pm) has been recognized as one of the best small museums in the United States. It is truly spectacular, with interactive displays, remote wildlife cameras, some contemporary art, and a wonderful pioneer cabin—walls still partially blackened by an old fire—that has been restored to showcase the challenges of life in early Homer.

Kilcher Homestead Living Museum

Fans of the reality-TV show *Alaska: The Last Frontier,* which features the adventures of the Kilcher family in Homer, will love a visit to the historic cabin and 600-acre homestead that they've converted into the **Kilcher Homestead Living Museum** (Mile 12 East End Rd., 907/235-8713). So will non-fans of the show, who may be entertained to see that the Kilchers live only a few miles out of

the homestead cabin annex outside Homer's wonderful Pratt Museum

town—nowhere near as remote as the show makes it appear.

Their homesteading credentials are very much the real deal, though, and you can sign up for guided hikes, music lessons, and workshops on rustic skills from birding to making wild berry jam and building fences.

★ Cooking School at Tutka Bay

Chefs Kirsten and Mandy Dixon exemplify the type of world-class talent that is drawn to Alaska, whether from a sense of curiosity or a thirst for adventure. These Le Cordon Bleu-trained chefs have netted an impressive set of national and international accolades for their food, thanks to their habit of innovating with fresh, local ingredients and the best seafood in the world. Just to make things more challenging, they also do their most inspired creating at backcountry lodges in the Alaskan wilderness.

If you'd like to absorb a fraction of their knowledge and artistry, visit the **Cooking School at Tutka Bay** (907/274-2710, withinthewild.com, day workshops $250 pp including water taxi). The school is housed in a World War II-era troop carrier that was repurposed into a crabbing boat before it became the cooking school, with space for up to 12 students at once.

RECREATION

Hiking

Homer offers some modest walking trails, most of them quite close to town; ask for a trail map in the visitor center However, the real highlight of hiking in this region is the system of maintained trails on the far side of Kachemak Bay.

The most popular trek is **Grewingk Glacier Trail** from the Glacier Spit/Grewingk Lake trailhead to **Grewingk Glacier,** then out via the **Saddle Trail** trailhead in Halibut Cove; the terrain is mostly easy, except for some steep stairs leading down to the Saddle Trail trailhead, and most people can easily do the trip in half a day with plenty of time to lounge beside the glacier lake. Any water taxi on the pit can arrange a drop-off and pickup for you (**Mako's Water Taxi,** 907/235-9055, is a longtime local favorite), and most cell phone providers actually have some degree of service near the two trailheads.

Biking

The sandy shoreline around Homer lends itself to exploring on a fat-tire bike, an unusual

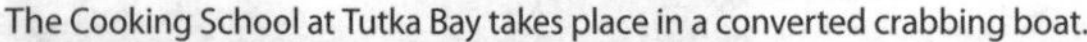

The Cooking School at Tutka Bay takes place in a converted crabbing boat.

a rustic footbridge on a hiking trail across Kachemak Bay

cycling phenomenon that was largely developed in Alaska. The bikes' enormously wide tires distribute your weight so you can pedal smoothly over sand and snow. Rent a bike, or take a guided tour through the area's intertidal region, with **Cycle Logical** (907/226-2925, cyclelogicalhomer.com).

Sea Kayaking

The scenic, wildlife-rich and generally calm waters of Kachemak Bay make for great paddling, no matter your level. Two of the best outfitters in town are **True North Kayak Adventures** (4287 Homer Spit Rd., 907/235-0708, truenorthkayak.com, from $115 pp for a half-day trip), which also offers stand-up paddleboarding and gear rentals, and **St. Augustine's Kayak & Tours** (Apr.-Sept. 907/299-1894, year-round homerkayaking@gmail.com, homerkayaking.com, from $110 for a half-day trip), which also offers paddle/hike combinations.

Bear Viewing and Flightseeing

Bear viewing might not be the first thing you think of in Homer, but the headquarters of Hallo Bay bear viewing are here, and the wild, remote **Hallo Bay Wilderness Camp** (888/535-2237, 907/235-2237, hallobay.com), in Katmai National Park, is just 120 air miles away on the Pacific Coast of the Alaska Peninsula. Day trips start at $650 per person, including air travel; overnight trips average $1,000 per night, with discounts for three nights or more.

TOP EXPERIENCE

Fishing

Homer is quite rightly the halibut fishing capital of the world, but that's not the only thing you can catch here. One of the most affordable trips you'll ever take is a $60 whitefish charter with **Rainbow Tours** (907/235-7272). Or they offer half-day and three-quarter-day halibut charters starting at $155 per person.

There are too many excellent charters out of Homer to list them all. Two more excellent choices that offer outings for both salmon and halibut include **Captain B's Alaskan C's Adventures** (907/235-4114, fishinghomeralaska.com, from $280 pp peak season, multiday charters available) and **Bob's Trophy Charters** (800/770-6400 or 907/235-6544, bobstrophycharters.com, from $235 for short trips in peak season, $275 pp for a six-person boat).

Don't forget to buy your entry ticket in the **Homer Jackpot Halibut Derby,** which runs from mid-May to mid-September; more than 100 tagged fish represent prizes up to $50,000 in cash. Each ticket costs $10 and is good for one day of fishing; you can buy tickets from sporting goods stores, many hotels, and B&Bs, some boat captains, and from the derby headquarters in the Homer Harbor (mid-May-Labor Day daily noon-9pm).

ENTERTAINMENT AND EVENTS

Bars

If you're looking to lift a beer in Homer, there is only one bar worth considering: the

Salty Dawg Saloon (4380 Homer Spit Rd., 907/235-6718, saltydawgsaloon.com). Don't just take pictures of the instantly recognizable lighthouse on the roof; step on in, belly up to the knife-etched bar, and make a new friend. Don't forget to sign a dollar bill and stick it to the wall.

Kachemak Bay Shorebird Festival

Homer is an unparalleled **birding** location, with more than 100,000 shorebirds migrating through Kachemak Bay every year. For many of these birds, the Homer Spit is a critical stopover location on their journey to Arctic breeding grounds, and birders have counted more than 130 species here. For the best of Homer's birding opportunities, visit the four-day **Kachemak Bay Shorebird Festival** (907/226-4631, kachemakbayshorebird.org) during peak migration in early May; there are more than 100 events, including guided hikes, keynote presentations, art and photography workshops, and presentations with live birds.

SHOPPING

Enjoy the small-town festival atmosphere with local crafts, produce, and ready-to-go food and drinks at the **Homer Farmers Market** (on Ocean Dr. across from the Washboard, 907/299-7540, homerfarmersmarket.org, July-mid-Sept. Wed. 3pm-6pm, late May-late Sept. Sat. 10am-3pm).

It's not hyperbole to say that every shop on the Homer Spit exemplifies the best of the art galleries and gift shops around the state; you can and should spend at least half a day exploring them. That said, if I had to choose a favorite, it'd be the **Sea Lion Fine Art Gallery** (907/235-3400, sealiongallery.com, Memorial Day-Labor Day daily 11am-9pm), which has a beautiful collection of artwork from easily recognizable Alaska artists and a collection of authentic Alaska Native artwork. It also has a couple of cozy rental rooms upstairs.

For year-round gift shopping, **Ptarmigan Arts** (471 E. Pioneer Ave., 907/235-5345, ptarmiganarts.com, summer daily 10am-6pm, winter daily 11am-5pm) is a co-op owned and operated by the local artists themselves.

the iconic Salty Dawg Saloon

FOOD

Fine Dining

If you want what's arguably the most famous (and best) meal to be had near Homer, hop a water taxi to the tiny community of **Halibut Cove** and **The Saltry Restaurant** (907/339-2683, thesaltry.com, daily 1pm-9pm, $30), where you'll find a mix of world-class, eclectic foods inspired by Alaska's seafood and other local ingredients.

On the Homer side of the water, locals love **Cafe Cups** (162 W. Pioneer Ave., 907/235-8330, cafecupsofhomer.com, dinner year-round Tues.-Sat. starting at 4:30pm, $28), a café-verging-on-bistro so quintessentially Homer that they couldn't help but plaster it with art and flowers. Casual fine-dining dinners and beer/wine are served in addition to the espresso, with 8-12 specials to choose from every evening. As you might imagine, it's often crowded during the summer; but you can phone in a takeout order to avoid the crush.

Baked Goods

Two Sisters Bakery (233 E. Bunnell Ave., 907/235-2280, twosistersbakery.net, Mon.-Fri. 7am-6pm, Sat. 7am-4pm, Sun. 9am-2pm, dinner Wed.-Sat. 5pm-9pm) is hands-down the best bakery in town, and its location—just up the street from the access to Bishop's Beach—is pretty great too. There's almost always a line, but it moves fast.

If you like bagels, head to **The Bagel Shop** (3745 East End Rd., 907/299-2099, thebagelshopalaska.com, typically daily 7am-4pm, opens later Sat.-Sun., $9) for freshly baked bagels, schmears, sandwiches, and soups with several options changing daily; they're happy to tell you about the specials over the phone and provide takeout orders.

Cafés

Homer's resident top chefs—the Dixon family of the Winterlake and Tutka Bay Lodges and the Cooking School at Tutka Bay—continue their string of "bests" with the best café in the whole town. The summer-only **La Baleine** (4460 Homer Spit Rd., 907/299-6672, labaleinecafe.com, Tues.-Sun. 5am-4pm, $13) serves breakfast and lunch using fresh organic and locally sourced ingredients. The result is a collection of hearty, generously portioned meals of seafood and unusual American-influenced sandwiches, plus a couple of specials every day.

Another local favorite is **K-Bay Caffe & Roasting Co.** (378 E. Pioneer Ave., 907/299-5750, kbaycoffee.com, Mon.-Sat. 7am-6pm, Sun. 8am-6pm), where you can get a great breakfast along with the best coffee in town.

Italian

If you love Italian food or wine by the glass, you'll enjoy **Fat Olive's** (276 Ohlson Ln., 907/235-8488, daily 11am-9pm, $12-25), which continues the long and distinguished Alaska tradition of repurposing buildings. This one used to be a garage but now serves as a year-round local favorite for the owners' calzones and pizza.

If you like cheese, you'll absolutely love the toppings on any **Starvin Marvin's** (1663 Homer Spit Rd., 907/235-0544, Mon.-Thurs. 3pm-10pm, Fri.-Sat. 11am-11pm, Sun. 11am-9pm, cash only, $18-23) pizza. The crust, however, draws mixed reviews; it's an unusual sweetbread-like creation that people either love or hate. They'll deliver to your campsite

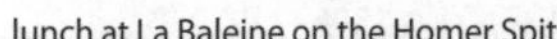
lunch at La Baleine on the Homer Spit

on the Spit, though, which does an awful lot to negate any doubts you might have about the crust. If you let them know how crisp you want the pizza to be, they'll cook it to order.

Seafood

There is no such thing as bad seafood in Homer, Alaska—and actually, there's no such thing as a restaurant here that doesn't serve *some* sort of seafood. But **Captain Pattie's Seafood Restaurant** (4241 Homer Spit Rd., 907/235-5135, lunch and dinner) is something special because they'll cook your own catch up for you, right on the spot.

Steakhouse

AJ's OldTown Steakhouse & Tavern (120 W. Bunnell Ave., 907/235-9949, daily 5pm-9pm, $15-50) is as much about the atmosphere as the food, with live piano music on some nights and entertainment from the likes of the famous "Alaska State Balladeer," Hobo Jim.

Breweries and Wineries

Alaska has one of the highest concentrations of craft breweries per capita—so perhaps it's little surprise that the state's artisan brewers have begun expanding their reach. **Bear Creek Winery** (60203 Bear Creek Dr., 907/235-8484, bearcreekwinery.com) uses freshly picked berries and other Alaskan ingredients in their wines; you're welcome to visit the tasting room, tour the facility, and walk the gardens.

True wine buffs will want to book one of the Bear Creek Winery suites for an overnight stay (from $275 summer season, two-night minimum). Your stay includes a complimentary bottle of wine, a free wine tasting, Alaska-made truffles, and breakfast at a local restaurant; the suites have kitchenettes, flat screen TVs, free Wi-Fi, and private baths.

Also enormously popular is the **Homer Brewing Company** (1411 Lake Shore Dr., 907/235-3626, homerbrew.com, typically daily noon-6pm, check Facebook for updates). Sip a tasting flight of their traditional country ales or just linger and see how the beer is made; you can buy straight from the tap in half-gallon growlers and 16- or 32-ounce bottles.

ACCOMMODATIONS

The iconic and appropriately named **Land's End Resort** (4786 Homer Spit Rd., 907/235-0400, lands-end-resort.com, from $249 peak rate, good winter specials) sits at the very end of the Homer Spit, with sweeping views over the water in every direction. The accommodations are comfortable enough, but it's really the location that draws people in. Amenities include free Wi-Fi, TVs, and a full private bath in each room; some suites come with private decks and mini-fridges.

Another beachfront option is the charming **Driftwood Inn** (135 W. Bunnell Ave., 907/235-8019, thedriftwoodinn.com). Rooms in the historical inn—read, older, with private sinks but shared showers—start as low as $100 during the peak season, while the more modern lodge typically starts at $189 in peak season. They also offer an RV park starting at $49 in the peak season.

For the greatest creature comforts in town, head to the **Homer Inn and Spa** (895 Ocean Drive Loop, 907/235-1000, homerinnandspa.com, from $249 for an oceanfront room in peak season); all rooms have en suite bathrooms, DVD players, kitchenettes, and Wi-Fi, and you don't have to be staying there to make use of the day spa.

Budget travelers who want to get away from the crowded campgrounds on the Spit should consider booking a bunk at **Mossy Kilcher's Seaside Farm Stay** (5 miles out on East End Rd., 907/235-7850, seasidealaska.com, bunks from $35, rooms from $90, tent spaces from $15).

Camping on the Spit

There is plentiful tent and RV camping in city-run lots along both sides of the spit; tent campers will need snow/sand stakes to set their tents up on the strip of sand between the road and the water, while RV users are restricted to the parking lots. The rates are affordable—from $10 for tents, $15 for RVs,

$5 for using the dump station; bring check or cash (exact change) and a pen to fill out the fee envelope, or pay in the camp office (907/235-1583) at the **Mariner Campground,** milepost 0.4 of the Homer Spit.

There's also a private campground, confusingly named the **Homer Spit Campground** (907/235-8206), which charges a little more but offers more amenities, including showers, electrical hookups, and water filling stations for RVs, as well as laundry facilities and a small snack shop on-site.

Spit Rentals

The **Sport Shed** (across from the fishing hole on the Homer Spit, 907/235-5562) has two simple but comfortable studio apartments for rent, from $159 with discounts for multiple nights or weekly stays. There is Wi-Fi, a fully equipped kitchen, and a private bathroom in each room, but no TV; these rooms are ideal for the fisher who just wants a place to lay his (or her) head in between casts.

The seasonal **Sea Lion Fine Art Gallery** on the Homer Spit (907/235-3400, sealiongallery.com, Memorial Day-Labor Day daily 11am-9pm) has two cozy rentals upstairs, with water views, kitchenettes, full baths, and a great location right in the middle of the Spit activity; $145 for the North room or $155 for the South, which has a jetted tub.

Wilderness Lodges

If you want to experience the ultimate in rustic luxury, book at the **Tutka Bay Lodge** (907/274-2710, withinthewild.com, May-mid-Sept., from $4,860 pp for three nights all-inclusive), one of National Geographic's Unique Lodges of the World. It sits at the head of a seven-mile-long fjord in Kachemak Bay; access is by helicopter or water taxi. While at the lodge, you'll have plenty of time for adventure activities, including day outings with the friendly lodge guides, fishing and clamming right off the docks, or relaxing in the lodge's spa. You'll also enjoy the award-winning cuisine of the Dixon family and ready access to their **Cooking School at Tutka Bay.**

INFORMATION AND SERVICES

If you need pamphlets, recommendations or a shot at free Wi-Fi, visit the **Homer Chamber of Commerce** (201 Sterling Hwy., 907/235-7740, homealaska.org); the friendly volunteers and small staff will be glad to help you out. Make sure to ask about the town walking tours, including an art map that calls out the town's wonderful art galleries and shops.

Public bathrooms—including flush toilets, a real luxury in Alaska—are available up and down the Homer Spit and in the larger visitor centers. Medical services come from the **South Peninsula Hospital** (4300 Bartlett St., 907/235-8101, sphosp.org), which has a 24/7 emergency department.

There are several gas stations just off the highway. The easiest ATM access is at the **Wells Fargo** (88 Sterling Hwy., 907/235-8151, wellsfargo.com) or the **First National Bank of Alaska** right next door. Drop your mail at the post office (3659 Heath St., Mon.-Fri. 8:30am-5pm, Sat. noon-2pm).

TRANSPORTATION

Getting There

There are four ways to get to Homer: driving (it's 220 miles or about 4 hours from Anchorage, and 170 miles or 3.5 hours from Seward); aboard the ferries of the **Alaska Marine Highway System** (800/642-0066, ferryalaska.com); as an increasingly popular stop in your cruise itinerary; or with the small regional airline **Ravn Alaska** (907/248-4422, flyravn.com), which offers multiple flights daily between Homer and Anchorage.

If you'd rather let somebody else do the driving, **Homer Stage Line** (907/235-2252, stagelineinhomer.com) offers twice-a-week shuttles from Anchorage to Homer and back again during peak season, and three-times-weekly shuttles from Seward to Homer.

Getting Around

It's easiest to get around Homer with a car, although if you arrive by cruise ship, you'll be met by representatives from the chamber of commerce and shuttled around to the town's biggest attractions for free. If you're traveling independently without a vehicle, you'll have to either pay $15 for a ticket on the hop-on, hop-off trolley that makes the rounds of the attractions (907/299-6210, homertrolley.com, mid-June-mid-Aug. daily 11am-6pm), rent a bike from **Cycle Logical** (3585 East End Rd., 907/226-2925, cyclelogicalhomer.com), or call a cab; **Kachekab** (907/235-1950) offers 24-hour service.

Around Homer

ANCHOR POINT

The tiny community of Anchor Point is at mile 157 of the Sterling Highway, which happens to be the westernmost point in the entire North American highway system; stop by the **Anchor Point Chamber of Commerce** (34175 Sterling Hwy., 907/235-2600, anchorpointchamber.org) to pick up a certificate commemorating your arrival.

Otherwise, the town's most notable feature is the **Anchor River,** which has the unusual distinction of being the most heavily fished stream on the southern Kenai Peninsula; watch for eagles that are there to fish, too. The river holds Dolly Varden, steelhead trout, silver salmon, and king salmon; see the *Roadside Angler* by Gunnar Pedersen (available in most Alaska sporting goods stores and bookstores, or on Amazon.com) for more details on fishing here. You can camp at the **Anchor River State Recreation Area** (Mile 157 Sterling Hwy., dnr.alaska.gov), which has 46 campsites ($12) for tents and campers; bigger RVs will have trouble maneuvering. Pit toilets, water, and picnic tables are available. If you want creature comforts, it's well worth continuing on to Homer, just 15 miles down the road.

DEEP CREEK

If you want to see something very unusual and very Alaskan, consider stopping by the beach in **Deep Creek State Recreation Area** (Mile 137.3 Sterling Hwy), where locals and commercial charters use a tractor-assisted boat ramp to launch and recover their boats from the beach. The boat is loaded onto a trailer, which is then pushed into the water until the boat can motor away. The challenge comes when it's time to reverse the process: The tractor backs the trailer down into the water and the boat captain gets a running start so the waves help carry him onto the trailer, while the very brave crew of the tractor launch stands there and secures the boat. When all goes well, this is poetry in motion. When things don't work so well, the video goes viral on social media.

SELDOVIA

Homer is a charming place already—but you can multiply the charm by taking a day ferry trip to the tiny seaside town of Seldovia across the bay; the population is about 255, with no malls and no crowds to distract you—just real, authentic Alaska life. Seldovia has year-round ferry service from the **Alaska Marine Highway System** (800/642-0066, ferryalaska.com), but if you don't want to take a vehicle with you, it's much easier to use the **Seldovia Bay Ferry** (seldoviabayferry.com, 907/435-3299, summer only), which costs about the same but gives you several hours to enjoy the town before your return trip.

HALIBUT COVE

This tiny, scenic residential community on the far side of Kachemak Bay from Homer has a population of about 75, although once upon a time it supported several dozen herring salteries and some 1,000 residents. Nowadays the population is made up of artists, craftspeople, fishers, and a few city folk who maintain weekend getaways here.

The only way to get here is by floatplane or

Homer and Kachemak Bay

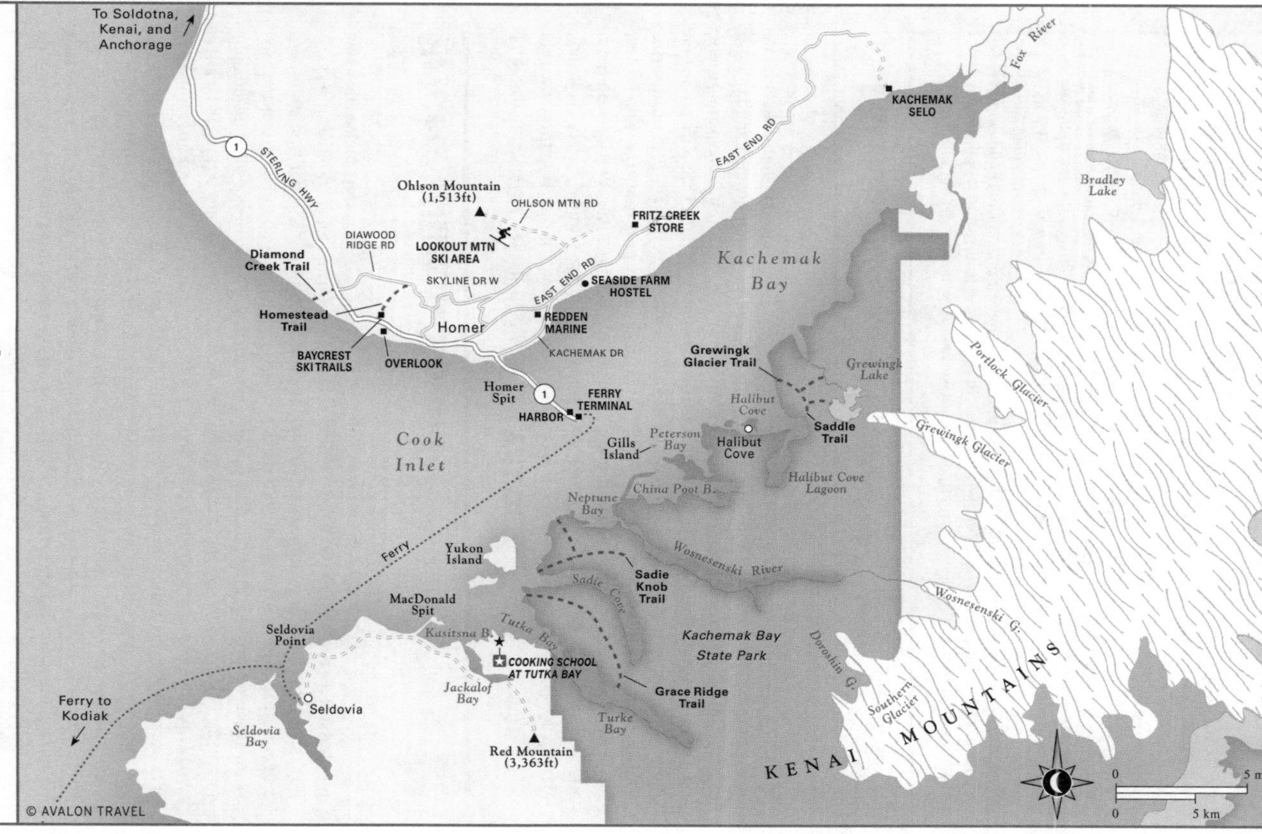

boat; you can hire a water taxi from Homer: **Bay Roamers Water Taxi** (907/399-6200 or 907/296-2257), **Mako's Water Taxi** (907/235-9055, makoswatertaxi.com), and **Ashore Water Taxi & Freight** (4246 Homer Spit Rd., 907/235-2341) all do a great job and offer comparable rates. Or book the **Danny J ferry** (907/226-2424, $63 noon departure, $38 5pm departure) to get here. Note that the *Danny J* is not a part of the Alaska state ferry system, and you won't be able to bring a vehicle with you; but it will swing by Gull Island, where thousands of seabirds nest in the summer. It stays for three hours before turning around to take you back to Homer.

That's plenty of time to see Halibut Cove's two biggest attractions: the **Halibut Cove Experience Fine Art Gallery** (907/296-2215, halibutcoveexperience.com, Memorial Day-Labor Day daily 1pm-4pm and 6pm-9pm), which displays the work of more than a dozen local artists in a variety of media, and then a lunch or dinner seating at the world-famous **Saltry** (907/339-2683, thesaltry.com, $30), where you can enjoy an eclectic mix of world-inspired foods based in Alaska's unrivaled fresh seafood and other fresh organic ingredients sourced from local farmers. You must make reservations or risk missing out on your meal.

Prince William Sound

The Gulf of Alaska, which lies between massive Kodiak Island to the west and the Southeast Alaska "Panhandle" to the east, is often described as the birthplace of storms. But Prince William Sound, a relatively calm, protected stretch of water that lies on the north edge of the gulf, between the Southcentral community of Whittier and the more remote community of Valdez, is a different proposition entirely.

VALDEZ

Sometimes known as Alaska's "Little Switzerland," Valdez is a picturesque little town perched at the feet of the lush, green 5,000-foot tall mountains that frame Prince William Sound. This community of about 4,000 people is about as rural as you can get without leaving the road system. It's also home to some of the state's most dramatic history, starting with its status as port of entry for

Earthquakes and Oil

Valdez was the site of two 20th-century tragedies. The first was a 9.2 magnitude earthquake, the world's second-largest ever recorded, that occurred on Good Friday in 1964. The resulting underwater landslide and tsunami inundated the town, sweeping away people and destroying many structures.

It was only 25 years before tragedy struck again: An Exxon tanker ran hard aground on Bligh Reef near Valdez, spilling almost 11 million gallons of oil into the pristine waters of Prince William Sound, launching four years and $2.1 billion of cleanup efforts to clean the thick oil off the beaches, as well as early efforts to rescue and clean oil-slicked animals whose natural waterproofing and insulation had been ruined by immersion in the oil; those who didn't receive human intervention died.

Nowadays, Valdez plays an important role as the southern terminus of the Trans-Alaska Pipeline System (TAPS), which pumps oil from the North Slope, high in the Arctic, down to this, the northernmost ice-free port in the state.

The Wrangells and Prince William Sound

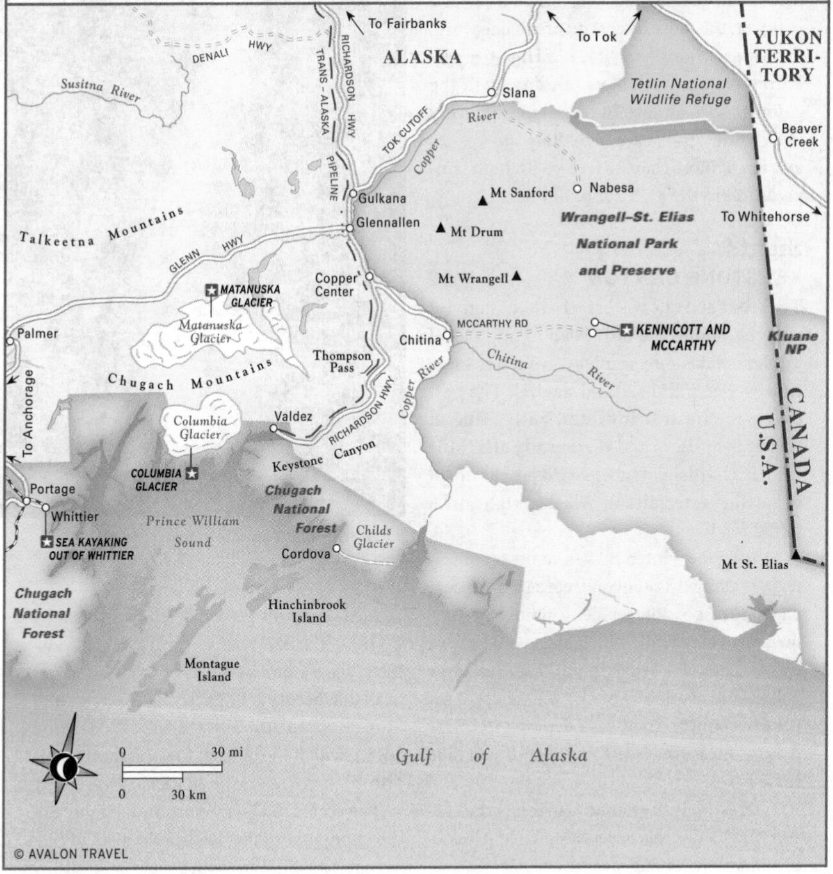

gold-hungry miners braving the passage over Valdez Glacier into Interior Alaska.

People come to Valdez for three reasons: to marvel at the terminus of the Trans-Alaska Pipeline, which ships oil from the Arctic North Slope to Valdez, at which point it's barged to refineries in the Lower 48; to take part in the unbeatable outdoor recreation opportunities, from boat tours to paddling and beautiful hikes in the summer, fat-tire biking and heli-skiing in the winter; or simply to enjoy a taste of life in a friendly, quiet small town that, despite its size, has been at the epicenter of some of the state's most significant history.

Gold mining isn't all that's happened here: The 1964 Good Friday earthquake caused an underwater landslide that swamped and destroyed most of the town. Twenty-five years later, a grounded tanker spilled some 11 million gallons of crude oil into the pristine waters near Valdez. But you'd never know about either disaster without stepping into the town's museums or taking a small turnoff to explore what little remains of Old Town Valdez.

Valdez is unusual in that the early season of the year—May, June, and July—tends to be nicer than the later season. The later in the summer, the more likely you are to have rain, and when it rains here, it *rains*. High temperatures average in the low 60s during in the summer with almost 70 inches of rain every year, while winters are incredibly snowy—an average of more than 27 feet—with high temperatures in the high 20s or low 30s.

Sights

KEYSTONE CANYON

This beautiful, waterfall-lined canyon stretches along the only road in and out of Valdez; make sure you leave yourself some time to just pull over and marvel. The best photo ops are at **Bridal Veil Falls** (Mile 14 Richardson Hwy.) and **Horsetail Falls** (Mile 13.5 Richardson Hwy.)—two of the most beautiful waterfalls in Alaska, right off a paved road.

During the winter, these and the other waterfalls along this canyon freeze into the best playground possible for ice climbing. By summer, the Goat Trail, which starts at the west end of the Bridal Veil Falls parking area, gives you scenic overlooks of the waterfalls. This is bear country, so always deploy full "Bear Aware" measures (see *Essentials*) if you take these hikes.

Interestingly, Keystone Canyon is the reason why Valdez was never designated Alaska's primary port; having just the one narrow, avalanche-prone route in and out of town was too big a risk to shipping, especially in the wintertime. Those concerns were borne out in 2014 when a series of massive avalanches closed the highway for more than a week, damming up flowing water and creating a lake in its place.

Bridal Veil Falls is one of the most iconic sights near Valdez.

BLUEBERRY LAKE STATE RECREATION SITE

Mind you, the entire drive is like one long pinball game through some of the state's most beautiful scenery, but if you had to choose just one place to sum up the beauty of the upper Chugach Range, dotted with high alpine lakes right at road level, this would be it. One of the best places to pull over, take pictures, have a quick picnic, or even camp out in all that beauty is 192-acre **Blueberry Lake State Recreation Site** (Mile 24 Richardson Hwy.), which looks back toward spectacular **Thompson Pass** (Mile 26 Richardson Hwy.).

The access road wraps around the shore of the eponymous lake, leading to a set of picnic shelters with sweeping views of nothing but mountains as far as you can see and a 25-site campground ($14) for both RVs and tent campers—there is no RV size limit. Amenities include wheelchair-accessible pit toilets, potable water, and good grayling fishing in Blueberry Lake.

WORTHINGTON GLACIER

In Thompson Pass is beautiful **Worthington Glacier State Recreation Site** (Mile 28.7 Richardson Hwy.), which showcases one of the most spectacular roadside glaciers in Alaska. Aside from its summer beauty, Thompson Pass also holds the record as the snowiest

Vicinity of Valdez

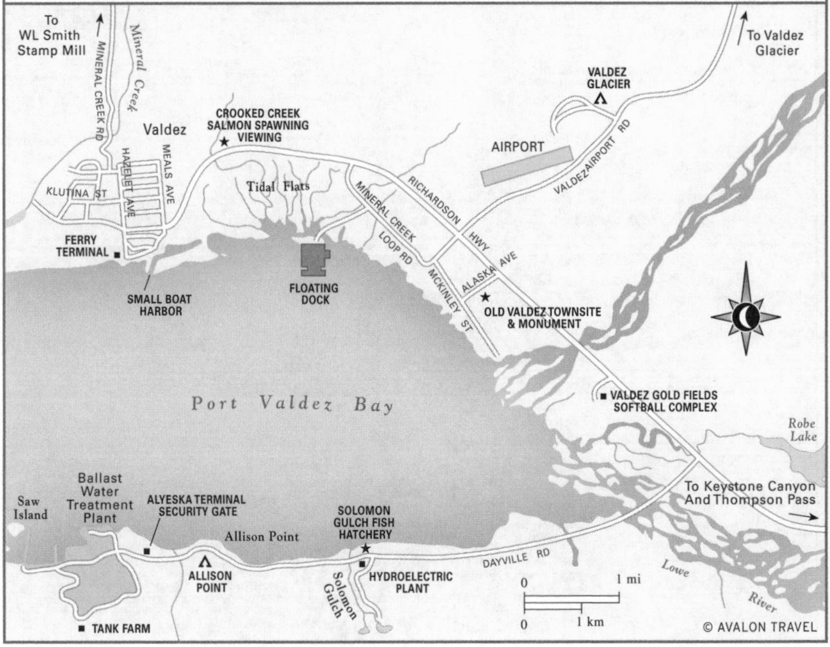

To WL Smith Stamp Mill
To Valdez Glacier
VALDEZ GLACIER
MINERAL CREEK RD
Mineral Creek
CROOKED CREEK SALMON SPAWNING VIEWING
Valdez
AIRPORT
HAZELET AVE
MEALS AVE
KLUTINA ST
Tidal Flats
VALDEZ AIRPORT RD
RICHARDSON HWY
MINERAL CREEK LOOP RD
FERRY TERMINAL
SMALL BOAT HARBOR
FLOATING DOCK
MCKINLEY ST
ALASKA AVE
OLD VALDEZ TOWNSITE & MONUMENT
VALDEZ GOLD FIELDS SOFTBALL COMPLEX
Port Valdez Bay
Robe Lake
Ballast Water Treatment Plant
Saw Island
ALYESKA TERMINAL SECURITY GATE
SOLOMON GULCH FISH HATCHERY
To Keystone Canyon And Thompson Pass
Allison Point
ALLISON POINT
DAYVILLE RD
HYDROELECTRIC PLANT
Solomon Gulch
Lowe River
TANK FARM
0 1 mi
0 1 km

up close with the half-buried edge of the Worthington Glacier

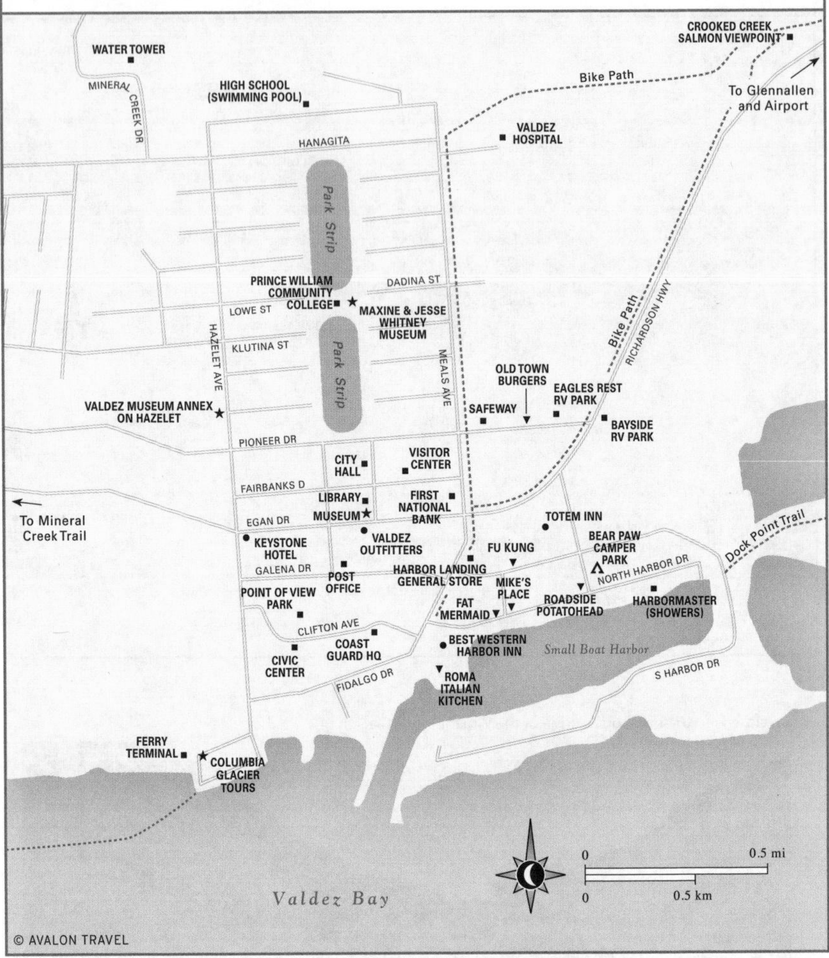

place in Alaska—which, in turn, helps buttress the glacier against a speedy retreat. Leave yourself about an hour to take a short, paved hike to a viewing platform with pedestal binoculars, where you can watch waterfalls gushing out of the glacier and down granite walls.

If you feel comfortable taking a two-mile hike on treacherously narrow and unstable terrain, you can hike up to an obvious lookout point over the glacier (when you're at the viewing platform, look for an obvious footpath to the left of the glacier's lowest point). You'll get spectacular pictures, but do take warnings about the terrain here seriously—it's nothing but unstable scree ground down and deposited by the glacier, and people have fallen and been seriously hurt.

VALDEZ MUSEUMS

Valdez has three small but excellent museums: the **Valdez Museum** (217 Egan Dr., 907/835-2764, valdezmuseum.org, daily 9am-5pm, $8

a cross-section of oil pipeline outside the Valdez Museum

adults, discounts for seniors, students, and military, free 13 and under) offers interactive displays and historic artifacts depicting life in early Valdez, including old city vehicles and a beautiful Fresnel lighthouse lens. It also has artifacts from Old Town buildings and exhibits on the Trans-Alaska Pipeline System, the 1964 earthquake, and the *Exxon Valdez* oil spill, along with a changing exhibit space.

Your admission to the Valdez Museum on Egan also gets you entry into the **Valdez Museum on Hazelet** (436 S. Hazelet, 907/835-5407, valdezmuseum.org, daily 9am-5pm) just down the road. This museum features a beautiful exhibit that remembers Old Town Valdez, along with tiny re-creations of the town depicting its growth over the years—and the destruction caused by the earthquake.

A separate facility, the **Maxine & Jesse Whitney Museum** (303 Lowe St., 907/834-1690, mjwhitneymuseum.org, May-Sept. daily 9am-7pm, free but donations accepted), displays one of the largest collections of Alaska Native art and artifacts in the world, plus a collection of wildlife mounts (including polar bears) and some natural history displays.

OLD TOWN VALDEZ

Many of the original town structures that survived the destruction of Old Town Valdez were relocated to the new (current) townsite, which was deemed to be on safer ground. Visiting the site of the old town is a poignant reminder of both nature's power and the resiliency of the people who rebuilt the community after that disaster. Look for a left turn to the southwest as you're driving into Valdez, just after the bridge over the stream coming out of Valdez Glacier; or, if you're stopping on your way out of Valdez, look for a right turn just after the airport road.

SOLOMON GULCH HATCHERY

The massive **Solomon Gulch Hatchery** (1455 Dayville Rd., 907/835-1329, valdezfisheries.org) rears and releases an astonishing 230 million pink salmon every year, plus a paltry-seeming 2 million silver salmon. They also imprint and release some 100,000 king salmon smolts from another hatchery. A self-guided tour walkway is open from May to October daily 8am-7pm. In July and August, ask when the hatchery will release water—this often attracts bears to the area.

CROOKED CREEK INFORMATION SITE

If you've never seen spawning salmon, stop by the **Crooked Creek Information Site,** 0.5 mile outside of Valdez, in July and August. You'll see dense runs of pink and chum salmon as they work their way up the creek, migrating birds and nesting waterfowl in the wetlands nearby, and maybe even a hungry black bear looking for fish if you're lucky. The information site is staffed from Memorial Day to Labor Day during business hours.

FLIGHTSEEING

During the winter, Valdez is one of the best places in the world for adventurous heli-skiing. During the summer, you can take to the air for sightseeing instead. There's nothing like helicopter flightseeing with **Vertical Solutions Helicopters** (300 Airport Rd., 907/831-0643, vshelicopters.com, $250-595 pp).

★ Columbia Glacier

Any cruise on Prince William sound is guaranteed to be beautiful, especially if you set out from Valdez. For whatever reason, even despite the oil spill a few decades ago, there tends to be more wildlife on this side of the sound's protected waters. Maybe animals come here, just like the people, because there tends to be less traffic. You can count on seeing lots of sea otters and harbor seals, but humpback whale sightings are common too. There are a few pods of resident orcas, and starting in June you might also get to see puffins.

Two excellent boat tours out of Valdez offer several trips; the most iconic is a visit to the tidewater **Columbia Glacier,** one of the fastest-moving glaciers in the world. It drops about 13 tons of ice into the water every day, and both companies navigate the surrounding icebergs to get you as close as (safely) possible to the face.

If you're on a strict tour schedule, go with **Stan Stephens Cruises** (866/867-1297, stephenscruises.com)—it's a tight, well-run operation that will have you back in plenty of time to catch your bus or cruise ship. If your schedule is a little more flexible, though, head straight for the ***Lu-Lu Belle*** (Kobuk and Chitina, 800/411-0090, lulubelletours.com), a mom-and-pop operation that runs the same route as Stan Stephens, with a flexible return time that gives you more opportunities to see wildlife. They'll also get you within 0.25 mile of the Columbia Glacier's face—ice allowing. Captain Fred Rodolf built the *Lu-Lu Belle* himself on a purchased hull; it's a beautiful

the Columbia Glacier ice field

ship with teak and mahogany fixtures and hard-wearing oriental carpeting. Rodolf is known for his colorful narration, and you're welcome to pop into the bridge to watch him navigate; a flying bridge with a plexiglass divider diverts the worst of the wind, but not the views.

Valdez Fly-In

Bush planes are still the lifeblood of travel in rural Alaska, just as they were during the early days of statehood. Celebrate that tradition with the **Valdez Fly-In & Airshow** (valdezflyin.com) over Mother's Day weekend in mid-May; pilots gather for competitions including short-field takeoffs and landings (STOL), flour bombing, and poker runs, with plane rides, vendors, and a free shuttle bus for spectators.

RECREATION

TOP EXPERIENCE

Sea Kayaking

For a more up-close-and-personal experience with the wildlife on your trip, consider taking a sea kayaking trip with **Anadyr Adventures** (800/865-2925 or 907/835-2814, anadyradventures.com, from $259 pp for 10-hour trip to Columbia Glacier) or **Pangaea Adentures** (107 N. Harbor Dr., 800/660-9637 or 907/835-8442, alaskasummer.com, from $259 pp for Columbia Glacier trip).

Both companies offer the same catalog of trips, many of which were pioneered by Anadyr Adventures, at similar rates, and they both have an excellent reputation. Again, the most iconic trip is a visit to paddle among the icebergs of the Columbia Glacier. You won't get anywhere near as close to the glacier face as on the bigger cruises, but the water taxi will drop you off close enough to paddle around the ice, and you'll have plenty of chances to see wildlife on the way back and forth too.

TOP EXPERIENCE

Fishing

If you want to fill your freezer with fish—especially big halibut caught in the deep, protected waters just offshore—Valdez is the place for you. **Valdez Outfitters** (104 Chenega Ave., 907/255-4555, valdezoutfitters.com, office daily 11am-7pm, from $225) and **Orion Charters** (535 W. Lowe St., 907/835-8610, orioncharters.com) both do a great job of halibut, ling cod, and salmon fishing trips.

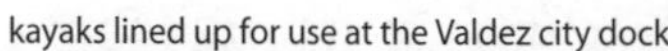

kayaks lined up for use at the Valdez city dock

Late-season visitors have the rare treat of a winter boat tour with Valdez Outfitters.

Lucky anglers stand to catch a lot more than "just" big fish out of Valdez: Before you go, make sure to buy a ticket for one of the competitive **fishing derbies** that run all summer long, starting with halibut in mid-May and moving on to silver and pink salmon derbies later in the summer. See valdezfishderbies.com for a calendar, information on purchasing derby tickets, and a list of prizes, which range all the way up to $15,000 for the largest halibut or silver salmon.

Hiking

Valdez's lush landscape makes for beautiful hiking in summer; stop by the **Valdez Visitor Center** (309 Fairbanks Dr., 907/835-2984, valdezalaska.org, Mon.-Fri. 8am-5pm) to pick up a short, to-the-point trail guide. The two best hikes to look out for are the 12.2-mile (round-trip) **Mineral Creek Trail,** which leads up to an old stamp mill, and the 3.8-mile (round-trip) **John Hunter Memorial Trail,** formerly known as the Solomon Gulch Trail, with rolling, forested hills and viewpoints over Solomon Lake and Valdez Bay.

Three notes on the Mineral Creek Trail: 1) Don't go here until avalanche hazard has passed; 2) most of the trail is actually a rough road still used by local miners, so you can shorten the hiking distance considerably if you feel comfortable driving the road or happen to have an ATV with you; and 3) you must ford a fairly fast-moving creek that's typically close to knee-high. Don't get caught on the wrong side of that creek during a heavy rain.

Snowkiting

If you're already capable on skis or a snowboard, up your game by tackling a characteristically extreme Alaskan hobby: snowkiting, or using a giant, parachute-like kite to power your glides across the snow or even loft yourself into the air. **Alaska Kite Adventures** (907/947-4775, alaskakiteadventures.com) offers lessons, workshops, and gear demos.

Climbing

In winter, the waterfalls in **Keystone Canyon,** just outside Valdez, transform into some of the world's biggest, most beautiful and dramatic ice-climbing terrain. Climbers come from all over the state (and sometimes Outside) to celebrate the stoke in the four-day, mid-February **Valdez Ice Climbing Festival** (valdezicefest.com).

The summer version of this festival, the **Valdez Rock Climbing Festival**, has traditionally been at the end of May, but starting in 2017 this three-day festival of rock climbing, workshops, and lessons will run during mid-June. Find it on Facebook for the latest details.

Food

Valdez is an anomaly in small-town Alaska because it has so many stellar food options; the only problem is figuring out which places serve which meals.

BREAKFAST

For breakfast, your best bet is **The Roadside Potatohead** (255 N. Harbor Dr., 907/835-3058, daily 8am-7pm), which serves breakfast burritos as big as your head. They also have some healthier options, including a salmon roll and a hummus wrap (both also huge); this is a great lunch spot too.

The **Totem Inn** (114 E. Egan Dr., 888/808-4431, toteminn.com, daily 5am-11pm) has the next-best breakfast in town. Their kitchen was damaged by a fire in September of 2016; check their Facebook page for updates on reopening.

BURGERS

Old Town Burgers (139 E. Pioneer St., 907/831-0999, daily 5am-7pm) is basically an old work-camp diner. This isn't fine dining, but it's a good value—think simple diner food in gargantuan portions that make it a great value. They do breakfast until 11am, then lunch and takeout after.

COFFEE

If you want a coffee fix, head for **Latte Dah** (130 Meals Ave. in Harbor Landing General

Store, 907/835-3720), the only real espresso stand in town since the wonderful Magpie's Bakery closed. They serve coffee from Kaladi Brothers (an Anchorage-based company) in both their espresso and drip drinks.

If you're of the organic persuasion, **Rogue's Garden** (354 Fairbanks Dr., 907/835-5880, roguesgarden.com, Mon.-Fri. 7:30am-6pm, Sat. 9am-5pm) is a health food store that also offers some organic baked goods along with good coffee and tea.

BREWPUBS

For lunch and dinner, you can't possibly do better than the **Fat Mermaid** (143 N. Harbor Dr., 907/835-3000, daily 3pm-11pm). The pizzas are stellar and creative—don't miss the smoked salmon—and the salads are enormous. Prices are a little higher here but, again, portions are huge, the service both behind the bar and at the tables is friendly, and the food is universally excellent.

Mike's Palace (205 N. Harbor Dr., 907/835-2365, $20-40) is a popular place to lift a brew with the people you just met on your tour, but the food is better (and more consistent) at the Mermaid.

CHINESE

Fu Kung (207 Kobuk Dr., 907/835-5255, fukungvaldez.com, Mon.-Sat. 11am-11pm, Sun. 4pm-11pm, $16) offers some of the best Chinese food you'll get anywhere, with a smattering of Thai offerings too. They have great lunch specials and the dinners are very reasonably priced; no MSG added.

ITALIAN

Also very popular is the **Roma Italian Kitchen** (100 N. Harbor Dr. beside the Best Western Valdez Harbor Inn, 907/835-9111, romaitaliankitchen.com); as you'd expect in a fishing town, they do an excellent job with any dish that includes seafood. If you choose to eat in the bar, you'll receive two separate checks, one for your drinks and the other for your food.

GROCERIES

The only place in town to stock up on groceries is **Safeway** (1313 Meals Ave., 907/461-3300, safeway.com, daily 4:30am-midnight). In general, prices range 25-50 percent higher than what you'll find in Anchorage.

Accommodations

All accommodations in Valdez are subject to a 6 percent bed tax. Even though Valdez is technically on the road system, it's small and remote enough that you should consider accommodations as you would for any other rural community: Sometimes, a clean, reasonably large room, comfortable bed, and lots of hot water are the best amenities you can ask for.

If you must have typical hotel accommodations, head straight for the **Best Western Harbor Inn** (100 Harbor Dr., 888/222-3440 or 907/835-3434, valdezharborinn.com, from $185), which is really the only conventional hotel in town. It's right by the harbor, so it's the perfect location for boat tours.

You can get a much better deal at the summer-only **Keystone Hotel** (400 Egan Dr.,

dinner at Fu Kung in Valdez

888/835-0665 or 907/835-3851, keystonehotel.com, from $95), an old work camp in a modular metal building. You don't get thermostat control, but the rooms are clean, the beds are comfortable, and each room has a private bathroom with great water pressure and lots of hot water. The Wi-Fi is sketchy in the lobby but acceptable in the rooms. The upstairs rooms can get hot during the summer. There's a very basic continental breakfast.

Be very careful about making reservations at the **Downtown Inn B&B** (113 Galena Dr., 800/478-2791, valdezdowntowninn.com, $110 for shared bath, $125 for private bath). Always ask to see the room before you pay (make sure you'll be able to sleep on the beds), and be warned that they may charge you for at least one night's stay, even if you decide that the room is unacceptable.

CAMPING

You have quite a few camping options in Valdez. One of the best RV campgrounds is **Bayside RV Park** (230 Egan Ave., 907/835-4425, baysiderv.com, $27-45), just off the highway as you arrive in downtown Valdez. They have 75 extra-wide full-service sites, including 35 pull-through sites; other amenities include cable TV, propane hookups, pull-through dump stations, and Wi-Fi.

Also excellent—and a little more remote—is the summers-only **Allison Point Campground** (Mile 5 Dayville Rd., 907/835-9866, allisonpointcampground.com, $15 tents, $20 RVs), with ocean views for almost every dry (no hookups) RV site and quaint tent sites close to the road; twice a day, there'll be a fair amount of traffic during the shift change at the Alyeska Pipeline (Trans-Alaska Pipeline System) Terminal. If you want to fish from shore, you can cast a line for salmon right from the campground. The amenities are very basic—multiple outhouses for each section of the campsites and a potable water station.

If you'd rather "camp" in a cute little cabin, book at **Eagle's Rest RV Park & Cabins** (139 E. Pioneer Dr., 800/553-7275, eaglesrestrv.com, $35-45 RVs, $143 per night cabins). The clean, comfortable 12-by-12-foot cabins each has a tiny deck, a bathroom (with shower), a cable TV, and an apartment-size kitchen sink and appliances (but no stove). A few of them have two beds or a bed and a bunk.

Information and Services

The main **Valdez Visitor Center** (309 Fairbanks Dr., 907/835-2984, valdezalaska.org, Mon.-Fri. 8am-5pm) doesn't pack the same type of interpretive exhibits you'll find in some other visitor centers, but the staff is friendly and helpful and can set you up with information about any local attractions or tours; make sure you ask for their pamphlet on local hiking trails, and check out their small showcases of representative goods from several gift shops. There's also a small taxidermied brown bear you can take photos with. If you're interested in shopping for yourself, the museum gift shops are one of your best options.

There is a gas station just behind the **Safeway** (1313 Meals Ave.) in town and two gas stations on the highway leading out of town. Always check which pump you're using—often, an entire pump is regular while another is premium—and have a credit card ready if you need to pay after hours.

Public Wi-Fi is almost nonexistent here, but you'll be able to get some sort of connectivity from most lodgings. Still, this isn't the place to come if you're on a business trip that requires high-speed Internet. You'll be much happier if you embrace the ability to unplug!

Transportation

GETTING THERE

Valdez is a long but beautiful drive of roughly 300 miles or 5.5 hours from Anchorage, or 360 miles and just over 6 hours from Fairbanks, both on the beautiful Richardson Highway. You can also get here on any of several daily 45-minute flights on **Ravn Alaska** (907/266-8394, flyravn.com)—think of them as mini flightseeing excursions—or by ferry aboard the **Alaska Marine Highway System** (800/642-0066, ferryalaska.com); the ferry dock is just a short walk out of town.

GETTING AROUND

Valdez is a truly walkable town, with broad sidewalks and courteous drivers who won't run you over. (That's a good thing, since there are no permanent stoplights in town.) Nothing is ever more than a mile away from any other attraction in town. That said, you can see a lot more—and explore some of the near-to-town attractions—if you have wheels. You can rent from **Valdez-U-Drive** (300 Airport Rd., 907/835-4402, valdezudrive.com, Mon.-Fri. 7:30am-6pm and during flight times on weekends), just outside the airport.

CORDOVA

This quiet fishing town of about 2,300 people is an ideal destination for anyone who wants to partake in the best of Alaska seafood—it's all over town—or just kick back and enjoy a taste of authentic, small-town life without the hustle and bustle that comes with being a part of the road system, however remote. The only way to get to Cordova is to fly, take the ferry, or arrive on a cruise ship.

This place was first settled by nomadic Eyak people. A permanent town sprang up around a cannery that was founded in the late 1800s, but it was Cordova's selection as the terminus for the Copper River and Northwestern Railroad, which transported more than $32 million of copper ore from the Kennecott copper mine near McCarthy, that really brought it into its own. When the mine closed in the late 1930s, Cordova's economy shifted to depend primarily on fishing, as it still does today.

Cordova sits perched between the magnificent Copper River Delta—the world's largest fully intact wetlands, drawing phenomenal numbers of waterfowl and migratory songbirds—and the east end of Prince William Sound, surrounded by the thick greenery of Chugach National Forest—mighty trees by Alaska standards, but only teenage saplings to anyone who's used to the giants of the Pacific Northwest.

Because of its location—sandwiched between the sea and part of Alaska's southerly coastline—Cordova enjoys a relatively mild maritime climate, with average high temperatures above freezing, even in the coldest months of December, January, and February. Summer highs tend to peak in the low 60s, and Cordova averages a whopping 148.37 inches of rainfall in a typical year—so definitely bring your slicker and your rubber boots. As long as you're dressed for the weather, rain won't stop you from having fun. Although the climate is mild, most tours and tourist services are still focused on the mid-May to mid-September busy season, so call to confirm availability before booking winter travel.

Sights

When you first get to Cordova, stop in at the **Cordova Chamber of Commerce and Visitor Center** (401 1st St., 907/424-7260, cordovachamber.com, Mon.-Fri. 10am-5pm) for more trail information and, while you're at it, ask for a self-guided walking tour map of the town. Don't let a little rain dissuade you; just take a rain jacket (it'll do much better than an umbrella in this climate) when you hit the trail—or the town—for the following sights.

CHILDS GLACIER

Historically, the biggest attraction in Cordova has been **Childs Glacier,** the only roadside glacier in Alaska where you could witness frequent calving. (Roadside might be a little bit of a misnomer, because a bridge closure means you have to take a boat ride before jumping back on a van or ATV shuttle to reach the glacier.) Two companies currently offer tours to Childs Glacier: **Orca Adventure Lodge** (2500 Orca Rd., 907/424-7249, orcadventurelodge.com, $200-275 pp, including lunch) and **Riverside Inn Tours** (riversideinncordova.com, from $150 pp, four-person minimum,

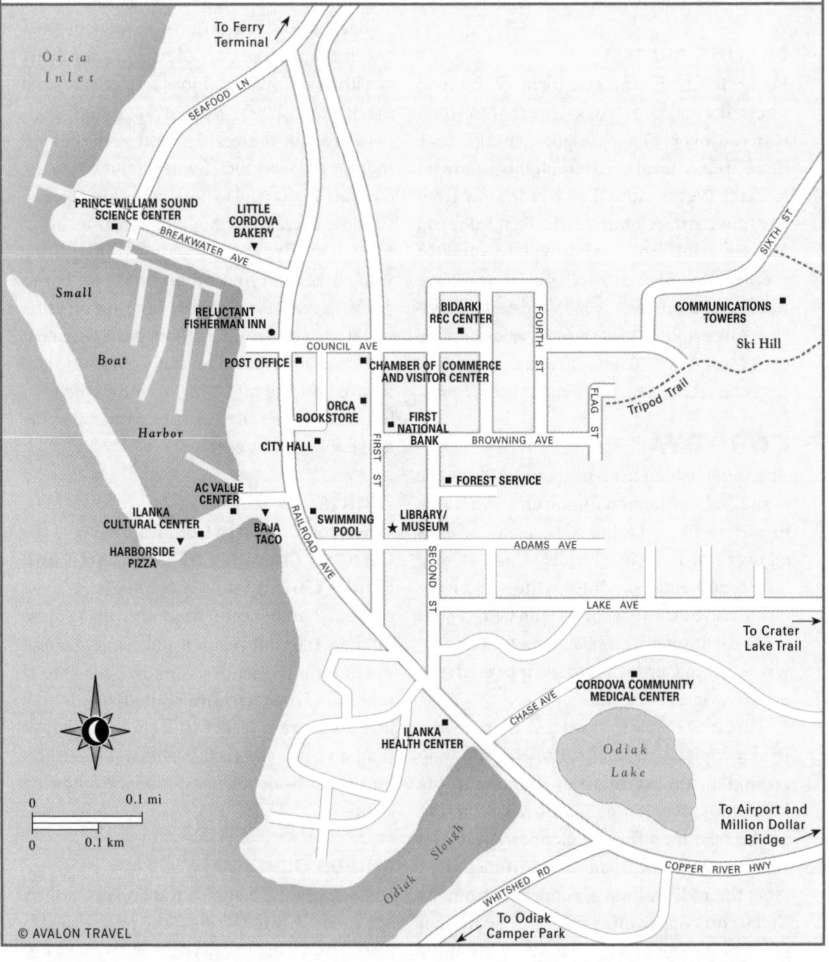

bring your own lunch). Orca Adventure Lodge's lower price is if you can meet them at mile 36 of the Copper River Highway to embark on the boat. Once at the glacier viewing area you'll have the benefit of covered picnic tables and rustic restrooms.

That said, in recent years the glacier has been a shadow of its former self and much less active. So, it's best to call one of the tour operators and ask how things are looking for the year before you book a trip based only on this.

A trip to Childs Glacier also includes a look at the **Miles Glacier Bridge,** a.k.a. the Million Dollar Bridge, which actually cost closer to $1.5 million. It was this bridge—one of the world's first true feats of Arctic engineering—that enabled ore from the Kennecott copper mine to reach Cordova, at which point it was loaded onto barges bound for smelters in Tacoma, Washington. The bridge was built in the depth of winter and designed to withstand amazingly difficult conditions, including 20-foot icebergs that were launched into the Copper River's seven-mile-an-hour current by the Miles Glacier upstream.

OTHER GLACIERS

Childs Glacier isn't the only one in town. If you have a vehicle, you can reach the "almost roadside" **Sheridan Glacier** with an easy walk of less than a mile. Take the Copper River Highway east of town; at mile 14, turn north on Sheridan Glacier Road. Don't head up the trail for Sheridan Mountain by mistake—that's a challenging (but beautiful) hike of almost three miles. If you don't want to go it alone, **Orca Adventure Lodge** (2500 Orca Rd., 907/424-7249, orcadventurelodge.com) offers a guided trip to the Sheridan Glacier that can be expanded to include a hike on the glacier itself—a fun, surprisingly non-scary adventure that every visitor to Alaska should try at least once.

It takes a little more doing to reach **Saddlebag Glacier,** namely, a mostly level 3.1-mile hike starting near mile 24.6 of the Copper River Highway; watch for mountain goats on the cliffs to either side of the glacier. This is also bear country, so make sure you brush up on your best "Bear Aware" tactics before taking either walk (see *Essentials* chapter).

COPPER RIVER DELTA

You may be familiar with Alaska's world-famous Copper River sockeye salmon, but that's not the only great thing the Copper River produces. Just east of Cordova it spreads out and runs into the sea, creating the 700,000-acre Copper River Delta, the largest contiguous wetland on North America's Pacific Coast. Estimates of how many shorebirds use the delta for staging or breeding range from 5 to 12 million.

You can survey much of the delta yourself from the U.S. Forest Service viewing station at mile 9 of the Copper River Highway (east of Cordova), then stop at Alaganik Slough at mile 17, where you can take in spring wildflowers, walk a short boardwalk to amazing views, and maybe have a chance of seeing browsing moose or mink playing.

This is a very easy sight to DIY, but if you want someone to give you a little more guidance, **Orca Adventure Lodge** (2500 Orca Rd., 907/424-7249, orcadventurelodge.com) offers a wonderful road tour, combined with hiking that can be modified from a short, easy

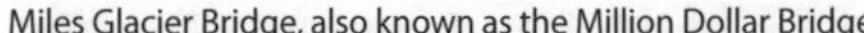

Miles Glacier Bridge, also known as the Million Dollar Bridge

walk on maintained gravel tread to up to 12 miles of hiking at the strenuous level.

CORDOVA HISTORICAL MUSEUM

Like many of Alaska's small-town museums, the **Cordova Historical Museum** (622 1st St., 907/424-6665, cordovamuseum.org, Mon.-Fri. 10am-6pm in summer) is a fascinating venture into the town's history—both recent and distant—with treasures like historical photos, a recently acquired master-built fishing boat, 100-plus-year-old schematics on the construction of the Copper River and Northwest Railway, and engineers' reports from the construction of the Million Dollar Bridge, one of the world's first great exercises in Arctic engineering. The museum is part of the town's 34,000-square-foot Cordova Center, a fully accessible multiuse facility that also houses the town library and city hall.

ILANKA CULTURAL CENTER

Don't miss a chance to visit the **Ilanka Cultural Center** (100 Nicholoff Way, 907/424-7903, nveyak.com, Mon.-Fri. 10am-5pm, also open Sat. in summer). This museum documents Alaska Native cultures around Prince William Sound and the Copper River Delta through a collection of tribal artifacts ranging all the way from the contemporary to prehistoric times. Look for a "shame pole" created in 2007 that depicts the events of the 1989 *Exxon Valdez* oil spill and a complete orca skeleton in the lobby, salvaged by the community after the whale was stranded and died in nearby Hartney Bay; it's one of just five on display in the world. The gift shop is great too.

Recreation

BIRDING

There really aren't any words for just how spectacular the birding can be in Cordova; the **Copper River Delta,** just east of town, is a magnet for millions of birds that either nest here or migrate through on their way north and return to stage their southerly migration in the fall, including nearly the world's entire population of western sandpipers and Pacific dunlin, more than half the world's tule white-fronted geese, and all of the world's dusky Canada geese—and that's just a tiny fraction of what you can see during the largest migration in the country.

Your birding opportunities peak in early May, which coincides with the **Copper River Delta Shorebird Festival** (copperriverdeltashorebirdfestival.com), four days of spectacular birding by foot, bicycle, and shuttle, and events that include the "Great Cordova Bird Count" and keynote speakers from around the country and the world.

HIKING

The **Chugach National Forest** around Cordova is heaven for hikers; see *Sights* for some of the most notable trails that take you to stunning views of the Sheridan and Saddlebag Glaciers, or visit the local ranger station, right in town (907/424-7661), for information on local trails.

WILDLIFE VIEWING

Sandwiched as remotely as it is between Prince William Sound—some of the richest waters in the world—and the pristine sweep of Chugach National Forest, Cordova offers amazing opportunities for wildlife viewing. The only catch is that your opportunities are just that—chances that can't be guaranteed—because the animals are completely wild and free to roam. So the longer you stay, and the happier you are just to be out watching for animals in this beautiful landscape, the more likely you'll be to have a wonderful outing.

Watch for trumpeter swans in the river delta and, if you're here in the spring or fall, millions of birds migrating through. You'll probably see eagles soaring overhead, and you might see bears, moose, beavers, minks, and more on land. If you want a little help in fulfilling your wildlife watching or photography goals, contact **Orca Adventure Lodge** (2500 Orca Rd., 907/424-7249, orcadventurelodge.com); they offer several wildlife and photography tours.

FISHING

At its core, Cordova really is all about the fish. If you're looking for some of the state's best runs of silver salmon, aim for a trip in mid-August or September. The **Orca Adventure Lodge** (2500 Orca Rd., 907/424-7249, orcadventurelodge.com) is the most prolific tour operator in town—including freshwater tours (both spin and fly fishing for salmon and trout) and saltwater fishing tours for salmon, halibut, and rockfish—and they do a wonderful job. They also offer fly-out trips to remote fish camps.

PADDLING

If you want to go paddling, you'll want to either rent a kayak from **Orca Adventure Lodge** (2500 Orca Rd., 907/424-7249, orcadventurelodge.com) or take one of their paddling tours. Heads up: Alaska's seaside communities have fast-moving tides and strong currents, the water is very cold, and the location is so remote that you're a long way from help. If you're not sure about your ability to handle any of the above, it's definitely best to take one of the guided tours.

SKIING AND SNOWBOARDING

If you're here during the winter, take advantage of Cordova's amazing snowcover to go skiing or snowboarding at the **Mt. Eyak Ski Area** (take 4th St. to Ski Hill Rd., less than a mile out of town, 907/424-7766, mteyak.org, Dec.-Apr. weekends, holidays, and most powder days, hours vary according to daylight), which uses a 1939 American Steel and Wire single-chair lift to stage riders for the 800-foot-vertical-drop run down to the base. The mountain regularly receives about 350 inches of snow in a year and offers mostly "more difficult" trails, with some easy and "most difficult" options. Lift tickets are $30, or get rental gear and your lift ticket for just $35. There's a full-service rental shop and food service.

If you'd like to turn the adventure up a notch, go heli-skiing with **Points North Heli-Adventures** (877/787-6784 or 907/424-7991, alaskaheliski.com), the only heli-skiing operation in this part of the Chugach Mountains; their expert guides, certified by the Heli Ski US Assocation, are some of the best in the business.

Events

Alaska's small towns host some of the best festivals, and the **Cordova Iceworm Festival** (cordovachamber.com) in early February certainly fits the bill. It started in the 1960s as a fun way to fight off the inevitable "winter blues," then grew into three days of local variety show performances, food stalls, arts and crafts, a Miss Iceworm pageant, the infamous Survival Suit Race to see who can get into the cold water fastest, and of course a parade through town showcasing the enormous Iceworm.

The **Copper River Bird Festival** (copperriverdeltashorebirdfestival.com) in early May encompasses four days of spectacular birding by foot, bicycle, and shuttle, a bird count, and notable keynote speakers.

Food

BAKED GOODS

Cordovans are a captive audience, so some of the food options are a little hit or miss—but there are a few gems, too. Don't miss the **Little Cordova Bakery** (203 Breakwater Ave., 907/424-5623, tlcbakerycdv.com, Thurs.-Sat. 5:30am-2:30pm, Wed. and Sun. 5:30am-6:30pm), where you'll get the best baked goods and coffee in town; gluten-free options may be available.

PIZZA

Also excellent is **Harborside Pizza** (131 Harbor Loop Rd., 907/424-3730, $28), where you can get amazingly good wood-fired pizzas, giant calzones, and sandwiches. Check out the AK 49er and Carnivore pizzas; they have reindeer sausage in the toppings.

SEAFOOD

For your seafood fix, head to the local favorite **Reluctant Fisherman Inn** (407 Railroad

Ave., 907/424-3272, reluctantfisherman.com), where you can devour everything from crab to halibut, salmon, and cod, all overlooking the water your food just came out of. The bar doubles as a sports bar during game season. The inn is also one of the best places to stay in town.

MEXICAN

You can get great Mexican-inspired tacos at **Baja Taco** (137 Harbor Loop Rd., 907/424-5599, bajatacoak.com, $10). Of course, it's hard to escape seafood in Cordova, but why would you want to? Try their fresh seafood tacos or the reindeer tacos. Seating is limited; the whole thing is built around an old school bus, but don't let that stop you from getting the best tacos in town.

GROCERIES

You can purchase groceries—although they'll be expensive, since you're off the road system—from Cordova's **AC Value Center** (106 Nicholoff Way, 907/424-7141) or **Nichols' Back Door Co** (512 1st St., 907/424-5219).

Accommodations

The rooms at the **Reluctant Fisherman Inn** (407 Railroad Ave., 907/424-3272, reluctantfisherman.com) are basic but clean and comfortable, with mountain and water views available. The restaurant serves amazing, freshly caught seafood.

Aside from their many tour offerings, **Orca Adventure Lodge** (2500 Orca Rd., 907/424-7249, orcadventurelodge.com) also offers a few rooms for rent (from $149) as well as all-inclusive adventure packages and package trips to remote fish camps. If you want to get your lodging, tours, and food (breakfast and lunch available on-site, with packed lunches available) all in one place, this is where you should stay.

If you're the independent sort, May-September you can rent a small two-bedroom, one-bathroom apartment from the **Riverside Inn** (Mile 6 1/4 Copper River Hwy., 907/424-7135, riversideinncordova.com, $150). On the downside, the inn is far enough out of town that you'll need a car; on the upside, you can fish right off the dock, and Riverside Inn offers the least expensive day tours to Childs Glacier, starting at $150 per person.

CAMPING

If you don't mind roughing it, **Skater's Cabin** sits on the shoreline of **Eyak Lake** (east of town) and costs just $25 for one night, $60 for two nights, and $110 for three (there's a three-night maximum stay). The cabin has electricity, a wood stove, a picnic table, a fire pit, and a barbecue; payments are made in cash or check only, and there's a refundable $35 cleaning deposit.

Tent campers and RV users are all welcome at the small **Shelter Cove Camping Area** near the town's ferry terminal (about a mile east of town): The 13 RV parking slots ($11) and three private campsites ($20) can be used for tents or RVs. You'll have access to restrooms and a fish-cleaning station, but no electrical hookups; showers and a dump station are available in the harbormaster's office. There's a three-day maximum for tent camping and seven days max for RVs; no long-term parking allowed.

If you want electrical hookups for your RV, join seasonal commercial fishers and their families at the **Odiak Camper Park,** which is open May-September and has some long-term spaces available (30-day limit). Sites cost $25 and you have access to restrooms, showers, water, and a children's play area on-site.

All three properties are run by the city and can be reserved in advance; contact Cordova Parks & Recreation in the **Bidarki Recreation Center** (103 Council Ave., 907/424-7282, cityofcordova.net) to arrange your rental. You can also camp for free in first-come, first-served campsites ranging up and down the Copper River Highway from mile 17 to mile 34 (both tents and RVs, very limited tent spaces in some sites), and you can camp for one night only, free of charge, in any pullout on the Copper River Highway from mile 13 to mile 26. (Unless designated, there is no camping in pullouts from mile 13 toward town.)

Information and Services

As you might imagine, an isolated community like Cordova has fairly limited services. There is, however, an excellent medical center with 24-hour emergency care, the **Cordova Community Medical Center** (602 Chase Ave., 907/424-8000, cdvcmc.com). Urgent-care facilities for all community members and visitors are available at the **Ilanka Community Health Center** (705 2nd St., 907/424-3622, nveyak.com, Mon.-Fri. 8am-5:30pm, Sat. 10am-2pm).

You can get free Wi-Fi and public access computer terminals at the **Cordova Public Library** (601 1st St., 907/424-6667, cordovalibrary.org, Tues.-Thurs. 10am-8pm, Fri. 10am-6pm, Sat. noon-5pm, Sun. noon-5pm), which is inside the beautiful new Cordova Center, which also houses the city museum and city hall.

If you want a workout, the **Bidarki Recreation Center** (103 Council Ave., 907/424-7282, cityofcordova.net) offers cardio equipment, a full weight room, a swimming pool, and a few group fitness classes; the locker rooms include saunas and showers. Day passes are available. Mail your postards at the town **post office** (502 Railroad Ave., Mon.-Fri. 10am-5:30pm, Sat. 10am-1pm).

Transportation

There are only three ways into Cordova: fly on one of the **Alaska Airlines** (800/252-7522, alaskaair.com) daily jets out of Anchorage, Juneau, or Seattle (the Cordova airport is almost a mile east from the heart of town); take a cruise ship; or take the **Alaska Marine Highway System** ferry (800/642-0066, ferryalaska.com); the ferry terminal is almost a mile out of town to the west. On the map, Cordova looks like it's awfully close to Valdez, but in truth, the two are almost seven hours apart by fast ferry service (regular ferries take about twice as long). You'll get there quicker on a fast ferry from Whittier, which only takes about three hours.

You can also fly from Anchorage on the small, regional airline **Ravn Alaska** (800/866-8394, 907/266-8394, flyravn.com), but I advise sticking with Alaska Airlines whenever possible: Their instrumentation is better, as is the airline's safety record.

If you're staying in town and only taking guided tours, you can easily get by without a car, but if you'd like to drive down the Copper River Highway to see the river delta or take advantage of the wonderful hiking near Cordova, rent a car from **Chinook Auto Rentals** (Mile 13 Copper River Hwy., 907/424-5279); they offer half-day and hourly rentals in addition to the more typical day rates.

GLENNALLEN

Glennallen's location makes it the perfect stopping point on a trip from Tok to Anchorage, Anchorage to Valdez, or as a staging point for an early-morning trip down the nearby McCarthy Road, and it's a great base for fishing trips to catch your very own sockeye salmon from the world-famous Copper River or king salmon from the Klutina and Gulkana Rivers.

Contact **Alaska River Wrangellers** (888/822-3967 or 907/980-6623, riverwrangellers.com) or **Copper River Guides** (907/960-0069, copperriverguides.com) to arrange a fishing charter for king, sockeye, or silver salmon and rainbow trout, or to book a river float that ranges from calm, placid water to boisterous white water.

Much of the surrounding land belongs to the Ahtna corporation, so land use permits are required for any use, including camping. You can purchase a $25 day camping permit (for one group/vehicle) online from permits/

ahtna-inc.com, or contact the Ahtna office in Glennallen at 907/822-3476.

The **Copper Country Discovery Tour** (907/822-3575, copperrivertours.org, $119 adults, $70 under 12) is also very popular, although you might have to meet their van at one of the Princess lodges in the area. You'll get great photo ops of the spectacular Wrangell Mountains, visit active beaver lodges, learn about the migration of Copper River salmon, plus gain hands-on learning about local plants and animals.

There aren't many services in Glennallen for the casual visitor: a couple of grocery stores and a soft-serve ice cream shop, all right on the main road; a few gas stations including a 24-hour **Tesoro** (Mile 189.5 Glenn Hwy., 907/822-3555); and the **Caribou Hotel** (Mile 187 Glenn Hwy., 907/822-3302, caribouhotel.com, from $160), which has earned a dubious reputation over the years but is supposedly under new management and being renovated as of late 2016.

For a more reliable housing experience, consider heading for one of the local bed-and-breakfasts. **Glennallen's Rustic Resort Bed & Breakfast** (Mile 187.5 Glenn Hwy., 907/259-2002, glennallenresort.com), which has three rooms with private baths and two rooms with shared baths, and **Antler's Rest Bed and Breakfast** (3rd St. in Glennallen, 907/822-4007, antlersrest.com, from $125 high season, $95 shoulder season), which has two rooms with shared baths and one room with a private bath, are both excellent.

Wrangell-St. Elias National Park and Preserve

Wrangell-St. Elias National Park and Preserve covers 13.2 million acres of pristine wilderness—as much as Yellowstone, Yosemite, and Switzerland put together. The park is a magnet for mountaineers (the crowning glory is 18,008-foot Mount St. Elias), birders, wildlife watchers, and serious backcountry hikers. But access is even more difficult than in the remote Arctic parks, with only two very small charter services offering flightseeing or landing service into the park.

Visitor services are found in four areas: the **Wrangell-St. Elias Visitor Center** near Glennallen (10 miles south of the intersection of Richardson Hwy. and Glenn Hwy., 907/822-7250, mid-May-mid-Sept. daily 9am-6pm, reduced winter/spring hours); the rugged, 42-mile **Nabesna Road** that leads south into Wrangell-St. Elias from the Tok Cutoff Highway; **Yakutat,** a Tlingit village in Southeast Alaska on the east side of the park; and **McCarthy and Kennicott.**

For most visitors, the latter area—McCarthy and Kennicott—offers the perfect window into a sweeping wilderness so vast and untouched, it's hard to comprehend, even when you see it spreading out in front of you. The road to McCarthy is fabled for its difficulty, but it's nowhere near as bad as it used to be, and minimal services are available once you reach McCarthy—just enough to make you comfortable as you revel in the wilderness around you.

★ McCARTHY AND KENNICOTT

McCarthy epitomizes the reality of life in small, remote Alaskan towns. Sure, getting there requires a 58-mile drive over a narrow, unpaved road that's notorious for tire-eating railroad spikes that lurk just below the surface—but that's what you get when you build a road on an old railbed, and I'm pretty sure the locals like it that way.

After all, they also agreed, as a community, to restrict visitors to one access point into town—a wide footbridge over the boiling Kennicott River that separates the McCarthy Road from the town—while the locals come and go, when necessary, via a gated vehicle bridge around the corner.

Don't get me wrong: It's not that McCarthy is an unfriendly place. In fact, if you go to the trouble of getting there, you'll find it to be one of the friendliest small towns in existence, where life slows down to a civilized, truly un-city-like pace and the real adventure is just being there. But the locals obviously like living in a place that's so far off the beaten path—smack in the middle of the nation's largest national park, actually—and visitors get the satisfaction of knowing they put in the not-unreasonable effort to actually get there.

Winters get very cold, with average low temperatures below zero and essentially no visitor services—but summers are balmy, peaking with highs that usually reach into the 70s by July.

Sights

Once you've conquered the McCarthy Road, the first thing you'll see—after the campgrounds, anyway—is the silt-colored **Kennicott River,** churning and boiling beneath the footbridge that leads toward town. **McCarthy River Tours & Outfitters** (907/554-1077, raftthewrangells.com, mid-May-mid-Sept. daily 7am-7pm, reduced winter hours, from $95 SUP, $115 white-water lake and river trip) specializes in safely taking you down these turbulent waters, with single- and multi-day trips on the mighty rivers of the Copper River Valley. They also offer calmer stand-up paddleboarding and kayaking trips in the lake at the foot of the Kennicott Glacier.

The historical, bright-red mine buildings in Kennicott are an eye-catching sight in and of themselves. You can hike or bike the five miles to the **ghost town,** which houses several tour operations and a big lodge during the summer season, or hop on the McCarthy-Kennicott shuttle van to get there (see *Transportation*). **St. Elias Alpine Guides** (888/933-5427 or 907/554-4445,

This sign in McCarthy is made of old railroad spikes.

Wrangell-St. Elias National Park and Preserve

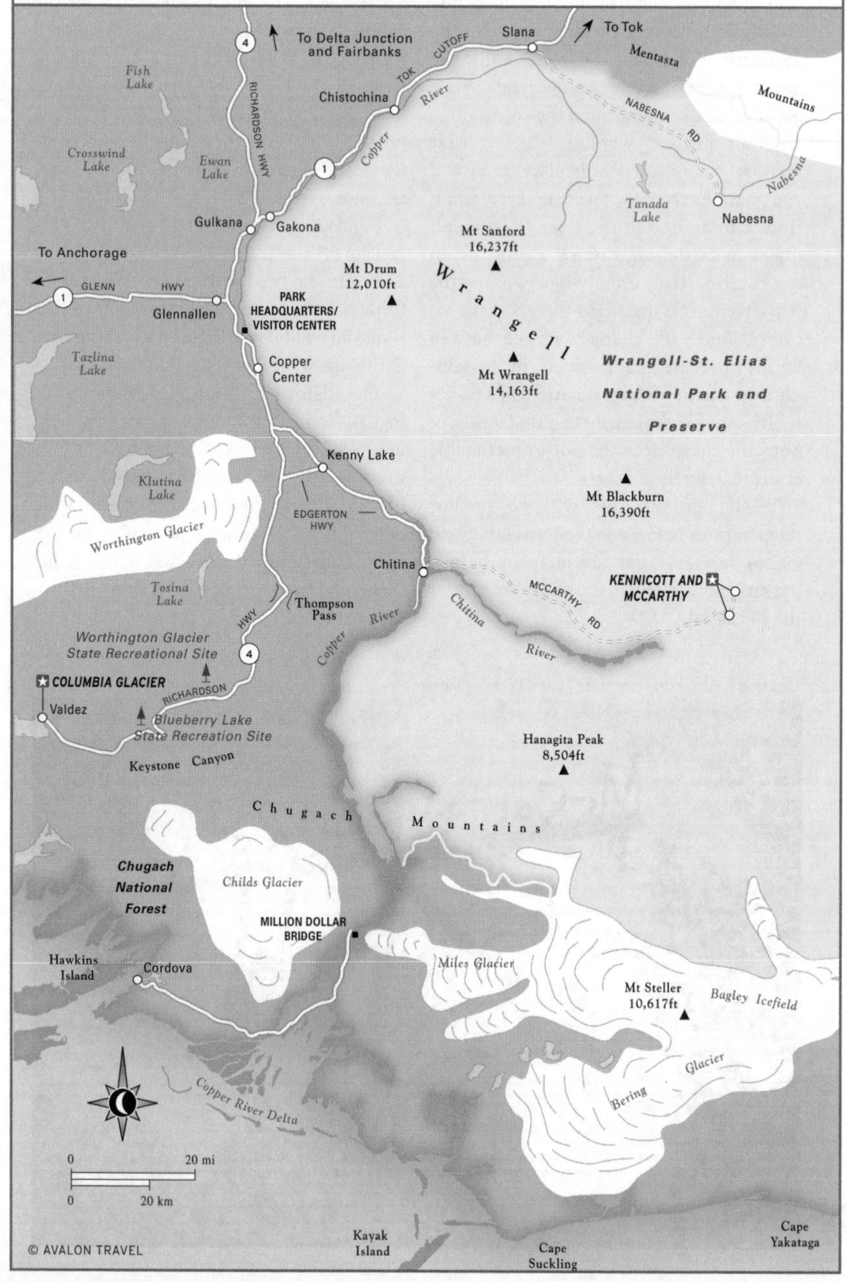

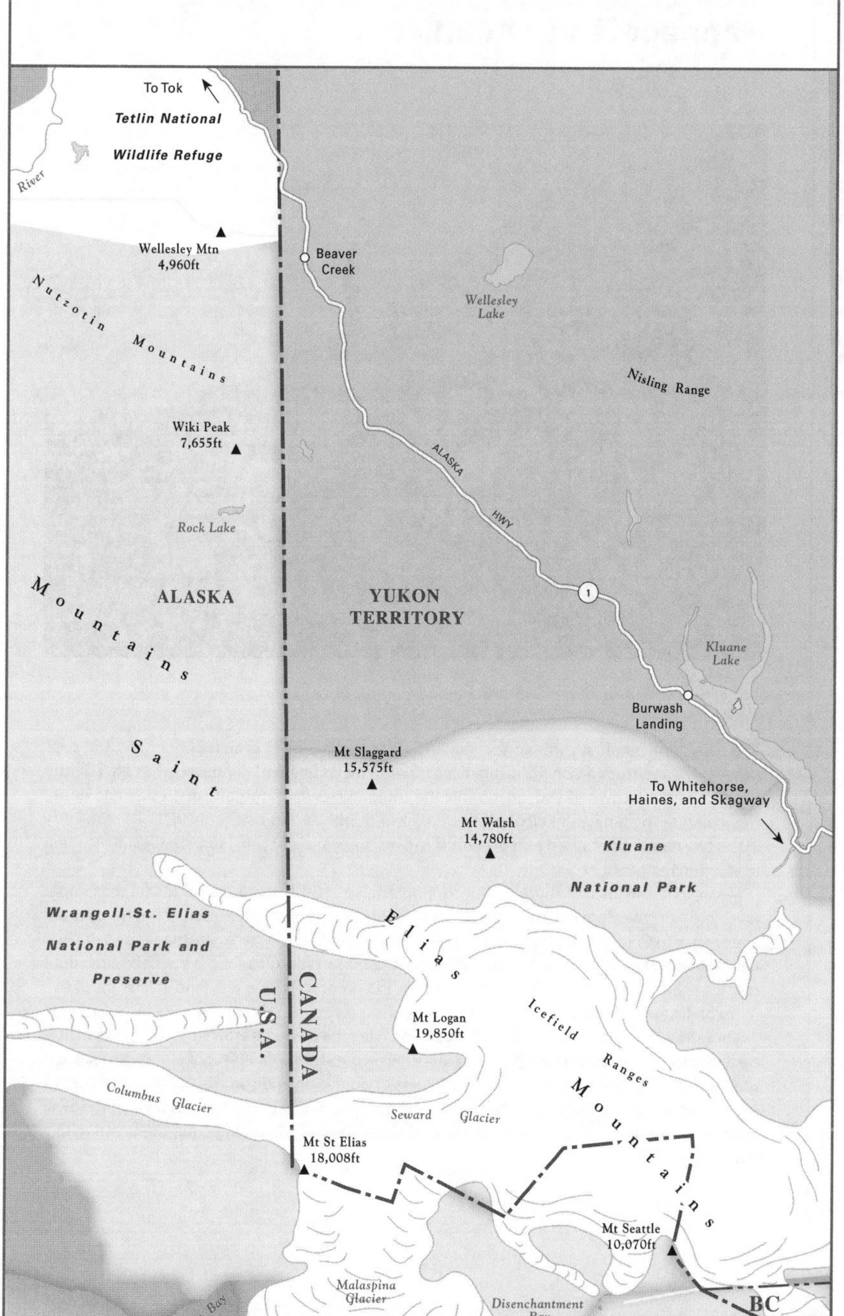
To Tok
Tetlin National
Wildlife Refuge
River
Wellesley Mtn
4,960ft
Beaver
Creek
Wellesley
Lake
Nutzotin Mountains
Nisling Range
Wiki Peak
7,655ft
ALASKA
HWY
Rock Lake
1
Mountains
ALASKA
YUKON
TERRITORY
Kluane
Lake
Burwash
Landing
Saint
Mt Slaggard
15,575ft
To Whitehorse,
Haines, and Skagway
Mt Walsh
14,780ft
Kluane
National Park
Wrangell-St. Elias
National Park and
Preserve
Elias
U.S.A.
CANADA
Mt Logan
19,850ft
Icefield
Ranges
Mountains
Columbus Glacier
Seward Glacier
Mt St Elias
18,008ft
Mt Seattle
10,070ft
Malaspina
Glacier
Disenchantment
Bay
Icy Bay
BC

Kennecott vs. Kennicott

the historic mining buildings of Kennicott

The early pioneers first came to the McCarthy/Kennicott area in search of not gold, but copper—and they struck a bonanza. The rich copper mine was named Kennecott with an "e," after the company that owned and ran it, while the company town that sprang up beside it to house the workers—no families or alcohol allowed—was dubbed Kennicott, with an "i." The similarity in the two names has caused a lot of confusion over the years, and you'll sometimes still see them used interchangeably.

Meanwhile, the town of Shushana Junction sprang up at the turnaround station for the Copper River and Northwestern Railroad, which crossed raging rivers and active glaciers as it transported copper ore to Cordova, where it could be shipped to Washington state. Shushana Junction was later renamed to McCarthy, and made up for all the guilty pleasures—from booze to a red light district—that the mine's work crew couldn't get in Kennicott. There was (and still is) about five miles of distance between the two communities.

There's still copper in these hills—in fact, if you have the time and effort to spare, you can hike up to the top of the **Bonanza Mine Trail** (9 miles round-trip, 3,800 feet of elevation gain) and grab a chunk of it for yourself. But after 27 years of operation and some $200 million in copper ore extracted, the Kennecott Mine could no longer *profitably* extract more. So it shut down, leaving the Kennicott company town a virtual ghost town, with mining equipment sitting idle where it was left.

steliasguides.com) is the only company with a concession to take you into the **Kennecott Mill** buildings, which are usually locked up against visitors; most of the equipment is still in surprisingly good condition, and quite a lot of it still works.

That said, it's the beauty of 13.2-million-acre **Wrangell-St. Elias National Park,** all around you, that'll really blow your mind. If you're a hardcore adventurer, McCarthy makes the perfect base camp for air-assisted expeditions into the park, or flightseeing with **Copper Valley Air Day Tours** (866/570-4200 or 907/822-4200, coppervalleyairservice.com) and **Wrangell Mountain Air** (800/478-1160, wrangellmountainair.com).

For most visitors, a day trip with **St. Elias Alpine Guides** (888/933-5427 or 907/554-4445, steliasguides.com) is enough. They offer guided expeditions to the spectacular **Root Glacier,** along with ice climbing, guided backpacking trips, air-assisted hiking trips, river rafting, and even mountaineering expeditions. During the early season, they play an integral role in maintaining the area hiking trails, which are also open for public use.

Food

CAFÉS

If you're staying on the McCarthy side of the footbridge, you're within easy reach of one of the state's best (and quirkiest) breakfast places: **The Roadside Potatohead** (90 Kennicott Ave., 907/554-1100), an espresso bar and purveyor of all things breakfast and lunch that involve potatoes, plus a few that don't (their food leans toward seafood and Tex-Mex).

If you're camping on the road side of the footbridge (before you cross into McCarthy), your breakfast place of choice is the **Slow Down Cafe** (Mile 59 McCarthy Rd., 907/554-2348, daily 7am-2pm, also Sat.-Sun. 5pm-9pm), where you can get a simple but filling breakfast made entirely from scratch by the amiable cooks.

This narrow footbridge over the raging Kennicott River is the only way for visitors to reach McCarthy.

FINE DINING

Believe it or not, you can get fine dining here in the **McCarthy Lodge** (101 Kennicott Ave., 907/554-4002, mccarthylodge.com), with an adventurous multi-course and à la carte menu that includes local yak meat, wild-caught Copper River sockeye salmon, and other ingredients.

Some people call the family-style dining fare at **Kennicott Glacier Lodge** (800/582-5128, kennicottlodge.com) "wilderness gourmet"; breakfast and lunch run $10-16, while dinner costs $33-40.

BARS

If you want to top your evening off with a few drinks, head for the only full-service bar in town: the **Golden Saloon** (101 Kennicott Ave., 907/554-4402, mccarthylodge.com) in the McCarthy Lodge, where you can get wine, liquor, and Alaska-made beer. The place really feels like a pub, where you (and all the rest of the town) go to socialize or take a turn at the weekly Thursday open mic.

GROCERIES

Your best bet for groceries—including produce—is the **McCarthy Center Stores,** also in the McCarthy Lodge (101 Kennicott Ave.), where you'll get everything from ready-made sandwiches to ice cream, liquor, hardware needs, and basic groceries.

Accommodations

The nicest accommodations in town are the **Kennicott Glacier Lodge** (800/582-5128, kennicottlodge.com, late May-mid-Sept., from $195 for a main lodge room with shared bathroom). There are a couple of common areas and a dining room; all the walls are lined with historical artifacts from the Kennecott copper mine.

Ma Johnson's Hotel (101 Kennicott Ave., 907/554-4002, mccarthylodge.com, from $229) offers quirky little rooms in an old boarding house, with shared bathrooms and electrical outlets down the hall (you'll find charging stations in the lobby). For more of a bargain, the **Lancaster Backpacker Hotel** (101 Kennicott Ave., 907/552-4002, mccarthylodge.com) offers rooms with shared bathrooms on a separate floor, starting at $129 for single or double occupancy.

a rustic wagon outside the Kennicott Glacier Lodge

For a cozier experience, try **Blackburn Cabins** (blackburncabins.com, year-round, from $150), which offers rentals of cabins with two full beds, a propane heater, a kitchen with running water, a filtration system for drinking water, free bike rentals, and other add-ons, from guided hikes to snowmachine rentals and trips (in winter only).

CAMPING

There are several pullouts where you can car camp along the McCarthy Road, and two campgrounds on the footbridge side of the road. Just one of them, the **Glacier View Campground** (glacierviewcampground.com, June-mid-Sept. only, $15 for one vehicle and one tent), takes reservations. It's worth trying to get a spot because you'll have a little more space there than at the massive first-come, first-served campground at the very end of the road. The Glacier View Campground also has a small open-air café that serves simple food like burgers as well as a bare-bones camp store that sells essentials like toiletries, cameras, and insect repellent. They rent bikes for $25/day.

Information and Services

There really isn't much here in the way of services—in fact, that's a big part of the town's appeal to locals and travelers alike. A general store in McCarthy has some limited grocery items, but you'd do best to plan on eating out or bring your own food; don't count on Wi-Fi in the lodging.

That said, for the first time in years there is excellent cell service in McCarthy and along the McCarthy Road from just one carrier, Verizon. AT&T service may also be available, but during a visit in 2016, I didn't have any luck.

There is sometimes gas and some limited vehicle service available on the McCarthy side of the road, but don't count on it. The last place you're guaranteed to find gas is Kenny Lake, so fill up before you make the trip.

Transportation

GETTING THERE

The unpaved 60-mile road from Chitina to McCarthy is legendary for being narrow and rough, full of sharp rocks and railroad spikes just waiting to puncture your tires. It's true that if you're unlucky, drive too fast, or are using bald tires, you can still have quite a few flats here—make sure you bring a full-size spare, patch kit or Fix-a-Flat, and air compressor.

That said, the road is nowhere near as bad as it used to be, and those stray railroad spikes only tend to pop up (with decreasing frequency) if the road has been recently graded. Still, there are plenty of sharp rocks, stretches of washboard, blind corners, and tire-eating potholes to be had; take your time and plan about three hours to make the drive; timid drivers might need even more time.

Leave yourself a few extra minutes to marvel at the Kuskulana bridge, a 775-foot expanse made even more impressive because it was built in 1910—oh, and because you have to drive across it! At least there's a guardrail now.

Be careful about bringing a rental car here; most large rental companies prohibit you from taking their vehicles on Alaska's gravel highways. **Alaska Auto Rental** (907/457-7368, 907/457-7368, alaskaautorental.com), with offices in Fairbanks and Healy and optional one-way rentals throughout Alaska for a sizable fee, is the most reasonable about taking their vehicles on this sort of unpaved roadway.

If you'd rather not drive, you can hop one of **Wrangell Mountain Air**'s (800/478-1160 or 907/554-4411, wrangellmountainair.com) thrice-daily flights from Chitina to McCarthy for about $260 round-trip, or board the **Kennicott Shuttle** (907/822-5292, kennicottshuttle.com, from $139 for a return trip on a different day) in Glennallen, Copper Center, Kenny Lake, or Chitina. They start early in the day, so you'll want to be staged at the pickup point the night before.

GETTING AROUND

It's easy to walk around tiny McCarthy, but Kennicott is five miles away. The easiest way to get around is to rent a bike (available from both campgrounds on the road side of the footbridge) or hop on the **McCarthy-Kennicott Shuttle** (mccarthykennicott-shuttle.com), which services McCarthy, Kennicott, and the footbridge (and the McCarthy airport when necessary) for a $5 ticket each ride. No bikes, and dogs are only allowed if there's space.

Denali, Fairbanks, and the Interior

Alaska's Interior is characterized by a mix of prominent, road-connected features and startlingly remote regions.

Fairbanks, Alaska's second-largest city, is the hub of commerce and transportation here. About 125 miles south of Fairbanks, you'll find the next biggest feature in this region, 6-million-acre Denali National Park and Preserve. Aside from its renown for stupendous landscapes and wildlife viewing, it is also home to the tallest peak in North America, 20,310-foot Denali. This mountain has always been "Denali" to Alaskans, but until 2015 was known as Mount McKinley in the rest of the country.

For the approximately 5 percent of intrepid Alaska visitors that drive up the Alcan Highway, another Interior community—the small town of Tok (rhymes with "poke")—will almost always be your first stop in the state. From there, you get to choose whether you continue northwest to Fairbanks or, ultimately, southwest to Anchorage and the Southcentral region.

Temperatures in the Interior tend to swing wildly from summer to winter. Lows of -40 during the winter aren't terribly uncommon, while summer highs range into the 80s with increasing frequency.

PLANNING YOUR TIME

The variety of communities and places you can reach by road in Interior Alaska makes exploring here a real joy, and all those road linkages mean you're in for relatively simple logistics—by Alaska standards, anyway, and as long as you're traveling from mid-May to mid-September. That peak season is when all services throughout the road system are operating at peak volume.

You can drive south to Anchorage, or Tok, or Valdez within a long day. But if you want to visit the traditional village of Anatuvuk Pass you'll have to hop on a small plane, and if you decide to drive the long Haul Road/Dalton Highway to Deadhorse in the Arctic (see *Arctic* chapter), you'll have to budget two days—each way.

Once mid-September rolls around, many tourist-oriented communities—chief among them the "town" just outside the entrance to Denali National Park—shut down almost completely. The exception is aurora viewing, especially around Fairbanks. You can't see the

Previous: grizzlies grazing on blueberries; bus tour in Denali National Park and Preserve.
Above: domesticated reindeer in Fairbanks.

Look for ★ to find recommended sights, activities, dining, and lodging.

Highlights

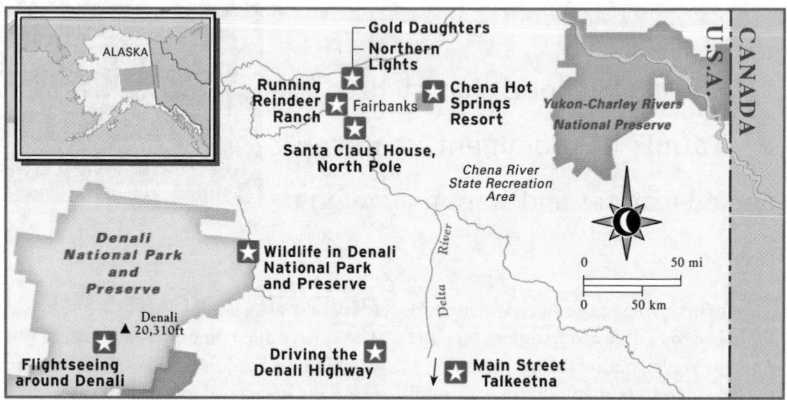

★ **Main Street Talkeetna:** Quirky Talkeetna is a charming, historical community with beautiful views of 20,310-foot Denali, the tallest mountain in North America (page 253).

★ **Wildlife in Denali National Park and Preserve:** Denali National Park and Preserve's sweeping wilderness is great for wildlife viewing (page 268).

★ **Flightseeing Around Denali:** One of the most awe-inspiring ways of seeing North America's tallest peak is from the sky; you can even land on a nearby glacier and take in the staggering grandeur of the entire massif (page 271).

★ **Driving the Denali Highway:** This 135-mile highway is a rough ride, but the incredible scenery is worth it (page 283).

★ **Running Reindeer Ranch:** Wander through the woods in the company of a small herd of domesticated caribou, a.k.a. reindeer, and their knowledgeable keeper (page 290).

★ **Northern Lights:** Fairbanks is one of the best places for viewing the northern lights; spend three nights here between September and April and you have an 80 percent chance of seeing them (page 294).

★ **Gold Daughters:** Pan for gold in a pleasant open-air setting, using real pay dirt and explore Fairbanks' largest display of historic mining equipment (page 294).

★ **Chena Hot Springs:** This luxurious resort powered by geothermal hot springs has a year-round ice museum (page 305).

★ **Santa Claus House, North Pole:** Yes, it's off-the-charts kitschy, but for the young and the young at heart, there's nothing like a visit to Santa (page 306).

Denali, Fairbanks, and the Interior

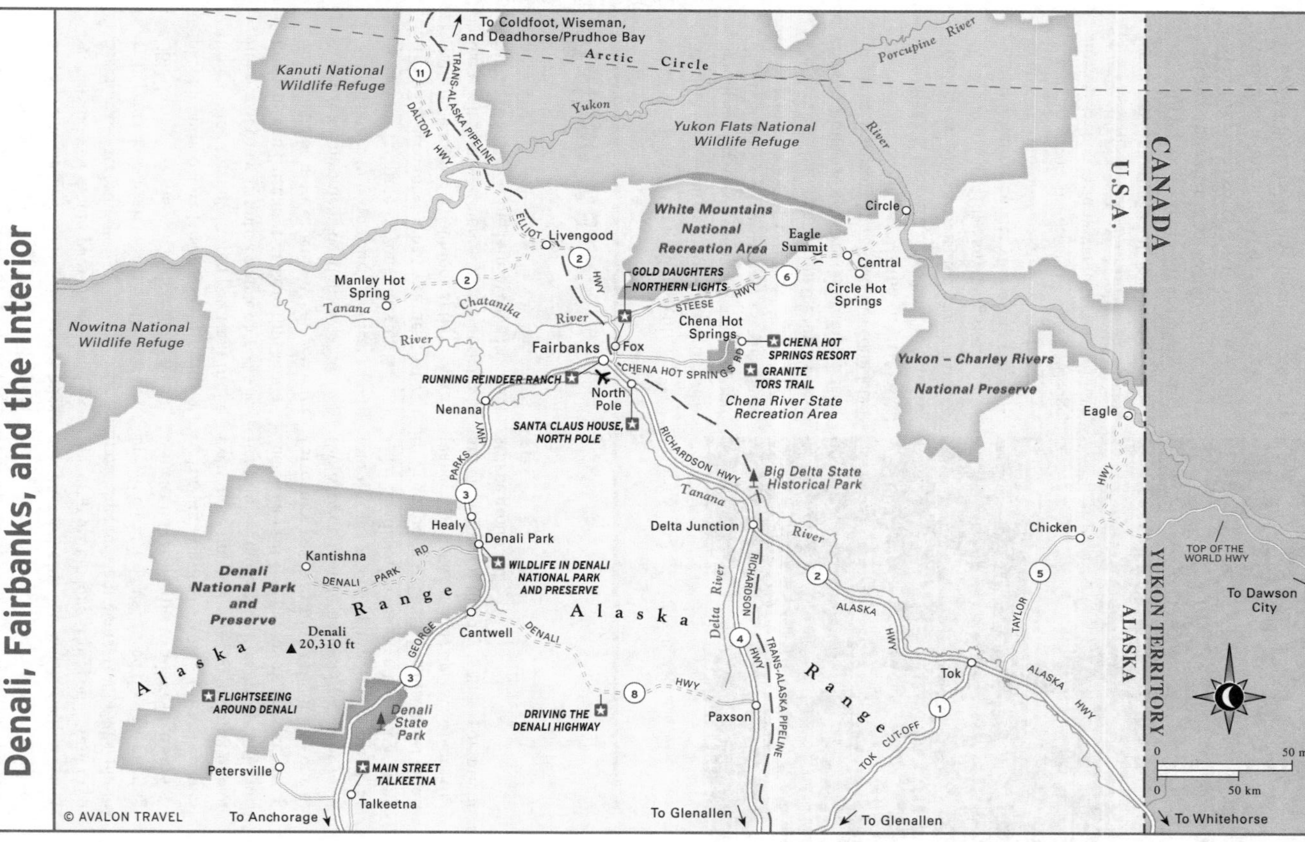

aurora during the traditional summer high season, because even at "night" it's too bright out. So for these operations, winter is the busy season and you should plan ahead—and expect to pay—accordingly.

In general, always book as far ahead as possible during any Alaskan high season. A couple of months beforehand is usually plenty of time to find the hotel room you want in the Interior. If you wait until a couple of weeks beforehand you'll usually be able to find a room, but it might be more expensive than you want or in a less convenient location.

Remember to leave yourself at least a day or two of flex time in your Interior Alaska trip. This accounts for bad weather that can stall some tours and outdoor activities, and there will always be more activities or sights to fill the time if nothing is delayed. Also, leave yourself at least an extra hour or two (depending on distance) for highway travel, to account for the inevitable construction delays that crop up. On long trips, you'll want even more time for sightseeing, rest breaks, photo ops, and traffic jams caused by slow-moving vehicles on the narrow two-lane highways.

Having a day or two of flex time becomes even more important if you're doing one of the more remote activities in the Interior, such as a visit to Anaktuvuk Pass, or using Fairbanks as a launching-off point to one of the Arctic's remote national parks or for a tour up the Dalton Highway, as known as the Haul Road, which takes you all the way up to Prudhoe Bay. That's because most small planes in Alaska can only operate when skies are clear; even if the day is nice, you might still be grounded.

Talkeetna

Talkeetna really is your quintessential quirky Alaskan town—but the floods of tour bus visitors during the day do change its character, and the vast majority of tourists have a strange habit of treating the locals as if they're part of the scenery. It's a big change from the town's early days as a railroad construction camp; in fact, until the Talkeetna Spur Road was completed in 1964 (the same year as the Great Alaska Earthquake), the only access was by train or small plane. Nowadays, it's tourism that drives the economy more than anything else.

You'll forever endear yourself to the residents—and probably make a few new friends—if you engage with them, or at least acknowledge their presence. And if you hang around into the evening once the buses have left, you'll get a peek into the jovial, joyous, and somewhat hippie character of the real Talkeetna.

Even though it's some 150 miles away from the entrance to Denali National Park, Talkeetna is one of the best places to see views of 20,310-foot Denali (the highest mountain in North America). Between that and its very

Every town in Alaska offers its own unique welcome.

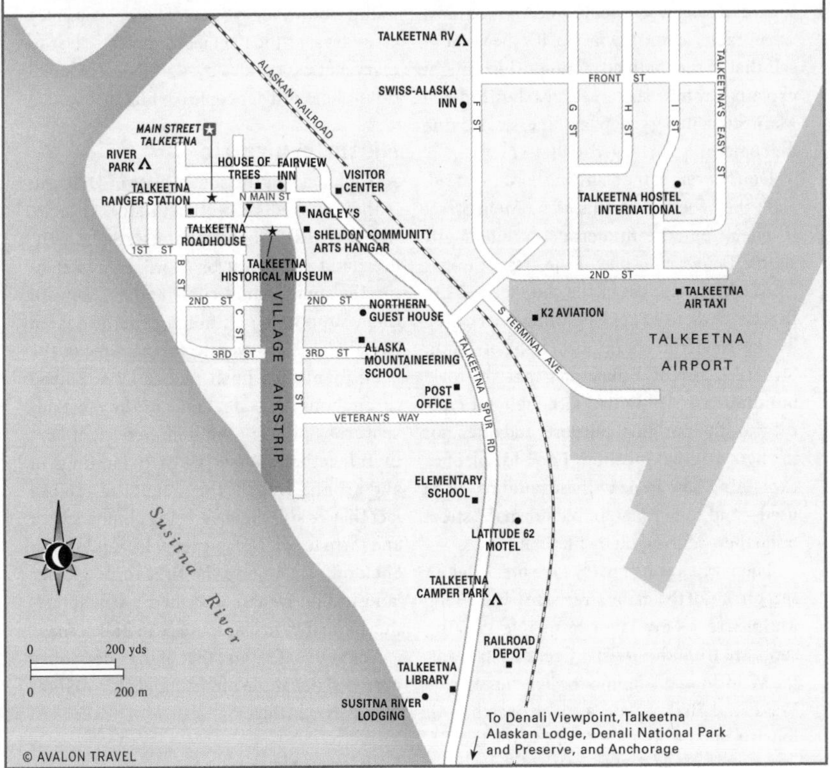

Alaskan character, it's no surprise that summer tourism is a big deal here. The town is so tiny—and parking so scarce—that it's easier to walk than to drive, especially when the tour buses are in town.

Heads up: Mapping apps aren't always accurate here, but most of the activity in town centers around East Main Street, which will be on your left as you follow the Talkeetna Spur Road into town. Temperatures are pretty mild by Alaska standards, with highs averaging in the 50s or 60s all the way from May through September, and only 28 inches of precipitation every year.

SIGHTS

Denali Viewpoint

Even though it's still a couple hours' drive from Denali National Park, Talkeetna is one of the best places for viewing 20,310-foot Denali, formerly known as Mount McKinley; in fact, when the mountain is "out," which means it's not obscured by clouds, you'll get an eyeful of it on the last stretch of road leading into town. You can get great photos of the mountain from a small turnout on the left at mile 13 of the Talkeetna Spur Road. It's the only turnout for miles, but if you're in doubt, just look for a big rock at one end that has, for one reason or another, been spray-painted gold.

★ Main Street Talkeetna

Taken individually, each of the attractions in Talkeetna—except maybe the views of Denali—is small and quaint. But this town is greater than the sum of its parts, and somehow that quaintness, powered by the determinedly free-thinking, free-spirited nature of the locals, creates one of Alaska's most memorable, iconic towns. So, it's the town itself that is the main attraction, which might explain why tourists sometimes shuffle down Main Street in big groups as if they are looking for something . . . bigger? Glitzier?

Don't be one of the shuffling horde. Instead, walk the pedestrian paths along Main Street to check out the numerous excellent gift shops. Talkeetna is one of the artsiest towns in Alaska, and most of the shopkeepers are fiercely devoted to keeping things local. Stop by the riverfront park (also right off Main Street). Many of Talkeetna's most historic buildings are still in use, although not typically for their original purpose, and often not in their original location. Look for plaques explaining how some of these buildings were used—and sometimes moved down the street or farther—during their "lifetime."

Then, when you're ready for a break, take a seat on one of the many streetside patios along Main Street—my favorite people-viewing spots are from the Twister Creek Restaurant, the Wildflower Cafe, and the benches outside Wake and Shake. Have a snack, watch both tourists and locals go by (can you tell the difference?), and weigh the merits of the popular notion that Cicely, the town setting of the TV series *Northern Exposure,* was actually modeled on Talkeetna.

Riverfront Park

The river park at the end of Main Street lets you walk along the banks of one of the most important salmon-producing rivers in the state, the **Big Susitna River,** known as "the Big Su" or simply "the Su River" to locals. Generally, the most important salmon rivers are those with the largest runs of fish; the Big Su contains all five species of Pacific salmon and has the state's fourth-largest run of king salmon, which are much more rare than the other species. Actually, three rivers come together just north of Talkeetna to form the Big Susitna drainage: the Su, the Chulitna, and the Talkeetna. Reaching the riverfront park, a favorite hangout of locals, really is as simple as walking down Main Street. There are no entry gates, fees, or the like, just a massive river to marvel at as it glides by, and the occasional raft or boat full of people passing through.

Historic Airstrip

A few blocks to the south, west of D Street, is the unpaved Talkeetna Village Airstrip, which is still in occasional use. Small children (and children at heart) will enjoy watching the small planes come and go, some of them supporting climbing expeditions on Denali. This is a wonderful example of the prominent role bush planes have played throughout the state. Some of the most adventurous pilots in the state were right here in Talkeetna, pioneering early landings in and around Denali, the mountain—and in fact they're still there, ferrying climbers back and forth today. Notable (late) local pilot Don Sheldon was among the first to do glacier landings on Denali, and there's still an airline named in his honor here in Talkeetna.

For your safety and that of the pilots, obey posted signs at the airstrip and stay well off the active runway.

Flightseeing

Speaking of airstrips, Talkeetna is one of the best places to catch a flightseeing tour of Denali, because this is where serious climbers set out on their trips up the mountain. The pilots are experts, well familiar with the area and the mountain, and if the mountain is out (not obscured by clouds) you can have splendid views of Denali from the instant your plane takes off. **Talkeetna Air Taxi** (14212 E. 2nd St., 800/533-2219 or 907/733-2218, talkeetnaair.com) is the favorite of locals; they offer flightseeing trips through Denali National Park, glacier landings on the Denali massif, and trips to Iditarod checkpoint tours in March, and they shuttle climbers back and forth from Denali base camp. **Sheldon Air Service** (22703 S. Terminal Ave., 907/733-2321, sheldonairservice.com) offers a similar selection of tours and

Talkeetna's Mayor Stubbs takes a break from his duties.

is also very popular, as is **K2 Aviation** (14052 E. 2nd St., 800/764-2291, flyk2.com).

Nagley's Store

Downtown Talkeetna—which is pretty much all of Talkeetna—is very picturesque. Most of the buildings have been moved at least once from their original location—literally being placed on a trailer and driven or hauled some distance—and they're often put to a new use with each move. This is the ultimate in practicality when resources are scarce, shipping is expensive and logistically difficult, and you all have more important survival tasks than building a whole new building.

Perhaps the most iconic building in town is the dark-red **Nagley's Store** (13650 E. Main St., 907/733-3663, nagleysstore.com, Sun.-Thurs. 7:30am-10pm, Fri.-Sat. 7:30am-11pm), which originally served as store, post office, and district territorial headquarters on the far end of Main Street. The store stayed open as it was moved to the current location, doing a brisk business from the back of the flatbed truck that transported it. Watch for plaques on some of the buildings—including Nagley's—that explain their various locations and the types of establishments they've housed over the years.

Because Talkeetna isn't an official township, it can't have an official mayor, but that didn't stop residents from electing an honorary one. Like most politicians, Mayor Stubbs has been caught up in the occasional scandal. Most notably, he made national headlines a few years ago when he was attacked by a dog. However, unlike most politicians, Mayor Stubbs is a cat. Mayor Stubbs is going

Nagley's Store is one of the most iconic sights on Talkeetna's Main Street.

on 20 years of public service (he assumed office when he was only a few months old). He still makes his home in Nagley's, but he rarely puts in public appearances.

Talkeetna Pedal Bus

For another way to see the town's historic sites, hop on to the **Talkeetna Pedal Bus** (907/733-7433 or 907/841-4878, talkeetnapedalbus.com), a giant bike-powered bus that uses human pedaling as the engine; it's fun and you might even become a tourist attraction yourself as you take the narrated tour through town. (Don't worry—if you're not up to pedaling, there's room for a couple of non-pedaling riders.) The company's second year in operation will be 2017, so they're still adjusting costs, tour times, and tour durations to suit the local market; it's best to call or email from the website for details.

Educational Centers

The closest thing to a nature center in Talkeetna is the **Susitna Salmon Center (SSC)** (13512 E. 1st St., 907/733-3474, arrialaska.org, Mon.-Sun. 10am-6pm), a nonprofit education center operated by the Aquatic Restoration and Research Institute. It's small but packed to the gills (sorry) with educational material, including tanks where you can see salmon fry (believe it or not, that's the word for the second stage in a baby salmon's

The Magical Salmon Life Cycle

Alaska's wild salmon are always appreciated when they show up on the dinner table, but their magical, transformative life cycle is less well known. A salmon's life cycle starts when the female digs a shallow nest, called a redd, in a gravel streambed. She and the dominant male salmon station themselves over the nest and release their eggs and milt (sperm), respectively.

When the baby salmon emerge from their eggs 3-4 months later, they're known as alevin or sac-fry, thanks to an attached yolk sac that may be twice the size of their own body. The alevin draw nourishment from that yolk sac as they hide out in the stream's gravelly bottom for a few weeks.

Once the fry are about an inch long and have developed camouflage markings that will help them hide from larger predators, they emerge from the gravel and start feeding independently on insects and other tiny organisms in the water. When they're about as long as your hand, they're known as smolt, and they're ready to follow the flow of their natal freshwater stream down to the ocean. The young smolt's body must undergo a series of astonishing metabolic changes to let them adapt to life in saltwater, where they stay for 1-5 years until it's time to migrate back to the freshwater stream where they were born. Nobody's entirely sure how they do this; the leading theory is that they use their phenomenal sense of smell to navigate.

While salmon live in the ocean, they're a sleek, bright silver; when they return to freshwater, they undergo another metamorphosis into their breeding form. Both sexes turn a bright color (depending on the species), some develop marked humps, and the males develop hooked "beaks" that they use to display dominance. They stop eating once they hit freshwater, so their stomachs dissolve and their flesh starts to soften and rot—spawning is always a one-way journey. Once the fish fight their way far enough upstream into their natal stream, against the current to find suitable conditions, they lay and fertilize their eggs, then die.

Some elements of that life cycle might sound tragic. After all, spawning is the hard stop to any individual salmon's life; by the time they metamorphose into their breeding forms their bodies are already starting to decompose, and by the time they've spawned they're so weak that they're very easy to catch—a fact that bears take ready advantage of. But those fish play an integral role not only in the health of their species—kicking off the remarkable, transformative life cycle to begin again—but also in the forest. It might help to think of the salmon as packets of ocean-nourished nutrients, which they carry back into the forested streams to be distributed by the bears and other predators that eat part of the fish, then leave the rest to decompose.

life cycle) and a tiny theater that shows short, award-winning nature documentaries on demand. They also offer guided walks along the Big Su River and sometimes to the confluence of the three nearby rivers (the Chulitna, Susitna, and Talkeetna) several times a week.

Like many businesses in small-town Alaska, the SSC is both a passion project and a labor of love, run by scientists from the neighboring Aquatic Restoration and Research Institute, which specializes in restoring streams and aquatic systems, and also collects data by monitoring local aquatic systems (rivers, streams, and fish populations). (Literally—those offices are right next door.) Although salmon don't play a leading role in Talkeetna's economy (that prize goes to tourism), they're a vital part of the ecosystem both here and around the state. The Susitna Salmon Center was created to promote the importance of this magnificent fish throughout all of Alaska.

Although it's not on the regular tourist circuit, **Northern Susitna Institute (NSI)** (13778 E. 3rd St., 907/733-7111, northernsusitnainstitute.org), a nonprofit that emphasizes "real learning in the real world," is a real gem in Talkeetna. Youth come from all over the country to participate in NSI's wilderness programs, which range from hands-on outdoor engagement for younger children to full-on expeditions for teens. NSI and one of its subdivisions, the Alaska Folk School, also offer craft classes for all ages, from building rocket mass heaters to creating birch bark baskets. If you want to engage with real Alaskans and learn an unusual hands-on skill while you're at it, this is a great place to do so.

Talkeetna Historical Society Museum

Another small but high-quality stop is the **Talkeetna Historical Society Museum** (22228 S. D St., 907/733-2487, talkeetnahistoricalsociety.org, early May-mid-Sept. daily 10am-6pm, winter limited weekend hours only, $3, free for 7 and under). The main museum is housed in the original Talkeetna school building, which opened in 1936; it has several exhibits that showcase aspects of historical Talkeetna life and its evolution into a climbing/flying/railroad town.

While you're in the museum, pick up the Talkeetna Historical Society's walking tour brochure, check out the book-heavy gift shop, and make sure to visit the scale model of Denali in one of the outbuildings. Interpretive rangers from the national park's **Walter Harper Talkeetna Ranger Station** (22241 B St., 907/733-2231, mid-Apr.-Labor Day daily 8am-5:30pm, winter Mon.-Fri. 8am-4:30pm) give daily talks about climbing the mountain

the re-created interior of a typical railroad cabin in the Talkeetna Historical Society Museum

here, usually around 1:30pm. You can also call the museum to book guided walking tours of the town for $10 per person, with at least a four-day advance notice.

If you're interested in mountaineering, the ranger station is also worth a visit; you can see photos of climbing history in the making, watch videos in the tiny theater, and check out a smattering of historical climbing gear.

RECREATION

Hurricane Turn Train

The Alaska Railroad's **Hurricane Turn Train** (800/544-0552, alaskarailroad.com, mid-May-mid-Sept. Thurs.-Mon., Oct.-May first Thurs. of the month) is your window into the true Alaskan experience, both then and now. This is one of the last remaining flag stop trains in the world; it'll stop for anyone who flags it down, anywhere along the line. Just as in the early days of homesteading, it's the only lifeline connecting a few rural residents to town.

Locals also use the Hurricane Turn Train for access to privately owned cabins, hunting opportunities, and paddling trips (inflatable boats only), and the conductor provides fun, family-friendly narration along the way, stopping the train for photo ops and to let you get out and stretch your legs or explore historical sites. There's no meal service and snacks are extremely limited, so bring your own food and plan to be out all day. Sit on the left side on the way out for beautiful views of the Big Su.

Another popular pastime is using the Hurricane Turn Train to haul camping equipment north, then catching a ride back a few days later. Again, before you go, make sure you have the right skills and equipment to camp in the Alaska backcountry. You won't have cell service, there will be no paths to civilization, and you may encounter wild bears, moose, wolves, and swarms of mosquitoes.

Jet Boat Tours

Another local favorite is **Mahay's Jet Boat Adventures** (on the right as you're driving into town, 907/733-2223, mahaysriverboat.com, $70-165 adults, $53-124 12 and under), which offers jet boat rides up and down the river. Ask about their River, Rail, and Trail trip, which as of this writing wasn't yet posted on the website; the 3.5-hour tour sends you up to the historic townsite of Curry on the Hurricane Turn Train in the company of a Mahay's naturalist. After a short tour through the old Curry townsite you then take a jet boat to the Mahay's "adventure site," where you can learn more about Alaska Native and trapping history in the area. Another popular trip is the Devil's Canyon Adventure, a ride through Class V white water in a 54-passenger jet boat.

ATV Tours

Visitors also rave about **DeVore's ATV Tours** (907/351-3914, talkeetna-atvtours.com, $195 pp for the full tour or $100 for shorter wilderness rides). The full tour includes the very Alaskan combination of a narrated tour of Talkeetna's historical district, an off-road trip to the owner's homestead, target shooting, and gold panning.

Ziplining

If adrenaline is your thing, check out the **Denali Zipline Tour** (13572 E. Main St., 855/733-3988 or 907/733-3988, denaliziplinetours.com, $149 adults, $119 youth). The nine ziplines, three suspension bridges, spiral staircase, and rappel aren't as tall or as long as you'll find in warmer locales, but they're a fun way to get a new perspective on this part of the state, and on clear days, you get amazing views of the Alaska Range (including Denali).

Fishing

Fishing is big on all three of the wild, scenic rivers that converge near town: the Talkeetna, the (Big) Susitna, and the Chulitna. Peak runs for sockeye and pink salmon typically run from late July to late August; they overlap with a run of silvers that typically lasts through August. Kings come first, from late June to mid July.

Family-owned **Phantom Tri River Charters** (907/733-2400, phantomsalmon charters.com) is the most popular fishing guide outfit in the area by a landslide.

Golf

Even in one of the bigger cities, Alaska's golf courses are delightfully unique. Check one major "must" off your list with a visit to the northernmost golf course in the nation, **North Star Golf Club** (330 Golf Club Dr., 907/457-4653, northstargolfclub.com, greens fees from $23 for 9 holes or $34 for 18, all-inclusive $74/$89). Your scorecard includes a checklist of the wildlife you might see, permafrost creates an ever-changing lay to the challenging terrain, and if a raven or fox steals a golf ball, you can replace it without penalty.

ENTERTAINMENT

Despite the fact that it's well inland, Talkeetna is a popular stop on the cruise ship circuit. By day, it's full of tourists who arrive by bus and stroll the streets; the real entertainment starts at night, and usually centers around the rocking, eclectic selection of live bands that play at the **Fairview Inn** (D St. and Main St., 907/733-2423). For daytime entertainment, watch for the Talkeetna Chamber of Commerce's **Live at 5** concert events (talkeetnachamber.org), every Friday at 5pm from Memorial Day weekend through Labor Day weekend.

Another uniquely Talkeetna—heck, uniquely Alaska—festival is the **Talkeetna Bachelor Society's annual auction** (talkeetnabachelors.com) on the first Saturday in December, which includes a **Bachelor Ball** and the wildly popular **Wilderness Woman Contest,** where single women 21 and older compete in rugged events like water-fetching, shooting, snowmachining, and opening beer for a lounging bachelor.

When the bachelors go on the auction block in front of a women-only audience, most of them perform a song, dance, or maybe even a striptease to entice bidders. Some of them bring their own "bonuses" too, like a bottle of wine or a hotel room. All proceeds benefit Women and Children in Crisis, and everything is, of course, done with tongue firmly in cheek. It's especially fun to ride the **Alaska Railroad** (800/544-0552, alaskarailroad.com) Aurora Winter train to Talkeetna that morning, stay overnight, then take another train back.

SHOPPING

Nagley's Store (13650 E. Main St., 907/733-3663, nagleysstore.com, Sun.-Thurs. 7:30am-10pm, Fri.-Sat. 7:30am-11pm) is more than "just" a historic landmark; it still functions as Talkeetna's general store, with basic toiletries, food, and fishing and camping gear. If you need outdoorsy clothing, the best selection in town is at the **Susitna River Trading Company** (13477 E. Main St., 907/733-7776, Mon.-Sun. 10am-6pm).

Talkeetna is full of good gift shops; even the booking offices for flightseeing operation K2 Aviation sell some basic gifts. It's well worth spending a couple of hours browsing up and down Main Street, where most of the gift shops are located.

That said, two stand out clearly as the best: **The Dancing Leaf Gallery** (13618 E. Main St., 907/733-5323, thedancingleafgallery.com, Mon.-Thurs. and Sat.-Sun. noon-5pm, Fri. noon-6pm) offers an enormous co-op of contemporary art from all-Alaskan artists, many of them from Talkeetna, and the gift shop in the **Susitna Salmon Center** (13512 E. 1st St., 907/733-3474, arrialaska.org, Mon.-Sun. 10am-6pm) has a great selection of beautiful aquatic- and nature-themed art.

FOOD

Housed in a circa 1917 log building, the **Talkeetna Roadhouse** (13550 E. Main St., 907/733-1351, talkeetnaroadhouse.com, café summer daily 6am-4pm, expanded winter hours, $15) has a reputation as *the* place to eat in town, and it does serve a great breakfast. The roadhouse's family-style dining room can get awfully rowdy during the evenings, though, and Talkeetna has plenty of other great food to choose from. So unless you're in it just for the experience, stick to breakfast or lunch.

The roadhouse has a small bakery, but I'd recommend you go to the **Flying Squirrel Bakery Cafe** (Mile 11 Talkeetna Spur Rd., 907/733-6887, flyingsquirrelcafe.com, summer Mon.-Wed. 7:30am-6pm, Thurs.-Sat. 7:30am-9pm, Sun. 8am-5pm) instead. They serve wonderful, hearty soups with a big chunk of fresh bread. Check their Facebook page to find out when their several-times-weekly wood-fired pizza night will be ($25).

Talkeetna is full of other great food. For the best pizza, hit **Mountain High Pizza Pie** (22165 C St., 907/733-1234, pizzapietalkeetna.com, summer daily 11am-10pm, reduced winter hours, entrées $15, pizzas $25), which also does phone-in "to go" orders. Go wild with the Mountain High pizza; it has more than 30 toppings. For decent brewpub fare and really good beer on an outdoor patio that overlooks Main Street—perfect for people-watching!—head to **Twister Creek Restaurant,** a.k.a. the **Denali Brewpub,** which is owned by **Denali Brewing Company** (13605 E. Main St., 907/733-2537, denalibrewingcompany.com, daily 11am-8pm, $15).

The **Wildflower Cafe** (13578 E. Main St., 907/733-2695, talkeetnasuites.com, Sun.-Thurs. noon-8pm, Fri.-Sat. noon-10pm) does just about everything well for lunch and dinner, with good burgers and pizza and great seafood; their deck is another great place for people-watching on Main Street.

For a touch of local sweetness, hit the **Wake and Shake** coffee/ice-cream stand (off E. Main St., just west of D St., 1 scoop $4), where the ice cream is homemade with milk from Alaska cows, using a 1927 John Deere engine to turn the drum. For another coffee option, head to **Conscious Coffee** (off the west end of E. Main St., 907/733-7473, daily 7am-6pm), a cozy little nook of a coffee shop in a tiny log cabin. Warning: This place is tiny, so you'll probably want to take your coffee outside.

If you want to splurge on a high-end meal, head for dinner at the **Foraker Dining Room** in the **Talkeetna Alaskan Lodge** (23601 Talkeetna Spur Rd., 877/777-4067, talkeetnalodge.com, $35), about a mile out of town on the spur road; they also have a more casual **Base Camp Bistro and Lounge** (breakfast, lunch, and dinner; lunch $16, dinner $20), although both restaurants are pretty laid back. After all, this is Alaska, where nobody bats an eye if you wear jeans to a black-tie event. The lodge is situated on a small ridge overlooking

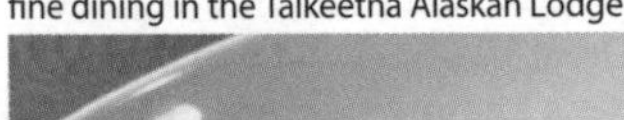

fine dining in the Talkeetna Alaskan Lodge

Talkeetna, with breathtaking views of the mountain if it's "out."

Groceries

Cubby's Marketplace (junction of Parks Hwy. and Talkeetna Spur Rd., 907/733-5050, Mon.-Sat. 8am-10pm, Sun. 9am-8pm) is large and inexpensive by rural Alaska standards, although if you're judging by Lower 48 standards, the selection will be limited and expensive. **Nagley's Store** (13650 E. Main St., 907/733-3663, nagleysstore.com, Sun.-Thurs. 7:30am-10pm, Fri.-Sat. 7:30am-11pm) has a basic, very limited selection of food.

ACCOMMODATIONS

If you're here to see Denali (the mountain), **Talkeetna Alaskan Lodge** (23601 Talkeetna Spur Rd., 877/777-4067, talkeetnalodge.com, from $199 or $265 for mountain side) offers splurge-worthy lodging with stunning views of the mountain from the "mountain side" rooms and all your standard high-end hotel amenities—the only thing that's missing is a day spa. **Talkeetna Denali View Lodge & Cabins** (15669 Coffey Ln., 907/733-4111, talkeetnadenaliviewlodge.com, from $195 summer, reduced winter rates) also offers great mountain views and a shot of full-on rustic Alaskana, from log-framed furniture to wood-paneled walls and wildlife mounts in the "trophy room." Each lodge room has a private bath, TV, and Wi-Fi, while the standalone cabin rentals offer the same plus microwaves, refrigerators, and outdoor decks.

At the other end of the price spectrum, the **House of Seven Trees** (north side of E. Main St., 907/733-7733, from $25/bunk) is a homey, clean hostel, with a few private rooms and a bunkhouse in a separate room out back. Or for $10, you can pitch a tent in Talkeetna City Park on the west end of East Main Street, just a stone's throw away from the Big Su River on one side and all of Main Street's shopping and restaurants on the other side. Bring exact change or a check, and a pen to fill out the form at the pay kiosk.

For very reasonable midrange rooms, check out the **Swiss Alaska Inn,** (22056 S. F St., 907/733-2424, swissalaska.com, from $130), which offers single, double, king, and cabin rooms with the cozy chalet feel its name suggests. Each room has a private bath, TV, and Wi-Fi, and two of the king rooms have Jacuzzi tubs. The on-site restaurant makes great breakfast omelets.

There are several cozy, small-scale accommodations to choose from. You'll find two clean, comfortable apartment-style suites that sleep four people (North suite) or six people (South suite) above the **Wildflower Cafe** (907/733-2695, talkeetnasuites.com, from $165). Keep in mind that you'll be sleeping above a very popular café, although it closes at a decent hour (8pm weekdays, 10pm weekends). The suites include private bathrooms, private entrances, free Wi-Fi, and kitchenettes.

The **Susitna Salmon Center** (907/733-3474, facebook.com/SusitnaSalmon, $150) also rents cabins just one block off Main Street, so they're a little quieter but still close to the action. Each cabin has a king or queen bed, full kitchen, and private bathroom; this is one of the most peaceful and comfortable accommodations in Talkeetna.

The **Talkeetna Northern Guest House** (13712 E. 2nd St., 907/715-4868, talkeetnanorthernguesthouse.com, from $60) offers one of the best bargains in town: small, clean rooms with their own bath for just $60 per night for the first person, $20 per night for each additional person. You also get discounts on some tours and have free use of bicycles to get around town, although all the main attractions are within an easy walk. The guesthouse is pet friendly if you have your pet pre-approved and pay a $25 pet deposit.

For RV campers, the full-service **Talkeetna Camper Park** (about 13.5 miles down the Talkeetna Spur Rd., 907/733-2693, talkeetnacamper.com, Apr.-Oct., from $40 during peak season) is very popular, although you're going to be parked in a gravel lot, not back in the woods. It's a short walk from here to the Alaska Railroad depot, and you're within reasonable walking distance of town. Reservations are highly recommended.

Another in-town option is **Talkeetna Boat Launch & Campground** (21889 S. F St., 907/733-2604, talkeetna-rv.com), which offers a more natural, riverfront experience with showers and Wi-Fi available. If this is full, the **Montana Creek Campground** (907/733-8255, montanacreekcampground.com, from $22 tents, $30 RVs) is very popular, with some electrical hookups and pull-through sites, although it fills up fast when the fishing is good. Montana Creek, which runs right past the campground, contains king, silver, and pink salmon in season, plus grayling, rainbow trout, and Dolly Varden.

If you don't mind a short drive into town and crave the quintessential rustic Alaska experience, check out **Susitna River Lodge** (23094 S. Talkeetna Spur Rd., 866/733-1505, susitnariverlodge.com, from $179 lodge rooms or $249 private cabin, winter rates discounted). You get your choice of private cabins, each with its own full bathroom, kitchenette, dining area, and overhead loft, or suites in the lodge building, three of which have their own lofts. Or book the delightful and very affordable **Talkeetna Wilderness Lodge & Cabin Rentals** (17351 E. Michele Dr., 907/733-8700 or 907/787-9663, talkeetnawildernesslodge.com, from $99). The cabins have full bathrooms, kitchenettes, Wi-Fi, screened porches, and TVs, and there's a spacious common room.

INFORMATION AND SERVICES

Talkeetna doesn't have a real visitor center, but the local chamber of commerce does stock a small kiosk with brochures and local information, on the west side of the Spur Road near Main Street.

Talkeetna's **Sunshine Community Health Center** (Mile 4.4 Talkeetna Spur Rd., 907/733-2273, Mon.-Sat. 9am-5pm) offers health services to the communities of Talkeetna, Willow, and Trapper Creek.

Most Talkeetna lodgings offer free Wi-Fi access. If you need another spot for Wi-Fi, try the **public library** (23151 S. Talkeetna Spur Rd., 907/861-7645, matsulibraries.org, Mon.-Sat. 11am-6pm).

There is a small cluster of gas stations at the Y, where the Talkeetna Spur Road meets the Parks Highway. Your last chance for gas on the way into Talkeetna is a credit-card-only Crowley gas station at mile 10.4 of Talkeetna Spur Road, with both diesel and unleaded.

TRANSPORTATION

Getting There

Talkeetna is 115 miles or about a two-hour drive north of Anchorage, or 275 miles (4.5 hours) south of Fairbanks. Denali National Park is just another 150 miles (2.5 hours of driving) to the north. All three areas are connected by the Parks Highway, which merges into the Glenn Highway as it nears Anchorage. The turnoff for the Talkeetna Spur Road is well-marked from either direction.

If you don't want to drive, you have a few bus options: **Alaska Bus Guy** (alaskabusguy.com, $74) departs Anchorage at 7am and arrives in Talkeetna at 9am, then starts the run back at noon. **Alaska/Yukon Trails** (907/479-2277 or 907/888-5659, alaskashuttle.com) offers an Anchorage-Talkeetna-Denali-Fairbanks run in comfortable passenger vans, and the **Alaska Park Connection** (alaskacoach.com) motorcoaches run all the way from Seward to Talkeetna and Denali.

Getting Around

Once you're in Talkeetna, you really don't need a car to get around, but there is one taxi service, **Talkeetna Taxi** (13765 E. 2nd St., 907/355-8294, talkeetnataxi.com). The rates range from a flat $4 within downtown Talkeetna to $3 per mile plus $2 per person for service all the way out to the Y, where Talkeetna Spur Road meets the Parks Highway. They also offer shuttle service to the Princess Lodge, Denali National Park, or Anchorage ($120-260).

Finally, there is one bike rental service currently housed in the Talkeetna Alaskan

Lodge: **Talkeetna Bike Rentals** (907/733-9500, 23601 Talkeetna Spur Rd., talkeetnabikerentals.com). They charge $15 for a half-day and $25 for a full-day rental, including safety vest and helmet, and also offer a shuttle from downtown Talkeetna to the lodge.

Denali National Park and Preserve

TOP EXPERIENCE

Denali National Park and Preserve is renowned for its stellar opportunities to see bears, moose, caribou, Dall sheep, and wolves in the wild; its pristine scenery set against the backdrop of the Alaska Range and 20,310-foot Denali (formerly known as Mount McKinley), the highest mountain in North America; and for being an intact, protected ecosystem on the forefront of wilderness research and education.

A visit to six-million-acre Denali National Park is the trip of a lifetime, offering the easiest possible access to a vast swath of trackless wilderness. There's only one road, running just 92 miles into a park that measures almost 9,500 miles square. With just a few exceptions (see *Winning the Road Lottery* page 276), you can only drive the first 15 miles of the road in a private vehicle—but you can go the entire distance in one of the park's many buses.

It's easy to think that the animals you see here are in some way trained or caged, but they're not. They're completely wild, beautiful, unpredictable, and potentially dangerous, which is why park officials insist that you follow key safety precautions.

There is a $10 per person fee for entering Denali National Park, or $40 for an annual pass that can cover up to three additional guests. The fee is collected as part of bus tickets and campground reservations; if you're not riding the bus or camping, you must pay the fee when entering the park or in advance at pay.gov. If you have a prepaid National Parks Pass you must still pay the entrance fee but can request a refund once you're in the park.

One Day in Denali National Park

If possible, you should schedule a minimum of two full days—or one full day and two partial days—in Denali National Park. If you only have one day, though, you can still hit the biggest highlights. Start with the earliest bus ride you can get into the park; in general, traveling in the early morning and late evening increases your odds of seeing wildlife.

Upon your return, if time allows, stop by the sled dog kennels, which are typically open until 5pm, and the Denali Visitor Center (Mile 1.5 Park Rd., mid-May-mid-Sept., daily 8am-6pm). During the peak of summer hours the sun never sets, so if you're still feeling peppy, go day hiking near the Savage River area (mile 14, take a shuttle bus) or Riley Creek Campground at the park entrance. Just make sure you remember your "bear aware" safety rules (see *Essentials*).

VISITOR CENTERS

Denali has three main visitor centers and a couple of secondary visitor stations. Most of them are open from mid-May to mid-September; visitor centers deeper in the park, where travel is restricted by shoulder-season road conditions, may open later. Just one visitor center, the Murie Science and Learning Center, is open year-round.

The **Backcountry Information Center** (mid-May-mid-Sept. daily 9am-6pm) and **Wilderness Access Center** (daily 5am-7pm for bus departures and coffee, 7am-7pm for tickets) are both at mile 1 of the Park Road. If you're here for a backcountry permit, head for the Backcountry Information Center; if you want bus tickets, need to board a bus, or want

Denali National Park and Preserve

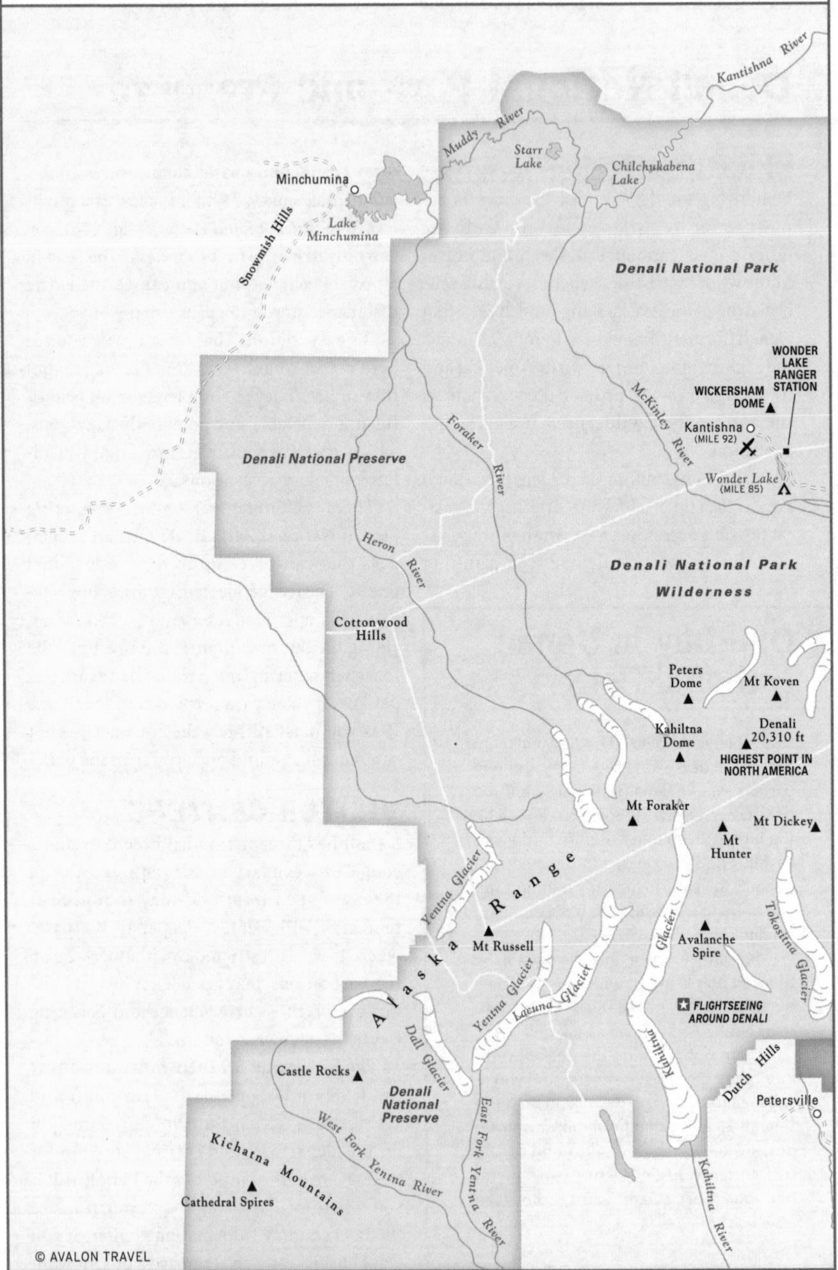

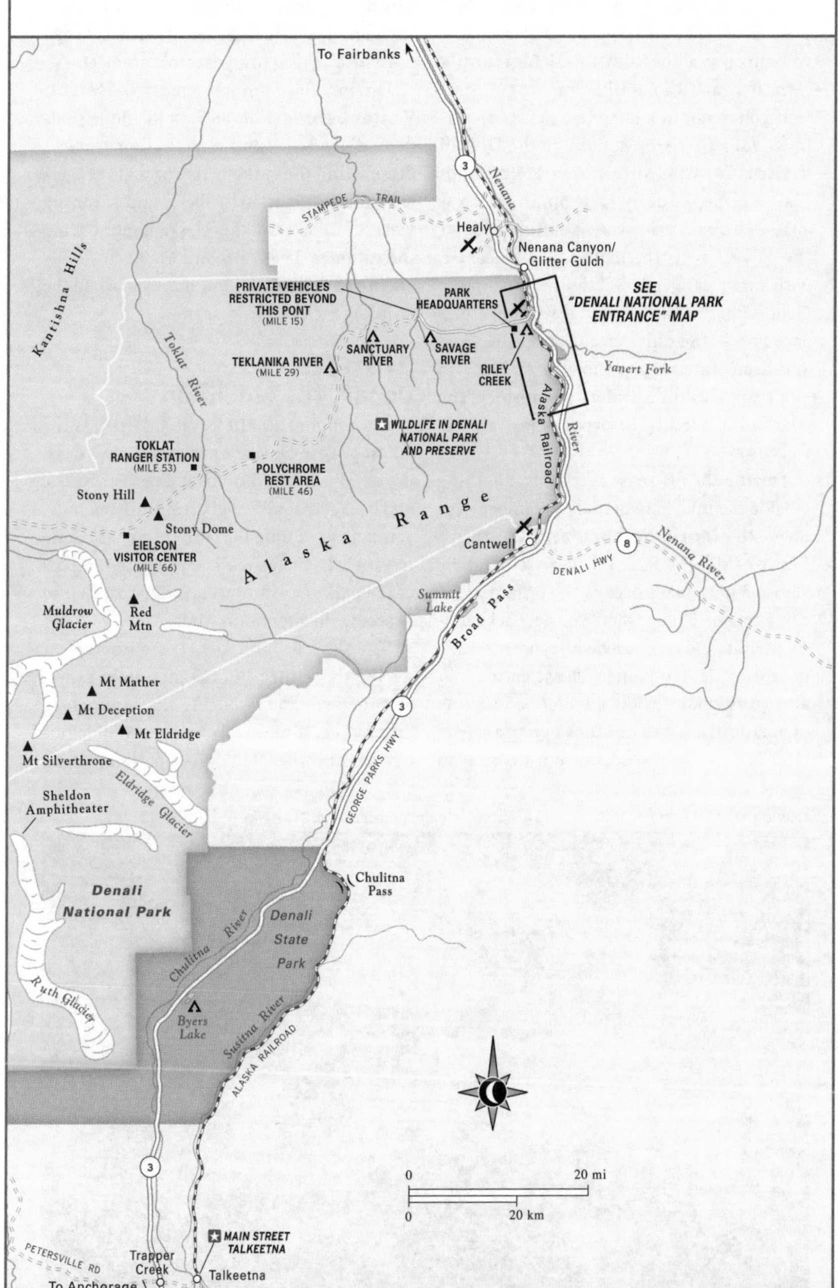
To Fairbanks
Nenana
STAMPEDE TRAIL
Healy
Nenana Canyon/
Glitter Gulch
SEE
"DENALI NATIONAL PARK
ENTRANCE" MAP
Kantishna Hills
PRIVATE VEHICLES
RESTRICTED BEYOND
THIS PONT
(MILE 15)
PARK
HEADQUARTERS
SANCTUARY
RIVER
SAVAGE
RIVER
TEKLANIKA RIVER
(MILE 29)
RILEY
CREEK
Yanert Fork
Toklat River
Alaska Railroad
River
WILDLIFE IN DENALI
NATIONAL PARK
AND PRESERVE
TOKLAT
RANGER STATION
(MILE 53)
POLYCHROME
REST AREA
(MILE 46)
Stony Hill
Stony Dome
EIELSON
VISITOR CENTER
(MILE 66)
Alaska Range
Cantwell
DENALI HWY
Nenana River
Muldrow
Glacier
Red
Mtn
Summit
Lake
Broad Pass
Mt Mather
Mt Deception
Mt Eldridge
Mt Silverthrone
Sheldon
Amphitheater
Eldridge Glacier
GEORGE PARKS HWY
Chulitna
Pass
Denali
National Park
Denali
State
Park
Chulitna River
Ruth Glacier
Byers
Lake
Susitna River
ALASKA RAILROAD
0
20 mi
20 km
MAIN STREET
TALKEETNA
PETERSVILLE RD
Trapper
Creek
Talkeetna
To Anchorage

to arrange a stay in a campground, go to the Wilderness Access Center. If you need tickets or to check into a campground after hours, you can do so at the **Riley Creek Mercantile** (Mile 0.5 Park Rd.) until 11pm.

If you're not in a hurry for tickets or permits, your first stop should be the **Denali Visitor Center** (Mile 1.5 Park Rd., mid-May-mid-Sept., daily 8am-6pm), which is also where you can pay your entrance fee for the park. This is the main welcome center, with many ranger-led activities, an Alaska Geographic bookstore and gift shop, a luggage check, the only restaurant in the park, and beautiful exhibits showcasing Denali's landscapes, wildlife, and natural history. The Alaska Railroad train depot is just a short walk away.

During the off-season—that is, anything outside the mid-May to mid-September window—the **Murie Science and Learning Center** (Mile 1.4 Park Rd., year-round daily 9am-4:30pm) takes over as the primary welcome center. This is where you get backcountry permits and can speak with rangers during the spring, fall, or winter. The science center also runs small-group interactive learning opportunities. Many of those programs are intended for local students, but if you plan ahead, you might be able to send young visitors on a once-in-a-lifetime field expedition through the **Alaska Geographic Field Institute** (akgeo.org/youth-programs/).

During the summer months, **Eielson Visitor Center** (Mile 66 Park Rd., June-mid-Sept. daily 9am-7pm) offers visitor services deep within the park, including daily ranger-led walks, a small art gallery, and stunning views of Denali and the Alaska Range during the summer. The restrooms are open all day and night during the summer, even when the building is closed.

SIGHTS

Denali, the Mountain

At a whopping 20,310 feet tall, Denali is the tallest peak in North America. On clear days, it is clearly visible from Anchorage, Fairbanks, and Talkeetna, although, ironically enough, you can't see it from the park entrance because terrain is in the way. Once you're past mile 9 of the park road, however, you have a chance of seeing the mountain—if it's "out."

The skies around Denali are often clear during the winter, but the mountain generates its own clouds during the summer, so on average, it may only be fully visible one day out of three. Don't give up, though—it's

Taking to the air is the only way to really appreciate the immensity of "The High One."

Denali National Park Entrance

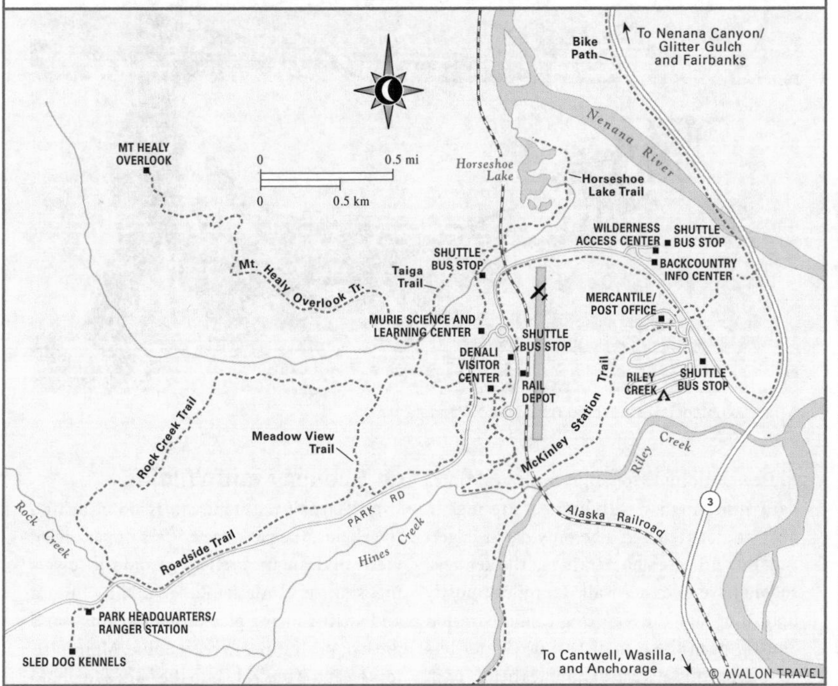

worth taking a chance to see it, and you have a better than 50-50 chance of getting at least a partial view of the mountain peeking out of the clouds.

It's hard to be precise because Alaska's climate is changing, but anecdotally you have a slightly better chance of seeing the mountain in the early summer rather than later in the year.

Don't forget to stop by the visitor centers for more information; if you take a bus all the way to mile 66 of the park road—and the Eielson Visitor Center—where there won't be any folds of land between you and *the* mountain—you might even get stunning views of Denali (again, if it's "out"). But it's absolutely worth the wait.

Here's one thing that you shouldn't do: Don't march up to the Denali National Park rangers and announce that you'd like to hike the mountain itself. Plain and simply put, most people can't; any trip up Denali is a high-level mountaineering expedition that requires technical skill, equipment, and quite a bit of fitness. People can and do *climb* it, though, and if you don't have the requisite skills, you can enlist the aid of a professional guiding service like the locally run **Alaska Mountaineering School** (13765 E. 3rd St., Talkeetna, 907/733-1016, climbalaska.org)—but you need to be willing to work hard, put in a lot of preparation and forethought beforehand, and learn a new skill set that might just save your life or that of your buddies. That sort of trip is anything but a day hike!

Sled Dog Demonstrations

Denali is the only national park with a working kennel of sled dogs; you can tour the park kennels and visit the working huskies

A park volunteer takes a sled dog team onto Wonder Lake.

in free, 30-minute tours given several times daily June-August, with limited offerings in May and September. The only catch is getting there. There's no parking at the kennels, so you have to either walk 1.5 miles (mostly uphill) or take the Sled Dog Demonstration Shuttle from the Denali Visitor Center bus stop, departing at least 40 minutes before each demonstration begins.

The kennels are also open year-round to visits even if a tour isn't scheduled, generally 8am-5pm, although during the winter, the kennels may be almost vacant when the dog teams are out working. Do not bring your pets to visit the kennel—this would not be a fun bonding experience for them or for the sled dogs.

For another type of sled dog experience, visit **Husky Homestead** (just outside the park, 907/683-2904, huskyhomestead.com), the kennel of Jeff King, the "winningest musher in the world." He has almost 30 first-place finishes in major races, including four Iditarod wins and the Yukon Quest. You can cuddle with puppies, watch adult sled dogs on their explosive summer training runs, and learn about the history of dog mushing, from heavy-duty freight haulers to lightweight racers.

★ Scenery and Wildlife

Even if Denali, the mountain, is hiding behind the clouds, the park itself offers unparalleled views of dramatic scenery—from the towering, snow-clad Alaska Range to high tundra and swift-flowing glacier-fed streams—and great opportunities to see wildlife. Many visitors treat the bus ride into the park as a photo safari and come back with memories to last a lifetime. You can take the same approach on any trip into Denali, even if it's "just" a short day hike.

Keep in mind that wildlife sightings here are never guaranteed. After all, the animals are truly wild and free to wander unfenced over Denali's six million acres—or more, since they can come and go from the park at will. That said, the park staff and concession staff (that's the people who run the buses) can tell you if there have been any consistent animal sightings as of late; that'll help you decide how far you should ride into the park on the bus.

Also, there are a few places you can direct your eyes—or binoculars—to help you find the specific animals that interest you. Keep a sharp eye out for moose on the first 15 miles of the roadway, especially near streams; watch for Dall sheep on rocky areas above treeline; and look for grizzly bears everywhere, but

Dall sheep resting in Denali National Park and Preserve

especially above treeline. There are black bears in Denali National Park, too, but they tend to stay below treeline and aren't often seen. Wolf sightings are unpredictable and, sadly, sometimes affected by hunting activity just outside the park's borders, but this remains one of the best places in the state to view them.

Bottom line: If you go into your tour with an open mind, you're guaranteed to see something awe-inspiring. It just might not be what you originally expected!

Ride the Park Bus

With the exception of the road lottery (page 276) and the early shoulder season when the road is partially plowed but buses aren't yet running, you can only drive to mile 15 of the park road. If you want to go farther than that, you must take a bus. Most of the road is very

A caribou dashes across the tundra in front of Denali.

Bear Viewing in Denali

Keep a safe distance between you and Denali's bears.

If you've ever been on a bear-viewing trip in Katmai or other coastal areas, you probably had a chance to get up very close to enormous bears with no negative consequences. That level of tolerance from a bear is completely unique to certain coastal areas, where resources are so plentiful that the bears are willing to tolerate other bears—and humans—in close proximity to get a shot at all that food.

In places like Denali National Park, the bears have much larger zones of "personal space" and have been known to charge from up to 0.25 mile away. Because of that, the National Park Service recommends that you stay at least 300 yards (274 meters) away from bears, and 25 yards (23 meters) from any moose. That can be hard to do when you're hiking in limited visibility; See *Essentials* for precautions you can take to reduce your risk of surprising big wildlife, and how to handle close surprise encounters with bears and moose.

If you remember only one thing, make it this: *Do not run* from a bear. Like all predators, they have an inborn chase instinct, so, as one expert memorably put it, "They may not want to eat you, but they'd love to chase you."

narrow, graded gravel with no shoulder, so it's a relief to let someone else do the driving while you keep an eye out for wildlife and scenery.

A number of buses run into Denali National Park; here are the different types, most of which run from mid-May to mid-September. The buses that go all the way to Kantishna, at the end of the road, usually don't start until June.

Tickets for all of these buses are sold through a park concessionaire and can be ordered as early as December 1 of the preceding year. This is also when the ticket prices, which fluctuate every year, are set. Get your tickets at reservedenali.com, 800/622-7275 or 907/272-7275, or at the **Wilderness Access Center** (Mile 1 Park Rd., 5am-7pm for bus departures and coffee, 7am-7pm for tickets).

Narrated tour buses are guided by the drivers, who are also trained naturalists. They do stop for photo opportunities, but don't stop to let people hop on and off the bus. Trips range 5-12 hours, depending on how far each bus goes into the park, and the prices range $77.25-194 (again depending on how far the bus goes), with steep discounts for youth 15 or younger. The bus schedules fluctuate throughout the summer, but the staff at the Wilderness Access Center can fill you in.

Shuttle buses aren't narrated, but they do stop for wildlife viewing and also to let people hop on and off along the road. Schedules and where the buses start and stop each run vary quite a bit, so always double-check to make sure you don't miss the last bus back! In 2016, prices peaked at $51 for a round-trip all the way to Kantishna at the end of the road. Kids 15 and under ride these buses for free, but Alaska's state laws apply to car seat requirements for kids.

Finally, the **camper bus** is available only to people who are staying at an established campground or in the backcountry; a round-trip ticket costs $34.

See *Transportation* for information on some of the other shuttle buses you'll see operating in and around Denali National Park. If you have accessibility issues that keep you from using the buses, you can apply for a road permit to drive yourself into the park.

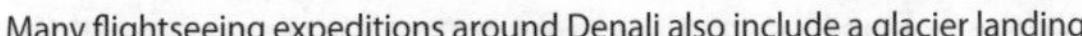
TOP EXPERIENCE

★ Flightseeing

Any trip into Denali National Park will be a phenomenal sightseeing adventure. But if you really want to see the park—and Denali, the mountain—at their best, take a *flight*seeing trip. Even the most jaded Alaskan will subside into awe when "The High One" is front and center in the windshield. Many flightseeing operations also include a landing on a nearby glacier, so you can get out and walk on ground that only the world's most intrepid explorers have ever reached by other means. This is truly a once-in-a-lifetime splurge that everybody should experience.

Only a few carriers are authorized to make glacier landings in Denali National Park. They are:

- **Fly Denali** (866/733-7768, flydenali.com); the only provider that can depart straight from the park entrance (they base their aircraft in Anchorage, Talkeetna, and Healy)
- **Talkeetna Air Taxi** (departing from Talkeetna; 800/533-2219, talkeetnaair.com)
- **Sheldon Air Service** (departing from Talkeetna; 907/733-2321, sheldonairservice.com)
- **K2 Aviation** (departing from Talkeetna; 800/764-2291, flyk2.com)
- **Kantishna Air Taxi** (departing from Kantishna; 907/644-8222 June-Sept., 303/449-1146 Oct.-May); also provides air taxi services between Kantishna and the park entrance

Many flightseeing expeditions around Denali also include a glacier landing.

Numerous other small airlines are authorized to operate in the park, but are not authorized to make glacier landings. If you've never flown in a small plane before, see *Essentials* for some useful information.

Era Helicopters (800/843-1947, eraflightseeing.com) also offers glacier landing tours to a glacier near the park and helicopter-supported hiking within the park. Small planes are an amazing adventure, but helicopters are even better: They can go closer, lower, and slower to terrain than a plane, and they can easily land in places that a plane pilot would never consider.

RECREATION

Denali National Park is a paradise for anyone who enjoys outdoor recreation. You can do almost anything here, but there are several backcountry experiences that will become a truly unforgettable part of your memories when you do them up "Denali style."

Horseback Riding

There's something special about seeing Denali's terrain from the back of a horse. You'll cover more ground with less effort (and a better vantage point) than if you were on foot, but you won't have the noise or emissions of riding an ATV, and you won't gouge tracks into the ground. Plus . . . horses. **Denali Horseback Tours** (907/322-3886, denalihorsebacktours.com, $110-260) in Healy is the closest outfitter to the park. They offer one-, two-, and four-hour rides in small groups and can accommodate most experience levels, from "never ridden" to "bona fide horse person."

Cycling

You can only drive the entirety of the park road if you're lucky enough to win the road lottery. But you can travel the entire Park Road—all 92 miles of it—on two wheels any time you like. You can rent a bike from most lodges near or inside the park, or use nearby **Denali Outdoor Center** (Mile 238.9 Parks Hwy., 888/303-1925 or 907/683-1925, denalioutdoorcenter.com). Make sure you bring proof that you paid your entrance fee at the Denali Visitor Center, or you may not get past Savage River at mile 15.

If you want to overnight anywhere along the road, you'll need to book at one of the pricey all-inclusive lodges along the way, stay in one of the park's six bike-rack-equipped campgrounds, or rough it like a backpacker (permit required). If you go the backpacking route you'll be required to carry a bear-resistant food container and conceal your bike off the road; if you lose your bike in the bushes, park officials won't help you hunt for it.

To extend your reach on a day trip, take a bus into the park to bike as far as you like on the road, then hop on a bus coming back. You can only take your bike on shuttle buses—not the narrated tour buses. Not all shuttles can take bikes, and those that do are limited to just two bikes at a time, so it's best to make reservations (reservedenali.com) or at least verify scheduling with a call to the shuttle operator (800/622-7275 or 907/272-7275).

For another suitably epic bike ride in the area, consider the 135-mile **Denali Highway.**

Hiking

Most of the maintained trails in Denali National Park are short, and the trails nearest the visitor centers are often crowded (by Alaska standards, anyway). But what these trails lack in length and sometimes privacy, they make up for in their beauty and scenic variety.

One of the most popular maintained trails in the park is the mostly level 1.7-mile **Savage River Loop,** which starts from the Savage River Day Use Area, accessible by private car or the free Savage River Shuttle. Or you can take the more strenuous four-mile **Savage Alpine Trail,** which goes up and over tundra slopes to the Savage River Campground.

Also popular is the **Horseshoe Lake Trail,** a 3.2-mile loop around a pretty lake of the same name; it starts just less than a mile into the park, near the railroad tracks. And if you go as far as the Eielson Visitor Center at mile 66, a couple of short, steep trails deliver great views in less than a mile: the **Eielson Alpine Trail** and **Thorofare Ridge.**

Venturing off the established trails and into the backcountry is one of the most glorious ways to see Denali, but due to the remote location and challenging terrain, which often involves crossings of swift, glacier-fed creeks, you should treat even a simple day trip as a serious backcountry expedition.

If you want some company on the trail, rangers often lead hikes on the maintained paths and "Discovery Hikes" that go off-trail; call the visitor centers or check nps.gov/dena for a list.

Backpacking

If you want to go backpacking in Denali—that is, sleeping in a tent somewhere off in the tundra, with the midnight sun or a spangle of stars and aurora borealis glimmering overhead—you're going to need a permit. The permits are issued in person only at the **Backcountry Information Center** (Mile 1 Park Rd., mid-May-mid-Sept. daily 9am-6pm), no more than 24 hours before your departure date.

The permits are free, and they're meant to help distribute traffic evenly throughout the park. It's best to treat the process of planning your backcountry trip as its own adventure, because the park is divided into numbered units, and there's no guarantee you'll get the unit you want. Hedge your bets by planning several trip possibilities in different sections or, if you must have a specific section, travel with flexible dates so you can make more than one attempt at getting it. You will also receive a loaner bear-resistant food container, which you are required to use while in the backcountry and then return within 48 hours of departing the backcountry. These hard-sided containers typically add 3-5 pounds to the weight of your pack.

A few hacks will help you speed through the permitting process, which takes about an hour and must be completed, in person, by all members of your party. You can watch the wilderness safety video in the Wilderness Access Center, which is also at Mile 1 of the Park Road but opens at 7am (two hours before the Backcountry Information Center opens). You can also grab a copy of the worksheet from the back door of the Backcountry Information Center and fill it out in advance; this gives details that can help park officials find you in an emergency.

Preparing ahead of time will position you to quickly complete the rest of the process once the Backcountry Information Center opens: Talking to a ranger, being assigned your unit number, buying maps, and finally buying any bus tickets needed.

Rafting

Denali's swift, restless creeks make for dangerous crossings on foot—but that also translates to lots of fun for rafters with **Denali Raft Adventures** (888/683-2234, 907/683-2234, denaliraft.com, from $94). They offer trips all the way from calm Class I water to boiling Class IV rapids. You choose between oar rafts, in which only the guide paddles, or paddle rafts where every client pitches in too, following commands from the guide.

Denali Outdoor Center (888/303-1925 or 907/683-1925, denalioutdoorcenter.com, from $92) is also excellent, with raft runs down Class III to IV rapids on oar or paddle rafts, plus lake and white-water kayaking trips.

Ziplining

The **Denali Park Zipline** (907/683-2947, denalizipline.com, from $139 adults, $99 kids 8-12) offers eight ziplines and six suspension bridges that might not be the biggest or longest in the world, but on clear days the scenery just can't be beat. Even if the mountain isn't "out," you still have the privilege of soaring over one of the world's greatest wilderness areas. Side-by-side ziplines mean you can even race a friend.

Off-Road Excursions

If you like your toys to have a motor in them, you might enjoy an off-road tour with **Denali**

From McKinley to Denali

Many visitors know the tallest mountain in North America as Mount McKinley, named after the 25th president of the United States, William McKinley, who was from Ohio. But to Alaskans, it's always been Denali, which derives from a Koyukon Athabascan phrase meaning "The High One."

Interestingly, the entire park was first named for the same president: Mount McKinley National Park was created in 1917 as a preserve for Dall sheep. In 1980, the park was enlarged to its current size and renamed Denali National Park and Preserve.

Alaska's legislature also changed the mountain's name at the state level in 1980. They first asked that it be changed on the federal level five years before that, in 1975. Forty years later, in August of 2015, the federal name change finally happened—although you might still see some businesses in the park that are branded with the name "McKinley."

Something else happened in 2015: The mountain's height was cut from 20,320 feet to 20,310 feet, thanks to new GPS technology that allowed a more exact survey of its altitude. It's still 759 feet higher than North America's second-highest peak, Mount Logan in Canada's Yukon Territory. The third-highest peak in North America is 18,008-foot Mount Saint Elias, an Alaskan peak that sits on the border with Canada.

ATV Adventures (907/683-4288, denaliatv.com); you can drive your own ATV or share a side-by-side double ATV. All that engine noise may reduce the amount of wildlife you see, but there's always the possibility, and it's thrilling to drive your own ATV around off-trail and see parts of the park that you otherwise wouldn't have seen. You'll be escorted at all times by a guide, of course, who'll keep an eye on how you're doing and adjust his or her speed, as need be, so everyone in the group is comfortable.

FOOD

There's just one real restaurant in Denali National Park: **Morino Grill** (Mile 1.5 Park Rd., mid-May-mid-Sept. daily 7:30am-5pm with limited hours during the shoulder season) is about 30 yards from the Denali Visitor Center. It offers boxed takeaway lunches and coffee all day long, plus made-to-order lunch and dinner.

You can also purchase a limited selection of snacks and food at the **Wilderness Access Center** (Mile 1 Park Rd.), which also has a small coffee stand. The **Riley Creek Mercantile** (Mile 0.5 Park Rd., 907/682-9246) sells sandwiches, snacks, and some limited groceries, along with fuel for camping stoves. The selection is very limited, so if you're looking for something specific, it's best to call first.

Happily, you have some excellent restaurant options within a short drive of the park entrance.

Fine Dining

For the best fine dining in the area, head to **Alpenglow** (Mile 238 Parks Hwy., 855/683-8600, denalialaska.com, breakfast daily 5am-10am, lunch 11am-4pm, dinner 5pm-10pm), the restaurant in the Grande Denali Lodge. You'll dine on all the best American food, from freshly caught wild seafood to steaks, pasta, soups, and salad.

Pizza

Prospector's Pizzeria and Alehouse (Mile 238.9 Parks Hwy., 907/683-7437, denaliparksalmonbake.com, 11am-late, kitchen closes at midnight, $31) is heavy on the typical Alaskan atmosphere, with lots of historical photos and taxidermied animals. The pizza is great, though, with dough that's aged 24 hours and very Alaskan toppings like salmon, halibut, crab, elk, and reindeer. Gluten-free and non-dairy options are available. The super-efficient staff is adept at handling big groups during the busy tourist season.

Asian Food and Vegetarian

Look for a little trailer, **Thai and Chinese Food 2 Go** (907/306-3534, $15), at one end of the scrum outside the park entrance. Everything is good, portions are generous, they offer lots of vegetarian options, and their prices are very decent by park standards. Seating is limited to a couple of benches and tables. Cash only.

Cafés

Black Bear Coffee House (Mile 238.5 Parks Hwy., 907/683-1656, denaliblackbear.com, daily 6am-8pm, $14) is a real gem, with big portions of tasty, typical American and Mexican foods: bagels, burritos, and scrambled eggs for breakfast, and tacos, paninis, and macaroni and cheese for lunch and dinner. They also offer baked goods, excellent local coffee, and vegan and gluten-free options. You can get Wi-Fi here.

ACCOMMODATIONS

There are various bed-and-breakfasts and lodges near the entrance to Denali National Park but only a few lodges within the park. Most of them offer all-inclusive rates, with no TVs, no phones, and limited satellite Wi-Fi if any. People come here to unplug from today's omnipresent technology or to splurge on a base camp experience that lets them hike, bike, or paddle deep into the park without having to take a long bus ride or secure a backcountry camping permit.

The **Denali Backcountry Lodge** (Mile 92 Park Rd., 855/581-3223, alaskacollection.com, from $529) is unique because it has no minimum stay. The rate includes lodging, three meals, twice-daily shuttle runs to nearby Wonder Lake, and extra activities like gold panning, mountain biking, morning yoga classes, and lake fishing. Ask for a room near the creek and if you want to avoid crowds of day trippers, and eat lunch early.

The **North Face Lodge** (907/683-2290, campdenali.com, from $1,800/3 nights) is the closest facility to the very popular backcountry camping destination of Wonder Lake, just 1.5 miles away on bicycle or by foot. The 15 hotel-style rooms all have electricity, private bathrooms, and running water, and an outdoor patio provides beautiful views of the Alaska Range. The all-inclusive rate covers meals, lodging, transportation from the railroad depot, day and night programs that are heavy on hiking, and the use of outdoor gear, including canoes, bikes, and fishing equipment. There's a fixed schedule for arrivals, with only three-, four-, or seven-night stays allowed.

The same company runs **Camp Denali** (907/683-2290, campdenali.com, from $1,800/3 nights), where you pay the same rate to stay in rustic cabins lit by propane lamps and woodstoves, with outhouses instead of flush toilets. A modern, shared bathroom and shower facility is available, but you'll have to take a five-minute walk to get there. Bonus: The camp sits right at treeline and has some amazing reviews, including Denali when it's "out."

Camping

There are six established campgrounds within Denali National Park. Some campgrounds can accommodate RVs of less than 40 feet, but they don't have electrical or water hookups. Unless otherwise noted, the only services you can expect are outhouses, potable water, and bearproof food lockers that you must use if you're not storing your food in a hard-sided vehicle (bikes and soft-sided trailers don't count).

Campground prices typically range $12-26 per night, and unless otherwise noted the campgrounds are only open mid-May to mid-September. Reservations are recommended in the Riley Creek Campground, located right inside the park entrance, and the other campgrounds occasionally do fill up. Call 800/622-7275 or 907/272-7275 or visit reservedenali.com to book a campsite.

The **Riley Creek Campground** (Mile 0.5 Park Rd.) has an RV dump/fill station during the summer only. Although it's open year-round, there are no services—and thus no fees—from late September-mid-May.

Winning the Road Lottery

The 92-mile road running into Denali National Park is only open to private vehicles until mile 15—unless you're lucky enough to win the yearly road lottery. Anybody at all (including visitors from out of state or out of country) can apply for the lottery, and the lucky winners can drive their own cars as far into the park as conditions permit.

The lottery entry period runs from May 1 to May 31 every year, and the winning tickets are drawn in mid-June; if you win, you'll be notified by email and your credit card will be charged a $25 fee for the road permit. The driving period runs for four days, and you're automatically assigned a day that your permit is valid. It's up to you to cover travel costs and logistics, and to provide the car.

Many rental car companies won't allow you to take their vehicles on gravel highways (including the park road), but **Alaska Auto Rental** (907/457-7368, alaskaautorental.com), which is based out of Fairbanks with a second office in nearby Healy, will. They also happily rent to drivers under 25 years of age.

The **Savage River Campground** (Mile 13 Park Rd.) can be reached on the free Savage River Shuttle. It offers 33 tent and RV sites and frequent ranger-led programs. This campground does sometimes book up completely. Technically this campground is open year-round, but there are no services after late September or October, and the 12-mile trip in—which requires skis or snowshoes during the winter—should be treated as a serious backcountry trip.

The last campground that accepts RVs is the **Teklanika River Campground** (Mile 29 Park Rd.). Officials do allow private vehicles here, making it an exception to the rule that you can't drive yourself past mile 15, but you must book for a minimum three-night stay, and once you reach the campground your vehicle must stay parked.

The **Sanctuary River Campground** (Mile 22 Park Rd.) offers tent sites only, as do the **Igloo Creek Campground** (Mile 35) and **Wonder Lake** (Mile 85). You can expect lots of mosquitoes anywhere in Denali during the summer, but they tend to be especially bad around Wonder Lake.

ENTERTAINMENT

Most of the entertainment in Denali National Park comes from the park itself; however, if you want a more conventional entertainment venue, in 2016 Holland American opened the **Denali Square** (877/932-4259, hollandamerica.com), a new addition to the 60-acre McKinley Chalet Resort, which is positioned at the park entrance. The square includes an outdoor amphitheater for ranger programs and musical performances, an artist-in-residence cabin, and a musical dinner theater show in the Gold Nugget Saloon.

INFORMATION AND SERVICES

Be aware that you get only limited cell service in Denali National Park, and only within the first few miles of the entrance. There is a small urgent care facility, **Canyon Clinic** (Mile 238.8 Parks Hwy., 907/455-6875), just outside the park entrance. Wi-Fi is essentially nonexistent at lodgings inside the park.

During the summer, public restrooms are available in all the park's visitor centers, with public-use pit toilets (basically, permanent outhouses) in the campgrounds. During winter, use the bathrooms in the **Murie Science and Learning Center** (Mile 1.4 Park Rd., year-round daily 9am-4:30pm) or the pit toilets in the Riley Creek Campground, which is just inside the park entrance.

There's a post office right next to Riley

Creek Campground (Mile 0.5 Park Rd.); you can also mail letters and packages from the nearby tiny communities of Healy and Cantwell. To arrange general delivery packages (for example, if you need to mail yourself backpacking gear), call the Denali **post office** at 907/683-2291.

Year-round gas stations are available in **Cantwell** (30 miles south of the park entrance) and **Healy** (11 miles north of the entrance). During the summer, you can also get gas at a seasonal station one mile north of the park entrance. The closest ATM is in Healy.

Basic camping items, including bear spray and sunscreen, are available at **Riley Creek Mercantile** (Mile 0.5 Park Rd., 907/682-9246). To rent or buy other backpacking equipment, contact **Denali Mountain Works** (Mile 239 Parks Hwy., 907/683-1542), which is 1.5 miles north of the park entrance along the Parks Highway; you can also rent gear from stores like REI, which has locations in both Fairbanks and Anchorage.

TRANSPORTATION

Getting There

Unless you're planning to drive the Park Road or staying outside the park, taking the **Alaska Railroad** (800/544-0552, alaskarailroad.com) to Denali is one of the best rides in the state. The trip takes about 4 hours from Fairbanks or 7.5 hours from Anchorage.

If you're coming by car, the trip is 238 miles from Anchorage, theoretically a little more than four hours, but leave yourself at least five to make it up the Parks Highway, which is often congested, by Alaska standards. The drive from Fairbanks is 125 miles or just over two hours if you don't run into construction or slow RVs.

You can also get to Denali on **The Park Connection** (800/266-8625, alaskacoach.com), one of the most-established bus services in the state, with service all the way from Seward to Denali. Fares start at $65 per adult for short trips, up to $155 for a Denali-to-Seward run (or vice versa); less-expensive express runs are available on some routes.

Finally, although it's rare, you can also charter a small plane from nearby communities to land at the McKinley Park Airstrip just inside the park.

Getting Around

You don't really need a car to get around once you've made it to the park. Most housing comes with a free shuttle that will pick you up from the train depot, airport, or bus stop, and if you're taking a tour, most tour operators will happily pick you up from your hotel or from one of the free shuttle bus stops near the park entrance.

There are three shuttle buses near the park entrances—not to be confused with the shuttle buses that run deeper into the park. The entrance shuttles all operate daily during the summer season (roughly mid-May-mid-Sept.), and they're all free and wheelchair accessible.

The **Savage River Shuttle** (which will bear a placard with that name on it, or be marked the "Woo Hoo!" bus with an image of bear cubs rolling down a mountainside) travels between the Denali Visitor Center, the Wilderness Access Center, and the Savage River area (Mile 14 Park Rd.). The round-trip takes about two hours.

The **Riley Loop Shuttle** (which may be marked as the "Nom Nom Nom!" bus, with an image of a browsing moose) travels a loop between all the visitor centers near the park entrance, the Riley Creek Campground, and the Horseshoe Lake/Mount Healy trailhead. Each loop takes about 30 minutes.

The **Sled Dog Demonstration Shuttle** is the only way to get to the park's sled dog demonstration other than walking. The shuttle picks up passengers at the bus stop just outside the Denali Visitor Center; make sure to be there at least 40 minutes before the sled dog demo is scheduled to start.

If you want to rent a car, either choose

from your many options in Anchorage or Fairbanks, or use one of these two local options: **Keys to Denali Car Rentals** (137 Healy Rd., 800/683-1239 or 907/683-1239, denalidomehome) is operated out of Denali Dome Home B&B in Healy, 12 miles north of the park entrance. They offer free pickup/delivery service in Denali, and have rentals available from May to mid-September. They will also loan you basic equipment like binoculars, walking sticks, and coolers. **Alaska Auto Rental** (907/457-7368, alaskaautorental.com) is based out of Fairbanks but also has a rental office in Healy, just north of Denali (Mile 248.6 Parks Hwy.). They will rent to people under 25 years old.

Outside Denali National Park

Many people choose to avoid the frenzied activity of the hotels near the Denali National Park entrance—dubbed "Glitter Gulch" by some—by overnighting in the much quieter, more rustic lodgings available in the nearby small communities of Healy, Carlo Creek, and Cantwell.

Although most tours and activities based in these communities are still pointed firmly toward Denali National Park, a long-term project is under way to develop more tours and attractions in **Denali State Park,** which butts up against the southeast corner of Denali National Park. If that happens, communities like Cantwell—which sits to the south of Denali National Park and to the north of the state park—will become excellent home bases for exploring both areas.

HEALY

Located 11 miles north of the entrance to Denali National Park, Healy is the closest community with year-round services. There are about a thousand year-round residents, most of whom make their living from coal mining and tourism.

Many visitors use Healy as a welcome escape from the crowds at the park entrance. Even if you don't have your own vehicle, many of the restaurants and attractions here and in Denali offer free or low-cost shuttles to take visitors back and forth. In fact, quite a few of the tours that operate in or near Denali originate here.

Sights

THE MAGIC BUS

One of the biggest attractions around Healy is the old *Into the Wild* bus where Christopher McCandless, a.k.a. Alexander Supertramp, famously perished in 1992. That's not necessarily a good thing: Every year tourists must be rescued after making a poorly planned pilgrimage down the muddy, 20-mile **Stampede Trail** to the bus. The trip includes two river crossings, tons of mosquitoes, and long stretches of flooded, muddy trail. If you're absolutely set on going, consult with the locals first; one of the last buildings before the Stampede Trail begins is **Earthsong Lodge** (907/683-2863, earthsonglodge.com). Also, keep in mind that the movie wasn't even filmed here, so the bus you see at the end of the trail is not the same one that was onscreen.

For a much safer photo op, you can visit the replica that was used for the movie at **49th State Brewing Company** in Healy (Mile 248.4 Parks Hwy., 907/683-2739, 49statebrewing.com). You can even go inside and take selfies to your heart's content.

Recreation

Most of Healy's recreational activities are exactly the same as what you'll find in Denali; in fact, quite a few Denali tours originate here.

That said, there are a few activities specific to Healy. The Stampede Ridge trip from **Denali ATV Adventures** (907/683-4288, denaliatv.com, from $195) doesn't actually take you to the *Into the Wild* bus where Christopher McCandless died, but it does give you a chance to survey the area and learn quite a lot about the impact of Mr. McCandless's journey on this area.

Another Healy ATV company, **Black Diamond ATV Tours** (907/683-4653, blackdiamondtourco.com), takes you out to the Dry Creek riverbed, which includes an **archaeological site** where ancient Athabascan artifacts have been discovered.

If you're the type of golfer who loves unusual courses, pay a visit to **Black Diamond Golf** (Otto Lake Rd. & Hilltop Rd., 907/683-4653, blackdiamondtourco.com, greens fees from $30). This 9-hole golf course is for those who eschew a refined experience in favor of unusual hazards like a ball-stealing fox, rough grass laid right over the Alaska tundra, and tee times until 10pm (because hey, it's light out anyway). You can choose an all-inclusive option, including transport, souvenirs, and greens fees, from $85 ($40 for under 16).

Food

The **49th State Brewing Company** (Mile 248.5 Parks Hwy., 907/683-2739, 49statebrewing.com, daily 11am-2am, kitchen closes at 11pm) is a staple, with good beer and classic brewpub food such as burgers, salads, and, because it's Alaska, fish-and-chips. They also serve some more adventurous local options—including Alaska-grown yak meat—and have recently opened a second location in Anchorage. A low-cost shuttle ($3 one-way, $5 day pass) makes regular trips between here and the Denali National Park entrance.

Rose's Cafe (Mile 249.5 Parks Hwy., 907/683-7673, rosescafealaska.com, daily 7am-9pm, $14) is an unpretentious but friendly diner with big portions of simple, hearty diner food at good prices. They also offer box lunches for adventures into the park.

Keep an eye out for the **Moose-AKa's** (907/750-4961, hours vary May-Sept.) food truck in the Healy and Denali National Park areas. They serve delicious Serbian cuisine and great crepes (both sweet and savory), and plan to upgrade to a full-fledged restaurant near the park entrance in 2017.

You can buy a limited selection of groceries and deli food at **Miner's Market and Deli** (Mile 248.5 Parks Hwy., 907/683-2379).

Accommodations

BED-AND-BREAKFASTS

All of these excellent lodgings are just a short drive from the entrance to Denali National Park.

Denali Dome Home B&B (137 Healy Rd., 800/683-1239, 907/683-1239, denalidomehome.com, from $205) offers eight rooms with private bathrooms and full cooked-to-order breakfasts, all set on six lovely acres. Wi-Fi is available and the homey common area has satellite TV. Bonus: A small car rental business, Keys to Denali, operates out of this B&B.

If you're willing to drive one extra bumpy, steep mile, **Ridgetop Cabins** (Mile 253.3 Parks Hwy., 907/683-2448, alaskaone.com/ridgetop, mid-May-late Sept., from $165) offers six simple, rustic frame cabins. Visitors are sometimes disappointed by the amount of brush between them and the mountains, although the views are still pretty and the setting is private and quiet. Each cabin has its own microwave and coffeemaker, and Wi-Fi is available in an enclosed porch area.

For large groups, **Denali Primrose B&B** (1 Stoney Creek Dr., 907/683-1234, denaliprimrose.com, from $142 for two guests, fees for additional guests) offers two suites set on 1.5 wooded acres. The upstairs suite has three bedrooms, the downstairs suite has one bedroom, and there's a common area/suite in between.

HOTELS

If you prefer a more traditional hotel experience, the **Motel Nord Haven** (Mile 249.5 Parks Hwy., 800/683-4501 or 907/683-4500, auroradenalilodge.com, from $169) is a good deal, with rooms set far enough off the highway to be nice and quiet. During the winter, their rates drop to just $89 for a single bed. The rooms are reasonably sized and very clean if a little dated, with a TV, phone, and free Wi-Fi; suites are available and there's a public computer in the lobby. During the summer, you can get a continental breakfast 6:30am-10am. Every so often you might see this property referred to as the Aurora Denali Lodge.

For a good deal try the **Denali Lakeview Inn** (Mile 1.2 Otto Lake Rd., 907/683-4035, denalilakeviewinn.com, from $159 peak season, from $99 winter). It's ridiculously peaceful here, with amazing views across Otto Lake to pretty Mount Healy and Mount Dora, but there are a few quirks. You might never see a staff member while you're here (you get your room number by checking a bulletin board), but they're around—the refrigerator in your room is magically restocked with a modest continental breakfast every day. There's also a communal snack bar and washer/dryer, each operated on the honor system.

Information and Services

You shouldn't have a problem getting cell service in Healy. There is a small **post office** (9998 Coal St., 907/683-2263, Mon.-Fri. 8:30am-12:30pm and 1:30pm-5pm, Sat. 8:30am-noon).

Gas stations are your best bet for public bathrooms; the owners will appreciate it if you make a small purchase in exchange for the use of their facilities. There's a **Tesoro** (Mile 249.5 Parks Hwy., 907/683-5500) with public restrooms and a deli, and a **Fisher's Fuel** (Mile 249 Parks Hwy., 907/683-2408).

You can also get gas, diesel, and propane at **Miner's Market and Deli** (Mile 248.5 Parks Hwy., 907/683-2379, daily 24 hours); just be warned that the RV park and campground next door, **McKinley RV Park and Campground,** has a poor reputation. Laundry, showers, and restrooms are available but historically aren't all that clean.

Transportation

Healy is just a 15-minute drive from the entrance to Denali National Park; if you're coming by train, many of the lodgings will send a shuttle to collect you. Another option for carless travel is **Alaska/Yukon Trails** (907/479-2277 or 907/888-5659, alaskashuttle.com), a series of passenger vans with very reasonable prices for travel up and down the Parks or Richardson Highway. Rates start at just $99 to go all the way from Anchorage to Fairbanks, and for a $10 reboarding fee you can hop off the van, overnight in a community like Healy, then hop back on another day.

If you want to rent a vehicle while in the area, you have two options: **Alaska Auto Rental** (Mile 248.6 Parks Hwy., Healy, 907/457-7368, alaskaautorental.com) has an office right in town and is great about renting to drivers under 25 and letting you take vehicles on gravel highways. That's a must if you're lucky enough to win the Denali Park Road Lottery.

Keys to Denali Car Rentals (137 Healy Rd., 800/683-1239 or 907/683-1239, denalidomehome, May-Sept.) also operates out of Healy, in the Denali Dome Home B&B. They offer free pickup/delivery service if you take the train into Denali, and they loan basic equipment like binoculars, walking sticks, and coolers.

CARLO CREEK

About 13 miles from the park entrance in the opposite direction (south), Carlo Creek offers an even smaller, quieter getaway from the hustle and bustle of "Glitter Gulch." Some consider this little hole-in-the-wall community to be an extension of Cantwell, which is another 15 miles to the south.

Food

STEAKHOUSE AND SEAFOOD

The **229 Parks Restaurant and Tavern** (Mile 229.7 Parks Hwy., 229parks.com, summer dinner hours Tues.-Sun. starting at 5pm, reservations recommended, Sun. brunch 9am-noon, box lunches available) is enormously popular, with American food in a lofty, wood-timbered building. The menu changes frequently to take advantage of the freshest and sustainable local offerings in creative selections like reindeer sausage flatbread. This is one of the few places in Alaska—much less the Denali area—where you can get grass-fed steaks to go with your wild-caught seafood.

Also good is **The Perch Restaurant and Bar** (Mile 224 Parks Hwy., 888/322-2523 or 907/683-2523, denaliperchresort.com), which offers excellent mountain views and prices that lean more toward what you'd find at Denali National Park. Everything on the menu—which includes steaks, burgers, lots of seafood options, and a few pasta selections—is excellent.

PIZZA

Many people list the **Panorama Pizza Pub** (Mile 224 Parks Hwy., 888/322-2523 or 907/683-2623, panoramapizzapub.com, summer daily 5pm-2am) as being in Cantwell, but it's actually in Carlo Creek. Heads up: The food is great but the service is often slow—but that leaves you time for a game of cornhole, horseshoes, or foosball in the cozy, pub-like atmosphere while you wait. (This is not a family-style pizza joint.)

CAFÉS

The **McKinley Creekside Cafe** (Mile 224 Parks Hwy., 888/533-6254 or 907/683-2277, summer daily 6am-10pm) really is right beside the creek. It's a cozy little place with a short but excellent menu of homemade food, heavy on the sandwiches, soup, and seafood, and baked goods including cinnamon rolls as big as your head. They even smoke the meat themselves. Hearty box lunches are available to take with you on your park excursions.

Accommodations

There are a couple of noteworthy lodgings. The first is **Denali Mountain Morning Hostel & Cabins** (Mile 224.1 Parks Hwy., 907/683-7503, denalihostel.com), which rents bunk beds (from $34 in three- to six-person dorms, some double beds available) and private cabins (from $99). Twice-daily shuttles to/from the park entrances also pick up train arrivals at the Wilderness Access Center (Mile 1 Park Rd., daily 5am-7pm).

The other is **McKinley Creekside Cabins** (Mile 224 Parks Hwy., 888/533-6254 or 907/683-2277, mckinleycabins.com, $149-179), a series of woodsy private cabins on the banks of the creek, with a hearty café that serves breakfast, lunch, and dinner and offers lunches to go. The cabins have almost everything you'd expect from a hotel, including private bathrooms, comfortable beds, small in-room refrigerators and microwaves, and free Wi-Fi. Most also have small, private decks.

Deneki Lakes BnB (Mile 227.1 Parks Hwy., 907/683-4188, denekilakesbedandbreakfast.com, from $230 one person, $285 two people) offers two spotless, quiet upstairs guest rooms with private baths. The beds are comfortable and the homemade breakfast, which goes far beyond the usual eggs and pancakes, is spectacular. You can look forward to things like homemade muffins or bread, homemade yogurt, freshly picked berries in season, plus of course eggs and potato hash as options. The owner will also, for a small fee, pack an excellent sandwich lunch to sustain you on day tours.

CANTWELL

This tiny community of approximately 200 people enjoys a central location: It's about a 30-minute drive south of Denali and sits near the western terminus of the rough but scenic Denali Highway, which joins the Parks Highway to the west and the Richardson Highway to the east. It makes a welcome refuge from the hustle and bustle near the park entrance, and is a great place to overnight before tackling the Denali Highway (or after finishing it).

Food

Cantwell is notorious for restaurants that open then quickly close again, but a couple of decent diners have withstood the test of time. **The Broad Pass Cafe** (Mile 209 Parks Hwy.) is attached to the Tesoro gas station. It offers a limited but reasonably eclectic selection of diner food at fair prices; you can pay much more for the same food 30 miles to the north, in the park.

A mile down the road, the **Denali Parks Cafe** (Mile 210 Parks Hwy., 907/768-2311) is open daily, usually at least 9am-9pm in the summer, with limited winter hours. Despite the name this is actually more of a steakhouse, with steak for dinner and burgers and sandwiches for lunch.

The **Cantwell Foodmart** (Mile 210.4 Parks Hwy.) inside the Chevron gas station offers a very limited selection of snacks and groceries.

Accommodations

RV parks in Alaska can be hit or miss, but **Cantwell RV Park & Cabins** (Mile 209.9 Parks Hwy., 907/888-6850, cantwellrvpark.wordpress.com, mid-May-mid-Sept.) is very well run, with cordial staff and a quiet, calm environment. Tent sites start at $18; RV sites are $28.50 for electrical or $31.50 for electrical and water hookups. You can also rent one of their (stationary) RVs or their "camper cabin" (from $75), which has electricity, two single beds, and a small refrigerator—no kitchen or running water. Amenities include a minimart, ice, free Wi-Fi, laundry facilities, and accessible restrooms and showers.

Backwoods Lodge (Mile 133.7 Denali Hwy., 907/987-0960, backwoodslodge.net, from $160 summer, $100 winter) offers very affordable rates for motel-style rooms in a beautiful log building and a few private cabins. Don't let the address on the Denali Highway throw you off; it's within two miles of the Parks Highway, which means you get all the beauty and almost none of the traffic. The clean, well-kept rooms come with updated pillowtop mattresses, satellite TV, free Wi-Fi, refrigerator, microwave, and gas barbecue.

Adventure Denali (Mile 214.5 Parks Hwy., 907/768-2620, adventuredenali.com, Beach Cabin $160, Maggie's Cabin $225) is a fishing lodge that also offers a couple of quaint cabin rentals with a two-night minimum stay and good discounts in the shoulder season. They also rent fat bikes and offer guided hiking trips.

Information and Services

Most travelers should have cell service here. There are a couple of gas stations in town; be warned that **Tsesyu Service** (Mile 209 Parks Hwy., 907/768-2302) has a very poor reputation for its aggressively eccentric owner (emphasis on the aggressive). Instead, head for **Cantwell Chevron** (Mile 210 Parks Hwy., 907/768-1168), just another mile up the road, for gas, diesel, an RV dump station, vehicle service, water, restrooms, and an ATM. There's even a pretty decent diner in the same building. (Here's a fun fact: The gas station exploded and burned down in 2011. It was rebuilt and reopened by late 2013.)

Transportation

It's easiest to get to and from Cantwell with your own vehicle. If you need to rent a car you have many options in Fairbanks or Anchorage, or two small operations in this stretch of the Interior.

Alaska Auto Rental (Mile 248.6 Parks Hwy., 907/457-7368, alaskaautorental.com) has an office in Healy and another in Fairbanks. They happily rent to people under 25 years of age and will usually let you take the car on gravel highways, including the unpaved portion of the Denali Park Road.

Keys to Denali Car Rentals (137 Healy Rd., 800/683-1239 or 907/683-1239, denalidomehome) is operated out of Denali Dome Home B&B in Healy, 12 miles north of the park entrance. They offer free pickup/delivery service in Denali and have rentals available from May to mid-September. They will also loan you basic equipment like binoculars, walking sticks, and coolers.

Passenger vans with **Alaska/Yukon Trails** (907/479-2277 or 907/888-5659, alaskashuttle.com, from $99 one-way between Anchorage and Fairbanks), or AYT, stop in Cantwell and many other small communities along the Parks Highway. For a $10 reboarding fee you can hop off the van, spend the night, then hop back on another van the next day. The AYT vans also run all the way to Whitehorse in the Yukon Territory; fares start at $385 per person from Fairbanks.

DENALI STATE PARK AND KESUGI RIDGE

With so many Denalis around, it can get a little confusing. There's the mountain, the national park and preserve, the highway, and then one more: the *state* park, which abuts the southeast corner of Denali National Park. Denali State Park sits about 85 miles down the Parks Highway from the national park entrance, and just 52 miles north from the turnoff to Talkeetna.

Officials have been working for several years to develop more recreational opportunities in this area, in hopes of easing congestion in Denali National Park. The first phase of that project, the **K'esugi Ken Campground** at milepost 135.4 of the Parks Highway, is perched in the perfect place to offer views of Denali (the mountain) on clear days. The campground is slated to open in 2017, with 32 RV sites, 10 walk-in sites, a couple of public-use cabins, and an alpine hiking trail.

Meanwhile, Denali State Park is already home to one of the state's very best hikes, 27.5-mile **Kesugi Ridge,** which most people hike in 3-4 days. This thru-hike offers stunning views of Denali but also leaves you completely exposed to the worst weather Interior Alaska can throw at you, including tent-crushing winds, sideways-blowing rain, and even snow in the middle of summer. Because of that, it's often used as a proving ground for expedition training programs.

That said, a day hike up from **Little Coal Creek trailhead** (Mile 163.9 Parks Hwy.) offers the potential for stunning views across the ridge and a peek at Denali if it's visible. It's a stiff ascent, gaining about 2,000 feet over 3.5 miles of rough terrain, but immensely rewarding.

★ DRIVING THE DENALI HIGHWAY

If you just can't get enough of Alaska's glorious alpine scenery, there is no drive better than the **135-mile Denali Highway,** which runs east-west between the small community of Cantwell, on the Parks Highway, and the minuscule community of Paxson on the Richardson Highway. In fact, *National Geographic Traveler* magazine named this trip the number two drive of a lifetime. They

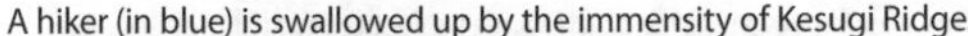
A hiker (in blue) is swallowed up by the immensity of Kesugi Ridge.

don't actually say why they chose it, but I can tell you that if you want the distinction of saying you drove one of Alaska's prettiest and loneliest roads—with nothing but a few roadhouses between you and the sprawling glory of Alaska's wildest, least-traveled mountains, this is it.

Because most of the road is above treeline, you'll be treated to nonstop views of glaciers, lakes, and the skirts of dense green trees that are slowly creeping higher on the peaks as the state warms. This place is a landscape photographer's dream (and of course you might see wildlife too), so don't forget to budget plenty of time to take in the views and take the photo album of a lifetime.

The road is mostly gravel and very rough in places, but tour buses can and do navigate it—so if you're careful, it is almost always drivable in passenger vehicles. There is no cell service, but a CB radio will allow you to communicate with other vehicles on the road. If you'd rather let someone else do the driving, **Denali Jeep Excursions** (907/683-5337, denalijeep.com) offers a wildly popular guided drive.

If you're driving yourself, the key to managing this and any other unpaved, minimally maintained road in Alaska is to take it slow, pay attention, and always have a full-size spare and the tools needed to change a flat—just in case. Depending on road conditions your max speed may be anywhere from 35 to 50 mph, and depending on the day you may see only a dozen or so people on the road.

Accommodations

If you get an early start you can easily do this drive in one day, but it's fun to stay overnight and enjoy being in the middle of such remote beauty, especially if you like landscape photography. There are three lodges along the road. All are very rustic with minimal luxuries, so keeping appropriate expectations is key. In this sort of remote, backcountry location, having a clean, comfortable place to sleep is all that really matters. Starting from Cantwell and going east to Paxson, the Denali Highway lodges are Alpine Creek Lodge, Maclaren River Lodge, and Tangle River Inn.

Alpine Creek Lodge (Mile 68, 907/743-0565, alpinecreeklodge.com) has small, cozy bunk bed rooms and private cabins (shared bathrooms are in the main lodge). There are also a couple of suites on the second floor. All meals are included in your rate, and they offer add-on tours that range from Jeep safaris to gold panning, dog mushing, and (when the skies are dark enough) aurora viewing.

The wild and remote Denali Highway takes you through some of the state's most beautiful landscapes.

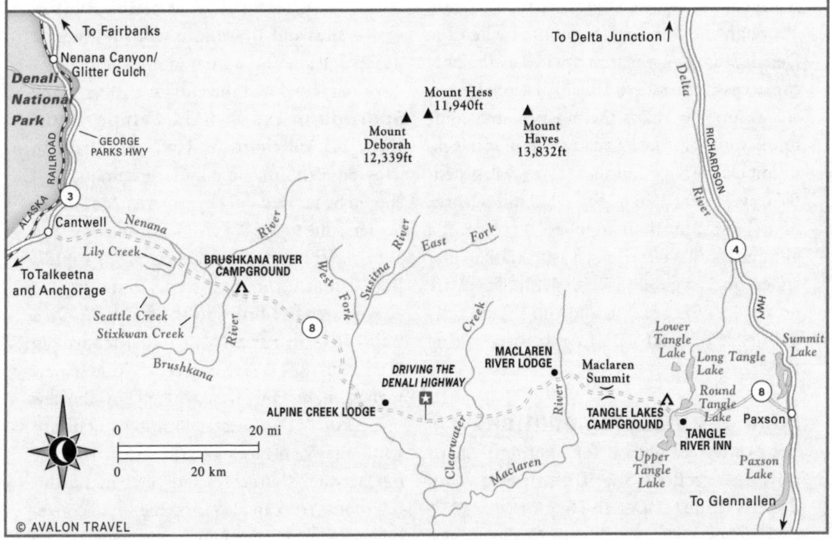

All-inclusive packages, including railroad transport from Anchorage or Fairbanks then ground transport from Cantwell, start at $1,750 for three nights.

Maclaren River Lodge (Mile 42, 907/269-4370, maclarenlodge.com, from $60 private rooms, $25 bunks, $100 private cabins) is the preferred stop of choice for most travelers, including large tour buses. The downside is that it can get very crowded when the buses are in, but the staff is friendly and skilled at handling the crush. The homemade food is simple but excellent, the rooms are clean but basic, and a few of them have private three-quarter baths.

The lodge also offers jet boat transport on the river and will taxi you up the river with a rental canoe, paddles, and life vests so you can float back. If you have a group of at least three, you can really go rustic by staying in their remote camp of wall tents 10 miles upriver. With overnight tent camp prices starting at $85 per person plus transport, it's really a great deal.

Tangle River Inn (Mile 20, 907/822-3970 summer or 907/892-4022 winter, tangleriverinn.com, from $48 bunks, $82.50 rooms, $159.50 cabins) is a true roadhouse; you get a bed and a room, that's about it. The huge bar is deliciously old school. Bunks and less-expensive rooms share a full bath; the more expensive rooms have private half baths and shared shower rooms. The Tangle River Inn also offers space for RVs, gas (sometimes; call to confirm availability), and basic towing/vehicle services. The latter two are a boon because the tiny community of Paxson, the next stop on the highway, offers no services at all.

You can tent camp anywhere along the road as long as you're not in any way obstructing traffic, and there are large, flat, RV-friendly pullouts every few miles. If you're a hiker equipped for backcountry travel, there are many trails to explore, and this is a delightful expedition for self-sufficient bikers. During the winter the road is closed to street vehicles but often used by snowmachiners.

PAXSON

Located where the east end of the Denali Highway meets the Richardson Highway, Paxson gives new meaning to the word "tiny": The latest estimates put Paxson's permanent population at about a dozen people. That's actually not too bad for what first started as a roadhouse along the Valdez-Fairbanks Trail, although the population boomed when the Denali Highway was first opened as the only car-accessible route to Denali National Park.

Paxson is perhaps the most remote community on the Alaska road system: It has no municipal services and no stores. Most people travel to Fairbanks, some 175 miles (three hours) away, for their supplies. If you want a glimpse into a true self-sufficient Alaskan lifestyle, this is a good place to get it. There are no services to speak of, and you should fully provision yourself with food before making the drive.

Food and Accommodations

Your only real option for lodging is, happily, an excellent one: **Denali Highway Cabins** (Mile 0.2 Denali Hwy. or Mile 185.6 Richardson Hwy., 907/987-0977, denalihwy.com, from $250 peak season, $180 for a tent cabin) sits on six acres at the headwaters of the National Wild and Scenic Gulkana River, just across the road from the Paxson Wildlife Reserve. They offer log cabins, tent cabins, and a small cottage for rent by the week.

The log cabins and cottage have electrical outlets and full plumbing—a real rarity in this part of the state—plus blackout curtains and in-room kettles. There's no TV, but you can take their mountain bikes out for a spin for free, rent kayaks, or borrow rain gear to try out the adage that there is no bad weather as long as you're adequately dressed. They also offer a few limited guided tours. The homemade breakfasts consisting of sweet and savory baked goods, egg casserole, steel-cut oatmeal, and house-made granola are excellent, and you can buy some very limited foodstuffs to complement whatever you brought with you from larger communities.

Ten miles to the south, the **Paxson Lake BLM Campground** (Mile 175 Richardson Hwy., $12 drive-in sites, $6 walk-in) offers 40 RV sites and 10 walk-in tent sites, with a dump station and a boat launch. The four-day float trip down the Gulkana River to the **Sourdough Creek BLM Campground** (Mile 147.5 Richardson Hwy., $12 drive-in sites, $6 walk-in) is a popular excursion that should be tackled only by experienced Alaska boaters, due to Alaska's cold, fast-moving, and silty waters and several sections of rapids. Both campsites are first-come, first-served.

Another five miles to the south, **Meiers Lake Roadhouse** (Mile 170 Richardson Hwy., 907/822-3151) is recently under new management. Only time will tell how the new owners do in this isolated location, but meanwhile they're off to a great start with simple but tasty fare (burgers, salads, etc.) in the dining room. You can also shop the small convenience store, do your laundry, and sometimes get gas or diesel; call to confirm availability.

Information and Services

There are no public services in Paxson: no library, no electrical grid, and no fire or police department. Forget about Wi-Fi. There's no guarantee you'll be able to get gas, either. The best places for a guaranteed fill-up are Cantwell if you're coming across the Denali Highway, Glennallen if you're coming from the south, or Delta Junction if you're coming from the north.

You can sometimes get gas at **Tangle River Inn** (Mile 20 Denali Hwy., 907/822-3970 summer or 907/892-4022 winter, tangleriverinn.com), which is 20 miles to the west of Paxson, or **Meiers Lake Roadhouse** (Mile 170 Richardson Hwy., 907/822-3151), some 15 miles to the south, but these sources are not guaranteed, so always call to verify availability.

Fairbanks

If you're driving into Alaska or taking a plane into the Arctic, you'll almost certainly pass through Fairbanks. This is the state's second-largest city, with a population of about 32,000. In the last few years, it's become quite the hip place to live or visit, full of art, music, and creativity.

Fairbanks is located in a relatively broad, flat stretch of the Interior, and its weather is usually calm and dry, which makes it easier to endure the broad temperature extremes; temperatures frequently sink to -40 (the temperature at which both Celsius and Fahrenheit scales are the same) in winter and can rise into the 90s during the summer. Those natural extremes may be part of why Fairbanks is such a warm, friendly city. As one local put it, "We all freeze just as fast."

Fairbanks is both a college town—with the University of Alaska Fairbanks and its various research centers impressively integrated into the community—and a military town, thanks to neighboring Fort Wainwright and Eielson Air Force Base. Mining is still a viable commercial enterprise, and tourism is a huge driver for the economy, so you have many well-honed activities to choose from. Although it's a short drive from Fairbanks, the neighboring community of Fox is so well-integrated (and the road between them so nicely paved) that Fox attractions are mixed in with Fairbanks in this chapter.

SIGHTS

Visitor Center

Your very first stop when you enter Fairbanks should be the **Morris Thompson Cultural and Visitors Center** (101 Dunkel St., 907/459-3700, morristhompsoncenter.org). The beautiful displays on local culture and history make it almost a museum in its own right. You can also watch free films in the theater or shop the Alaska Geographic Store and Public Lands Information Center, which are both in the same building. Together, the two are your best resource for maps and books in the entire city. There is a walking tour brochure, but it isn't always on display—you may have to ask for it.

Also housed in the Morris Thompson Cultural Center, the **Tanana Chiefs Conference** offers an excellent one-hour Cultural Connections show of music, dancing, and storytelling by Gwich'in Athabascan fiddler **Bill Stevens** (afternoon shows Mon.-Fri., donations appreciated; call 907/459-3741 for showtimes and information). You can also meet Alaska Native artisans and make and take your own porcupine quill earrings (Mon.-Fri. 11am-5pm, $10 pp, call to confirm availability).

Creamer's Field

Not far from the visitor center is **Creamer's Field Migratory Waterfowl Refuge** (1300 College Rd., 907/452-5162, creamersfield.org, trails always open, free guided walks year-round, call for times). This repurposed dairy farm has become near-legendary for the sandhill cranes that flock here during the summer; bring binoculars so you can view the birds without disturbing them, and bring bug repellent to help you survive the short nature hikes that showcase the beauty of Interior Alaska's wetlands and boreal forest.

Golden Heart Plaza

Also close by is the **Golden Heart Plaza** (530 1st Ave., between Cushman and Lacey), a charming riverside park built in the mid-1980s that sometimes offers live music, craft booths, and other festivals during the summer. It also has a clock tower, a looming statue titled the *Unknown First Family* that's meant to symbolize Alaska's pride and dignity, and tons of flowers in season; walk to the side and you get views over the placid, narrow Chena River, which is uncharacteristically docile for

Fairbanks

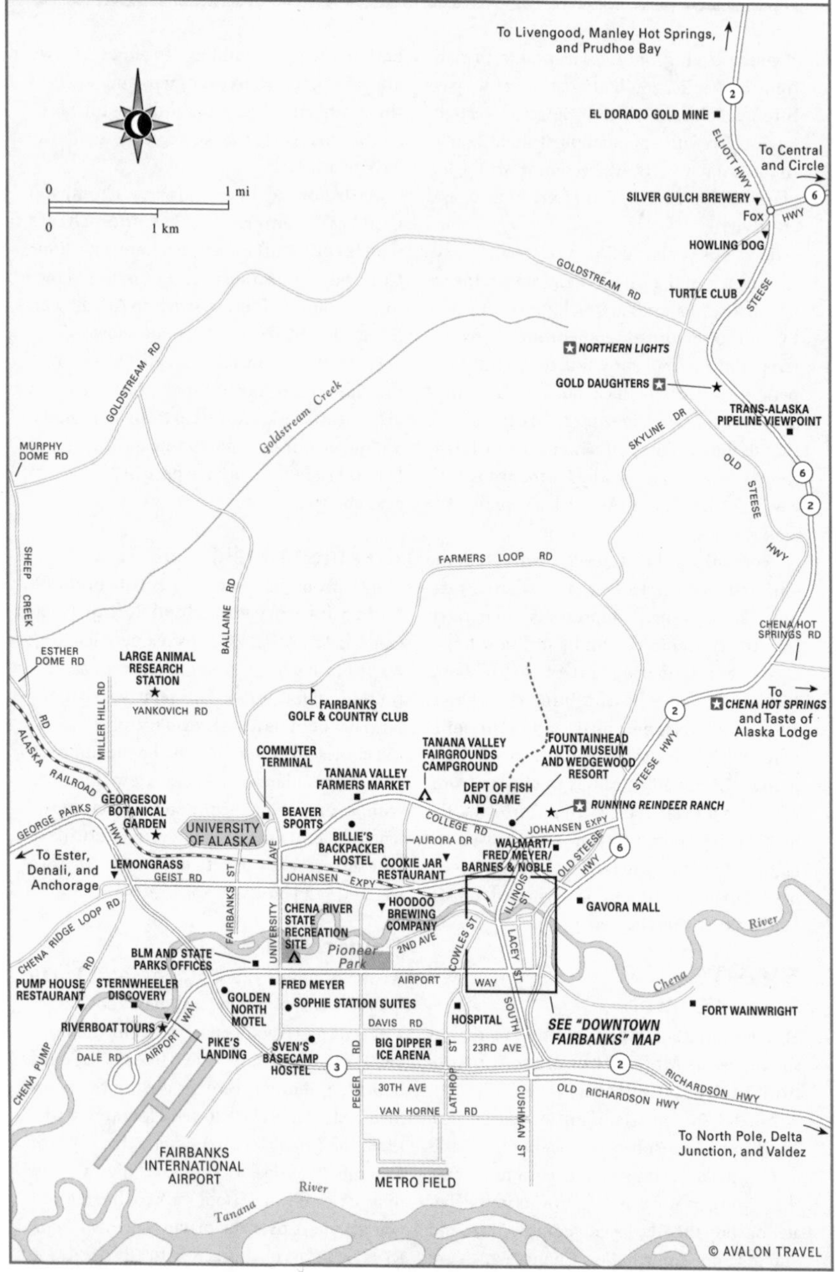

To Livengood, Manley Hot Springs, and Prudhoe Bay
EL DORADO GOLD MINE
ELLIOTT HWY
To Central and Circle
SILVER GULCH BREWERY
Fox
HWY
HOWLING DOG
GOLDSTREAM RD
TURTLE CLUB
STEESE
NORTHERN LIGHTS
GOLD DAUGHTERS
TRANS-ALASKA PIPELINE VIEWPOINT
SKYLINE DR
OLD STEESE HWY
0
1 mi
0
1 km
GOLDSTREAM RD
Goldstream Creek
MURPHY DOME RD
SHEEP CREEK
FARMERS LOOP RD
BALLAINE RD
CHENA HOT SPRINGS RD
ESTHER DOME RD
LARGE ANIMAL RESEARCH STATION
MILLER HILL RD
YANKOVICH RD
FAIRBANKS GOLF & COUNTRY CLUB
To
CHENA HOT SPRINGS and Taste of Alaska Lodge
RD
ALASKA RAILROAD
COMMUTER TERMINAL
TANANA VALLEY FAIRGROUNDS CAMPGROUND
FOUNTAINHEAD AUTO MUSEUM AND WEDGEWOOD RESORT
STEESE HWY
TANANA VALLEY FARMERS MARKET
DEPT OF FISH AND GAME
GEORGESON BOTANICAL GARDEN
RUNNING REINDEER RANCH
GEORGE PARKS HWY
UNIVERSITY OF ALASKA
BEAVER SPORTS
BILLIE'S BACKPACKER HOSTEL
COLLEGE RD
JOHANSEN EXPY
AURORA DR
WALMART/ FRED MEYER/ BARNES & NOBLE
OLD STEESE HWY
To Ester, Denali, and Anchorage
LEMONGRASS
COOKIE JAR RESTAURANT
GEIST RD
JOHANSEN EXPY
FAIRBANKS ST
UNIVERSITY AVE
ILLINOIS ST
GAVORA MALL
CHENA RIDGE LOOP RD
CHENA RIVER STATE RECREATION SITE
HOODOO BREWING COMPANY
River
2ND AVE
COWLES ST
LACEY ST
Pioneer Park
BLM AND STATE PARKS OFFICES
Chena
AIRPORT
WAY
PUMP HOUSE RESTAURANT
STERNWHEELER DISCOVERY
FRED MEYER
GOLDEN NORTH MOTEL
SOPHIE STATION SUITES
HOSPITAL
SOUTH
FORT WAINWRIGHT
RIVERBOAT TOURS
AIRPORT WAY
DAVIS RD
SEE "DOWNTOWN FAIRBANKS" MAP
PIKE'S LANDING
BIG DIPPER ICE ARENA
DALE RD
SVEN'S BASECAMP HOSTEL
PEGER RD
23RD AVE
CHENA PUMP RD
AIRPORT WAY
30TH AVE
LATHROP ST
CUSHMAN ST
RICHARDSON HWY
OLD RICHARDSON HWY
VAN HORNE RD
To North Pole, Delta Junction, and Valdez
FAIRBANKS INTERNATIONAL AIRPORT
METRO FIELD
River
Tanana
© AVALON TRAVEL

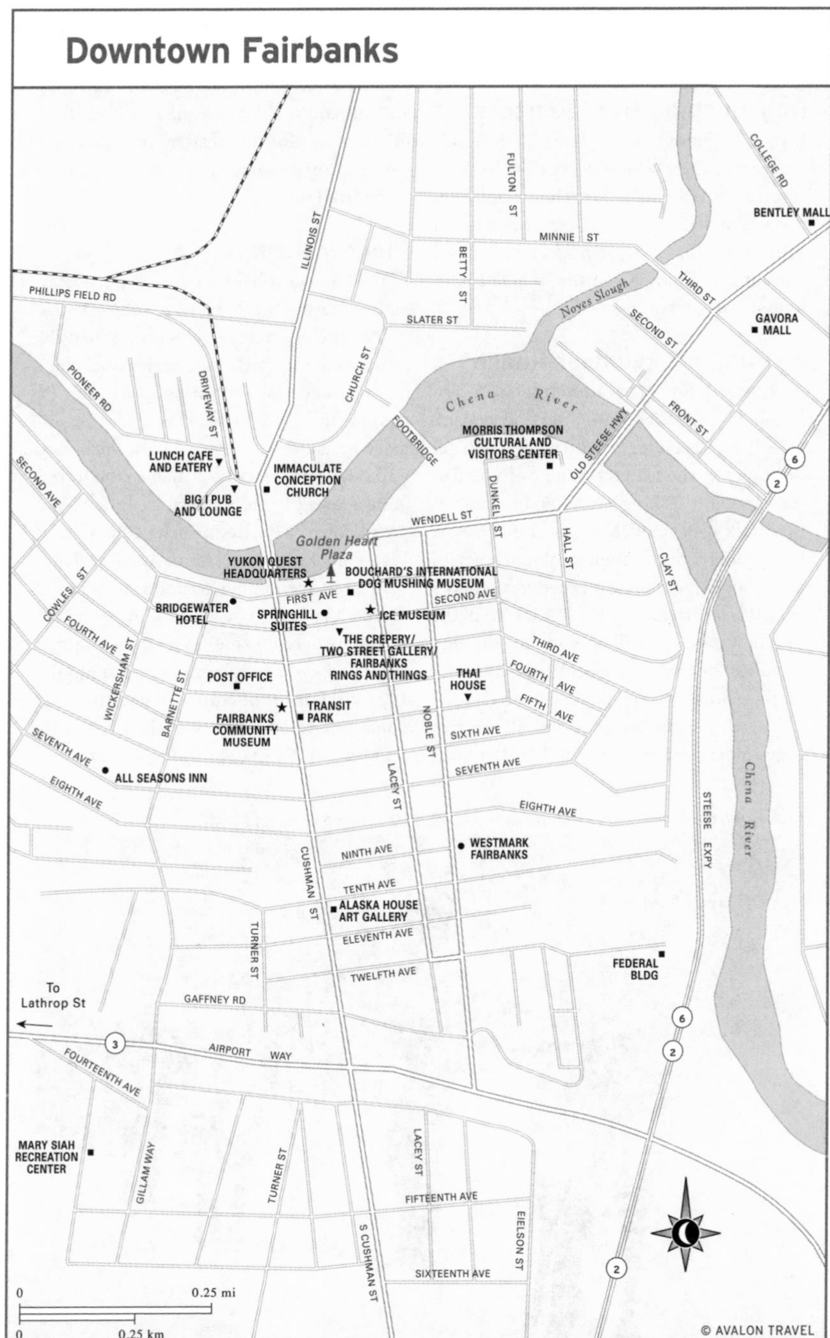
Downtown Fairbanks
FULTON ST
COLLEGE RD
BENTLEY MALL
MINNIE ST
BETTY ST
ILLINOIS ST
THIRD ST
PHILLIPS FIELD RD
Noyes Slough
SECOND ST
GAVORA MALL
SLATER ST
CHURCH ST
PIONEER RD
DRIVEWAY ST
Chena River
FRONT ST
FOOTBRIDGE
MORRIS THOMPSON CULTURAL AND VISITORS CENTER
LUNCH CAFE AND EATERY
OLD STEESE HWY
SECOND AVE
IMMACULATE CONCEPTION CHURCH
BIG I PUB AND LOUNGE
DUNKEL ST
WENDELL ST
HALL ST
Golden Heart Plaza
YUKON QUEST HEADQUARTERS
BOUCHARD'S INTERNATIONAL DOG MUSHING MUSEUM
CLAY ST
COWLES ST
FIRST AVE
SECOND AVE
BRIDGEWATER HOTEL
SPRINGHILL SUITES
ICE MUSEUM
FOURTH AVE
THE CREPERY/ TWO STREET GALLERY/ FAIRBANKS RINGS AND THINGS
THIRD AVE
WICKERSHAM ST
BARNETTE ST
POST OFFICE
THAI HOUSE
FOURTH AVE
FIFTH AVE
TRANSIT PARK
FAIRBANKS COMMUNITY MUSEUM
NOBLE ST
SIXTH AVE
SEVENTH AVE
ALL SEASONS INN
LACEY ST
SEVENTH AVE
EIGHTH AVE
EIGHTH AVE
STEESE EXPY
Chena River
CUSHMAN ST
WESTMARK FAIRBANKS
NINTH AVE
TENTH AVE
ALASKA HOUSE ART GALLERY
TURNER ST
ELEVENTH AVE
FEDERAL BLDG
TWELFTH AVE
To Lathrop St
GAFFNEY RD
AIRPORT WAY
FOURTEENTH AVE
MARY SIAH RECREATION CENTER
GILLAM WAY
TURNER ST
LACEY ST
FIFTEENTH AVE
EIELSON ST
S CUSHMAN ST
SIXTEENTH AVE
0 0.25 mi
0 0.25 km
© AVALON TRAVEL

an Alaska river. See festivalfairbanks.info for an events schedule.

Dog Mushing Headquarters

If you're a fan of mushing, stop by the headquarters of the **Yukon Quest** (550 1st Ave., summer usually Mon.-Sat. 11am-6pm, Sun. noon-4pm, free, daily visits from mushers and dogs), where they'll happily answer any and all questions you have about the "other" 1,000-mile sled dog race.

★ Running Reindeer Ranch

At **Running Reindeer Ranch** (book for location, 907/455-4998, runningreindeer.com, $55 adults, $35 children 4-12) you get to stroll through the woods in the middle of a herd of tame reindeer. Taking what amounts to a nature walk with reindeer might sound a little hokey, but for most people (including me) it's an eye-opening, magical experience; there's something surreal about seeing a herd of the next best thing to caribou go leaping through the forest or browsing placidly within arm's reach, especially when they have calves.

The owner does a great job of explaining reindeer behavior, the mild differences between these animals and their wild cousins the caribou, and many of the plants you'll see on your walk. You will be outdoors for about an hour and you'll climb one short but steep hill, so dress for the weather, but you don't have to worry too much, because you never go far from the house.

Pioneer Park

Alaskans have a habit of both repurposing and relocating their older buildings. Think of it as the ultimate in recycling: When resources are extremely limited, logistics challenging, and transportation costs high (if possible at all), practicality demands that you make use of whichever resources—including buildings—are already available. You'll find quite a few of them in the rustic little theme park known as **Pioneer Park** (2300 Airport Way, daily noon-8pm), formerly Alaskaland. It's fun to spend an afternoon reading the plaques that identify each building's original use and where it came from. Some of them are still open for exploration, including the 1904 **Wickersham House Museum** (free, donations accepted), one of the first frame buildings in Fairbanks. Judge and explorer

Explore the forest with a herd of domesticated caribou at Running Reindeer Ranch.

James Wickersham played an enormous role in Alaska history, so you'll see buildings and land features with his name on them all the way from Fairbanks to Juneau.

University of Alaska Fairbanks

The **University of Alaska Fairbanks** is beautifully integrated into this community and easily reached on the bus system. Its campus contains quite a few pleasant walking paths, several interesting research facilities, including a geophysical institute, and the International Arctic Research Center, where scientists from around the world collaborate to monitor and predict how the Arctic is changing in response to climate change.

The biggest attraction is the stellar **Museum of the North** (907 Yukon Dr., 907/474-7505, museum.uaf.edu, June-Aug. daily 9am-7pm, winter Mon.-Sat. 9am-5pm, $12 adults, discounts for youth and Alaska residents). This is a must-visit while you're in town for its beautiful displays on all five of Alaska's major geographic regions; look for traveling visits and Blue Babe, the only mummified steppe bison on exhibit anywhere in the world. Make sure you leave some time to visit *The Place Where You Go to Listen,* a plain-walled room where you have the unearthly experience of hearing our planet's natural processes turned into sound, or to view one of the movies typically shown on the hour. A movie ticket costs $5.

Fountainhead Auto Museum

Auto enthusiasts will love the **Fountainhead Auto Museum** (212 Wedgewood Dr., 907/450-2100, fountainheadmuseum, summer Sun.-Thurs. 10am-8pm, Fri.-Sat. 11am-6pm; $10, $5 ages 6-12). Of particular note, every single car in their fleet of 80-plus can be (and is!) driven around town with some frequency. Accompanying displays of ladies' formal wear from the same eras as the autos help bring home the reality that people really once used these vehicles as part of their everyday life. Even if you're not a car lover, this place is enthralling; it's easy to spend a couple of hours reading all the information provided, and there's a big picture window into the shop, where you can watch cars being actively restored.

the University of Alaska Fairbanks' Museum of the North

Fairbanks Community Museum

Perhaps the smallest museum in town, the **Fairbanks Community Museum** (535 2nd Ave. Ste. 215, 907/457-3669, fairbankshistorymuseum.com, donations accepted) has a tiny art gallery and a much larger room dedicated to the early history of Fairbanks, including incredibly detailed packing lists, ledgers, and the like, showing what each adventurer had to pack, carry, or buy on their way here in hopes of surviving the gold rush.

Pipeline Viewing Station

Many tours out of Fairbanks give you some sort of glimpse of the **Trans-Alaska Pipeline System,** or just "the pipeline" to locals, but you can get your own up-close glimpse at the **Pipeline Viewing Station** (Mile 8 Steese Hwy.) 10 miles north of Fairbanks.

The sight is impressive for two reasons: One, it's a feat of engineering that stretches 789 miles from Prudhoe Bay to Valdez, where the oil is then barged to the Lower 48 states for refining; it's cleverly engineered to withstand everything from the seasonal freeze/thaw cycle to melting permafrost and the nation's largest earthquakes, and is maintained in large part by "pigs," or automated/semi-automated cleaning machines, that are sent through the pipes at intervals. Two, the construction of this pipeline fueled some of the wildest days in Alaska history, from the 1970s, when workers came to the state—especially Fairbanks—to reap amazing wages in even the most menial jobs. Alaska has always had a certain frontier spirit, but those who lived through "the pipeline days" remember it as one of the wildest, most uncontrolled periods in the state—and in all truth, the effects of the relationships made during that period, both business and personal, continue to shape our state's path in modern days—sometimes for better, sometimes for worse.

There's no charge, no staff, and no entrance gate; you can walk right up to the pipeline and its H-shaped support/cooling stanchions, which help keep the permafrost underneath frozen and create a safe surface the pipeline can slide around on in case of an earthquake. You'll also see examples of the pigs used to clean the pipeline.

Visit Rural Communities

Fairbanks is the air travel gateway to many rural Alaska communities. **Warbelow's Air** (888/280-0582 or 907/474-3520, warbelows.com) offers guided tours, or for a truly

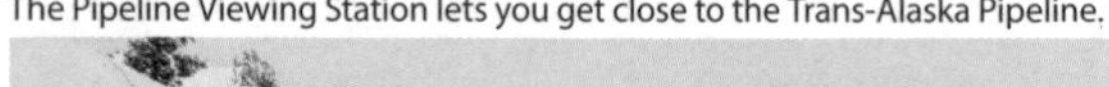
The Pipeline Viewing Station lets you get close to the Trans-Alaska Pipeline.

unusual experience, ride along on one of their scheduled mail flights to any of 12 rural communities, some of which are above the Arctic Circle (from $309).

Both Warbelow's and **Northern Alaska Tour Company** (800/474-1986 or 907/474-8600, northernalaska.com) offer guided day tours to the traditional community of **Anaktuvuk Pass** (from $769 pp); Warbelow's also offers a visit to **Fort Yukon.** For most visitors (and quite a few longtime Alaskans), a trip to one of these rural communities—whether you're taking a formal tour or visiting with the mail plane—is unlike anything you can experience anywhere else in the state. The trappings of everyday life in these communities might look fairly familiar: Most people wear Western clothes, live in houses that resemble yours or mine, and drive familiar-looking vehicles. But once you look past the surface, the way of life here is very different.

During a quick visit, you'll see those differences most in two aspects: One is the simple logistical burden of living in a place where a half gallon of orange juice or a gallon of gas can cost $10 (if either is available at all) and any fresh produce has to be flown in. The other is in the strong foundation in Alaska Native culture and mannerisms that often underlies these communities. The differences aren't always immediately obvious, but you can look for clues in the way people speak or, more to the point, the way they listen, and the way they conduct the delicate balancing act of interpersonal relations that it takes to survive in near-Arctic villages where your survival may depend on being able to work with a neighbor that you either love or hate.

Polar Bears

Warbelow's Air (888/280-0582 or 907/474-3520, warbelows.com) and **Northern Alaska Tour Company** (800/474-1986 or 907/474-8600, northernalaska.com) offer air/ground expeditions to tiny **Kaktovik** (population 250), the only community in the Arctic National Wildlife Refuge, for polar bear viewing (from $1,599 pp, 4-person minimum, all day). The trip reads like a "lifetime adventure" checklist for any Alaska traveler: You get to fly across the Arctic Circle in a small plane, see the wild, untracked Brooks Range and Gates of the Arctic National Park from the air, land in a remote Iñupiat Eskimo village, and then take either a boat or land-based trip to see the bears. A boat trip is best, because you're able to both see the bears at the whale boneyard near town and get close to a nearby island where they spend much of their time. There's just one catch: There need to be at least four people for the tour to go. If that minimum number isn't met, you'll be notified about two weeks out.

The Dalton Highway

Fairbanks is also the launching-off point for a fly-in adventure that takes you halfway up the rugged Dalton Highway, past the Arctic Circle to the tiny work camp of **Coldfoot** or **Wiseman**. You then either fly or drive back down to your starting point. Like many experiences in Alaska, the tour sounds very simple on the surface—it's the scale and the place that really make it special.

You'll get to cross the Arctic Circle twice, at least once from the air, with only the single road below you and the occasional zigzag piping of the Trans-Alaska Pipeline to show that humans are nearby; meet the handful of people who live and work in camps so remote, a shared bathroom is considered a luxury; and sample wild vistas that few people in the world will ever see. Driving back is an adventure, too, as your competent, personable van driver dodges big trucks hauling equipment north. Just remember to pack a lunch (or order from the tour company in advance), and when your driver offers mosquito repellent, say yes—those things can bite through Gore-Tex boots!

Northern Alaska Tour Company (800/474-1986 or 907/474-8600, northernalaska.com) does an excellent job with this trip; see page 381 for more information on the Dalton Highway, a.k.a. the Haul Road.

★ Northern Lights

Fairbanks is one of the very best places for viewing the northern lights, or the aurora borealis (but we just call it "the aurora"). The lights, which are caused by electrically charged particles from the sun colliding with Earth's atmosphere, can be seen directly overhead in Fairbanks, as opposed to down low on the horizon as you'd see them from the southern part of Alaska. One study showed that if you spend three nights actively looking for the northern lights in Fairbanks from September to April, when it's dark enough to actually see them, you have an 80 percent chance of success.

The lights are at their brightest when you're away from the pollution of the city lights, and almost all hotels offer a call service to wake you up when the aurora is out. Interestingly, winter—not summer—is the busy season for many hotels here, because visitors flock from Asia—especially Japan—to see the northern lights.

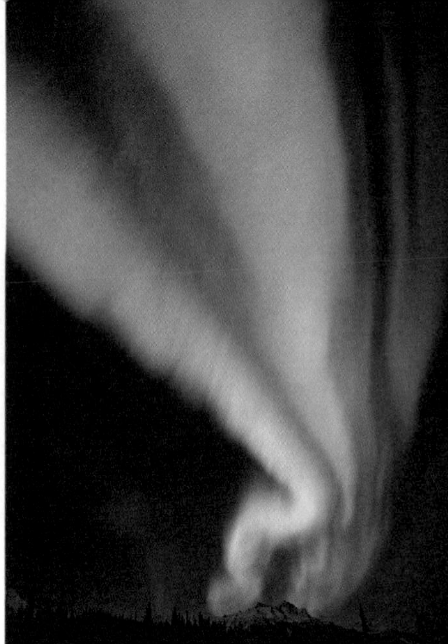

spectacular northern lights

You'll see many stunning photographs of the northern lights for sale when you're in Alaska. You can take your own photographs by getting as far as possible from the light pollution of the city, placing your camera on a tripod, setting it for the longest exposure possible, then using a two- or three-second delay on the trigger button so the motion of your hand doesn't blur the image.

RECREATION

TOP EXPERIENCE

★ Gold Panning

For the most authentic gold-panning experience, visit **Gold Daughters** (1671 Steese Hwy., 907/347-4749, golddaughters.com, $20 for all-day gold panning, hours limited in fall), which is run by the daughters of the family that originally established the attraction at Gold Dredge No. 8; you may have seen them on the National Geographic show *Goldfathers*. Here, you scoop your own panfuls of the real deal: pay dirt that's hauled here by a mining company. When you want a break, you can explore the largest collection of historical mining artifacts in the state, or browse their rustic gift shop. If you're carless, round-trip shuttle service is available for $25 from **Alaska Affordable Taxi** (907/987-5546).

If you're a fan of big machinery, you may also enjoy a trip to historic **Gold Dredge No. 8** (1803 Old Steese Hwy. N, 866/479-6673 or 907/479-6673, golddredge8.com). Dredges are massive machines that carved gold out of the gravel, reshaping the landscape in the act. However, be aware that the entire tour is geared toward a cruise ship audience, so you'll be shuttled from each attraction by train with a long wait in the gift shop, and you'll be panning for gold that's placed in each poke bag by management.

Hiking

Fairbanks has many excellent hiking trails, and the community makes frequent use of many miles of walking trails on the University of Alaska Fairbanks campus, too. There are two clear standout hikes for visitors.

ANGEL ROCKS

The shorter of the two is **Angel Rocks** (trailhead access from Mile 48.9 Chena Hot Springs Rd.), a 3.7-mile loop that poses a short, stiff climb onto a series of granite tors that are slowly emerging from the eroding landscape around them; you gain and lose about 900 feet of elevation, but it's all in a little less than a mile.

GRANITE TORS TRAIL

The longer hike is the 15-mile loop at **Granite Tors,** which is one of the biggest highlights in the area. Granite Tors Trail takes you from boggy black spruce forest to towering chunks of granite plopped improbably on the tundra. These rock formations, which are millions of years old, emerged from the land as the ground around them was slowly weathered away.

On a clear day, this trail also provides stunning views of the Alaska Range and over the Chena River Valley; on days with low visibility you may have trouble finding the trail, even with the help of cairns. Be ready for steep and rocky stretches of trail, especially on the West Trail portion of the loop.

For a more gradual ascent up the roughly 2,900 feet of elevation gain, hike the trail clockwise, starting with the East Loop. Trailhead access is from the Granite Tors Campground (Mile 39.5 Chena Hot Springs Rd.). You can get more information on this hike and other area trails at the Public Lands Information Center inside the **Morris Thompson Cultural and Visitors Center** (101 Dunkel St., 907/459-3700, morristhompsoncenter.org).

Paddling

Locals and visitors alike love taking a leisurely two-hour float down the tranquil **Chena River,** which runs straight through the middle of town, to the Pump House Restaurant. For a full-day adventure, you can ask to be shuttled 12 miles upstream to the Nordale Road Bridge, then float 5-7 hours back downriver to the outfitter.

Float the Chena with **Canoe Alaska** (1101 Peger Rd. behind Pioneer Park, 907/457-2453, canoealaska.com, daily Memorial Day weekend-Labor Day, from $50 for 8 hours), which rents canoes, kayaks, inflatable kayaks, and stand-up paddleboards. They also offer instruction and a fun "bike and boat" combo—float one way, drop off your boat, then cycle back.

If you want a custom shuttle trip for an

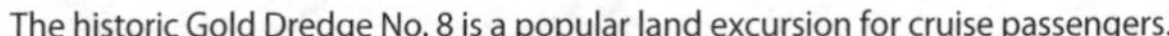

The historic Gold Dredge No. 8 is a popular land excursion for cruise passengers.

Interior Alaska water adventure, this is your outfitter of choice for renting an easy-to-transport inflatable canoe or kayak and booking a shuttle. You may sometimes see the same service advertised as Alaska Outdoors Rentals and Guides, but it's the same company.

For an entirely different type of paddling, consider a tour aboard the **Riverboat *Discovery*** (1975 Discovery Dr., 866/479-6673 or 907/479-6673), a stern-wheel paddleboat that includes a chance to see a floatplane pilot in action, a visit to the kennels of the much-beloved late Iditarod champion Susan Butcher, and a staged recreation of a "Native village." It's interesting, and the young people working the boat do a stellar job, but please remember that the Indian village is a curated, very narrowly focused re-creation—it doesn't actually showcase everyday Native life in Alaska.

Dog Mushing

Believe it or not, dog mushing is a year-round occupation up here. The dogs need to run to stay fit and healthy, but they're too powerful to run without the weight of a sled—so instead the mushers hitch them to wheeled carts and use the brakes to keep the team under control. You can take a kennel tour or ride in a cart/ATV with **Black Spruce Dog Sledding** (book for address, 907/371-3647, blacksprucedogsledding.com), or take a dog cart ride with the kennel of retired and rescued dogs at **Chena Hot Springs Resort** (Mile 56.5 Chena Hot Springs Rd., 907/451-8104, chenahotsprings.com).

For a truly once-in-a-lifetime splurge, **Arctic Dog Sledding Adventures** offers dog sled tours of the Brooks Range out of the remote **Bettles Lodge** (800/770-5111, bettleslodge.com, fly-in access only); the rates are expensive but all-inclusive.

ENTERTAINMENT AND EVENTS

If this is your first time in Fairbanks, run—don't walk—to the ***Golden Heart Revue*** (2300 Airport Way, akvisit.com/the-palace-theatre, mid-May-Sept. nightly at 8:15pm, $22/adult, $11/child) in the Palace Theatre at Pioneer Park Plaza. This musical comedy is a polished, hilarious, locally written send-up of Fairbanks's history and the eternal question: Why would anybody want to live here?

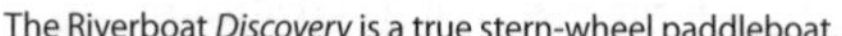
The Riverboat *Discovery* is a true stern-wheel paddleboat.

During the June-September summer season, **Festival Fairbanks** puts on live music acts several times a week in **Golden Heart Plaza** (530 1st Ave., between Cushman and Lacey). Typical showtimes are 12:30pm on Tuesday and Friday, 7pm on Wednesday, but they do vary and there are often extra acts throughout the week—check festivalfairbanks.info for an events schedule and to see which bands will be on. The same organization also offers a selection of local vendors in their **Market Festival** (June-early Sept. Mon. noon-8pm).

Annual Festivals

In mid-November every year, the **Athabascan Fiddle Festival** showcases a surprising facet of Alaska Native culture in this region: The Athabascan people absorbed fiddle music traditions brought by immigrating gold seekers and trappers and made them into a vital part of their own culture, complete with "jigging" and square dancing. The festival has split in two to accommodate the varied sensibilities about this music; the **Fiddle Festival** features the more modern, rock-and-roll side, although there's at least one fiddle in every group. You'll find the more traditional music and dances at the **Gwich'in Old Time Athabascan Fiddle Dance,** which is held at the **Morris Thompson Cultural and Visitors Center** (101 Dunkel St., 907/459-3700, morristhompsoncenter.org).

The **Fairbanks Summer Arts Festival** offers a slew of international music and dance at venues all over town, usually during the last two weeks in July; most of the events are free. See fsaf.org for a full schedule of dates, times, and entertainment types.

Every August, the **Tanana Valley State Fair** (1800 College Rd., 907/452-3750, tananavalleyfair.org) erupts with more than 300 food and craft booths, mind-blowingly huge cabbages, livestock and horse shows, games, a modest amusement park, and live entertainment on two outdoor stages.

Bars and Brews

The **Big I Pub and Lounge** (122 Turner St., 907/456-6437, bigi.alaskansavvy.com), an Irish-style pub with a cozy, dark-wood interior, brings in great bands on weekend evenings in a variety of styles, with a modest cover; find them on Facebook to see who's performing and when. If you're staying at the Bridgewater Hotel just across the water, you'll be able to hear the music clear as a bell for free.

If you want to hang out and lift a pint with the locals, head to the **HooDoo Brewing Company** (1951 Fox Ave., 907/459-2337, hoodoobrew.com, Tues.-Fri. 3pm-8pm, Sat. 11am-8pm), where it's perfectly acceptable to sidle up to a stranger and ask, "So, what's your story?" They don't serve food, but you can bring your own. Note that although it's located on Fox Avenue, HooDoo is not in the community of Fox—it is in Fairbanks.

If you're a real beer aficionado, you should visit both HooDoo and the **Silver Gulch Brewery** (2195 Old Steese Hwy. N, 907/452-2739, silvergulch.com, Mon.-Thurs. 4pm-10pm, Fri. 4pm-11pm, Sat. 11am-11pm, Sun. 11am-10pm). The latter, which *is* in Fox, is the northernmost brewery in the country. It offers good pub food plus fresh seafood and, sometimes, just-harvested oysters from Kachemak Bay (the waters just off Homer, Alaska).

Also enormously popular with both locals and visitors is the **Howling Dog in Fox** (2160 Old Steese Hwy., 907/456-4695, howlingdogsaloonak.com, Sun.-Thurs. 4pm-1am, Fri.-Sat. till 3am). Just 11 miles north of Fairbanks on paved road, the Howling Dog is notorious for its laid-back vibe and sand volleyball court out back; it also has good pub food and great musical acts on weekend evenings.

SHOPPING

Like many of Alaska's other large communities, Fairbanks has a problem with fake or "replica" Alaska Native art that creeps into the gift shops. Shop at trusted shops like the **Alaska House Art Gallery** (1003 Cushman

St., 907/456-6449, thealaskahouse.com, Mon.-Sat. 11am-6pm or by appointment), where you'll find a beautiful selection of fine Alaska Native and contemporary Alaska art in all price ranges, all showcased on equal footing. The owner's mother, Claire Fejes, penned an excellent series of journals on her visits to remote Arctic villages in the mid-1900s. You can buy her books, which are still in print, here at the shop.

Fairbanks also has beautiful contemporary galleries that focus on local art. Two of my favorites are in the same downtown minimall, which also happens to hold **The Crepery** (see *Food*). **Two Street Gallery** (535 2nd Ave. Ste. 102, 907/455-4070, 2streetgallery.com, Mon.-Sat. 10am-6pm, Sun 11am-5pm, reduced winter hours) features a beautiful, eclectic collection of fine art from local artists. **Fairbanks Rings & Things** (535 2nd Ave. Ste. 103, 907/699-7792, Mon.-Sat. 9am-8pm, Sun. noon-8pm) is a small community co-op offering the craftier end of the art spectrum; gifts range from $5 up to several hundred, and the friendly shopkeeper can tell you the story behind every artist and work of art in the shop. This is also the only place in town where you'll find a real penny-candy counter.

Gulliver's Books (3525 College Rd., 907/474-9574, shopgulliversbooks.com, Tues.-Fri. 10am-8pm, Sat. 11am-6pm) is a charming little independent bookstore and community touchstone, with a mix of new and used stock and a great selection of area guidebooks for travelers.

The open-air **Tanana Valley Farmers Market** (2600 College Rd., tvfmarket.com) is open Wednesday, Saturday, and Sunday from early May through mid-September. This is a fun place to shop local art booths, sample local foods, and ogle the giant vegetables that start showing up in late summer.

Because Fairbanks is Alaska's second-largest city, it has several handy big-box stores, including **REI, Fred Meyer,** and **Safeway.** If you want a local gear outfitter, head for **Beaver Sports** (3480 College Rd., 907/479-2494, beaversports.com). They sell gear for everything from camping to paddling and biking and rent camping gear.

FOOD

Thai Food

Thai food is popular all over Alaska, but the folks in Fairbanks have taken it to an extreme with more than 20 restaurants (no exaggeration!) that all seem to be thriving. The three most popular are **Pad Thai** (3400 College Rd., 907/479-1251, Mon.-Sat. 11am-9:30pm, Sun. 11:30am-9pm), which offers large servings at a great price, but extremely limited parking in the back, perhaps because the clientele is often college students; the very traditional **Thai House** (412 5th Ave., 907/452-6123, thaihousefairbanks.com, daily 11am-4pm and 5pm-9:30pm); and **Lemongrass** (388 Old Chena Pump Rd., 907/456-2200, lemongrassalaska.com, Mon.-Sat. 11am-4pm and 5pm-10pm), which incorporates fresh Alaska seafood into cuisine so authentic, they have a branch location in Chiang Mai, Thailand.

Surf and Turf

If you like surf and turf, the **Turtle Club** (Mile 10 Old Steese Hwy., 907/457-3883, alaskanturtle.com, Mon.-Thurs. 5pm-2am, Fri.-Sat. 5pm-3:30am, Sun 4pm-2am) serves great steaks, prime rib, and seafood in a cozy, dim setting. They offer three seatings every evening, seven days a week during the summer. Reservations are highly recommended, and keep your wallet handy—entrées typically run $30-40 and higher.

Visitors love **The Pump House** (Mile 1.3 Chena Pump Rd., 907/479-8452, pumphouse.com, summer Mon.-Sat. 3pm-11pm, Sun. 10am-11pm) for its reconstructed gold rush ambience; it's a featured attraction on the Riverboat *Discovery* cruise (866/479-6673 or 907/479-6673, riverboatdiscovery.com). The food—a combination of steakhouse, seafood, pub grub, and weekend brunch—is good and the servers are friendly.

Vicinity of Fairbanks

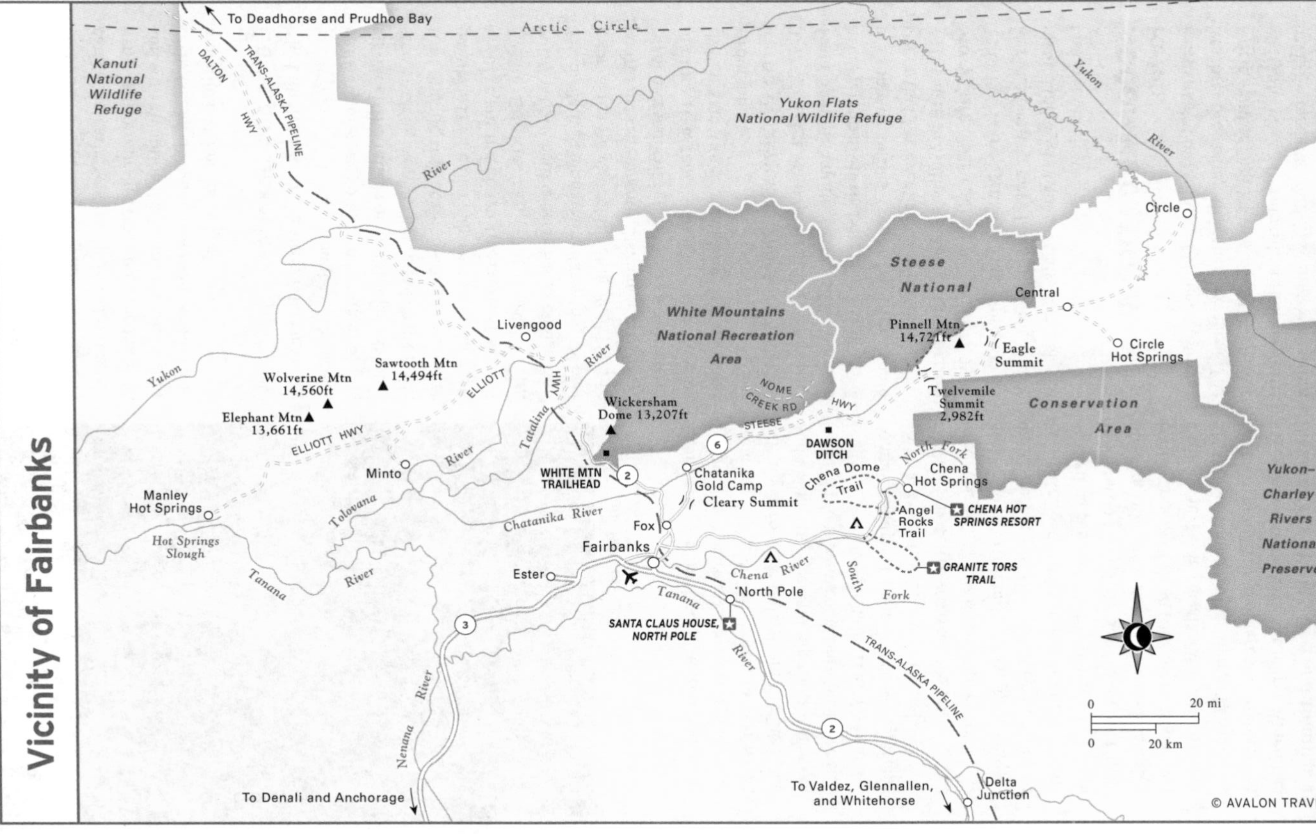

The all-you-can-eat **Alaska Salmon Bake in Pioneer Park** (2300 Airport Way, 800/354-7274 or 907/452-7274, akvisit.com, early May-early Sept. daily 5pm-9pm) offers king salmon, prime rib, and beer-battered cod with an optional add-on of Alaskan snow crab. The food is good, but keep in mind that quantity is the primary goal here.

Alaska Salmon Bake in Pioneer Park

Cafés and Bakeries

The **Lunch Cafe and Eatery** (206 Driveway St., 907/455-8624, timeenoughforlunch.com, daily 10am-4pm, longer in summer, $14) is an under-the-radar community favorite that serves salads, sandwiches, and kebabs made with organic and local ingredients whenever possible. Their bakery also offers a wide variety of vegan and gluten-free creations.

The **Cookie Jar** (1006 Cadillac Ct., 907/479-8319, cookiejarfairbanks.com, Mon.-Sat. 6:30am-8:30pm, Sun. 8am-4pm) is best known for its chocolate chip cookies and enormous cinnamon rolls, but this bakery-turned-restaurant also serves a full menu of diner-style food, plus a few very popular Italian selections, including calzones and stromboli.

The Crepery (535 2nd Ave., 907/450-9192, Mon.-Fri. 7am-7pm, Sat. 9am-6pm, Sun. 11am-5pm) isn't quite a café and isn't quite a bakery, but this little hole in the wall turns out some of the best crepes, both savory and sweet, that I've ever had. Don't miss out.

If you're in Gulliver's Books, the **Second Story Cafe** (3525 College Rd., 907/474-9574, Tues.-Fri. 10am-6pm, Sat. 11am-5pm, $8) offers inexpensive, tasty fare, including wraps, salads, and weekly hot specials, with a side of fast, free Wi-Fi.

ACCOMMODATIONS

Hotels

Fairbanks's Fountainhead Hotels group offers three properties, all of them excellent. The **Bridgewater** (723 1st Ave., 800/528-4916 or 907/456-3642, fountainheadhotels.com/bridgewater-hotel, mid-May-mid-Sept., from $126) offers the best budget accommodations in downtown Fairbanks, just across the street from the Chena River. Expect to hear music drifting across the water from the Big I Pub and Lounge on weekend nights. If you're not a fan, the staff hands out complimentary earplugs. Amenities include free Wi-Fi and a complimentary 24-hour shuttle to the airport and train depot. Staff is very friendly.

The **Wedgewood Resort** (212 Wedgewood Dr., 800/528-4916 or 907/456-3642, fountainheadhotels.com/wedgewood-resort) is the most resort-like of Fountainhead's properties, set on 30 landscaped acres, with the private, 75-acre Wedgewood Wildlife Sanctuary just next door, including wheelchair-accessible lakeside trails. Creamer's Field Migratory Waterfowl Refuge is just a short walk away. Rates start at $154 for enormous suites with fully equipped kitchens, or $143 for a large, comfortable room in the Bear Lodge on the property. Amenities include free Wi-Fi, air conditioning, a workout room, and a complimentary 24-hour courtesy van to the airport and railroad depot.

Finally, **Sophie Station Suites** (1717 University Ave. S, 800/528-4916 or 907/456-3642, fountainheadhotels.com/sophie-station, from $154) offers enormous, comfortable suites situated very close to the airport, complete with full kitchens; this is a great place for families or business travelers to set up shop. It has a restaurant and a lounge with a good selection of Alaska beers and wine. Amenities include free Wi-Fi and a 24-hour complimentary courtesy van.

If you're looking for a hotel with character, visit **Pike's Waterfront Lodge** (1850 Hoselton Rd., 877/774-2400 or 907/456-4500, pikeslodge.com). It has a fun blend of rustic decor and luxury, with spacious, comfortable rooms and several decks overlooking the river. Other amenities include an aromatherapy sauna, fitness center, and free Wi-Fi in the public areas and most rooms. The restaurant, **Pike's Landing** (907/479-6500 for reservations), serves produce grown in a hydroponic greenhouse.

Budget Options

For the hostel crowd, the summers-only **Sven's Basecamp Hostel** (3505 Davis Rd., 907/456-7836, svenshostel.com, $30/bunk in a shared wall tent, private cabins from $70), formerly known as the Base Camp Hostel, offers a European hostel feel with a touch of quirky Alaska. That quirkiness is helped along by the presence of a literal treehouse on the property ($100/night, king bed, accessed by a short suspension bridge) and a giant tipi in the middle of the grounds ($25/bed). You can also pitch your own tent for $14 per person per tent. The hostel is a five-minute taxi ride from the airport, within walking distance of a Fred Meyer supermarket, and there's a bus stop right outside the door. Free Wi-Fi, showers, bike and canoe rentals, a TV room, and volleyball field are included, and there's a bus stop just outside. There's no curfew or lockout, and no chores are required.

Billie's Backpackers Hostel (2895 Mack Blvd., 907/479-2034, alaskahostel.com, $34/dorm bed) is an excellent year-round option, with shared bunks in a repurposed home that has a cozy, community-driven feel. There's also a gazebo ($27/bed), or you can pitch a tent for $20. The hostel is convenient to bus lines, within walking distance of the Museum of the North, and just a short drive from the Alaska

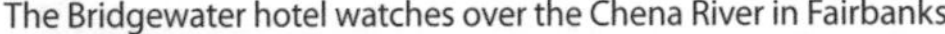

The Bridgewater hotel watches over the Chena River in Fairbanks.

Railroad Depot. Wi-Fi, linens, hot showers, and local phone calls are included; there's no curfew and no chores are required.

If all you want is a place to lay your head that's near to the airport, the **Golden North Motel** (4888 Old Airport Rd., 907/479-6201, goldennorthmotel.com, from $69) offers small, extremely basic but clean rooms with friendly management. It's directly under the flight path from the airport, though, so bring your earplugs.

Bed-and-Breakfasts and Resorts

If you're a fan of us quirky Alaskans, head straight for the **Taste of Alaska Lodge** (551 Eberhardt Rd., 907/488-7855, atasteofalaska.com, from $185). The private rooms and suites are enormous, clean, and comfortable, with beautiful handmade quilts and a hodgepodge of vintage collectibles that give the place great character. The wooded grounds are beautiful, the beds are comfortable and breakfast is simple but delicious; you get the privacy of a hotel but the atmosphere of a B&B. There is free Wi-Fi and a TV in each room, and an enormous common space upstairs.

Some people feel that the accommodations at **Chena Hot Springs Resort** (Mile 56.5 Chena Hot Springs Rd., 907/451-8104, chenahotsprings.com, from $209) to the east of Fairbanks are overpriced, but if you want a single, remote place to unplug—or to take in spectacular views of the starry sky and aurora borealis during fall and winter—this is it. The rooms are spacious and come with a hot springs swim pass. Wi-Fi costs $8 per 24 hours and there is only limited cell service on the ACS Alaska and Verizon networks.

INFORMATION AND SERVICES

You won't have any problem finding gas stations or auto service in Fairbanks, and public bathrooms are available in all big-box stores and at the **Morris Thompson Cultural and Visitors Center** (101 Dunkel St., 907/459-3700, morristhompsoncenter.org, summer daily 8am-9pm, winter daily 8am-5pm, reduced holiday hours). You can also get free Wi-Fi at the visitor center.

The **Fairbanks Memorial Hospital** (1650 Cowles St., 907/452-8181 or 907/458-5000 for the switchboard, fmhdc.com) offers

the Taste of Alaska Lodge in Fairbanks

Scenic Drives: the Steese and Elliott Highways

There's so much going on in Fairbanks that your first priority should be covering your favorite attractions. But if you want a low-key rest day or are in town long enough to take in the scenery, there are three beautiful, scenic—and sometimes challenging—drives.

The **Steese Highway** runs 162 miles northeast to the tiny Yukon River community of Circle, which, despite its name, is still a few dozen miles short of the Arctic Circle. Take binoculars with you for the excellent wildlife viewing, as the highway takes you from heavily wooded river-bottom land to alpine tundra and over two summits: **Twentymile Summit** (2,982 feet, 76 miles from Fairbanks) and **Eagle Summit** (3,685 feet, 107 miles from Fairbanks).

Along the way, there are half a dozen campgrounds, plus basic services, lodging, food, and amenities available at roadhouses and in **Circle,** at the end of the road, and **Central,** which is 128 miles from Fairbanks. A spur road used to lead from Central to the Circle Hot Springs Resort, but that resort is now closed.

The **Elliott Highway** runs 150 miles north then west from Fairbanks, offering beautiful views as it follows the gentle inclines and declines along ridges through the White Mountains. The road ends at the small community of Manley Hot Springs, where geothermal energy makes year-round farming a possibility. The first 75 miles are paved but rough and prone to frost heaves; the rest is gravel and chip seal, which requires slow, careful driving.

The road roughly parallels the Trans-Alaska Pipeline for the first 50 miles, offering periodic views of the four-foot-diameter pipe as it snakes across the terrain on its H-shaped supports. The supports are designed to radiate heat from fins at the top of each pylon, helping cool and stabilize the permafrost beneath. The pipeline's zigzag path gives the pipe room to flex and slide on the supports in response to earthquakes or the natural expansion and contraction due to the area's extreme temperatures.

Make sure you stop at the **Arctic Circle Trading Post/Wildwood General Store** (Mile 49, 907/474-3507, arcticcircletradingpost.com) for coffee, snacks, and Arctic Circle crossing certificates, even though you haven't crossed the Arctic Circle yet; 24 miles farther down the road, you'll have the option of turning north onto the notoriously rough and narrow **Dalton Highway**, which can take you all the way to Deadhorse/Prudhoe Bay on the shores of the Arctic Ocean.

If you make it all the way to the tiny community of **Manley Hot Springs** (population about 100) at the end of the road, you deserve a soak in the natural hot waters—but it's best to call ahead to verify access to the cement bathing tubs (907/672-3231). You can place the call from the **Manley Roadhouse** (100 Front St. in Manley Hot Springs); food and lodging are also available at the roadhouse.

comprehensive, around-the-clock emergency service. There are multiple post offices in town; see usps.com to find the location closest to you.

TRANSPORTATION

Getting There

Fairbanks is about 350 miles from both Anchorage (via the Parks Highway) and Valdez (via the Richardson Highway). Google Maps will tell you that's a six-hour drive, but in real-world terms it usually works out to at least eight hours, once you've factored in rest stops, traffic or construction delays, and a little sightseeing for the dramatic scenery along the way.

If you're in a hurry, **Alaska Airlines** (800/252-7522, alaskaair.com) offers daily jet flights between Anchorage and Fairbanks; you spend just an hour in the air. **Ravn Alaska** (800/866-8394 or 907/266-8394, flyravn.com) also offers daily flights that clock in a little over an hour, but I always try to fly Alaska when I can—they have bigger planes, a better safety record, and are better able to deal with bad weather.

If you don't want to fly or drive yourself, a few bus systems can get you here from other communities on the road system. Most allow one or two checked bags and a carry-on per passenger, but always inquire about luggage limits beforehand.

Alaska/Yukon Trails (907/479-2277 or 907/888-5659, alaskashuttle.com) offers a $99 one-way trip from Anchorage to Fairbanks, with lower fares at pickup points along the way, including Talkeetna, Denali, and many other smaller communities. For an additional fee ranging $5-8, they'll drop you off or pick you up at your hotel, the airport, or the train depot. You can also hop off at almost any Parks Highway community, then hop back on the next day for a $10 reboarding fee, or explore their other route, which runs all the way to Whitehorse in the Yukon Territory (fares run $385 pp from Fairbanks).

Interior Alaska Bus Line (800/770-6652, interioralaskabusline.com) makes year-round runs between Anchorage, Tok, Fairbanks, and the small community of Northway on Monday, Wednesday, and Friday. Rates start at $20 from Anchorage to Palmer and range up to $160 for Anchorage to Fairbanks.

Getting Around

Once you're in Fairbanks, it's best to have a car. If you don't, **MACS Transit** (907/459-1010, fnsb.us/transportation, $1.50 fare or $3 day pass, reduced for youths, seniors, and active military) offers decent bus service by Alaska standards, with 10 lines serving Fairbanks and the nearby communities of North Pole and Fort Wainwright, but they won't be able to get you to all the attractions.

Some of the best taxi services are **King Cab** and **Alaska Cab** (907/452-2222, kingalaskacab.com) and **Arctic Taxi** (907/455-0000, arctictaxi.com, also offers roadside service), both of which offer 24/7 service. Smaller operations include **Greatland Taxi and Tour Service** (907/490-2405, greatlandtaxiandtourservice.com, reservations preferred, also offers roadside assistance) and **Call Roy Taxi** (314/556-0596). The latter is a particular favorite for being honest and easy to work with, and he's open 24 hours a day.

Your rental car options include national chains like **Hertz** (907/452-4444), **Thrifty** (907/451-1048), **Avis** (907/474-0900), **Budget** (907/474-0855), and **Dollar Rent-a-Car** (907/451-4360), all at the airport, plus locally run **Alaska Auto Rental** (2375 University Ave. S, 907/457-7368, alaskaautorental.com), **Arctic Outfitters** (3920 University Ave., 907/474-3530, arctic-outfitters.com), and **GoNorth Car and Camper Rental** (3713 S. Lathrop St., 907/479-7272, gonorth-alaska.com), which also rents RVs.

Arctic Outfitters and GoNorth are the only two companies that don't mind if you drive their vehicles on gravel highways, including the unpaved Dalton Highway, which runs all the way to Prudhoe Bay. GoNorth is of particular note because they also have rental locations in Anchorage; Whitehorse (Yukon Territory); and Seattle, Washington; and allow one-way rentals. Whichever service you use, reserve as early as possible because the cars often sell out, especially from the smaller companies.

Bike rentals are available from **Canoe Alaska** (1101 Peger Rd. behind Pioneer Park, 907/457-2453, canoealaska.com, Memorial Day weekend-Labor Day weekend, 11am-7pm). Prices start at $20 for a half day, and you may sometimes see this company also advertising as Alaska Outdoors Rentals and Guides.

Around Fairbanks

★ CHENA HOT SPRINGS

The "ring of fire"—a ring of volcanoes around the Pacific Ocean—runs right through Alaska, so it's no great surprise that the state is full of geothermal energy. Most hot springs are either off the road system or not developed for tourism, but **Chena Hot Springs Resort** (Mile 56.5 Chena Hot Springs Rd., chenahotsprings.com) is the exception.

If you don't mind the 60-mile drive to get there on paved, permafrost-buckled road, the outdoor, 18-and-over hot springs rock pool ($15 for a daily swim pass) is one of the best things going in the Fairbanks area. There's a mildly heated swimming pool indoors for kids, and add-on tours include ATV rides, horseback rides, hiking tours, and, my favorite, a dog cart ride with their kennel of retired sled dogs and shelter rescues.

There's also a spectacular ice museum—literally, a building carved of ice by the husband-and-wife world champion ice carvers, Steve and Heather Brice. It's well worth the $15 admission fee, and you can also have an appletini served in a glass made of ice.

Heads up: Cell service is extremely limited (currently only ACS Alaska and Verizon phones get reception), and if you want Wi-Fi, you're going to have to pay $8 per day; treat it as a chance to unplug and unwind. Winter is actually the busy season here, driven largely by Japanese tourism to watch the northern lights. Although the hot springs are exceptional and many of the resort tours are great fun, some locals feel the accommodations are overpriced, so if you have your own transportation, consider stopping in for a day pass at the hot springs and checking out the popular three-mile **Angel Rocks Trail,** starting from **Chena River State Recreation Area** (Mile 48.9 Chena Hot Springs Rd.). If you're willing to make an 8.3-mile round-trip, you can use a connecting trail to hike all the way to Chena

The outdoor rock lake at Chena Hot Springs is open year-round.

Hot Springs and back again; make sure you leave yourself time to soak in the hot springs before you head back.

★ SANTA CLAUS HOUSE, NORTH POLE

Are you on Santa's good list? Find out with a visit to North Pole, a small Alaska community about 20 minutes (14 miles) southeast of Fairbanks, where it's all Christmas all the time. **Santa Claus House** (101 St. Nicholas Dr., 800/588-4078 or 907/488-2200, santaclaushouse.com) is a giant, lovable, and gleefully kitschy year-round gift shop.

You can get your picture taken in the giant sleigh, pose in front of a 40-foot Santa sign or with a nearly 50-foot Santa statue, or insert yourself into a life-size nativity scene—or make your child's day with a personalized letter from Santa, bearing a real "North Pole, Alaska" postmark and the customized text you provide, along with a real physical address they can write back to (although not every letter is answered).

Play it cool like a local by getting this community's name right: It's "North Pole." If you say "*the* North Pole," you're talking about the northern axis of the Earth's rotation.

NENANA

This old railroad town, just 55 miles south of Fairbanks on the Parks Highway, is home to only a couple hundred people. But it has a big name, thanks to the **Nenana Ice Classic** (907/832-5446, nenanaakiceclassic.com), the closest thing Alaska has to a lottery.

Every year the Tanana River, which runs right past town, freezes over. During a three-day festival in March the locals place a wooden tripod out on the ice, then charge $2.50 for each guess at the date and time the ice will break up, causing the tripod to fall over. The closest guess to the minute wins, and the pot often exceeds $300,000 and is shared among however many participants made the winning guess. Anybody can participate, as long as you buy your tickets in Alaska.

When the river thaws it becomes a workhorse, with shallow-draft barges transporting goods to remote villages. If you're lucky, you might get to see a fish wheel—a traditional means of subsistence fishing—in action on the water.

Sights

Stop in to the **Nenana Visitor Center** (907/832-5435, daily Memorial Day-Labor

the Santa Claus House in North Pole

Yukon Quest

The Iditarod sled dog race gets lots of worldwide press. But Alaska is home to another yearly 1,000-mile test of sled dog and musher endurance: the **Yukon Quest,** which follows historical gold rush and mail delivery dog sled routes between Fairbanks and Whitehorse in Canada's Yukon Territory. Mushers cross four mountain summits along the way and are required to take a 36-hour layover in Dawson City.

There's also a 300-mile version of the quest for mushers who want to experience a milder taste of the trail and a junior race for mushers 14-17 years old; the former is recognized as a qualifying race for both the full-fledged Yukon Quest and the Iditarod. The Yukon Quest starts the first full weekend of February, a month before the Iditarod starts. In odd years it starts in the Yukon, and in even years it starts in Fairbanks.

Many of the same big mushing names run in both races, although the rules are slightly different. Only twice has someone won both races in the same year: Lance Mackey in 2007, then again in 2008. In fact, he won the Yukon Quest four years in a row (2005-2008) and the Iditarod four years in a row (2007-2010). The current record-winning time is 8 days, 14 hours, and 21 minutes, held by Allen Moore in 2014 on the Fairbanks to Whitehorse route.

Day) for a quick orientation to the area. It's near where the Parks Highway meets 6th Street and is a sight in and of itself; during the summer, the log cabin's sod roof is planted with flowers.

Best for railroad buffs, the **Alaska State Railroad Museum** (900 A St., at the end of the road when you drive into town) is a quick exhibit on the ground floor of the Nenana train depot. This building is listed in the National Register of Historic Places, and interested visitors may enjoy the historical feel of sleeping in one of the four upstairs rooms with a shared bathroom (from $99; call 907/832-5500 9:30am-5pm, or visit tripodgs.com). Nearby, you'll find a monument marking the spot where President Warren G. Harding drove the golden spike that commemorated the completion of the Alaska Railroad.

Just down Front Street from the depot, on the water side of the railroad tracks, you'll find the **Alfred Starr Nenana Cultural Center** (415 Riverfront, 907/832-5520, summer daily 10am-6pm, donation requested). This small museum showcases local culture, including traditional Athabascan life, riverboat racing, and dog mushing; it also has an excellent gift shop with locally made Native art. Your other gift shop option is **Palmer's Cabin Fever Gifts** (105 8th St., corner of Parks Hwy. and 8th, 907/982-7715, winter hours Fri. and Sat. or other days by appointment, expanded summer hours). They specialize in antler, horn, and bone carvings, with a smattering of jewelry, ulus, and other gifts.

Food and Accommodations

You can get basic groceries, including dairy and frozen meat, at **Coghill's General Store** (907/832-5422, Mon.-Sat. 9am-6pm). The **Chevron** gas station (Mile 304.5 Parks Hwy. 907/832-5823) offers a deli, restrooms, essential groceries, and an ATM.

If you end up overnighting here, the charming, bright red **Fireweed Roadhouse** (Mile 288.5 Parks Hwy., 907/582-2224, fireweedroadhousedenali.com) serves as both inn and restaurant. The owners are famous for their friendly, laid-back attitude, and their generous portions of home-cooked food are excellent.

Transportation

Because this town is so small, most people only stop over during their drive between Anchorage and Fairbanks. If you're carless, there are two easy ways to get here: Either take **Alaska/Yukon Trails** passenger vans (907/479-2277 or 907/888-5659, alaskashuttle.com, reservations required), which stop in small communities between Anchorage and Fairbanks, or ride the **Alaska Railroad** passenger trains (800/544-0552, alaskarailroad.com) from Anchorage or Fairbanks.

Along the Richardson Highway

The paved **Richardson Highway** stretches all the way from Fairbanks southeast to Valdez, the northernmost ice-free port in the United States. It's an easy, mostly smooth and mostly two-lane drive, as long as you don't mind the roller-coaster-like frost heaves that crop up every year around Fairbanks. They're great fun to zoom over, until you bottom out your car's suspension and scrape off the oil pan or transmission—so take your time.

Starting from Fairbanks and working southeast, the Richardson Highway passes through several communities of note: **Delta Junction; Paxson,** which is also the junction with the **Denali Highway; Glennallen;** and then **Valdez.** If you were to turn east from Delta Junction or Glennallen you'd reach **Tok,** which in turn leads southeast to the Canadian border.

Also of particular note is a pipeline viewing area at mile marker 216, 146 miles southeast of Fairbanks, where you can get an up-close look at the deceptively simple-looking **Trans-Alaska Pipeline System,** which carries crude from the Prudhoe Bay oil fields to Valdez, where it's barged to out-of-state refineries. If you've already seen the Pipeline Viewing Station north of Fairbanks, it's basically the same.

During the gold rush days, the Richardson Highway was the primary route into the Interior—so when you drive it, you're retracing the steps of thousands of hopeful gold miners, only a few of whom actually struck it rich. If Valdez had achieved its bid to be the state's primary port, this conduit would no doubt be one of the most heavily traveled in the state. As it is, it's a tranquil, beautifully scenic drive with only a fraction of the traffic you'll find on the Parks Highway, which connected the Glenn Highway out of Anchorage with Fairbanks.

You'll find small rest stops and public restrooms (pit toilets—basically, permanent outhouses) dotted sporadically along the highway; it's best to have your own hand sanitizer and toilet paper with you, just in case. Most roadhouses and gas stations will have bathrooms also, but usually only for paying customers.

DELTA JUNCTION

Initially founded as a telegraph station in 1904, Delta Junction was kick-started as a farming community when the government chose it as the base for a buffalo importation program in the 1920s, using stock imported from Montana. By 1947, the herd had grown to some 400 animals. At the same time, Delta served—and continues to serve—as an important crossroads for farmers, gold miners, the military, and, nowadays, travelers like you.

This sleepy agricultural community of about 1,000 people sits roughly two hours south of Fairbanks, right at the junction of the Richardson Highway and the Alaska Highway, the only road that connects the state to Canada and the Lower 48.

If you've driven up from the Lower 48, make sure to take your picture in front of the 1,422-mile marker, where the Alaska Highway and the Richardson Highway meet. This area is known as "The Triangle," and it's also where you'll find the **Delta Junction Visitor Center** (junction of Alaska Hwy. and Richardson Hwy., 907/895-5063, open year-round), where you can get a certificate for completing the nation's most epic road trip.

Sights and Recreation

HISTORIC BUILDINGS

Across from the visitor center is the **Sullivan Roadhouse Historical Museum** (Memorial Day-mid-Sept. Mon.-Sat. 9am-5:30pm, free), circa 1905, one of the last remaining roadhouses from the original Valdez-to-Fairbanks trail. The museum showcases the history of this early mining and military trail that eventually became the Richardson Highway, with beautifully re-created rooms to give you a feel for life in Alaska during the early 1900s.

You'll see many other old roadhouses eight miles north of Delta Junction in **Big Delta State Historical Park** (Mile 274.5 Richardson Hwy.). The park centers around the 1913 **Rika's Roadhouse.** Once a center of activity for gold stampeders and freighters, the roadhouse is now a reconstructed museum of area life during the 1920s and 1930s.

The park also contains a military **cable and telegraph station that you can explore**—until its construction, it took a year to send a message from Interior Alaska to Washington DC, and then get an answer back! By the mid-1920s, the telegraph had been replaced with a 50-watt radio; during World War II, the buildings were used for soldiers.

East of town on the Alaska Highway, you'll see the **Alaska Homestead and Historical Museum** (1 mile south on Darshorst Rd. from Mile 1,415.4 Alaska Hwy., 907/895-4431, unpredictable hours, so call first), a preserved homestead that gives great insight into how the early farmers in Alaska scratched a living from the land.

WILDLIFE

Bison from Delta Junction have been used to start three other herds in near the Copper River, the Chitina River, and Farewell. Hunting permits are issued to keep the Delta Junction population down to a manageable population of about 300 animals that roam freely on 90,000 acres of sanctuary land around Delta.

Note that these imported wild bison are not the same as the native wood bison, a native species that was believed to be extinct until a small herd was discovered in Canada in 1957. In 2015, a herd of wood bison was reintroduced to the tundra near the remote Western Alaska community of Shageluk, after more than a decade of effort from the **Alaska Wildlife Conservation Center** (alaskawildlife.org) and the U.S. Fish and Wildlife Service.

The Delta Junction bison roam freely but tend to linger on the flats south of Delta, near Donnelly Dome, an unmistakable hump of land rising out of the trees, during the late April to early June calving season. Several trails lead to the dome's summit, and it makes a good vantage for watching for the small Macomb caribou herd in late summer and fall.

The fields southeast of Delta are one of the state's more spectacular places for viewing sandhill cranes; 200,000-300,000 of these elegant birds pass through from May to September. Moose are common along the flats north of town, and also near the road—so drive carefully.

MARKETS AND FAIRS

Get a taste of Delta's excellent local produce—which includes cereal grains, a crop that's very unusual in Alaska—at the **Highway's End Farmer's Market** (junction of Richardson Hwy. and Alaska Hwy., 907/322-2896), which is held 10am-5pm on Wednesday and Saturday during the summer, right across the street from the visitor center. If you're passing through during the **Deltana Fair and Music Festival** in late July (2755 Nistler Rd., deltanafair.com, $7 adults, discounts for seniors, students, and children) you can enjoy the best of small-town farming fun with food stands, carnival games, and down-home events like tractor pulls.

HIKING AND PUBLIC-USE CABINS

If you like hiking, stop by the **Quartz Lake State Recreation Area** (Mile 277.8 Richardson Hwy.), about 10 miles north of Delta Junction. Five short trails in the area give you access to great views of the Tanana River Valley, the Alaska Range, and several pretty lakes. It also has a swimming area, campground, fishing dock, and picnic area, plus two public-use cabins that you can reserve through dnr.alaska.gov: the **Quartz Lake Cabin,** right off the parking lot, and the **Glatfelder Cabin,** which is 0.5 mile in along the shore of Quartz Lake.

Shopping

You'll find lots of Alaska-made gifts in **Rika's Roadhouse Cafe and Gifts** (Mile 275 Richardson Hwy., 907/895-4201, mid-May-Labor Day daily 10am-4pm), a great little gift shop. The **Knotty Shop** (6565 Richardson Hwy., 907/488-3014) is a little bit of a tourist trap, but they have a lot of fun Alaska-related trinkets, a selection of very memorable animals made of giant wood burls (knots), and great ice cream.

Local hunters take their game to **Delta Meat and Sausage** (Mile 1,413 Alaska Hwy., 800/794-4206 or 907/895-4006, deltameat.com, Mon.-Fri. 8am-5pm, Sat. 10am-4pm, Sun. hours during the summer) to be processed, but for visitors it's a fun stopover to sample and purchase sausages made from local meat, including reindeer, buffalo, elk, yak, and of course beef and pork. This sort of meat agriculture is unusual in Alaska, so they make great gifts to take home.

Food

FAST FOOD AND CAFÉS

For a fun (and fast) blast to the past with good burgers, fries, and dreamy milk shakes, visit the **Buffalo Center Drive-In** (Mile 265.5 Richardson Hwy., 907/895-4055, mid-May-Labor Day Mon.-Sat. 11am-10pm, Sun. noon-10pm). It's a true drive-in, with no indoor seating; you can order from and eat in your car, or walk up to the window and dine outdoors under a protective awning. Cash only.

You can get homemade café fare at **Rika's Roadhouse Cafe and Gifts** (Mile 275 Richardson Hwy., 907/895-4201, mid-May-Labor Day daily 10am-4pm), such as sandwiches, soups, and baked goods.

PIZZA

Pizza Bella (Mile 265 Richardson Hwy., 907/895-4841 or 907/895-4524, pizzabellarestaurant.com, entrées $24, pizzas $20) is a surprisingly decent hole-in-the-wall. It's better on the inside than it looks on the outside, and they make an excellent thin crust pizza. Portions are generous but prices are a little high, as should be expected in any rural Alaska community.

THAI FOOD

Nobody knows why Alaskans love Thai food so much, but we do—and **JB's Thai Food** (2455 Craig St., 907/895-2222, Tues.-Sat. 11am-8pm, Sun. noon-6:30pm) is a nice break from the mostly American food available in Delta Junction. Portions are generous, prices are reasonable, and all the food is made fresh, so service can be a little slow.

GROCERIES

For groceries, visit the **IGA Food Cache** (Mile 266 Richardson Hwy., 907/895-4653, igafoodcache.com, Mon.-Sat. 6:30am-9pm, Sun. 8am-8pm), but brace yourself for fairly high prices.

Accommodations

RV travelers can camp in one of 23 spots in the **Big Delta State Historical Park** (Mile 274.5 Richardson Hwy.); toilets, water, and a dump station are available. Also popular are the **Delta State Recreation Site** (Mile 267 Richardson Hwy.) and the **Quartz Lake State Recreation Area** (Mile 277.8 Richardson Hwy.), which is about 10 miles north of Delta Junction. Quartz Lake has a handful of wooded camping areas for RVs or tents, plus a huge paved lot for RVs.

There are a couple of more conventional hotels in town, but you'll have a much better experience if you stay in one of the excellent B&Bs. **Garden Bed & Breakfast** (3103 Tanana Loop Extension, 907/895-4633, alaskagardenbnb.com, from $89) offers private cabins with full kitchens, plus a selection of quiet rooms in the main house. Other amenities include home-cooked breakfast every morning, Wi-Fi, and a beautiful flower garden during the summer. The deluxe queen suite even has a jacuzzi.

Hillcrest Bed & Breakfast (3474 Hillcrest Rd., 907/895-6223, hillcrestbnb.com) offers four rooms, with two shared baths between them; the upstairs rooms and a big deck have nice mountain views, while the ground floor has an accessible room and bathroom. You also get Wi-Fi and a beautiful home-cooked breakfast every morning.

TOK

If you're driving to Alaska, Tok (rhymes with "poke") will be the first community you hit on this side of Canada. Just 93 miles west of the border, this town was an Athabascan community that was settled as a camp for the Alaska Road Commission in the 1940s. Nowadays it has a year-round population of more than 1,000 people, with an economy that depends heavily on summer tourism.

Nobody can agree on exactly how Tok was named or why it's pronounced this way; one theory is that the name is shortened from "Tokyo Camp," a change that would have taken place in the 1940s during World War II—or it might be named for a husky.

Most businesses are open year-round—make reservations during busy season May-September. Summer highs easily reach into the 60s or 70s; typical winter highs are a positively frigid -7 degrees Fahrenheit, and winter lows can easily dip far below -50 degrees. A drive through here in the winter requires full survival gear, just in case your car breaks down.

Sights and Recreation

Tok itself is a beautiful sight, with its log homes sporting sod and wildflower roofs in the summer, old fish wheels by the river, log caches, and historic mining equipment. Make sure you stop by the **Mainstreet Visitor Center** (junction of Alaska Hwy. and Tok Cutoff Hwy., 907/883-5775) for exhibits on the area's history, wildlife, and construction of the Alaska Highway. The enormous log building is impossible to miss.

TOP EXPERIENCE

SCENIC HIGHWAYS

Tok sits in an incredibly scenic location between the Alaska Range and the Tanana River. If you have a vehicle and the time, drive north on the **Taylor Highway,** a designated National Scenic Byway through the "Forty-Mile" region that so inspired Jack London. This region is still gold mining country, with many active claims along the road, so be sure to respect private property. You might also catch a glimpse of the Forty-Mile caribou herd that sometimes wanders through this area.

Some people like to make the 77-mile drive to the tiny community of **Chicken,** Alaska, just to say they've been there, but there isn't much else to do there. If you're intent on seeing Chicken, try pairing it with a trip to the iconic gold rush town of **Dawson City** in Canada's Yukon Territory. Just keep going past Chicken and take the turnoff to the **Top of the World Highway,** which will take you into Canada; the whole drive is 185 miles or at least six hours one-way, so you'll want to spend the night there before you come back.

NORTHERN LIGHTS

Because Tok is so isolated, it's a great place for viewing the **northern lights** when the sky is dark enough (Aug.-May). Be sure to let the staff at your lodgings know you want to be woken up if the lights come out. As in Fairbanks, you can take beautiful photos of the Aurora by getting as far away as possible from any light sources, setting up your camera on a tripod with the longest exposure possible, and using either a remote trigger or a short timer delay on the shutter to keep the movement of your finger on the button from blurring the image. Two or three seconds is plenty. You may need to turn off your camera's autofocus and manually focus it on a distant object to help you get a clear shot.

FLIGHTSEEING AND WILDLIFE VIEWING

Tok couldn't be situated in prettier country, with the foothills of the mighty Alaska Range starting just to the south and the Tanana River running to the north. While you're here, keep an eye out for the Nelchina caribou herd, which winters in the area, and for plentiful moose along the highway corridor.

This is also prime country for **birding,** with nearly 200 species documented in the nearby Tetlin Wildlife Refuge. Keep an eye out for sandhill cranes in the fields along with resident trumpeter swans. Birders, beware: You may never want to leave Tok. The birdwatching checklist for this region (the Upper Tanana Valley) notes 186 different species, with spring and fall being the best times to see migratory species passing through. Keep an eye out for waterfowl in wetlands and lakes alongside the Alaska Highway between mileposts 1,221 and 1,289.

All **flightseeing** trips in Alaska are, arguably, spectacularly beautiful, but they're also expensive. If you only do one, it's probably best to save your money for flightseeing around Denali. If you can spare $135 to $200 per person for an hour's flight (depending on group size), though, this is a great chance to look for moose and Dall sheep from the air, flying past some of the giant mountains and spectacular glaciers of the Alaska Range (which continues all the way west to its crowning glory, Denali); **40-Mile Air** (907/883-5191, 40-mileair.com) offers flightseeing and wildlife-viewing flights in the region.

Tok is a recreationist's paradise—but guided tours are limited when compared to places like Denali National Park. For the hardcore adventurers, **Tok Air Service** (907/322-2903, flytokair.com) offers small-plane support for true backcountry paddle trips, hikes, snowboarding/skiing trips, and mountaineering. These are not guided trips; you are responsible for your own adventure and safety.

GOLD PANNING

Panning for gold is one of the highest-ranking items on most visitors' Alaska bucket lists. But in a place like Tok that isn't brimming with commercial gold panning tours, it's hard to tell which areas are fair game for recreational gold panners. If you stop by the **Public Lands Information Center** (1314 Alaska Hwy., 907/883-5667, alaskacenters.gov/tok), they'll be able to point you in the right direction.

FISHING

If you want to fish, head north along the Taylor Highway to Four Mile Lake, which is actually 4.5 miles up the road; in exchange for a 0.5 mile hike, you get good fishing for sheefish and rainbow trout. Fishing licenses and gear are available at **Three Bears Outpost** (Mile 1,313.3 Alaska Hwy., 907/883-5370, threebearsalaska.com, daily 7am-11pm).

HIKING AND HORSEBACK RIDING

There are very few maintained hiking trails here, but it's worth making the one-mile boardwalk trip to lovely **Hidden Lake;** the trailhead is at mile 1,240 of the Alaska Highway. If you're an experienced backcountry hiker, stop in at the **Tetlin National Wildlife Refuge Visitor Center** (Mile 1,229 Alaska Hwy., 907/883-5312, tetlin.fws.gov, mid-May-mid-Sept. 8:30am-4pm) for advice on local land use regulations and the best destinations. This is also how you reserve the smattering of public-use cabins on refuge land, although hunters generally reserve them far in advance through a lottery system during moose season (late Aug.-mid-Sept.).

This is great country for a horseback adventure, but we're not talking trail rides. Master guide Terry Overly with **Pioneer Outfitters** (907/734-0007, pioneeroutfitters.com, starting at $2,500/person for five days) in nearby Chisana offers five- to seven-day adventures that take you deep into the wilderness around Tok.

SNOWMACHINING

During the winter, **snowmachining** (known as snowmobiling elsewhere in the world) is immensely popular here, but due to winter temperatures that can easily drop below -30 degrees, you should not venture out without an experienced companion who's familiar with the area.

Shopping

For outfitting, go to the **Three Bears Outpost** (Mile 1,313.3 Alaska Hwy., 907/883-5370, threebearsalaska.com, daily 7am-11pm).

They sell a full line of hunting, camping, and fishing gear, plus hunting and fishing licenses. A new convenience store add-on sells hot food, ice cream, and other amenities.

Entertainment and Events

Mukluk Land (Mile 1,317 Alaska Hwy., 907/883-2571, mukklukland.net, June-Aug., $5) lives up to its billing as "Alaska's most unique destination." It's also a little hard to explain: There are a few carnival games like skee ball, a bouncy castle, 18 holes of mini golf, and some truly unusual, often kitschy historical items on display around the grounds. If you packed your sense of humor, you'll enjoy it.

On a more serious—and competitive—note, much of Tok's population is involved in dog mushing, and in late March (once the Iditarod is over) the whole community turns out to celebrate a marvelously deep field during two days of sprint races in the **Race of Champions** (tokdogmushers.org).

Food

THAI

Even though Tok has only a handful of restaurants, its residents love Thai food just as much as the rest of Alaska. Case in point, the stationary "food truck" **Jen's Thai Food** (corner of E. Slana Ave. and Center St., just north of the Tok Cutoff Hwy., 907/883-3362) offers excellent food at fair prices, considering the location. You might want to bring your own camp chairs if there's not room at the picnic table.

PIZZA AND AMERICAN

Fast Eddy's Restaurant (Mile 1,313 Alaska Hwy., 907/883-4411, fasteddysrestaurant.com, $32) is a staple for travelers; they serve pizza and American food, including steak, crab, and of course halibut. Prices are high, though not unusually so for rural Alaska, and breakfast and lunch are more reasonably priced.

GROCERIES

If you want to shop like a local, head for **Three Bears Food Center** (Mile 1,314 Alaska Hwy., 907/883-5195, threebearsalaska.com, daily 7am-9pm), the Alaskan version of Costco, for groceries, including meat and fresh produce.

Accommodations

MOTELS

The rooms at **Young's Motel** (Mile 1313 Alaska Hwy., 907/883-4411, youngsmotel.com) don't offer much in the way of amenities, but they're very clean, comfortable, and a good deal for the region. If you want out of the hotel they also have new private cabins for rent, and one of the town's better restaurants, Fast Eddy's, is on the grounds.

The **Alaska Range Motel** (Mile 1,312.7 Alaska Hwy., 855/282-6246 or 907/883-6246, mainstreetmotelalaska.com) offers modest rooms with good Wi-Fi, satellite TV, mini fridges, coffeemakers and microwaves in each room, and laundry facilities on-site.

CABINS

Caribou Cabins (907/883-8080, cariboucabins.info, from $159) is a peaceful, beautifully kept getaway on 10 forested acres. Each cabin has good Wi-Fi, satellite TV, and a private bathroom. Most also have lofts, and some even have jacuzzis that are available year-round. Pets are allowed for an extra $20.

BED-AND-BREAKFASTS

Mooseberry Inn (3 Mae's Way, 907/883-5496, from $139) is a quiet, comfortable little bed-and-breakfast with spacious rooms and good continental breakfasts. The couple who started this B&B has since moved to Willow, Alaska, and started a second B&B there, leaving this one to be managed by a family friend.

Cleft of the Rock (0.5 Sundog Trail, 907/883-4219, from $120 with discounts for multiple nights) offers four distinct cabins and a guesthouse room; two of the cabins have kitchenettes. The simple, homemade breakfasts are delicious, and pets are welcome for an additional fee of $25.

CAMPING

If you don't need much in the way of services, you can't beat the small, family-run **Alaska**

Stoves Campground (Mile 1,313 Alaska Hwy., 907/883-5055, alaskanstovescampground.com, tent sites from $16, RV sites from $20). There are just a few RV spots—four with electric, one full-service, and a couple of pull-throughs—plus hosteling options just up the road that range from a bunk in a wall tent ($12) and private rooms from $45 to $55.

Three Bears Outpost (Mile 1,313.3 Alaska Hwy., 907/883-5370, threebearsalaska.com, daily 7am-11pm) has a clean, well-run RV park and also offers 24-hour gas.

The National Fish and Wildlife Service offers two public-use campgrounds in Tetlin National Wildlife Refuge along the Alaska Highway: **Deadman Lake Campground** (Mile 1,249.3 Alaska Hwy.) has 15 campsites, 4 of which can accommodate RVs up to 40 feet. **Lakeview Campground** (Mile 1,256.7 Alaska Hwy.) has 11 campsites but cannot accommodate trailers, fifth wheels, or RVs over 30 feet. Both campgrounds open when the roads are clear (typically April) and close when the roads are no longer passable (typically October) and do not take reservtions; all sites are first-come, first-served.

NEAR THE BORDER

If you can't quite make it all the way to Tok (or to the border, if you're heading out of state), stay at the **Alaska Border City Lodge** (Mile 1,225.5 Alaska Hwy., 907/774-2205, alaskabordercitylodge.com, from $100). It's just three miles northwest of the border, with clean rooms, an excellent café, and very helpful staff. You can also get gas, and they rent RV spaces from $50.

Information and Services

The **Tok Visitor Center** (Mile 1,314 Alaska Hwy., 907/883-5775) is where the Alaska Highway and Tok Cutoff Highway meet. Just to the east is an **Alaska Public Lands Information Center** (also Mile 1,314 Alaska Hwy., 907/883-5667, alaskacenters.gov/tok), which offers invaluable assistance for trip planning on public lands around the state, including camping trips and all manner of outdoor recreation.

There are four gas stations along the Alaska Highway as it runs through town. Of particular note, **Young's Chevron** (Mile 1,314 Alaska Hwy., 907/883-2821) is a **NAPA AutoCare Center** that also offers gas, diesel, and propane plus a limited selection of food items and coffee. **Three Bears Outpost** (Mile 1,313.3 Alaska Hwy., 907/883-5370, threebearsalaska.com, daily 7am-11pm) offers 24-hour gas pumping.

The small community clinic is the **Upper Tanana Health Center** (907/883-5855), located on the Tok Cutoff Highway, just south of the Tok Cutoff/Alaska Highway junction.

Most gas stations offer ATMs, but there's also a **Denali State Bank** (1314 Alaska Hwy., 907/883-2265, denalistatebank.com, Mon.-Fri. 10am-6pm) with an ATM.

The most convenient **public restrooms** are in the Mainstreet Visitor Center and the Public Lands Information Center; most gas stations will also let you use their restrooms with a purchase.

Transportation

GETTING THERE

Tok is 320 miles (about a six-hour drive) from Anchorage and 200 miles (about 3.5 hours) from Fairbanks. If you're just traveling into Alaska, you have two popular options to choose from: Either continue up the Alaska Highway to its terminus in Delta Junction, then head north on the Richardson Highway to Fairbanks, or head southwest on the Tok Cutoff Highway, which then joins with the Glenn Highway and takes you the rest of the way to Anchorage.

If you're heading for Canada, the border is 93 miles away on the Alaska Highway. The next large community in Canada, Whitehorse, is a whopping 385 miles away, or a little more than a seven-hour drive if you were to go non-stop. Once you're in Canada, you can reach two small Southeast Alaska communities by road: Turn south from Whitehorse through Carcross to reach **Skagway** or head south on the Haines Junction, before Whitehorse, to reach **Haines.**

This is the only all-year route connecting Alaska to Canada, but during the summer you can also leave the state via the rough **Top of the World Highway,** which runs north from Tok to the tiny community of Chicken, Alaska, and then into Dawson City in Canada's Yukon Territory. If you started in Alaska and want some real road-trip cred, you can reach Whitehorse in about two days via the Top of the World Highway (more than 12 hours of driving if you went nonstop), then make a giant loop by coming back on the Alaska Highway. The total distance for the loop is about 900 miles and almost 20 hours of drive time.

You have two options for reaching Tok by bus. One is **Interior Alaska Bus Line** (800/770-6652, interioralaskabusline.com), which makes runs from Anchorage to Tok and Fairbanks to Tok—plus most small communities in between—three times a week year-round. Fares start at $115 from Anchorage to Tok, and $80 from Fairbanks to Tok.

Your second option is **Alaska/Yukon Trails** (907/479-2277, alaskashuttle.com), which does not offer scheduled service directly to Tok but passes through on the way to Dawson City and Whitehorse; this is a good choice if you want to continue on to those Canadian communities. You can hop off at any point in the line (including Tok), spend the night, then hop back on the next shuttle for just a $10 reboarding fee each time. Both companies also offer service up and down the Parks Highway between Fairbanks and Anchorage.

If you'd rather fly, the only scheduled air service is from the very small **40-Mile Air** (907/883-5191, 40-mileair.com), which offers service several times weekly between small eastern Interior communities, including Tok, Fairbanks, and Delta Junction.

GETTING AROUND

Technically there are no car rental services in Tok, but if you got here by air or on a bus line and want to do a little sightseeing, you might be able to rent a small truck or van from the **U-Haul** dealership (Mile 1,314.5 Alaska Hwy., 907/883-4285, uhaul.com, Mon.-Fri. 7am-5pm, Sat. 9am-5pm). This sort of untraditional use is up to the franchise owner, although they're usually pretty mellow if you explain what you're up to—in fact, you'd do well to reserve a pickup truck or van before they all sell out. Keep in mind that you'll pay a mileage fee of almost a dollar a mile and be aware that if you rent anything larger than a cargo van or pickup, your regular liability auto coverage probably won't cover any damage to the vehicle.

Kodiak and Southwest Alaska

Kodiak Island is, quite rightly, known as Alaska's "Emerald Isle." When your plane, ferry, or cruise ship arrives, you'll be greeted by more than 3,500 square miles of lush, rolling green hills and mountains, carpeted in dense trees and, higher up, tiny tundra plants and wildflowers that cluster together just as thickly. Meanwhile, Kodiak, the city—the largest community on the island—is a hardworking commercial fishing area with just enough grit around the edges to fascinate visitors from out of town.

You'll find that "work hard, play hard" commercial fishing lifestyle in almost every single Southwest Alaska community, from Kodiak west to the Alaska Peninsula, which then breaks apart into the treeless, tundra-clad, cliff-ringed islands of the Aleutian chain. The cities, towns, and villages in these places might not be as pretty on the surface as places where tourism is the prime economic driver, but they exemplify the "come as you are" mentality that makes the entire state (even the big cities) special—a willingness to judge people not by whatever happened in the past but by the way they carry themselves in the moment.

Southwest Alaska is also rich with World War II history. In fact, the tiny Aleutian Islands of Attu and Kiska were the only U.S. territory to have been occupied by the Japanese (or any Axis country) during the war, and the naval base—and later, airfield—at Dutch Harbor played an important role in the campaign to take them back and defend against further attacks in Alaska.

With the exception of Kodiak Island, which is relatively well-connected, with multiple jet flights and frequent ferry service from the mainland, every community in Southwest Alaska is very remote, reached only by small to midsize airplanes, the state ferry, and occasionally cruise ships. A trip to some of these places—say, Dutch Harbor/Unalaska in the Aleutians or the tiny, isolated Pribilof Islands in the middle of the Bering Sea—feels like you're paying a visit to the ends of the earth, where you'll be greeted by a profusion of exotic wildlife that's difficult to see anywhere else in the world and a horizon more distant than many people ever see in their lives.

Previous: wild horses of Kodiak; hiking on Unalaska. **Above:** bald eagle in Dutch Harbor.

Look for ★ to find recommended sights, activities, dining, and lodging.

Highlights

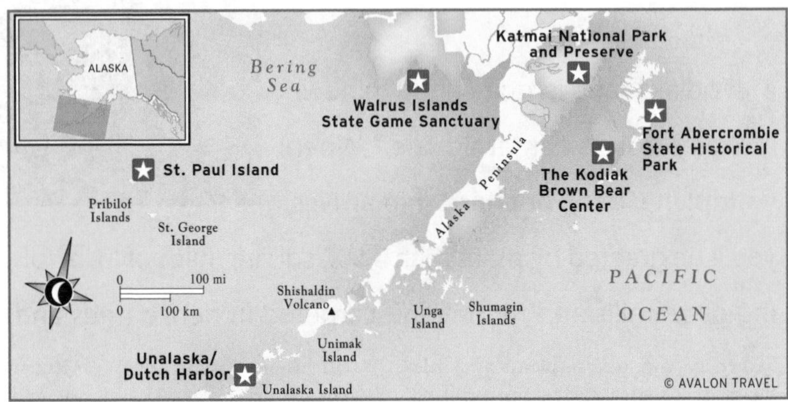

★ **Fort Abercrombie State Historical Park:** Dramatic coastal cliffs and mossy forestlands are dotted with the remains of World War II buildings and gun emplacements; a number of relics, many of them still in working order, are gathered in a small museum (page 324).

★ **The Kodiak Brown Bear Center:** Step up your bear-viewing game at this remote facility, where only six visitors at a time are allowed on the grounds (page 325).

★ **Katmai National Park and Preserve:** Tour some of the world's most epic bear-watching areas and the incredible desolation left over by the largest volcanic eruption of the 20th century (page 332).

★ **Walrus Islands State Game Sanctuary:** A lucky few get to see up to 14,000 wild walruses at one time while roughing it on these wild, windswept islands (page 341).

★ **Unalaska/Dutch Harbor:** This Navy port that withstood Japanese air attacks in World War II is now best known for spectacular hiking, camping, and birding—and as the home port for *Deadliest Catch* (page 342).

★ **St. Paul Island:** This tiny, remote island is known as the "Galapagos of the North," thanks to its isolation and profusion of rare species (page 350).

You won't find many big-city comforts in these remote towns, so they're not for the luxury traveler. But if you're enchanted by the idea of treeless, windswept islands, getting a glimpse into Alaska's most dangerous industry (commercial fishing) or if you simply want to see nature at its wildest and most unspoiled, Southwest Alaska is the place for you.

PLANNING YOUR TIME

Travel in Southwest Alaska is governed by the weather. If the cloud cover is too thick, the seas too rough, or the winds too high for your plane or boat to make it safely through, you'll end up cooling your heels until conditions improve. Plan a little flex time into your schedule so that you don't miss out on a once-in-a-lifetime opportunity because your flight or boat was delayed by a few hours or—in a worst-case scenario—a few days.

Never plan tight travel connections in this part of the state. Also, keep in mind that if a flight or ferry is delayed, the airline or ferry service won't charge you extra—but they won't pay for your hotel room while you wait, either. Trip insurance is an excellent investment, and it's a good idea to budget extra for those additional nights, just in case you find yourself stranded in a remote community. The airports and ferry terminals are open only when a plane or boat is coming in, so you won't be able to sleep there.

July and August are usually the nicest months to visit Southwest Alaska, although the limited travel and visitor services in these small communities are usually available starting in June (sometimes earlier) and into September.

TRANSPORTATION

All of Southwest Alaska's communities are off the road system; you can only get there by airplane or by boat. Having a vehicle is useful once you're there, but it's almost always easier—and cheaper—to rent a car once you arrive. If you want to take your own car you'll have to ferry it across on an Alaska Marine Highway System ship, which limits your options to Kodiak and the Aleutian Islands.

Be aware that in many Southwest communities, the airport and ferry terminal may be several miles out of town. Happily, in the communities frequented by tourists, it's easy to get a taxi—although in smaller communities, you may have a short wait—and many accommodations offer free shuttles to and from the airport and ferry terminal.

Travel Costs

Travel in these rural areas can be even more expensive than a trip to the Arctic. It's not unheard of for a round-trip plane ticket from Anchorage or Fairbanks to some of these smaller communities to cost $800 or $1,000 per person. You don't get much choice in price range with the limited accommodations, and grocery prices can be ridiculously high; it's not unusual for a gallon of milk to cost $8 or more in some of these communities.

The one exception is Kodiak; because it's very close to heavily populated Southcentral and well-connected with multiple daily flights and frequent ferries, both travel and the cost of living are much cheaper than in other, more isolated Southwest communities.

If you're not in a rush and don't have a vehicle, Alaska Marine Highway System (800/642-0066, ferryalaska.com) ferry tickets are often the most inexpensive way to travel, especially if you're willing to camp in the solarium or are traveling in a group that can split the cost of a cabin with multiple bunks. (The cabins are sold per trip, not per person.) You'll be cut off from cell service and Wi-Fi during the trip, but it also provides some of the best sightseeing you'll ever experience in your life, at no extra charge. You might even make friends with some of your fellow passengers, who are usually a mix of locals and other savvy visitors.

Southwest Alaska

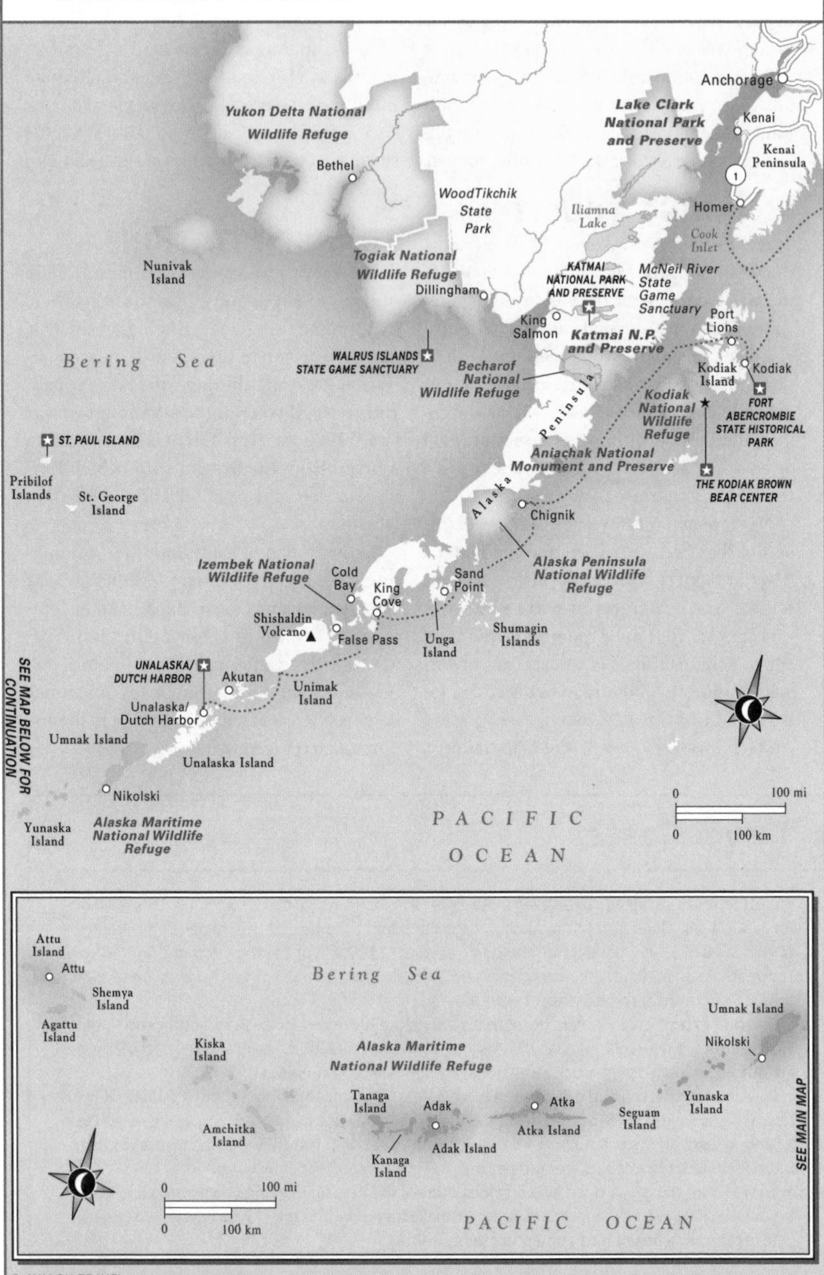

Air

Southwest Alaska communities are served by one major airline, **Alaska Airlines** (800/252-7522, alaskaair.com) and two smaller airlines, **Ravn Alaska** (800/866-8394 or 907/266-8394, flyravn.com) and **PenAir** (800/448-4226 or 907/771-2640, penair.com). You can use Alaska Airlines miles to purchase tickets on either of the smaller airlines, but you should fly Alaska whenever you can because their jets have the best safety record and better instrumentation for flying in poor visibility, so they're more likely to make it through when weather is marginal.

Note that three Southwest Alaska communities—Dillingham, and St. Paul and St. George in the Pribilofs—can only be reached by plane and very occasional cruise ships. Anything that can't be flown in, including vehicles, is delivered by barge.

Boat

The **Alaska Marine Highway System ferries** (800/642-0066, ferryalaska.com) run from Homer and Whittier down to Kodiak. From there, the seaworthy ferry *Tustumena* makes twice-monthly trips down the Aleutian Islands from late April to early October. When the *Tustumena* is not available, the other seaworthy ferry, the *Kennicott,* makes the trip instead. The ferries stop at Chignik, Sand Point, King Cove, Cold Bay, False Pass, and Akutan during their four-day trip to Dutch Harbor. Of these, the best destination for tourists is Dutch Harbor.

There is no ferry or passenger boat service to the Pribilof Islands in the Bering Sea, 300 miles off Alaska's west coast, although occasionally small cruise ships do visit; vehicles are delivered by occasional barges, while produce, mail, and the like are usually delivered by plane.

Kodiak Island

The minute your plane drops down for its low-to-the-water approach to the Kodiak runway or your ship pulls up to the port, you'll understand why this giant island—second in the United States only to Hawaii's Big Island—has been nicknamed Alaska's "Emerald Isle." Its lower reaches are carpeted in rich green spruce trees and, just above them, rolls of tundra that bloom with more variegated green and a riot of wildflowers, all dotted with crystal-clear mountain tarns and wrapped up by dramatic cliffs that drop straight into the sea.

Kodiak is home to about 6,400 people living in a city of the same name, with about double that population in the borough, which includes the entire island, a narrow strip of the mainland on the far side of Shelikof Strait, and some neighboring islands. Kodiak is a sterling example of how renewable energy systems can serve rural communities; since 2014, their utilities have been 99.7 percent powered by a combination of enormous wind turbines (which you'll see on your approach if you fly in) and hydropower.

The weather in Kodiak is usually fairly mild and wet, with summer temperatures peaking in the 60s and winter lows averaging in the mid-20s. The island receives about 70 inches of rain every year and another 70 inches of snow, but don't let that stop you from enjoying your visit. Just do as the locals do: Put on your wet-weather gear and go.

KODIAK CITY

At first impression, Kodiak (the town) is a gritty little fishing town; everybody looks worn around the edges, and people drive as if they're on a racetrack, sometimes playing chicken with the people in crosswalks. But the longer you stay, the friendlier the people seem and the more the island works its spell on you. Most attractions are either clustered in the downtown area—close to the cruise ship, ferry, and fishing docks—or so far flung that you must rent a car or take a taxi to visit them.

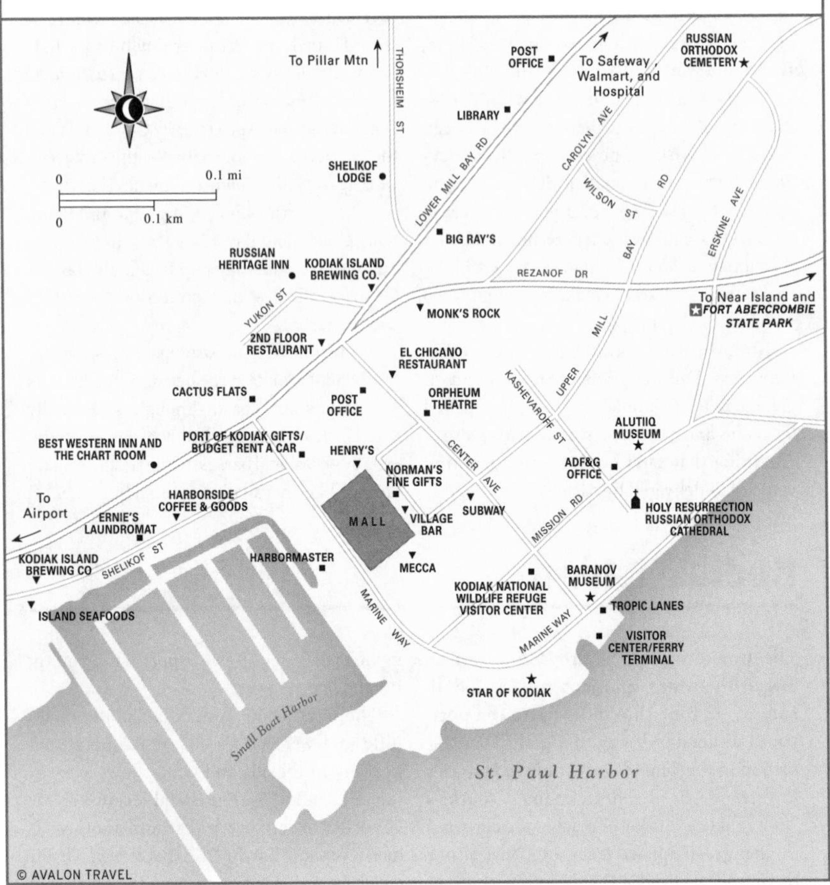

Sights

ST. PAUL HARBOR

St. Paul Harbor, right in the middle of downtown Kodiak, is one of the oldest harbors in the entire country; it was established in 1792. A small gazebo overlooks the harbor, and an open-air "museum" with interpretive signs explains the history and types of commercial fishing that drive the town's economy. Loiter on the harbor walk for long enough and you'll see everything from huge, 125-foot crabbers (yes, you might recognize one or two from the Discovery Channel's *Deadliest Catch*) and relatively small 32-foot gillnetters and jig vessels, not to mention a few sea lions cruising in hope of fish scraps.

Much as in Petersburg in Southeast, the trash cans in Kodiak have historical fish can labels on them; it's a charming touch that turns an ugly necessity into something photo-worthy.

ALUTIIQ MUSEUM

The **Alutiiq Museum** (215 Mission Rd., 907/486-7004, alutiiqmuseum.org, Tues.-Fri. 10am-4pm, Sat. noon-4pm, $7) is a must-see.

It has a traditional kayak that dates all the way from the 1800s, plus more than 25,000 collected artifacts of beautiful regalia, masks, and everyday items once used by the Native people in this area. It also has a small gift shop with a good selection of books, videos, fine Native art, and smaller keepsakes like postcards. The museum is small, but there are so many exhibits—including a very interesting video about recovering Alutiiq traditions—that you can easily spend an hour or more here.

BARANOV MUSEUM

Also interesting—although very different from the Alutiiq Museum—is the **Baranov Museum** (101 E. Marine Way, 907/486-5920, baranovmuseum.org, Mon.-Sat. 10am-4pm, $5, 12 and under free), where you can see re-created kitchen and living areas that depict life in the early days of Russian settlement in Alaska. Every artifact in this quaint but fascinating museum showcases either a piece of Russian life that made its way across the Bering Strait (visitors are often enthralled by the large samovar, a traditional Russian chimney-cum-teapot used to boil water) or a snapshot—sometimes literally—of the everyday life of people in more recent years. One of the most interesting parts of this museum is a looped video of stories from locals, paired with handwritten notes from them that are papered along the walls of one exhibit, and it's easy to spend an hour leafing through notebooks full of historical photographs.

HOLY RESURRECTION RUSSIAN ORTHODOX CATHEDRAL

Kodiak is home to the well-kept **Holy Resurrection Russian Orthodox Cathedral** (385 Kashevaroff Ave., 907/485-5532), which is supposedly open to visitors during the week, but that isn't always the case. You'll have better odds of getting in when cruise ships are in town.

If you've never seen the inside of a Russian Orthodox church, it's fascinating to compare the relatively austere, onion-domed outside with the inside's ornate icons (religious portraiture) and the partially screened-off altar room—the holiest of the holy spaces in this tradition. The Kodiak parish was founded in 1794, but this particular church—the fourth in the parish—has only been here since the 1940s; its predecessor was destroyed in a terrible fire.

Visitors are welcome to attend services, although you should know a few things first. Attendees are expected to stand throughout the entire service (any chairs or pews around the edge of the room are expressly reserved for the elderly or infirm). I understand that in some Orthodox traditions you may also be asked to kneel occasionally, and some Orthodox churches in other parts of the country might even have pews for the public, but in every Alaska church I've visited, you stand. Both men and women should dress modestly (cover your shoulders, no tight or unusually short clothing) and nicely, as a demonstration of respect.

Everything in a Russian Orthodox service is usually chanted or sung, and the services are typically conducted in a mix of languages, including the local Native dialect. So you probably won't understand much, if anything, of what's being said—but as long as you stand quietly and respectfully and do *not* take photos during the ceremony or try to enter the screened-off altar room, you will be welcome. Local clergy post the weekly list of services on Facebook; look for the morning liturgy services or the evening vespers.

Even if the church isn't open, **Sargent Park** right next door is a lovely place to stretch your legs or linger for a few minutes; it's a broad, open stretch of grass, complete with a couple of picnic tables and trees, one of which has an improvised rope swing.

KODIAK FISHERIES RESEARCH CENTER

Learn more about the sea life and fisheries of this area inside the public portion of the **Kodiak Fisheries Research Center** (301 Research Court, 907/481-1800, summer

Mon.-Sat. 8am-4:30pm, winter Mon.-Fri. 8am-4:30pm, free), a working fisheries research laboratory that's also designed for public outreach. It has a massive, cylinder-shaped 3,500-gallon aquarium that showcases the cold-water species living around Kodiak, touch tanks where you can gently handle aquatic species like sea stars and crabs (exactly which species are on hand varies), and educational displays about the species that are most important to local fisheries in this part of the world.

KODIAK NATIONAL WILDLIFE REFUGE VISITOR CENTER

The **Kodiak National Wildlife Refuge Visitor Center** (Mission St. and Center St., 907/487-2600, fws.gov/refuge/Kodiak, daily 9am-5pm through late August, reduced fall and winter hours, free) has a beautiful exhibit hall that showcases local wildlife and habitat. Don't miss the complete 36-foot skeleton of a gray whale. Other features include an Alaska Geographic bookstore, lots of great kids' programs, and on-demand showings of an award-winning 12-minute film on bears. Ask for a handout on the many Sierra Club hikes in the area.

Of course the refuge itself is well worth exploring, but there are no roads or maintained trails. The best way to see it is with a floatplane trip to one of the nine public-use cabins you must reserve well in advance; call or visit the refuge headquarters for more information.

★ FORT ABERCROMBIE STATE HISTORICAL PARK

If you're even remotely interested in World War II history, this is a must-see. The sprawling 182-acre park is made up mostly of woodland, with narrow footpaths connecting old military fortifications that are being colonized by moss, with occasional fragments of artifacts—including gun emplacements and the tracks that were used to run giant spotlights out of their protective housings—dotted throughout. The surrounding coastline is beautifully dramatic, with waves breaking over rocky pinnacles and rugged beaches. Park admission is $5 cash or check, payable to the "iron ranger" pay station (you'll need a pen or pencil to fill out the pay stub).

A small gem within the gem, the **Kodiak Military History Museum** (follow signs once in the park, 907/486-7105, Fri.-Sun. 1pm-4pm or by appt., $5 cash, 12 and under free), inside an old magazine bunker between two gun emplacements, has a collection of

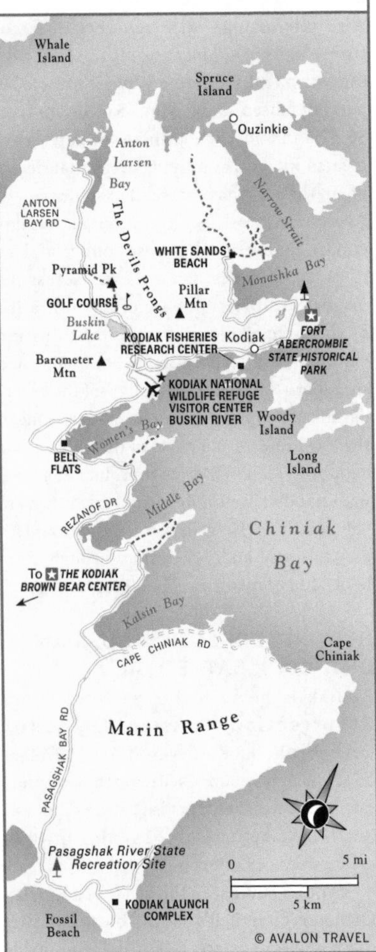

an overgrown bunker in the rainforest of Fort Abercrombie State Historical Park

artifacts of military history. Most of the artifacts are from World War II, almost all of them are meant to be handled, and many of them are still in working condition.

The entire museum is volunteer-run and maintained. Some of their treasures include working teletype machines, a WWII Army Jeep that still runs (with a collection of period uniforms and helmets you can wear for photo ops), semaphore flags you can practice with, a working half-scale plotting table, a re-created barracks, a piece of a P-38 Lightning wing, and uniforms from both Japanese and American soldiers of the period.

★ THE KODIAK BROWN BEAR CENTER

Bear viewing anywhere in Alaska is a once-in-a-lifetime adventure for most visitors. But if you're ready to elevate the experience to its ultimate realization, head for the exclusive **Kodiak Brown Bear Center** (KBBC, 877/335-2327, kodiakbearcenter.com, from $4,225 for 4 days/3 nights), a 45-minute floatplane flight from Kodiak. You'll be one of just six guests at a time allowed on the 112,000-acre KBBC grounds. The KBBC and its surrounding land are owned and managed by the Kodiak region's Alaska Native corporation, Koniag Incorporated, and butt up against the 1.9-million-acre Kodiak National Wildlife Refuge, which has no maintained trails or roads.

Even though you're in a remote location, your cabin contains all the comforts of home—including on-demand hot water and Internet access—and the staff are either born and raised on the island or have spent decades here. The season runs from late July through mid-October, with good discounts for visits later in the year. Prices include all meals, lodging, transport from Kodiak city, and daily guided bear-viewing trips.

BEACHES

Kodiak has some beautiful beaches. **Whitesand Beach** is nice (even though the sand is actually gray, and there's a lot of rock), as is **Fossil Beach.** You'll need a car—or a ridiculously generous taxi budget—to get to any of these. Whitesand Beach is north of Kodiak city; drive northeast of town and follow the (two-lane) "highway" as it winds past Fort Abercrombie State Historical Park, then back west to the clearly signed beach. Fossil Beach—where, yes, you can sometimes see fossils—is more than an hour's drive south of Kodiak, past Pasagshak State Recreation Site.

The **Bells Flats** area, about 10 miles south of

A baby brown bear practices its climbing skills.

Kodiak on the Chiniak Highway, where Sargent Creek runs into the ocean, is also nice; during late summer you'll sometimes see bears fishing for salmon. The bears and fish are on their own schedule, so there are no guarantees, but you're most likely to see them at low tide (the lower water makes it easier for the bears to get at the fish), and if you see a bunch of vehicles at the side of the road, they're almost always there because the bears are out. Please remember that these bears are wild animals that may react unpredictably to your presence, so don't approach them; use a zoom lens or binoculars to get that great view or shot.

KODIAK VAN TOURS

For a laid-back, six-hour tour that takes you to Kodiak's most beautiful places on the road system, with no rental necessary, try the immensely popular **Kodiak Island Van Tours** (907/631-2571, kodiakislandvantours.com), with chances to see bears, Sitka blacktail deer, mountain goats, foxes, whales, harbor seals, sea otters, and sometimes even whales feeding off the coast. But it's Janet, the experienced local guide who clearly loves what she's doing, who is the real high point of the tour. There's just one tour departure per day, usually around 9am, with a light lunch, bathroom breaks as necessary (although be warned, facilities are few and far between, and will usually be pit toilets), and courtesy pickup at the airport, ferry terminal, and most hotels. Kodiak's roads are actually in great shape, but if you get carsick easily, ask to sit up front or in the first row back. It's smart to book in advance when the salmon are running and bears are most visible, usually July-August and into September.

Recreation

Want an up-close view of Kodiak's dramatic, surf-pounded cliffs? **Kayak Kodiak** (907/512-5112, kayakingkodiak.com) can take you **sea kayaking** or **stand-up paddleboarding** on a trip that suits your ability level. If you truly have the chops to create your own trip in Kodiak's frigid coastal waters, they'll also rent you the gear—but if in doubt, always go for the guide. Not only will you be safer, but you'll also understand more of what you're seeing. Challenges for DIY paddlers include cold water (usually it's not lack of swimming ability that kills you, but hypothermia or the gasp reflex that causes you to inhale when you hit the water); busy boating traffic; the remote location; sheer cliffs that often present no easy landing area; and wildlife like orcas and sea lions that, while thrilling to see up close, can also be scary.

Whitesand Beach

For a totally different perspective on the island, take a **flightseeing** trip. Both **Deckload Aviation** (907/512-0744, deckloadaviation.com) and **Kingfisher Aviation** (866/486-5155 or 907/486-5155, kingfisheraviation.com) have great reputations, offering half-day plane trips for bear viewing or shorter sightseeing trips over the spectacularly beautiful island. Deckload Aviation offers the added bonus of helicopter trips. There's nothing like being able to land in places a plane would never consider or flying low and slow over the beautiful Kodiak coastline.

Flightseeing trips typically cost about $300 per person for a one-hour trip, while longer bear-viewing trips start at about $525. Be aware that weight limits are a serious issue with small aircraft, so you should expect to be weighed along with the minimal luggage you're allowed to bring (usually limited by weight), and some pilots will charge according to the total weight of passengers and luggage in the plane. Be sure to reserve as far in advance as possible for the busy July-September bear-viewing season.

If you're working on your "remote Alaska golfing" punch card, don't miss a chance to visit the U.S. Coast Guard's **Bear Valley Golf Course** (907/487-5323, kodiakmwr.com/golf.shtml, late Apr.-mid-Oct., weather permitting), a nine-hole course with a driving range and putting greens. (Yes, it's open to the public.) Golf clubs and pull carts are available for rent, but there are no motorized carts. Greens fees for civilians are $19 for 9 holes or $29 for 18 holes, and tee times are available anytime during open hours (Mon.-Thurs. 11am-7pm and Fri.-Sun. 10am-7pm).

Some people come to Kodiak not to see bears, but to compete with them for some of the best wild-caught seafood in the world. **Fish n' Chips Charters** (907/539-6135, fishingkodiak.net, from $350 pp, max 6 people) is one of the most popular charters on the island. They offer full-day trips on the custom-built 33-foot *Fish Hawk,* with a heated, fully enclosed cabin and a private bathroom, guided by a Kodiak native with more than 25 years of experience fishing these waters. Target species include halibut, king and silver salmon, lingcod, Pacific cod, and rockfish.

For a land-based fly-fishing excursion, hit up **Reel Extreme Alaska** (907/942-1356, reelextremealaska.com, from $350 pp for a full-day off-road trip, or $150 pp for a half-day trip on the road system), where you can take an off-road vehicle to some of Kodiak's best backcountry fishing spots, soaking up the

helicopter flightseeing over Kodiak with Deckload Aviation

beautiful scenery along the way. Target species include red salmon, which run from mid-June into August, and silver salmon, which start arriving in August, plus Dolly Varden, steelhead, and rainbow trout and the possibility of seeing bears.

Entertainment

The modest downtown **Orpheum Movie Theater** (102 Center Ave., 907/486-5449) shows new releases. There's also a bowling alley in town: **Tropic Lanes** (102 E. Marine Way, 907/486-6257).

If you'd rather watch sports, **The Village Bar** (408 W. Marine Way, 907/486-3412) is a decent sports bar that serves a good variety of drinks and breakfast late at night. But the best beer in town is at **Kodiak Island Brewing Co** (117 Lower Mill Bay Rd., 907/486-2537, kodiakbrewery.com, daily noon-7pm). It closes early, so this is one case where you might want to go for beer first, dinner second—there are a couple of decent restaurants within walking distance.

Shopping

Interestingly, the best Russian gift shop in town is **Monk's Rock** (202 E. Rezanof Dr., 907/486-0905, Mon. 11am-3pm, Tues.-Fri. 8:30am-3pm, Sat. 8:30am-1pm), a great little coffee shop that also has a collection of icons, nesting dolls, hairpieces, and trinkets for sale.

If you're looking for authentic Alaska Native art, the gift shop inside the **Alutiiq Museum** (215 Mission Rd., 907/486-7004, alutiiqmuseum.org, Tues.-Fri. 10am-4pm, Sat. noon-4pm) is excellent (no charge for visiting the gift shop). The **Baranov Museum** (101 E. Marine Way, 907/486-5920, baranovmuseum.org, Mon.-Sat. 10am-4pm) also has a small gift shop that's worth a visit. For books, maps, and a few gift selections, visit the small Alaska Geographic store inside the **Kodiak National Wildlife Refuge Visitor Center** (Mission St. and Center St., 907/487-2600, fws.gov/refuge/Kodiak, daily 9am-5pm through late August, reduced fall and winter hours).

For a more regional gift selection, **Norman's Fine Gifts** (Mon.-Sat. 10:30am-6pm, Sun. noon-5pm) just off the harbor offers a nice selection of items mostly made in the Pacific Northwest; the selection includes jewelry, charming children's books, and Christmas ornaments. If you're shopping for a crafter, pay a visit to the lovely **The Rookery** (104 Center Ave., 907/486-0052, Mon. noon-5pm, Tues.-Sat. noon-6pm), where you'll find yarn, fabric, and other crafting materials.

Port of Kodiak Gifts (518 Marine Way, 907/486-8550, Mon.-Fri. 10am-5:30pm, Sat.-Sun. 10am-6pm) is bigger than it looks from the outside, with a modest selection of fairly generic gifts like shirts, bumper stickers, and stuffed animals with a few higher-end items throughout. This is also the downtown office for **Budget Rent a Car.**

If you need an outfitter, **Big Ray's** (212 Lower Mill Bay Rd., 907/486-4276, bigrays.com, Mon.-Sat. 7am-7pm, Sun. 8am-6pm) has everything you need for your outdoor adventures, from fishing to hunting and photography. For more mundane personal needs, there's a **Walmart** a few miles from downtown (2911 Mill Bay Rd., 907/481-1670, daily 7am-10pm).

Finally, if you didn't catch enough fish, **Kodiak Island Smokehouse** (1011 Mill Bay Rd., 907/486-6455, kodiakislandsmokehouse.com) will sell you smoked salmon, halibut, and cod. If you did catch your fill, they'll also happily process your fish and ship it to you, so you don't have to worry about it thawing out on the flight home.

Food

FINE DINING

For a truly one-of-a-kind dining experience that makes the most of Kodiak's beautiful scenery and its just-caught-five-minutes-ago seafood, **Galley Gourmet** (907/486-5079, galleygourmet.biz, $150) offers 3.5-hour dinner and sightseeing cruises aboard the 42-foot yacht *Sea Breeze*. The food is delicious, with a heavy focus on seafood and organic, locally grown green salads, but they're happy to serve non-seafood meals and work around any dietary restrictions you may have—just let them know when you book your tickets. Alcohol is not served on the boat, but you can bring your own. Although the atmosphere on the boat is "Kodiak casual" (which basically means dress for the weather), the elements all combine to create one of the best meals you'll ever have; if you've had a good experience, don't forget to show your appreciation by leaving a tip.

MEXICAN

The casual **El Chicano Mexican Restaurant and Cantina** (103 Center Ave., 907/486-6116) serves typical Mexican food, from fajitas to burritos and enchiladas, at very decent prices, with a few local beers on tap—just be patient, because sometimes the food is slow in coming. The ambience is laid-back and I've never seen it crowded—presumably it fills up only when cruise ships are in town. I'm a fan of their "healthy bowls," which lean heavily on generous servings of brown rice, seasoned meats, pico de gallo, and the like.

CAFÉS

Monk's Rock (202 E. Rezanof Dr., 907/486-0905, Mon. 11am-3pm, Tues.-Fri. 8:30am-3pm, Sat. 8:30am-1pm, sandwiches $12-15) is a little bookstore that also sells sandwiches, omelets, and smoothies, with takeaway lunches available on the honor system ($15, cash only). All their sandwiches are great. This place is especially charming because starting at 11am you can take your lunch upstairs to High Tide Treasures, a cozy thrift shop that feels like your best friend's living room.

Harborside Coffee & Goods (210B Shelikof Ave. and 1715 Mill Bay Rd., 907/486-5862 and 907/486-5864, both locations Mon.-Sat. 6am-6pm, hours vary Sun.) has two cozy little coffee shops on the island with coffee, tea, a limited selection of baked goods, and some pretty good ice cream. Prices are typical of anywhere in Alaska—a few dollars each for baked goods or that first scoop of ice cream.

Cactus Flats Natural Foods (146 Rezanof Dr. W, 907/486-4677, Mon.-Fri. 10am-7pm, Sat. 10am-6pm, Sun. noon-6pm) is really more of a health food/supplements store than a café, but they do offer organic smoothies made with real fruit.

BURGERS

The **Chart Room** (236 W. Rezanof Dr., 907/486-5712, kodiakinn.com, daily 4pm-9pm, $18-20), inside the Best Western Kodiak Inn, has decent beer and strictly average pub grub. It's an option if you're hungry after

one of the great sandwiches from Monk's Rock

most other places have started closing down. If you're not picky, the Wednesday burger and brew combination for $11 is hard to beat.

GROCERIES

There used to be a large grocery store in downtown Kodiak, Alaska Food for Less, located right next to the harbor. It's since closed, so your only option that's even remotely nearby is **Safeway** (2685 Mill Bay Rd., 907/481-1500, daily 6am-midnight). Prices range anywhere from on par with Anchorage to twice as much. The shop is more than two miles away from downtown through a fairly boring residential district, so most travelers will want to take a cab or catch one of the rare local bus (KATS) runs.

Accommodations

For the nicest B&B experience in Kodiak, aim for the year-round **Cliff House B&B** (galley-gourmet.biz, from $190 for a single room with private bath, $375 for a three-room suite with private bath and kitchen), which backs up to a spruce forest and looks out over the action at Kodiak's largest harbor. You stand to see almost anything in the water, from leaping salmon to killer whales, from that lofty perch. It's run by the same family that offers Galley Gourmet dinner cruises, so you know you're in for a great meal, and the laid-back, homey ambience—complete with organic gardens maintained by your master gardener host—is a shining example of the bucolic life Alaska offers to the resourceful. That said, amenities include just about everything you'd expect in a hotel, including Wi-Fi, TV, hair dryers, and so on.

If you're traveling on a budget, the **Shelikof Lodge** (shelikoflodgealaska.com, from $140) is dated but clean with refrigerators and microwaves in most rooms, complimentary airport/ferry shuttle, and a small-town friendly staff. Each room has a private bathroom, and it's pet friendly ($10/day fee). The walls are a little thin, but the place is reasonably tranquil, although some visitors might feel strange about the fact that the room doors don't have deadbolts—just thumb locks. The Wi-Fi is reasonably fast, given the location.

The overpriced **Best Western Kodiak Inn** (236 Rezanof Dr., 888/563-4254 or 907/486-5712, bestwestern.com, from $183) is one of two conventional hotels in town; the other is the newly renovated **Comfort Inn** (1395 Airport Way, 907/487-2700, choicehotels.com, from $180), which is near the airport.

Information and Services

If you're not sure how to prioritize your time in Kodiak, make your first stop the main **Kodiak Visitor Information Center** (100 Marine Way, 800/789-4782 or 907/486-4782, year-round Mon.-Fri. 8am-5pm, expanded summer hours), right beside the ferry terminal. You'll find **public restrooms** a short walk away at the Kodiak harbor, near the corner of Marine Way and Shelikof.

There are two **post offices** in Kodiak; the main branch (419 Lower Mill Bay Rd., Mon.-Fri. 9am-5pm) and the more convenient downtown station (111 W. Rezanof Dr., Mon.-Sat. 10am-1pm and 2pm-6pm), inside the giant, gutted Alaska Food for Less building (look for the illuminated Open sign).

There are also two **Wells Fargo** branches in Kodiak. The downtown branch (202 Marine Way, 907/486-3126, Mon.-Fri. 10am-5pm, Sat. 10am-2pm) has package drops for both FedEx and UPS outside and a 24-hour ATM; the other branch (2645 Mill Bay Rd., 907/486-6900, Mon.-Fri. 10am-6pm) doesn't have Saturday hours. The **KeyBank** (422 W. Marine Way, 844/433-2070, Mon.-Thurs. 9am-5pm) closes at 5:30pm on Friday.

The area hospital, **Providence Kodiak Island Medical Center** (1915 E. Rezanof Dr., 907/486-3281) offers 24-hour emergency care; dial 911 for emergencies.

Finally, you won't have to worry about gas stations; they're all over the place, including one smack in the middle of downtown and another right next to Safeway, which also has its own gas station. Prices may be as much as 50 percent more per gallon than in Anchorage.

Transportation

GETTING THERE

Kodiak can only be reached by sea or air. It's a frequent stop for cruise ships; passengers usually appreciate its gritty realism, the lack of a defined "cruise ship alley" full of generic shops, and of course the stunning scenery and wildlife viewing. If you come on the **Alaska Marine Highway System** (800/642-0066, ferryalaska.com), it's a 9- to 10-hour trip from Homer.

For air travel, your options are two flights from **Alaska Airlines** (800/252-7522, alaskaair.com) or a handful of flights on **Ravn Alaska** (800/866-8394 or 907/266-8394, flyravn.com). Take the Alaska flights when you can, because they have better instrumentation for landing in fog. No matter which airline you take, visitors are sometimes surprised by the low approach to the runway, which is right at sea level. I'll never forget hearing one visitor blurt out, "Is this a floatplane?" Only if the pilot messes up!

GETTING AROUND

Kodiak has a very rudimentary public transit system: **Kodiak Area Transit System** or **KATS** (907/486-8308, katsbus.org). Currently, it only makes two stops a day at the airport and three to five stops a day at places like the library, Safeway, and Walmart, but it might grow in the years to come. Each ride costs $2 one-way, and you have to buy a fare ticket in advance at either Senior Citizens of Kodiak (302 Erskine Ave.) or First Student (2014 Mill Bay Rd.).

You have two options for rental cars: **Budget Rent-a-Car,** which has a location in the airport (1647 Airport Way, 907/487-2220, open until 10:30pm) and another downtown in Port of Kodiak Gifts (428 Marine Way, 907/486-8550, Mon.-Fri. 10am-5:30pm, Sat.-Sun. 10am-6pm). Call 907/487-2220 to secure an after-hours rental at the downtown Budget. I've heard some stories about cars in pretty bad condition, so always check out the condition of your car—especially the tires—before you accept the rental.

Your other option is **Avis,** which has only an airport location (1647 Airport Way, 907/487-2264, daily 6:30am-11pm). Their cars are more expensive but tend to be better quality.

If all the rental cars are sold out (as frequently happens) or if you don't have a credit card to rent with, you can rent a pickup or cargo van from the local **U-Haul** franchise

(1213 Mill Bay Rd., 907/486-1767). The office is behind the coffee cart. Remember that if you rent a vehicle that's larger than a cargo van—in other words, anything that's a legitimate moving truck, albeit a small one—it almost definitely won't be covered by your private insurance, so buy the add-on insurance from U-Haul.

Kodiak has lots of cab companies that will pull up and wait when a plane comes in (the ferry terminal is so close to the middle of town, it's not such a big deal). One of the biggest and most permanent-looking is **Kodiak City Cab** (907/486-5555, kodiakcitytaxi.com). These sorts of providers—private individuals who usually don't advertise—tend to rotate in and out of business fairly quickly in rural communities, so call the visitor center (100 Marine Way, 800/789-4782 or 907/486-4782, year-round Mon.-Fri. 8am-5pm, expanded summer hours) to see who'll be in business during your trip.

Alaska Peninsula

This peninsula of land sits between Kodiak Island to the east and Dillingham to the west. The peninsula stretches southwest, eventually fracturing into the volcanic Aleutian Islands, which stretch some 1,200 miles along a curve that follows part of the Pacific Ring of Fire. The biggest attraction is bear viewing at Katmai National Park and Preserve, although Lake Clark National Park sits just north of Katmai and also offers excellent bear-viewing opportunities.

★ KATMAI NATIONAL PARK AND PRESERVE

Katmai National Park and Preserve may be the best-known bear-viewing location in the entire world, but that isn't all it has to offer. This four-million-acre park includes phenomenal sea kayaking along its coastline, world-class fishing, and one of the most stunning sights you'll ever see, the **Valley of 10,000 Smokes**. Alaska Native people also lived here for thousands of years, leaving hundreds

brown bears in Katmai National Park and Preserve

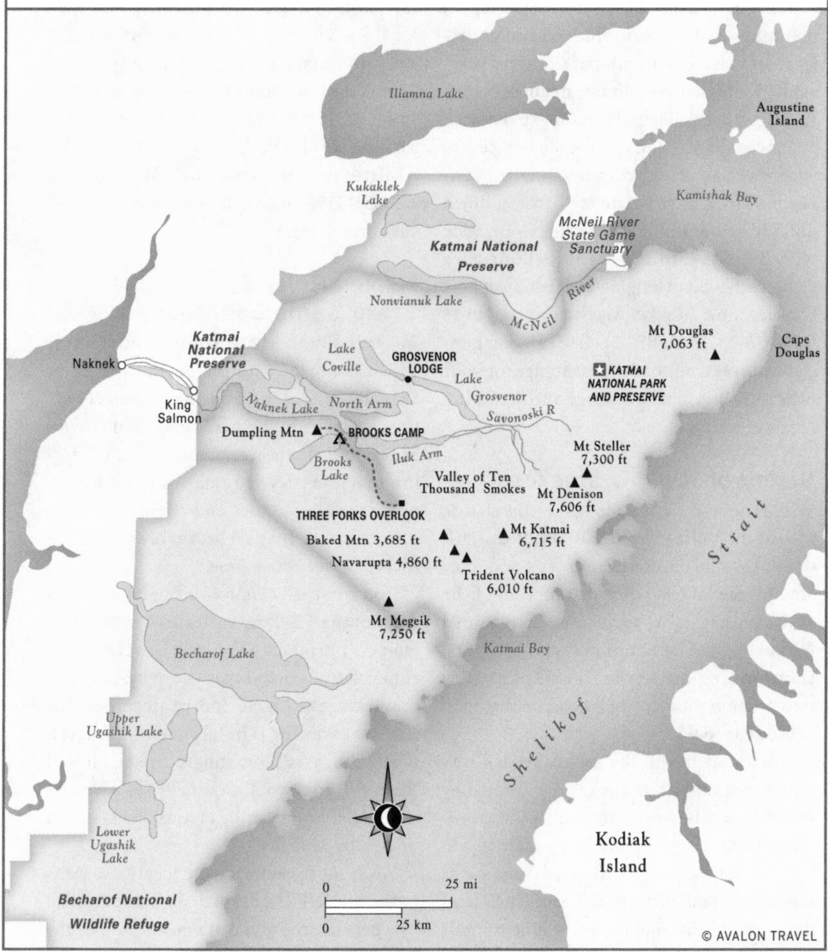

of depressions along the river from their ancient homes.

If you're going bear viewing, the most popular destination in Katmai is, far and away, **Brooks Camp.** This is also one of the hottest spots for fishing. Here, you'll find the park visitor center, an established campground, an auditorium where rangers lead nightly chats in addition to their daytime guided hikes, and of course **Brooks Lodge** (katmailand.com, from $916 for lodging, including airfare from Anchorage) if you want to spend the night within four walls.

You can also make this an easy—although long—fly-in day trip from Anchorage or Dillingham, or stay in either of the two other lodges operated by the same park concessionaire, Katmailand. These seasonal activities all take place from early June to mid-September. As a general rule the bear viewing is best from mid-June to early August, while fishing is often better in the shoulder seasons before and after prime bear viewing.

Can't quite make it to Katmai yet? Keep on planning—in the meantime, you can participate in video chats with park rangers year-round and also view a live bearcam of bruins fishing at Brooks Falls, both via explore.org.

A bewildering number of guide services are authorized to operate within Katmai for various purposes. If you want to narrow it down quickly and ensure a good experience, stick with **Brooks Camp** or **Brooks Lodge** for right-at-the-camp lodging and fishing opportunities, and **Alaska Alpine Adventures** (877/525-2577 or 907/351-4193, alaskaalpineadventures.com) out of Anchorage for your other hiking, backpacking, and paddling needs in Katmai.

Valley of 10,000 Smokes

While you're in Katmai, don't miss the chance to visit the **Valley of 10,000 Smokes.** This desolate, ash-covered landscape was created by the largest volcanic eruption of the 20th century, from a volcano later named **Novarupta.** The eruption lasted 60 hours, transforming the fertile Ukak River valley into a smoking, desolate landscape that took decades to cool.

The valley is a stark reminder of nature's power, not only from the change created by the eruption but from the very gradual return of life to this region. The easiest way to visit is a daylong tour with park concessionaire Katmailand (katmailand.com); their trips depart daily through the early June to mid-August visiting season, require advance reservations, and cost $88 (add $8 for a sack lunch).

If you want to camp in or near the valley, you can arrange a one-way drop-off with Katmailand, starting at $51. Some backcountry camping spots are available around the fringes of the valley, where you're more likely to see wildlife, or it's a 12-mile hike (one-way) to the Baked Mountain huts that you can share with other campers (no reservations or fee required and no services available, except for a three-sided outhouse).

The trek requires you to cross two rivers that can run deep and swift, and you probably won't have access to water once seasonal snowfields melt. See nps.gov/katm for more information to help you plan your visit (there's a subsection for the Valley of 10,000 Smokes). If you want company on a backpacking trip through the valley, try **Alaska Alpine Adventures** (877/525-2577 or 907/351-4193, alaskaalpineadventures.com) out of Anchorage.

McNeil River State Game Sanctuary

McNeil River State Game Sanctuary, which is tucked into the northern edge of Katmai National Park, was established in 1967 to protect the highest concentration of wild brown bears in the world. As you might imagine, that leads to some amazing bear-viewing opportunities; guides and researchers have counted more than 70 brown bears near the McNeil River at one time.

You can easily charter a flight here from Anchorage (250 air miles to the east) or Homer (100 miles to the east); however, make sure you understand that you're heading to a roadless area with no modern amenities. The best bear viewing is in July and mid-August, when chum salmon congregate at McNeil River Falls, but you can usually see a smaller number of bears during an early sockeye run up nearby Mikfik Creek.

As at most bear-viewing locations, visits to the McNeil River sanctuary are controlled by a permit program that's meant to offer the best of both worlds for everybody: People get a chance to see wild bears up close without fighting through a crowd, and the bears aren't disturbed by the limited number of people. Only 10 guided viewing permits are issued per day from early June to late August.

Guided viewing permits are assigned by lottery, which starts on March 2 of the prior year and ends on March 1 of the viewing year; each permit is valid for four days and requires a four-mile round-trip hike to get to the falls. If you don't win a guided viewing access permit, you might win a camp-standby permit, which is also valid for four days. This allows you to stay in the sanctuary campground (tents only) and view bears from the campground and beach area. If somebody no-shows for their guided viewing trip during your stay, you can take their spot.

To apply, go to adfg.alaska.gov. It costs $25 to enter the lottery, and if you win a viewing permit, you pay $350 for the permit itself (Alaska residents pay $150). Standby permits cost $175 for nonresidents or $75 for residents. For questions about the permit lottery program, contact the **Alaska Department of Fish and Game** office in Anchorage (907/267-2189, dfg.dwc.mcneil-info@alaska.gov).

KING SALMON

The tiny, 275-person community of **King Salmon** sits 290 miles southwest of Anchorage on the Alaska Peninsula, a stout finger of land that reaches out toward the Aleutian Islands; you can only get here by plane. It's just off the west flank of Katmai National Park and holds the park's headquarters. For many people, the grizzly-viewing trip of a lifetime starts with the seasonal daily Alaska Airlines flight to King Salmon or one of a handful of PenAir flights; after that, they hop an air taxi (which must be reserved in advance) into the park. You can also fly directly from Kodiak, which is on the other side of Katmai National Park.

Because King Salmon is so small and isolated, despite its wonderful location relative to Katmai, you can see all of its tourist-oriented sights—and sample all of its amenities—in just a few hours. The flip side is that because amenities are so sparse, you should never board a flight to King Salmon (or any rural Alaska community) without having confirmed your lodgings in advance. Otherwise, you might find yourself stuck with no flights out and literally nowhere to stay.

Sights

The **King Salmon Visitor Center** (4 Bear Rd., next to the airport, 907/246-4250, fws.gov/refuge/Becharof, summer daily usually 8am-5pm but may vary) offers educational displays on the Alaska Peninsula's Native cultures and traditions, wildlife, and the fishing (sport and commercial) that drives the region's economy. This is not the place to go to arrange lodging or other services in King Salmon. In a community this small, you must have all that confirmed before you arrive.

The visitor center also serves as the headquarters of 1.15-million-acre **Becharof National Wildlife Refuge,** which is just south of King Salmon, wrapped around Becharof Lake. At more than 300,000 acres this is the second-largest lake in Alaska, home to some of the world's richest salmon runs up from Bristol Bay.

The truly intrepid and well-prepared might consider hiking the **Kanatak National Recreation Trail,** which crosses from Becharof Lake to the Pacific Ocean. Only people with broad experience in Alaska wilderness travel, survival, and navigation should even consider attempting this; the spectacular scenery comes with lots of bears and other wildlife on the trail, but you're unlikely to see another human being—you'll be entirely on your own in a remote land with no services, cell service, roads, or other trails. Access is by floatplane to Becharof Lake on the east end, and by boat or airplane on the west end. Contact the visitor center or Becharof National Wildlife Refuge (907/246-3339) before planning this trip.

Food and Accommodations

There's just one hotel in King Salmon: the **Antlers Inn** (471 Alaska Peninsula Hwy., 888/735-8525 or 907/246-8525, antlersinnak.com, from $195 for a private bedroom with shared common area and bathroom in peak season). The rooms are bare-bones but always clean and comfortable, and the amenities are pretty good for a community of this size: You'll have free (but slow) Wi-Fi, cable TV, a refrigerator and microwave, and a full kitchen if you rent a suite or apartment. Suites and apartments also have private bathrooms.

Other amenities include a free shuttle to/from the airport, laundry facilities, and some limited freezer space if you've been fishing.

The inn is next door to the only restaurant in town, **Eddie's Fireplace Inn** (1 Main St., 907/246-3435, typically open daily 8am-8pm but call to confirm hours, burgers $18-20), where you can almost always get foods that come frozen, like hamburgers, french fries, and onion rings, but the availability of anything else is governed by when the last shipment of fresh food came in. Parts of the interior are held together by duct tape, but the food is good given the location (especially the nachos), the servers are friendly, they have beer on tap, and they don't mind if you want to loiter while you're waiting on a flight.

Information and Services

Cell phone service is limited to nonexistent in King Salmon; the only coverage is from the local company GCI, so your phone won't work unless your carrier contracts with them. You can rent a local cell phone from **Alaska Eagle Eye** (907/246-2277), though, or bring a calling card to use on the landline phones. Your best bet for Wi-Fi is the hotel, but be aware that wireless Internet is always slow—and sometimes simply nonexistent—in rural communities like this.

Medical services are very sparse as well: A small village **health clinic** (907/246-3322) is generally open 9am-3pm, and a larger clinic, the **Camai Community Health Center** (2 School Rd., 907/246-6155, open Mon.-Fri. 8am-5pm except 1pm-7pm on Wed., closed noon-1pm for lunch) is in **Naknek,** a 15-mile drive to the west. For medical emergencies, dial 911. The nearest **post office** is also in Naknek (1/2 School Rd., usps.com, Mon.-Fri. 8am-4:30pm, Sat. 9am-11:30am).

Transportation

The only way to King Salmon is by air. During the summer, **Alaska Airlines** (800/252-7522, alaskaair.com) offers one flight a day, while **PenAir** (800/448-4226 or 907/771-2640, penair.com) offers five or six. (Make things easy on yourself by booking either airline through alaskaair.com.) The hotel offers a free shuttle from the airport and is within an easy walk of just about anything you could need, including an ATM, the town visitor center, and the only restaurant.

That said, if you'd like to drive to nearby Naknek you can rent a car from **Alaska Eagle Eye** (907/246-2277); they also rent outdoor gear, including kayaks, mountain bikes, satellite phones, Spot Trackers, snowmachines, and ATVs. They'll deliver your car to you at the airport, so make sure you know your flight information when you call. Some taxi service will be available, although in small communities like this the taxi operators come and go very quickly; ask the staff at the airport or hotel whom you should call.

LAKE CLARK NATIONAL PARK AND PRESERVE

Lake Clark National Park and Preserve sits a short distance north of Katmai National Park, on the far side of Lake Iliamna; it's about 120 miles southwest of Anchorage and 65 miles northwest of Homer. The more than four-million-acre park is most famous for three things: brown bear viewing, fly-fishing, and the cabin of naturalist **Richard Proenneke,** which he built himself using only hand tools. Proenneke then lived in the cabin for 30 years with no modern conveniences. He documented the building process in videos that have been collected in a DVD, *Alone in the Wilderness,* and his journals have been published in book form as *One Man's Wilderness.*

The three top brown bear-viewing opportunities in the park, all best accessed by floatplane, are **Chinitna Bay, Crescent Lake,** and **Silver Salmon Creek;** bear viewing is at its best from June to early September. You may also see black bears at Crescent Lake.

Lodging options in Lake Clark are all privately owned and operated. You can't go wrong with any of them, but **Silver Salmon Creek Lodge** (888/872-5666, silversalmoncreek.com, from $875 pp per night with transport from Homer, or $1,075 pp per night with transport from Anchorage) and **Redoubt Mountain Lodge** (907/776-7516, redoubtbaylodge.com, from $1,370 pp per night including transport from Anchorage, guide service, and equipment) are two of the best.

For a slightly less rustic experience, stay at a lodge or inn in tiny **Port Alsworth** (population 175) on the shore of **Lake Clark.** Two of the best are **General Lodge** (121 Flight Line Rd., 907/781-2323, generallodge.com, from $1,995 for 3 days, all inclusive including airfare from Anchorage) and, if all you want is a room and maybe the use of a kayak, **Alaska's Back Country Inn** (77 Paradise Pl., 907/351-2387, alaskasbackcountryinn.com, from $150, $75 per extra person, tours cost extra). The town also has the park's visitor center, and your lodge can offer water-taxi service to get you to Richard Proenneke's cabin.

The lodges in Lake Clark and Port Alsworth cater as much to fishing, kayaking, and other activities as to bear viewing specifically, and their rates include use of all the necessary gear.

Tulchina Adventures (907/781-3033, tulchinaadventures.com) also rents camping and paddling equipment (or even motorized skiffs), if you're prepared to be entirely self-reliant during backcountry explorations in this remote location, or play it safe in their maintained campground and cabin rentals. For a guided backcountry trip that can include hiking, backpacking, kayaking, and rafting, contact excellent **Alaska Alpine Adventures** (877/525-2577 or 907/351-4193, alaskaalpineadventures.com) out of Anchorage.

Transport to Lake Clark is easy from Anchorage and Homer; in fact, there are dozens of carriers authorized to fly into the park, most of which also offer guided bear-viewing trips, as do all the local lodges. You can see the entire list, organized by which towns they fly out of and whether they land on wheels or floats, in the Plan Your Visit section of nps.gov/lacl; click on Directions.

DILLINGHAM

Just west of the Alaska Peninsula and some 350 miles southwest of Anchorage, the 2,400-person community of Dillingham is the only other large community serving the attractions in the Alaska Peninsula. It sits within easy reach of the spectacular bear viewing in Lake Clark National Park and Katmai, although if you're coming straight from Anchorage you are more likely to make a short stop in King Salmon on your way to Katmai, and may go direct to Lake Clark. Dillingham also serves as the hub for medical services, transportation, freight, and shopping for smaller communities in the area, and if you get weathered out partway through a flight to the tiny, remote **Pribilof Islands**, you may find your plane landing here instead.

This multicultural fishing town—perched at the head of **Bristol Bay,** the world's largest sockeye salmon fishery—packs a few stunning natural attractions of its own, including access to once-in-a-lifetime walrus viewing at Round Island. That said, it's fishing that draws most people here. Dillingham sits at the nexus of the Nushagak and Wood Rivers where they flow into Nushagak Bay, and then into Bristol Bay. It's also a hotbed of alternative fuel development; look for windmills, solar panels, and wood-fired boilers as residents experiment to see which renewable fuel services will work best for them.

The town was originally the site of Yup'ik and Athabascan settlements for many thousands of years. Eventually a permanent town was set up as a trading post by the Russians, then renamed for a U.S. senator. Nowadays, Dillingham's population is bolstered by seasonal workers on the fishing boats and in the canneries that process the fish that in turn power the entire region's economy, which also depends on government work and is often supplemented by a subsistence lifestyle.

Seasonal highs peak in the low 60s during July, while winter highs linger around 20 degrees and lows may dip to almost zero. The weather can be notoriously awful here, so weather delays are almost inevitable; plan as much flexibility into your schedule, preferably at least a few days, so that you don't miss out on your opportunities because of the weather.

Sights and Recreation

CANNERY TOURS

During the summer you can take a free, 1.5-hour tour of the oldest continually operating cannery in Alaska. The **Peter Pan cannery** (1 Denny Way, 907/842-5414) employs more than 300 people to harvest from the Bristol Bay run—the largest sockeye fishery in the world—in a frenzy of activity that starts in June and lasts all the way through July.

SAMUEL K. FOX MUSEUM

The **Samuel K. Fox Museum**—which is housed in the city library (306 D St. West, next to the University of Alaska, 907/842-5610, dillinghamak.us, Mon.-Tues. and Thurs. 10am-5pm, Wed. 10am-6pm, Fri. 11:30am-6:30pm, Sat. 10am-2pm, free, donations appreciated)—offers a beautiful collection of Yup'ik artifacts and art. It's named for a carver, artist, and teacher who was much beloved by the community and his students.

WOOD-TIKCHIK STATE PARK

If you rent a car, you can make the paved 25-mile drive to the tiny community of **Aleknagik,** which is the portal to 1.6-acre **Wood-Tikchik State Park.** The park is named for its network of large, interconnected clear-water lakes, perched at the transition zone between coniferous forest and tundra. All five species of Pacific salmon spawn here, and the freshwater fishing opportunities are stupendous. That said, the park facilities are very limited and extremely rustic; you're essentially on your own, and permits are required for camping and river floats in much of the park. Call the **Aleknagik ranger station** (907/842-2641) for details. If you don't want to drive, you can also charter a private floatplane from Dillingham into the park.

TOGIAK NATIONAL WILDLIFE REFUGE

If you're in a plane-chartering mood, you can also hire a floatplane to take you into massive 4.7-million-acre **Togiak National Wildlife Refuge,** which lies just west of Wood-Tikchik State Park. There is no road access for this park, but you get to see a variety of landscape types, from craggy mountains to "typical" fast-flowing Alaskan rivers, tundra, and marshy wetlands. A wide range of animals inhabit this refuge or at least visit it, from walruses to seals, migratory birds, and herring.

WILDLIFE VIEWING

Wildlife sightings are never guaranteed, but you have very good odds in both **Togiak National Wildlife Refuge** and **Wood-Tikchik State Park.** Look out for large wildlife like moose, caribou, and brown bears; black bears are present but not as common, and tend to stick to wooded areas. Even if you don't go into the parks, keep your eye out for wildlife while you're near the water in Dillingham. You might see belugas (small white whales) and, on rare occasions, orcas chasing salmon, plus lots of waterfowl, including trumpeter swans, geese, terns, bald eagles, and a plethora of migratory songbirds. From Dillingham, you can charter a small plane to visit some of Alaska's best-known bear-viewing sites, **Katmai National Park** and **Lake Clark National Park.** Both parks also offer stupendous fly-fishing opportunities. You can also visit both of these destinations directly from Anchorage.

Food

As in all rural communities, everything in Dillingham has to be either barged or flown out. As a result, restaurants and grocery stores are very pricey, and it's a rare treat to get truly fresh ingredients. If you're going to be here for a couple of days, you can save a lot of money by shipping yourself the ingredients to cook your own food. When you do eat out, it's very common for the restaurants to be open at unpredictable hours. So always check their

Facebook pages (Spruce Kitchen and The Racks have them) or call before heading down.

ITALIAN

Spruce Kitchen (805 Kanakanak Rd., 907/842-4453, Tues.-Fri. 11:30am-7pm), formerly known as the Bristol Bay Eagle, makes giant calzones and really great pizza from scratch. Like everything else in rural communities, they're on the pricey side; expect to pay at least $30 for a large pizza. They're sometimes open at unpredictable hours, so check their Facebook page before heading down.

CHINESE

Locals love **Twin Dragon** (732 Airport Rd., above Grant Aviation in the airport, 907/842-2172) for their great Chinese food; they also serve burgers and fries. Like most restaurants in Dillingham they're sometimes open at unpredictable hours, so call before heading down for lunch or dinner.

BREWPUB

The Racks (3310 Nina Way, 907/843-3789 or 907/842-1825, Tues.-Sat. 5pm-9pm) is a new addition, serving only dinner in a brewpub atmosphere with giant moose racks all over the walls. So far, the reception has been great, especially for the flame-broiled steaks and seafood.

GROCERIES

Locals often purchase produce through **Full Circle Farms** (which is flown in every two weeks) or order by phone from Anchorage or Fairbanks, then have it shipped in by plane. There are two grocery stores in Dillingham: **N&N Market** (10 Main St., 907/842-5283) and the **AC Value Center** (295 Main St., 907/842-5444, acvaluecenter.com). Both stores also offer a selection of clothing and household items. Brace yourself for high prices: It's not unusual for a half gallon of orange juice to cost more than $10.

There is also a bulk store, **Bigfoot LGM Inc** (1307 Nerka Dr., 907/842-4707), that probably won't be of interest unless you're staying for a while.

Accommodations

All lodgings in Dillingham are subject to a 10 percent room tax. Heads up: Even when Wi-Fi is promised, it's often very slow or limited to a very low data cap.

Bristol Bay Inn (104 Main St., 800/764-9704 or 907/842-2240, bristolinn.com, from $210) is the closest thing to a traditional hotel in town. The rooms are clean and basic but reasonably modern (last renovated in 2008), and the inn is within easy walking distance of the museum, restaurants, and grocery stores. It also houses the **Bayside Diner** (summer Mon.-Sat. 7am-8pm, Sun. 9am-7pm). You do get Wi-Fi, but it's slow and limited to just 100 MB per day.

The **Bear Paw Inn** (formerly Thai Inn) (dillinghamlodging.com, from $180) is clean, cozy, and a little faded around the edges, but the owners have invested in some serious renovations. Almost every room has a TV and a full kitchen. You also get free (slow) Wi-Fi and free access to a washer and dryer. If you're traveling with a large group, the same owners also rent out a four-bedroom house starting at $500.

Beaver Creak B&B (866/252-7335 or 907/842-7335, dillinghamalaska.com, from $340 summer, $220 winter) offers three lodging options (the Birch Circle House, the Caribou Cottage, and the Main House) on four acres of wooded property. Amenities include an airport courtesy shuttle, Wi-Fi, cable or satellite TV, laundry machines, and fully equipped kitchens in most units, with breakfast foods and snacks stocked in the rooms. They also offer some limited off-site accommodations for longer stays and rent cars and trucks to visitors.

LODGES

Tikchik Narrows Lodge (907/243-8450, tikchiklodge.com, $8,550/week double occupancy, $8,850/week singles) is located in Wood-Tikchik State Park; the staff will send a floatplane to pick you up from the Dillingham airport. The floatplane transport is included in your lodging rates, along with guided fly-in fishing every day, all the gear you need (except fishing licenses), and all your gourmet meals, which of course go heavy on the seafood. The guides maintain a very low client-to-guide ratio, so you'll always get lots of attention. They might be willing to take you bear viewing in nearby Katmai or Lake Clark National Park—just ask.

Bristol Bay Lodge (907/571-6524 in summer, 907/570-1459 in winter, bristol-bay.com, from $3,780 for 3 nights, $7,180 for 6 nights), on the shore of Lake Iliamna, takes in only eight guests a week. The lodging rates include all meals, lodging, most of the equipment you need, guided fly-in fishing trips every day, and transport from the Iliamna airport, which can be reached only by small plane; if you ask, they might be willing to arrange transport from the Dillingham airport. You'll also need to provide—or purchase—terminal tackle, including flies, lures and lines, and of course your own fishing license. Slow Wi-Fi is available. The lodge also offers side trips for bear viewing in Katmai or Lake Clark, and for touring Richard Proenneke's famous cabin in Lake Clark National Park.

Information and Services

There is very limited cell service in Dillingham; even AT&T, which is pretty good about cellular service in rural Alaska, doesn't offer service there. If you must have cell service, your best bet is to buy a SIM card from the Alaska provider **GCI** (414 2nd Ave., 800/800-4800, Mon.-Fri. 9am-6pm), which does offer service in this area. Just be prepared for limited or no data service.

Wi-Fi is also extremely limited in Dillingham; you can get limited service through most lodgings, but it's often slow and may be limited to as little as 100 MB per night—enough to check email but not to send or download pictures. If you need more Wi-Fi, try stopping by the **Dillingham Public Library** (306 D St. West, next to the University of Alaska, 907/842-5610, dillinghamak.us, Mon.-Tues and Thurs. 10am-5pm, Wed. 10am-6pm, Fri. 11:30am-6:30pm, Sat. 10am-2pm), which also offers limited computer access if you didn't bring your own.

There are a few small, private health clinics in the area. The major hospital, which also serves as the medical services hub for surrounding communities, is the small, 16-bed **Kanakanak Hospital** (6000 Kanakanak Rd., 907/842-5201), which does have a 24-hour emergency room.

There is one **post office** in Dillingham (114 D St., 907/842-5633, Mon.-Fri. 9am-5pm, Sat. 9am-noon).

Transportation

GETTING THERE

Between **Alaska Airlines** (800/252-7522, alaskaair.com) and **PenAir** (800/448-4226 or 907/771-2640, penair.com), there are several flights daily between Dillingham and Anchorage, seven days a week. The flight takes a little more than an hour in one of PenAir's turboprop planes, and tickets typically cost $600-700 for a round-trip, although they can be more expensive. Fly Alaska Airlines when you can; their jets have better instrumentation, which means better odds of still making the flight when weather is marginal.

GETTING AROUND

Dillingham is fairly spread out, and there is no public transportation. Most tour operators will come pick you up at your lodging, but if you plan on doing anything independently, it's a good idea to rent a car from **Beaver Creek Auto Rentals** (3905 Bea Ave., 907/842-7335).

You can also take a taxi. In rural communities like this small providers usually come and go, so it's best to call the local **Chamber of Commerce** (348 D St., 907/842-5115) before your trip to see which cab providers are in business. Unlike in many other rural communities, taxi fares in Dillingham are not regulated by the local government, so always ask the rate for your destination before you get in the cab, and ask if they charge per person or by the trip. Fuel is expensive, so if a local offers to give you a ride somewhere, you should offer to pay for the gas.

TOP EXPERIENCE

★ WALRUS ISLANDS STATE GAME SANCTUARY

Walruses are one of the species being heavily affected by climate change. They depend on sea ice as a resting place or haulout while foraging, and the ice is thinning and drifting away from the relatively shallow areas where they can feed. One of the most obvious effects of this is that large groups of them are now popping up in places where they'd never been seen before.

This causes quite a disruption for everybody in the area, because despite their bulk, walruses tend to be panicky, and something as simple as an airplane passing by can easily provoke the whole herd into a deadly stampede. As a result, when walruses crop up in new places, the flight paths that form the lifeblood of transport in rural Alaska must be adjusted. Because pilots are asked not to overfly the walrus herds, it's surprisingly difficult for visitors to see them.

Now the good news: If you want to see this fragile species in the wild, you can see as many as 14,000 walruses at a time in one place—Walrus Islands State Game Sanctuary, a set of seven rugged, remote islands in northern Bristol Bay, 65 miles west and slightly south of 2,400-person Dillingham. To get there, charter a plane or boat from Dillingham. The plane trip is usually more pleasant, because Bristol Bay's waters can be rough in any season.

You typically do not need a permit if you're coming to the game sanctuary for fishing, hiking, general camping, or wildlife watching. If you want to see the walruses, though, you need to get to Round Island; that requires a permit. The only facility is a rough campground, and you'll be far away from any medical facilities in weather that tends to be extreme. Nobody's going to wait on you—you're expected to be fully self-sufficient.

If that rugged, once-in-a-lifetime opportunity sounds like fun to you, you can apply for one of the coveted Round Island permits beginning on September 1 of the preceding year. Applications can be submitted online through the Round Island section of adfg.alaska.gov. Only 252 permits are issued on a first-come, first-served basis, separated out into 21 five-day periods, ranging from early May to mid-August; each person in your group must apply individually and submit a

Walrus Islands State Game Sanctuary

$50 check or money order for the permit. If your desired time periods are not available, your payment will be returned to you.

See **adfg.alaska.gov** for more permitting information, and call the **Dillingham Chamber of Commerce** (907/842-5115) to see which local providers might be able to provide transport out to the islands; always confirm transport availability before you go.

The Aleutian Islands

Formed some 40 million years ago by volcanic activity, Alaska's Aleutian Islands stretch 1,250 miles south and west from the mainland. Sea and air are only two ways to visit these tiny, remote islands. The island best suited to tourism, with the best infrastructure and services, is tiny Unalaska, the point farthest west on the Alaska Marine Highway System's twice-monthly summer ferry run from Homer to Kodiak and along the Aleutians.

★ UNALASKA/ DUTCH HARBOR

If you're a diehard angler, dedicated birder, or World War II buff, Unalaska is a must-visit. This remote village, 800 miles southwest of Anchorage, was inhabited for at least 10,000 years by the Unungan (Aleut) people before Russian fur traders arrived in the 18th century.

For 18 years, this has been the nation's number one port for seafood landings by weight, and the number one or two port for landings in terms of dollar value. This is the only community in the Aleutian Islands with the capacity to provide full support services to a commercial fishing fleet, from repair and maintenance to gear replacement, freight forwarding, vessel haulouts, and welding, all based out of the only year-round, ice-free, deep draft port in this part of the state.

In a typical year the Unalaska docks bring in more than 700 million pounds of fish and crab; valuable species that form the base of this economy include pollock, Pacific cod, halibut, sablefish, sole, rockfish, herring, salmon, and, of course, crab; after all, Dutch Harbor is the headquarters for some very famous crabbing boats that you may recognize from the Discovery Channel's show *Deadliest Catch*.

Despite those impressive numbers and résumé, when you book your tickets and accommodations, keep in mind that you're traveling to one of the most remote communities in the world. Services are limited, food is pricey, and high-tech connectivity is hard to get.

The town's population is currently about 4,750 people. The weather is cool, breezy, often foggy or rainy, and prone to changing quickly; bring layers and waterproof boots. July and August are prime months for visiting, although average temperatures typically remain in the 50s—and may even reach into the 60s—from June through September. Wintertime highs are typically in the high 30s.

Sights and Recreation

WORLD WAR II VISITOR CENTER AND HISTORIC AREA

The **Aleutian World War II Visitor Center and Historic Area** (right next to the airport, 907/581-9944, nps.gov/aleu) explores the complicated history of the World War II campaign in the Aleutian Islands, from Japanese attacks on Dutch Harbor to their occupation of Attu and Kiska and the ill-advised American decision to evacuate almost 900 Unungan Native people from their villages and send them to makeshift camps in Southeast Alaska, where harsh living conditions resulted in many deaths.

The name of this facility is a little unfortunate. Because it's the first thing you see

Unalaska/Dutch Harbor

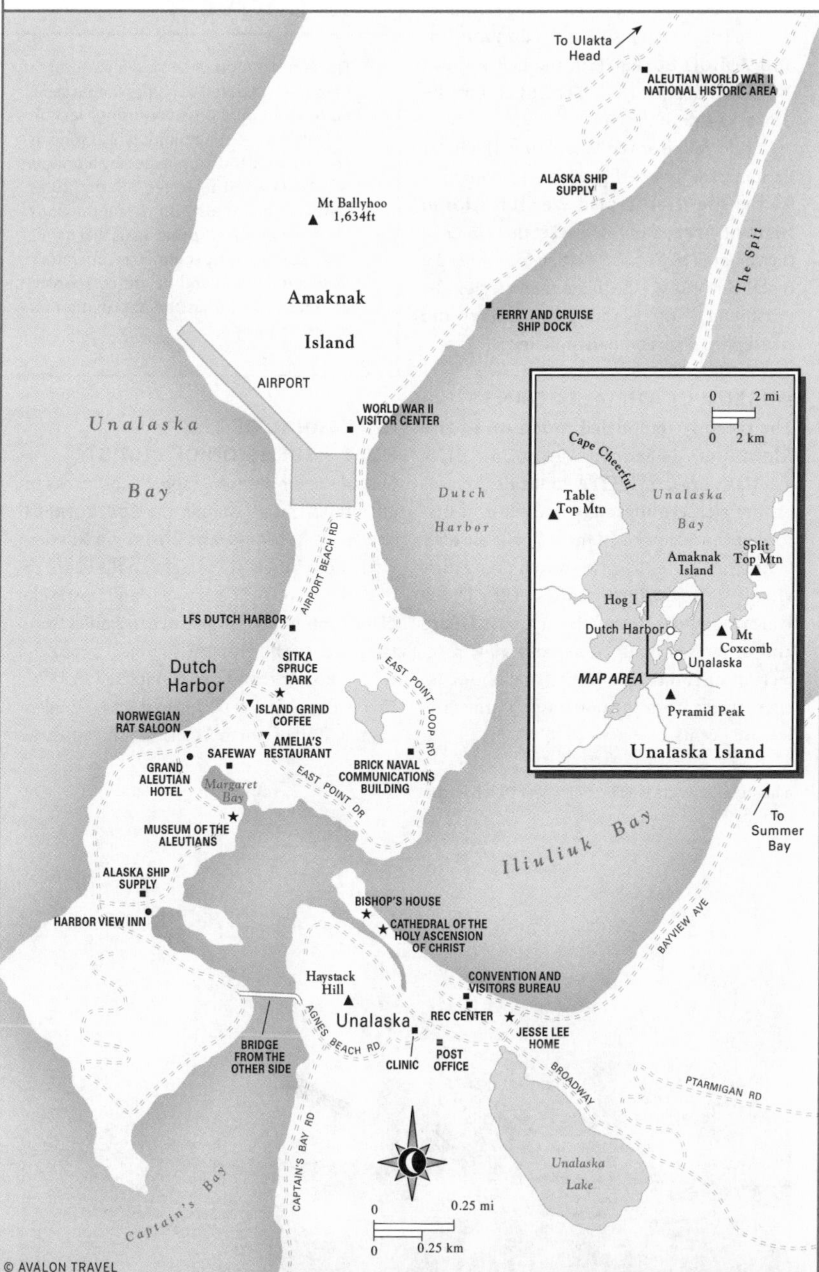

when you get off the plane, visitors often assume that it's a general visitor center, but it's really a museum. The closest thing Unalaska has to a true visitor center is the **Convention and Visitors Bureau** (5th and E. Broadway, 907/581-2612 or 877/581-2612) on the Unalaska side of the city.

While you're at the World War II Visitor Center, pick up a self-guided tour pamphlet for the **Aleutian World War II National Historic Area,** a 134-acre tract that contains the remains of Fort Schwatka. You'll need a rental car or taxi ride to get there: It's on the north end of the island, past the ferry and cruise ship docks on Ballyhoo Road.

MUSEUM OF THE ALEUTIANS

The recently remodeled **Museum of the Aleutians** (314 Salmon Way, 907/581-5150, aleutians.org), or MOTA to locals, focuses on the rich ethnography and natural history of the Aleutian Islands. You'll see artifacts from more than two dozen prehistoric village sites within two miles of the Dutch Harbor airport, learn about Coast Guard and other sea operations, and view a selection of rotating exhibits that showcase everything from local art and artifacts to lecture events.

Which Name Is Correct?

The combination of Unalaska and Dutch Harbor—two different names for the same place—can be a little confusing. Technically the whole community, which spreads across two islands connected by a bridge, is Unalaska, but it's often referred to as Dutch Harbor or just "Dutch" for the body of water just offshore that bears that name. Interestingly, most commercial operators, including airlines and freight companies, use Dutch Harbor as the designation for the community.

CATHEDRAL OF THE HOLY ASCENSION OF CHRIST

One of the most photographed landmarks in all of the Aleutian Islands, the **Cathedral of the Holy Ascension of Christ** is a Russian Orthodox church. It sits right on the beach of Iliuliuk Bay, on the Unalaska Island (east) side of the community. It's almost three miles from the hotel to the church, so you'll probably want a taxi or rental car. Completed in 1896, this is the oldest cruciform-style Orthodox church in all of North America. The cathedral

a humpback whale waving hello near Dutch Harbor

may be open for viewing when cruise ships are in port, but it's not guaranteed. Visitors are welcome to attend services, held on Saturday at 6:30pm and Sunday at 10am. Attendees are expected to stand, and services are conducted in a mix of English, Unangam Tunuu (Aleut), and Old Church Slavonic.

HIKING

Unalaska's rolling, treeless landscape is unlike almost anything else you'll see in the world. There are no bears, so you can feel perfectly comfortable wandering the hills looking for World War II artifacts—Quonset huts, barracks, and old gun emplacements—scattered across the landscape. There are also 38 miles of back roads and ancient Unungan trails you can explore with a rented vehicle.

Most of the land around the village is owned by the local Native corporation, **Ounalashka** (400 Salmon Way, 907/581-1276, ounalashka.com). Visit their headquarters for information on hiking trails and to purchase a land-use permit, which you need for any recreational purpose, including hiking or camping. Permits cost $6 per person per day or $10 per family; weekly permits are $15 per person or $20 per family.

Keep in mind that you'll be hiking in a remote area where fog, wind, and rain can all set in suddenly and stay for days. Most trails are unmaintained and unmarked, and cell service is extremely limited. It's a very good idea to take some sort of emergency beacon with you, just in case; Spot beacons (findmespot.com) work well here.

WILDLIFE VIEWING

There are no bears in Unalaska, but you might see a herd of feral horses that run wild—they can get pretty pushy if they think you might have food. During the fall, keep an eye out for salmon running in Iliuliuk Creek, which passes right through town. If you get tired of walking, sit down on one of the benches near the harbor to watch whales feeding in the bay or fishing and crabbing vessels coming and going. You might just recognize a few famous craft from the Discovery Channel TV show *Deadliest Catch*.

BIRDING TOURS

The birding is spectacular too; Dutch Harbor's sheltered waters host myriad overwintering waterfowl, and blustery winds often bring Asian birds to the islands during migration season. For the best birding trip in town, contact **Suzi Golodoff** (907/581-1359 or sgolodoff@gmail.com), a longtime birder

Iliuliuk Bay seen over the Russian Orthodox cathedral

An Unalaska bald eagle makes off with its lunch.

who's lived in Dutch Harbor for more than 40 years.

EXTRA MILE TOURS

Bobbie Lekanoff with **Extra Mile Tours** (907/581-1859, unalaskadutchharbortour.com) offers tours that encompass everything from local culture to World War II history, hiking, birds, and wildflowers. Prices start at $50 per person for a two-hour tour, or $90 per person for a four-hour tour, with discounts for seniors and children 12 and under. Cruise passengers can request a special rate that includes stops at both local museums and the Russian Orthodox church, if it happens to be open.

FISHING

If you're an angler, there is no better place for fishing than the wild, untamed waters of the Bering Sea. But don't worry: You won't be braving the ocean *Deadliest Catch* style, as long as you stick to the calm waters near Dutch Harbor's shores. Common species for sportfishing include **salmon, halibut,** and **cod;** you can get a fishing license and check local regulations at adfg.alaska.gov.

The real challenge is finding a charter that can take you out on the water. Tourism in this area fluctuates enough that people rarely pursue charters as their sole source of income. Instead, they operate tours on the side and may not choose to offer them every year. Call the **Unalaska/Dutch Harbor Convention and Visitors Bureau** (907/581-2612 or 877/581-2612; the toll-free number may not always work) to see who's offering fishing and sightseeing charters during your visit.

Food

CAFÉS

Margaret Bay Cafe (907/581-7122, Mon.-Sat. 7am-3pm, express lunch buffet 11:30am-1:30pm, breakfast $15, lunch $18), one of several restaurants in the Grand Aleutian hotel, offers breakfast and lunch fare along with specialty drinks, including espresso.

If all you want is coffee, head to **Island Grind Coffee** (2141 Airport Beach Rd., 907/581-3054, Mon.-Sat. 6:30am-8pm, Sun. 8am-8pm), where you can get espresso and other specialty drinks.

MEXICAN

Like most restaurants in rural Alaska, **Amelia's Restaurant** (907/581-2800, E.

Point Dr. and Airport Beach Rd.) serves a little bit of everything, including sandwiches, soups, and burgers. Their specialty, however, is Mexican food, and it's excellent, especially given the setting. Breakfast is good, too, and the portions are generous. Keep an eye out for captains and crew from *Deadliest Catch* refueling their bodies when they're in town.

SEAFOOD

The **Chart Room** (498 Salmon Way, 907/581-7120, Mon.-Sat. 6pm-11pm, Sun. 10am-2pm and 6-9:30pm, $35-40) in the Grand Aleutian hotel is the closest you'll get to fine dining in Unalaska. If you're looking for a romantic night out, this is it. The food is a little pricey, as is everything in a community this remote, but the seafood is fabulous (as are the views), and the all-you-can-eat seafood buffet on Wednesday night is a can't-miss.

BARS

The **Norwegian Rat Saloon** (1906 Airport Beach Rd., 907/581-4455, Mon.-Sat. 11am-2am, Sun. noon-10pm) is a sports bar that also serves the best pub grub and beer in town. The pizza is expensive but also excellent, tourists especially love the crab plate (about $30), and they do great fish-and-chips too. Service can be very slow and Wi-Fi nonexistent when a cruise ship is in town, so kick back and play a game of pool or enjoy the views over the beach from the back deck.

For the town's most refined lounge experience, head to the **Cape Cheerful Lounge** (498 Salmon Way, 907/581-7130, Mon.-Sat. 3pm-midnight, Sun. noon-10pm, $20), also located in the Grand Aleutian hotel. Cozy up to the fireplace and flat-panel TVs or enjoy their open mic nights and July-August Friday night barbecues.

GROCERIES AND FISH

Safeway (2029 Airport Beach Rd., 907/581-4040, safeway.com, daily 7am-11pm) offers groceries, produce, baked goods, and a hot-and-cold deli. Brace yourself for extremely high prices and "gently aged" produce. If you're going to be here for any stretch of time, you can save a lot of money by shipping yourself groceries or bringing them as luggage.

Alaska Ship Supply (487 Salmon Way, 907/581-1284, alaskashipsupply.com, daily 7am-10pm) offers groceries, produce, espresso, liquor, beer and wine, plus other products, including hardware and clothing. You can buy phone cards if you need to use a landline to communicate with the outside world.

If you want to take fish back with you or send it to loved ones, you can buy freshly caught seafood from **Aleutian Fresh Seafoods** (on Airport Beach Rd. south of the airport, 877/581-1864 or 907/581-1864, aleutianfreshseafood.com), either in person or online.

Shopping

For authentic Unungan artwork, make an appointment with **Gert Svarny** (907/581-1597 or Samandi@arctic.net); he works in bone, ivory, baleen, wood, and stone.

If you need serious foul weather gear, seasonal outdoor gear, and some great Bering Sea-themed logowear, head to **LFS Marine Supplies** (2315 Airport Beach Rd., 907/581-2178, lfsmarineoutdoor.com, Mon.-Sat. 8am-8pm, Sun. 8am-6pm).

Alaska Ship Supply (487 Salmon Way, 907/581-1284, alaskashipsupply.com, daily 7am-10pm) also functions as a general outfitter, with hardware, clothing, and health and beauty products in addition to its groceries, espresso, and alcohol. You can also buy phone cards.

For local art, jewelry, and other charming gifts, visit **Carolyn Reed Art & Framing Boutique** (179 Gilman Rd., 2nd floor of the Dutch Harbor Mall, 907/359-4679, Wed.-Sat., noon-6pm).

Accommodations

The only hotel in town, **The Grand Aleutian** (498 Salmon Way, 907/581-3844, grandaleutian.com) offers more than a hundred rooms and suites, with complimentary airport shuttle and a half dozen restaurants either inside the hotel or within walking distance. The gift shop is very good, but be ready to pay extra for Wi-Fi access.

The Grand Aleutian also offers economy rooms (and a free shuttle service) at their sister property, the nearby unstaffed, bare-bones **Harbor View Inn** (185 Gilman Rd.), which most travelers agree is nothing but a place to lay your head at night. If you go that route, get a room overlooking the water—it'll be quieter.

If you're staying longer—which you absolutely should, to take in the island's natural beauty—consider booking at **Windy Island Bungalows** (907/359-5722), which offers weekly and month rates in two-bedroom rentals.

Information and Services

Most of the land on Unalaska, Amaknak, and Sedanka Islands is privately owned by the Ounalashka Corporation. All recreational uses, including hiking or camping, require a permit in advance, which can be obtained from **Ounalashka Corporation** (400 Salmon Way, 907/581-1276, ounalashka.com).

You'll find **public bathrooms** in most of Unalaska's public buildings, including the Aleutian World War II Visitor Center, the Museum of the Aleutians, the grocery stores, the community recreation center, and down by the Carl E. Moses Boat Harbor (very nice bathrooms!), on the south end of Amaknak Island (the Dutch Harbor side).

The **community recreation center** (5th and E. Broadway, 907/581-1251) is where you can access a swimming pool, weight room, indoor track, racquetball, yoga, and other fitness and health needs. There's also a small medical clinic, **Iliuliuk Family and Health Services** (34 Lavalle Ct., 907/581-1202, after hours 907/581-1233, 911 for emergencies, ifhs.org).

You'll find **ATMs** at the airport, in the hotel, at Harbor View Bar & Grill (Unisea complex on Gilman Rd., 907/581-7246, Mon.-Thurs. 11:30am-2pm, Fri.-Sat. 11:30am-3am, Sun. noon-10pm), and of course at **KeyBank** (487 Salmon Way, 907/581-1300, Mon.-Fri. 9:30am-5:30pm).

Expect **cell service** to be very limited here; AT&T and GCI users may get some reception, but it's limited and sporadic at best, with no data—only basic phone service. If you absolutely must have a data connection, you can purchase 1 G data cards to be used at hot spots around town from **OptimERA** (123 Loop Rd., 907/359-1121, optimera-wifi.com)—it's slow and expensive, but the best Internet you can possibly get out here. If it's not a data emergency, just go to the **Unalaska Public Library** (64 Eleanor Dr., 907/581-5060, Mon.-Fri. 10am-9pm, Sat.-Sun. noon-6pm) for free Wi-Fi and computer workstations.

There are two **post offices,** one in the west side of the city, near the hotel and most restaurants (1745 Airport Beach Rd., 800/275-8777, Mon.-Fri. 9am-12:30pm and 1:30pm-5pm, Sat. 1pm-5pm), and the other across the bridge on the east side of the city (82 Airport Beach Rd., 800/275-8777, Mon.-Fri. 9am-11:30am and 12:30pm-5pm, Sat. 9am-1pm).

Transportation

GETTING THERE

Weather allowing, Unalaska receives at least two flights daily from **PenAir** (800/448-4226 or 907/771-2640, penair.com); you can book through **Alaska Airlines** (800/252-7522, alaskaair.com) and use frequent flier miles if you have them; a one-way in-state ticket is only 7,500 miles. It's always possible that your checked baggage will be delayed due to weight and balance limits on the plane, so make sure you pack all the necessities for a couple of days, including medication and extra clothing, in your carry-on.

The **Alaska Marine Highway System**'s seagoing ferry, the *Tustumena* (800/642-0066, ferryalaska.com), travels down the Aleutian Chain from Kodiak to Unalaska/Dutch Harbor twice a month from late April to early October; it takes about four days to make the trip, with very short stops in Chignik, Sand Point, King Cove, Cold Bay, False Pass, and Akutan along the way; you won't have time to get off, unless you want to catch a plane or wait two weeks for another ferry to go by. Still, this is one of the most glorious (and inexpensive) sightseeing cruises you'll ever take.

The only other way to reach Dutch Harbor is on a cruise ship or private yacht. Short- and long-term moorage is available for private vessels up to 200 feet in length. Cruise visits to this ice-free, deep-draft port are slowly increasing; in 2016 they had 10 ships visit, with at least a dozen sailings confirmed for 2017 before the year was out. If you're coming on a cruise ship, remember that you'll get the best weather June-August or early September; by October, the weather is starting to get windy and unpleasant.

GETTING AROUND

The Dutch Harbor airport is about a mile away from the hotel, with the ferry deck about a mile beyond that. If you're not renting a car, all of the services you'll need are on the Dutch Harbor side of the city (on Amaknak Island), within easy walking distance of the hotel.

If you want to extend your reach and go hiking, camping, or sightseeing on your own, there are two car rental companies: **BC Vehicle Rental** (105 Airport Beach Rd., 907/581-6777, checker@arctic.net), which also offers cellular phone rentals, and **North Port Rentals** (907/581-3880, northportrentals.net). Both are located at the airport and offer 24/7 service, with free delivery and pickup. There are also quite a few taxi services in town, although there is a fair bit of turnover; your best bet is to get taxi numbers at the airport or from the hotel.

The Pribilof Islands

The tiny, isolated **Pribilof Islands** have been called the Galapagos of the North for their remote location in the middle of the Bering Sea, 300 miles off Alaska's west coast, and their rich profusion of wildlife, much of which is difficult—if not impossible—to view anywhere else. Between them, the two inhabited islands in this tiny cluster contain many tens of thousands of fur seals, millions of seabirds, and approximately 600 people, many of them Alaska Native.

The human history of these islands is a hard story: Some of the Aleut people of the Aleutian and Commander Islands were forcibly relocated here by Russian fur traders through the early 1800s, used as slave labor to harvest the fur seals that come here every summer to breed. Commercial harvests ended in the early 1980s, and now the only harvests are small subsistence takes. The communities are driven primarily by the government sector, fishing and crabbing (you may recognize some boats from the Discovery Channel's wildly successful show, *Deadliest Catch*), and some tourism.

The weather is cool, windy, and frequently foggy, with average temperatures ranging from about 20 degrees in winter to 50 degrees during the summer, which is also filled with the growling barks and groans of fur seals in their shoreside rookeries. Heavy fog is also very common during the summer; it can come in suddenly and last for days, causing unpredictable travel delays. You'll have to pay for the hotel room if you get weathered in, so trip insurance is a must. When you're packing, take the time to review information (see *Essentials*) on how to layer for wet and windy weather, and bring XtraTuffs or other similar calf-length rubber boots; it's the only way your feet will stay dry out on the tundra.

This is not the place to bring your pets. If you're traveling with a dog, you'll do well to board him or her at a kennel in Anchorage or some other major city during this leg of your trip.

★ ST. PAUL ISLAND

St. Paul is the name of both an island in the Pribilofs and its small village, which contains some 400 people. It contains the world's largest population of the rare northern fur seal and a staggering number of seabirds (there are even more on neighboring St. George) but has extremely limited infrastructure and services for visitors.

That doesn't mean you'll be unhappy here—it just means that, as in all small, remote Alaska communities, you need to approach the trip with realistic expectations. This is one case where, no matter how independent you are, it's best to visit with a tour company; I recommend **St. Paul Island Tours** (877/424-5637, alaskabirding.com), which is owned by the local Alaska Native corporation, TDX. Rates start at $2,329 for three days/two nights, which includes round-trip airfare from Anchorage (which can easily cost $1,000 on its own), ground transportation, and guide and sightseeing services. There is only one hotel, one restaurant, and one bus to take you around, so even if you book through a more expensive third-party tour operator, you're still going to get the same experience.

Sights and Recreation

St. Paul is in and of itself a can't-miss attraction for its remoteness and incredible biodiversity of animals. That said, there are a few catches. The island is so remote that there's only one hotel, one place to eat, and one tour company that shuttles everybody around (even if you book through another company, you'll end up on the same bus). The weather is also notoriously foggy, which means there's always a chance of being weathered in—or out—for a day or more as you make your way to and from the island. So if you must have a clockwork schedule or lots of creature comforts, this island—and the Pribilofs in general—really aren't for you.

But roughing it in Alaska comes with many perks of the natural sort. The adventurous souls who brave a trip to St. Paul will be rewarded with visits to the world's largest rookeries of **northern fur seals**—for most people, the only chance to see this enormous animal, whose pelt was once one of the most prized commodities in the state. (To view the seals, you must secure a permit from the tribal office.)

St. Paul also has sheer cliffs teeming with some of the world's largest seabird colonies

The roads on St. Paul Island are made of crushed volcanic rock.

(neighboring St. George has even more seabirds but fewer seals), not to mention the drama of waves booming at their feet. If you're a fan of migratory songbirds instead, this is the place to catch Asian migrants that were blown off-course by the high winds that haunt this region almost as much as the fog. The village is picturesque, too, a short arc of weather-beaten A-frame houses along the shore, and the island's stretches of black-sand beach would be the nicest in the state if only it weren't a little on the chilly side, even in the summer.

St. Paul's treeless landscape, dramatic cliffs, and relatively gentle, tundra-clad hills also make for beautiful walking—as long as it's clear out. Pay attention to what the locals say and don't go walking in the fog, which can come in very quickly and stay for days. It's all too easy to accidentally wander too close to one of those cliff edges, which can crumble underfoot even on clear days.

For a real sightseeing treat, rent a car or truck from one of the locals (there are no formal car rental services, but the hotel front desk can help you connect with someone for an informal rental) and drive the scant miles of roadway, lined with crushed volcanic rock, that lead to the corners of the island. You'll never see a more remote, windswept, and achingly beautiful place in your life.

WILDLIFE VIEWING

Fur seal viewing is best from early June, when the smaller females arrive to join the males already on shore, through September. The bulls aggressively defend their harems as the mothers give birth in late spring; the pups play ashore while the mothers go into the water to feed. Some 70 percent of the world's population of northern fur seals breeds in these islands.

You can view the seals from either of two designated blinds, but first you need a permit from the **tribal office** (2050 Venia Minor Rd., 907/546-3200, Mon.-Fri. 8am-5pm) and also a car—yet another reason it's much easier just to go with the tour.

When you're near seals, stick to the designated boardwalks and walkways. The males can easily weigh up to 600 pounds and may look unwieldy, but they're astonishingly fast on land, very territorial, sometimes come farther inland than expected, and can easily take your arm off with their sharp teeth. Most longtime residents have

Most of the world's northern fur seals come to the Pribilof Islands to raise their young.

at least one story about being chased by a fur seal.

You may also see harbor seals, Steller sea lions, orcas, and even gray whales in the area, although ironically, everything except the rare gray whale is easier to see elsewhere in Alaska. On land, keep your eyes peeled for blue foxes, a subspecies of Arctic fox that appears a dark, slate gray, and keep your car windows rolled up; if you don't, they seem to take a perverse delight in urinating in your vehicle. Finally, about 1,000 reindeer—domesticated caribou introduced by the Russians in 1911—roam freely across the island.

BIRD-WATCHING

Birds that are very hard to find anywhere else are absurdly common here. You can expect to see seabirds like tufted and horned puffins, kittiwakes, cormorants, and crested and least auklets, but the biggest draw is Asian "vagrants" that are blown off-course during their migration, along with birds blown here from the Alaskan mainland. A number of birds on the North American birding checklists were first seen in St. Paul.

Food

There is only one restaurant—such as it is—on the island: the **Trident Seafoods cafeteria** in the fish processing plant, which is right next to town. The good news is that it offers surprisingly good salads and even fresh fruit at decent prices for rural Alaska. The bad news is that the cafeteria is on the upper floor of the plant, it isn't wheelchair accessible, and meals are only available in limited, sometimes unpredictable time windows. It also shuts down from October to May in order to feed the cannery workers during fishing season. Talk to the locals at the hotel or **St. Paul Island Tours** (877/424-5637, alaskabirding.com); they'll be able to tell you when the cafeteria is open and whether you'll need to call ahead for reservations.

GROCERIES

You can shop for food in the **AC Value Center** (134 Tolstoi Blvd); there's also an ATM. However, prices are very expensive, and fresh produce, which must be flown in, is fairly rare. If you're going to be here for any period of time, you can save a lot of money by shipping groceries to yourself.

Accommodations

There is just one hotel in St. Paul, the thin-walled but spotless **King Eider Hotel** (at

one of many Arctic foxes on St. Paul Island in the Pribilofs

Birding Heaven

The Pribilofs' remote location and the rich sea life in the Bering Sea make the islands the perfect haven for seabirds; the steep, dramatic cliffs hold the largest seabird colonies in the world. The resident blue foxes—a color phase of the Arctic fox—scavenger seabird eggs and young, but the steep cliffs help protect against this predation.

The islands' location also makes them perfect for spotting Asian/Siberian vagrants blown off their migratory course by the winds. There've been almost 250 distinct species sighted on this island, a number of them first-time sightings in North America. This one-of-a-kind habitat is protected as part of the 3.4-million-acre **Alaska Maritime National Wildlife Refuge,** which also includes land in the Aleutian Islands and just off the Chukchi Sea in the high Arctic.

You may be surprised to see that there are no dogs at all on either of the populated Pribilof Islands. This is to protect the seabirds, although some residents do keep cats in their homes (but they're never allowed outside). Currently, the biggest threat to the island's seabirds is the risk of rats from a visiting ship.

the airport, 907/546-2477, $125 per person per day). Note that the prices are per person, so sharing a room doesn't actually save you money. The accommodations are spartan at best—just a bed—with shared bathrooms and shower stalls down the hall, and a little common area with a microwave, refrigerator, and coffeepot.

The hotel sometimes fills up when large tour groups are in town or travelers are held up because planes can't make it through the fog, so always make—and confirm—reservations before you arrive. Laundry is free and there's limited, unreliable Wi-Fi; if you're lucky, you might be able to stream radio.

The hotel presents a little bit of a conundrum: It's three miles from town, so unless you've hired St. Paul Tours, which will arrange for you to eat, you may have to pay $30 round-trip for a cab. The cabs in St. Paul are operated by locals and aren't always the most reliable. You can also rent duplex units that are actually in the village, though, for the same price ($125 per person per day).

Information and Services

There is limited GCI **cell service** here. (GCI is a local provider; don't assume that your national or international provider will be able to use their towers.) If you want to be sure to stay connected with the outside world during your stay, take a prepaid phone card to use on the shared landline phone in the hotel.

Internet access is sometimes available, but it's very slow and may be data limited.

There is a small **Community Health Center** (1000 Polivenia Turnpike, 907/546-8300) and a volunteer EMT squad; call 911 in an emergency.

Transportation

GETTING THERE

St. Paul is served by **PenAir** (800/448-4226 or 907/771-2640, penair.com) turboprop planes from Anchorage, offering at least three flights per week. The tickets usually cost $800-1,100 round-trip, take about four hours, and book up fast. The planes travel under visual flight rules only, so weather delays and cancellations are not unusual; be sure to purchase travel insurance that will cover part or all of the hotel cost if you're required to stay extra nights. The only other way to reach the island is by small cruise liner.

GETTING AROUND

The only really convenient way to get around the island is with the help of the **St. Paul Island Tours** (877/424-5637, alaskabirding.com) tour bus; they'll shuttle you to seal blinds and wildlife-viewing areas, and also arrange for you to get to and from the cafeteria for meals. If you want to travel independently, contact the **tribal office** (2050 Venia Minor Rd., 907/546-3200, Mon.-Fri. 8am-5pm) and ask them to connect you with a local who's willing to rent you their car. You can also take a cab, but those are also operated by private individuals; they're expensive, and they aren't always reliable.

ST. GEORGE ISLAND

There is a second, smaller community on neighboring St. George Island, which has a population of about 150 people and more spectacular bird cliffs than St. Paul, some of them rising more than 1,000 feet above the booming sea. Again, there's just one place to stay: the **Aikow Inn** (907/859-2255, tanaq.com/travel-accommodations, $220), which can house up to 18 guests in 10 basic rooms.

There are six fur seal rookeries within easy reach (you'll be able to hear the seals from your hotel room), although they're not as large as those on St. Paul; you may be able to hire a local to guide you or you can explore on your own. Talk to the hotel about meals when you make your reservations; it's usually best to bring your own food.

The Arctic

Look for ★ to find recommended sights, activities, dining, and lodging.

Highlights

★ **Visit the Iditarod Finish:** Every March, Nome booms with visitors who come to watch mushers and their dogs complete the iconic 1,000-mile dogsled race (page 364).

★ **Bird-watching:** Migratory birds flock to this region from all seven continents, mating and raising their young in the endless bounty of the Arctic summer (page 366).

★ **Iñupiat Heritage Center:** Equal parts museum, visitor center, and cultural conduit, this is the best possible introduction to Iñupiat cultural values and history (page 375).

★ **Polar Bear Tours:** Although you can see polar bears in Barrow, the tiny village of Kaktovik offers your best chance of seeing North America's largest land predator (page 377).

★ **The Dalton Highway/Haul Road:** This road's 414 miles of rugged, unpaved adventure will take you past the Arctic Circle and through some of the state's most beautiful, remote scenery—and highest concentrations of mosquitoes (page 381).

★ **Arctic National Wildlife Refuge:** This refuge encompasses more than 19 million acres of hotly contested, resource-rich wilderness, home to one of the last fully intact ecosystems in the world (page 384).

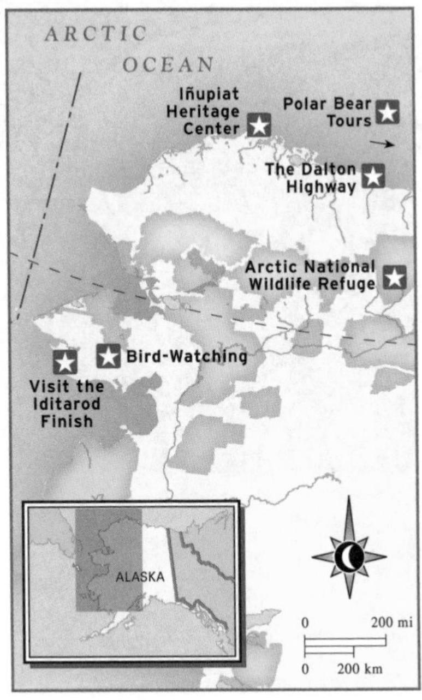

Most of what you've heard about Alaska's Arctic regions is true.

The sun really does shine all day from mid-May to early August, and it never makes it over the horizon from mid-November to mid-January, although there's still a period of twilight and the moon provides a surprising amount of light when full. The Arctic is populated by far more caribou than people, and the isolation of its small communities has helped preserve deep roots in traditional Iñupiat culture.

The only viable way of visiting these isolated communities is by air; you can take a jet or large turboprop plane to hub communities like Nome or Barrow. Smaller six- or eight-passenger commuter planes and tiny bush planes offer service from those hubs to outlying villages.

During your flight you may pass over or through the Interior's rugged mountains, particularly the Brooks Range, which stretches across Alaska like the arc of a smiley face, roughly parallel with the Arctic Circle. But Alaska isn't all mountains, and your view from the air will give you a new perspective on the millions of acres of spruce forest, endless marshes, boreal forest, and braided, gravel-clad rivers that make up the rest of the land.

The Arctic is also home to some of the last remaining intact ecosystems in the world, and you may see some familiar avian faces while you're there; migrating birds come from every continent of the world to take advantage of the endless summer light.

Arctic Alaska's remoteness presents some logistical challenges for visitors: Prices for gas and groceries are often outrageous, lodgings tend to be spartan but pricey, and Wi-Fi and cell service are often spotty at best. And yet those are small hurdles indeed when compared to the opportunity to visit communities where the land, the weather, and the wildlife all determine life's rhythm. There simply aren't many places like this left on earth.

Even though the vehicles, clothes, and weather-battered homes may look familiar to city dwellers, subsistence living is still an important way of life in the Arctic, and Alaska Native traditions run deep, as does the harm caused by forced assimilation. However, those same traditions are a point of well-justified pride in these communities,

Previous: the Arctic Divide, near the village of Anaktuvuk Pass; musk oxen in Cape Krusenstern National Monument. **Above:** Trans-Alaska Pipeline along Dalton highway to Pudhoe Bay.

Western and Arctic Alaska

and if you approach your visit with a sincere, open interest in learning about the cultures you visit—and a willingness to look beneath the superficial similarities and actually *see* those cultures—you will be warmly welcomed.

PLANNING YOUR TIME

Traveling in Arctic Alaska is a constant balancing act. Weather can impact—or even completely cancel—travel plans, even during the summer, so it's good to leave at least a day or two of flex time in your schedule. However, because communities are small and isolated, there's usually not much to do once you've exhausted local attractions.

Services and amenities are very limited in the smallest villages—visitors often end up sleeping on the floor of the school gym—so always coordinate and confirm your plans well in advance. In hub communities, you can look forward to modern plumbing, electricity, and vehicles. Wi-Fi and cell service are there, but often spotty.

With that said, traveling to a remote community off the road system is an eye-opening experience that everybody should do at least once. Bring your best, most flexible travel attitude and an interest in learning about the Alaska Native culture that runs deep here, and you'll have a fabulous time. Three or four days is plenty for the independent traveler in a single hub community, and most guided tours that focus on a single place or activity run 2-4 days.

Never run your budget out to the ultimate limit while in "the bush," because both food and lodging are very expensive, and you'll have to pay for more of both if you get weathered in. Plan to spend about $200 per night on lodging, and be prepared to pay $7-8 for a loaf of bread in the grocery store and $15 or more for a gallon of orange juice in some communities. Restaurant prices are correspondingly high; it's not unheard of to pay $60 or more for a large pizza and a few soft drinks. If you're staying for any length of time, you can save a *lot* of money by booking lodgings with a kitchenette and mailing groceries to yourself in advance.

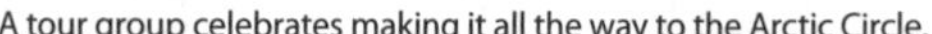

A tour group celebrates making it all the way to the Arctic Circle.

Nome

If you take only one trip off the main road system, make it a visit to Nome, the most cosmopolitan of Alaska's remote regional hubs. Although the town's biggest moment comes every March when it serves as the finish line for the 1,000-mile Iditarod Sled Dog Race (it also serves as halfway point for the Iron Dog snowmachine race in February), this is a fascinating place to visit at any time, especially during the summer. Like many rural Alaska communities, this is a particularly heavenly destination for migratory birds and the people who love watching them, and if you stay on Front Street, the Bering Sea will be right outside your door.

Although Nome isn't actually above the Arctic Circle—it's at roughly the same latitude as Fairbanks—it still gets near-endless sunlight from mid-May to late July. It's easy to spend a full day exploring the town's small but rich museums, hiking nearby trails, or driving on scenic roads to nearby communities. This sort of rudimentary road network is a true rarity in rural Alaska. Nome also has an unusually good assortment of restaurants to choose from—a huge accomplishment in a community where all the fresh produce has to be flown in.

Be aware that Nome is also a "wet" community. Rural communities are either wet (you can buy alcohol there), damp (you can have alcohol but can't buy it), or dry (it's illegal to bring alcohol with you into town). People often come to wet communities—like Nome—with the specific intent of indulging in drink, which often turns to overindulgence and causes a lot of problems, both personally and socially. If you wish to minimize noise and encounters with people who've been drinking, book lodgings away from bars.

SIGHTS

Every village in Alaska is surrounded by stunning scenery, but Nome actually has roads that can take you into those landscapes—that's a rare thing indeed! But before you saddle up, check out the offerings in town.

You can easily spend a couple of hours at the **Carrie M. McLain Memorial Museum** (223 Front St., 907/443-6630, Tues.-Sat.

a gold dredge on the tundra near Nome

Nome

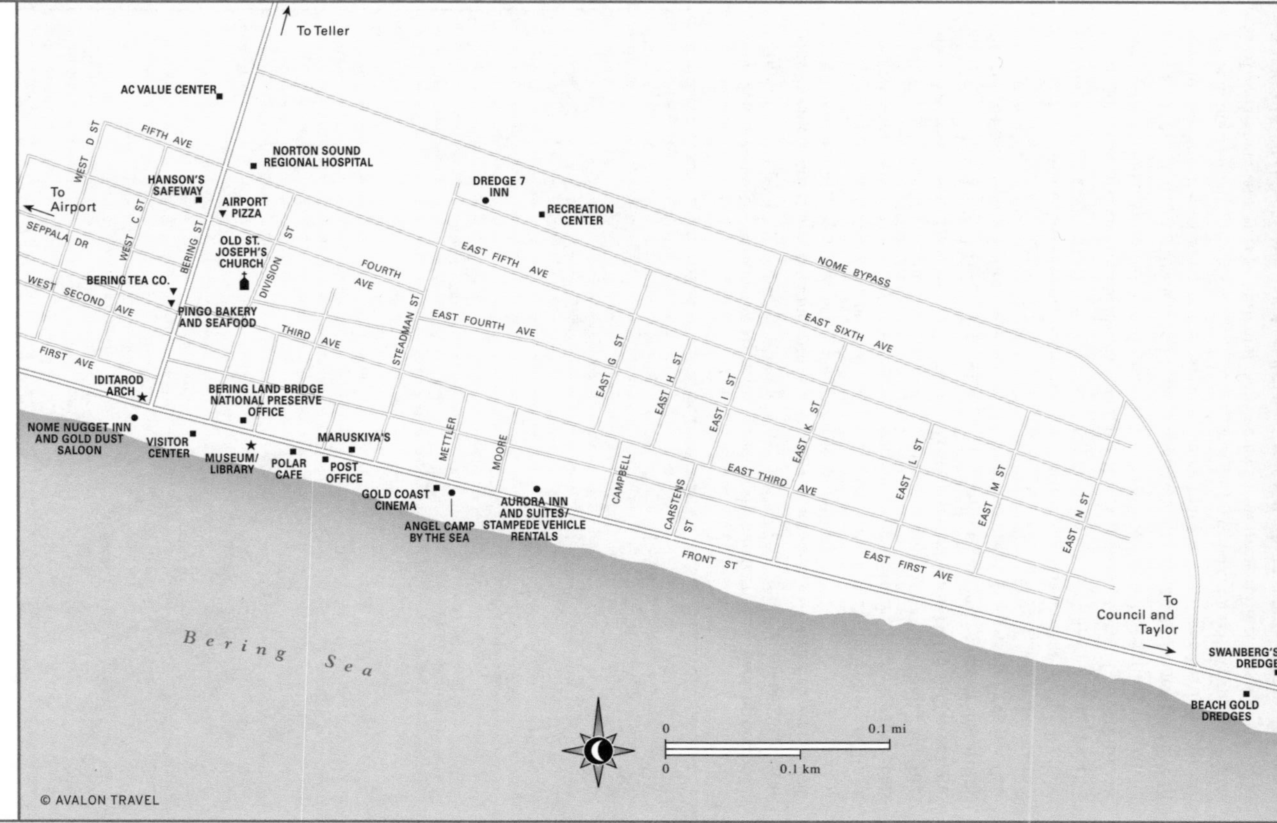
To Teller
AC VALUE CENTER
WEST D ST
FIFTH AVE
NORTON SOUND REGIONAL HOSPITAL
HANSON'S SAFEWAY
To Airport
AIRPORT PIZZA
DREDGE 7 INN
RECREATION CENTER
SEPPALA DR
WEST C ST
BERING ST
OLD ST. JOSEPH'S CHURCH
DIVISION ST
FOURTH AVE
EAST FIFTH AVE
NOME BYPASS
BERING TEA CO.
WEST SECOND AVE
PINGO BAKERY AND SEAFOOD
STEADMAN ST
EAST FOURTH AVE
THIRD AVE
EAST SIXTH AVE
FIRST AVE
IDITAROD ARCH
BERING LAND BRIDGE NATIONAL PRESERVE OFFICE
EAST G ST
EAST H ST
EAST I ST
EAST K ST
NOME NUGGET INN AND GOLD DUST SALOON
VISITOR CENTER
MUSEUM/ LIBRARY
POLAR CAFE
POST OFFICE
MARUSKIYA'S
METTLER
MOORE
CAMPBELL
CARSTENS ST
EAST THIRD AVE
EAST L ST
EAST M ST
EAST N ST
GOLD COAST CINEMA
ANGEL CAMP BY THE SEA
AURORA INN AND SUITES/ STAMPEDE VEHICLE RENTALS
FRONT ST
EAST FIRST AVE
To Council and Taylor
SWANBERG'S DREDGE
Bering Sea
BEACH GOLD DREDGES
0 0.1 mi
0 0.1 km

Southern Seward Peninsula

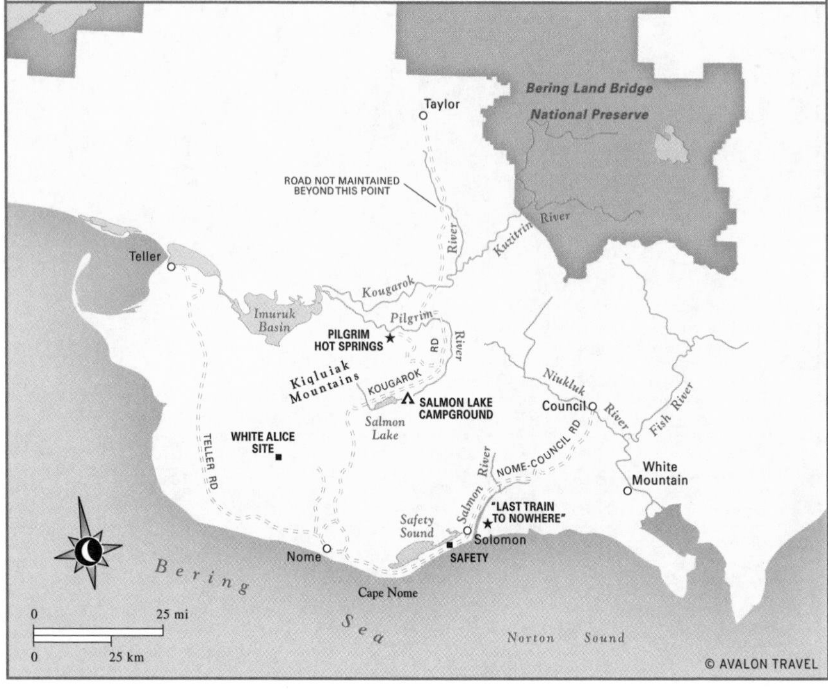

noon-6pm, free, suggested donation $1), in the bottom floor of the town's library building. This tiny museum is full to bursting with artifacts that tell the history of indigenous people along the Bering Sea, the 1900 gold rush that shaped Nome, local aviation, and of course long-distance mushing, which started with the All Alaska Sweepstakes.

The **Bering Land Bridge National Preserve Park Service Office** (214 Front St., 907/334-2552, nps.gov/bela, Mon.-Fri. 10am-4:30pm, free) also doubles as a small museum, with maps, giant fossils, a nice gift shop, and short movies on local culture and history. You can't miss this building; just look for the polar bear sculpture atop the entrance, and make sure to ask about the schedule for free ranger presentations and nature walks.

If you're here late August-April and happen to look up at night, you might get lucky and see the northern lights dancing overhead. But you'd better bundle up, because clear skies that let you see the lights also mean cold temperatures.

If you visit Nome in the winter and think you see a spruce forest on the ice that coats Norton Sound, you're not hallucinating. That's just the **Nome National Forest,** the community's customary way of discarding Christmas trees. It's a yearly custom that died out for several years when the original instigators passed on, but Mayor Richard Beneville has been working to revive this lighthearted, playful way of discarding the trees, which are usually cut from around the community of Council, the nearest place to Nome that has trees. The "national forest" and the plywood cutouts that pepper it—from ducks to walrus, reindeer, and bears—also create something entertaining for the locals to look at besides their usual horizons of tundra and winter sea.

Mayor Beneville also happens to be the person who has run the town's best value in tours, **Nome Discovery Tours** (907/304-1453 or 907/443-2814, discover@gci.net), for almost 30 years. A self-described old gypsy from New York, Beneville is a real character, so don't miss the unique opportunity to have a town's mayor pick you up from the airport in a heated van, talk fishing and gold dredging, show you the town's best sights, and regale you with local history. As of 2016 he charges $120 for this "generic" day tour, with plenty of custom options available.

Although Mayor Beneville doesn't consider himself a professional birder, he's the go-to resource for independent, traveling birders who want advice from a local. **Birding** in Nome is best from mid-May to mid-June when migratory species are arriving, although you can have an excellent birding experience all the way into August.

One of Beneville's other very popular trips is a day excursion to **Teller,** a small village of about 250 people with one of the most beautiful natural harbors in existence—but you can also drive there yourself (see *Driving the Nome Roads*). One of the upsides to going with Beneville is that he can tell and show you how climate change has affected these communities.

You can also take yourself to some of the other stops on Beneville's day tour, although you'll be deprived of his entertaining and knowledgeable company. The first is the **White Alice site** atop Anvil Mountain, giant parabolic antennae left over from a communications system that spanned Alaska during the Cold War. The drive up to the top of the mountain is about 4.5 miles from Nome, and the last part of the road is steep and rough enough that you might want to borrow or rent a four-wheeler, or just walk. The wildflowers are beautiful and on a clear day you'll get spectacular views over Nome, the Bering Sea beyond, and maybe a herd of musk ox too—make sure you give them plenty of space.

The other can't-miss site is the **Safety Roadhouse,** which sits 22 miles—or a day's travel by dog team—along the coastal Nome-Council road. It's open only during the summer and for a brief spell in March, when it serves as the second-to-last checkpoint along the Iditarod Trail. Expect basic food and bar service, with a healthy side of fascinating memorabilia; this is the type of place you go just to say you've been there. The walls are

the remains of the White Alice installation on Anvil Mountain

literally wallpapered with signed dollar bills, so don't forget to add yours and take a picture with it before you go.

RECREATION

During the summer, don't miss a visit to **Salmon Lake,** a favorite recreation area that sits 38 miles down the Kougarok Road. The maintained lakeside campground (open late June-mid-October, depending on snow and road conditions) is the terminus of the northernmost red salmon run in the country and has six campsites plus picnic tables, outhouses, and grills for public use.

If you have your sights set on the same gold that so dramatically shaped this seaside community, try your hand with George Foot of **Nome Tour and Marketing** (907/304-1038). For $150 he'll take you on a three- to four-hour tour that includes gold panning, a tour of the city and nearby area, and a slideshow on the town's history. He can also take you sluicing for gold, fishing, or on an ATV tour.

Your hotel won't have a gym, but you can always work out in the **Nome Recreation Center** (208 E. 6th Ave., 907/443-5431, summer Mon.-Fri. 5:30am-10pm, winter hours vary, day-use $7 adults, $6 youth 2-18 and seniors 55 and up), which has a full-size gym, weight room, racquetball facilities, and even a rock-climbing wall. A bowling alley is open only during the winter. The locker rooms have showers and saunas. When you visit, keep in mind how meaningful this sort of activity space can be when there's literally nothing else to do in town. Winter hours vary enormously, so it's best to call.

TOP EXPERIENCE

★ The Iditarod Finish

Nome's biggest moment comes every March, when it serves as the finish line for the 1,000-mile **Iditarod Trail Sled Dog Race.** The race has its ceremonial start in Anchorage on the first Saturday in March, with dog teams running an 11-mile course through town that ends at the Campbell Creek Airstrip. The ceremonial start has a carnival atmosphere, with spectators hauling lawn chairs and sometimes even barbecue grills to stake out their favorite viewing points along the trail. Mushers throw dog booties or candy to children in the crowds, and each musher hauls an Iditarider who bid on the privilege in a fundraising auction.

Animal-rights groups sometimes protest the Iditarod as being cruel to dogs. It's true

the iconic burled arch at the Iditarod finish

Driving the Nome Roads

mile 12.5 of the Teller Highway

One of Nome's most unusual features is its rudimentary road system. You still can't drive here, but once you *are* here you can rent a car to explore beautifully scenic drives, both along the coast and inland. The unpaved roads are very rugged, traffic is minimal, and services are limited, so make sure not to go too fast—you'll definitely get a flat!—and travel with extra food, water, and warm clothes in case you have car problems and need to shelter in the vehicle until help arrives.

Take it slow and that will increase your odds of spying big wildlife like musk oxen, reindeer, moose, and grizzly bears, not to mention the area's plentiful birds and maybe even some marine wildlife when you're along the coast. Bring your binoculars.

You have three options, all of which make good day trips, but leave plenty of time to turn around and get back to Nome before night falls. Gas service is unreliable and commercial lodgings nonexistent, so always leave Nome with a full tank of gas.

- The **Teller Highway** (technically the Bob Blodgett Nome-Teller Memorial Highway) runs 72 miles northwest to this tiny seaside community, which has a beautiful natural port and a few small stores offering local crafts and food items, but not much else. Running water is a luxury. On a clear day, the trip down this road offers great views of the Bering Sea to the west and the tundra-clad Kigluaik Mountains to the east.

- The 72-mile **Nome-Council Road** takes you through beaches, wetlands, and high tundra on the way to this tiny gold-rush-era community. Well, almost there—Council is on the far side of the river from the road's end. Locals cross in four-wheel-drive vehicles with high clearance, but there are deep holes, so only try this if you have a local guide and good insurance. You'll have better luck turning right at the river and hitching a boat ride with a local. Respect the seasonal camps you pass along the way, which are private property regardless of whether they're currently occupied.

- The 86-mile **Kougarok Road,** a.k.a. the Nome-Taylor Highway, actually peters out about 25 miles before it gets to Taylor. It offers spectacular passage through the Kigluaik Mountains and can take you to **Salmon Lake** (mile 38), a popular picnic and camping spot with locals, or the ruined ghost town of **Pilgrim Hot Springs** (mile 65, plus about 8 miles of unmaintained back road—bring rubber boots for scouting through pools of standing water). Pilgrim Hot Springs has been a gold rush town and a Catholic mission/orphanage, and is under consideration as a source of geothermal energy; meanwhile, you can still soak in what's left of rudimentary tubs that hold the natural spring water.

that if you took Rover and Fido out of your living room and put them in the traces to run 1,000 miles, it would be cruel; as would using dogs that aren't bred for the trail conditions they encounter. But these sled dogs are bred to thrive in Alaska's challenging conditions, and anybody who knows even the slightest thing about dog behavior can see that running is the one thing they love most. It's not a matter of making the dogs run: The mushers simply get out of the way and *let* them run. It's keeping them from running that would be cruel.

From the ceremonial finish line, the dogs are trucked out to Willow for the restart, which takes place the following day and marks the start of the real race to Nome.

It's impossible to predict exactly when the frontrunners will finish, but for the last couple of decades, the winner has reached Nome in eight or nine days. As of 2016 the record for fastest finish is 8 days, 13 hours, 4 minutes, and 19 seconds, set by Dallas Seavey in 2014. Northwest Alaska's temperamental weather can affect both racers and air travel, so plan to come a day or two early and stay a day or two after the expected finish; otherwise, you risk making your way all the way up here just to miss the winner's arrival.

Finally, keep in mind that the racers are released from Willow with staggered start times. So if it's a close race, the first team across the finish line in Nome might not be the winner, depending on when they started.

Best places to watch the Iditarod finish: Nome has an average high temp of 19 degrees in March, so spending all day outside waiting on the mushers isn't realistic. Your best options are to either wait until the city blows a horn to signal mushers closing in on the finish—then bundle up and head out—or, better yet, stake out a comfortable indoor viewing area in the **Nome Nuggett Inn**'s saloon, which has the closest indoor viewing area. The **Subway** sandwich shop, on the other side of the finish line, also offers good indoor viewing.

You can also head to the **Nome Recreation Center** for the awards/finishers banquet and rub elbows with the tired, jubilant mushers. Tickets go on sale in Nome's Iditarod Headquarters at the **Mini Convention Center** (409 River St., 907/443-6874) only *after* the first musher has crossed the finish line.

More than 1,000 people pour into Nome to see the finish, so make your travel reservations as early as possible; they can book up a full year in advance. Some residents open their homes to visitors; contact the **Nome Visitor Center** (907/443-6555, visitnomealaska.com) to get on the wait list.

You don't need a guide to watch the Iditarod finish, but if you want a more behind-the-scenes experience, consider booking a tour from one of these reputable companies: Anchorage-based **Planet Earth Adventures** (907/717-9666, discoverak.com), Juneau-based **Wild Alaska Travel** (855/294-5325, wildalaskatravel.com), and Wasilla-based **Sky Trekking Alaska** (907/315-6098, skytrekkingalaska.com). The tours typically last 4-9 days and start at about $4,000, but they can get you places that'd be challenging to coordinate alone, like visits to nearby checkpoints, Sno-Cat tours, mushing your own dog team, driving a snowmachine, and (hopefully) seeing the northern lights. (Okay, the last one is easy enough to do on your own—just look up!)

★ Bird-Watching

Bird-watching is one of the biggest and best summer draws in Arctic Alaska, especially mid-May-mid-June, when migratory species come winging back to their mating and breeding grounds. Independent birders will get the best possible value from Nome mayor and tour guide Richard Beneville, who runs **Nome Discovery Tours** (907/304-1453 or 907/443-2814, discover@gci.net). If you'd rather take a guided tour based Outside, **High Lonesome Bird Tours** (443/838-6589, highlonesometours.com) has a great reputation for small groups and experienced guides.

Fishing

If there's water in Alaska, rest assured there

bird-watching in the Arctic

will be some spectacular fish inhabiting it. Your hottest opportunities in Nome include staying at a former subsistence camp and fishing for trophy grayling with **Alaskan NW Adventures** (907/443-3971, akadventure.com), or floating and fly-in fishing with **Twin Peaks Adventures** (907/443-2398, twinpeaksadventures.com).

ENTERTAINMENT

The newly redone decor in the **Gold Dust Saloon** (315 Front St., in the Gold Nugget Hotel, 907/443-4612) harkens back to the saloons of yesteryear. This place is equal parts bar and pub, with good drinks, a full kitchen, live music, karaoke, and a cozy atmosphere that encourages conversation. The average dinner entrée runs about $20; less-expensive sandwich options are also available.

You should at least visit **Mark's Soap'n'Suds** on Front Street (907/443-6943) for the novelty factor; after all, who hasn't wished for a good stiff drink in a laundromat at least once? Another interesting combination you won't find anywhere else is Nome's **Gold Coast Cinemas** (135 Front St., 907/443-8100, $12/adult, $9/child), which happens to be inside the Subway sandwich shop.

SHOPPING

Nome is a great place to shop for authentic Alaska Native artwork. Visit **Maruskiyas** first (247 Front St., 907/443-2955, maruskiyas.com), then stop by **Chutkotka-Alaska** (309 Bering Ave., 907/443-4128). The **Bering Land Bridge National Preserve Park Service Office** (214 Front St., 907/334/2552, nps.gov/bela) also has a small but nice gift shop with a naturalist bent.

FOOD

Grocery prices can be outrageous in Nome, and restaurant food is correspondingly pricey. Still, there are some good values to be had. For a solid breakfast check out the omelets at the tiny **Polar Cafe** (204 Front St., 907/443-5191), upstairs from the Polar Bar. The café offers basic but tasty diner food with a side of Wi-Fi and sweeping views of the Bering Sea. It also has the only salad bar in town, since all fresh produce has to be flown or barged in. Breakfast typically runs around $16, and there's a $10.50 soup-and-sandwich special.

For a more conventional café experience, head to the delightful **Bering Tea Co.** (310 Bering St., 907/387-0352), a cozy coffee shop with stellar baked goods and pastries, and one of the few places in town where you'll find organic breakfast options. If you need a place to strum a guitar or cozy up with a good book gleaned from the take one/leave one rack near the door, this is it. The Bering Tea Co. transferred ownership but will hopefully remain just as great.

The **Bering Sea Bar and Grill** (305 Front St., 907/443-4900, beringsearestaurant.com, entrées $25) offers a mature take on the usual eclectic blend of food, with beautifully presented steaks, seafood, burgers, pasta, and Korean/Japanese fare, including sushi and sashimi; they serve breakfast, too.

Another great dinner option is **Pingo Bakery and Seafood House** (308 Bering St., 907/387-0654, pingobakery-seafoodhouse.com), which has the best baked goods and seafood meals in town. It's pricey, though, and small, so during busy times you might share a table with others.

Finally, **Airport Pizza** (406 Bering St., 907/443-7992) is worth mentioning because they've gotten a lot of press for delivering pizza to small outlying communities by plane. The service isn't what it used to be, though, and as with everything else in Nome, prices run high; a regular cheese pizza with no toppings is $18. The enormous calzones ($17-25) are the best value, and the reindeer sausage pizza is still great.

Groceries

Grocery stores are always expensive in rural communities; it's not unusual to pay $7 for a loaf of bread, so, if you're staying for any length of time, it's worth shipping food to yourself before your trip. While in town, your two food shopping options are the **AC Value Center** (1 Nome-Teller Rd., 907/443-2243) or **Hanson's/Safeway Grocery** (415 Bering St., 907/443-5454).

ACCOMMODATIONS

Like all wet communities in rural Alaska, Nome has its problems with alcohol. Limit late-night noise and drunken encounters by asking for a room away from the bar.

Most hotels and bed-and-breakfasts are within walking distance of everything downtown, but if you find one of the few outlying places, you'll probably prefer having a rental car. Add 6 percent room tax to all prices, and beware that some places bump up their lodging costs during Iditarod season.

Rooms at the **Aurora Inn & Suites** (302 Front St., 800/354-4606 or 907/443-3838, aurorainnome.com, $160-265) are simple but large, modern, and clean, with very friendly service. Some rooms have kitchenettes; front rooms have great views over the Bering Sea. The Wi-Fi is free but spotty (which is par for the course in any rural community). This hotel is also home to Stampede Vehicle Rentals ($126/day car, $201/day 14-passenger van); they'll rent to you no matter where you're staying.

The **Dredge No. 7 Inn** (1700 Nome-Teller Hwy. or 608 D St., 907/304-1270, dredge7inn.com, $155) offers a hodgepodge of clean, spacious rooms in several buildings, most of which have kitchen access and a private bathroom. Amenities include free Wi-Fi and cable. If you're not staying in the downtown location, you'll want a rental car—$100 for 8am-8am rental from the inn, which rents only to its own customers during the winter. Fees bump to $185 per day during Iditarod season and part of June.

If you prefer a B&B, visit **Angel Camp by the Sea** (922 E. Front St., 907/304-2633, angelcampbythesea.com, from $149). This place is clean, cozy, and modern, with comfortable beds, access to a common room, and plenty of options for breakfast and snacks. Watch for waterbirds just out the door. Wi-Fi is intermittent as always, but the hospitality is great.

If you're really on the cheap, ask the **Ukpeagvik Iñupiat Corporation** (1250 Agvik St., 907/852-4460, uicalaska.com), which owns most of the surrounding lands, for permission to camp on the beach or tundra, where you might just find yourself next to serious gold miners. You should also check with the corporation before exploring out of town to see if you need a permit. There are no polar bears here, but you may encounter grizzly bears.

INFORMATION AND SERVICES

Your first stop in Nome should be the **Nome Visitor Center** (301 Front St., 907/443-6555); ask for a free walking tour pamphlet to familiarize yourself with the town, or for a brochure of nearby hiking trails if you're feeling peppy.

Two banks in town offer ATM access in addition to their usual Monday-Friday teller services: **Credit Union 1** (406 Warren Pl., 800/478-2222) and **Wells Fargo Bank** (109A Front St., 907/443-2223). The Credit Union 1 branch is also open on Saturday.

Internet access can be sketchy, but Nome is better than many other rural Alaskan communities, with public Wi-Fi access in the **AC Value Center** (1 Nome-Teller Rd., 907/443-2243) and the **Kegoayah Kozga Library** (223 E. Front St.), plus a few restaurants and most hotels and B&Bs.

TRANSPORTATION

For the casual visitor Nome is accessible only by airplane, with three flights per day from Anchorage on **Alaska Airlines** (800/252-7522, alaskaair.com). You can also get here on **Ravn Alaska** (907/443-7595, flyravn.com) with a stop in Unalakleet. Once you're in Nome, both Ravn and **Bering Air** (800/478-5422 or 907/443-5464, beringair.com) offer travel to nearby rural communities. Bering Air also offers chartered flights to the Russian Far East.

The Nome airport is 1.4 miles out of town; expect to pay about $7 for the one-way trip with either **Checker Cab** (907/443-5211) or **Mr. Kab** (907/443-6000). Once in town, you can either take cabs just about anywhere for a flat rate that's regulated by the city (topping out at around $7 one-way). Be prepared to share the ride. You can also rent a car at either the **Dredge No. 7 Inn** (1700 Nome-Teller Hwy. or 608 D St., 907/304-1270, dredge7inn.com, $100 for 8am-8am rental; the inn rents only to its own customers during the winter) or **Stampede Vehicle Rentals** at the **Aurora Inn & Suites** (302 Front St., 800/354-4606 or 907/443-3838, aurorainnome.com, $126/day car, $201/day 14-passenger van). Make your reservations in advance, because the rental cars do sell out.

In the coming years, climate change may make boat travel a viable means of transport to Nome; 20 years ago they only had 30-odd ships docking per year, but nowadays the port has some 700 annual dockings, including a handful of cruise ships.

Kotzebue

This remote Iñupiat community of almost 3,300 people, 33 miles north of the Arctic Circle on the shores of the Chukchi Sea, is the largest community in all of Northwest Alaska. That means that people from the Northwest Arctic Borough's 11 smaller villages come to Kotzebue for shopping, services, medical care, and transportation options that aren't available in their home communities. Government and transportation services help drive Kotzebue's economy, along with commercial fishing and, to a declining degree, mining.

Kotzebue's biggest draw for out-of-state visitors is its status as gateway and headquarters to several remote national parks. This is where you come to charter a small plane to Kobuk Valley National Park and its staggering sand dunes, Noatak National Preserve and its mighty river, or Cape Krusenstern National Monument. If you want to have your National Parks passport stamped, you do that during a visit to the Northwest Arctic Heritage Center on your way back through Kotzebue.

Kotzebue's tourist amenities have expanded somewhat in recent years but remain minimal. However, a visit here is still awe-inspiring for the simple fact that Kotzebue—traditionally known as Kikiktagruk, or "place that is shaped like a long island," in an area that's been inhabited by the Iñupiat Eskimo people for more than 9,000 years—is the oldest settlement in all of the North and South American continents. The sweeping views of Kotzebue Sound from smack in the middle of town are beautiful, too.

An important note for visitors: Kotzebue is a damp community, which means you can buy alcohol at the city-owned liquor store, but there are severe restrictions over transporting your own alcohol into the community, and selling or bartering alcohol is a criminal offense. Respect the rules established by the community and play it safe by not bringing any alcohol with you at all.

Kotzebue's winters last for most of the year; typically, high temperatures only peep above freezing in May, then soar—relatively speaking—into the 50s and even 60s June-August. Like all Arctic communities, Kotzebue is also quite dry, receiving 61 inches, or about five feet, of snow every year. The only way to get here is by plane; multiple flights are operated by Alaska Airlines almost every day.

SIGHTS

One of the most impressive sights in Northwest Alaska is right off Kotzebue's main street: Kotzebue Sound, one arm of the frigid Chukchi Sea, which, together with the Beaufort Sea, cradles Alaska's northern coastline. You can stroll the beach and dip your fingers in the water, or marvel at the city's ongoing efforts to combat erosion when storm-driven waves wash right over the vestigial beach and into town.

National Parks

Kotzebue is surrounded by some of Alaska's most remote and beautiful national parks, including Noatak National Preserve, Cape Krusenstern National Monument, and Kobuk Valley National Park with its stunning sand dunes (see *Remote Arctic Parks*, page 383). There are no roads into these parks, and there are no established trails or amenities, although sufficiently experienced outdoorspeople can enjoy floating the mighty Noatak River and easy stretches of the nearby Kobuk River. This is wilderness in its truest sense, so unless you're prepared for authentic backcountry travel and navigation (which are

looking down on the Arctic regional hub village of Kotzebue

A Word About Liquor

Because Kotzebue is a damp community, if you want to buy and consume alcohol, you must do so at the city-owned **Jailhouse Liquor** (258 4th Ave., 907/442-4000, cityofkotzebue.com, Mon.-Sat. 3pm-9pm), so named because it's right next to the jail. You'll have to purchase a permit before you buy alcohol (residents must have a permit too). Visitor permit costs vary by length of stay; call the liquor store for more information.

more remote and challenging in Alaska than almost anywhere in the world), you should hire a guide service.

Arctic Wild (907/479-8203, arcticwild.com), based in Fairbanks, is authorized to conduct guided trips into all three parks, while **Arctic Backcountry Flying Service** (907/442-3200, arcticbackcountry.com), out of Kotzebue, offers air taxi to all three; they also offer flightseeing tours.

Northwest Arctic Heritage Center

The multiagency **Northwest Arctic Heritage Center** (171 3rd Ave., 907/442-3890, Mon.-Fri. 9am-6:30pm, Sat. 1pm-5pm) serves as visitor center, nature center, and museum, plus headquarters for Kobuk Valley National Park, Noatak National Preserve, and Cape Krusenstern National Monument. Educational programs for both kids and adults include classes in traditional Native crafts. Expect to spend at least an hour here, taking in all the exhibits.

Nullaġvik Kotzebue Tour

Consider booking a day tour through the corporation-owned **Nullaġvik Hotel** (306 Shore Ave., 907/442-331, nullagvikhotel.com). The tour starts upstairs in the hotel's observation lounge, overlooking Kotzebue Sound, then shuttles you to local points of interest that showcase the history, culture, and way of life of the region's Iñupiat people.

LaVonne's Fish Camp

For a very Alaskan experience indeed, consider a visit to **LaVonne's Fish Camp** (fishcamp.org), just a few miles out of Kotzebue. This is a very rare opportunity to spend time with local Iñupiat people, learning about traditional subsistence activities by participating in them. You might get to help catch, cut, and dry fish or gather other foods. Other activites include bird-watching, hiking, and beachcombing. The camp and its accommodations are extremely rustic: simple cabins with water jugs and electric heat (sometimes). There's a shared outhouse and shower, and a dining room/kitchen cabin where meals are eaten family style at a shared table.

This is a working fish camp and the site of many cultural activities; visit fishcamp.org to read about what life is like in the fish camp and for contact information for arranging your visit.

FOOD

As you can imagine, shipping anything to Kotzebue, including food, is very expensive. That drives costs up—way, way up to the tune of $10 for a half gallon of orange juice—in both the grocery stores and the restaurants. If you're going to be here for any length of time, it's smart to bring your own groceries, either as luggage on the plane or by shipping them to yourself.

The good news is that if you do need to eat out, the **Nullaġvik Restaurant** (in the Nullaġvik Hotel, 306 Shore Ave., 907/442-331, nullagvikhotel.com, entrées $20) is very good and the prices are surprisingly decent, too. Try the reindeer stew. Service hours can be a little confusing. Breakfast is offered Monday-Friday 6:30am-9:30am, with brunch Sunday 10am-2pm. Lunch is offered Monday-Friday 11am-2pm, and dinner is daily 5pm-9pm except for Saturday and Sunday, when dinner ends at 8:30pm.

Your next-best option in town—although

you must approach it with the recollection that you're in one of the world's most remote communities—is the family-owned **Bayside Restaurant** (303 Shore Ave., 907/442-3600), which serves decent but pricey Chinese and American food. However, the family was recently looking to sell, so there's some question of how long the restaurant will remain open.

Groceries

You now have three options for groceries in Kotzebue, although it's still cheaper to bring your own if possible. The **North Star Market** (175A 3rd Ave., 907/442-3333, daily 8am-midnight) is working to drive down the very high price of groceries in this remote community by choosing the most cost-effective versions of products—for example, shipping up bleach tablets, which are much lighter and less expensive to transport, instead of gallon jugs of bleach. Your other options are the **AC Value Center** (395 Bison St., 907/442-3285, acvaluecenter.com, daily 7am-10pm) and **Rotman Stores** (500 Shore Ave., 907/442-3123).

ACCOMMODATIONS

There's really just one place to stay in Kotzebue: The **Nullaġvik Hotel** (306 Shore Ave., 907/442-331, nullagvikhotel.com, from $259), whose name means "a place to sleep" in Inupiaq. The previous hotel was fairly spartan, but this newer incarnation, built in 2011, is modern and, dare I say, luxurious, with European-inspired decor and touches of Alaska Native art throughout. Many rooms offer beautiful views over the water, and on one of the upper floors there's an observation room overlooking Kotzebue Sound. Amenities include free (but slow) Wi-Fi, a fitness center, a laundry center, flat-screen TVs, mini fridges and microwaves in some rooms, and, just as important, private bathrooms.

INFORMATION AND SERVICES

Wi-Fi in Kotzebue recently got faster, thanks to an undersea fiberoptic cable laid to several Arctic communities in 2016—but it's still slow by any means. The hotel will have the best connection in town, but if you can't get Wi-Fi there, you can try in the **Chukchi Consortium Library** (604 3rd St., 907/442-2410, open Tues.-Sat., call for hours).

Medical care is provided at the **Maniilaq Health Center** (436 5th Ave., 907/442-7777, maniilaq.org), which is owned and run by the local Native corporation. Take care of postal needs at the Kotzebue **post office** (333 Shore Ave., 800/275-8777, usps.com, Mon.-Fri. 9am-11am, Sat.-Sun. noon-4pm).

TRANSPORTATION

The only way to get to Kotzebue is by air; during summer, there are daily **Alaska Airlines** (800/252-7522, alaskaairlines.com) flights from Anchorage and Nome. If you're trying to visit one of the nearby national parks or a smaller village, you'd need to charter a flight with **Bering Air** (800/478-3943 or 907/442-3943 or 907/442-3187, beringair.com). The airport is just 0.5 mile from the Nullaġvik Hotel—an easy walk—or you can hail a cab for around $7.

Taxi service is run at a per-person flat rate; try **Kobuk Cab** (907/442-4444), or ask the staff at the airport to help you find whoever may be driving a cab that day. Services like taxicabs tend to fluctuate in and out in rural communities with almost no predictability, depending on demand and how busy the drivers are with their other jobs or daily activities.

Barrow/Utqiaġvik

Barrow, or in the Inupiaq language Utqiaġvik (roughly pronounced "oot-key-ahk-vick"), is one of the oldest inhabited townsites in the United States, with archaeological evidence dating back to AD 800. It's also the farthest-north community in the country and the largest community in the North Slope Borough, with a population just under 4,400.

Barrow is cold, dry, and often windy in the winter, with the Arctic Ocean on three sides and hundreds of miles of flat tundra to the south. High temperatures are only above freezing for about a third of the year, and the sun remains below the horizon for two full months in the winter, offering about three hours of limited twilight at the winter solstice.

The converse is also true during the summer; the sun stays up for almost three months straight and the tundra explodes with life, including many migratory bird species that come here to rear their young before flying back to their winter grounds. That said, high temps in the summer typically peak at just 47 degrees in July—but you might be surprised by just how warm that feels when the sun is out.

Polar bears, snowy owls, and local culture are all big draws for visitors, as are other wildlife species, including walrus, bearded seals, whales, caribou, foxes, and Steller's eider. Another type of visitor—scientists—comes in droves because Barrow is considered to be ground zero for climate change, although "climate change" tours for the public aren't big business here . . . yet. I'd wager that as our climate continues to shift, more people will come to Barrow just to see its effects firsthand.

Most homes in Barrow are heated by natural gas, with modern sewer and water service. They also all look drab and weather-beaten on the outside, but you'll sometimes be surprised by the contrast with how they look on the inside.

In late 2016, the residents of Barrow voted to change the city's name back to the traditional Inupiaq name of Utqiaġvik. It's not entirely clear how long it may take for businesses and signs to be changed over, or when Alaska Airlines and other, smaller air carriers to the region will update their airport and flight information, so you may see both names used interchangeably for a while.

SIGHTS

Barrow is far enough north that you can get spectacular views of the **northern lights** from August to April when skies are dark and clear. In fact, Barrow and Fairbanks are the best places for viewing the aurora in the entire state.

While you're in Barrow, make sure not to miss a visit to the northernmost point of land in the United States, **Point Barrow**—just 10 miles northeast of the town. You can get close to the point by taxi or with a rental car, but it's best to take an organized tour because this is also one of the places you might encounter polar bears.

When you first fly in, look for the **Will Rogers and Wiley Post Monument** near the airport; the two stars died when their plane crashed 15 miles southwest of Barrow in 1935. Post was the first pilot to fly solo around the world; Rogers, a performer in many disciplines, has been described as the most popular and beloved man in America during his lifetime. There's another monument at the actual crash site, which you can visit by four-wheeler or on a tour.

Don't miss your chance at the standard Barrow photo op: The **whalebone arch**—made of the jawbones of a bowhead whale, a species that is still hunted for subsistence here—sits on the coast near the corner of Brower and Tahak Streets. Once you have your photo, bundle up and take a stroll on the windy, rocky beach.

A small company called **Touch Alaska Interactive Media** (touchalaska.com)

Barrow/Utqiaġvik

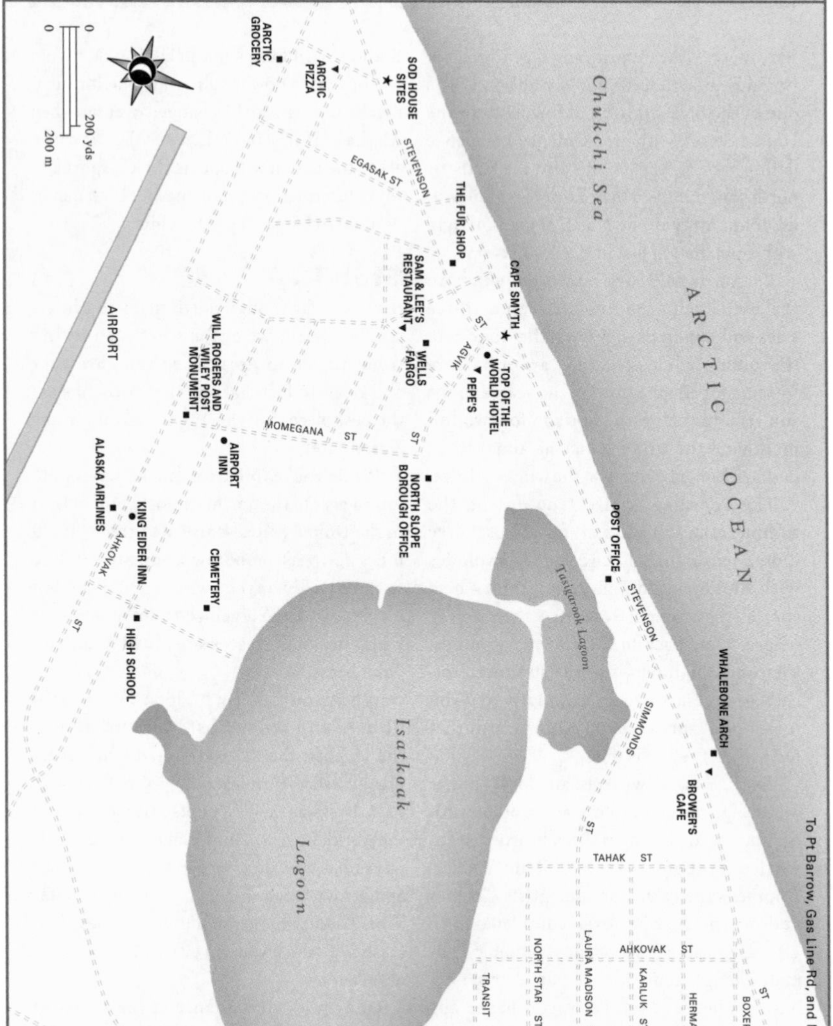

Barrow's iconic whalebone arch sits on the shore of the Arctic Ocean.

produces an excellent walking tour that will take you to the sites just mentioned, plus several ancient house mounds and archaeological sites and the 1893 **Cape Smythe Whaling and Trading Station** (Building 3220, Browerville), the oldest frame building above the Arctic Circle. You can pick up a free copy of the tour brochure at the **Iñupiat Heritage Center** or many other sites around town.

If you'd rather take a guide, you can book with **Tundra Tours** (3060 Eben Hopson St., 800/478-8520 or 907/852-3900, tundratoursinc.com), run out of the Top of the World Hotel, which charges $150 for a tour that lasts about five hours, including a walk on the tundra to see the remains of ancient sod huts.

★ Iñupiat Heritage Center

The **Iñupiat Heritage Center** (5421 North Star St., 907/852-0422, nps.gov/inup, Mon.-Fri. 8:30am-5pm, closed noon-1pm, also summer weekends 1pm-5pm, $10 adults, $5 youth

the main entrance of the Iñupiat Heritage Center

The Reality of Remote Living

a neighborhood in Barrow

Barrow and other North Slope communities exemplify the reality of remote living in Alaska. Subsistence hunting, fishing, and whaling are still immensely important in these communities; whale, seal, polar bear, walrus, fish, caribou, and waterfowl are still common foods. If you're lucky enough to be in Barrow when whaling captains return from a successful hunt, the entire town—including you—will turn out to help haul in the catch.

It may be tempting to romanticize this sort of lifestyle, but there are downsides. Residents have to pay for the ammunition and gas they use for hunting, and monetary income can be very scarce in communities where local government, utilities, and services are the largest employers. Homes must be built on pilings to protect them from the permafrost. Weather can be a serious danger anywhere in Alaska, but that's especially true in Barrow and other communities in the North Slope Borough, thanks to their exposed northerly location.

When you live a subsistence lifestyle, your dinner—and your survival—depends on an intimate understanding of the land, the weather, and the wildlife. That understanding is passed from one generation to the next and greatly challenged by the rapid effects of climate change, which is changing the character of the sea ice—which also plays a huge role in life near the Arctic Ocean—and the weather.

Other side effects of remote living include transport in small craft—the smaller your destination, the smaller the plane you'll ride in—and absurdly high prices on groceries, gas, and other basic goods, since everything has to be barged or flown in and there's very little competition to drive prices down.

Although these aspects make living here challenging, they're just the flip side of the reason you must come. You will never see another place like this on planet Earth, and nowhere else in the nation can you see this degree of subsistence living and indigenous traditions still intact. After all, there's no better way to gain an understanding of a given culture than to experience the place where it was born—and still lives.

7-17, free age 6 and under) showcases the traditional practice of whaling and other elements of a subsistence lifestyle in this part of the state. You'll also see demonstrations (and teaching) of traditional crafts. Monthly gatherings celebrate local Native customs.

RECREATION

Basketball is a big deal in rural Alaska, and especially big in Barrow. The community turns out in droves to watch the Barrow Whalers high school team play their fierce, relentless style during home games. If you'd rather stay fit yourself, head for the **Piuraagvik Recreation Center** (2026 Ahkovak St., 907/852-2514). It costs $5 for adults to use the gym or weight room, with other facilities priced à la carte (rock-climbing wall, racquetball courts, sauna, and an inflatable dome for outdoor sports like soccer, ice-skating, and hockey).

If you're feeling especially daring, head out to the Arctic Ocean and jump in; it's called the **Polar Plunge,** and the Top of the World Hotel gift shop (3060 Eben Hopson St., 800/478-8520 or 907/852-3900) will happily sell you a certificate to commemorate the occasion.

When the weather's nice, **bird-watching** is a great way to pass the time; with binoculars and a good handbook, you can see birds that have migrated in from all seven continents to take advantage of the Arctic Circle's endless summer paradise. Don't forget to watch for snowy owls, which nest in the ground and are especially plentiful in this area.

★ Polar Bear Tours and Kaktovik

There's a short list of things you can see and do only in the Arctic: dip your toe in the Arctic Ocean, watch the sun circle the horizon without setting, and see a polar bear, the largest land carnivore in the world. Male bears can measure 8-9 feet from nose to tail and weigh up to 1,300 pounds. Females are typically about half that size.

Make no mistake about it: You're about the right size to be a polar bear appetizer, so you should only seek these animals out in the company of an expert guide who's properly armed and trained to defend you, preferably from the safety of a substantial vehicle.

You might be able to see a polar bear in a guided tour from Barrow. Smaller tour companies tend to come and go somewhat unpredictably; as a perennial fixture, Tundra Tours at Top of the World Hotel is one of your best

See polar bears with Northern Alaska Tour Company.

bets—but your odds are even better in the tiny community of **Kaktovik**, sometimes called **Barter Island.** This is the only village within the Arctic National Wildlife Refuge. Peak whaling season in September is also peak bear-viewing season, when fresh whale carcasses draw the giant predators close to town. Visitors are sometimes surprised to see that the normally white bears can get very dirty during this snowless season, but they're still stunning creatures to behold.

For an all-in-one day tour that includes transport from Fairbanks to Kaktovik in a small plane (the only way to get there), a guided tour, a buffet lunch and a return flight in time for a late dinner, you can book through **Northern Alaska Tour Company** (800-474-1986 or 907/474-8600, northernalaska.com) or **Warbelow's Air** (888-280-0582 or 907/474-3520, warbelows.com). The 2017 price for the tour is $1,799 (it will probably increase a little bit in 2018 to account for fuel costs), and there must be a total of four guests for the tour to go on a given day.

You can also fly yourself to Kaktovik, which has a year-round population of about 250 people, on **Ravn Alaska** (800-866-8394 or 907/266-8394, flyravn.com) from Fairbanks or Barrow. Budget $800 to $1,100 for round-trip tickets if you book well in advance. You can then stay at the modest but clean **Marsh Creek Inn** (907/640-5500, marshcreekinn.net, $325 d, meals included), and book a tour with local Iñupiat guide Robert Thompson of **Kaktovik Arctic Adventures** (907/640-6119, kaktovikarcticadventures.com).

If you book another tour operator, visit www.fws.gov/refuge/arctic/pbguide.html to make sure they're on the list of permitted operators, and make sure you get a clear safety briefing before leaving on the tour.

ENTERTAINMENT

Tundra Tours (3060 Eben Hopson St., 800/478-8520 or 907/852-3900, tundratoursinc.com)—operating out of the pricey Top of the World Hotel—includes traditional Iñupiaq drumming and dancing as part of their city tour. Sometimes, the tour may include an opportunity to try Alaska Native foods like dried fish, seal, or whale. The guides say some people have trouble adjusting to these traditional foods, but this is one experience that comes around just once in a lifetime for most people, if at all. So if you're offered the chance to try traditional foods, say yes!

The **Nalukataq Barrow Whaling Festival** is a traditional community celebration of a successful spring whaling season, usually conducted in late June. It features events like traditional singing and dancing and a blanket toss, and the successful hunters share their harvest with the entire community.

The Messenger Feast is a three-day midwinter festival, usually held in late January or early February. Participants come from all over the Arctic Circle, including Russia and Canada and Greenland, for dancing, trading, storytelling, feasting and traditional games.

SHOPPING

Your first stop should be the **Iñupiat Heritage Center** (5421 North Star St., 907/852-0422, nps.gov/inup) which, in addition to serving as a museum and educational center, also offers Native arts and crafts for sale.

If you want to go authentic Alaska, you can always stop by **The Fur Shop** (936 Stevenson St., 907/852-2900). It's not so much the hanging pelts that make the place authentic as how it fills so many functions: It's a gift shop, dry cleaner, florist, water service, Western Union station, and yarn/fabric/craft shop, all under one roof.

FOOD

Restaurant food is expensive in Barrow, just like everything else. However, portions are usually generous, almost everyone offers some sort of great seafood dish, and most places offer a smorgasbord of different styles, so you can shift cuisines without even getting up from your chair.

Arctic Pizza (125 Apayauk St., 907/852-4222, entrées $25) is a favorite of locals and tourists alike; the great views over the Arctic Ocean don't hurt either. The seafood is good and the pizza is excellent. Good lunch specials; also open for dinner.

Sam & Lee's (1052 Kogiak St., 907/852-5555, 6am-2am daily, entrées $20) is within easy walking distance of the town's three best hotels, with a waterfront view of Barrow's famous whalebone arches. You can get both Chinese and American food, plus American breakfast options and a great all-you-can-eat lunch buffet on weekdays. Head straight upstairs to eat, then go downstairs when you're ready to pay (don't wait for your check—it'll never come).

Groceries are available at the **AC Value Center** (4725 Ahkvoak St., 907/852-6711), but you might feel better just taking a picture of the price tag and walking out. A gallon of milk can cost at least $10, a loaf of bread can cost $7 or more, and so on. (Gas prices at the single station—Eskimo, Inc.—can easily run around $7 a gallon.)

ACCOMMODATIONS

Accommodations are, like most things in Barrow, pricey, reflecting a range between winter and summer rates. Add a 5 percent city room tax. Heads up: Although most lodgings offer free Wi-Fi, it's almost always spotty or slow. Every hotel should also have blackout curtains to keep the summer sun out at night, but it's a good idea to bring a sleeping mask with you, just in case.

The family-run **Airport Inn** (1815 Momeganna St., 907/852-2525, airportinnak.com, $163-189) is just one block from the airport and offers a homey atmosphere at a great price for the area. Rooms are clean and comfortable, with a microwave, mini fridge, flat-screen cable TV, free Wi-Fi, and a private bathroom in every room. Upstairs rooms have kitchenettes, and the free continental breakfast includes great homemade bread.

The **King Eider Inn of Barrow Alaska** (1752 Ahkovak St., 907/852-4700, kingeider.net, $169-209) is a block from the airport. The inn is clean and well-maintained, with great hospitality and free Wi-Fi, although you're on your own for meals. Kitchenette rooms are available ($10 extra); double rooms are $25 extra. They'll ask you to take your shoes off at the door but will provide slippers if you want them. The suite with in-room jacuzzi is $269 (winter) or $309 (summer).

Barrow's **Top of the World Hotel** (3060 Eben Hopson St., 800/478-8520 or 907/852-3900, tundratoursinc.com, $250-295 standard room, $289-329 deluxe room, add $20/day per extra occupant) is one of the newer lodgings in town. The previous Top of the World Hotel suffered heavy smoke damage when the iconic restaurant Pepe's burned down in 2013; the new hotel is within easy walking distance of the heritage center and the AC Value Center and has a free shuttle to/from the airport, which is one mile away. Staff are helpful and you can get good meals in the restaurant downstairs. Deluxe rooms have a kitchenette and waterfront views. Basic Wi-Fi is free, or you can buy faster access for $15 per day.

The very newest hotel in Barrow is the **UIC Tukkumavik Suites** (5665 C Ave., 907/852-5280, uicguest.com), which opened in 2016. The rates alone are impressive given the region, starting at $175 for up to two people in a fully furnished one-bedroom suite with a queen bed during peak season, or $210 for up to four people in a two-bedroom suite with two queen beds. Each suite has a kitchen and dining area—so you can save a lot of money by cooking for yourself—plus cable TV, Wi-Fi, and a private bathroom; laundry facilities are on-site. An ADA-accessible suite is available on request.

Some residents in rural Alaska use Airbnb as a long-term business plan to open their homes to visitors. This lets you mimic the travel strategy most local visitors use—renting a house or part of a house—while giving the operators a nice income in an area where job diversity can be quite scarce. So far, Barrow's best option that books through Airbnb is **Latitude 71 B&B** (5725 B St., 907/855-1210, latitude71bnb.com), a custom-built 10-bedroom, six-bathroom home that is now back in business after having been rented to an oil company for about three years. Rooms range from single twin beds to double-queen suites with kitchenettes; common space is shared and laundry facilities are free. A single queen room averages $175 in the summer and $150 in the winter.

INFORMATION AND SERVICES

Barrow is a damp town, which means you can legally bring alcohol into town, but you can't buy it here. The town has electricity, water, and sewer services that will be familiar to any city dweller. There is also a **Wells Fargo Bank** (1078 Kiogak St., Mon.-Thurs. 10am-5pm, Fri. 10am-6pm, with a 24-hour ATM).

The public **Tuzzy Consortium Library** (5421 North Star St., 800/478-6916, Mon.-Thurs. 9am-9pm, Fri.-Sat. noon-6pm, tuzzy.org) offers computer workstations and free Wi-Fi access. There's also a **post office** (3080 Eben Hopson St., 907/852-6800, Mon.-Sat. 9am-5:15pm). The **Samuel Simmonds Memorial Hospital** (7000 Uula St.) is a modern Level IV trauma center that also includes outpatient clinics and services.

TRANSPORTATION

With Arctic Sea ice receding, it's possible that the rarest of the rare events—a cruise ship docking at Barrow—will become more common. But until then, this remote community is accessible by air only, with several jet flights daily from Anchorage and Fairbanks on **Alaska Airlines** (800/252-7522, alaskaair.com), or a more circuitous route on **Ravn Alaska** (907/266-8394, flyravn.com).

Once you're in town, you could walk from one side of town to the other in about half an hour, but you don't have to. Use taxis as "mass transit" instead. There are plenty of them; Barrow has the highest concentration of taxis per capita in the United States. Taxi fares are regulated by the city and cost just $6 one-way to anywhere in town; the cabbie can charge $1 each for extra passengers. Because the taxi fares are set by the city, you're not expected to tip the driver. It might help to think of this more like a bus service than a taxi.

Driving North to Prudhoe Bay

If you want to be able to say that you drove the most rugged and remote road in all of Alaska, head straight for the Dalton Highway, a.k.a. the Haul Road, which starts 84 miles north of Fairbanks at an intersection with the Elliott Highway. The road ends 414 miles later at the North Slope community of Prudhoe Bay, a few miles short of the Arctic Ocean off Alaska's north coast.

Prudhoe Bay is a company town that exists for only one reason: to produce oil. It's also the start of the 800-mile Trans-Alaska Pipeline System (TAPS), which ships oil south from the North Slope to Valdez, Alaska, the northernmost ice-free port in the United States. The pipeline will parallel your route for most of the Haul Road, with the exception of portions in the Brooks Range, where it's buried to protect it from avalanches and falling rocks. You can't tour the Prudhoe Bay oil fields yourself or go through them to get the Arctic Ocean on your own, but you can book a tour company to take you.

The Haul Road is remote and rugged enough that you have no option but to take your time. It's not for everybody, so make sure you read all of this section before you plan a trip. With that said, the ruggedness is also thrilling, and this road cuts straight through some of the most remarkable and otherwise untouched wilderness on the planet, taking you over the Yukon River, past the Arctic Circle, and through the Brooks Range. You'll see all sorts of wildlife, and visitors to

Prudhoe Bay are almost always surprised to find that the "residents"—oil workers and the people who provide services for them—are very friendly.

The North Slope area is very flat and exposed, and weather delays can happen even in summer, so plan accordingly. Bring a head net for mosquitoes and a good sleeping mask, too; the sun doesn't set from mid-May to mid-July.

★ THE DALTON HIGHWAY/HAUL ROAD

Before you drive up the Haul Road, make sure you understand what you're getting into: It's extremely rough and almost completely unpaved, with only two gas stations and essentially no services between Fairbanks and Prudhoe Bay. If you have any loose fillings, do yourself a favor and skip this trip.

The Dalton Highway is also full of big trucks, and they have the right of way; in a few places the road is narrow enough that you'll have to pull over to let those big rigs pass as they build up enough momentum to make it up the steeper hills, or maintain that momentum as they head downhill on the other side.

Budget at least 15 hours for a one-way drive on the Haul Road; that's a ridiculously long day of bouncing around, so you'll want to split the trip into at least two days. You can find lodgings in the tiny communities of Coldfoot or Wiseman (miles 175 and 189, respectively), or there are several campgrounds along the way. You should have cell service in Prudhoe Bay, but don't expect it along the highway.

Make sure you fill up the gas tank every chance you get, carry extra gas—especially if you don't get great mileage—and consider carrying a CB radio so you can communicate with passing truckers and hear their updates on road conditions or wildlife. The truly hardcore can even bicycle this road; sometimes a passing big rig driver will help you out with a lift.

The following are notable mile markers along the Haul Road, measured from its intersection with the Elliott Highway:

- **Mile 56:** Cross the Yukon River. You can get food, gas, showers, basic camp-style lodging, and access to a phone (credit card or calling card required) at Yukon River Camp (907/474-3557, yukonrivercamp.com).
- **Mile 60:** Five Mile Campground (no fee, undeveloped, although a dump station is available).
- **Mile 115:** Cross the Arctic Circle. It's

the Dalton Highway

marked by a big sign that makes a great photo op.

- **Mile 175:** The tiny community of Coldfoot, which offers basic lodgings and camping. Budget some time to visit the Arctic Interagency Visitor Center here. This is also your last gas opportunity before Prudhoe Bay.
- **Mile 180:** Marion Creek Campground (fee applies).
- **Mile 189:** Another tiny community, Wiseman, with limited lodging available.
- **Mile 275:** Galbraith Lake Campground (no fee, undeveloped; very flat with nothing to buffer you against the wind).

For more detailed information on the Dalton Highway, see blm.gov/ak/dalton or call the Arctic Interagency Visitor Center at 907/678-5209 or 907/678-2014. You can also get a great downloadable Dalton Highway guide from alaskageographic.org.

PRUDHOE BAY AND DEADHORSE

Also known as Deadhorse (although the official zip code designation is Prudhoe Bay), Prudhoe Bay is a straight-up company town with no tourist facilities, services, or nightlife to speak of. Average high temperatures during the "tourist" season run from about 20 degrees in May to a little over 50 degrees in July; during the winter, temps can easily dip to 25 degrees below zero. There are no grocery stores, no street signs (time to get comfortable with asking for directions), and no booze; this is a dry community.

Sights and Recreation

If you (and your dental work) are willing to brave the Haul Road, it's your ticket to some of the best **wildlife viewing** in the world. Once you're in Prudhoe Bay, you may see beautiful arctic foxes, caribou, musk oxen, swans, and even polar bears. The **northern lights** are also visible overhead, but only on the late fringe of the driving season, when the skies are dark.

If you want to **tour Prudhoe Bay's oil fields** or **visit the Arctic Ocean** (which requires going through the oil fields), you can only do so with the help of an authorized tour operator. Arctic Ocean tours are currently available from **Deadhorse Camp** (Mile 412.8 Dalton Hwy., 800/474-3565 or 907/474-3565, deadhorsecamp.com, $69), **Northern Alaska Tour Company** (800/474-1986 or 907/474-8600, northernalaska.com, $219), **Alaska Tours** (866-317-3325, alaskatours.com), **Tours of Alaska** (800/439-5780, prudhoebay.com), and **Go North Alaska** (855-236-7271 or 907/479-7271, gonorth-alaska.com). Whichever tour you book, register at least 24 hours in advance so you can make it through the security checks, and be prepared to show your U.S. driver's license or, for international visitors, your passport.

Accommodations

When you visit Prudhoe Bay, you'll be sharing the same bunkhouse ambience the workers live in as they work shifts of a few weeks at a time, then a few weeks off. In fact, you'll probably be staying in one of their rooms, which are held first for oil workers, then released to civilian visitors when the oil worker is out of town on his or her time off. Make your reservations as far in advance as possible, then call back a week before your trip to see if any better rooms have been released.

Because there are no real town services to speak of, life in Prudhoe Bay revolves around the hotels/bunkhouses. Almost all hotel rates include three cafeteria-style meals a day and offer a gym, laundry facilities, and surprisingly good Internet access for such a remote location. Each hotel will also ask you to either remove your shoes at the door or put on shoe covers to help keep the area clean.

The **Prudhoe Bay Hotel** (100 Airport Rd., 907/659-2449, prudhoebayhotel.com) is just across the street from the airport—great if you're flying in, but it also means your views will be of oil fields instead of wilderness. Most rooms are dorm style, with two twin beds, no TV and no phone; they cost $135 for one person or $115 each for two, and shared bathrooms are down the hall. A single room with a private bath costs $160. There's a small gift shop, and the food in the restaurant is very good.

Aurora Hotel and Suites (123 Lake Colleen Rd., 907/670-0600) is the most hotel-like of the properties and offers the most luxurious, modern accommodations; there are even big-screen TVs in each room, all of which are single occupancy only. Rates range from $150 for a "Jack and Jill" room with a twin bed and shared bathroom to $170 for a "mega-style" queen room with a private bath. Amenities include free laundry, a gym, a game room, and a library. Ask for a room with a lake view.

Information and Services

You should have cell service while in Prudhoe Bay, though not on the Haul Road. For basic needs while in Prudhoe Bay, visit the **Prudhoe Bay General Store** (1 Old Spine Rd., 866-659-2550 or 907/670-5160) for snacks, books, household/beauty supplies, clothing, and more. This also functions as a gift shop of sorts, with Native arts and crafts for sale.

The post office is in the same building and credit cards are usually accepted, although you must pay cash for postage or a hunting or fishing license. An ATM at the **Prudhoe Bay Hotel** is the closest you'll get to a bank.

There is a **Tesoro gas station** (100 Sag River Rd., 888/659-3198 or 907/659-3198), and tire and vehicle repairs are available. All other services in Deadhorse center around the hotels; there isn't even a grocery store in town, although the hotels let you pack a generous bag lunch for yourself if you need to travel. They can also sell you basic amenities like toothpaste or shampoo.

Transportation

You have two options for getting to Prudhoe Bay. There are several jet or turboprop flights daily from Fairbanks or Anchorage on **Alaska Airlines** (800/252-7522, alaskaair.com) and **Ravn Alaska** (907/266-8394, flyravn.com), or you can drive the 500 miles north from Fairbanks.

If once up or down the Dalton Highway is plenty for you, most of the tour operators offer an option that takes you up the Dalton Highway one way, then brings you back by air (or vice versa). Some also offer side trips to **Barrow** or to **Kaktovik,** the only community that's inside the Arctic National Wildlife Refuge, for polar bear viewing—see the section on Barrow for more information.

Remote Arctic Parks

The Dalton Highway is bordered by massive wilderness areas on both sides. To the east, the far western tip of the **Arctic National Wildlife Refuge** nearly touches the highway; to the west, you have the option of forging your own rough, undeveloped overland access into **Gates of the Arctic National Park.** Otherwise, visitor access is by bush plane only. To the west of Gates of the Arctic lies the massive **Noatak National Preserve,** and just to the south of that is the smaller **Kobuk Valley National Park.**

These parks serve variously as migratory routes, summer breeding grounds, or winter feeding grounds for the state's largest caribou herds. Other fascinating wildlife denizens include musk oxen, with their foot-thick coats, hibernating grizzly bears, and color-changing arctic foxes and collared lemmings. Black bears appear in the more southerly, forested regions, with polar bears to the north and grizzly bears in between; meanwhile, hundreds of bird species migrate from all over the world to take advantage of the long Arctic summers.

All of these wilderness areas are devoid of

established trails, roads, campgrounds, and services—it's that very wildness, along with the chance to see wildlife, that is the draw. Winters are unforgivingly harsh, and temperatures can drop well below freezing, even in summer. The varied terrain, numerous water crossings, and lack of trails make travel difficult; even experienced backpackers are lucky to make five or six miles in a day, and you must carry bear-resistant containers for storing food. Only people adept at wilderness survival, travel, and navigation should come here on their own.

For the less-experienced wilderness traveler, professional guide services offer a safe—though pricey—way to experience the once-in-a-lifetime wonder of the intact ecosystems and untouched wilderness that stretch across Arctic Alaska. Although several outfitters serve these parks, I recommend **Alaska Alpine Adventures** (300 E. 76th Ave., 877/525-2577 or 907/351-4193, alaskaalpineadventures.com), based in Anchorage, for their excellent service and some of the best food you'll ever eat on the trail. It's so good, in fact, that it spawned a whole separate business that's run out of the same building: **Adventure Appetites** (907/868-1749, adventureappetites.com). Carl Donohue of **Expeditions Alaska** (770/952-4549, expeditionsalaska.com), based out of Anchorage, also has an excellent reputation for his competence and extensive knowledge, and he's tops at guiding photo tours.

★ ARCTIC NATIONAL WILDLIFE REFUGE

Originally established as the Arctic National Wildlife Range in 1960, today's **Arctic National Wildlife Refuge (ANWR)** includes 19.64 million acres of land and water, more than 200,000 caribou, an unthinkable horde of mosquitoes, and exactly one human settlement—the Iñupiat village of **Kaktovik,** population about 250, which can be reached by air from Barrow or Fairbanks. There are also grizzly bears, musk oxen, the highest concentration of nesting golden eagles in Alaska, and of course polar bears too (only in the northern portion of the park).

ANWR is bordered by Canada to the east, the Arctic Ocean to the north, and, to some degree, the Dalton Highway to the west. It's so large that it spans five ecological regions, from boreal forest in the south to an alpine zone, coastal plain tundra, and the coastal marine region that borders the Arctic Ocean.

ANWR is also believed to be rich in oil, and whether or not to allow drilling here has been

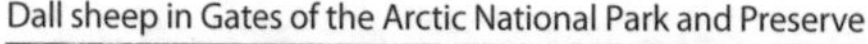
Dall sheep in Gates of the Arctic National Park and Preserve

Travel in Alaska's Arctic National Parks

Alaska's Arctic national parks are like nothing you'll ever find in the Lower 48 states. They're vast, remote, and trackless wildernesses where the weather and the animals still rule; we are simply transient visitors. The wildness and remoteness make them such special places to visit—the big attraction is the land itself. However, that also means that these parks are not a place for the unprepared or inexperienced.

You will spend most of your time alone and you won't have cell phone service. In some places you won't even be able to use a satellite phone, because tall mountains block access to satellites low on the horizon. With only occasional, rambling animal trails to follow, you'll have to navigate your own way, in the truest sense, through numerous water crossings and loose, unstable terrain. If you get yourself into trouble, rescue is not guaranteed—and even if it comes, it can take a long time. With just one exception, you don't get to these parks by road; you have to fly in, and you must be prepared to survive a little extra time on your own if weather or mechanical troubles keep the pilot from returning for you.

The rangers who serve in these parks are more than happy to field questions about what sort of conditions and terrain to expect and how to prepare. After all, they want people to see the parks they safeguard—but they also want to make sure you do so safely.

Does that mean that only hardcore backpackers and survivalists should head into our Arctic parks? No! In fact, I'd argue that places like this have the greatest impact when they're open to everybody. But if you're not already experienced at remote backcountry travel and navigation on Alaskan terrain, and confident in your ability to handle wild animals and rugged terrain completely on your own, you should hire a guide. The guides handle all the logistics (including air travel to access the park) and will provide a packing list so you know what to bring.

Even on a guided backpacking trip, you need to have a base level of fitness, be ready to carry your own gear, and be comfortable traveling over rough terrain for days at a time. Float trips are a little easier on you because most of the time the raft carries both you and your gear, but you should still be ready to deal with rough conditions and take an active role in ensuring your own comfort.

If that sounds like a stretch outside your comfort zone, you're not alone! But as anyone who's been into the Arctic can tell you, being willing to push the edges of your comfort zone just a little bit—in the company of seasoned professionals who make it their business to keep you safe and reasonably comfortable—results in a true once-in-a-lifetime adventure. I say that a little bit tongue in cheek, because once you experience the true wilderness that is Alaska's national parks, you're going to want to come back for another adventure.

an ongoing conflict for more than a decade. Those in favor of development say we need the domestic source of energy, while those against it argue it would present an unacceptable risk to one of the planet's few remaining truly intact ecosystems.

For more information about a visit to ANWR, call the U.S. Fish and Wildlife Service Office in Fairbanks at 800/362-4546 or 907/456-0250. Only about 1,500 people visit per year and, like most of Alaska's national parks, ANWR remains a vast, largely trackless wilderness. There's just one thing to do here: explore. You'll be able to say you've seen the only conservation land in North America that protects a truly complete, undisturbed spectrum of Arctic ecosystems, but a visit to ANWR goes deeper than that: It shows you the sort of landscape that most people will never see in their lifetime and opens up a whole new perspective on the world.

GATES OF THE ARCTIC NATIONAL PARK AND PRESERVE

Located in the central Brooks Range at the foot of the needle-like Arrigetch Mountains, **Gates of the Arctic National Park and Preserve** is another vast, untouched wilderness that spans about 8.4 million acres. It stretches west from the Dalton Highway, with no established roads, trails, or campgrounds and no established services at all. This park's dense vegetation, marsh, frequent water crossings, and soaring granite peaks make travel very challenging but beautifully remote.

Be prepared to navigate in varied terrain, including remote arctic and subarctic tundra. The best access is by air taxi from Fairbanks (**Ravn Alaska,** 907/266-8394, flyravn.com) to the tiny gateway community of **Bettles** (which houses the park visitor center) or **Anaktuvuk Pass.**

For more information, see nps.gov/gaar or call 907/692-5494 (summer) or 907/459-3730 (winter), or stop in at the **Arctic Interagency Visitor Center** in Coldfoot, at mile 175 of the Dalton Highway. There's no one at Gates of the Arctic to stamp your National Parks passport, but you can catch an air taxi to the headquarters of Kobuk Valley National Park, located in Kotzebue, and get it stamped there.

NOATAK NATIONAL PRESERVE

Perched between the northern coniferous forest and tundra, massive **Noatak National Preserve** serves as a migratory pathway for the Western Arctic caribou herd—about 450,000 animals. It contains more than 250 miles of the slow-moving Noatak River, along with one of North America's largest ecologically intact mountain-ringed river basins. Rafting, canoeing, kayaking, and fishing (for grayling, salmon, arctic char, and whitefish) are all popular activities on the river. This is also a great place for hiking or backpacking along the ridges, where travel is easiest; watch for animals like brown bears, moose, lynx, and Dall sheep. More than 150 songbird species migrate through this area.

As with the other parks listed here, there are no services or developed areas in Noatak National Preserve. Park access is by small plane or boat from nearby communities (Kotzebue or Bettles), and the headquarters are located in Kotzebue's **Northwest Arctic Heritage Center.** Call 907/443-3890 for help getting oriented to the park and arranging travel logistics.

KOBUK VALLEY NATIONAL PARK

The 1.8-million-acre **Kobuk Valley National Park (KVNP)** is most notable for its 25 square miles of massive sand dunes, which can reach as high as 100 feet, a relic of the glaciers that ground their way through the land. Other major features include the slow-moving Kobuk River—an exquisite wilderness float—and the Onion Portage site, where people still gather to harvest caribou as they cross the water, just as they did 10,000 years ago.

KVNP's headquarters are in the **Northwest Arctic Heritage Center** in Kotzebue; call 907/442-3890 for more information.

Alaska Wildlife

Alaska's wildlife is every bit as varied as our wild, diverse landscapes, which range from sandy beaches and temperate rainforests to tundra-clad mountains, glacier-fed waters, and of course the treeless stretch of the high Arctic, which transforms itself into one of the world's richest ecosystems for a few months every year. In fact, summer in Alaska is the destination of choice for many migratory animals, from songbirds to enormous gray whales.

It would be impossible to cover every single animal or bird that you'll find here, but the following are some of the most common, distinctive, or fascinating animals in this amazing state. Of course, we can't guarantee that you'll see these animals—nobody can, they're wild!—but we'll give you as much information as we can to help you increase your odds.

A black bear sow waits patiently as her cubs play at Anan Creek Wildlife Observatory.

Land Mammals

BEARS

If there's one animal that people associate with Alaska, it has to be bears. We have three types of bears, and, believe it or not, there are quite a few differences between them. The good news is that, for the most part, they don't want anything to do with us and will usually make themselves scarce unless you're unlucky enough to surprise one or get between a mother and her cubs. See page 456 for information on safety in bear country.

Black Bears

Black bears *(Ursus americanus)* are the shiest, smallest, and most abundant of Alaska's bears. Still, adult males (called boars) can weigh up to 350 pounds, and the females are, like any mammal, fiercely protective of their young. So they're still plenty intimidating if you come nose-to-nose with one in a surprise encounter. Black bears are agile climbers, and the female (called a sow) will send her cubs up a tree for safety, while she remains at the base to defend them.

Black bears can sprint up to 35 mph for short stretches, and they can be efficient predators of baby moose during the spring calving season. But typically they're opportunistic omnivores, eating a mix of roots, grasses, grubs, insects, berries, fish, meat, and scavenged carrion. Sometimes rich salmon runs will lure black bears to fish shoulder to shoulder with brown bears, but under normal circumstances they try to avoid brown bears, which sometimes prey on their smaller cousins.

Despite the name, black bears aren't always black. They can be brown, cinnamon-colored, blond, an unusual blue-gray color phase called a glacier bear (most common in Southeast Alaska), and even white. So, instead of depending on color to distinguish one bear species from another, look at their face and body shape. Black bears have prominent ears and long, straight noses, and they lack the pronounced shoulder hump that you'll see on a grizzly or brown bear.

Like their bigger brown cousins, black bears stuff themselves to build up reserves of body fat during the summer and fall, when food is plentiful, then hibernate through the winter when food supplies are scarce. Black bears are most likely to den in forested areas and may occupy rock cavities, hollow trees, the empty space underneath tree roots, or holes they've dug. (You might be surprised by the small spaces these bears can squeeze into!)

Cubs are born during hibernation—blind, hairless, and weighing a pound or less—although they grow quickly as they nurse in the den. Cubs typically hibernate with mom through the next winter; families stick together for a couple of years before the cubs go their own way.

WHERE TO SEE THEM

An estimated 100,000 black bears range widely throughout Alaska; you'll find them almost everywhere **south of the Brooks Range** or, to put it another way, everywhere **south of the Arctic Circle.** The only places you usually will not see them are the Seward Peninsula (near Nome), the Alaska Peninsula south of Lake Iliamna (around Katmai National Park), and on a few islands, including Kodiak and Admiralty Island. It's no coincidence that the places you won't find black bears usually have high concentrations of brown bears, which sometimes prey on the smaller black bears.

That said, if you're interested in going to a black bear viewing spot, where spawning

Opener: bears fishing at the Kodiak Brown Bear Center; wolf in Denali National Park. **Above left:** moose crossing sign on highway.

salmon draw them to congregate in unusually high numbers, you're best off heading to **Southeast;** you'll get excellent black bear viewing at the **Anan Creek Wildlife Observatory** and at a few little-known locations on **Prince of Wales Island.**

WHEN TO SEE THEM

You can encounter a black bear at any time of day or night, although they tend to be more active around **dawn and dusk.** They typically emerge from their hibernation in March or April (females who gave birth may stay denned up into April) then go back into hibernation in October or November (pregnant females usually den up sooner). That said, the bear's denning behavior is influenced by the weather, so off-kilter winter weather can also translate to bears that go to sleep earlier or wake up sooner.

Brown Bears and Grizzly Bears

Let's get a bit of terminology straight: Except for the brown bears of Kodiak, which are genetically distinct because of their geographic isolation, **brown bears** and **grizzly bears** are the same species, *Ursus arctos horribilis.* The two names distinguish between the bears' habitats: Brown bears live on the coast and tend to be larger and more tolerant of other bears in close proximity because food is more abundant, while grizzly bears live inland, tend to be smaller, and are also grumpier about bears (or humans) being close by because they need a larger territory to support themselves. When in doubt, just call it a brown bear. That is always correct, while grizzly is only correct if you're dealing with an inland bear.

Like black bears, brown bears are omnivorous opportunists and scavengers, although their greater size and power give them better odds of hunting large animals like moose. They can sprint up to 30 mph over short distance. When a brown bear does kill a moose or other animal, it buries the carcass and will aggressively defend it until it's finished eating, which may take a couple of weeks.

Still, a brown bear can also be attracted by food sources as small as birdseed or as inelegant as your neighborhood trash (the same goes for black bears). As you might imagine, a bear of either species that learns to associate humans or human places with food quickly becomes dangerous and often ends up being killed as a result.

Like black bears, brown bears come in a spectrum of colors from dark brown to a very light blond. They're easy to recognize in part because of their size—a big grizzly boar can weigh up to 600 pounds, while a Kodiak brown bear boar can weigh up to a staggering 1,500 pounds—and their body shape. Brown bears and grizzlies have a pronounced hump of muscle over their shoulders, which gives them the power to dig for food and of course to hunt as well. They have a shorter nose and more dish-shaped face than black bears, and less prominent ears.

Because brown bears are at the very top of the food chain, they're much less shy than black bears and a lot more entertaining to watch. Stick around for long enough and you'll see that individual bears have distinct personalities, and the species as a whole has developed a complex system of body language and social interactions to help minimize conflicts between these powerful, potentially deadly animals.

In coastal areas where rich food sources are available year-round, brown bears may stay awake all year. But in most parts of the state, they stuff themselves during the summer to build up stores of body fat and then hibernate through the long winter when food sources are scarce. As you might imagine, this apex land predator can sleep anywhere it likes, but brown bears typically den in alpine and subalpine areas when possible.

When bears hibernate, their body temperature drops and their metabolic rate drops as they live off their fat reserves. They stop eating, drinking, urinating, and defecating, and they sleep for long periods. That said, every so often a hibernating bear does get up and shuffle around during the winter, not unlike people who stumble out of bed during the night. There's nothing quite like finding fresh bear tracks in the snow to get your adrenaline going.

WHERE TO SEE THEM

You'll find brown bears almost everywhere in Alaska, extending up to the **Brooks Range;** they can even interbreed with the polar bear, creating a hybrid that's variously known as the pizzly or grolar bear. However, guided **bear-viewing trips**—which are the safest way to see a bear in the wild—take place in coastal areas where profuse rich food sources mean the bears are more tolerant of humans and other bears in their "personal space." Some of the most common places for brown bear viewing include **Katmai National Park, Lake Clark National Park,** the **McNeil River State Game Sanctuary, Kodiak Island** in Southwest Alaska, and **Admiralty Island** in Southeast.

WHEN TO SEE THEM

Like black bears, brown bears are usually most active at **dusk and dawn,** although you can encounter them any time of day or night. Mating can occur throughout the summer but typically peaks in May or June, depending on the season; the bears typically hibernate on a similar schedule as black bears, denning up in October or November and emerging in late March, April, or even May.

Peak bear activity—and thus the best opportunities for bear viewing—typically lines up with the salmon runs, which are timed slightly differently around the state, but typically run from **June-September.** The last few years of unusual weather have also caused some unusually timed salmon runs; it's smart to call and chat with a tour provider and ask about their best guess for bear-viewing times this year, before you book a trip.

CHECK THE TRACKS

If you come across bear tracks, you can usually tell what made them by looking at the shape of the toes and the pad of the front foot. The pads on a black bear's feet are more curved than those on a brown or grizzly bear, with shorter claws and toes spaced a little wider apart. The pads of the brown bear's feet are straighter, their claws are longer, and the toes tend to be closer together.

A grizzly bear catches a salmon in Katmai National Park.

Polar Bears

The **polar bear** (*Ursus maritimus*) is a streamlined version of its land-going brethren, so well-suited to life in and around the water that many countries classify it as a marine mammal. Polar bears generally live on any coastal land above the Arctic Circle, with populations on the northern and northwest shores of Alaska. They feed primarily on seals, which they catch when the seal comes up to a breathing hole in the sea ice. However, they will also feed opportunistically on anything else they encounter, including the carcasses of whales brought in by Alaska Native hunters.

Polar bears are listed as a threatened species because the sea ice they depend on for hunting is vanishing. Interestingly, when they move inland in search of other food sources or simply on a wandering exploration, polar bears can meet and interbreed with grizzly bears, creating a hybrid that's known as either a pizzly or a grolar bear.

a polar bear seen on a tour with Northern Alaska Tour Company

Nobody knows exactly how many polar bears there are; the best estimates are between 20,000 and 25,000 in the world. Some scientists speculate that because there are more grizzly bears than polar bears, polar bears will eventually vanish as a distinct species because of interbreeding.

Polar bears can get as large as some of their coastal brown bear cousins—a big male can weigh almost 1,000 pounds—and their fur may be stained, so they don't always appear white. But you can recognize them by their streamlined shape and lack of the prominent shoulder hump that grizzlies use for digging.

Only pregnant female polar bears den up in the winter. They birth 1-3 cubs over the winter, then emerge in the spring when the cubs are strong enough to accompany their mother on the trek to the sea ice.

WHERE TO SEE THEM

During winter, polar bears may wander as far south as St. Lawrence Island and the Kuskokwim Delta (near Bethel, in Western Alaska), but as a general rule, they're found only in the **Arctic.** You might occasionally see a polar bear on Point Barrow, the northernmost point of land in the United States, just outside of **Barrow.** But the best place to see them is in the tiny village of **Kaktovik,** the only human settlement in the Arctic National Wildlife Refuge. Hopefully it goes without saying that you should not, under any circumstances, go searching for polar bears yourself. Take a guided tour so that you'll have proper (armed) protection and a suitably strong vehicle to ride in.

WHEN TO SEE THEM

Male polar bears and non-pregnant females don't hibernate, so you can see them year-round. The **fall whaling season** is the best time to see bears near Kaktovik. The bears are attracted by the whale carcasses, although there is no guarantee of when (or if) the captains will land a whale. **Spring** usually offers better than usual chances of sighting bears, thanks to the usual lighting and ice conditions.

TOP EXPERIENCE

MOOSE

Moose *(Alces alces)*, the largest members of the deer family, range throughout all of Alaska. In fact, our Alaska-Yukon subspecies *(Alces alces gigas)* is the biggest moose of them all, with females typically weighing up to half a ton while males may weigh up to 1,600 pounds. Interestingly, the same animal we call a moose here is called an elk in Europe.

A moose's favorite food is willow, birch, and aspen twigs, although they'll strip bark off tree branches during the winter. You can tell a moose has been browsing because the bark is chiseled off the branches in long scrapes—as opposed to the vertical scrapes on the trunks sometimes made by bears—or when you see the ends of twigs that look like they were sawed off crudely. (If they're chiseled off neatly, it's the work of a hare or possibly a porcupine.)

There may be as many as 200,000 moose distributed throughout most of Alaska. Their presence in Southeast Alaska's islands is limited but becoming more common; they are strong swimmers that can travel several miles in the water if need be, and they may live more than 16 years in the wild.

Only male (bull) moose grow antlers. They form during the bull's first year of life, then are shed that winter. They grow a new pair of antlers every summer, and use them to spar with other males in shoving matches to determine who is most dominant during the rut, or breeding season, which takes places in late September or early October.

Cows birth their calves in the spring—typically May and June, although it can vary—and are incredibly protective. New calves weigh 25-30 pounds and can walk within a few hours of birth. They can grow to be several hundred pounds by the time they're five months old, and are typically weaned in the fall. The following spring, the mother will chase them off so she can breed again.

Where and When to See Them

Moose range throughout the **entire state,** except for the Arctic coast and some islands

Only male moose have antlers.

in Southeast and Southwest Alaska. They can go anywhere—I've even seen nugget-like moose droppings atop mountain ridges—but the most common places to see them are anywhere that **dense growth** of their favorite willow, aspen, and birch browse occurs. Favorite spots for moose usually include recently burned or deforested areas, places where streams meet **brushland,** and **wetlands,** which their long, slender legs make them marvelously suited to navigate. Unfortunately, brushy and wet areas near roads are also popular moose habitats, which causes predictable problems when these giant animals dart into the roadway unexpectedly.

DALL SHEEP

Believe it or not, a wish to protect Dall sheep helped spur the creation of Denali National Park and Preserve. The majestic **Dall sheep** *(Ovis dalli dalli)* can weigh up to 300 pounds and lives in the craggy alpine regions of Alaska's subarctic mountain ranges. They're closely related to bighorn sheep and in the same genus as domestic sheep.

Both male and female wild sheep have horns, but it's the males' horns that usually draw the most attention. By the age of about eight years old, a Dall sheep ram's curved horns will have grown so long, they form a full circle. These horns become both weapon and armor as the rams engage in fierce head-butting contests to establish their pecking order of dominance. The head-butting takes place year-round but is especially intense during the November-December mating season. Dall sheep ewes have horns too, but they're more of a curved, slender sickle shape.

Dall sheep lambs are born in late June or early July, in rocky cliffs that help protect them from predators. They start eating tundra plants soon after birth and are usually weaned by October. During the winter, sheep typically move to windswept areas where they can access feed like lichen, moss, and frozen grass or sedges. During the spring, they may travel great distances to eat mineral-laden soil at mineral licks. Twelve is considered "old" for a Dall sheep, although ewes have been documented as living to 19 years old.

Where and When to See Them

Spring and **summer** are the best to see Dall sheep in the wild. Look for them in **mountainous areas** along the **Kenai Peninsula**, around **Tok,** the **Chugach mountains** of Southcentral; the central and eastern **Brooks Range;** and in the **Tanana Hills** and **White Mountains** near Fairbanks. However, perhaps the most famous place of all for seeing Dall sheep is **Denali National Park**. Make sure you bring your binoculars, and look for moving spots of white on the mountainsides.

MOUNTAIN GOATS

If you see a white spot moving around on the mountainside and it's not a Dall sheep, it's a **mountain goat** *(Oreamnos americanus).* Both genders of this wild goat have long, shaggy coats, including long hair on the legs, and a distinct "beard" under the chin, with black, sharp, and spiky horns. They start shedding their winter coats in June and by July will have a softer and sleeker summer coat; by mid-October, they've grown a full winter coat again.

The males are called billies and travel alone or in small bachelor groups; the females, called nannies, birth their young, called kids, in rugged nursery cliffs that provide protection against predators. The goats' hooves have a hard outer sheath and a soft inner pad that helps them grip onto sheer rock faces, letting goats traverse seemingly impassable cliffs.

Even if you can't get a clear view with binoculars, use body shape to help you differentiate between mountain goats and Dall sheep, which also inhabit steep, rocky mountainsides. If the moving white shape you see is barrel-shaped, it's probably a Dall sheep. If it's more of a rectangular blob, it's a mountain goat.

Billies can weigh up to 280 or 300 pounds, but females usually top out at about 180 pounds. They spend their winters in high alpine forest or windswept ridges, eating rough forage like mountain hemlock and blueberry bushes. During the summers they spend their time browsing on a multitude of tiny plants in the alpine tundra.

Where and When to See Them

Mountain goats are most common in **Southeast** and the **Chugach** and **Wrangell Mountains** of **Southcentral** Alaska. During the summer, look for them in the cliffs along the **Seward Highway** south of Anchorage, in **Wrangell-St. Elias National Park,** and on **wildlife cruises** out of **Seward,** and almost anywhere in **Southeast;** you might even see them from a plane during a flightseeing trip.

Finally, you can also find introduced populations of mountain goats on **Kodiak Island** and **Baranof Island,** which is best known for housing the community of **Sitka.**

CARIBOU AND REINDEER

Caribou *(Rangifer tarandus)* are one of Alaska's most enigmatic animals. They may live in herds that number 100,000 strong or as few as 100 animals. Every year, caribou migrate en masse from their winter ranges to summer calving grounds. Each band of caribou has set migration routes that they've traveled for hundreds of years, and in places where caribou are common, Alaska Native lifeways were often built around that migration.

Caribou subsist on leaves and mushrooms during the summer and lichens, sedges, and shrubs during the winter. They typically weigh up to 350 or 400 pounds for a bull, or roughly 200 pounds for a cow. Both male and female caribou grow antlers and then shed them every winter, although the females' antlers are smaller and more dense than those of the males. The males use their antlers for shoving matches to establish dominance, much as moose do.

Cow caribou typically calve in the spring, dropping all their babies—called calves—within a 10-day period. This serves as a survival strategy both by maximizing their access to summer resources and "flooding the market," as it were, for predators. The calves can run well within just a few hours, and quickly become strong swimmers too.

Interestingly, the tendons in a caribou's feet make a snapping sound when they walk. A small herd of them walking together sounds a little bit like bacon frying. Every hair in a caribou's coat is hollow, making them buoyant

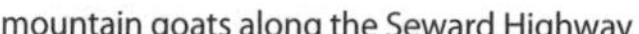
mountain goats along the Seward Highway

A herd of wild caribou crosses the road.

and giving them great insulation; you won't find anything warmer than traditional Alaska Native clothing made of caribou hide.

You'll occasionally find reindeer throughout Alaska, either being deliberately farmed or in feral herds that are managed for hunting. Reindeer are essentially domesticated caribou, but because of that domestication, there are a few differences between the species: Reindeer are typically shorter, stouter, and have slightly smaller antlers, with a thicker, denser coat than caribou. Reindeer will usually have ear tags, too. Reindeer cows weigh about the same as a caribou cow, but the reindeer bulls tend to be smaller than their caribou cousins.

A note on terminology: In Europe, both subspecies just discussed are known as reindeer. A European "wild reindeer" is what Americans would call a caribou, and a "domesticated reindeer" is what we call a reindeer too.

Where and When to See Them

Caribou live throughout the state, except for Southeast Alaska and most of the Aleutian Islands. Many of them spend their winters in the mountains or the boreal forest, but you'll have a much easier time finding them in their summer calving grounds, which, again, spread all over the state. You'll find some of the best potential for caribou-viewing in places like **Denali National Park,** especially around mile 15 of the Park Road and the Savage River Loop Trail, east of the Bridge Access Road in **Kenai** (mile 10.8 of the Kenai Spur Highway), and on the tundra near **Arctic** communities. You can also see them at the **Alaska Wildlife Conservation Center** in Southcentral.

In some places—especially the roadways near **Nome**—you may see herds of reindeer instead of caribou. There are also feral reindeer on the **Pribilof Island** of **St. Paul**.

MUSK OXEN

Although the name is a little counterintuitive, the species of musk ox found in Alaska is the **Greenland musk ox** *(Ovibos moschatus),* descendants of 34 animals transported here from Greenland in 1930. (Musk oxen were indigenous to Alaska but died out here by the early 1920s.)

Nowadays, several thousand musk oxen exist in northern and northwestern Alaska and on a few islands. They have a coarse outer coat and a very short, fine undercoat called qiviut that keeps them warm through the Arctic winter. Bulls can grow up to five feet tall at the

A musk ox grazes near the Chugach Mountains.

shoulders and weigh as much as 800 pounds; cows can stand four feet tall at the shoulders and weigh some 500 pounds. They subsist by grazing on small plants, grasses, and shrubs, and cows generally give birth to one calf a year in the spring. The calves weigh around 30 pounds at birth and may weigh almost eight times that by the time they're a year old.

Both sexes have horns (although the bull's horns are much larger and heavier). When threatened, the herd forms a ring around their young, horns facing out to address the threat. During the rutting season (generally August-October), the bulls hold spectacular "jousting" matches in which they charge full-speed at each other from a distance of up to 50 yards (50 meters) and collide headfirst at full force. Four inches of horn and three inches of the bone, layered directly over the brain, help absorb the force of the impact. The collisions continue until one of the bulls turns tail and runs.

Qiviut can be harvested and turned into yarn; you'll find it at the Musk Ox Farm in **Palmer,** where you can also see the musk oxen themselves. You can also find qiviut (but not the actual musk ox) at the **Oomingmak Musk Ox Co-op** in Anchorage and in other stores around Alaska.

Where and When to See Them

If you want an absolutely guaranteed musk ox sighting, head to either the **Alaska Wildlife Conservation Center** south of Anchorage or the **Musk Ox Farm** in Palmer. The best place to see them in the wild is near **Nome,** where you'll often see them on or near the scenic roads leading to nearby villages. There are a few musk oxen in the **Arctic National Wildlife Refuge** too, although their population has diminished so much—and the refuge is so enormous—that your odds of seeing them are minuscule.

WOOD BISON

The **wood bison,** which once ranged across both Alaska and Canada, was thought to be entirely extinct by the early 1900s. However, a small population was found in Canada and, after several years of concerted effort from the Alaska Wildlife Conservation Center and the Alaska Department of Fish and Game, 130 wood bison—descendants of that surviving Canadian herd—were, with the community's agreement and support, released near the tiny Western Alaska town of Shageluk.

Wood bison look very similar to the plains bison of the Lower 48 states, and both sexes have short, upward-curving horns. Bulls can stand up to six feet tall at the shoulder and weigh more than a ton (2,000 pounds); females generally weigh around 1,200 pounds. Both sexes have most of their weight concentrated in the forward halves of their bodies, with a massive head and hair on their chins that looks like a goatee. A large hump in front of the shoulders helps wood bison sweep their heads back and forth, using them as brooms to brush away the snow from winter feed (mostly grass and sedges).

Wood bison are very social and, given the opportunity, tend to live in groups of 20-60 cows and their young, with bulls living in smaller bachelor groups until they rejoin the cows for the late-summer breeding season. Cows typically bear two calves every three years; the young can stand within 30 minutes and run and kick within hours. Both genders keep warm with a dense winter coat of soft, warm hair; they shed that winter coat in the spring and will have grown a completely new summer coat by midsummer.

Where and When to See Them

So far almost all the wood bison have stuck fairly close to the town of Shageluk, which has no tourist infrastructure to speak of—so there really is no easy way to see them. That might change over time.

WOLVES

Denali National Park may contain the most famous **wolf packs** *(Canis lupus)* in Alaska, but if you're very lucky you might see them almost anywhere in the state—including coastal bear-viewing areas (some wolves have learned to catch salmon, just like bears) and the densely populated area around Anchorage.

The Alaska Department of Fish and Game estimates that there are between 7,000 and 11,000 wolves dispersed throughout Alaska. Depending on the environment, they may prey on everything from squirrels and hares to larger animals like deer and moose. These long-legged animals can sprint up to 40 mph or sustain a ground-eating lope for long periods.

Wolves in Interior Alaska typically weigh up to 115 pounds for a male, with females just a little smaller; both sexes of wolves in Southeast are a little smaller yet. Alaska wolves typically live in packs of 6-7 animals with an intricate social hierarchy that's topped by a dominant male and a dominant female. These two typically form the breeding pair that produces pups each year, although occasionally another female will bear pups too.

Where to See Them

Wolves are intelligent, adaptable creatures. As such, they range widely over mainland Alaska, all the way from the tundra near the Arctic Ocean to most of the forested islands of Southeast; you might even see them hanging around the outskirts of big cities like Anchorage, Fairbanks, or Juneau. Perhaps the most stories of wolf pack sightings are in **Denali National Park**, but the density of wolves is actually highest in **Southeast**, where Sitka black-tailed deer are a plentiful

a mother wolf and her cub in Denali National Park

food source. There is no guaranteed or "suggested" way of finding these typically shy animals, but keep your eyes open **near bear-viewing** areas; sometimes wolves catch salmon working their way upstream, just like the bears do.

When to See Them

There is no ideal or peak time for viewing wolves. That said, keep a particular lookout in mid- to late summer, when the pups of the year are old enough to travel with the rest of the pack.

FOXES

There are two fox species in Alaska: the **red fox** *(Vulpes fulva),* which is found throughout much of the state, and the **arctic fox** *(Vulpes lagopus),* which is uniquely suited to life on the treeless tundra of the Arctic and Aleutian Islands.

The red fox can weigh up to 15 pounds and measure up to 32 inches long, including a 15-inch tail. Red foxes are only sometimes monogamous, although both parents care for the young. Their food of choice seems to be voles, but they are omnivorous and will eat everything from muskrats and squirrels to carrion, insects, eggs, and birds.

Arctic foxes look stouter than red foxes, thanks to their shorter limbs and luxurious winter coat; but they're actually notably lighter, weighing only up to 10 pounds. Arctic foxes are monogamous, and both parents help to feed and rear the pups. They typically hunt small mammals, including lemmings and voles, and in coastal regions seabird eggs and young birds figure heavily into the arctic fox's diet. Like red foxes they are omnivorous, and will even eat berries.

Arctic foxes molt twice yearly, shedding their white winter coat for a mottled summer coat, or vice versa. White arctic foxes are common in northerly parts of the state, while in the more southerly Aleutian and Pribilof islands you may see a blue color phase, which really looks dark gray. The "blue" foxes are a darker gray during the summer, while the white foxes turn brown during the summer.

Both species of foxes have been known to cache food for later use when prey is abundant, and may even dig up their cache, inspect it, and then rebury it in the same place.

Where to See Them

The arctic fox typically lives in the **Arctic** and the windswept **Aleutian islands.** The red fox

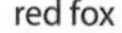

red fox

is native in some parts of Alaska, but thanks to fox farming operations its range was expanded to encompass most of the state. The red fox prefers to live in **marshes, hills,** and other **broken country,** although it sometimes shares tundra range with arctic foxes. When this happens, the largest red foxes are dominant to—and sometimes prey on—arctic foxes.

When to See Them

Both foxes are active year-round and are so widespread that, if you're in the correct type of habitat, they could pop up anywhere. Just keep your eyes open. The one exception to that is St. Paul and St. George Islands in the **Pribilofs,** where an unusual blue/black phase of arctic fox is so common near towns that they can be considered a real pest.

Birds

Alaska is home to a fascinating variety of birds, especially when migratory songbirds fly in for the rich summer season. The following birds are some of the most notable, unusual, or distinguished of the state's inhabitants, but this isn't even a tithe of the state's bird population.

I cheerfully refer you to the excellent Cornell Lab of Ornithology (allaboutbirds.org) or your favorite birding guide for help with identifying the many other birds you'll encounter here. Local birders have also told me that the iBird app is excellent for use in Alaska.

TOP EXPERIENCE

EAGLES

You'll find both bald and golden eagles in Alaska, although bald eagles are by far more common, with an estimated 30,000 throughout the state. Despite their noble image, bald eagles are in fact accomplished scavengers. So, although you may see them swooping down from the sky to pluck a fish out of the water, you're just as likely to find them dining on carrion or picking over a dumpster, right next to the ravens.

Bald eagles can weigh up to 12 pounds and have a wingspan of 7.5 feet; the females are larger than the males. They prey primarily on fish and can even swim—albeit badly—if they latch onto a fish too big to lift and would rather tow it to shore than let go of it. Bald eagles also take small mammals, waterfowl, and sea creatures like urchins, clams, and crabs that are exposed by the tide.

Bald eagles mate for life and the female lays two or three eggs in the spring, but usually just one fledgling survives to leave the nest after a couple of months. The immature bald eagle doesn't get its trademark white head and tail until it's four or five years old; until

a raven and a bald eagle near the Chilkat River

then, it's a mottled brown. A mating pair may return to the same nest year after year, enlarging it each time until it weighs as much as two tons.

Golden eagles, on the other hand, are finely tuned killing machines, although they won't hesitate to scavenge carrion when it's available—but perish the thought of ever seeing a golden eagle in a dumpster. Golden eagles can weigh up to 12 pounds and have a wingspan of up to seven feet. As with bald eagles and most raptors, the females are usually larger than the males.

Golden eagles can prey on young Dall sheep and caribou and will even team up to hunt much like a wolf pack, with one eagle flushing out prey while the other descends to make the kill. In very rare cases a golden eagle can even kill an adult caribou by striking it repeatedly. That said, they also prey on hares, birds, and other small game.

You can easily tell the difference between mature bald eagles and golden eagles, thanks to the bald eagle's characteristic white head and tail. But immature bald eagles and their mostly brown plumage can look quite a bit like a golden eagle. The easiest way to tell them apart, if you're lucky enough to get up close or catch them in your binoculars, is by looking at their legs and wings: Bald eagles have bare legs and a whitish underside on the front edge of their wings, while golden eagles have feathers all the way down their legs.

Golden eagles pair-bond for several years at a time and breed once a year, but their young face a mortality rate as high as 75 percent. Both bald and golden eagles are thought to live up to 20 or 30 years old in the wild.

Where and When to See Them

You can live in Alaska for decades and never see a golden eagle—so if you do see one, you're very lucky! That said, your best odds of seeing one are at the **Gunsight Mountain Hawkwatch,** which takes place in early to mid-March; the migration continues through May.

Bald eagles are easier. From October through February, thousands of eagles congregate to feed in the open water of the **Chilkat Bald Eagle Preserve**. In April, eagles again congregate en masse near the mouth of the mighty **Stikine River** near Wrangell, also in Southeast, to feast on an oily fish known as hooligan or euchalon.

Bald eagles are also plentiful along almost all of Alaska's coastline, especially when there are rich runs of salmon, herring, hooligan, or other fish the eagles can dine on. You'll even see bald eagles perched on trees or light posts in the middle of some Alaska towns, and if some poor fisherman is foolish enough to leave his catch uncovered in the back of a pickup truck, you might be treated to the unusual sight of the eagles mobbing the truck and eating the fish. They also hang out near dumpsters in regular fishing towns, and for some reason during the winter they often perch like Christmas ornaments in the trees along the road to Portage Glacier in Southcentral.

OWLS

Alaska is host to 10 species of **owls,** from the tiny saw-whet owl that you might see perched atop roadside light poles in broad daylight to great gray and great horned owls, which can stand two feet tall or more. These birds have enormous eyes, hearing so acute they can pinpoint a small animal moving around beneath the snow by sound only, and special feathers that let them glide soundlessly. They're beautifully suited for hunting at night, although some species are active during the day.

Perhaps the most interesting owl in Alaska is the snowy owl, which nests on the Arctic tundra, depending on their speckled white feathers to help them blend in. (If you see an owl that's almost completely white, it's a male.) They typically hunt lemmings and voles, although they can take prey as large as ducks. When game is scarce in their home range, snowy owls will sometimes migrate to other hunting grounds, sometimes venturing as far south as the Lower 48 states.

Because owls are nocturnal, you will most frequently find yourself birding for them by

Birding Bonanza

Hundreds of species and millions of birds flock to Alaska every spring. With that in mind, there is no such thing as a bad place for birding in Alaska. However, there is a "best" time for seeing migratory songbirds—typically May and June—and there are a few places around the state that stand out as particularly good for birding.

Wherever you find yourself for your Alaska birding trip, you'll want to bring spotting scope and tripod, binoculars, camera with telephoto lens, rain jacket for yourself, and waterproof covers for spotting/camera gear.

Most communities offer downloadable birding checklists for their area; check the website for the local convention and visitors bureau or chamber of commerce. You can also participate in the Alaska Department of Fish and Game's **Wings Over Alaska** birding program, which includes birding checklists and certificates for the number of species you've seen in Alaska. See adfg.alaska.gov for more information.

SOUTHEAST

More than 300 species of birds nest up and down the "Panhandle," an affectionate nickname for Southeast Alaska. In general, June is the best time to observe nesting birds and hear their songs anywhere in Southeast, and hundreds of species have been seen/identified in every town up and down the Inside Passage.

Birding Festivals in Southeast

- **Ketchikan's Alaska Hummingbird Festival** (April): This low-key event runs through the month. Although it celebrates the return of all migratory birds, the focus is on the lovely rufous hummingbird.
- **Wrangell's Stikine River Birding Festival** (late April, wrangell.com): Watch millions of shorebirds arriving to the Stikine River delta area. An astonishing number of eagles also congregate to feast on oily hooligan (also called euchalon or candlefish).
- **Cordova's Copper River Delta Shorebird Festival** (early May, copperriverdeltashorebirdfestival.com): A massed migration of millions of shorebirds, raptors, waterfowl, and songbirds passes through the Copper River delta in early May.
- **The Haines Alaska Bald Eagle Festival** (mid-November, baldeagles.org): This festival celebrates one of the world's largest concentrations of bald eagles; from October through February, they congregate to feed in the open water of the nearby Alaska Chilkat Bald Eagle Preserve.

SOUTHCENTRAL

Birders all flock to Homer for the **Kachemak Bay Shorebird Festival** (kachemakshorebird.

ear, or identifying them by their calls. Many mobile apps for birding and birding CDs have recordings of owl calls to help you differentiate between the species. You can also listen to recordings of each owl species in the Alaska Department of Fish and Game e-Library (adfg.alaska.gov).

Where and When to See Them

Your best chance of seeing owls is where forest meets a cleared area or a waterway, and the best time to see them is around dusk or dawn. Their distribution throughout Alaska, however, varies greatly between species. You'll almost never find the northern pygmy owl, northern saw-whet owl, barred owl, or western screech owl outside Southeast Alaska, while the unusual snowy owl lives only in Arctic tundra and, more rarely, in the tundra along the Western Alaska coastline. The org) in early May; more than 130 species usually migrate through. Another legendary Southcentral birding festival is the **Gunsight Mountain Hawkwatch** (hawkwatch.org) in early to mid-March, when birders gather to watch **raptors** migrating through a mountain pass some 120 miles northeast of Anchorage. (The migration continues through May.)

INTERIOR

Interior Alaska's real spectacle is **sandhill cranes.** You can see these stately birds—and hear their strange croaking, rattling cry—as they stage in the legendary **Creamer's Field Migratory Waterfowl Refuge,** which just happens to sit smack in the middle of Fairbanks, Alaska's second-largest city. There are two festivals to celebrate the birds' passage: **The Spring Migration Celebration** (creamersfield.org) in late April/early May, and the **Tanana Valley Sandhill Crane Festival** (creamersfield.org) in August, as the cranes are heading back south. Both festivals are great chances to see and hear migratory songbirds, too.

SOUTHWEST

If you're interested in seabirds, there is no better place to visit than the remote, windswept **Pribilof Islands,** where during the summer you'll see millions of seabirds cascading into the air or the water every morning; the seabird colonies on **St. George Island** (one of the Pribilofs) are among the largest in the world. Meanwhile, a springtime or fall trip to **St. Paul** (the only other inhabited Pribilof Island) is a great place to find Asian species that have been blown off their migration course by the ever-present winds.

Unalaska—better known as **Dutch Harbor**—is another spectacular place for seeing Asian strays during the spring and fall migration. But Unalaska is also the best base for seeing some 40 million seabirds nesting up and down the Aleutian Islands in the summer, and great flocks of **waterfowl** overwinter in these ice-free waters.

ARCTIC

These remote tundra towns are the ideal destination for spring and summer birding trips because the nearby area is the goal for many migratory species who then set up shop to breed and raise their young. The hundreds of miles of roadway around Nome make it particularly suited for bird-watching from mid-May to mid-June, when hundreds of migratory species are arriving or passing through.

The bird-watching in **Barrow** isn't as diverse, but this is the only reliable place for seeing the enormous **snowy owl,** and the Arctic shoreline is the ideal summer habitat for a number of shorebirds.

short-eared owl, however, is found throughout all of Alaska, and you'll find the northern hawk owl and great horned owl everywhere in Alaska except the Arctic. The boreal owl and the great gray owl occupy Southeast, Interior, and Southcentral Alaska.

RAVENS

If you ever hear unexplainable noises coming from the trees in Alaska—ranging from croaking and cawing to the mews of a cat, the "glook" of big stones falling into a pond or the rasp of two wood pieces being knocked together—odds are good that they're coming from a **raven** (*Corvus corax*). These clever members of the crow family are accomplished mimics and have even developed calls to alert land predators to the presence of prey so they can feed on the leftovers.

Ravens are omnivorous, dining on carrion,

small mammals and birds, grains, berries, and fruits. The biggest ravens you'll ever see are in and around large towns like Anchorage, Fairbanks, and Homer, where they dine richly on fish scraps and other trash discarded by humans.

Ravens are extremely intelligent, capable of reasoning their way through problems with logic and recognizing individuals of various species, including humans. It's not unusual to see them playing in the air currents generated around tall buildings or rock formations; they also play "fetch" with sticks and feathers in the air, and they'll interact playfully with other species. It's no wonder that Alaska Native mythologies give Raven the attributes of both Creator and Trickster; depending on his whims he may act with great generosity or cause great mischief, or both.

Nobody's exactly sure how long ravens live in the wild, but captive birds have lived to be almost 30. The male and female mate for life (although infidelity is common) and breed once a year in the spring.

Where and When to See Them

You'll find ravens all over Alaska at any time of year. That said, they tend to congregate more in human areas during the winter, when they take advantage of plentiful food from dumpsters and trash cans; during the summer they are still common but more widely dispersed. You may see groups of ravens "commuting" in and out of town from backcountry roosting spots, where dozens (sometimes even hundreds) of ravens may gather to sleep in a single tree.

PTARMIGAN

There are three species of **ptarmigan** in Alaska: the **willow ptarmigan** (*Lagopus lagopus*), the **rock ptarmigan** (*Lagopus muta*), and the **white-tailed ptarmigan** (*Lagopus leucura*). All three are about the size of a small chicken, and their chicks are adorable, fast-moving balls of yellow fluff with brown stripes. All three species typically migrate very short distances when compared to other Alaskan animals, moving from higher-elevation breeding grounds to lower-elevation winter grounds. Ptarmigan chicks usually hatch in mid- to late June. They double or triple their weight within a couple of weeks as they follow their mother around, learning to eat berries, leaf buds, and the tips of twigs.

All ptarmigan change colors with the season, developing mostly white feathers in October and then molting to a variety of speckled browns in the spring, from May to July, depending on species and gender. The males also develop breeding plumage, although it's relatively subtle when compared to songbirds and other species. For example, the male willow ptarmigan (called a cock) develops a cape of chestnut-red feathers.

Where and When to See Them

You can see ptarmigan all year-round throughout Alaska, although some of the best spots are **Thompson Pass** on the way to Valdez; the **Haines Highway** as it goes through **Chilkat Pass**, 65 miles north of Haines; around **Nome;** and sometimes along the **Steese** and **Taylor Highways** north of Fairbanks. Listen to hear their strange mix of croaking/cackling calls in alpine or subalpine valleys near dusk or dawn, or watch to see flocks startled from cover by your approach in fall or winter.

During the summer, you're more likely to see a lone female floundering away from you, seemingly wounded. Rest assured that she does not need your help; she does this to lure predators away from her nest. So, count yourself lucky to have seen her, then politely give her plenty of space.

SANDHILL CRANES

Alaskans know spring is here when great Vs of sandhill cranes fly overhead, long necks thrust straight forward, legs trailing behind their six-foot wingspan. The best description for their very distinctive call is the sound of rocks being rattled in a tin can, although they're very elegant once they're on the ground.

The stately gray wading birds measure almost three feet tall and have bright red foreheads. They're omnivorous ground feeders that devour frogs, rodents, insects, seeds, and berries, and although the parents do feed the young, a baby crane can also hunt for itself within about a day of birth.

All dignity is abandoned when sandhill cranes meet for their breeding display, usually in late winter or early spring. The pair take turns making deep bows followed by dramatic, ungainly leaps into the air and a series of hops, skips, and turns. Scientists think cranes probably mate for life, and they're believed to live as much as 20 years in the wild.

Where and When to See Them

Two distinct populations of sandhill cranes nest in Alaska, using two migratory pathways to get to their traditional nesting grounds. If you're fascinated by these birds, you can take an early May or mid-September trip to the Copper River Delta to see the smaller Pacific Flyway population, which numbers 20,000-25,000 birds, or to the Tanana Valley near Delta Junction to see the Mid-Continent population, which easily numbers 10 times as many. Creamer's Field in Fairbanks is also a near-legendary place to see these birds congregating and staging for their migration.

LOONS

If you've ever heard a strange, cackling laugh or wail crossing over the water in Alaska, especially near dusk, don't worry: The only thing haunting you is a **loon,** also known as the "spirit of the wilderness." There are five species of loons in the world (common, yellow-billed, red-throated, Pacific, and Arctic), and Alaska has every one of them.

Loon parents take turns incubating the eggs, and the newly hatched young ride on their parents' backs for much of their first week. Loons are spectacular divers, staying underwater more than a minute and diving hundreds of feet deep as they feed on fish, insects, aquatic vegetation, and even frogs. They're also strong divers, although when they land they coast to a stop on their breasts instead of their feet, which are set far back on their bodies.

Where and When to See Them

Loons spend the winter in coastal waters, then migrate to inland waters to breed and raise their chicks. You'll typically find common and Pacific loons throughout Southcentral and Interior Alaska, with red-throated loons appearing in these waters less commonly. Yellow-billed and arctic loons are most commonly found along the Arctic coast.

PUFFINS

Puffins are sometimes called sea parrots, although I always think of these funny little birds as a cross between penguins and toucans—they just got shorted a little bit in the beak department! You'll find two species here: the **horned puffin** *(Fratercula corniculata)* and the **tufted puffin** *(Fratercula cirrhata).* Unlike penguins, puffins can fly through the air, but like penguins they are at their best

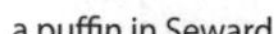

a puffin in Seward

when they "fly" under the water, using their wings for propulsion, diving to feed on fish and zooplankton.

Most of the pictures and souvenirs out there show horned puffins; during the summer they have bright yellow, red-tipped beaks, white faces and chests, and a small, fleshy "horn" over each eye. Tufted puffins have black bodies, white faces, and tufts of feathers curling back from either side of the head.

Puffins beat their wings up to 400 times per minute when they fly, reaching speeds of up to 50 mph. I love the description given of them on Audubon's Project Puffin (projectpuffin.audubon.org): a flying puffin sometimes looks like a black -and-white football.

Puffin parents nest underground and work together to carefully raise a single chick in the burrow. Nobody knows exactly how old puffins can get, but they can keep breeding up to 10 years old, and at least one Atlantic puffin is known to have lived for almost 40 years.

Mosquitoes

Yes, mosquitoes are present throughout the Americas—but I guarantee you've never seen anything like Alaskan mosquitoes. We're only half-joking when we call them the unofficial state bird. We have several species of mosquitoes, all of which are much larger than the mosquitoes you'll see in other states or countries. They'll swarm anywhere, especially if there's stagnant water—their preferred breeding ground—within easy reach. Only the female mosquito bites, using the protein in blood to grow her eggs; the male mosquito subsists peacefully on nectar.

Mosquitoes are particularly dense and bothersome in Interior and Arctic Alaska, and it's no exaggeration to say that their bloodthirsty swarms can drive caribou to run madly in a blind attempt to escape. They'll even bite through clothing, and thicker material, such as GORE-TEX boots.

Where and When to See Them

Puffins spend most of their lives out at sea, but you can see them when they come to land to breed during the summer. Almost any **sightseeing cruise** in **Southeast** or **Southcentral** has good odds of spotting puffins breeding on islands and headlands starting in June, until the chick fledges in September or October and the whole family heads to open water for the winter. Some of the best starting spots for these cruises include Seward and Valdez in Southcentral, Kodiak in Southwest, and cruises out of Gustavus into the Southeast Alaska waters of Glacier Bay National Park.

Aquatic Wildlife

ORCAS

It's impossible to mistake the sight of an orca's tall, black-and-white dorsal fin cutting through the water; it can be up to six feet high on a male. Also called killer whales or wolves of the sea, the **orca** *(Orcinus orca)* is the largest member of the dolphin family. These highly intelligent predators feed on fish and marine mammals, and will even briefly beach themselves to grab a seal or sea lion from shore.

A male killer whale can be up to 27 feet long and weigh up to 13,300 pounds; by any measure, they're the most powerful predator on earth. Females grow up to 23 feet long and may only weigh half as much. Their upright dorsal fins are unique to each individual, so they play a crucial role in helping scientists and observers identify individual whales. The male, or bull, killer whale's dorsal fin is much taller than that of the females.

Not much is known about the complex social lives and structure of the clever orca, although they've earned their nickname by hunting in a pack to kill larger animals, or working cooperatively to drive schools of fish into other waiting orcas. They might even regulate their reproduction to maintain a stable group size, and each pod (family group) has its own distinctive noises that can be recognized from a distance—although the killer whales that specialize in hunting other marine mammals don't vocalize as much. Male killer whales may live to be as old as 50 in the wild, while females may live to be 80.

Where and When to See Them

Orcas live throughout Alaska's waters, although they're most common in the waters between and throughout **Southwest, Southcentral,** and **Southeast** Alaska, with **Prince William Sound**—especially near **Valdez** and **Cordova**—and Southeast Alaska providing some of the best viewing. During the spring they tend to move northward through the Bering Strait, then head back south when the pack ice (old sea ice) encroaches.

HUMPBACK WHALES

Also called the ballerinas of the sea, **humpback whales** *(Megaptera novaeangliae)* show a variety of eye-catching behavior, from breaching to sky hopping, lob-tailing, tail-slapping, and flipper-slapping—not bad for an animal that can be 49 feet long and weigh 35 tons (that's for a female; the males are a little smaller). Aside from this behavior, humpbacks are instantly recognizable by their very long flippers, which can measure up to one-third of their body length.

Nobody knows exactly why humpbacks engage in such spectacular behavior, although it's thought that at least some of it is males vying for a female's attention. But both sexes perform these behaviors throughout the year, even during the summer months when all they want to do is feed in Alaska's frigid but rich waters. (They do nothing but feed here, then fast while at their winter breeding grounds in Japan, Hawaii, or Mexico.) Quite a few scientists speculate that both genders perform these acrobatics simply because they can, or for the fun of it.

Surprisingly, the giant humpback survives on one of the smallest creatures in the ocean:

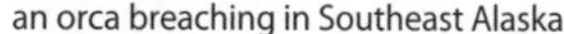

an orca breaching in Southeast Alaska

krill, along with a few species of schooling fish. They feed by taking in a big mouthful of seawater, closing their mouth, and pressing that water out through their baleen, which acts as a sieve; the water can make it out, but all the food is trapped in the humpback's mouth. A single humpback can eat up to 1.5 tons of krill in a day. They also engage in bubble-net feeding, a cooperative behavior in which several whales encircle a school of fish by blowing bubbles, forcing the fish together. Then, at the leader's audible cue, all the whales lunge up through the middle to grab a mouthful of food.

Humpbacks are the only baleen whales that vocalize. While they might be most famous for the long, intricate songs that males perform—again, thought to be related to mate selection—they also growl or bellow, sounds that people are sometimes surprised (or spooked!) to discover can be heard from dry land.

Here's another fascinating aspect of humpback behavior. They've long been listed on the endangered list, mainly due to human whaling activities. But the species is bouncing back, and with numbers noticeably higher, scientists have started seeing humpbacks deliberately—and repeatedly—protecting smaller marine mammals, like seals, from killer whales. Some speculate that these agile giants may be engaging in true altruistic behavior as they forgo opportunities to feed, rest, and socialize in order to rescue the smaller creatures, sometimes deliberately homing in on the orcas' feeding calls to do so.

Where and When to See Them

The humpback whales you'll see in Alaska are part of the North Pacific population, which spends its winters in breeding grounds near Japan, Hawaii, or Mexico. Alaska's waters are part of a summer feeding ground that stretches all the way from the Chukchi Sea (off the north coast of Alaska) all the way south to Washington State. Perhaps the very best place in all of Alaska to watch humpback whales is in **Frederick Sound,** just north of Petersburg. The whale-watching out of **Juneau** is also very good. Quite a few whales also feed in **Prince William Sound,** although the wildlife-watching (including whales) is usually better in the northern part of the sound near **Valdez.**

STELLER SEA LIONS

Although you will sometimes see the smaller California sea lion in Southeast Alaska (listen

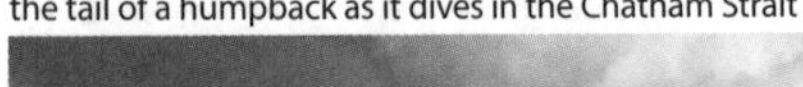
the tail of a humpback as it dives in the Chatham Strait

for its distinctive barking call), most of the sea lions you see in Alaska are the much larger Steller, or northern, **sea lion** *(Eumetopias jubatus)*. Instead of barking, Steller sea lions groan, growl, and roar.

These "eared seals" have long, flipper-like forearms, external ear flaps, and hind flippers that they can pull under their feet to "walk" with, as if they were legs. Sea lions move surprisingly fast on dry ground and can even climb up cliff faces. The males may weigh up to 1,200 pounds, be almost 11 feet long, and live up to 20 years in the wild. Meanwhile the much smaller females, who typically weigh half as much as the males, may live up to 30 years.

Sea lions eat fish, octopus, and squids, and in turn may be eaten by killer whales or sharks. They congregate in rookeries, where predator access is limited; the females leave the pups on dry land as they forage for food, then return to nurse the young. In the water, sea lions use their front flippers for propulsion and their rear flippers to steer, as opposed to seals, which use their hind flippers for propulsion and their front flippers to steer.

Where and When to See Them

Sea lions are a very common sight in all coastal Alaska communities. They're here year-round but tend to frequent shoreward protected waters in the winter. During the summer, you'll see them hauled out in exposed rookeries or even sunning themselves on harbor buoys, or trolling harbor waters for fish scraps.

SEALS

Alaska has several species of seals. The most common is the **harbor seal** (*Phoca vitulina*). This adorable, torpedo-shaped creature wriggles awkwardly on land because it can't move its flippers underneath its body to walk, but it's the epitome of sleek grace in the water.

Harbor seals are curious and very widespread, so it's not unusual to see them pop their heads out of the water and watch you with interest. They eat a variety of fish, and it's not unusual to see the females and pups hauled out on icebergs shed by Alaska's tidewater glaciers. Adult seals typically measure 5-6 feet long; females typically weigh about 180 pounds, while males can weigh almost 300 pounds.

On the more exotic end of the seal spectrum, Alaska is also home to **northern fur seals** (*Callorhinus ursinus*), which are actually related to sea lions. Like sea lions, fur seals have vestigial ear flaps and can pull their hind

a colony of northern fur seals on St. Paul Island

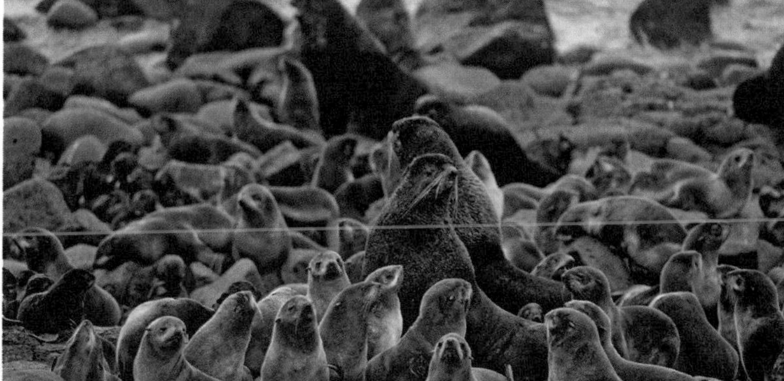

flippers underneath their body to "walk" on land. Males may weigh up to 600 pounds, while females only weigh about 100 pounds.

You may see some of these animals in the Aleutian Islands, but more than 75 percent of the world's entire population of northern fur seals congregates in breeding rookeries in the remote Pribilof Islands. Males come ashore in late May to establish territories, which they aggressively defend against other males. Pregnant females come ashore in June, birth their pups, then mate again within a week.

Male fur seals fast until they're done breeding and may lose up to 25 percent of their body weight. Female seals need nourishment for their pups, however, so they will leave their pups for up to a week at a time to feed. Researchers have found female fur seals that have lived for more than 25 years. The lives of the fur seals are intimately entwined with those of the Aleut, or Unungan, people of the Pribilof Islands, because the Unungan were taken from their native Aleutian chain and transported to the Pribilofs by Russian fur traders, who used them as slave labor to kill the seals for their fur.

Where and When to See Them

The summer is the best time to see harbor seals, especially in protected waters near glacier fjords, where the females haul out on drifting icebergs to birth and raise their young starting in the months of May and June. There's no clear pattern of migration—some seals seem to move seasonally or in pursuit of food, while others don't—but you will consistently see seals closer to shore during the spring and summer. Sometimes they even swim up rivers. If you see a curious, large-eyed head observing you from the water and it doesn't have vestigial ear flaps like sea lions, it is almost definitely a harbor seal.

Fur seals, on the other hand, have a very clearly established movement pattern. They spend about 80 percent of their lives out at sea foraging, but the other 20 percent is spent in land-based breeding rookeries. One of the best places in the world to see fur seals is the **Pribilof Islands** from June to October, although you'll need a permit from the tribal government to do so.

SEA OTTERS

Sea otters *(Enhydra lutris)* are the largest members of the weasel family, and their beautifully dense, plush fur almost led to their extinction at the hands of fur hunters. The average sea otter has between 800,000 and one

a sea otter floats in icy water

million hairs per square inch in its fur. The species has bounced back, however, and they are now plentiful in many parts of Alaska, especially the eastern section of Prince William Sound.

Sea otters are up to five feet long, and males can weigh up to 100 pounds, while females typically average about 60. They live to be 15-20 years old and are unusual among sea mammals because they depend on their fur to keep warm instead of blubber (body fat). That made sea otters in Prince William Sound especially vulnerable to the effects of the 1989 *Exxon Valdez* oil spill, because contamination with oil robbed their fur of its insulating quality. In addition to their fur, a very high metabolism also helps sea otters keep warm—they have to eat an amazing 25 percent of their body weight every day to keep that metabolism going.

Sea otters eat fish and invertebrates, including sea urchins, octopus, crabs, clams, and mussels. They use rocks as tools to crack open the shells of their prey, although their teeth are nicely adapted for crushing through shells too. Females birth just one pup in a season; the baby rides on the mother's chest as she swims on her back. Sea otters are very social and gather together in groups known as rafts. The exception is breeding males, who aggressively defend a territory where females are concentrated.

Where and When to See Them

You'll typically see Alaska's sea otters in Southeast, Southcentral, and Southwest Alaska. They tend to stay close to their home range year-round. Some of the best places to see them are in the waters of **Prince William Sound** (you can take a day cruise into the sound from Valdez, Cordova, Whittier, or Seward and in most Southeast communities. That said, the highest and most consistent concentration of sea otters I've ever seen is in eastern Prince William Sound near Valdez.

PACIFIC SALMON

There are five species of **Pacific salmon,** each of which has two names: **king** (chinook), **red** (sockeye), **pink** (humpy), **silver** (coho), and **dog** (chum). Often, multiple species of salmon will spawn in a given stream, with their runs spaced out throughout the year. In almost any part of Alaska, peak salmon runs occur in July and August, although the species' timing and availability vary by region.

jumping salmon in Katmai National Park

Salmon are extraordinary creatures that start out in freshwater, migrate to the ocean for 1-4 years, then return to their freshwater stream of origin to spawn (breed) before they die; see page 257 for more information on their life cycle.

All salmon are a bright silvery color (sometimes called "ocean bright") when living in saltwater. When they return to freshwater, they metamorphose into a breeding phase that's usually easy to identify, especially among the males. Sockeye salmon become a bright red with green heads, a moderate back hump, and a prominent upper jaw; pink salmon turn dull gray and the males grow an enormous hump. Silver salmon turn dark brown with greenish-black heads; dog salmon turn a dull green, with irregular red stripes; and chinook salmon turn a drab brown or dark red color.

By the time fish have reached this spawning phase, their bodies have already started to decompose. They're very easy to catch but not any good to eat (except for bears, which play an important role in scattering the nutrients left in each salmon's body throughout the forest). Most spawning streams are also protected once you've gone a certain distance upriver; if the fish aren't allowed to spawn the species won't continue, and you can be fined for harassing them in these protected areas.

Identifying the various salmon species while still in their ocean phase is more difficult. The best resource for this is the Alaska Department of Fish and Game's free sportfishing regulations booklet, which you can download from adfg.alaska.gov or pick up anywhere fishing licenses are sold. Rules for fishing vary greatly from region to region and sometimes stream to stream, so always check the regs before you go.

Where and When to See Them

Salmon-spawning streams are distributed throughout Alaska, and the timing of the salmon runs depends on both species and location. The best way to time a fishing trip (or a bear-viewing trip, where the best times coincide with the salmon runs) is by going to adfg.alaska.gov and searching for "sport fish run timing." This will bring up an interactive calendar that shows you the timing for both freshwater runs and saltwater fish in various parts of the state.

That said, most spawning areas are protected from fishing (or even bothering the fish)—and even if you were allowed to catch spawned-out fish they'd only be wasted, because by the time they reach the spawning grounds their bodies are literally decomposing from the inside out. And just because there are plenty of fish in the ocean doesn't mean you can legally catch them. So if you're looking to catch salmon, you'll have to consult the Alaska Department of Fish and Game's fishing regulations, available online at adfg.alaska.gov or in any Alaska store that sells fishing licenses and gear, for the timing of fishing openings.

HALIBUT

For many anglers, catching a "barn door" halibut—that is, a fish that's big enough to be a barn door—is the dream of a lifetime. But as tasty as it is, the **halibut** *(Hippoglossus stenolepis)* is also a mighty strange fish. Salmon are known for the incredible series of metamorphoses they undergo in their lifetime, but a young halibut undergoes something even more drastic. By the time the halibut larva is about an inch long, the left eye has migrated over to the right side of the head. This becomes the "top" of the fish, which spends most of its life on the ocean floor, while the coloration on the left side of the fish (which becomes the "bottom") fades to white. The mouth never migrates, though, so the adult halibut ends up looking a little bit like a Picasso painting.

Young halibut (around six months old) spend their time in shallow, near-shore waters feeding on plankton. As they get older and larger they start feeding on small crustaceans and small fish, working their way up

Things We Don't Have

You might be surprised by some of the animals we don't have in Alaska. Although there are reports of ticks making inroads in some of the more temperate parts of the state—presumably due to our increasingly shorter, milder winters—we remain, for the most part, blissfully tick free.

Also, although we have more than our fair share of mosquitoes, we are almost completely free of the ailments their bite transfers, from West Nile virus to yellow fever and Zika. Ditto for tick-borne illnesses like Lyme disease and Rocky Mountain spotted fever—at least so far. We don't have heartworm (which affects pets) up here either, although infected pets are sometimes brought up from the Lower 48.

We don't have any native poisonous spiders or snakes in Alaska. In fact we don't have any snakes at all, except for a few reports of harmless garter snakes in Southeast Alaska. In most of the state we have just one native species of frog. The adorable little wood frog is a truly astonishing creature that goes dormant and freezes solid in the winter. Even its blood and eyes freeze; the frog's heart stops beating and it stops breathing. When spring comes, the frog thaws out from that state of suspended animation and goes about its business as usual.

Ports in Alaska are extremely fastidious about staying rat free. That's because rats can easily prey on—and even exterminate—the seabirds that nest in the ground and along cliffs near many a seaside town, an issue that's been very problematic on some of the remote Aleutian Islands.

to larger prey—and inhabiting increasingly deeper water—as they get bigger. Those gigantic halibut people so prize catching are females; according to the Alaska Department of Fish and Game, male halibut rarely reach three feet long. Although people love catching these fish as trophies and they do make an awful lot of good eating, most locals feel that smaller "chicken" halibut actually taste better.

The official state record for the largest halibut is a 459-pound monster caught in 1996 near Dutch Harbor, but there's been at least one larger fish—482 pounds, caught in the deep, little-traveled waters near Gustavus in Southeast Alaska—that was disqualified from the record because it was shot before being brought into the boat. As you might imagine, this is an important safety measure. A fish that big can injure people in the boat or even sink the boat with its thrashing around.

Where and When to See Them

Halibut move toward deep offshore waters from November through March to spawn, then back toward shallower near-shore waters to feed in the spring. **Homer** and **Valdez** are two of the most popular halibut fishing ports but, because of that popularity and because of commercial fishing boats trailing long lines of baited hooks, giant halibut here aren't as common as they are in little-fished waters like the area around tiny, remote **Gustavus** in Southeast.

Background

The Landscape

GEOGRAPHY AND ECOSYSTEMS

If you were to think Alaska's 663,300 square miles of land area are made of nothing but glaciers, mountains and fjords, it would be perfectly understandable—after all, that's what makes it into most of the pictures. But our state is so very big that it spans five distinct ecosystems: tundra; boreal forest; coastal rainforest; wetlands, rivers, and lakes; and marine/coastal. Here's a look at the defining characteristics of each landscape region.

Tundra

There are two types of tundra in Alaska: lowland or **Arctic tundra,** which takes place at high latitudes (farther north), and **alpine tundra,** which takes place at high altitudes (up in the mountains). In either case, tundra is characterized by a lack of trees, generally chilly temperatures, and windy conditions.

You'll find alpine tundra in mountain ranges throughout Alaska and in some treeless coastal islands, while the Arctic tundra forms a great broad, flat plain that extends north from the Brooks Range—which cuts east and west across the northern third of Alaska—to the shore of the Arctic Ocean. There's also a band of tundra along Alaska's northwest, west, and southwest coastline, where average temperatures are low enough that larger plants won't flourish, but tiny tundra plants still can. The Aleutian Islands, the Pribilof Islands, and most of massive Kodiak Island are also clad in tundra.

Although tundra might look barren from a distance or during the winter, it's actually a lush landscape full of tiny shrubs, mosses, sedges, and lichens. That rich biodiversity draws a profusion of birds north to feed and rear their young on the summer tundra, and although it might seem impossible, some animals—including musk oxen, wood bison, and caribou—even spend their winters on the tundra, feeding in the windswept areas where it takes less effort to get down to the tiny tundra plants.

Tundra also tends to be fairly dry. For example, the city of Barrow, which is situated on a broad tundra plain, receives less annual precipitation than the Mojave Desert. But you wouldn't know that by looking at the summer tundra, which is dotted here and there with jewel-like lakes and sometimes a squishy, marshy wetland in its own right.

In the alpine tundra, those conditions are fueled by snowmelt, glacier runoff, and sometimes springs of water. In the Arctic tundra, the wetness is a result of permafrost, a layer of ground that stays frozen all year long, even during the summer. That layer of permafrost helps trap water near the surface, where it's readily accessible to both plants and animals, and, in fact, when the permafrost melts, it sometimes causes entire lakes to disappear as it opens a channel for the water to flow out through.

Boreal Forest

It might be easiest to think of Alaska's boreal forest—also called taiga—as several types of forest cobbled together. You'll find a little bit of everything here, from sunny aspen groves to tall black spruce trees, spreading white and Sitka spruce, hemlock, birch, and cottonwoods, all tangled together. Dense shrubs grow beneath the trees—groundcover like horsetail ferns, devil's club, moss, and lichen—while the "glue" for this forest mosaic

Previous: the Richardson Highway leading into Valdez; a caribou in Gates of the Arctic National Park and Preserve.

is a mix of wetlands, lakes, and rivers that wind through it.

The **boreal forest** is the largest terrestrial ecosystem on the earth, covering some 11 percent of the planet's entire landscape. In Alaska, boreal forest covers almost the entirety of the Interior, filling the land south of the Brooks Range and north of the Talkeetna, Chugach, Wrangell, and St. Elias mountains.

More than Alaska's other landscapes, the boreal forest is shaped by fire. Tall, spindly black spruce trees are better able to thrive in moist, boggy areas that boreal forest sometimes covers, and they've adapted to the point that they actually need fire to reproduce: The flames open their spruce cones, which are sealed with a resinous tar, which then allows the seeds held inside the cones to spread.

Although the trees in a boreal forest are small and the wildlife sparse when compared to a rainforest, there are very few animals that don't pay a visit to Alaska's boreal forest, from brown and black bears to migratory waterfowl, foxes, caribou, moose, hares, porcupines, grouse, ptarmigan, and songbirds.

Coastal Rainforest

Alaska might not be the first place you think of when the word "rainforest" comes to mind, but the 16.8-million-acre **Tongass National Forest** in Southeast Alaska is the largest temperate rainforest remaining in the world. (It's also the largest national forest in the country.) The Tongass is made up primarily of evergreens like cedar, hemlock, and spruce; in old-growth areas, the trees can be 800 years old.

Like all rainforests, the Tongass teems with life, hosting all the "expected" Alaska wildlife, such as black and brown bears, wolves, moose, Sitka black-tailed deer, and plentiful sealife, including Steller sea lions, sea otters, orcas, and humpback whales. All five species of Pacific salmon spawn here, and there are more than 125 glaciers creeping down through the rainforest to the tide line. You'll even find a few species that are unique to this place in the world, like the Alexander Archipelago wolf.

Wetlands, Rivers, and Lakes

It might seem like walking from one end of Alaska to the other should mean striding through only mountains, forests, and maybe a few glaciers for effect, but our state is so woven through with **wetlands, rivers,** and **lakes** that you would, at some point, run into a wall of water. These waters are truly the lifeblood of not only the land but also her people, with rivers acting as transport corridors that help rural residents travel between villages or to and from seasonal subsistence camps.

Meanwhile, the rivers are also highways that allow life-giving salmon to stream deep inland, where predators like bears, eagles, and wolves help distribute the nutrient-rich bodies of the spawned-out fish. All told, Alaska holds more than 40 percent of the nation's surface water resources, with more than **12,000 rivers** and **three million lakes** larger than five acres in size.

Alaska's rivers not only help people, fish, and nutrients move through the land, but they also move the land itself, alternately eroding their banks, redistributing sediments, and building new sand and gravel bars, which are then colonized by plants and animals.

Our rivers also feed the complex wetlands that make up almost half the state's surface area, including massive river deltas that provide ideal havens for migratory birds to raise their young and provide plenty of places for young fish and waterfowl to hide from predators. Moose also stop by to feed, ducking their heads under the water to browse on submerged plants.

Marine/Coastal

Alaska has some 47,000 miles of **coastline**—that's more than twice as long as the East and West Coasts combined. This is where you'll find the sheer walls and deep waters of glacier-carved fjords, the seemingly endless **mudflats** where eagles snatch fish trapped in the muddy channels, rich kelp beds where otters feed, and fascinating **tidepools** on the shoreline.

Humans depend on these coastal areas for

food and transportation; most of the state's settlements are either on the coast or along rivers that run down to the coast. Meanwhile, those coastal regions also serve as important migration routes and breeding grounds for a number of animals—sometimes a significant portion of the entire world's population.

For example, more than half the world's population of fur seals assemble in summer rookeries on St. Paul Island in the remote Pribilofs, and 80 percent of the world's red-legged kittiwakes nest in the cliffs of the other inhabited Pribilof Island, St. George. You'll also find many thousands of walruses hauled out in the Western Alaska rookeries of the Walrus Islands State Game Sanctuary.

Major Geographic Features

Alaska's landscapes are marked—and often separated—by rivers and mountains. The biggest mountain ranges include the **Brooks Range,** which divides the massive **Arctic tundra plain** to the north from the boreal forest to the south; the staggering **Alaska Range,** an arc that corrals Southcentral Alaska from the rest of the state and includes 20,310 foot **Denali,** the tallest peak in North America; and the **Chugach Mountains,** which embrace Anchorage, Valdez, and Cordova before blending with the Wrangell and **St. Elias Mountains** to form the **Coast Range** of Southeast Alaska.

Major rivers include the **Yukon River,** which flows west from the Canadian border to **Norton Sound** in Western Alaska; the **Koyukuk River,** which travels southwest to flow into the Yukon; the **Colville River,** which flows down from the north edge of the Brooks Range and into the **Beaufort Sea,** north of Alaska; the Noatak, which winds west and south from the Brooks Range until hitting the sea near Kotzebue; and the mighty **Stikine River,** which flows into the sea near Wrangell in Southeast Alaska.

Islands are also key features of the land in Southeast Alaska—where most communities are housed on islands, or on chunks of land isolated from the mainland by tall mountains and glaciers—and in Southwest Alaska, where the unmistakable **Aleutian Islands** stretch so far west that they cross the international dateline, making Alaska simultaneously the most easterly and westerly state of the country.

What Shapes the Landscape

Alaska's landscape is shaped by the continual push-pull of several forces. We sit atop the meeting point of two massive tectonic plates: the **North American Plate** and the **Pacific Plate,** which is slowly diving under the North American Plate. The pressure of that movement builds mountains. In fact, the Wrangell-St. Elias Mountains, which sit atop a portion of the earth's crust called the Yakutat Block, are being slowly pushed upward by the pressure of the Pacific Plate against that block.

Every so often **earthquakes** have a more dramatic effect on Alaska's landscape. The "Great Earthquake" on Good Friday of 1964 is a prime example. Among many other effects, this massive earthquake "dropped" a portion of Anchorage's downtown terrain, creating a steep hill where none had existed before; it also caused land along Turnagain Arm to sink so low that you can still see the skeletons of trees, mummified by the sudden influx of saltwater, and the scattered remains of a building or two poking up from the ground.

But if plate tectonics (the movement of the plates that make up the earth's crust) are building mountains, glaciers slowly grind them down. Think of the glacier as a giant scouring pad that's carving its way through the land in super-slow motion; the silt in Alaska's glacier-fed rivers and the piles of moraine (ground-down rock) left in a glacier's path are just one sign of their passage.

Tidewater glaciers—that is, glaciers that reach all the way to the sea—have carved out deep, steep-walled fjords along the coast, while terrestrial glaciers scoop giant valleys out of the mountains. You can tell if a valley was formed by a glacier because it'll have a wide, U-shaped bottom. If the valley was carved by a stream it'll have flatter walls that meet in a sharp "V" at the bottom.

Alaska's **rivers**—all 12,000 of them—are another land-shaping force to be reckoned with. They're like freight trains hauling sediment down to the coastal river deltas, but along the way they carve out land and drop some of that sediment, periodically flooding lowland areas and fueling the wetlands that drive so much of the state's ecology.

Finally, Alaska has more than 40 **active volcanoes** that trace the arc of the Aleutian Islands on up into the mainland—some 80 percent of all the volcanoes in the United States. (A volcano being "active" means it has erupted at least once since 1760.) One of Alaska's volcanoes, Novarupta, erupted in 1912 and buried more than 40 square miles of land under ash that piled up 700 feet deep, creating the desolate landscape now known as the Valley of Ten Thousand Smokes. But that was the largest volcanic eruption of the 20th century. A more typical volcanic eruption in Alaska lobs clouds of fine, abrasive ash particles into the air. The ash disrupts air travel and causes eye and respiratory problems when it falls on nearby communities.

CLIMATE

Alaska's climate roughly parallels its geography, thanks in large part to the mountains that channel—or block—the flow of moisture throughout the state. The Arctic region is chilly even during the summer, with seasonal highs hovering in the 40s, thanks to the Brooks Range stolidly disrupting airflow on the southern edge of the Arctic plain.

Arctic weather is dry, too; the northernmost city in Alaska, Barrow, receives just 4 inches of precipitation per year. That said, Barrow averages 29 inches of snow every year. How are those two figures possible? It's because precipitation is measured by rainfall and the water equivalent of snow, not the depth of the snow itself. Snow has an awful lot of air in it, so when you measure the amount of water you'd have if the snow melted, you end up with a much smaller figure for precipitation.

So, although the snow might make it look like there's more water flying around, Barrow actually gets less annual precipitation than the Mojave Desert.

Much of Alaska's southerly coastline, including Southeast Alaska and the islands of Southwest Alaska, has a mild maritime climate. That means summer highs typically peak in the 60s (although our highs are getting hotter) while lows linger around the very civilized temperature of 20 degrees.

There's plenty of precipitation to go around

hikers on the Root Glacier near Kennicott

in a maritime climate: The island communities of Southeast Alaska get up to 200 inches of precipitation per year, while the islands of Southwest Alaska—including the Aleutian Islands—typically get closer to 60 inches per year. Southwest Alaska is also notoriously windy, and in the Aleutians and the Pribilofs, this is exacerbated by an almost completely treeless landscape.

South of the Brooks Range but north of the Alaska Range is Interior Alaska, which has a continental climate characterized by great temperature extremes—summer temperatures may soar as high as the 80s and 90s, while low temperatures plunge to -30 or lower. Those extremes are made more bearable by the dry, calm environment. Interior cities may average only 12 inches of precipitation per year, and there usually isn't much wind.

To the west of the Interior, Alaska's sparsely inhabited western coast has a mix of milder summer highs, moderated by the cool waters of the Bering Sea, and fierce, continental-style low temperatures that are egged on by the presence of pack ice offshore.

Finally, Southcentral Alaska has a blend of climates. The southerly coastal regions enjoy a mild maritime climate, much like what you'll find in Southeast Alaska. The inland portions of Southcentral have more extreme temperatures, with summer highs easily ranging into the 70s and winter lows that typically dip below zero for short periods at a time. But, because the water is never terribly far away, the weather is still milder than what you'll find in the Interior.

DAYLIGHT HOURS

Alaska's almost **endless summer sun** and **short winter days** are a continual source of fascination for visitors. They're caused by the way the earth tilts on its axis as it circles the sun. During the summer the northern hemisphere is tilted toward the sun so, the farther north you are, the longer the days will be. But we get the flip side of the coin in the winter when our hemisphere tilts away from the sun, giving northerly cities a much shorter day than what you get as you near the equator.

In Southeast Alaska, the summer solstice (longest day of the year) offers about 19 hours of daylight, plus an hour of twilight in the morning and another in the evening. Go north to Southcentral and you'll get about 20 hours of daylight (not counting the twilight), and in Fairbanks you get about 22 hours of daylight. If you include the twilight, you can make a solid case for usable light all night long.

Of course in Barrow, Alaska's northernmost city, you don't have to do any fudging about twilight hours to get your endless midnight sun. There, the sun rises in mid-May and doesn't set again until early August. Instead, it circles the sky above the horizon like the hand of a clock. In the winter it does the opposite, dipping below the horizon in late November and not coming back up until late January, although it lingers close enough below the horizon that you get a bit of twilight each "day."

The long winter night is a little more forgiving in other parts of the state. In Fairbanks you get almost four hours of daylight on the winter solstice, the shortest day of the year. In Southcentral you get above five hours of daylight, and Southeast gets a whopping six hours of daylight on the winter solstice.

ENVIRONMENTAL ISSUES

Here in Alaska, **climate change** is not a theory but a reality. The U.S. Environmental Protection Agency says that in the last 60 years, average temperatures across Alaska have increased by about 3 degrees Fahrenheit, or more than twice what you'll see in the rest of the United States. Winter temperatures have increased by an average of 6 degrees.

Although that kind of change might not sound like much, it's enough to cause earlier breakup of river ice, which in turn affects travel and subsistence hunting throughout the state. Likewise, fast-melting sea ice affects the livelihood of subsistence hunters in coastal communities, whose deep understanding of the weather allowed them to know when it was safe to travel and hunt on the ice. But now the ongoing, fast-moving changes make both the weather and the ice harder to predict, so travel is becoming more dangerous.

Another prominent effect of climate change on Alaska's people is **coastal erosion,** with the small Northwest Alaska village of Shishmaref as a prime example. This community is located on a small barrier island some 120 miles north of Nome, but it won't be for much longer: Their island has been steadily eroding into the sea for more than a decade, leaving buildings to crumble off the advancing edge and into the water. In August 2016, the entire community voted to relocate five miles inland, although they're going to have to find an estimated $180 million to make the move happen.

Alaska's coastal animals are struggling too. Although this has immediate impacts on the subsistence hunters and their families who are so intimately connected to the welfare of the land and the animals, it's also a clue to how things are already changing for the rest of us, even if we haven't quite yet recognized the consequences.

Both polar bears and walruses depend on old, stable sea ice to hunt; as the ice melts, thins, and drifts farther from land, they're both faced with longer swims to reach their feeding grounds. In some cases, the distances are becoming impossible and the animals are left to starve or swim until they drown.

Ice and coastlands aren't the only places Alaska's climate is changing. The permafrost that forms such an integral part of the Arctic ecosystem (and to a lesser degree, the Interior) is melting. This destabilizes the land in a very literal sense, causing entire hillsides to slough away and trees to tip at crazy angles. Lakes are disappearing as the layer of permafrost that helped contain the water melts and opens a channel for the water to drain out. As the permafrost melts it also releases gases that were trapped in the frozen earth, which in turn makes the remaining permafrost melt faster.

The plant life is changing too, as milder winters allow more insects to survive and those infestations kill off large swaths of trees. Fewer live trees means less water being taken up, which translates to more surface runoff that in turn destabilizes the landscape and washes away nutrient-rich topsoil. The dead trees are also the perfect fuel for forest fires, which, paired with hotter, drier conditions, are becoming bigger, more frequent, and more catastrophic in their effects.

Plants

I am very pleased to report that we don't have poison oak or poison ivy in Alaska. That said, we do have a few plants you should be aware of. First, let's start with the unfriendly plants.

DEVIL'S CLUB

This perennial plant is a powerful herbal remedy in Alaska Native healing traditions, and if you catch the plant at just the right stage, its spring shoots are an edible vegetable. But if you make the mistake of brushing up against the spiky stem of **devil's club,** its thorns will break off and fester in your flesh. They'll also "bite" through clothes—I've ended up with patches of devil's club thorns in both thighs while wearing three layers! Even the leaves have tiny thorns on them.

Most Alaskans wear tough gloves if they know they're going to have to handle or move through devil's club, although of course it's better to avoid this plant entirely. You shouldn't have to worry about it if you stick to cleared, maintained trails.

COW PARSNIP

Cow parsnip, also known as pushki or wild celery, looks a lot like devil's club without the thorns. But that doesn't mean it's harmless:

For many people, exposure to the sap of the cow parsnip plant causes terrible blistering burns that are made worse by exposure to the sun. Some people are so sensitive that just brushing up against a cow parsnip plant causes them to blister, while others don't seem to be immediately affected, although increased exposure (say, breaking open a stem and smearing the sap on your skin) could still cause burns.

Again, you're better off just avoiding this plant and, as with devil's club, you shouldn't have to worry about it if you stick to cleared, maintained trails. You won't find cow parsnip or devil's club in Alaska's major cities, except perhaps in the understory of densely wooded greenbelts.

BANEBERRY

Alaska has many delicious edible berries; I encourage you to pick up a copy of Verna Pratt's excellent book, *Alaska's Wild Berries and Berry-Like Fruit,* to help you identify which are safe to eat. Or, better yet, take a guided nature walk. With that said, there is one highly poisonous berry you absolutely must know about. **Baneberry** comes in both white and red varieties, with each berry springing sideways off a single upright stem.

Just a few baneberries are enough to make someone very sick, and they can potentially kill. Happily, protecting yourself is easy: Never eat berries unless you're positive they are edible, and teach your children not to eat anything they've picked unless you've okayed it first. (You should ask to see the entire plant—not just isolated berries or leaves—before saying okay.)

MONKSHOOD AND LUPINE

Both **monkshood** (also known as wolfsbane) and **lupine** form beautiful flowers, despite their poisonous nature. They won't hurt you if you touch them—but don't even think of eating them!

These two are a little tricky because they both bear some resemblance to flowering plants that are both beautiful and edible. The upright, circular flowering stalks of lupine look quite a bit like the lovely (and edible) fireweed, which is one of the first species to spring up in recently burned areas. Meanwhile, the foliage of the monkshood plant looks very much like the edible wild geranium, although their flowers look quite different.

Again, the solution is simple: Don't harvest or taste anything unless you're absolutely positive it's safe to eat. Another book by Verna Pratt, *Field Guide to Alaskan Wildflowers*, is very helpful in making good identifications.

FIREWEED

The tall, round spikes of pink/purple **fireweed** may just be Alaska's most iconic bloom, surpassing even the official state flower, the forget-me-not. Fireweed grows throughout Alaska, and is named for the fact that it's one of the first plants to spring up in recently burned areas. But you could also say that the bright flowers, which tend to grow thickly together in those recently burned areas, make an entire hillside look like it's on fire. You'll also find a dwarf version of fireweed growing in the alpine and subalpine tundra, and areas where the forest gives way to rocky bluffs.

Fireweed flowers are edible, and fireweed honey is a local delicacy. You can also eat the young leaves of fireweed while they're still tender. However, be very careful when harvesting this plant, because it bears quite a few similarities to the beautiful but poisonous lupine.

SPRUCE TREES

Those lush evergreens you see growing across most of Alaska aren't pine trees. They're three species of spruce: **black spruce, white spruce,** and the towering **Sitka spruce.** If you remember the beautiful U.S. Capitol spruce tree in 2015, that was a hybrid of white spruce and Sitka spruce.

If you have trouble telling Alaska's various spruce trees apart, you're in great company—even experienced botanists struggle to

detail of a spruce in Denali National Park and Preserve

differentiate among them. Here are some clues that can help you narrow things down.

Sitka spruce are the largest spruce trees in Alaska, growing up to 225 feet tall and 8 feet in diameter. They are very common in Southeast and Southcentral Alaska and into the Alaska Peninsula of Southwest Alaska and have a blue-green tint to their sharp needles, which grow on all sides of the branches. The cones on a Sitka spruce usually grow in the top quarter of the tree.

White spruce grow up to 115 feet tall and 30 inches in diameter, and can grow (in a much smaller version) all the way up to the treeline. Its needles are usually crowded onto the upper side of the branch and aren't sharp to the touch.

Black spruce typically grows up to 30 feet tall and is tolerant of wet, cold, and boggy sites, which often makes it tall and spindly. Some people say they look like pipe cleaners or cotton swabs, and they actually need fire to reproduce; it unseals the resinous pitch that otherwise binds the black spruce cones shut and allows them to release their seeds.

BIRCH TREES

The **white birch,** or **paper birch,** is an unmistakable inhabitant of Alaska's boreal forests. It typically grows slender and tall (up to 45 feet high), with a distinctive papery, peeling bark that ranges from white to a subdued rainbow of neutral pastels. This hardy plant often grows near black spruce trees in poorly drained soil and alongside white spruce in areas with better drainage; you'll find it all the way from Kodiak in Southwest to the Brooks Range, which forms the northern border of the Interior.

Birch sap is made into a delicious syrup that you can buy in many craft markets and local gift shops. The buds and leaves are used in healing salves, and the papery-thin bark makes an amazing fire-starter. The bark has also been used traditionally by Alaska Native peoples to create watertight containers—including watercraft!—and decorative baskets.

BLUEBERRIES

Regarding fruit, Alaska is perhaps best known for its **blueberries,** which thrive all over the state except in the extreme Arctic. We have multiple strains of blueberries, ranging from tiny alpine blueberry plants to "highbush blueberries" in the temperate rainforest that reach as tall as a person. Alaskans of all walks of life turn out to harvest these delicious berries once they're ripe—usually in July or August, depending on the region and the weather—and you can do so, too, if you happen to be here at the right time. I guarantee that they're much better than anything you might buy in the store, and, as long as you're not on private or tribal land, you don't need a permit to harvest these berries.

CROWBERRIES

If you go out picking blueberries on a mountainside, you will almost always find the crowberry, also called a mossberry or blackberry, growing nearby. **Crowberries** are black in color, but they bear absolutely no resemblance to the blackberries of the southern United States. Instead, they're a valuable, traditional subsistence food for Alaska Native peoples. Many blueberry pickers eschew the crowberry, which grows on a shrubby little evergreen plant that's usually mixed in with alpine blueberries. But some people love these black berries in their own right or collect them as an easy way to extend their blueberry harvest.

OTHER EDIBLE BERRIES

Alaska is full of other **edible berries,** although I refer you to a good berry book (see *Suggested Reading*) to make a positive confirmation of the berries you're looking at before you harvest or taste anything. Some of our most popular berries include high-bush cranberries; raspberries (which look just like the raspberries you get in the supermarket, only much smaller); wild strawberries (ditto the previous remark); watermelon berries, which have a mildly melon-like taste when ripe; dangling red and black currants; and low-brush cranberries, which are tiny versions of the same cranberry you'd see in the supermarket; they grow close to the ground in boggy areas.

MEDICINAL HERBS

If you're fascinated by **medicinal herbs,** Alaska offers a wealth of natural medicines. (Bonus: Some of them are edible, too!) We have both white-flowering and pink-flowering yarrow, which helps stop bleeding; copious amounts of plantain (the plant, not the fruit), which is also called "white man's foot" for its tendency to grow on disturbed ground and provides a soothing salve to put on skin irritations; and wormwood, which is poisonous but still used—with proper care—as a tonic and to treat soreness, arthritis, and infection. A great starter resource on how to harvest and use our medicinal plants is *Alaska's Wild Plants: A Guide to Alaska's Edible Harvest*, by Janice Schofield.

History

EARLY HISTORY AND FIRST CONTACT

Alaska's history begins not with the arrival of Russian explorers and fur traders, but with the indigenous people who have called this place home since time immemorial, developing sophisticated seafaring and land-raging cultures that were—and still are—supremely adapted to thrive in Alaska's challenging conditions.

Alaska's 11 distinct indigenous cultures can be divided into five cultural regions (never pass up a chance to visit Alaska Native cultural centers while you're here). These cultures were (and still are) anything but primitive, making use of highly evolved and adapted technologies to thrive in the challenging and varied conditions presented by this immense state.

Alaska's first peoples were typically nomadic, moving between camps to follow their seasonal food sources, which included salmon, land animals, and, in the coastal regions, large sea mammals, including seals, sea lions, and whales. However, that began to change with first contact from Russian explorers.

The acknowledged first contact is from a Cossack, Mikhail Gvozdev, who was

ancient Alaska Native petroglyphs on Wrangell's Petroglyph Beach

approached by an Alaska Native in a kayak near King Island on the northwest coast of Alaska in 1732, although the "discovery" of Alaska is usually credited to a 1741 expedition of the explorer Vitus Bering, whose crew met and traded with the Unungan (Aleut) people during the course of their explorations.

THE FUR YEARS

It wasn't long before wealthy Russian investors gave fur traders the stakes they needed to travel to Alaska and collect pelts. Sea otter, fur seal, and fox furs were all valuable, but instead of killing the animals themselves, the traders forced the Alaska Native people they encountered—especially Unungan people, who lived in the path of their exploration—to do the work for them, often holding the women and children as hostage.

As with other cases of European contact in North America, the Russians also brought diseases that they had developed immunity or resistance to but the indigenous people had not. The Unungan people in particular were decimated by these illnesses and mistreatment.

Russian explorers and fur traders quickly spread their explorations in search of more resources to exploit. Alaska Native groups periodically resisted their advances but were subdued by the Russians' superior armament.

On your travels through Southwest and Southcentral Alaska, you may notice quite a few Russian Orthodox churches. Although of course the Russian occupation led to the presence of missionaries in the late 1700s, it's the way the missionaries in many cases defended the Alaska Native people from poor treatment, and the way that their customs were able to flex and be adapted to Alaska Native beliefs, that helped the churches stay. To this day, services are often held in a mix of Russian and Alaska Native languages. One of the most central figures of this time was the Russian missionary Ioann Veniaminov, who later became Bishop Innocent, the first Russian Orthodox bishop in Alaska.

SALE TO THE UNITED STATES

By the mid-1850s, Russia had thoroughly probed Alaska's resources, found fur to be the only viable money-maker, and—by proxy and slave labor—hunted many fur-bearing animals into scarcity. In addition to these dwindling resources, they faced ongoing fierce resistance from the Tlingit people of Southeast Alaska.

When Russia decided to turn its attention to fur resources on the Asian continent instead, the United States expressed an interest in purchasing Alaska. Once the American Civil War was over, U.S. Secretary of State William H. Seward arranged the purchase on October 18, 1867: Just $7 million for all 663,300 square miles of Alaska. Because of the land's remoteness and perceived barrenness, the sale was criticized as "Seward's Folly" or "Seward's Icebox" . . . until explorers struck gold.

THE GOLD RUSH

From this point on, a surprising amount of Alaska's past and present was shaped by the lust for a particular mineral—in this case, gold. One of the first documented gold strikes was at Telegraph Creek in Southeast Alaska, in the year 1861. A series of small strikes followed, spurring thousands of prospectors to flock north from the West Coast and resulting in the creation of Juneau as a mining town.

But it was the Klondike gold strike of 1896—in Canada, not Alaska—that really ignited gold fever. An estimated 80,000 people participated in the rush to the Klondike, using several routes through Alaska to get there. Some traveled up the Yukon River, while others took grueling and often deadly overland routes, including the Chilkoot Trail (which hikers still travel to this day), the White Pass route (which you can retrace from the comfort of a historical narrow-gauge railcar), or a rough trail over Valdez Glacier.

Many of the people who came rushing for gold were turned around by conditions and weather that were much more brutal than they'd expected, and quite a few died. If those who turned back missed the last steamboat heading back to the continental United States, they'd have to wait out the winter. Towns began to spring up, providing services to the miners or, to put it a little more colloquially, "mining the miners" as a resource themselves.

By 1899, news of a gold strike on the Seward Peninsula (which, confusingly, is

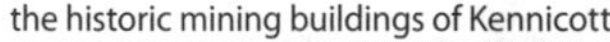
the historic mining buildings of Kennicott

nowhere near the town of Seward—it's actually in Northwest Alaska) sent thousands of people flocking to the area in a single week. Thus Nome was born. When placer gold was found in the beach sands and a judge ruled that the beach couldn't be staked, more than 2,000 people camped on 30 miles of beach, mining 24 hours a day with any means available to them. Ultimately, they extracted more than $46 million of gold in an 11-year period.

Gold strikes resulted—sometimes incidentally—in the founding of other Alaska towns, most notably Fairbanks, thanks to a strike by Italian immigrant Felix Pedro in 1902. Gold fever also spurred the spread of transportation networks, including the Alaska Railroad, which was completed in 1923. Anchorage (now Alaska's largest city) started as a railroad construction camp located on the shores of Ship Creek, which still runs through downtown Anchorage today.

However, World War II put a stop to the mining-spurred exploration of Alaska, thanks to an executive order closing all mines that weren't essential to the war effort. Once the war ended, the fixed price of gold (set by the U.S. government) wasn't enough for companies to turn a reasonable profit, so gold mining in Alaska stopped until the price-fixing stopped too, in the 1970s. Since then, mining exploration has varied along with the price of gold and concerns about environmental damage and water pollution as a result of the mining techniques.

WORLD WAR II

By the time the Japanese attacked Pearl Harbor in Hawaii on December 7, 1941, the U.S. government had recognized Alaska's strategic importance as an air base overseeing the Pacific Ocean and within a long-range flight of Japan.

What followed was, from an ethical and human rights standpoint, one of the bleakest chapters in American history. Not only Japanese citizens living in Alaska but also Japanese-Americans and Alaska Natives from the Aleutian Islands and Pribilofs were arrested and placed in internment camps, the latter for "their own protection," although in fact they suffered greatly and many of them died.

War came to Alaska six months after the Japanese strike at Pearl Harbor that brought the United States into the war, when the Japanese dispatched a naval fleet to attack American bases in the Aleutian Islands. Their radio messages were intercepted, however, so United States Navy ships and Army aircraft were relocated to defend the islands. The complicated geography of the Aleutian Islands was both a help and a hindrance to both sides, as the Japanese had mistaken information about where to find the U.S. airfields and naval bases, but the U.S. Navy had trouble locating some of the Japanese ships.

In June of 1942, the Japanese made landfall and occupied the Aleutian Islands of Attu and Kiska—the first time American territory had been occupied by an invading force since the War of 1812. Evicting the Japanese from this toehold became a priority, as the Aleutian bases allowed long-range Japanese seaplanes to patrol the Pacific and also put them within a long-distance bombing run of Seattle.

The United States retook Attu in May of 1943, with more American casualties due to frostbite and exposure than Japanese resistance. In August of 1943 the Americans and Canadian allies landed to retake Kiska. Nearly 100 troops were killed by friendly fire or booby traps before they realized that the Japanese had snuck off the island.

That ended Alaska's starring role in the war, although the Aleutian Islands were used as operating bases for long-range American bombing flights and patrols until the war ended in 1945. You can still see many artifacts of this time—ranging from bunkers and forts to searchlight emplacements, foxholes, abandoned garrison towns, and communications emplacements—scattered throughout the Aleutian Islands, Western Alaska, and even Southcentral.

Perhaps one of the most lasting effects of the World War II effort in Alaska was the construction of the Alcan (Alaska-Canada) Highway. Once Alaska's strategic importance was understood, military engineers laid some 1,500 miles of unpaved roadway in less than eight months. The roadway officially opened to military traffic in November of 1942. Over the next few years the roadway was paved, and in 1948 it was opened to civilian traffic.

STATEHOOD

By the end of World War II, Alaskans' collective independent streak—which continues to this day—had already asserted itself as a finely tuned resentment for regulations imposed from afar, especially from a national government that really didn't "get" the unusual conditions of life in Alaska. (To put this in perspective, the state's entire population in 1945 was about 100,000 people—and remember, there still was no road access open to civilians.)

In a bid for a greater degree of self-governance, the citizens of Alaska—then a territory—set out to prove that they could satisfy the conditions for statehood, principally their population's law-abiding nature and ability to sustain the state economically. Having such a small population made the last point problematic, so when Alaska was granted statehood in 1959, Congress imposed two extra conditions upon that status.

First, they set aside 60 percent of Alaska as federal land and paid Alaska 90 percent of profits from mineral rights on that land. (Oil remains a significant, although perhaps fading, component of Alaska's economy today.) Next, they set aside more than a quarter of the land in Alaska for ownership by the state, which allowed the state to keep revenue from that land. Again, this provision became very valuable because of the discovery of oil on that land.

THE PIPELINE DAYS

Just as the gold rush and then World War II changed the landscape of Alaska, the 1967 discovery of oil in Prudhoe Bay—also called Deadhorse, in a region known as the North Slope—forever changed life in Alaska again. It wasn't the first oil strike in Alaska—in fact, the first oil claims in Alaska were filed in the 1890s. But the enormous North Slope fields took Alaska's oil production to another level; historically, they've produced about a fifth of the country's domestic oil, earning an average of $2 billion a year for the state, although that income has fallen off in recent years.

In order to make use of the North Slope oil, it had to be transported to refineries in the Lower 48. Workers flocked to the state in the 1970s to construct the 800-mile Trans-Alaska Pipeline, which transports the crude oil from Prudhoe Bay to Valdez, where it's collected in holding tanks and barged to refineries in Washington state.

Both Fairbanks and Anchorage became oil boomtowns, with people sleeping in sheds and cars when no housing was available. More than 28,000 people worked directly on the pipeline during the peak of its construction, and even support workers doing menial jobs—say, housecleaning—could gross $40,000 a year, or the equivalent of $250,000 in today's dollars. The crime rates were correspondingly high, including plenty of high-level organized crime. Drugs and prostitution were also rampant, although these side effects of the "high-living" lifestyle as Alaska's economy went into a slump following the initial boom of the pipeline days.

THE ALASKA NATIVE CLAIMS LAND SETTLEMENT ACT

If you remember, Russia sold Alaska to the United States in 1867. But did Russia have the right to sell, since it never purchased the land from Alaska's indigenous people? Alaska Native groups began to coordinate among themselves and protested the land selection process that had been one condition of the statehood granted in 1959, effectively stalling the process of economic development.

Thanks to fierce, coordinated advocacy from Alaska Native negotiators, the federal and state governments agreed to give Alaska

Native peoples clear title to the lands they had historically used, and would pay them to surrender any potential claims on other lands. That payment was used to form regional corporations, with all Alaska Native peoples having the right to opt in as shareholders for their region. The corporations would be tasked with investing the money they received for profit and then paying out dividends to their shareholders, thus ensuring a continuing income for the Native peoples of that region.

The resulting agreement, the **Alaska Native Claims Settlement Act** (ANCSA), was signed into law in 1971, giving Alaska Native tribes title to 44 million acres of land in Alaska and almost $1 billion dollars in cash as settlement for their prior claims on other land. This, in turn, freed the state to finish selecting the acreage designated as a condition of statehood and continue with its own economic development.

The ANCSA was not without controversy and has been amended several times to address the issues of land taxation and inheritance/assignment of shares in the Native corporations. You might say that the agreement—and the corporations it created—are still evolving, and exactly what role the corporations should play in Alaska Natives' lives remains a point of debate.

Still, the corporations have proven to be powerful drivers in aspects of the state's development, from providing hard-won dignity and recognition to the Alaska Native tribes to combined worldwide assets totaling several billion dollars and some 58,000 employees worldwide, including 16,000 jobs in Alaska. There's a very good chance that during your trip through Alaska you will stay at more than one hotel owned by an Alaska Native corporation or otherwise make use of their services, although the connection isn't always obvious.

Local Culture

DIVERSITY

Alaska rural communities generally have large Alaska Native populations, but they're also quite diverse, thanks in large part to seasonal workers who came to work in fish canneries and then stayed, or people from all over the world who went literally to the ends of the earth to start a new life for themselves.

Two examples of the populations you might see in rural communities include the fishing port of Unalaska/Dutch Harbor (41 percent white, 30 percent Asian, 15 percent Alaska Native/American Indian, 14 percent Hispanic/Latino) and the fishing community of Dillingham (70 percent Alaska Native/American Indian, 18 percent white, 3 percent Hispanic/Latino, 9 percent two or more races).

That said, Alaska's greatest diversity is in its cities, which have traditionally welcomed refugees from all over the world. Anchorage is the best example, with more than 100 languages spoken in the Anchorage School District. Spanish is the most common minority language here, but only by a nose. It's followed very closely by Samoan and Hmong, then Filipino and Yup'ik.

ALASKA'S FIVE INDIGENOUS CULTURAL REGIONS

In Alaska, the indigenous tribes are known collectively as Alaska Natives. The capitalization is important: "Native" or "Alaska Native" designates a person with blood that is indigenous to Alaska; "native" or "native Alaskan" without the capital "N," simply means the person was born here, but doesn't say anything about their bloodline.

Some of the tribes in Southeast Alaska describe themselves as Indians, and some of the northern and northwest Alaska Native tribes choose to describe themselves as Eskimos, reclaiming what has been used as a derogatory term and turning it into a point of pride.

So, how do you know if it's okay to call someone an Eskimo or an Indian? Easy: Listen to how they refer to themselves, or just ask! As long as you approach the conversation with good intentions and open curiosity without making assumptions, people will usually appreciate your inquiry and respond in kind. Many people are happy to share some aspect of their culture with visitors. When in doubt, the umbrella term "Alaska Native" is entirely appropriate and correct.

If you see people in regalia ("reh-GAY-lee-ah"), or traditional finery, and you're not bothering or interrupting them, you can also ask about their clothing—in fact, you really should! Just don't call it a costume. A costume is something you put on while pretending to be something you're not. Traditional regalia, on the other hand, is meant to showcase an integral aspect of who an Alaska Native person is, representing the lineage and traditions that shape the way they experience and move through the world.

The following gives you a brief background on the five main Alaska Native cultural regions.

Iñupiaq and St. Lawrence Island Yupik

The Iñupiaq people and the St. Lawrence Island Yupik people occupy Arctic and northwestern Alaska. Many of them still live a hunting and gathering lifestyle that's heavily dependent on animals like the whale, walrus, seal, caribou, and fish, although they're more likely to use snowmachines instead of dogsleds and rifles instead of harpoons.

Nowadays, you'll usually find people of this (and every) Alaska Native region living in Western-style houses. However, traditionally, the people of this region lived in semi-subterranean structures made of sod blocks, with an underground entrance tunnel to help trap cold air. Communities were organized into cooperative family groups that made survival in these harsh conditions possible. The men lived in a community house, or *qargi*, that also served as a working and gathering area, while women and children lived in separate family homes.

Community decisions about governance—say, punishments or rewards for things done well or wrongly—were made as a group. Traditional clothing for both men and women included pullover parkas and pants made of caribou skin; the hollow hairs on the caribou hide make it a marvelously lightweight and warm insulation. The intestines of sea mammals were used to make waterproof outerwear.

The extreme climate of north and northwest Alaska might seem forbidding to an outsider, but the Iñupiaq people have developed such an intimate understanding of the climate, through thousands of years of observation and experience, that they know how to live with it. For example, they use their knowledge of the ice and the weather to know when and where it's safe to go out on sea ice that's been shoved up against the land by the tide and the winds (but can easily be lifted away again). And they know how to find seal breathing holes and how to wait patiently for a long time, in such a way that the seal can't tell the hunter is there (in which case it would avoid the breathing hole).

That traditional knowledge is just as deep and varied as any scientist's understanding of the world—probably much more so. Even as this cultural relationship to Alaska's northern shores is challenged by a changing climate that disrupts the normal ways of life, observations and historical knowledge from Native elders provide very useful information on how things used to be and how they've changed.

Yup'ik and Cup'ik

The Native peoples of Southwest Alaska are called Yup'ik or Cup'ik, depending on which dialect of the language they speak. Traditionally the Yup'ik and Cup'ik were also a migratory people, traveling in small groups of extended family to follow the animals and plants that made up their food sources. Many Yup'ik and Cup'ik people still live subsistence lifestyles today; the modern villages used to be seasonal settlements they used in their travels.

Yup'ik and Cup'ik people typically lived off the sea and inland waters, hunting whales, seals, sea lions, and walrus, or harvesting salmon, herring, halibut, whitefish, crabs, and other seafood. People at inland settlements sometimes hunted moose and caribou too.

In some communities the men and boys, once they were old enough to leave their mothers, all lived together in a men's house that also served as a community center for ceremonies, singing, and dancing. Women and children lived in a smaller communal house that also had space for cooking food (which was then taken to the qasgiq, or men's house, where the women also participated in ceremonies and dancing).

Tasks were divided by gender, with women traditionally handling the children, food, and sewing. Clothing was made of bird, fish, and land animal skins, with intestines and fish skins to make waterproof outerwear, and there was intense trading between coastal and inland villages. Winter was a time for ceremonies and community life that emphasized the closely intertwined relationships of the people, animals, and spirit world.

Unungan (Aleut) and Sugpiaq (Alutiiq)

The Unungan and Sugpiaq people, perhaps better known by their Western names Aleut and Alutiiq, were perhaps the most sophisticated seafarers of all Alaska Native cultures, using enclosed, split-bow kayaks and larger, open, skin-covered boats for hunting and transport. They lived intimately with the water—both saltwater and freshwater—and viewed it as a living thing. Unungan and Sugpiaq communities stretched all the way down through the Aleutian Islands, Kodiak, and a little bit of the Southcentral Alaska shoreline around Prince William Sound.

The Unungan people also moved to the Pribilof Islands, but not by choice; they were forcefully relocated by the Russians, who used them as a slave labor force to harvest fur seals for their pelts. Those slave labor conditions continued for years under the American government, even after the purchase of Alaska from Russia—a very dark but little-known spot on our country's ethical record.

The Unungan and Sugpiaq people lived primarily in coastal villages, in semi-subterranean, single-room homes called barabaras; they were made of sod on a driftwood or whalebone frame, and you climbed down through a log with notches cut into it to be used as steps. Two of the most distinctive markers of these cultures were their fine sea craft, built to flex and bend with the waves, and their long bentwood hunting visors, decorated with sea lion whiskers.

Most of the materials Unungan and Sugpiaq people used for clothing, utensils, and tools came from sea mammals, although bears, birds, and small land mammals like squirrels were sometimes harvested for clothing as well. Grass was used to weave baskets with stitching so fine, there may be thousands of stitches in a single square inch.

In certain parts of the Unungan and Sugpiaq teritory, caribou and deer were also an important part of the subsistence lifestyle. Waterproof clothing made of skin and gut was critical to survival in this wet maritime environment. Hunters would tie themselves into the kayak with a special waterproof outer garment, forming a waterproof seal to keep the boat from filling up if it was swamped by a wave.

Athabascan

The Athabascan people traditionally lived in Interior Alaska along major rivers, moving nomadically to follow the seasons and their food sources. Materials such as birch bark, moose hide, and cottonwood were used to make canoes for traveling on water; sleds and snowshoes were used to travel on snow, and dogs were used as pack animals. Key foods included moose, caribou, mountain goats, sheep, salmon, and migratory waterfowl.

Athabascan families are traditionally organized along the mother's clan lines, with just a few exceptions. Uncles (literally, the

one of the two totem poles outside the Petersburg city hall

mother's brother) took a prominent role in rearing children to understand traditional customs and ways of life. Actually, the teaching role of uncles or grandparents is a prominent factor in most Alaska Native traditions. Sharing also plays a prominent role in Alaska Native traditions, but it's particularly key for the Athabascan culture, with each hunter participating in—and providing for—a kin-based sharing network.

Traditional Athabascan clothing is typically made of either moose or caribou hide, with women doing most of the sewing. Beaded decorations, especially flowers, are very common; before first contact, embellishments were made with feathers, porcupine quills, skin fringes, and fur.

The Athabascan language is closely related to that of the Dené or Diné peoples of Canada and the United States, a lineage that stretches all the way through Canada and into the American Southwest. You might be familiar with two of the tribes in this language family, the Navajo and the Apache.

Eyak, Haida, Tsimshian, and Tlingit

If you're familiar with Northwest Coast Indian art, the motifs of Eyak, Haida, Tsimshian, and Tlingit cultures may look familiar; there is a strong, shared heritage. Each of these cultures has a complex social system—Eyak, Tlingit, and Haida society are each divided into two moieties, while Tsimshian society is divided into four phratries, creating a societal structure that cleverly kept people from accidentally marrying one of their own relatives. Babies inherited their clan affiliations from their mother.

Traditionally, homes in this region were made of wood—usually either red cedar, spruce, or hemlock, then roofed with bark or spruce shingles—with a central fire pit and a hole in the roof to let the smoke escape.

Wood figured, and still figures, prominently in the utensils, construction, tools, and even regalia of these Southeast cultures, and many traditional foods are still harvested, including eulachon, or hooligan (a small, oily fish that is both eaten and dried to burn as a candle), herring, and herring eggs. Salmon was a key food, and in some areas sea mammals were eaten too.

The artwork of all four cultures—which includes the distinctive totem poles and clan houses that most people associate with Southeast Alaska—is extremely elevated. Fine baskets, mats, and hats were made with spruce roots and cedar bark, and very fine Chilkat weaving, the only weaving style that creates perfect circles, is believed to have originated with the Tsimshian people from the region of the Nass River. (They used mountain goat wool for their weaving.)

In addition to the moieties and phatries, these cultures were also highly stratified into royalty, commoners, and slaves, the latter usually captives from war raids on other villages. The moieties and phatries of these cultures still, to this day, form an important, reciprocal part of the community's social structure, with a complex give-and-take that's carried out through highly ceremonialized exchanges including potlatches, ceremonies that were both a show of wealth and a way to pay off social debts to the other clan. A potlatch might be held to celebrate the naming of a child, the completion and naming of clan regalia, or as a thanks to the other clan for their support during a difficult time, such as grieving the loss of a loved one.

RELIGIONS AND SUBCULTURES

Alaska has a strange mix of hard-nosed conservatism and open-minded tolerance. As a general rule you can get by with anything up here as long as you're not bothering somebody else, so in the bigger cities, the varied religious and cultural groups generally live and let live. Anchorage is the best example of this, with populations that range from Old Believers (a Russian Orthodox sect) to Orthodox Jews, Muslims, Buddhists, and Christians. Occasionally there is friction caused by intolerance, but usually people all just live their lives.

Subcultures that have been accepted into the national mainstream, such as bodybuilders, bikers, gamers, and even goths, tend to feel comfortable in Alaska's largest cities. Less-mainstream groups—including cosplayers, "otherkin," punks, and fetish groups—are here too, but tend to fly under the radar; they're all but invisible in hyper-conservative rural Alaska, where safety can be a real concern. If your best Google skills can't get you an in with the locals, your best bet is to work your own local community for a word-of-mouth referral.

LITERATURE

As with most of the arts, the art of literature—including writing and poetry—thrives here in Alaska. Perhaps one of our best-known literary exports at the moment is the extremely talented Eowyn Ivey, the Pulitzer Prize-nominated author of *The Snow Child, Last Days in Hunting Camp,* and *To the Bright Edge of the World.*

Other well-known Alaska authors include Dana Stabenow (author of the Kate Shugak mystery series) and nonfiction authors Seth Kantner (*Ordinary Wolves, Shopping for Porcupine,* and *Swallowed by the Great Land*), Nick Jans (*A Wolf Called Romeo* and *The Giant's Hand*), and Heather Lende (*If You Lived Here, I'd Know Your Name* and *Find the Good*).

We also have some amazing Alaska Native authors who have used literature as a way to share insights into their cultures, including the struggle for recognition and equal rights. One of the best books in this genre is *Fifty Miles from Tomorrow,* by William L. Iggiagruk Hensley.

Finally, of course, the number of books inspired by Alaska is almost endless—from much of Jack London's writing to *Into the Wild* by Jon Krakauer, which told the sad story of a young man who journeyed to Alaska with intentions of re-creating himself in the wilderness, but eventually died there instead.

VISUAL ARTS

Alaska inspires creativity, or perhaps creative people simply thrive here; it's hard to tell which comes first. Sometimes you'll find unique media being used to make Alaska art, from clay tiles made of glacial silt to "fish prints" (literally using a fish to "stamp" prints onto paper) or wallets made of fish skin. Other times, it's the subject matter that is uniquely Alaskan, from paintings of songbirds to beautiful watercolor images of bears or photographs of the northern lights.

There is no single defining style that depicts Alaska in the visual arts. The closest we might get is a deep willingness to experiment and innovate, and a tendency to focus on the natural world for subject matter or inspiration. After all, even those of us who live in the cities are keenly aware of our connection with the land and, sometimes, our vulnerability to it.

MUSIC AND DANCE

Alaska Native Music and Dancing

If you're very lucky, you might get to see traditional Alaska Native drumming, singing, and dancing during your stay. Sometimes cruise ships are met by traditional dancers; otherwise, your best chance to see these performances is at Alaska Native cultural centers and events that are sprinkled throughout the state.

Each Native culture has a distinct way of making music or songs and dancing, just as each culture and region has its own distinct regalia. In the northwest part of the state, drums were traditionally made of walrus or seal stomach; now they're often made of airplane fabric, which mimics the same properties but doesn't need to be wet down before playing. The drum skins may be struck directly with a long, thin beater, or the drummers may strike the beater against the frame of the drum.

In other parts of the state, you're likely to see frame drums with an animal skin stretched over them, a similar look to the American Indian hand drums of the Lower 48 states. The frames are made by steaming wood to bend it, and sometimes the beaters are made this way too. The drums are sometimes painted with traditional designs, and you may also see rattles carved or painted to depict figures from traditional myths and legends.

Perhaps the most unusual traditional music and dancing you'll find in Alaska is Athabascan fiddling, a result of the Athabascan people of Interior Alaska adopting old-timey fiddling techniques and folk dances brought to the state by white settlers in the 1800s and making them their own. The best time and place to see this is during the **Athabascan Fiddle Festival** and **Gwich'in Old Time Athabascan Fiddle Dance** in Fairbanks every November.

Other Music and Dancing

In a more general sense, you'll find a rich variety of music and dance in Alaska's largest communities, primarily Anchorage, Fairbanks, and Juneau. In these cities you can enjoy anything from Latin dancing to old-timey music, Irish folk dancing, ballroom dancing, square dancing, contra dancing, line dancing, and some "go out to the club and shake it" dancing, although we usually lag a few years behind the hottest music trends of the Lower 48—if they ever catch on here at all.

In the smaller communities, there just isn't enough of a population to drive much in the way of music trends. But you'll find a very strong bent toward folk music and folk rock throughout the state, perhaps due in part to folk music's culture of informal, person-to-person teaching and making the music your own, something that suits self-sufficient, independent Alaskans very well.

There are annual folk festivals in most major Alaskan cities, including Anchorage, Fairbanks, and Juneau. Southcentral Alaska, in particular, is rife with multiday festivals celebrating folk music of all sorts. Perhaps the most famous is the three-day Salmonfest in the Kenai Peninsula community of Ninilchik, with four stages, lots of food vendors, and plenty of social gathering space.

CUISINE

If there's a single defining cuisine in Alaska, it's seafood. The sort of fresh, wild-caught seafood that people pay high prices for in the Lower 48 is downright commonplace here, and you'd be hard-pressed to find a restaurant that can't serve at least one excellent seafood dish during the summer. If you've been fishing, some restaurants will even take what you've caught and cook it up for you.

That said, some of Alaska's major towns and regions have developed distinct signature foods. In Fairbanks, that's Thai food; nobody knows exactly why, but this Interior town of about 33,000 people has about 20

Thai restaurants, all of them successful, and doesn't seem to have hit the saturation point yet.

In Anchorage, the food of choice is pizza—sometimes with crazy toppings, ranging from artichokes to salmon—and pho (pronounced "fuh"), a delicious Vietnamese soup. If you travel down the Kenai Peninsula the food of choice seems to be barbecue, and it's pretty darn good.

If there's one single cuisine (beyond seafood) that unites Alaska, it's not food but beer. We have an estimated 5.3 breweries per 100,000 adults over the age of 21, which ranks us eighth in the nation for density of breweries—and they're still coming. Each brewery has its own unique recipes, ranging from hoppy to bitter or sweet, and loyal local followings. If you're a fan of beer, sampling as many breweries as possible is a great way to travel the state—just make sure you remember to bring a designated driver or call a cab. Wineries and cideries are slowly starting to catch on across the state, too.

Essentials

Transportation

GETTING THERE

Despite the real possibility of travel delays between smaller communities in Alaska, getting here is very easy. Southeast Alaska is a major destination for many cruise lines, or independent travelers can hop on an Alaska Marine Highway System state ferry from Bellingham, Washington, or Prince Rupert, Canada, and take a delightful, inexpensive sightseeing cruise up the coast on the way to Southeast Alaska.

Most cruise ship docks are right in town, and if they're not, the cruise line will help you get to your lodgings and tours. Ferry travelers, however, sometimes have to deal with ferry docks that are several miles out of town and rarely serviced by public transit, so make sure to budget for the cost of a taxi.

If you'd rather come by air, **Alaska Airlines** (800/252-7522, alaskaair.com) offers the most frequent service and widest choice of destinations within the state, but you can also get a ticket to major Alaska cities year-round from **Delta** (800/221-1212, delta.com), **United** (800/864-8331, united.com), or **Iceland Air** (800/223-5500, icelandair.us). Several airlines, including **Jetblue** (800/538-2583, jetblue.com) and (for European visitors) **Condor** (866/960-7915, condor.com), offer seasonal service to Alaska.

Finally, you always have the option of driving the beautiful Alaska-Canada, or Alcan, Highway—a mere 1,390 miles of mind-blowing scenery and wildlife sightings—through Canada to either Anchorage or Fairbanks. Most people take at least a week to make the drive. If you don't want to drive both directions, you can always take the ferry back to Washington or Canada. Just book your ferry ticket early, because vehicle slots fill up very quickly.

Cruise Travel

If you're on a cruise tour, you have the easiest logistics of all: Just sit back and let the ship take you to top destinations throughout Southeast Alaska. If your cruise includes stops in Southcentral Alaska, you'll be loaded onto motorcoaches at one of the Southcentral ports—probably Seward or Whittier—and bused to your land excursions.

Cruise ship visits to the Aleutian Islands and villages in Western and Arctic Alaska are rare but becoming more frequent. In fact, in 2016, the 1,000-passenger *Crystal Serenity* became the first large cruise ship to travel the Northwest Passage, going from the Pacific Ocean off Alaska over the top of North America to the Atlantic Ocean, calling in small Alaska villages along the way.

GETTING AROUND

If you're traveling between Alaska communities by plane or boat, all you have to do is plan your schedule with a little flex time in case of weather delays—and remember, no tight connections—then sit back and enjoy the ride.

If you're getting around by car, travel here really isn't very different from the Lower 48, except for the narrowness of the highways (most are only two lanes wide) and the relative sparsity of the road system. That said, here are a few tips to make your Alaska highway travels easier and more enjoyable:

- Keep your headlights on at all times, even during the day.
- If you want to slow down and enjoy the scenery or look at wildlife, pull over so people won't have to pass dangerously to get around you.
- If you see a lot of traffic backed up behind

Previous: cruise ship at the Juneau docks; Prince of Wales Island aerial view.

you, please pull over for the same reason. The official (although rarely enforced) law is that if there are five or more cars behind you, you must pull over and let them pass.

- If you have to pass somebody, wait until you have good visibility and leave yourself plenty of leeway. Seeing a broken yellow line means you can legally pass, but it doesn't mean it's always a good idea.
- Watch for wildlife, especially moose. Like all deer, they're prone to darting across the road unexpectedly. Believe it or not, bears are sometimes road casualties too.

Highway Names and Numbers

Alaska highways do have numbers, and if you use a GPS for navigation it'll probably identify the roads by their numbers. That said, the numbering system is actually very confusing, with one number sometimes applying to multiple highways, and some highways receiving multiple numbers. For example, part of the Richardson Highway is designated as Alaska Route 1, while another part is Alaska Route 2; meanwhile, Alaska Route 1 can also apply to the Seward Highway, the Sterling Highway, and the Glenn Highway.

If you talk to locals using the highway numbers, most of them will be confused. But if you use the names, they'll know exactly what you're talking about. With that in mind, I've used the highway names—not numbers—as designators, following the excellent example set by that most distinguished of Alaska road guides, *The Milepost,* and every print map published of the state. It's just less confusing that way.

Rental Cars

Rental cars can be very expensive during peak tourism months in Alaska, and they often sell out quickly. Locally run rental car providers usually offer better rates than the big chains and may be more flexible about letting young people or those without credit cards rent, but even they sell out in the high summer.

If you find yourself marooned with no rental car options, consider giving the local U-Haul provider a call and reserving a pickup or van. Unless you're taking a long trip, renting a U-Haul will usually be less expensive than a typical rental, even after the hefty mileage charges. And although you might earn a few surprised looks when you roll up to the grocery store or hotel in your trusty U-Haul, people will appreciate your ingenuity. (I know, because I've done this!)

One last thing: If you end up renting an actual moving truck for transport, buy the extra insurance. Many people are surprised to discover that while their car insurance typically covers a pickup or van rental, it usually won't cover damage to a moving truck.

Getting Around Rural Alaska

Although travel in and around Alaska's larger communities works pretty much as you might expect, visitors are sometimes surprised by several aspects of travel in rural Alaska. Here's what you need to know to get oriented.

Limited visitor services. Visitor services are variable and may not be available year-round (or even all summer long). Because of that, it's imperative that you always book and confirm your accommodations beforehand. I personally am a big fan of a loose itinerary while traveling, but rural Alaska is not the right place for that approach. Services may come and go unexpectedly. Because tourism to Alaska's smallest rural communities is relatively sparse, some travel services—in particular, taxi operators, car rentals, and some tours—are offered on an informal basis and may not be available all the time. The local convention and visitors bureau, chamber of commerce, or tribal government (in that order) is your best resource for learning who's offering which services when.

Travel delays. Air travel between small communities is often governed by the weather and visibility. Hearing that your flight has been cancelled due to cloud cover might be frustrating, but it's much better than dying in a plane crash. Fatalities can occur when planes fly in marginal conditions.

Airport location. Visitors are sometimes

Traveling in Small Planes

For many residents of rural Alaska—that is, the small communities that exist off the state's very limited road system—traveling in small planes is the only way to get from community to community.

For visitors, boarding a small plane is a thrilling glimpse into another way of life or an exotic way of reaching the next adventure. Of course, the act of getting into a small plane can be either scary or exciting, because it's so unlike any jet you've ever flown in. With that in mind, here are a few things you should know about traveling in small aircraft:

- **Limit your luggage.** Weight and balance is a crucial matter for small planes, and the storage compartments—either to the aft or in the wings—are small, so passengers are usually allowed just one small hand-carry item (typically limited to 10 pounds. or less and small enough to fit under the seat in front of you). If you're allowed checked luggage it will be very limited, both in size and weight. So, no big suitcases!
- **Expect to be weighed.** This doesn't always happen, but you should expect to be weighed, along with your luggage, before you get on any small plane. If the airline doesn't weigh you, they will probably ask your weight and then weigh your luggage. Some tour operators and small airlines set passenger weight limits (typically around 300 to 350 pounds). If you are over this limit, you may be asked to buy more than one seat.
- **Expect to be separated from your luggage.** Because weight and balance are so crucial in a small plane, luggage is sometimes left behind to keep the plane's weight within safe limits. It'll catch up to you—eventually—but that can take up to a couple of days, depending on how frequent the flights are. So always pack enough essentials into your carry-on to get by until your bags catch up. That includes clothes, toiletries, and essential medications.
- **Small planes are limited by weather.** Most small plane flights in Alaska are limited to visual flight rules—they don't fly on instruments alone—so they can't take to the air when visibility is bad at the starting point or the destination. Pilots have crashed because of flying in marginal conditions so, even though it's frustrating to have your flight delayed or cancelled, it's a good sign that the pilot or company you've chosen is safety-conscious... and it's much better than the alternative.
- **Alaska planes are almost always old.** Nobody cares what a bush plane looks like—the important thing is that it flies. With that in mind, one of the most beloved planes for use in Alaska is the deHavilland Beaver, a rugged workhorse that's so functional, you can actually refill the engine oil from inside the cockpit—as you're flying! The deHavilland Beaver was first flown in 1947 and ceased commercial production in 1967. So, if you're lucky enough to fly in one, it'll be anywhere between 50 and 70 years old. They're still in service because they're still the best you can get for Alaska's challenging flying conditions.
- **Check airline safety records.** Some people are terrified by the prospect of flying in a small plane, and the truth is that for every Alaskan with his or her own pilot's license and plane, there's another who will only get into a small plane if there's no other alternative. One of the best ways to soothe any safety concerns you have is by looking up the safety record of the

surprised to find the rural airports may be several miles away from the actual town. If you're staying in a hotel or bed-and-breakfast, they might or might not offer a shuttle service. Always check first. If your lodgings can't offer a shuttle, they can tell you who to call for taxi service.

Small plane logistics. Both luggage space and people space are limited commodities in the small planes that provide service between Alaska's rural communities. Always check the airline's size and weight limits on baggage before you pack, and be aware that you and your baggage might be weighed,

These 6-8-person aircraft are the most common means of transport between small communities.

airline or tour operator you're considering on both the National Transportation Safety Board (ntsb.gov) and Federal Aviation Administration (faa.gov) websites. You can also talk to the tour operators about your concerns. Don't worry—they're used to fielding these questions!

- **Some turbulence is normal.** When you're in a small plane, you'll feel every bump or bounce of turbulence much more significantly than you would feel while flying through the same air patterns in a large plane. Don't worry: A little bit of bouncing around is perfectly normal, especially when traveling over rugged or mountainous terrain, and for the most part your flight should still be smooth.
- **Bring a jacket.** I always bring at least a light jacket with me on an airplane, even in the summer, because, hey, the air gets chilly up there!
- **Ask about the view.** Most tour planes carry 6-8 passengers, depending on the configuration, and are set up so that every seat has a window to look out. They also don't sell assigned seats: Everyone just walks onto the plane and chooses where they'll sit. Sometimes one lucky passenger even gets to sit up front with the pilot (the cockpit is completely open, so you'll get to watch what they're doing even from the back). But, every once in a while you'll see a plane where a couple of the seats, usually toward the back, don't have a good view. If you're concerned about this happening, talk to your tour operator beforehand.
- **Think ahead on airsickness.** I have never been airsick on a small plane, nor have I ever seen another passenger feeling airsick, but it can happen. If you know you're prone to getting airsick, take your motion sickness remedy of choice before getting into the plane.

together or separately. You might also be separated from your luggage—it could be left behind without notice if the plane is too heavy or full—so pack your carry-on with anything you need for a day or two, including medication and clothing, so you can get by until the airline gets your bag to you.

Food and produce. Groceries (and restaurant food) tend to be absurdly expensive in rural Alaska, because everything has to be flown in or (depending on the community's location) shipped in on barges that may come only once or twice a year. It's not uncommon to see prices in the neighborhood of $10 for a half gallon of orange juice or milk. As you might imagine it's hard to get high-quality produce in such remote places, although some communities are making great inroads with geothermal greenhouses or hydroponic farming. If you're going to stay for long, you can save a lot of money by shipping food to yourself in advance instead of shopping in the stores or eating out.

The price of gas. Much like groceries, gas, heating oil, and other types of fuel also have to be barged in and prices are usually very high. If a local offers to drive you around or take you out on a boat, it's polite to offer to chip in for the gas. This does not apply to tours; their prices are adjusted to account for the price of fuel, which is why they often fluctuate from year to year. However, tour operators and their staff are always grateful for tips if you feel they've offered excellent service.

Remote National Parks

Alaska has some of the country's most beautiful national parks, and some of them, like Denali National Park, Kenai Fjords National Park, and the Klondike Gold Rush National Historical Park, have well-developed visitor services. But many of our parks are so remote that they offer no amenities and services at all, and their visitor centers are usually located in a nearby community instead of the park itself.

That does make access challenging and expensive; in most cases, the best way in to these parts is by small plane. Because there are no roads, trails, services, or amenities, all but the most seasoned wilderness travelers will need to hire a guide. On the upside, this remoteness also preserves a true wilderness character that you won't find anywhere else in the country, and is becoming increasingly scarce throughout the world.

Travel Delays

Transportation is the most tenuous aspect of life in Alaska, with just one year-round road link that connects the state to Canada and, beyond it, the contiguous 48 states (the "Lower 48," or simply "Outside" to Alaskans). Even our biggest cities have just one or two highway links connecting them to the road system, so a single traffic accident can block travel in one or both directions for hours. Then there are the inevitable delays for road construction, which kicks into high gear during the short summer months.

And that's only on the road system. The big Alaska Airlines jets that service most major communities in the state can fly in almost any weather, but the smaller airlines, like Ravn Alaska and PenAir, can only fly when visibility is good. That goes double for the small bush planes that provide services between the state's smallest, most remote communities or out to isolated lodges.

Avoid frustration by doing as the locals do: When you're on the road system, always leave a little bit early, and bring enough clothing, water, and snacks to be comfortable if you have to sit through a short delay. (Happily, long delays are very rare, although they do happen.) I like to bring a book to read, just in case, although I've never had to use it.

The general rule with air or sea travel is to never, ever plan tight connections. Although boats and ferries aren't outright cancelled nearly as frequently as planes are, you should expect them to arrive late, even when they leave the previous port on schedule. (The exception is tour boats and chartered fishing boats—in most cases, they're very reliable.) If you're traveling on a small airline that can't fly in limited visibility, it's best to leave yourself at least a day of flex time so you don't miss out entirely on side trips and adventures because of a weather delay.

In Southeast Alaska, where air and sea are the *only* way to get between communities, it's not a question of *if* weather delays will happen on your trip, but when and how often. Again, Alaska Airlines jets are the most reliable mode of transport here, but in some communities there's only one jet flight per day, and half the plane may be given over to cargo containers.

If you're traveling by ferry with a vehicle, consider giving yourself at least a couple days of flex time, because that's how long it usually takes for the next ferry—and the only way of moving your car off one island and on to the next—to come along. If you don't have a vehicle, at least you have the option of hopping on a plane or even chartering a small boat if the ferries are delayed.

Travel Tips

VISAS AND OFFICIALDOM

Even though it's geographically separated from the rest of the country, Alaska is indeed part of the United States, so if you're a U.S. citizen, have a U.S. visa, or are otherwise authorized to live or travel in this country, you don't need any additional documents or permissions to visit Alaska.

As of late 2016, 38 countries participate in a Visa Waiver Program that allows their nationals to visit the United States (including Alaska) for up to 90 days without a visa, and vice versa. Those countries include European Union members, Australia and New Zealand, Iceland, South Korea, Japan, Singapore, Taiwan, and Chile; see dhs.gov/visa-waiver-program-requirements or your country's equivalent for a comprehensive list.

If you plan to drive through Canada to Alaska, however, be aware that you must pass through Canada and as such you'll be subject to their laws, which may restrict people with felony convictions—especially driving while impaired—from entering the country, whether you're coming from the Lower 48 states or from Alaska. See cic.gc.ca/english/information/inadmissibility for more information.

Finally, you might think that because Alaska is so geographically remote from the rest of the country, we'd have our own foreign consulates and domestic passport office—but that isn't the case. At the time of this publication there is a Japanese consular office and a Korean consular office in Anchorage, but that's it; the Mexican consulate was closed several years ago. If locals want to acquire or renew a passport, they must either travel to the other states to do so or send it out by mail.

TRAVEL INSURANCE

For most visitors, every aspect of their Alaska trip will go smoothly. But when travel delays do happen, you may find yourself paying peak rates for lodgings until your next shot at transport arrives. In smaller communities, you can't use sleeping in the airport or ferry terminal as a contingency because they're only open for a short time before and after the planes or boats come in.

With all that in mind, purchasing travel insurance that will reimburse you for the cost of travel delays is a very good idea. The more remote your trip, the more valuable that insurance becomes.

SAVING MONEY

While it's true that certain aspects of travel in Alaska can get pretty pricey, there are also lots of ways to save money. One of the best is by traveling in the early shoulder season, which in Southeast begins in mid-April; for the rest of the state, the shoulder season typically begins in May.

You can also get great deals at the end of the tourist season—early-mid-September in most parts of the state, sometimes late September or early October in Southeast—although some services may already be shut down at that point; always check to confirm availability first.

The prices listed in this guide were current at the time of the writing in 2016, but they may fluctuate somewhat from year to year, depending on fuel costs and the price of supplies (food for catered or sack lunches, for example). This sort of fluctuation is especially common in rural areas where fuel prices can fluctuate wildly.

If you're traveling with at least one other person, two coupon books offer great 2-for-1 deals and discounts. They are the **Northern Lights Entertainment Coupon Book** (888/563-2618, alaska-discounts.com, $55) and the **Alaska TourSaver** (toursaver.com, $99.95, also available as a smartphone app). Although both have a bit of an up-front cost, you can quickly recover that cost with the savings after just one or two tours or nice meals out. Both list their contents online, so you can make sure you're buying coupons that you'll actually use.

Finally, if you're not too picky, you can travel Alaska on a shoestring, even in the high season. Here are some of my favorite tricks for saving money so you can put more of your funds toward the experience of a lifetime.

Use hostels . . . carefully. Staying in hostels is a great way to save money, as long as you realize that Alaska hostels aren't like the hostels you'll find throughout Europe and other parts of the world. Here, they're more likely to be in converted homes or churches, and daytime lockouts are common. Some of the people running Alaska hostels can be pretty quirky, so be sure to check *Accommodations* section in each city listing for my recommendations or screen reviews carefully (check TripAdvisor, Yelp, and hostel-specific sites like hostelz.com for honest reviews).

Pack or ship your own food. As in many places, you can save a lot of money in Alaska by cooking for yourself in hostels. If you're traveling to remote small communities, groceries and meals out are especially expensive; so you can save a lot of money by packing your own food for the trip, or even shipping it to yourself in advance if you plan to be there for a while.

Walk on the ferry. Taking the ferry as a walk-on passenger (without a vehicle or a cabin berth) is one of the cheapest and most enjoyable ways to get around Southeast Alaska and some communities in Southcentral and Southwest Alaska. If you want to extend your reach, you can carry on a bike for a small fee. Along the way you'll also get to see great swaths of Alaska's beautiful coastline—and sometimes a lot of wildlife—at no extra charge. If the ferry is an overnight trip, pack your sleeping bag and a set of earplugs and board early enough to snag one of the reclining loungers in the upper deck solarium. Between the fresh air and the surprisingly soothing, muted hum of the engines, it's the best night's sleep you'll ever get.

Take the train. Having a car is definitely the easiest, most versatile way to get around Alaska. But if your list of destinations includes Anchorage, Seward, or Fairbanks, you can get back and forth by train for about the same or less than what you'd pay for one of the limited shuttle bus services—and it won't cost you much to haul a bike along so you can get around once you're in town.

Share taxi fares. Public transit is limited in most small Alaska communities, and airport and ferry docks are usually a few miles out of town. Taxi fares add up fast, especially if there's traffic. If you make a few discreet inquiries, you can usually find somebody who's heading in the same direction and will happily split a taxi fare with you.

Use the libraries. Visitors are often surprised by how hard it is to find free Wi-Fi in Alaska. You can always head to the local library for free, albeit slow, Wi-Fi; most libraries also have computer terminals you can use for free if you didn't bring a tablet or laptop with you.

WHAT TO PACK

What you pack will depend, to some degree, on which part of the state you're visiting. I've included average temperatures and precipitation in each city description but, as a general rule, you can expect summer temperatures in the 50s and 60s throughout most of Alaska, dipping into the 40s in Arctic communities and sometimes rising into the 70s—and more rarely the 80s—in Southcentral and the Interior. With that in mind, here are the essentials you'll need on your Alaska trip.

- A **waterproof, windproof jacket** with a hood. If the weather gets bad, a simple "windbreaker" won't be enough. If you're traveling in a chillier part of the state or will be outside in all weather conditions, a lightweight, packable "puffy" (down or synthetic-fill) jacket is also handy. You won't need a heavy parka unless you're going to a cold part of the state in winter.

- **Non-cotton insulating layers** that you can adjust to keep yourself warm in changing temperatures. Wool and synthetics like capilene are excellent choices.
- **Calf-length rubber boots** (sometimes called "Alaska sneakers") are great for keeping your feet dry on boat docks or while fishing or hiking in the tundra.
- **Sturdy walking shoes.** Trust me, you won't want to walk everywhere in those rubber boots.
- **Sunglasses** and **sunscreen.** Believe it or not, you're almost guaranteed to need them at some point!
- **Insect repellent.**
- **Sleeping mask.** Many hotels have blackout curtains, but some travelers are still bothered by how bright the summer skies can be, even at midnight).
- If you wear glasses, a **ball cap** is invaluable for keeping rain and snow off your eyewear.
- Any **medications** you need during your trip.
- Don't forget your **camera** and extra batteries/chargers for it and your smartphone or tablet.
- Don't bother with an umbrella unless you want to brand yourself clearly as a tourist; locals never use them, and a **rain jacket** will do a better job of keeping you dry.
- **Light summer clothing.** Recent summers have been warm and dry.
- **Fishing license.** You can buy this online from adfg.alaska.gov.

Optional items include a swimsuit (some hotels have pools, hot tubs, or saunas, and on warm days Alaskans will swim in the lakes) and gallon-size zip-close freezer bags for holding wet clothing layers until you get to a place where you can dry them out. I also like having a trash bag along to sit on in wet weather; you can also put it over your backpack as a rain cover or use it as an impromptu rain poncho. It might not be stylish, but it's better than being wet!

Layering

By now, most people know that you're supposed to dress in layers when you visit a place like Alaska, but not everyone is clear on what that means. The idea is to "dress like an onion"—in multiple layers—so you have the option of adding or removing layers to stay comfortable, no matter what the weather does.

For my travels around Alaska, which usually involve spending a lot of time outside, I pack a lightweight, long-sleeved shirt, a medium-weight long-sleeved shirt and a fleece vest. If things look to be especially chilly or you know you're prone to feeling cold, a lightweight, packable puffy jacket comes in handy too; but if you're spending most of your time inside, you won't need it.

Add a hat, cap or hood, a pair of light gloves, and whatever non-cotton socks you prefer, and you can adjust your clothing to be comfortable in absolutely anything Alaska throws at you.

ACCESS FOR TRAVELERS WITH DISABILITIES

You will find very good wheelchair accessibility in Alaska's larger communities on the road system, especially Anchorage, Fairbanks, and most good-size communities. The mass transit buses "kneel" to make it easier to get on board and usually have wheelchair lifts and fold-up seats that create space for wheelchair users; most businesses have wheelchair-accessible entrances.

Most walk/crosswalk signals in these cities have not yet been updated to speak for the visually impaired. However, most of the larger businesses and tourism agencies have telecommunication devices for the deaf (TDD) communication lines for the hearing impaired.

Alaska State ferries are also wheelchair-accessible, with elevator access and wheelchair-friendly staterooms and bathrooms on every boat. All of the Alaska Railroad passenger cars are wheelchair-accessible, and a few of their rail routes offer periodic narration that may be helpful to those with limited sight. Small planes, by virtue of their size, do not come with wheelchair lifts; however, if you give the carrier advance notice, they may be able to accommodate you and carry the wheelchair as cargo.

Increasingly, outdoor attractions on public lands—such as the beautiful rail-access-only Spencer Glacier Whistle Stop, one of the highlights of Southcentral Alaska—are being designed to be partially or completely wheelchair accessible; the Alaska Public Lands Center in whichever part of the state you're visiting will have more information.

Accessibility is variable in other communities throughout Alaska, including Southeast communities, which are frequently built into coastal hillsides and use steep staircases as shortcuts for pedestrians. You'll usually have good access to local museums and other recently remodeled attractions, but reaching them can involve steep grades, so it may be easiest to use a taxi to get around.

Often, local nonprofits exist to help provide accessibility for a variety of differently abled people, and if you give advance notice, most museum docents will happily interpret exhibits for anyone who is visually impaired. They may also have wheelchairs on-site for those with mobility impairments.

Your best bet for getting connected to these local resources—which, unfortunately, must be done on a community-by-community basis—is by calling the local chamber of commerce or visitor center. Many local chambers or convention and visitors bureaus also list accessibility resources on their websites.

TRAVELING WITH CHILDREN

Coming to Alaska is an adventure most children will never forget—in a good way. Take these tips into consideration to keep the trip from being unforgettable in a bad way for you:

Be careful about putting your kids in

A young girl and a young brown bear enjoy a sunny day at Pack Creek in Admiralty Island National Monument.

situations where they'll be confined to a small space for long periods and forced to sit still. Bear viewing is a prime example: As thrilling as it is to see the bears, you're often asked to sit quietly in limited space for an extended period of time.

Are your kids able to handle the weather delays—sometimes lasting for a day or more—that crop up in rural Alaska communities? If not, you should avoid the most remote communities or lodges that can only be reached by small plane or bush plane. If your kids aren't comfortable in a commercial jet, they probably won't be comfortable in a small plane either.

Not all tours to remote areas accept small children; ask about age limits when you book. On the upside, almost all tours in Alaska that do accept children do so at a discounted rate.

Always check out cruise ship land excursions before you take your children along. Cruise ship excursions are usually finely tuned operations designed to whisk you smoothly from one place to the next, so once you get started on the tour you're fully committed to going through with the whole thing.

WOMEN TRAVELING ALONE

I frequently travel through Alaska by myself, and have met many women from all states, countries, backgrounds, and ages who feel comfortable doing the same. That said, you should be aware that Alaska does have one of the highest rates of sexual assault in the nation, both in urban centers and in remote communities.

In the big cities (Anchorage, Fairbanks, and Juneau), locals will give you an honest read on which neighborhoods or trails might not be safe for a woman alone, especially after dark; just ask. If you're traveling by yourself to a remote community with a particularly rough reputation—for example, Bethel, which I have not featured as a destination for that reason—you should definitely choose your lodgings with an eye toward safety first.

SENIOR TRAVELERS

Although Alaska might have a rightly earned reputation as an adventure traveler's paradise, seniors make up the largest visitor sector overall and are very welcome here. Most tour operators are good about disclosing how much walking or other physical exertion may be required on their trips, along with giving periodic rest and bathroom breaks; all you have to do is ask.

Most major Alaskan towns on the road system, or in large island communities like Juneau and Ketchikan, have at least one pharmacy where you can get commonly requested medications. However, it's best to come prepared with enough medication to last the duration of your trip, and if you think you might need a refill while traveling through smaller communities, call ahead well in advance to see if the medication you need will be available.

Similarly, all the big cities will have a hospital with a 24-hour emergency room and trauma capabilities. However, medical treatment in the smaller communities is much more limited and may consist only of a small, local clinic. Serious cases that can't be handled locally may be medevaced to a larger hospital.

GAY AND LESBIAN TRAVELERS

Alaska is a strangely mixed bag when it comes to serving gay, lesbian, bisexual, transgender, and queer travelers. On one hand, Alaskans are known for their easygoing "live and let live" lifestyle. We tend to accept people as they come and take them at face value, regardless of where you came from, what you've done in the past, or the choices you make in your personal life.

On the flip side of the coin, Alaskan politics tend to be very conservative, and lifestyles tend to be both conservative and aggressively macho in most rural areas. To give you a couple of points of reference, it wasn't until 2015 that the Anchorage Assembly finally passed an ordinance making it illegal to discriminate on the basis of sexual orientation or gender identity within the city. This was the first civil rights ordinance of its kind in Alaska, despite the fact that according to a 2013 report from the University of California, Los Angeles School of Law's Williams Institute, we have the third-highest proportion of same-sex couples raising biological, adopted, or stepchildren in the nation: 23 percent, right behind Mississippi (26 percent) and Wyoming (25 percent).

There is also at least one "megachurch" in Anchorage, the Anchorage Baptist Temple, that has actively promoted discrimination in the past. Its pastor is widely acknowledged as leading the decades-long fight to keep the aforementioned antidiscrimination regulations from being passed. Because of that prevailing attitude, Alaska's gay and lesbian population tends to fly slightly under the radar, living a little less visibly "out" than you might see in communities like San Francisco or Portland. As one friend puts it, it's important to know where the safe spaces are where you can really express yourself. Also, because our population is so small, the LGBTQ population is correspondingly small as well; as such, the various LGBTQ populations tend to blend together more here than in larger communities.

Those safe spaces tend to be concentrated in the larger population centers, so, unfortunately and unless a trusted source advises otherwise, discretion is a smart default in the more rural areas. That said, there are LGBTQ-friendly lodgings, tour providers, and travel agents operating throughout Alaska that can help you create that safe space as you travel.

LGBTQ Resources

Although Alaska's LGBTQ resources tend to be quite localized, they can help you find similar organizations—when they exist—in other parts of the state. Here are some notable resources for LGBT travelers.

Identity, Inc.'s Gay and Lesbian Community Center (336 E. 5th Ave., Anchorage, 907/929-4528, identityinc.org, typically Mon.-Fri. 3pm-9pm and Sat.-Sun. noon-6pm, but hours may vary) is a safe place to hang out in Anchorage and meet others in the community.

PFLAG (pflag.org) is not geared specifically toward travelers, but their mission statement includes providing support for LGBTQ individuals in an adverse society, and their events are some of the best places to meet other members of the community. There are PFLAG chapters in Anchorage, Fairbanks and Juneau; you can find contact information on their website.

The SEAGLA (seagla.org), or **Southeast Alaska LGBTQ+ Alliance,** holds regular socials and other events in Juneau. Other good resources for LGBTQ travelers in Alaska (although most are primarily focused on the gay community) include purpleroofs.com (an excellent resource for gay-owned and gay-friendly lodgings, travel agents, and tour operators) and outinalaska.com (a tour company that specializes in gay-owned and gay-friendly tour operators, accommodations, and services).

Anchorage has two notable, full-time LGBTQ bars. **Mad Myrna's** (530 E. 5th Ave., 907/276-9762, madmyrnas.com) is wildly popular and generally seen as a friendly, inclusive place for all comers; they offer wonderful variety shows on Friday nights and are regularly voted the best place to dance in town.

The Raven (708 E. 4th Ave., 907/278-9672) is the longest-running gay bar on the West Coast, and Anchorage also has a wonderful week-long **PrideFest** in mid-June (alaskapride.org).

Although other Alaska communities don't have "out and proud" bars that cater to the LGBTQ community, there are usually low-key gathering places known to locals. Contacting the nearest LGBTQ organization is a good place to start.

Gender-Neutral Bathrooms

As part of the Anchorage Assembly's antidiscrimination ordinance, facilities can still provide gender-segregated locker rooms, restrooms, and dressing rooms, but you are allowed to use the facilities that are consistent with your gender identity. That said, if you want to go to the toilet without worrying if an intolerant jerk is going to give you a hard time—or if you're in other Alaska cities, which have yet to pass their own antidiscrimination ordinances—you might be more consistently comfortable in gender-neutral restrooms, where nobody will bat an eye about who goes where.

The best place to find gender-neutral restrooms throughout Alaska is in coffee shops; when in doubt, look for a Kaladi Brothers or a Starbucks. Also, although roadside and campground toilets are occasionally marked according to gender, when the only thing behind the door is a single-stall pit toilet and a dubious supply of toilet paper, they're effectively unisex. Nobody cares which door you go through as long as you're not cutting in line.

Conduct and Customs

Longtime Alaskans can easily spot a tourist at 100 yards. That's not always a bad thing; Alaskans are generally friendly and helpful, and many will go out of their way to give you directions or help out if they realize you're from out of town. Still, if you don't want to stand out so much, there are a few tricks you can use to blend in.

- Leave the umbrella and rain poncho at home. (Alaskans use rainproof jackets instead—they offer better coverage and leave your hands free.)
- Don't tuck your shirt in.
- Don't carry a giant camera in the most mundane of places (e.g., downtown Anchorage, Fairbanks, or Juneau). Your smartphone should be more than adequate for photos in those spots.

With all that said, here are a few more things every tourist should know, all based on questions I've received over the years.

AREA CODES

Visitors are sometimes surprised to find that even though all of Alaska has only one area code, you still pay in-state long distance charges for calling to towns in another region of the state. For most, this is only an issue if you use a hotel, bed-and-breakfast, or hostel landline to dial other parts of Alaska.

CURRENCY

Yes, we use American dollars in Alaska; in fact, that's the only currency accepted. You'll have ready access to ATMs throughout the state, in all but the smallest communities. Credit cards are accepted almost everywhere, although you will find a few cash-only businesses, particularly in small communities.

DRESS CODE

Alaska is notoriously casual; we're more concerned with practicality and comfort than style. It's not uncommon to see people in jeans, flannel, or Carhartt clothing (a brand of workwear) out on the town, even at touring theater shows. So, with the exception of a very few nice restaurants, you don't need to worry about meeting a dress code.

LANGUAGE

English is spoken in every Alaska community. You will find people who speak only Alaska Native languages—primarily Yup'ik—in some remote communities, but most of the younger generation speaks English too.

ELECTRICITY

Yes, we have electricity in every Alaska community! We use a 120-volt current, just like the rest of the United States.

SILVER HAND STICKER

Every year, some tourists experience the heartbreak of taking the trip of a lifetime to Alaska and thinking they've walked away with a piece of authentic Alaska Native artwork as a souvenir, only to discover that they've been duped into buying an imitation.

Protect your purchase and make sure you're getting an authentic piece of Alaska Native art by looking for the Silver Hand sticker or tag, which signifies that the artist is in fact Alaska Native.

Not every Alaska Native artist chooses to use the Silver Hand sticker, but, in those cases, the shopkeeper should still be able to give you biographical information about who the artist is and where they come from. If you see a row of souvenirs that look like they've been mass-produced or are made with rough craftsmanship, they probably aren't authentic; true Alaska Native workmanship really is a fine art.

MADE IN ALASKA STICKER

If you're shopping for general Alaska-made art or other goods, keep an eye out for the Made in Alaska sticker. This sticker means the product was made or assembled in Alaska, but doesn't say anything about who did it—so if you see it on something that looks like Alaska Native artwork, the Made in Alaska sticker is not a guarantee of authenticity. Ask for biographical information about the artist before you buy.

If you're looking for authentic artwork or crafts made by Alaskan artists in general, however, the Made in Alaska sticker is a great help, so definitely keep an eye out for this indicator that you're buying locally made goods.

ACCOMMODATIONS

Alaska's larger communities have many chain hotels that will look familiar to most visitors, including Aspen Suites, Hilton, Marriott, Best Western, Day's Inn, and Comfort Inn. In smaller communities, a modest hotel like Best Western will often be the best en masse lodging available in town, although some bed-and-breakfasts can be very nice.

Be warned that air-conditioning is not a common amenity in Alaska, although I expect it'll become more common as our summers get hotter and drier. At the moment, Fairbanks—which tends to be hot and dry in the summer—is the place you're most likely to find air-conditioning in a hotel room.

Many hotels have blackout curtains to help cut down on the amount of midnight sun that leaks into your room at night, but not all of them do, so always ask first if this is important to you. If you think the light might bother you it's a good idea to bring a sleeping mask, just in case.

In smaller communities, lodgings are usually modest at best and may even be in a repurposed work camp from the pipeline or railroad days. If you go into your hotel, inn, or B&B expecting a big-city experience, you'll probably be disappointed. But if you go into it with the knowledge that in a small community, having a private bathroom with lots of hot water and a comfortable bed with great pillows is at least a midrange amenity, you'll be in a better position to enjoy the adventure. Television reception can be dodgy in the more remote communities, so, again, if this is important to you, ask about it when you book your room.

Hotel Prices

Unless otherwise noted, hotel prices in this book are given per room, not per person, based on double occupancy. In Alaska, that means that you can put up to two people in the room for the price given; there's an extra charge, often quite small, for every additional person beyond that. You don't have to pay a singles supplement unless otherwise noted (usually only at some remote lodges and on some cruises). Even ferry cabins don't require a singles supplement, although of course you'll save money if you split the cost of the cabin by as many people as there are bunks.

ALCOHOL AND TOBACCO

Alaska's minimum ages for drinking (21) and smoking (19); you'll need to show government identification to purchase either. Even if you are obviously well beyond the minimum age, you will probably be turned away if you can't show government ID. If you're not a U.S. citizen, you might be denied the purchase of alcohol or tobacco if the clerk doesn't recognize your country's ID. If you want to be absolutely sure of getting your drink or smokes, be ready to show your passport.

Both breweries and brewpubs are very popular in Alaska, but they have different rules about selling alcohol and food. Breweries are restricted in how much alcohol they can serve to you for consumption on-site in a given day, although they can fill growlers or bottles for you to take away with you. Breweries cannot serve their own food, although they often station food trucks outside or will happily let you bring your own eats. In general if you want a true pub atmosphere—where people go primarily to socialize—you're more likely to get it in a brewery, although it's still not quite the community center you'd expect from a European pub.

Brewpubs, on the other hand, do serve their own food—it's often quite good—and don't have the daily limit on how much they can serve you for consumption on-site, although any institution that serves alcohol is required by law to refuse sale to anyone who's obviously had too much.

Bars in Alaska, which can include late-night restaurants where alcohol is served, typically close between 2am and 3am. In some regions they have the option of staying open later, but they can't continue serving alcohol during that extra window of time, which is designed to help patrons get home safely.

The legal limit for drunk driving in Alaska is a blood alcohol concentration (BAC) of 0.08 percent. You can drive with closed and sealed containers of alcohol in the car, but you're not allowed to drive with open containers that could indicate you were consuming as you drove.

Wet, Dry, and Damp Villages

If you travel to rural Alaska, be warned that alcohol abuse has caused quite a few problems in these remote communities. As a result, some communities have elected to be wet (you can bring alcohol in, and it's sold freely), damp (you can buy alcohol in very limited circumstances, but you can't bring it into town without the proper permit), or dry (no alcohol allowed under any circumstances).

Make sure you respect the rules of the community you're visiting. If you're caught smuggling contraband alcohol it is a crime, and in some communities they'll turn you around at the airport and send you back home.

MARIJUANA

In 2015, Alaskans voted to legalize marijuana for recreational use, making it the third state to do so. That said, as of early 2017 we're still slowly picking our way through the maze of regulations and implementation for exactly how that'll look on a community-by-community basis.

Just to make it more complicated, according to federal law it's still a crime to possess marijuana unless you have a medical marijuana card. So it's illegal to travel through or into other states with marijuana, and you can't use it on federal lands like national parks or national forests. But by the time this book is published, you will probably be able to buy it. Here's what you need to know about marijuana regulation in Alaska so far:

- You must be at least 21 years old to use marijuana products. Giving marijuana to a minor (under 21) is a crime.
- You can possess up to one ounce of marijuana for personal use with no state penalty, but possessing more—or having any quantity with intent to distribute—can be prosecuted as a misdemeanor or felony, depending on the circumstances.
- It's illegal to take marijuana products out of Alaska.

- Possession of marijuana in a school zone may be considered a crime.
- Driving while under the influence of marijuana is a crime, just like driving while under the influence of alcohol.

You cannot smoke or otherwise consume marijuana in public places, including businesses, entertainment venues, parks, sidewalks, and the like. It's limited to use in private places, although hotels, landlords, and entities may have rules in place that prohibit its use. Once the wrangling over rules is complete, there will probably be some private clubs created where you can smoke with others. (There are some now, but they're operating in a legal gray zone.)

Recreation

If you're experienced enough to DIY your own outdoor recreation in Alaska, most communities have at least one outfitter that can provide rental gear for most pursuits, including paddling, camping, and fishing. However, please keep in mind that each region has its own particular considerations or hazards for outdoor recreation, and Alaska is no different.

Some of the things you must be aware of here include frequent sweepers and strainers (for river paddlers); one of the highest tidal differentials in the world (for sea kayakers and anyone recreating in intertidal zones); wildlife hazards, including bears and moose; and cold, silty, swiftly flowing waters.

But perhaps the biggest hazard that many recreationists aren't prepared for is the sheer remoteness of Alaska's wilderness. The old adage of "just follow water downhill and you'll end up at a town" doesn't always work out here—you might find yourself lost in the mountains or end up in Canada! There is also limited to nonexistent cell phone service in most wilderness areas, and in some places even satellite phones won't work. Most of our parks and recreation areas have little to nothing in the way of amenities, services, and facilities (beyond the occasional campground), and rescues may be delayed in remote areas, if they're possible at all.

None of that is meant to keep you from participating in outdoor recreation; in fact, the sheer size and wildness are a big part of Alaska's appeal. But you should definitely be well-prepared and well-informed before heading out on an adventure by yourself, preferably with a satellite phone or rescue beacon that you know works in your area (talk to the local outfitters to find out what works and what doesn't). Just in case.

If you don't feel ready to tackle an outing on your own, you can—and should!—hire a guide to take you on the adventure of a lifetime. Finally, regardless of whether you're going with a guide or without, make sure you read through the bear safety section.

CAMPING SAFETY

There are three types of camping in Alaska: Car camping in an established campground, just a short walk from the car; cabin camping in a public-use hut that may be right off the road or miles into the backcountry; and backpacking. The latter doesn't refer to the travel term, but instead to carrying all your camping gear on your back and setting up a tent in the backcountry.

Whichever type of camping you're doing, there are three aspects that set camping in Alaska apart from most other places: weather, terrain, and wildlife. Even if you're not camping out, it's good to keep these three things in mind. Here are the basics. If any of this is unfamiliar to you, I'd encourage you to do more research on a guided trip or with an excellent print resource like *Mountaineering: The Freedom of the Hills* (Seattle: Mountaineers Books, 2010).

Weather

Perhaps the most defining characteristic of weather in Alaska is that it changes . . . constantly. Just to make things a little more challenging, in a state this big, with such extreme topography and relatively few weather stations, weather forecasting is iffy at best—so do pay attention to the forecasts, but don't bet your comfort or safety on their being accurate.

The *Climate* section in the *Background* chapter will be helpful in figuring out what general conditions to prepare for in any given part of Alaska. In very general terms, the Interior region (between the Brooks and Alaska ranges) has greater extremes of temperature in summer and winter and a profusion of mosquitoes. Exposed areas in both Interior and Southcentral Alaska are prone to very high winds—gusts can reach up to 100 mph—so you should carry a strong tent and know how to stake it out to withstand those winds.

The wind may be accompanied by blowing rain or snow (yes, even at the peak of summer, although it's rare), so it's important that you don't skimp on weatherproof and insulating layers or your sleeping bag. Of course, it's always possible that you might go packed for cold weather and run into hot weather instead. That's why it's so important to dress in layers so you can adjust your clothing to stay comfortable, and to carry a sleeping bag that's cold enough to handle a worst-case scenario, but not overkill.

For example, I usually carry a beat-up zero-degree bag that's probably more like a 20-degree bag nowadays. I know from experience that I get chilled easily when I sleep outside, so that sleeping bag keeps me very comfortable down to about 40 degrees, and safe (if not necessarily comfortable) down to about 20. If you don't sleep cold or aren't camping in exposed areas with some elevation, you might be comfortable with a lighter-weight bag. Experience really is the key to figuring this out; if you're just starting out, get a feel for your personal tolerances by doing your camping in areas close to your car or other shelter so that if you find out your sleeping bag isn't warm enough or your tent isn't strong enough, you can seek shelter or grab an extra blanket from the car.

Summer highs tend to be a little milder in Southeast Alaska and chillier in Southwest Alaska, thanks to the masses of nearby water. In Southwest Alaska, you're likely to encounter both strong winds and still days with lingering fog; in Southeast, foggy or misty days are very common but don't tend to linger as

a well-stocked van at one of Alaska's alpine lakes

persistently as Southwest Alaska fog banks can. And finally, even at the peak of summer, temperatures in Arctic Alaska tend to be chilly; plan and pack accordingly for that and the exposure of camping in a treeless landscape.

Terrain

Although some areas do have quite a few maintained hiking trails (for example, Sitka or Southcentral), the vast majority of Alaska remains a trackless wilderness. So be aware that if you're planning a true backcountry trip that doesn't involve maintained trails, you will probably end up bushwhacking—literally, crawling through the bushes. Even the strongest hikers struggle to make four or five miles of progress in a day under such conditions, so plan your routes accordingly.

Often, you'll find much easier walking on ridgelines and above treeline. You might also get lucky and find an animal trail that leads in the right direction—just keep in mind that wildlife uses those paths (and people paths too), so you have heightened chances of an encounter.

People are often surprised by our rivers and streams. In some other states and countries, a river is a relatively small thing; here they usually come in three varieties: mighty, wide rivers that it's foolhardy to cross without a boat; relatively shallow, braided rivers that split into multiple channels; and narrow, fast-moving and turbulent streams that are dangerous to cross because of their swiftness and the risk of a fall. The cold temperature of the water and the limited visibility from heavy silt or mineral content often come as a surprise to travelers, too.

Always follow backcountry basics like undoing the straps of your pack before crossing so that if you fall, you can slip out of the pack before it drags you down. Scout for a crossing point that offers the shallowest, slowest-moving water possible, and scope out the possible consequences of a fall at your crossing point of choice. If a bad step would send you tumbling down rocky rapids or under a cluster of half-submerged tree limbs, that's not the place to cross.

Obviously, it's safer to cross with a friend, linking arms for balance or using trekking poles for extra stability. Finally, beware of changes in depth; there may be deep "holes" near rocks that create turbulent water or on the outside of curves where the river undercuts its banks. Again, I refer you to *Mountaineering: The Freedom of the Hills* for more detailed information and techniques.

WHAT TO PACK

Exactly what you end up carrying into the Alaska backcountry is going to vary depending on which part of the state you're in, where you're going, the length of your trip, the weather forecast, and your skill and comfort level with the expedition. As a general rule, you should always approach your trips with the mindset that you're going to be on your own out there, and take a proactive approach to ensuring you're ready to handle any emergencies that could reasonably come your way.

That said, you don't have to carry a 60-pound pack on an overnight trip. Instead, start by covering the "Ten Essentials" as laid out in the book *Mountaineering: The Freedom of the Hills.* This is what you need to stay alive in case of emergency—or, to put it another way, plan for the worst but hope for the best, so that if something ever does go wrong, you'll be prepared to save yourself or others. Here's a sample packing list, starting with which "essential" you're satisfying and then what you should carry.

1. Navigation: Bring GPS, maps, and a compass with you. GPS is not always reliable in the truly remote areas, so do not depend on it as your exclusive means of navigation.

2. Sun Protection: Believe it or not, you do need both sunblock and sunglasses in Alaska!

3. Clothing/Insulation: The idea is that you can add or remove layers to help you stay comfortable in changing conditions or as your activity level changes. For a summer trip, I usually pack lightweight long underwear top and bottoms, a midweight wool or fleece top, a fleece vest, plus light gloves, a light hat, and a waterproof/windproof jacket and pants.

For colder trips I'll include a lightweight, packable puffy jacket and a midweight insulating layer for my legs—and of course warm, non-cotton socks, too. The non-cotton bit is important. If you wear cotton into the Alaska backcountry and it gets wet, it'll hold that water against your skin and chill you instead of making you warmer. In fact, cotton clothing can and has contributed to hypothermia in the backcountry. Top it all off with a waterproof, windproof outer layer.

If you're planning to stay overnight, don't forget your sleeping bag and a sleeping pad, too. The sleeping pad is not optional: You need the extra insulation to keep you from losing body heat to the cold ground.

4. Illumination: Even in the summer, it's a good idea to have some source of illumination. Headlamps are more convenient than a flashlight because they leave your hands free.

5. First Aid Supplies: You can buy travel/outdoors first aid kits in almost any sporting goods store.

6. Fire: I carry windproof matches in a watertight container and a few small firestarters—usually packets made of wax and sawdust—to help get a fire going in case of emergency.

7. Repair Kit and Tools: Unless you're carrying a camp stove or air mattress that requires specialized repair gear, a knife/multitool, duct tape, and either zip ties or cordage is usually plenty. Safety pins or needle and thread, or some lightweight wire, can also come in handy. I also like to carry a pair of tweezers for removing devil's club thorns or porcupine quills.

8. Nutrition: This just means extra food. This is for more than just comfort: Food gives you energy and also keeps you warm when you're outdoors.

9. Hydration: Although Alaska's waters look pristine, you can still get backcountry parasites like giardiasis (a.k.a "beaver fever") and cryptosporidium by drinking untreated water. Bring either a backcountry water filter or an ultraviolet (UV) purifier designed for camp use, and use it to treat water before drinking. If you're in an RV, don't use a household-style water filter unless it's specifically advertised for removing backcountry contaminants as well.

10. Emergency Shelter: Depending on the trip you have in mind and your comfort level, this could be anywhere from a foil "space blanket" that folds down to the size of a deck of cards or a full-on tent or bivvy bag.

That might sound like an awful lot, but I can put most of my survival gear into a quart-size zip-close freezer bag; add food, water, clothing, and shelter to the backpack and I'm ready to go. Usually, one or two car camping trips are all you need to figure out what you should carry to feel comfortable and safe. Sticking close to the car for those first few trips minimizes the consequences of any missteps; you always have the car as a shelter option, and if you've forgotten something important, you can just grab it from the car or even drive off to get it, if it was really important.

PERSONAL HYGIENE

Most established campgrounds and some hiking trailheads in Alaska have pit toilets, but if nature calls while you're out on the trail, you're going to have to handle it on the fly. The general rule is to do your business at least 200 feet away from camp, a cooking spot, or a water source. If you have to defecate, dig a hole that's 6-8 inches deep, then fill it in once you've done your business.

If you have to urinate, you don't have to dig a hole—but if you use toilet paper, please put it in a zip-close freezer bag and pack it out with you. That might sound gross, but you don't ever have to touch any bodily fluids—and it's nowhere near as gross as finding sodden blots of white paper left by careless visitors, still hanging around the forest a year after the initial deposit. It might be tempting to think that toilet paper will just dissolve into nothing like it does in your toilet, but cool weather and relatively limited microbial activity in the soil mean nothing decomposes that fast in Alaska.

Think about it: If you don't want to mess with your used toilet paper, neither does the next person to come by the same spot! If you'd rather avoid the paper fuss already, you can always choose a place with plenty of soft vegetation and use that instead. Just make sure you're not reaching for devil's club, cow parsnip, or anything else that looks remotely spikey!

LICENSES AND PERMITS

If you go fishing or clamming in Alaska, you must have a state-issued fishing license on your person at all times. You can buy your fishing license online from adfg.alaska.gov, anywhere that fishing equipment is sold, and from many (but not all) tour operators that offer fishing expeditions.

Backcountry permits may be required for travel or camping in some of the state's largest and wildest national parks, including Denali National Park; it's best to check each park's rules before you go.

TIPPING FOR TOURS

Alaska tour guides are service workers, just like a waiter or waitress. So, although tips are not required, they usually make up a good portion of the guide's take-home pay and are always appreciated. Tipping is appropriate if you feel that the guide has done a good job or otherwise positively affected your experience.

As a general rule, anywhere from 10 to 20 percent of the tour price is considered a good tip. That doesn't mean you have to tip every worker 20 percent of the entire cost; sometimes there can be 10 or more workers on the bigger tours! Instead, aim for a total tip that adds up to the percentage you want, and either give it to the person you feel has most earned it or, if you want it to be split up among the entire staff, just give it to the manager/leader and let them know.

When in doubt—or if you'd like to tip but can't afford to tack an extra 10-20 percent onto an already expensive tour price—nobody will ever be offended if you slip them $20 with a discreet smile and a "thank you."

Health and Safety

Alaska is, for all intents and purposes, free of mosquito- and tick-borne illnesses that are common in the Lower 48 states, including Rocky Mountain spotted fever, Lyme disease, malaria, and Zika. No special immunizations are required to visit. That said, there are a few key facts you should know about health and safety, as well as a few unusual hazards to be aware of.

CLINICS AND HOSPITALS

Every large city in Alaska has a hospital with a 24-hour emergency room and trauma care capabilities. However, medical care in smaller communities may be limited to a single small clinic. Alaska state ferries don't carry shipboard doctors, and most hotels don't have a doctor on staff either. If you're concerned that you might need access to specific medical care in a given town, you should contact local medical providers—or, failing that, the local convention and visitors bureau or chamber of commerce—to see if they have the facilities to meet your needs.

WATER SAFETY

Many of Alaska's best activities take place on or near the water, and yes, our cold, swift-running, and silty water can kill you. But believe it or not, it's not lack of swimming ability that causes most people to drown; it's the gasp reflex that causes you to automatically inhale when you go under, which is one reason everyone should wear a personal flotation device, regardless of how strong a swimmer you may be. Even if you make it out of the water, if you inhaled water you should seek medical care immediately because you could still die of "dry drowning."

MUDFLATS

Throughout Alaska's coastline, low tides reveal long stretches of mud that may seem firm underfoot. But that mud is made of very fine, silty particles ground up by the passage of a glacier, and as the water table rises, those fine particles can turn to quicksand, trapping you to be covered by the tide.

Rescue is sometimes possible—but only if first responders can reach you with the right equipment before you succumb to the cold water or simple drowning. In a few heartbreaking cases, rescuers have stayed with victims as they slowly drowned, trying until the very last moment to free them from the water.

WILDLIFE SAFETY

Wildlife

Here's the big one that most people (understandably) worry about. The good news is that, just like in the city, wild bears and moose really don't want anything to do with you. As long as you make enough noise for them to hear you coming, they will generally get out of the way so quietly that you'll never even know they were there. If you see a bear or a moose and it hasn't noticed you, you can quietly back up and choose another route around it, giving it plenty of space. And, of course, the guideline that you should never, ever get between any animal and its young still applies.

With that said, what do you do if you accidentally surprise a moose or a bear, or if one surprises you? Here are the basics.

MOOSE

Believe it or not, many locals agree that moose are more frightening than bears. Moose may be "just" giant deer, but think about it: They can weigh half a ton and are designed to withstand attacks from bears and wolves. They can and have killed people with their sharp hooves. They're also notoriously cantankerous and sometimes even seem to hold a grudge, so you never know if a moose you're encountering for the first time might already be irritable because of harassment from a bear, wolves, or a dog. Play it safe by always giving them lots of space.

Signs that you're too close or that a moose is already agitated include a lowered head, flattened ears, and raised hackles. If a moose does charge you, the best approach is usually to put something solid—say, a car or a tree—between you; to climb a tree if it's available; or, if there's space and time, to run away. You cannot outrun a moose, but they don't have the chase instinct that predators do, so if you get far enough away from a moose, it'll lose interest in you.

BEARS

If you've ever been on a bear-viewing trip in coastal Alaska, you were probably able to get shockingly close to the bears with no consequences. Please remember that this is only possible in areas where food is extremely plentiful, and the bears have become accustomed to human proximity, and people as a group follow certain rules that keep current and future visitors safe, and the guides are always prepared to handle an aggressive bear, just in case.

Or, to put it another way, don't expect bears in other situations to react the same way. Grizzly bears in Denali National Park have been known to charge humans from up to 0.25 mile away—a far cry from the few feet of distance you may have enjoyed during coastal bear viewing.

However, even though coastal, inland, and non-human-habituated bears tend to have different definitions of the "personal space" that might trigger a charge, you use the same techniques to avoid and defuse surprise encounters, no matter where the bears are. The following techniques have long been recommended by the Alaska Department of Fish and Game and other bear experts.

First, have and carry an effective bear deterrent. A can of bear spray costs $35-50 and is well worth the expense if you're going to be hiking in bear country. The TSA won't let you carry bear spray in your checked or carry-on luggage, so plan to buy it while you're here.

Next, if you do see a bear but it hasn't seen you, quietly back away, keeping your eyes on the bear so you can see if it suddenly notices you or changes its behavior. Never approach a bear deliberately.

If you see a bear and it also sees you, but doesn't seem concerned by your presence, you can speak to it in a calm voice (to help it recognize you as human) and slowly back away. Do not run because like all predators, bears have a chase instinct that kicks in automatically. Even if they don't want to eat you, they would love to chase you if you run. Traveling in a group greatly reduces your chances of being charged by a bear, even if you surprise it; there are no documented cases of a group of four or more people being attacked by a bear, as long as they stuck close enough together for the bear to perceive them as a group (as opposed to walking scattered apart).

If the bear follows you, stop, hold your ground, and prepare your deterrent. Hopefully you won't need it, but get it ready just in case. Group together with others, if possible, to make yourselves look bigger. If the bear continues to approach, get louder and more aggressive; hikers may yell, wave their arms to look bigger, or bang pots and pans to scare a bear away. Despite what the movies show us, a bear that stands up on its hind legs isn't acting threatening; it's just trying to figure out what you are. Be ready to use your deterrent if appropriate. The Alaska Department of Fish and Game (adfg.alaska.gov) has an excellent video on how and when to use bear spray properly; it's basically mace for bears. You should start spraying when the bear is at least 20 or 30 feet away, aiming for its nose and eyes, and be aware of wind direction so you don't accidentally spray yourself.

If a bear makes contact with you out of a defensive instinct—which is the norm if it's been surprised, or if you've gotten between a mother and her cubs—the experts recommend playing dead, lying flat with your belly on the ground, legs splayed for stability and hands clasped over your neck for protection. A defensive bear will soon stop attacking if it feels you are no longer a threat. Movement may provoke another defensive attack, so try your best to keep still until you're sure the bear has left the area.

If the attack is prolonged or seems to be of a predatory nature—which is extremely rare, but does sometimes happen—the experts recommend fighting back, concentrating on the bear's face and nose. People have successfully fought off bears in this manner.

Sound scary? Don't worry. This is "just in case" information, and if you're traveling with a guide service, they'll go over anything you need to protect against bears, and the guides will be

Bear Defense

Many people derive a sense of greater security from having a gun on hand for bear protection in Alaska, but in many cases that's a false sense of security. Statistics show that bear spray is almost always effective at stopping a bear charge without injury to the people or the bear. It's very hard to shoot a bear accurately enough to kill it, especially if it's charging at you at 30 mph; if you shoot the bear but don't kill it, you've made your situation worse instead of better.

While bear spray can affect you adversely if you spray it into the wind or accidentally spray it at a friend or a dog, it probably won't kill you. A poorly handled gun or a panicked shot, however, certainly can. If you kill a bear even in self-defense or by accident, you must salvage the carcass and surrender it to the Alaska Department of Fish and Game; you won't get to keep it.

So, although a gun can be a very useful last resort in remote situations, unless you've practiced extensively with your gun in situations that simulate a bear attack, it's usually better to hike in a group and carry bear spray instead.

armed for extra protection—again, just in case. I've spoken to bear guides with more than a decade of experience that say they've never had to use their guns, despite many up-close encounters. For many visitors to Alaska, getting to see a bear in the wild is the absolute highlight of their visit.

Most national parks require that you carry bear-resistant food canisters—sometimes called bear canisters, bear barrels, or abbreviated to BRFCs—while traveling overnight in the backcountry, and it's a good practice for travel in state parks, too. If you're traveling with a guide, they'll help you with this aspect of the trip. If you're on your own, many state and national parks offer bear canisters on loan.

These hard-sided canisters are designed to be too slippery for a bear to grip with its paws, too large for them to carry off in their jaws, and too strong to break when the bear does the only thing they can do with it—basically, kicking it around. Bears are hugely scent-motivated, so you put not just your food into the canisters but anything with a smell that might interest them, including soap, sunblock, scented insect repellents, deodorant, and any other toiletries you brought with you.

Bears are smart enough that once they realize they can't get into the canisters, they'll usually give up on them as a source of food. That's good for you—you get to keep your food, and bears learn that humans aren't a food source—and good for the bear, because "problem bears" that learn to associate humans with food usually end up having to be killed.

In some areas, bear-bagging—hanging a bag of food from a tree limb so that a bear can't reach it from the ground or by climbing up the tree—is an acceptable option, but in many parts of Alaska the trees are not suitable for this. The bag needs to be at least 15 feet off the ground and 10 feet away from the trunk or nearest branch. (You'll find varying recommendations for exact distances—this is one of the more conservative.

Wherever you store your food and other scented items—whether it's in a bear-resistant food container or bear-bagged—it should be at least 200 feet downwind from your camp. Do all your cooking at least 200 feet downwind from camp, too, so that your sleeping area doesn't become contaminated by food smells. Some people even go as far as storing the clothes they ate or cooked in with their food—on the theory the clothes are contaminated by food smells—but I usually don't worry about this unless I cook something smelly or spill food on myself.

FOOD POISONING

The restaurants in Alaska's cities and towns are all subject to health inspections, so food poisoning is no more of a concern here than anywhere else in the United States. Even in small towns, most restaurants do a good job of food handling and safety.

In terms of water quality, you are almost always in excellent hands here in Alaska. Even in Anchorage we have some of the country's best water, courtesy of beautiful glacier-fed Eklutna Lake, which acts as a drinking water reservoir for the town.

That said, if you're traveling in the backcountry, you should always filter, UV-treat, or boil water sources before drinking, no matter how pristine they may appear; even fresh-tasting Alaska water can harbor parasites like cryptosporidium or giardia. If you find yourself in the remotest and tiniest of rural villages, there may or may not be running water, and there may or may not be a water treatment facility that makes the water supply safe. You'll have to ask somebody or, when in doubt, discreetly filter your water before drinking it.

DEHYDRATION

Once upon a time, dehydration was only a concern in Alaska if you went for a long, physically strenuous trip on an unusually hot day. But our summer conditions through much of the state are getting hotter and drier, so dehydration, heat exhaustion, and heat stroke are starting to become more frequent hazards.

As anywhere else, you can avoid dehydration by drinking plenty of water and consuming electrolytes—that is, the minerals your body needs to actually make use of that water. Electrolytes are more likely to be an issue for people who are sweating profusely for a long time or engaged in strenuous, prolonged physical activity. Don't forget to also wear sunblock or sunscreen to protect from sunburn.

In really extreme cases you might need to seek shade or shelter from the sun, but in the city that's as easy as ducking into a nearby shop or restaurant. Not very many of our buildings have air-conditioning—yet—but at least you'll be out of the direct sun, and you'll probably start seeing air-conditioning more frequently if the weather continues its warming trend.

Finally, you should know the symptoms of dehydration, heat exhaustion, and heat stroke—just in case—so that you can recognize if you or someone in your party is having a heat-related problem. Symptoms of dehydration include reduced urine output that's darker than usual; irritability; very dry mouth, skin, and mucous membranes; sunken eyes; and extreme thirst.

If you notice that you're mildly dehydrated, experts recommend resting in a cool, shady area if possible and rehydrating with both water and electrolytes. Cases of severe dehydration or shock setting in as a result of dehydration (mild or otherwise) require evacuation and medical treatment.

Symptoms of heat exhaustion and heat stroke are similar. They include confusion, dehydration, dizziness, fainting, fatigue, headache, muscle or abdominal cramps, a racing heart rate, rapid breathing, a change in how you sweat (or stopping sweating altogether), altered mental state, and an elevated body temperature.

HYPOTHERMIA

Hypothermia is a life-threatening condition when your body temperature gets too low. Although it is certainly a hazard during the Alaska winter, most people are surprised to hear that it can also strike during the summer. The general guideline is that any time temperatures are below 60 degrees—which is all summer long in some parts of Alaska—hypothermia is a possibility. Symptoms include shivering, clumsiness, slurred speech or mumbling, drowsiness, and confused behavior. (The classic example of confusion is somebody pulling clothes off when they're already far too cold.)

Happily, hypothermia is also easy to avoid if you're properly prepared for the weather and the amount of time you'll be outside. The things that will chill you are getting wet, exposure to wind, exposure to cold air, and contact with cold ground (or other cold surfaces). Most of these aren't an issue if you're in a well-populated city or just stepping outside your tour bus, but the farther you go from shelter or the longer you spend outside, the more they matter.

So, to keep safe you should dress in insulating layers made of non-cotton material, wear a waterproof/windproof outer layer to keep you warm and dry, and bring a camp chair or piece of foam to separate and insulate you from the cold ground if you plan to sit down for a while. In a pinch, even a garbage bag will help protect you from a little bit of the chill, even if it's not entirely ideal.

Knowing your limits is just as important. If you're tuned in to all the particulars of your situation—starting with how your body is feeling, what the temperature is like, the weather forecast, and how far you are from shelter—you can make smart decisions about when to go back and head inside. And if you happen to be in a heavily populated part of the city, you can almost always duck inside to warm up.

If you're here on a winter trip, it's always smart to have some emergency supplies in your car—blankets, extra clothing layers, and even a sleeping bag are a good place to start—just in case you have mechanical issues and can't get where you're going right away.

The treatment for mild hypothermia is to rewarm the body; the classic example is swapping out wet clothing for dry clothing, then putting the victim and another person into a sleeping bag. (The other person's body acts as a heat source, while the sleeping bag provides insulation.) But moderate to severe hypothermia is a medical emergency that requires immediate evacuation and hospitalization, and mild hypothermia has the potential to devolve quickly. Factoring that into the fact that rescues can be delayed by rough terrain or bad weather, even in Alaska's frontcountry, should drive home the point of why it's so important to be proactive about your health and safety outdoors.

FROSTBITE

If you're spending your time in the cities or under the care of a guide on outdoorsy trips, you should never have to worry about frostbite. That said, you should know what it is and how it happens, just in case—and if you are traveling unguided outdoors when temperatures dip below freezing, you absolutely must know what it is.

Frostbite is what happens when your skin or underlying body tissues start to freeze. The ice crystals that form can severely damage your tissue; that's why some people lose fingers, toes, or even limbs that have become severely frostbitten.

The early symptoms of frostbite include skin that's turning pale yellow or white and itches, stings, or feels like it's burning. As the frostbite advances the skin may go numb or start feeling hard to the touch and looking shiny or waxy, and with advanced frostbite it may look blue or later turn black.

Frostbite is easy to prevent if you're carrying the proper clothing and gear for winter conditions. Alaska's winter weather changes quickly, so the general rule is to plan for the worst possible scenario, just in case. That said, if you don't have enough experience to know what sort of clothing layers you need to carry for a given low temperature, you definitely shouldn't be out on your own during the winter.

One last tip: Make sure that all your clothing layers, including any layers you're wearing on your hands and feet, are loose enough to allow easy blood flow. The sort of reduced circulation you get from wearing tight clothing, especially on your extremities, makes it much easier for frostbite to set in.

People often rush to put on thick, heavy socks when their feet are cold, and while this is often the right solution, if it doesn't help you might actually have the opposite problem: socks that are so thick or tight, they're cutting off circulation to your feet and making you colder instead of warmer. Again, the key here is prevention. If you've developed frostbite, deciding whether or not to thaw out the affected body part becomes part of a complex calculation; it's best to take proactive steps to avoid the situation, and seek evacuation and medical help immediately if you suspect you're developing frostbite.

CRIME

If you look at the national rankings for "most dangerous state" you will, surprisingly, usually see Alaska within the top three. That's due to our horrendously high rate of sexual assault, which falls under the umbrella of "violent crimes." Our rate of forcible rape is typically 2.5 times the national average, and the rate of child sexual assault is up to 6 times the national average.

These statistics are both sickening and frightening, but there's an extra layer of complexity because the highest rates of assault per capita are often in isolated, rural villages. Alcohol is very often involved. Our sky-high assault rates are part of a series of complicated social problems that our state has been wrestling with for decades.

Alaska's bigger cities are also wrestling with the fact that the police forces have not been expanding to keep up with population growth. This is a particular problem in Anchorage, where one of the recent city administrations made severe cuts to the police force. The current mayor, Ethan Berkowitz, is working to restore the force to operating levels but, in the meantime, the reduced force is also contending with increased rates of violent crimes, robberies, and burglaries around the city.

All that might make Alaska, or Anchorage in particular, sound like the Wild West. But the truth is that most visitors won't notice any of these issues, and the places tourists frequent are all quite safe, with the exception of some out-of-the-way downtown Anchorage spots that attract a disproportionate amount of crime.

In 2015, the highest per-capita concentration of violent crimes and sexual assaults reported in rural communities was in Western Alaska, including the exceedingly rough community of Bethel. In most parts of the state, however, the small towns are very safe, although you should look for lodgings away from bars for the sake of quiet and not accidentally getting embroiled in anybody else's drunken conflict.

Resources

Suggested Reading

ALASKA NATIVE CULTURE

Alaska Native culture is diverse, complex, and still evolving. These are some of the best books relating to Native culture—both contemporary and historical.

Fejes, Claire. *People of the Noatak*. Volcano, CA: Volcano Press, 1994. A young artist documents her travels to Arctic villages to sketch and paint the people going about their traditional lifeways, along with the friendships she made while there.

Hensley, William. *Fifty Miles from Tomorrow: A Memoir of Alaska and the Real People*. New York: Picador, 2009. The author tells the story of being raised in a traditional, seminomadic Iñupiaq lifestyle and how he became a fearless advocate for Native land rights.

Napoleon, Harold. *Yuuyaraq: The Way of the Human Being*. Fairbanks: Alaska Native Knowledge Network, 1996. A short and honest book in which the author reflects on the damage caused by cultural and physical traumas to his Yup'ik people, and on hope for the future.

TRAVEL BOOKS/MAPS

If you're going to be doing a lot of your own driving, nothing beats the detail of the *Milepost* (themilepost.com), a literal mile-by-mile log of Alaska's highways. If you don't buy it before you come, you can pick up a copy in almost any Alaska bookstore that also sells maps.

Also useful and available in most Alaska bookstores (and online) is the *DeLorme Alaska Atlas & Gazetteer*, a collection of maps for the entire state.

FISHING

Kleinkauf, Cecilia "Pudge." *Fly-Fishing for Alaska's Grayling: Sailfish of the North*. Portland, OR: Frank Amato Publications, 2010. To my knowledge, this is the only book in existence on fishing for Alaska grayling.

Kleinkauf, Cecilia "Pudge." *Rookie No More: The Flyfishing Novice Gets Guidance from a Pro* (Kenmore, WA: Epicenter Press, 2016). For novice fly fishers who want a great pocket book of advice, Kleinkauf recently published this easy-to-read "beyond the basics" introduction to everything from gear, casts, and skills to when and how to hire a guide.

Pedersen, Gunnar. *The Highway Angler: Fishing Alaska's Road System*. Anchorage: Fishing Alaska Publications, 2013. Much like the land, Alaska's fishing opportunities are enormously varied. If you're traveling anywhere near the road system, pick up a copy.

CLIMBING

Gray, Kelsey. *Alaska Rock Climbing Guide*. Anchorage: Azimuth Adventure Publishing, 2009. For rock climbers, this is the single most comprehensive print resource in existence. It's usually updated every couple of years and is available on Amazon.com, or inquire at the excellent Alaska Rock Gym in Anchorage (665 E. 33rd Ave., 907/562-7265) or contact Gray on the Alaska Rock Climbing Guide Facebook page. He and several others also published the Alaska Bouldering Guide (for shorter climbs that don't involve a rope).

HIKING

Maloney, Lisa. *50 Hikes Around Anchorage.* Woodstock: Countryman Press, 2010. I wrote this book—although it has unfortunately gotten out of date. I'm hoping to make an update soon. It details hikes close to Anchorage.

Nienhueser, Helen and John Wolfe Jr. *55 Ways to the Wilderness in Southcentral Alaska.* Seattle: Mountaineers Books, 2002. Although it's gotten a little out of date, this guidebook is still considered the bible of hiking in Southcentral Alaska. It even has a few good paddling trips in it.

Shepherd, Shane. *50 Hikes in Alaska's Chugach State Park.* Seattle: Mountaineers Books, 2001. This book is also excellent, and tackles more peak hikes/climbs than the others. However, it, too, is fading out of date. (Notice a trend?)

Littlepage, Dean. *Hiking Alaska: A Guide to Alaska's Greatest Hiking Adventures.* Helena: Falcon Publishing, 2006. This is the best statewide hiking resource I know of, although as you might imagine the coverage is spread fairly thin to cover as much ground as possible. Still, it hits high points in areas that other guidebooks don't.

Mountaineering: The Freedom of the Hills. Seattle: Mountaineer Books, 2010. This enormously useful tome is, quite rightly, considered the bible of all things backcountry travel.

PLANTS, FLOWERS, AND BERRIES

Verna Pratt is the undisputed queen of all things plants in Alaska. If you want to identify a berry, flower, or plant, pick up any of her excellent books:

Pratt, Verna. *Alaska's Wild Berries and Berry-Like Fruit.* Anchorage: Alaskakrafts, 1995.

Pratt, Verna. *Field Guide to Alaskan Wildflowers.* Anchorage: Alaskakrafts, 1990.

Pratt, Verna. *Wildflowers of Denali National Park.* Anchorage: Alaskakrafts, 1993.

INTERIOR ALASKA RECREATION

Joly, Kyle. *Outside in the Interior: An Adventure Guide for Central Alaska.* Fairbanks, AK: University of Alaska Press, 2007. If you're going to be spending some time in Interior Alaska and want a single guide to all the best outdoor adventures, this is your go-to reference.

FAMILY TRAVEL

Aist, Jennifer. *Babes in the Woods: Hiking, Camping & Boating with Babies and Young Children.* Seattle: Mountaineers Books, 2010. This book (written by an Alaskan) is another wonderful resource for getting outside, well worth a read even if you never come to Alaska.

Kirkland, Erin. Alaska on the Go: Exploring the 49th State with Children. Fairbanks: University of Alaska Press, 2014. If you're considering traveling through Alaska with children, this book is an indispensable resource. The author also has a great website, AKontheGo.com.

Internet Resources

Although I've done my best to make this book both comprehensive and selective, the Alaska travel and tourism business is in a constant state of flux. In between book updates, you'll find updated information, Alaska travel news, helpful packing lists and longer articles about tour experiences on my website, cometoalaska.net, and on moon.com.

Many Alaska businesses, especially those in smaller communities, don't have websites—but the majority of them do have Facebook pages. These Facebook pages are great for checking when businesses open for the season and for updates on their open hours and days. That's especially helpful in rural communities where hours and availability fluctuate frequently.

LODGING OPTIONS

airbnb.com

It's no secret that hotels in Alaska are very expensive during the summer. Airbnb is a viable option for finding relatively affordable accommodations, although those options still book up quickly and cost more in the summer than in the off-season.

vrbo.com

Vrbo.com, vacation rental by owner, is also useful, particularly if you're looking for a place that's pet-friendly, although its use isn't as widespread as Airbnb.

WEATHER FORECASTS

wunderground.com

Weather Underground is the most useful forecast site in Alaska, although of course the coverage for highly localized forecasts is much more sparse in Alaska than in more densely populated states.

TRAVEL

travelalaska.com
alaska.org

Both these sites are diverse and fairly comprehensive resources, but I'm not sure how often they're updated. The state's official vacation planning website (alaska.org) is tailored toward individual travelers.

FISHING AND HUNTING

http://adfg.alaska.gov

If you're interested in fishing or hunting, you can purchase permits and download regulations online from the Alaska Department of Fish and Game (ADF&G). But that's not all it offers. ADF&G also has videos on how to properly use and carry bear spray and how to free your dog if it blunders into a trap, as well as links to in-person camps and skills clinics that are open to people from out of town (look under the Education tab) and reports on current hunting and fishing conditions. It's also one of the most comprehensive sources for advice on handling wildlife encounters and traveling safely in bear and moose country, and it has interesting species profiles on almost any animal that's common in Alaska.

AURORA FORECASTS

gi.alaska.edu/auroraforecast

If you're here from September to April, when the sky gets dark enough for seeing the northern lights, keep an eye on the University of Alaska Fairbanks Geophysical Institute's aurora forecast page. Although it's not an exact science, they forecast both the intensity of the aurora display and where it might be visible across the state. Also very useful—and fun—is the Facebook page Aurora Borealis Notifications, where you'll find news about the aurora forecast and posts from across the state and the Lower 48, reporting when and where they see the aurora.

HIKING

alaskahikesearch.com

This is best single resource for finding

information on Alaska hikes. The webmaster is an avid hiker who writes great trail reports, including photos and maps, and he also accepts trail reports from others. His database of trails is easy to search, and even when the information is a few years old, it's still useful. For more generalized packing lists and skills information I'm partial to my own website, hikingalaska.net.

NEWS AND MEDIA

adn.com

The state's largest daily newspaper, based in Anchorage.

newsminer.com

The daily newspaper for Fairbanks and the Interior.

juneauempire.com

The largest daily newspaper in Southeast Alaska.

thebristolbaytimes.com

The largest newspaper for the Southwest Alaska region.

thearcticsounder.com

The largest newspaper for the Arctic.

Index

A

B

C

D

E

F

G

H

I

J

K

L

M

N

OP

QR

S

T

UV

WXYZ

List of Maps

Front Maps:

Juneau and Southeast Alaska:

Anchorage and Southcentral Alaska:

Denali, Fairbanks, and the Interior

Kodiak and Southwest Alaska

The Arctic

Photo Credits

Title Page: one of the totem poles at Ketchikan's Totem Bight State Park © Lisa Maloney; page 4 © Jeanninebryan | Dreamstime.com; page 5 NPS photo by Jacob W. Frank; page 6 (top left) © Kodiak Brown Bear Center/Steve Goodman, (top right) © Manonringuette | Dreamstime.com, (bottom) © Cpsphotos | Dreamstime.com; page 7 (keynote) © Lisa Maloney, (bottom left) © Lisa Maloney, (bottom right) NPS photo by Tim Rains; page 8 NPS photo by Jacob W. Frank; page 9 (top) © Jose Ramos | Dreamstime.com, (bottom left) © Lisa Maloney, bottom right © Explore Fairbanks/Jade Frank; pages 10-11 © Calexgon | Dreamstime.com; page 12 (top) © Arkrogan | Dreamstime.com, (bottom) © Lisa Maloney; page 13 © Cpsphotos | Dreamstime.com; page 14 (top) Unalaska CVB, (bottom) © Lisa Maloney; page 15 NPS Photo by Alex Vanderstuyf; page 16 (top) NPS Photo by Jacob W. Frank, (bottom) © Lisa Maloney; page 17 (top) © Lisa Maloney, (middle) NPS Photo by William M. O'Neill, (bottom) © Nouseforname | Dreamstime.com; page 18 (top) © Lawrence Weslowski Jr | Dreamstime, (bottom) © Lisa Maloney; page 19 © Francis O'Brien | Dreamstime.com; page 21 © Bradcalkins | Dreamstime.com; page 22 © Lisa Maloney; page 23 © Lisa Maloney; page 25 © Lisa Maloney; page 26 © Lisa Maloney; page 27 © Lisa Maloney; page 28 © Chena Hot Springs/Denise Ferree; page 30 © Jerry Murphy | Dreamstime.com; page 31 © Rinusbaak | Dreamstime.com; page 32 © Lisa Maloney; page 33 © Lisa Maloney; page 34 © Driley | Dreamstime.com; page 35 © Lisa Maloney; page 36 © Lisa Maloney; page 39 © Chena Hot Springs/Travis Knauss; page 40 © Lisa Maloney; page 41 © Tab1962 | Dreamstime.com; page 42 © Mscornelius | Dreamstime.com; page 43 (top) © Lisa Maloney, (bottom) © Lisa Maloney; page 45 © Lisa Maloney; page 51 © Lisa Maloney; page 57 © Lisa Maloney; page 58 Courtesy of alaska.gov; page 59 © Lisa Maloney; page 66 (top) © Lisa Maloney, (bottom) © Lisa Maloney; page 68 © Lisa Maloney; page 73 © Lisa Maloney; page 74 © Lisa Maloney; page 75 © Lisa Maloney; page 76 © Lisa Maloney; page 77 © Lisa Maloney; page 80 © Adeliepenguin | Dreamstime.com; page 82 © Lisa Maloney; page 84 © Lisa Maloney; page 85 © shakzu/123RF.com; page 87 © Lisa Maloney; page 92 © Lisa Maloney; page 94 © Lisa Maloney; page 95 © Tank_bmb | Dreamstime.com; page 97 © Bjorn Dihle of Pack Creek Bear Tours; page 99 © Lisa Maloney; page 102 NPS; page 105 NPS; page 108 © Lisa Maloney; page 109 © Lisa Maloney; page 110 © Lisa Maloney; page 112 © Lisa Maloney; page 115 © mfron/123RF.com; page 117 © Surz01 | Dreamstime.com; page 124 (top) © Lisa Maloney, (bottom) © Perry Solmonson/Sound Paddler; page 125 © Lisa Maloney; page 129 © Chilkoot | Dreamstime.com; page 133 © Michael Dinneen Photography; page 135 © Lisa Maloney; page 137 © Lisa Maloney; page 138 © Lisa Maloney; page 140 © Lisa Maloney; page 144 © Lisa Maloney; page 147 © Lisa Maloney; page 149 © Lisa Maloney; page 154 © Lisa Maloney; page 160 © Eqroy8 | Dreamstime.com; page 161 © Lisa Maloney; page 163 © Alaskakaren09 | Dreamstime.com; page 167 © Maxfx | Dreamstime.com; page 168 © Grayfoxx1942 | Dreamstime.com; page 169 © Lisa Maloney; page 172 © Lisa Maloney; page 173 © Lisa Maloney; page 175 © Lisa Maloney; page 177 © Perry Solmonson/Sound Paddler; page 178 © Lisa Maloney; page 179 © Lisa Maloney; page 180 © Lisa Maloney; page 183 © Lisa Maloney; page 184 © Lisa Maloney; page 187 © Lisa Maloney; page 188 © Lisa Maloney; page 194 © Yibbish | Dreamstime.com; page 195 © Bounder32h | Dreamstime.com; page 197 © Lisa Maloney; page 204 © Lisa Maloney; page 205 © Eric Menck; page 211 © Lisa Maloney; page 213 © Lisa Maloney; page 214 © Tyrone Potgieter/Within the Wild Adventure Company; page 215 © Lisa Maloney; page 216 © Lisa Maloney; page 217 © Lisa Maloney; page 224 © Lisa Maloney; page 225 © Lisa Maloney; page 227 © Lisa Maloney; page 228 © Lisa Maloney; page 229 © Lisa Maloney; page 231 © Lisa Maloney; page 235 © Lorpic99 | Dreamstime.com; page 241 © Lisa Maloney; page 244 © Lisa Maloney; page 245 © Lisa Maloney; page 246 © Lisa Maloney; page 248 (top) NPS photo by Jacob W. Frank, (bottom) NPS photo by Jacob W. Frank; page 249 © Lisa Maloney; page 252 © Lisa Maloney; page 255 (top) © Jenni Konrad, (bottom) © Lawrence Weslowski Jr | Dreamstime; page 257 © Lisa Maloney; page 260 © Lisa Maloney; page 266 NPS photo by Tim Rains; page 268 NPS phobo by Jacob W. Frank; page 269 (top) NPS photo by Katie Thoresen, (bottom) NPS photo by Daniel A Leifheit; page 270 © Porbital | Dreamstime.com; page 271 © Rickmcmillin | Dreamstime.com; page 283 © Lisa Maloney; page 284 © Kamchatka | Dreamstime.com; page 290 © Explore Fairbanks/Running Reindeer Ranch; page 291 © Lisa Maloney; page 292 © Lisa Maloney; page 294 NPS photo by Jacob W. Frank; page 295 © Lisa Maloney; page 296 © Lisa Maloney; page 300 © Lisa Maloney; page 301 © Lisa Maloney; page 302 © Lisa Maloney; page 305 © Chena Hot Springs/Denise Ferree; page 306 © Santa Claus House/Explore Fairbanks; page 316 (top) © Unalaska CVB/Brett Richardson, (bottom) © Unalaska CVB/Sam Zmolek;

page 317 © Jmaentz | Dreamstime.com; page 325 © Lisa Maloney; page 326 © Kodiak Brown Bear Center/ Steve Goodman; page 327 © Lisa Maloney; page 328 © Lisa Maloney; page 330 © Lisa Maloney; page 332 NPS; page 341 © Alaskakaren09 | Dreamstime.com; page 344 © Unalaska CVB/Ross Enlow; page 345 © Unalaska CVB; page 346 © Unalaska CVB/Ross Enlow; page 350 © Lisa Maloney; page 351 © Olga N. Vasik | Dreamstime.com; page 352 © Lisa Maloney; page 355 (top) NPS photo by Sean Tevebaugh, (bottom) NPS photo/Doug Demarest; page 357 © Aivoges | Dreamstime.com; page 359 © Explore Fairbanks; page 360 © Leon Boardway; page 363 © Leon Boardway; page 364 © Gregoir | Dreamstime.com; page 365 © Leon Boardway; page 367 NPS photo by Stuart Leidner; page 370 NPS photo by Neal Herbert; page 375 (top) © Steven Prorak | Dreamstime.com, (bottom) North Slope Borough, Iñupiat, History, Language and Culture Department; page 376 © Andrew Gildersleeve; page 377 © Northern Alaska Tour Company; page 381 © Marchello74 | Dreamstime.com; page 384 NPS photo by Zak Richter; page 387 (top) © Kodiak Brown Bear Center/Brad Starry, (bottom) NPS Photo by Tim Rains; page 388 (keynote) © Urbanraven | Dreamstime.com, (bottom) © Lisa Maloney; page 391 © Photographerlondon | Dreamstime.com; page 392 © Northern Alaska Tour Company; page 393 © Birdiegal717 | Dreamstime.com; page 395 © Jhvephotos | Dreamstime.com; page 396 © Raymona | Dreamstime.com; page 397 © Brinat | Dreamstime.com; page 398 © Jerryway | Dreamstime.com; page 399 © 19838623doug | Dreamstime.com; page 400 © Surz01 | Dreamstime.com; page 405 © Jerryway | Dreamstime.com; page 407 © davidhoffmannphotography | Dreamstime.com; page 408 © Arkrogan | Dreamstime.com; page 409 © Photographerlondon | Dreamstime.com; page 410 © Chrisboswell | Dreamstime.com; page 411 © Sekarb | Dreamstime.com; page 414 (top) © Lisa Maloney, (bottom) NPS photo by Zak Richter; page 418 © Lisa Maloney; page 422 © Lstonekim | Dreamstime.com; page 424 © Lisa Maloney; page 425 © Lisa Maloney; page 431 © Lisa Maloney; page 435 (top) Lisa Maloney, (bottom) © Izanbar | Dreamstime.com; page 439 © Lisa Maloney; page 444 © Bjorn Dihle of Pack Creek Bear Tours; page 451 © Oksanaphoto | Dreamstime.com.

Photos on foldout map: (front) An Alaskan brown bear catches a sockeye salmon in the Brooks River at Katmai National Park © Chris Richardson; (foldout) Katmai National Park & Preserve © Calexgon | Dreamstime.com; Whale-watching © Arkrogan | Dreamstime.com; Glaciers © Lisa Maloney; Northern Lights © Cpsphotos | Dreamstime.com; Iditarod © Lisa Maloney; Denali National Park & Preserve NPS photo by Alex Vanderstuyf; Bird-watching NPS photo by William M. O'Neill

Also Available

MAP SYMBOLS

Expressway
Primary Road
Secondary Road
Unpaved Road
Feature Trail
Other Trail
Ferry
Pedestrian Walkway
Stairs

City/Town
State Capital
National Capital
Point of Interest
Accommodation
Restaurant/Bar
Other Location
Campground

Airport
Airfield
Mountain
Unique Natural Feature
Waterfall
Park
Trailhead
Skiing Area

Golf Course
Parking Area
Archaeological Site
Church
Gas Station
Glacier
Mangrove
Reef
Swamp

CONVERSION TABLES

°C = (°F - 32) / 1.8
°F = (°C x 1.8) + 32
1 inch = 2.54 centimeters (cm)
1 foot = 0.304 meters (m)
1 yard = 0.914 meters
1 mile = 1.6093 kilometers (km)
1 km = 0.6214 miles
1 fathom = 1.8288 m
1 chain = 20.1168 m
1 furlong = 201.168 m
1 acre = 0.4047 hectares
1 sq km = 100 hectares
1 sq mile = 2.59 square km
1 ounce = 28.35 grams
1 pound = 0.4536 kilograms
1 short ton = 0.90718 metric ton
1 short ton = 2,000 pounds
1 long ton = 1.016 metric tons
1 long ton = 2,240 pounds
1 metric ton = 1,000 kilograms
1 quart = 0.94635 liters
1 US gallon = 3.7854 liters
1 Imperial gallon = 4.5459 liters
1 nautical mile = 1.852 km

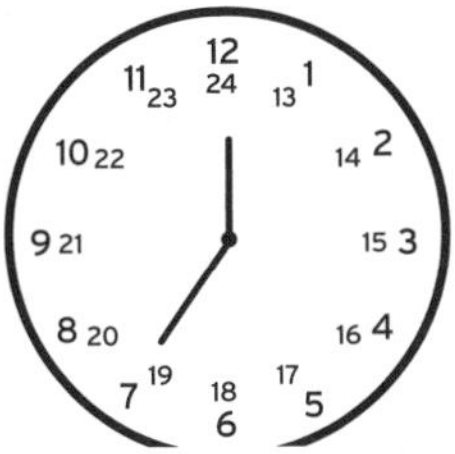

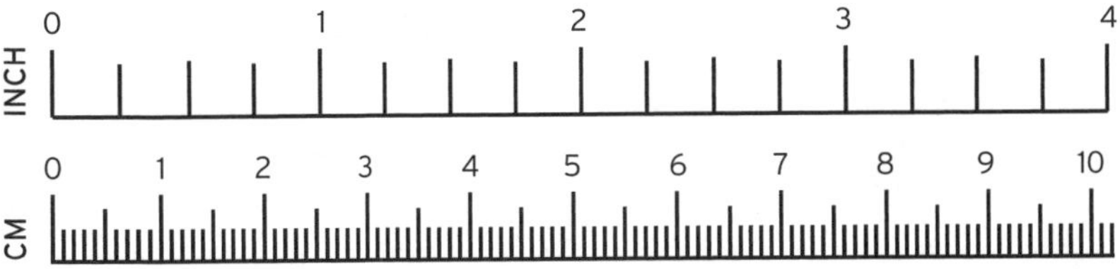

12 24, 1 13, 2 14, 3 15, 4 16, 5 17, 6 18, 7 19, 8 20, 9 21, 10 22, 11 23

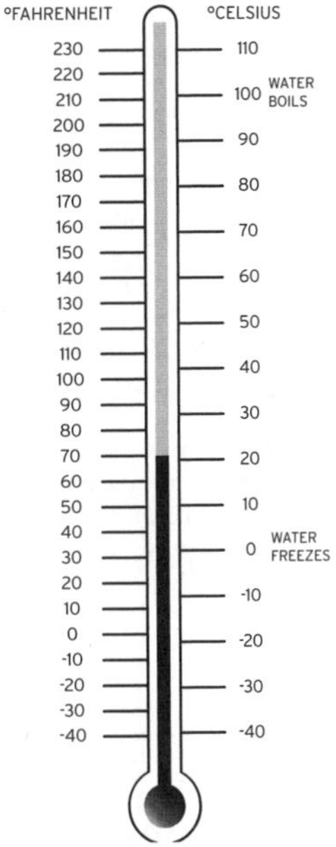

°FAHRENHEIT: 230, 220, 210, 200, 190, 180, 170, 160, 150, 140, 130, 120, 110, 100, 90, 80, 70, 60, 50, 40, 30, 20, 10, 0, -10, -20, -30, -40

°CELSIUS: 110, 100 WATER BOILS, 90, 80, 70, 60, 50, 40, 30, 20, 10, 0 WATER FREEZES, -10, -20, -30, -40

INCH: 0, 1, 2, 3, 4

CM: 0, 1, 2, 3, 4, 5, 6, 7, 8, 9, 10

MOON ALASKA
Avalon Travel
An imprint of Perseus Books
A Hachette Book Group company
1700 Fourth Street
Berkeley, CA 94710, USA
www.moon.com

Editor: Kimberly Ehart
Series Manager: Kathryn Ettinger
Copy Editor: Deana Shields
Graphics and Production Coordinator: Elizabeth Jang
Cover Design: Faceout Studios, Charles Brock
Interior Design: Domini Dragoone
Moon Logo: Tim McGrath
Map Editor: Mike Morgenfeld
Cartographers: Brian Shotwell and Mike Morgenfeld
Proofreader: Rosemarie Leenerts
Indexer: Greg Jewett

ISBN-13: 978-1-63121-496-7

Printing History
1st Edition — June 2017
5 4 3 2 1

Front cover photo: An Alaskan brown bear catches a sockeye salmon in the Brooks River at Katmai National Park. © Chris Richardson

Back cover photo: photographing Alaska's northern lights © Rena Tan | Dreamstime.com

Printed in Canada by Friesens

KEEPING CURRENT

If you have a favorite gem you'd like to see included in the next edition, or see anything that needs updating, clarification, or correction, please drop us a line. Send your comments via email to feedback@moon.com, or use the address above.